FOREST ENTOMOLOGY
Ecology and Management

ROBERT N. COULSON
Department of Entomology
Texas A & M University

JOHN A. WITTER
School of Natural Resources
The University of Michigan—Ann Arbor

A Wiley-Interscience Publication
JOHN WILEY & SONS
New York • Chichester • Brisbane • Toronto • Singapore

Library of Congress Cataloging in Publication Data:

Coulson, Robert N. (Robert Norris), 1943–
  Forest entomology.

"A Wiley-Interscience publication."
  Includes bibliographies and indexes.
    1. Forest insects. 2. Forest insects—Control.
I. Witter, John A.   II. Title.
SB761.C68 1984   634.9'67   83-23492
ISBN 0-471-02573-9

Printed in the United States of America

10 9 8 7 6 5 4 3 2 1

PREFACE

Forest entomology is a subject that draws on knowledge from several different academic specialties, including general entomology, forestry, and ecology. Forest entomology involves consideration of the roles that insects play in forest ecosystems, specialized forestry settings such as seed orchards and nurseries, and urban forests. Insects can have both positive and negative effects in these forest situations depending on the value system we use in judging their activities. Most forest insects play beneficial functional roles, which have been identified through basic studies in forest insect ecology. In some cases insects disrupt our planned uses of forests and are considered pests. During the last two decades our knowledge of forest insect ecology has increased dramatically. We have also witnessed the development of a component of forest management termed "integrated pest management" (IPM), which is the philosophy, concept, and methodology for dealing with insects when they threaten or actually damage our forests.

The subject of forest entomology is taught in departments of entomology and schools of forestry at both undergraduate and graduate levels. The course is presented under several different formats: as a service course for undergraduate forestry students, as a section of an undergraduate forest protection course, and as a specialty course for entomology undergraduate and graduate students. In some cases a laboratory is offered as part of the course. Therefore, a textbook in forestry entomology can serve a number of different purposes.

Our goal in this text is to address the fundamental issues of forest entomology. The book consists of 18 chapters divided into three sections. Each chapter contains a table of contents at the beginning, which is intended to serve as a guide to the subjects discussed; figures and tables to illustrate key points; and a contemporary literature cited section, which is intended to reference the work of other scientists and serve as a guide for further study. The first section consists of four chapters dealing with general entomology. The subjects covered include: introduction to insects (Chapter 1), insect structure and function (Chapter 2), insect classification (Chapter 3), and insect damage and sign categories (Chapter 4). This section is intended for students who have not had training in entomology and as a review for students with previous knowledge. The second section consists of six chapters dealing with principles and concepts of integrated pest management of forest insects. Chapter 5 provides a general overview of the subject of integrated pest management and is the focal point of the section. The basic components of integrated pest management are defined in Chapter 5, and these components are discussed in detail in the remaining chapters in the section. The subjects discussed include population dynamics of forest insects (Chapter 6), population dynamics of forest trees in relation to phytophagous insects (Chapter 7), principles of population modification and regulation using artificial and natural agents (Chapter 8), impact assessment (Chapter 9), and monitoring pest populations and forest stands (Chapter 10). The third section consists of eight chapters dealing with the principal forest insect feeding groups: defoliators (Chapter 11); sapsucking insects (Chapter 12); terminal, shoot, twig, and root insects (Chapter 13); seed and cone insects (Chapter 14); phloem feeding insects (Chapter 15); wood boring insects (Chapter 16); gall forming insects (Chapter 17); and insects affecting recreational uses of forests (Chapter 18). The goal of Section III is to provide an overview of the primary insect species that impact on forest ecosystems, specialized forestry settings, and urban forests. We emphasize the ecological functions of the insects covered, examine case history examples for major pest species, define the treatment tactics and strategies used in regulating or modifying populations, and provide a contemporary reference section for each feeding group.

The organizational format for this text was selected to accommodate the various ways that forest entomology is taught. We have cross-referenced the chapters in each section in order to direct the student to pertinent definitions and concepts.

ROBERT N. COULSON
JOHN A. WITTER

College Station, Texas
Ann Arbor, Michigan
March 1984

ACKNOWLEDGMENTS

Numerous individuals have helped in the preparation and production of this text. Our colleagues have reviewed drafts of each chapter and made suggestions on content and have provided photographs and figures. We acknowledge and thank D. C. Allen, R. J. Allen, J. R. Baker, B. V. Barnes, C. W. Berisford, A. A. Berryman, R. F. Billings, J. H. Borden, M. H. Brookes, S. Buthman, R. S. Cameron, I. S. Cantrall, W. M. Ciesla, S. P. Cook, J. E. Coster, D. A. Crossley Jr., G. L. Curry, G. E. Daterman, G. L. DeBarr, C. J. DeMars, M. E. Dix, A. T. Drooz, N. Dubois, L. J. Edson, W. S. Fargo, C. W. Fatzinger, R. M. Feldman, M. D. Ferguson, R. O. Flamm, J. L. Flexner, J. L. Foltz, R. T. Franklin, J. A. Gagne, N. Gosling, P. B. Hennier, G. D. Hertel, W. Houser, K. M. Hughes, R. L. Hyde, P. J. Iwai, S. Jones, R. Kelly, C. S. Koehler, P. W. Kovarik, H. M. Kulman, D. Loh, R. Long, P. L. Lorio, A. M. Lynch, L. A. Lyons, C. T. Maier, B. Manoulian, W. J. Mattson, F. G. Maxwell, M. S. McClure, M. W. McFadden, J. R. McGraw, M. M. McKnight, J. A. McLean, R. Merritt, B. A. Montgomery, H. L. Morton, T. E. Nebeker, I. Otvos, T. L. Payne, F. W. Plapp, P. E. Pulley, R. B. Ryan, E. J. Rykiel, L. Safranyik, T. D. Schowalter, C. P. Schwalbe, P. J. H. Sharpe, G. A. Simmons, K. Simpson, L. Simpson, G. A. Snyder, J. D. Solomon, F. M. Stephen, M. W. Stock, R. L. Talerico, R. C. Thatcher, L. C. Thompson, H. Trial, R. H. Turnbow, S. B. Vinson, T. L. Wagner, W. E. Wallner, W. E. Waters, D. P. Webb, D. S. White, M. L. Williams, L. F. Wilson, S. L. Wood, and H. O. Yates III.

Special thanks are due to R. W. Stark and F. P. Hain for their candid review of the manuscript of this text, to Nancy Witter for providing artwork, and to M. M. Conway for her perseverance with us and expert editorial service.

We especially acknowledge and thank A. M. Bunting for her conscientious and thorough attention to the details of preparation of the manuscript. She assisted in preparation of figures and tables, editing, file management, and numerous other vital details.

We are indebted to and dedicate this book to our parents and families (Frances, Karah, and Amy Coulson and Nancy and Leslie Witter) for their encouragement and commend their patience during the preparation of this textbook.

                                                                                          R.N.C.
                                                                                          J.A.W.

CONTENTS

FOREST ENTOMOLOGY

I | GENERAL ENTOMOLOGY

Section I contains four chapters that provide an overview of general entomology. Chapter 1 is an introduction to the science of entomology. Chapter 2 considers basic principles of insect structure and function. Chapter 3 provides a treatment of classification of insects and other arthropods. Chapter 4 defines the various types of damage that insects cause to forest trees.

These four chapters serve as a basic course in general entomology for the student without training in entomology and a review for students with previous knowledge of entomology.

1 | INTRODUCTION TO INSECTS

INTRODUCTION

This chapter is divided into four parts: (1) forest entomology, (2) shade tree entomology, (3) insects beneficial to human beings, and (4) insects harmful to human beings and their perceived needs.

FOREST ENTOMOLOGY

Definitions

Forest entomology is concerned with insects that affect the forest and forest products. Smith et al. (1973) provides information on the history of forest entomology in North America, whereas Coulson (1981) discusses the evolution of forest pest management. Wood product entomology is concerned with the protection of wooden structures, poles, posts, and wood by-products from insect damage. Although usually considered as part of forest entomology, its problems are quite different from most of those in forest entomology and is sometimes considered a separate field (Chamberlin 1953, Hickin 1975). This textbook emphasizes insects affecting live trees. Some of the important insects affecting wood products such as termites, powderpost beetles, carpenter ants, and the old house borer, however, are covered in Chapter 16.

The Forest Entomologist

The forest entomologist studies insects in the forest, their damage to trees and shrubs, and the interaction of the insects with plants, animals, and the physical environment. The results from these studies in applied forest insect ecology must then be incorporated with the silvicultural, management, policy, and economic goals of forestry and resource management. Forest entomologists, therefore, need strong academic training and practical experience in both forestry and entomology. Although specific goals of forest entomologists are influenced by their employers, most of them would list some or all of the following as major goals: (1) collection of ecological information to reduce insect damage through forest management and silvicultural practices, (2) development of methods and conducting surveys to determine insect abundance and insect impact, (3) development or use of natural enemies and other pest management techniques—excluding chemical insecticides—to reduce insect damage, (4) public education on forest insect pests and sound pest management programs, and (5) development and/or use of chemical insecticides to reduce insect damage. Goals 1–3 usually provide a more permanent type of pest management program, whereas goal 4 involves the transfer of information from the literature and current research to the user groups. The last goal is primarily a temporary stopgap method in pest management and is used with more specialized crops such as Christmas trees, planting stock, and seed orchards.

In the United States forest pest management operations are the responsibility of the following organizations: (1) the U.S. Department of Agriculture, Forest Service, State and Private Forestry, Forest Pest Management; (2) state forestry or natural resource departments; and (3) forest industry. These organizations plan and conduct insect surveys and insect impact evaluations and organize, supervise, and evaluate forest pest management techniques. Research work on forest insect problems in the United States is handled primarily by personnel at Forest Insect and Disease Units of Forest Service Experiment Stations and at state and private universities. Some land grant universities have entomologists involved in forest entomology extension work. For example, North Carolina State University has a very effective extension program in forestry, including forest entomology. Presently, very few forest entomologists are employed full-time as extension specialists. Most forest entomologists are involved with some extension duties as part of their total job responsibilities. A few forest industries have their own forest entomologists.

The Forester

The field forester or forest technician, who is in direct contact with the forest resource, is often the first person to notice new insect problems. The field forester or forest technician must be trained to recognize potential forest pest problems and must have the ecological training necessary to plan and carry out sound forest management and forest pest management practices. Specifically, a forester should be trained to (1) recognize and identify the common types of insect damage; (2) identify the common insects found in the forest; (3) recognize insect damage and the various stages of the most common forest pest problems in their region; and (4) understand the seasonal history, population dynamics, impact, and management strategies for the most common forest insect pests. A forester trained in the above skills will be able to recognize and identify the common types of insect damage present in the particular region and will be able to properly integrate many forest pest management techniques into the forest management practices used in the region.

SHADE TREE ENTOMOLOGY

Differences between Forest and Shade Tree Entomology

Shade tree entomology is concerned with insects affecting individual trees or groups of trees in the urban forest, including park trees, street trees, and yard trees. The insects present on these trees are generally the same species that occur in forest stands. However, the unit involved, ecological conditions, economic values, and the amount of damage tolerated differs between trees in the urban forest and forest stands.

In shade tree entomology, the homeowner, city forester, or arborist is managing and caring for an individual tree or a small group of trees while the forester is managing and caring for a forest stand. A city forester is responsible for maintaining all trees on city property, including trees on lawn extensions. The city forester may be involved in managing a reasonably large number of trees, but is interested in the maintenance of individual trees. The homeowner is interested in individual trees that provide shade and aesthetic beauty on the home property. The forester or natural resources manager is rarely concerned about an individual tree within a forest stand. There are a few exceptions such as large highly prized trees within a forest stand such as black walnut or redwood, individual trees that provide nesting sites for endangered animal species (e.g., a large white pine tree with a bald eagle nest), and trees selected for seed sources.

The economic value of an individual tree in the urban environment is normally much greater than one tree in a forest stand. The homeowner or city forester is often willing to spend a considerable amount of time and money to maintain individual trees. The value of a city tree is determined by its size, condition, species, and location. For example, the value of a 63-cm DBH sugar maple tree and a 88-cm DBH elm tree in a city in the eastern United States in good condition and in a prime location are valued at $4909 and $1924, respectively (International Society of Arboriculture 1975). The costs of treatment, such as removing a large dead tree from a city lot, are much greater than any comparable action in the forest. The current costs of removing a large dead American elm or sugar maple tree from an urban environment varies from about $150 to $2000 depending on the size and location of the tree.

Ecological conditions normally vary considerably between urban forests and managed or unmanaged forest stands. Soil disturbances, changes in drainage patterns, damage to tree roots, nutrient deficiencies, air pollution, and mechanical injury to trees are much greater in urban areas than in forest stands. The urban areas are warmer and less humid than the surrounding rural areas because of the extensive asphalt surfaces and the massive combustion of fuels in cities. Also, trees are often planted in an urban environment on poor sites, or species are planted outside their native range.

The amount of insect damage normally tolerated by most homeowners and the general public on trees in the city is much less than the amount of damage tolerated by foresters on trees in forest stands. Many homeowners and the general public envision a "perfect tree" or "perfect leaf" with no damage, or they believe in the dead insect syndrome (i.e., the only good insect is a dead insect) or have an entomophobia problem. For these reasons, insect species normally not considered forest pests, such as many species of aphids, scales, and mites, are considered to be pests in urban areas.

The City Forester or Arborist

The city forester or arborist is involved with planting, growing, maintaining, and protecting urban trees, whereas the shade tree entomologist concentrates on the protection of urban trees. The goals of these professionals are similar to the goals of a forest entomologist or forester. In the urban environment, professionals in the past often relied more on chemical insecticides as a control tactic because very little insect damage and low numbers of insects were tolerated by the general public. Shade tree extension specialists or horticultural extension specialists are employed by city, state, and federal governments. They provide information on shade trees and ornamental plants to the general public. Research on shade tree pests has been limited. The only two shade tree pests that have received substantial federal research support have been Dutch elm disease, *Ceratocystis ulmi* (Buisum) C. Moreau, and gypsy moth, *Lymantria dispar* (Linnaeus). There will be increasing emphasis on research in shade tree pest management programs as the public uses and places more value on urban forests, including protection of shade and park trees. The minimal research work on shade tree insect problems has been conducted primarily by scientists at USDA facilities and at various state and private universities.

The Nonforester and Nonarborist

Some students and individuals are not planning careers in forestry or arboriculture. The information in this textbook will give these readers a better understanding of insect interactions within our environment. It will enable them to be more informed regarding insects and insect pest management and help them to cope better with insects in the urban and rural forest environment. For example, the public is becoming more involved in issues such as the broad-scale use of pesticides and the effects of pollution on public lands. The U.S. Forest Service must consult with the public (requirement of the National Forest Management Act) before any major land use activity occurs.

INSECTS BENEFICIAL TO HUMAN BEINGS

This textbook concentrates on and emphasizes insects that cause damage to forest and shade trees. It is erroneous to regard all insects as pests. Estimates of the number of insect species that occasionally cause damage in the United States vary from about 500 to 1000 species depending on the evaluation criteria used. Less than 1% of all the described insect species in North America are major insect pests. The majority of insects are either directly or indirectly beneficial or neutral in their relationship to human beings. Insects pollinate plants; provide food for other animals and products for human consumption; serve as natural control agents of other pests, including insects and weeds; enrich the soil; and contribute to the aesthetic and educational experience of human beings.

Insects as Pollinators

Sexual reproduction in flowering plants occurs when wind or insects transfer pollen from the anther of a male flower to the stigma of a female flower. Well-known examples of wind-pollinated plants are many species of trees such as oaks, willows, pines, and many species of cereals such as corn and wheat. Most of our fruit crops; many ornamental flowers; many vegetables such as beans, peas, tomatoes, and onions; and many field crops such as alfalfa, clover, cotton, and tobacco depend on insects for pollination. There are thousands of species that pollinate plants. Most insect pollinators are found in the orders of Hymenoptera (bees), Lepidoptera (butterflies), Diptera (true flies), Coleoptera (beetles), and Thysanoptera (thrips). The flowers of plants and the insects that visit them have co-evolved. Wild pollinating insects were sufficient to pollinate our food crops until recently. Large monocultures, clean cultivation, and the intensive use of chemical insecticides in agriculture have reduced the numbers of wild pollinating insect species so that they cannot now maintain an adequate level of pollination in many of our commercial crops. Provision of pollinators is now a big business. Honeybees, alkali bees, and leafcutter bees are commonly reared for pollination of approximately 80% of our commercial crops. Insect pollination is a very important and complex subject that covers many ecological and evolutionary principles (Proctor and Yeo 1972, Gilbert and Raven 1975, Daly et al. 1978).

Insects as Food

Insects are an important source of food for other insects and for many other animals such as birds, fish, mammals, amphibians, and reptiles. Swan (1964) reported that at least 50% of the food consumed by North American land birds consists of insects. Most land birds are primarily insectivorous while rearing their young regardless of their food habits during the rest of the year. It is probably not a coincidence that the nesting period of most birds parallels the peak emergence periods of many insects. Insects are rich in proteins and lipids necessary for the rapid growth of young birds.

Immature and adult insects such as midges, mayflies, stoneflies, and caddisflies are an important food source for fresh-water fish. Many anglers have spent hours studying the aquatic ecology of a favorite fishing area to increase the chance of a successful fishing trip. Insects have been used as models for fishing flies since the second century (Atkins 1978).

Insects have been eaten by human beings for thousands of years. The Europeans and their descendants are the only major group of humans who do not readily enjoy a delicious meal of insects. For many human beings in the world, insects are an important source of protein and fat. Many insects such as house fly pupae, termites, and locust contain a rich food source of protein, fat, and vitamins (Taylor 1975). The use of insects as a source of food in developing countries is not adequately exploited. It may be a few years before we are willing to use insects in our diet or in the diet of our domesticated animals. Nevertheless, it would be wise if we were to increase our research endeavors so that good insect protein supplements are available for human and domesticated animal consumption. For example, the solid waste generated by cattle feed lots in the United States could easily be converted to fly protein that can then be fed to poultry and other livestock. Human beings will turn to insects as a protein source for themselves and their domesticated animals when the supply of high-quality protein becomes more limited.

Insect Products

A number of insect products are used by human beings in today's society. We have chosen to mention only those products from insects that are currently being managed as a renewable natural resource. These insect products are silk, shellac, dyes, and bee-associated products.

A lepidopterous caterpillar known as the *silkworm, Bombyx mori* (Linnaeus), has been domesticated for over 4000 years. The silk industry was developed in China, and the methods used to produce silk remained a secret until the Japanese obtained the eggs and rearing techniques in 195 AD (Smith et al. 1973). Two monks smuggled eggs and rearing techniques from China in 555 AD and brought the silk industry to Europe. The silk industry has become an important industry in China, Japan, Italy, France, and Spain. Silkworm larvae are reared on mulberry leaves. A silken filament is produced by a proteinaceous secretion from the salivary glands in the mouth of a mature silkworm larva. The larva constructs a cocoon from this silken filament, in which it molts to the pupal stage. Cocoons are collected, the filament unraveled, and the filaments woven together to produce silk fibers. Approximately 25,000 cocoons produce one pound of silk. Cheaper synthetic fibers are now available, but natural silk will always be available as an exquisite cloth for those willing to pay the price.

Shellac is produced from lac sticks, which are tree branches covered with a resin material (lac). Lac is secreted by the Indian lac insect, *Laccifer lacca* (Kerr), a common scale insect found on trees in India and Burma. Heavy infestations of the lac scale may occur on a single tree since they are sedentary during most of their life cycle, and many generations may develop on the same tree. A branch is collected when it is entirely encrusted with lac. Metcalf et al. (1978) presents a description of the production of shellac along with a list of other manufacturing processes and products that use lac. Many other scale insects produce resinous coverings that can be extracted, but none produce a substance of the quality of lac. Also, none of these other resinous materials have been used as a commercial product.

Dyes have been produced in a limited manner from a number of scale insects by cultures throughout the world. Cochineal, the only dye presently being produced, is a vivid red pigment obtained from the cochineal scale. This dye is now being produced in the Canary Islands from the dried, ground bodies of the cochineal scale that inhabits prickly pear cactus.

The major products derived from the honeybee are honey, beeswax, pollen, royal jelly, and queens and packages of worker bees. Primitive humans collected honey from wild beehives. The honeybee, *Apis mellifera* Linnaeus, is the only wild bee that has been domesticated and used for commercial production of honey, beeswax, and other products. Worldwide honey production has grown to over one million metric tons per year (Morse 1975).

Beeswax, an important by-product of apiculture, is secreted by specialized hypodermal glands located on the abdomen of worker bees. Honeybees use beeswax to construct the honeycomb in which they store honey and rear their young. Beekeepers collect the surplus combs, which are melted down and manufactured into frames for commercial beehives, candles, cosmetics, furniture polish, car wax, and other products.

In some areas, the honeybees collect more pollen than is necessary to rear their young. Excess pollen is collected and sold to other beekeepers and health food stores. Royal jelly, a specialized food that bees feed to their young, is used to treat some skin disorders and is an ingredient of certain expensive cosmetics. Queens and packages of worker bees are sold to establish new colonies.

Insects as Natural Enemies

Most insect species seldom reach epidemic population levels because they are kept at endemic population levels primarily by natural enemies. The role of insects as natural enemies of phytophagous insects is so important that it is discussed in detail in Chapter 8.

Insects as Destroyers of Weeds

Close to 50% of all insect species are herbivores (plant feeders). Nature's strategy and human strategy are not always completely compatible in plant–insect interactions. Insect herbivores that feed on unwanted plants or weeds are considered beneficial to human beings, whereas insect herbivores that damage our crops and forests are considered insect pests. Successful introductions of phytophagous insect species to reduce populations of exotic weed pests such as the prickly pear cacti in Australia and the Klamath weed in the United States are discussed in Chapter 8.

Insects as Scavengers

Scavengers are organisms that feed primarily on dead plants or animals, decaying vegetation, or animal excrement. The food of a scavenger is not all dead material because microbes such as bacteria and fungi flourish in the kind of food consumed by scavengers and are incidentally ingested. The diet of scavengers varies considerably. Scavengers are usually specific to either plant or animal material. For example, some scavengers bore into and feed on decaying wood and others feed on dead animals or animal feces, whereas some feed exclusively on materials such as microbial organisms, diatoms, algae, and yeast. Some species of scavengers feed only on very small pieces of animal and plant material.

Many species of insects feed on various kinds of dead plant and animal material found in the environment. These insect scavengers play a very important role in the decomposition of plant and animal material, including a role in the recycling of nutrients. We often forget the beneficial role that termites and many species of bark beetles, wood boring beetles, and carpenter ants play in the decomposition of dead woody material. Likewise, insects such as blow flies, rove beetles, and carrion beetles are important in the decomposition of dead animals.

Numerous soil fauna and soil microflora live on the dead organic material found in terrestrial environments. The ultimate breakdown of this forest litter is accomplished primarily by soil microflora (primarily protozoans) interacting with soil animals (insects and other arthropods, molluscs, and earthworms). Through these interactions, nutrients are released from the organic material to the soil. Many soil animals (e.g., earthworms, many species of immature insects) facilitate the oxygenation of the soil through burrowing into the soil and also help to facilitate the movement of capillary water in the soil. Wallwork (1970), Crossley (1977), and Mattson (1977) present additional information on the ecology of soil animals and the roles of insects and other arthropods in forest soils. Wagner et al. (1977) present a thorough coverage of soil invertebrates in a deciduous forest.

Aesthetic and Educational Value of Insects

The aesthetic value of insects is unlimited and priceless because of the number, kinds, variations, and behavioral patterns of insects. Most philosophers agree that an aesthetic experience is a basic human need. The concepts regarding aesthetic experiences have primarily been developed in the fine arts, but additional emphasis is now being placed on the beauty of our natural surroundings and the potential of natural history in providing healthy aesthetic experiences. The increased emphasis on using natural history to provide an aesthetic experience in the United States can be explained as follows: (1) approximately 85% of us will live in cities by the year 2000 (Salter 1974); (2) it is becoming more difficult for human beings to have experiences on natural or seminatural lands; and (3) it is felt that a daily contact with nature in some form is an inherent biological necessity (Treshow 1976). Insects have provided aesthetic beauty and aesthetic experiences to human beings for thousands of years. Most human beings have marveled at the inherent beauty in many insects such as butterflies and certain beetles (Sandved and Brewer 1976, Dalton 1975). Butterflies, other brightly colored insects, and insects in general are of considerable interest to collectors, educators, naturalists, and artists who collect them, use them for teaching purposes, and use them as models or in various crafts. Singer and Gilbert (1978), Kulman (1977), and Pyle (1976) present excellent coverages on the ecology, production management, and conservation of butterflies.

The aesthetic and educational values of insects will increase immensely during the twenty-first century. The effect of changing living and land-use patterns on the aesthetic value of insects already has been mentioned. Emphasis on insect zoos or live insect displays has increased recently following the opening of the live insect zoo in 1976 at the U.S. Museum of Natural History in Washington, D.C. Insects have been underused as an educational tool. Insects are extremely useful as aids in teaching various biological concepts such as survival, adaptability, diversity, population dynamics, and plant–animal interactions. The number of articles in general teaching magazines and increased sales of insect supplies from biological supply houses indicate that insects are now being used more as a teaching aid at the elementary and secondary levels (see Volume 38, issue No. 4 of *The American Biology Teacher*).

Scientific Value of Insects

Fruit flies, flour beetles, blow flies, house flies, cockroaches, honeybees, wax moths, and reduviid bugs have been used for many years in numerous basic studies on genetics, developmental biology, and population dynamics. Insects were chosen over other animals because they are easily collected and reared; some produce many generations per year; most can be manipulated easily and stored in small areas; and these insect species provide a tremendous diversity of form, function, and habits.

Insects are good organisms to use as an index of environmental change. Almost any prolonged change in an environment will bring about changes in the community of organisms that occupies that environment. The potential applicability of insect indicators to monitor changes in environmental quality is unlimited. Insects can serve as indices of change in specific parameters such as oxygen content, pH, salinity, soil moisture content, soil compaction, and concentration of a contaminant that accumulates in the tissues. They may also be used to indicate broader changes in environmental quality or community structure.

Indicator organisms can be used singly or in combination with several species. They are generally used in one of three ways: (1) to demonstrate the presence of organisms that experience has shown to be significantly characteristic of a particular condition such as kinds and degree of pollution; (2) to demonstrate the absence of organisms known to be highly intolerant of a particular environmental condition; and (3) to monitor changes in population density, relative abundance of several species, or community change over time. Many aquatic insects such as certain species of midges, mayflies, caddisflies, and stoneflies have narrow environmental tolerances to certain parameters. The presence or absence of these species have been used for some time to indicate the quality of particular streams. Resh and Unzicker (1975) presented an excellent review on the use of aquatic insects as indicator species. Lenhard and Witter (1977) discuss the advantages and disadvantages of insects as biological indicators of environmental change. They also developed a list of criteria to be considered when selecting "ideal" insect indicator species or groups of species for a particular study. The National Forest Management Act recommends the use of indicator species to measure the effects of various management actions.

INSECTS HARMFUL TO HUMAN BEINGS AND THEIR PERCEIVED NEEDS

Insects harmful to human beings can be divided into three groups: insects that injure growing plants; insects that annoy and injure human beings and domesticated animals; and insects that destroy products produced by human beings.

Insects That Injure Growing Plants

In North America, all economically important plants are damaged by insects. Metcalf et al. (1978) and Pfadt (1978) present reasonably complete coverages of many different insects that attack economically important plants. Chapters 11–17 of this textbook present detailed coverage on the most important forest and shade tree pests in North America.

Insects That Annoy and Injure Human Beings and Domesticated Animals

Insects that annoy or injure human beings and their domesticated animals can be divided into three general groups: household pests; insects of medical importance; and pests of livestock, poultry, and domestic pets. Nobody needs to be reminded about the furor that household insect pests such as cockroaches, ants, flour beetles, carpet beetles, termites, powderpost beetles, and carpenter ants can cause in an individual's home. Information on these household insect pests is presented by Metcalf et al. (1978), Pfadt (1978), and Ebeling (1975). Piper and Frankie (1978) provide an interesting review of integrated pest management of urban cockroach problems. The most common household pests that attack wood products are presented in Chapter 16 of this textbook.

Insects of medical importance include insects that either bite, sting, feed on blood or other tissues, induce allergies, invoke entomophobia, are parasites, or are vectors and intermediate hosts of diseases and parasites. Harwood and James (1979) provide a thorough coverage on insects of medical importance. A thorough review of the common pest problems, primarily biting and stinging insects, in urban and rural forest recreational areas is provided in Chapter 18 of this textbook.

Many insect pests attack livestock, poultry, and domestic pets. Information on insects attacking domesticated animals is provided by Harwood and James (1979), Metcalf et al. (1978), and Pfadt (1978).

Insects That Destroy Products Produced by Human Beings

Many insects attack various products produced by human beings. We often forget that storage losses caused by insect attack may be as great or greater than the losses sustained while growing the crops. Insect damage causes an approximate annual loss of 5–10% of the world's supply of stored grain (Wilbur and Mills 1978). They also reported an estimated loss in stored grain of 300–600 million dollars per year in the United States. Most people in North America are aware that certain insects (e.g., grain beetles, Khapra beetles, flour beetles, meal moths, flour moths) damage stored grain products. However, few of us living in North America comprehend the amount of insect damage of stored products in tropical areas and in underdeveloped countries. Other insects such as clothes moths and carpet beetles attack clothing, rugs, and other fibers. Termites, powderpost beetles, and carpenter ants are examples of insects that cause damage to wood products. Further information on wood products insects is presented in Chapter 16.

REFERENCES

Atkins, M. D. 1978. *Insects in Perspective*. Macmillan, New York.

Chamberlin, W. J. 1953. Insects Affecting Forest Products and Other Materials. Oregon State Coop. Assoc., Corvallis.

Coulson, R. N. 1981. Evolution of concepts of integrated pest management in forests. *J. Georgia Entomol. Soc.* **16**:301–316.

Crossley, D. A., Jr. 1977. The roles of terrestrial saprophagous arthropods in forest soils: Current status of concepts. In Mattson, W. J. (Ed.), *The Role of Arthropods in Forest Ecosystems.* Springer-Verlag, New York.

Dalton, S. 1975. *Borne on the Wind. The Extraordinary World of Insects in Flight.* Dutton, New York.

Daly, H. V., J. T. Doyen, and P. R. Ehrlich. 1978. *Introduction to Insect Biology and Diversity.* McGraw-Hill, New York.

Ebeling, W. 1975. *Urban Entomology.* University of California, Division of Agricultural Sciences, Berkeley.

Gilbert, L. E. and P. H. Raven (Eds.). 1975. *Coevolution of Animals and Plants.* University of Texas Press, Austin.

Harwood, R. F. and M. T. James. 1979. *Entomology in Human and Animal Health.* Macmillan, New York.

Hickin, N. E. 1975. The Insect Factor in Wood Decay: An Account of Wood-boring Insects with Particular Reference to Timber Indoors. Assoc. Bus. Prog., London.

International Society of Arboriculture. 1975. *A Guide to the Professional Evaluation of Landscape Trees, Specimen Shrubs, and Evergreens.*

Kulman, H. M. 1977. Butterfly production management. In Kulman, H. M. and H. C. Chiang (Eds.), *Insect Ecology—Papers Presented in the A. C. Hodson Lectures.* University of Minnesota Agricultural Experiment Station Technical Bulletin 310.

Lenhard, S. C. and J. A. Witter. 1977. Insects as biological indicators of environmental change. *Bull. Entomol. Soc. Am.* **23**:191–193.

Mattson, W. J. (Ed.). 1977. *The Role of Arthropods in Forest Ecosystems.* Springer-Verlag, New York.

Metcalf, C. L., W. P. Flint, and R. L. Metcalf. 1978. *Destructive and Useful Insects.* McGraw-Hill, New York.

Morse, R. A. 1975. *Bees and Beekeeping.* Cornell University Press, Ithaca, New York.

Pfadt, R. E. (Ed.). 1978. *Fundamentals of Applied Entomology.* Macmillan, New York.

Piper, G. L. and G. W. Frankie. 1978. Integrated management of urban cockroach populations. In Frankie, G. W. and C. S. Koehler (Eds.), *Perspectives in Urban Entomology.* Academic Press, New York.

Proctor, M. and P. Yeo. 1972. *The Pollination of Flowers.* Taplinger, New York.

Pyle, R. M. 1976. Conservation of the Lepidoptera in the United States. *Biol. Conserv.* **9**:55–75.

Resh, V. H. and J. D. Unzicker. 1975. Water quality monitoring and aquatic organisms: The importance of species identification. *J. Water Pollut. Control* **47**:9–19.

Salter, P. S. 1974. Toward an ecology of the urban environment. In W. H. Johnson and W. C. Steere (Eds.), *The Environmental Challenge.* Holt, Rinehart, and Winston, New York.

Sandved, K. B. and J. Brewer. 1976. *Butterflies.* N. Abrams, New York.

Singer, M. C. and L. E. Gilbert. 1978. Ecology of butterflies in the urbs and suburbs. In Frankie, G. W. and C. S. Koehler (Eds.), *Perspectives in Urban Entomology.* Academic Press, New York.

Smith, R. F., T. E. Mittler, and C. N. Smith (Eds.). 1973. *History of Entomology.* Annual Reviews, Palo Alto, CA.

Swan, L. A. 1964. *Beneficial Insects.* Harper & Row, New York.

Taylor, R. L. 1975. *Butterflies in My Stomach—Or: Insects in Human Nutrition.* Woodbridge Press, Santa Barbara, CA.

Treshow, M. 1976. *The Human Environment.* McGraw-Hill, New York.

Wagner, T. L., W. J. Mattson, and J. A. Witter. 1977. A survey of soil invertebrates in two aspen forests in northern Minnesota. USDA Forest Service General Technical Report NC-40.

Wallwork, J. A. 1970. *Ecology of Soil Animals.* McGraw-Hill, London.

Wilbur, D. A. and R. B. Mills. 1978. Stored grain insects. In Pfadt, R. E. (Ed.), *Fundamentals of Applied Entomology.* Macmillan, New York.

2 | INSECT STRUCTURE AND FUNCTION

INTRODUCTION

An understanding of insect structure is necessary for distinguishing insects from each other and from other animals. It is also important to know how insects function, live, and move about the environment. This chapter is divided into four parts: (1) external structure and function, (2) internal structure and function, (3) insect growth and development, and (4) adaptive features of insects.

The coverage on the external and internal structure and function of insects is concise because of the applied nature of this text and because the information is provided in other references. Excellent presentations on the structure and function of insects are found in general entomology texts by Ross et al. (1982), Romoser (1981), Borror et al. (1981), Gillott (1980), Atkins (1978), and Daly et al. (1978). Chapman (1982), Richards and Davies (1977), and Snodgrass (1935) provide detailed information on insect morphology, whereas Chapman (1982), Rockstein (1973–1974), and Wigglesworth (1972) present a thorough coverage of insect physiology.

EXTERNAL STRUCTURE AND FUNCTION

The Generalized Insect

Insects display a wide diversity in form. Therefore, it is necessary to use a generalized model (Figure 2.1) in discussing insect structure. Adult insects normally have three distinct body regions: head, thorax, and abdomen. The head bears the mouthparts and a number of sensory organs: antennae, palps, and eyes. The thorax is the middle region of the insect's body and bears the legs and wings (when present). The abdomen is the posterior body region and also consists of segments.

Head

The head is the anterior capsulelike structure that bears the eyes, antennae, and mouthparts. Head shape varies considerably in relation to how the insect feeds. Insects with chewing mouthparts normally have large heavy heads that are directed downward or forward. Insects with piercing–sucking mouthparts have small heads that are quite variable in appearance and position.

Eyes

Most adult insects and many nymphs have a pair of compound eyes and three ocelli (simple eyes). The compound eyes are complex and variable. Generally, they are large and located dorsolaterally (at the top and to the

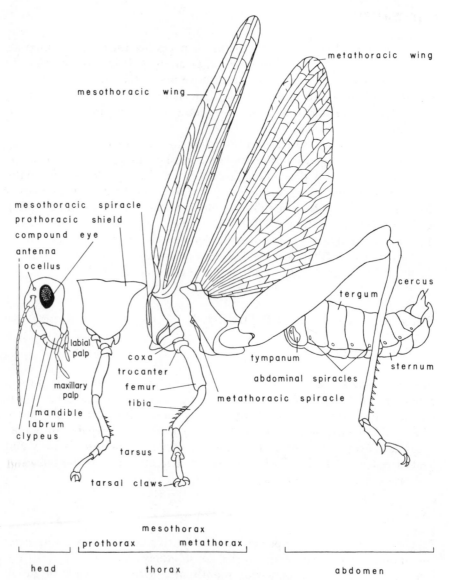

metathoracic wing

mesothoracic wing

mesothoracic spiracle
prothoracic shield
compound eye
antenna
ocellus

cercus

tergum

labial
palp

coxa
trocanter
femur
tibia

maxillary
palp

tympanum

abdominal spiracles

metathoracic spiracle

sternum

mandible
labrum
clypeus

tarsus

tarsal claws

mesothorax
prothorax   metathorax

head   thorax   abdomen

Figure 2.1 Generalized insect model (Orthoptera, grasshopper).

side) on the head. Each compound eye is composed of individual sensory units called *ommatidia*. The number of ommatidia varies from one in some ants to 30,000 or more in some flies, beetles, and dragonflies. Each ommatidium contains a lens and sense cells. An individual ommatidium can perceive only a small portion of the environment. However, the combined images of all ommatidia give a mosaic view of the insect's environment. This system can perceive movement faster than the human eye.

Most adult insects and nymphs have simple eyes, called *ocelli*, located on the dorsal portion of the head. The number of ocelli per insect varies from zero to three. The function of the ocelli is not fully understood. They are not important as image formers but are light sensitive and act as "stimulatory organs" in reaction to major changes in illumination.

Another visual organ is the *stemma*. It is present only in larvae with complete metamorphosis. Stemmata are normally found in single groups of one to six on both sides of the head. The structure and function of the stemmata are between that of the light-sensitive dorsal ocelli and image forming ommatidia. Larvae with stemmata have weak form perception, but side-to-side head movement allows more detailed perception.

Antennae

All insects except Protura possess a pair of antennae located on the anterior portion of the head near the compound eyes. However, antennae are greatly reduced in some insects (e.g., larval forms). The primary function of the antennae is sensory. Various types of small hairs (sensilla) located on the antennae act as tactile, odor, temperature, humidity, and sound receptors. Antennae often play an important part in the mating process of many insects. For example, the comblike antennae of a male moth perceives the odor (pheromone) of a female moth of the same species. Sexual dimorphism of antennae is common, with the male antennae often more complex than the female.

Antennae are commonly used as a taxonomic characteristic in identifying insects because of the distinctive variations in their size and shape. The most common antennae types are illustrated in Figure 2.2.

Mouthparts

A basic understanding of the mouthpart types is important because it indicates the type of feeding and damage caused by insects in the environment. It is also extremely important to recognize mouthpart types since they vary considerably and are always used in classifying insects. Mouthparts are generally divided into two major types: chewing and piercing–sucking.

Chewing Mouthparts

There is considerable similarity in mouthpart structure between insects with chewing mouthparts and closely related arthropods such as centipedes and symphylids. Chewing mouthparts occur in the generalized, more primitive insect orders such as Orthoptera and Thysanura. It is generally accepted that all other types of insect mouthparts evolved from the chewing mouthparts. Grasshoppers and lepidopterous larvae are common examples of insects with chewing mouthparts. Chewing mouthparts are normally recognized by the heavily sclerotized mandibles that move laterally. Insects with chewing mouthparts bite and chew their food.

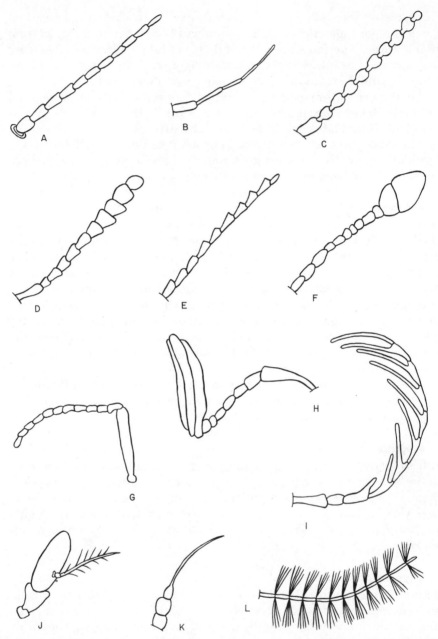

Figure 2.2 Types of antennae: (A) filiform, (B) setaceous, (C) moniliform, (D) clavate, (E) serrate, (F) capitate, (G) geniculate, (H) lamellate, (I) pectinate, (J) aristate, (K) stylate, (L) plumose.

Chewing mouthparts (Figure 2.3) generally consist of labrum, mandibles, maxillae, labium, and hypopharynx. The *labrum,* often called upper lip, covers the mandibles, closes the mouth in front, and helps to pull food into the mouth. *Mandibles* are the first pair of jaws located directly behind the labrum and vary considerably in size by species. A single mandible is pyramidal in shape and usually almost solidly sclerotized cuticle with teeth. The mandibles move from side to side while performing the major function of chewing, cutting, and grinding food. *Maxillae* are the segmented, second pair of jaws located directly behind the mandibles. Each maxilla bears a feelerlike organ called the *maxillary palp.* The maxillary palp, which functions as a sense organ, is antennalike in shape, with five or six segments. Great variation in structure of the maxillary palp and the terminal lobes (galea, lacinia) causes much of the variation in the maxillae. The maxillae

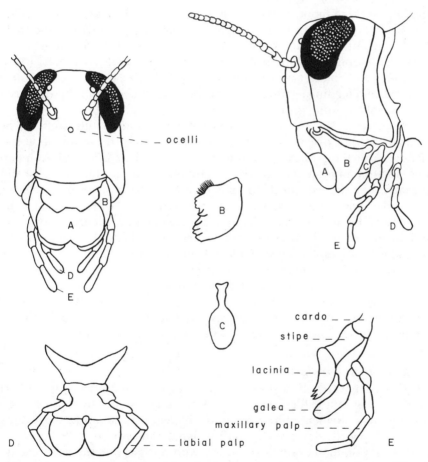

Figure 2.3 Grasshopper head showing chewing mouthparts: (A) labrum, (B) mandible, (C) hypopharynx, (D) labium, (E) maxillae.

move from side to side while holding, manipulating, pushing, and tasting the food being eaten. A single structure called the *labium*, lower lip, lies behind the maxillae. The primary function of the labium is to close the mouth from below or behind; this pushes the food into the esophagus. The *hypopharynx* is a tonguelike structure located in front of or above the labium.

Insects with chewing mouthparts are normally recognized by the mandibles and by the absence of a beak. Weevils and scorpionflies are two major exceptions. The front part of the head of a weevil is prolonged into a snout, but tiny laterally moving mandibles occur at the tip of the snout. The head of the scorpionfly is prolonged ventrally into a beaklike structure, also with laterally moving mandibles.

Piercing–Sucking Mouthparts

Piercing–sucking mouthparts usually appear as a rodlike beak, often called a *proboscis* (Figure 2.4) and are adapted for piercing plant tissues and sucking the sap. Insects with piercing–sucking mouthparts are found in orders such as Homoptera (aphids, scales), Hemiptera (true bugs), Anoplura (sucking lice), and Diptera (some of the true flies). The exact shape, structures involved, and feeding techniques of the piercing–sucking mouthparts varies considerably in some groups.

The piercing–sucking mouthparts of Hemiptera and Homoptera will be used for further discussion [see Borror et al. (1981) for additional information on piercing–sucking mouthparts]. The rodlike beak of Hemiptera and Homoptera is an enlarged labium that has become elongated, sheathlike, and tube shaped. Inside this labium are two pairs of slender, delicate, needlelike stylets, the *mandibular* and *maxillary stylets*. During feeding the outer pair, the mandibular stylets, cut a small opening into the plant tissue and the inner pair, the maxillary stylets, are inserted into the opening. This alternating process, of cutting plant tissue followed by insertion of the maxillary stylets, continues until the insect reaches suitable sap-containing tissues. The maxillary stylets interlock and form a *salivary channel* and a *food channel*. During feeding, saliva is pumped into the plant tissues through the salivary channel. This saliva helps facilitate the extraction of sap from the plant tissue. The sap is ingested through the food channel.

Variations in Mouthparts

Mouthparts have evolved over time and some are modified (Figure 2.4) for siphoning (butterflies, some moths), sponging (house fly) or chewing–lapping (many hymenopterous insects). Some insects do not feed as adults and have poorly developed, nonfunctional mouthparts called *vestigial mouthparts*. Common examples of insects with vestigial mouthparts are mayflies, most caddisflies, and many moths.

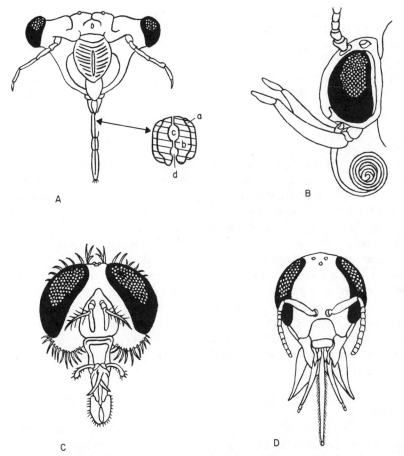

Figure 2.4 Insect mouthparts: (A) piercing–sucking mouthparts of cicada—front view of head showing beak; diagrammatic view of cross section through stylets—a = mandible, b = maxillae, c = food channel, d = salivary channel; (B) siphoning mouthparts (peach tree borer); (C) sponging mouthparts (house fly); (D) chewing–sucking mouthparts (honeybee). (Redrawn with slight modifications: A and B from Snodgrass 1935; C and D from Metcalf et al. 1962.)

Thorax

The thorax is the middle body region of an insect and is usually composed of three segments: *prothorax* (first anterior segment), *mesothorax* (middle segment), and *metathorax* (last segment). Each thoracic segment normally bears a pair of legs. Most insects have a pair of wings attached to the mesothorax and a second pair attached to the metathorax. Two *spiracles*, external slitlike openings of the respiratory system, are present on each side of the thorax. One is located between the prothorax and mesothorax;

the other is situated between the mesothorax and metathorax. The chief function of the thorax is locomotion.

Each thoracic segment consists of four major groups of sclerites: *notum* (dorsal), *sternum* (ventral), and a pair of lateral *pleura* (sing., pleuron). Each group is often divided into two or more sclerites. A specific sclerite is indicated by attaching the proper prefixes (i.e., pro, meso, meta). In other words, the pronotum refers to the top sclerite on the prothorax.

Legs

The walking leg is the generalized leg from which all other types evolved. It consists of (Figure 2.5) a *coxa* (basal segment), *trochanter* (small segment, rarely two segments, distal to the coxa), *femur* (first long leg segment), *tibia* (second long leg segment), *tarsus* (one to five small segments beyond tibia), and *pretarsus* (last leg segment, normally consists of a pair of claws and one or more padlike structures). Insects have legs adapted for jumping, grasping, swimming, and digging (Figure 2.5). Leg characteristics are often used in insect identification owing to the great variations in leg size, shape, number of tarsal segments, and the number, shape, and location of spines.

Immature insects may have legs as just described, may be legless, or may have jointed thoracic legs and fleshy, unjointed abdominal appendages called *prolegs*. The tips of the prolegs in lepidopterous caterpillars contain hooked spines (*crochets*, pronounced croshays) that help the caterpillar attach itself to silk.

Wings

Most adult insects have two pairs of membranous wings located dorsolaterally on the mesothorax and metathorax. Wings are often used in identifying insects because they vary in number, size, shape, texture, venation, and position held while at rest. Some, such as true flies, have only one pair of wings that arise from the mesothorax while others such as springtails and fleas are wingless. Springtails and silverfish never developed wings, whereas fleas and bird lice had ancestors that were winged but evolved into wingless forms.

Insect wings are unique because they evolved as skeletal outgrowths (projections) from the insect's body wall instead of from appendages such as vertebrates. The adult wings are solid structures except for the veins that are hollow structures containing tracheae, blood, and nerves. The wings are powered primarily by muscular contractions and expansions of the thorax. The muscles that move the wings are primarily attached to sclerites in the body wall of the thorax instead of attached directly to the wings like birds.

The major function of wings is flight, but the front wings of some insects such as beetles have evolved into thickened, hard, horny wings called *elytra* (singular, *elytron*) that act as protective armor. In the true bugs, order

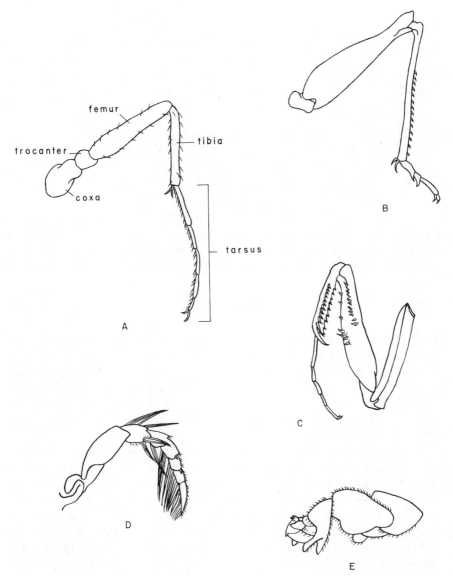

Figure 2.5 Modification of insect legs: (A) walking, (B) jumping, (C) grasping, (D) swimming, (E) digging.

Hemiptera, the apical portion of the front wing is thickened and the distal portion membranous; this is called a *hemelytron* (plural, *hemelytra*) wing.

Wing venation is an important taxonomic characteristic because of the great variation in insect wings. A widely used terminology for naming veins has been developed. See Borror et al. (1981) for a complete description of wing venation. The generalized wing venation is illustrated in Figure 2.6.

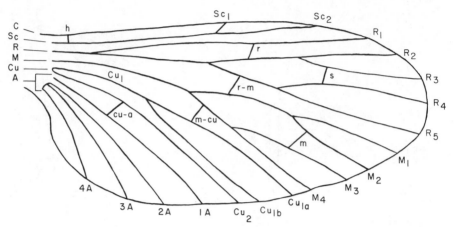

Figure 2.6 Generalized wing venation: longitudinal veins—costa (C), subcosta (Sc), radius (R), media (M), cubitus (Cu), anal (A); cross veins—humeral (h), radial (r), sectorial (s), radiomedial (r-m), medial (m), mediocubital (m-cu), cubitoanal (cu-a). (Redrawn from Borror et al. 1981.)

Abdomen

The abdomen is the posterior body region of an insect. The generalized insect abdomen consists of 11 rather uniform segments with the last segment forming appendages. Many insects have eight or fewer distinct abdominal segments owing to the fusing or telescoping of some segments. Each abdominal segment consists of a top sclerite (*tergum*) and a bottom sclerite (*sternum*). A pair of spiracles is usually present on each side of the first eight abdominal segments.

Abdominal appendages are absent from most insects except for structures located at the posterior end of the abdomen. Major exceptions are (1) *gills* on the abdominal segments of mayfly immatures, (2) simple abdominal appendages called *styli* found on thysanurans, (3) abdominal appendages (*collophore, furcula,* and *tenaculum*) of springtails, and (4) *prolegs* present on lepidopterous caterpillars and some sawfly caterpillars.

Many insects have a number of structures such as cerci, epiproct, paraprocts, and genitalia at the posterior end of the abdomen. These perform copulative, respiratory, or defensive functions and probably other unknown functions. *Cerci* are a pair of clasperlike (e.g., earwigs) or feelerlike (e.g., stonefly immatures) structures arising from the dorsal side of the last abdominal segment of certain insects. The *epiproct* is an appendage or process rising directly above the anus. It may be filamentous (e.g., the media caudal filament of mayflies), clasperlike (e.g., male dragonflies) or inconspicuous. The *paraproct* varies in shape and arises lateroventrally (to the side) from the anus. It may consist of rounded lobes (e.g., dragonflies) or as many leaflike structures (e.g., lateral gills of damselfly immatures).

Genitalia provide valuable taxonomic characteristics for many insect groups, especially at the species level. In many insect species, the sex can be distinguished by external genital structures. The male genitalia are extremely complex, with more variation at the species level than any other insect structure. The female *ovipositor*, which is the egg-laying organ, is also external in many species and varies in size and shape. The sex may be determined easily in some insects with internal genitalia by using other taxonomic characters such as size or color markings. It is impossible to sex some individuals, such as weevils, without dissecting them.

Exoskeleton

The exoskeleton (also called *integument*) is the hard, outer covering of insects and other arthropods. It is the insects' counterpart to the endoskeleton of humans and other vertebrates. The exoskeleton is composed of three major layers: cuticle, epidermis, and basement membrane (Figure 2.7). The *cuticle* is the noncellular outer layer of the integument, which comprises three layers: (1) *epicuticle*—a very thin layer that contains waxes and oils and acts as a "waterproofing" layer, (2) *exocuticle*—the second layer, which varies in thickness but adds hardness and strength to the cuticle, and (3) *endocuticle*—the third layer, which is comparatively thick and adds strength and flexibility to the cuticle. The *epidermis* is the living layer that produces all other layers, whereas the *basement membrane* is a lining that separates the exoskeleton from the rest of the insect.

The major functions of the exoskeleton are (1) a shield for the internal

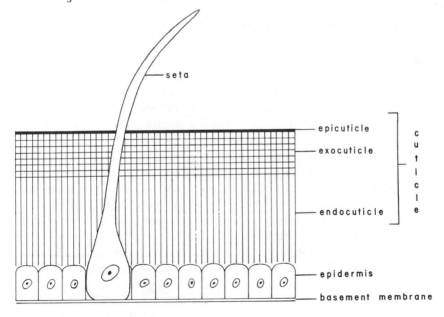

Figure 2.7 Diagrammatic view of insect exoskeleton.

organs against external mechanical injury, pathogens, insecticides, and a barrier which greatly retards water movement into and out of the insect's body; (2) a framework for muscle attachment; and (3) a surface for the sensory receptor system that keeps the insect in contact with the environment. Major disadvantages of the exoskeleton are (1) it restricts the organism to a small size, (2) it must be shed in order for the insect to grow, and (3) the insect is quite vulnerable when it is molting from one stage to the next.

The major constituents of cuticle are chitin, structural proteins, and pigments. Chitin contributes 25–50% of the dry weight of the exocuticle and endocuticle; it is not present in the epicuticle. The hardness of the cuticle is caused by the interaction of the protein sclerotin with tanning agents. The process of hardening is called *sclerotization*. The surface of the exoskeleton is composed of a number of hardened plates called *sclerites*. These sclerites are separated from each other by means of soft membranous areas or by sutures, which are external linelike grooves. This covering of hardened plates and membranous areas allows the insect to move its body and appendages.

There are a number of external and internal projections of the exoskeleton. Common external projections are setae (also called *bristles* or *hairs*), spines, horns, and warts. The internal projections, called *apodemes*, are spinelike or ridgelike; they function as places for muscle attachment and also add strength to the exoskeleton.

INTERNAL STRUCTURE AND FUNCTION

Digestive System

Diverse and unique feeding habits of many insects have led to enormous variation in their digestive systems. Digestion and absorption of food occurs in the alimentary canal. The generalized alimentary canal of insects with chewing mouthparts is illustrated in Figure 2.8. The somewhat coiled *alimentary canal* extends from the mouth to the anus and is divided into three distinct regions: *foregut, midgut,* and *hindgut.* Food is gathered and prepared for digestion by the mouthparts and then passed into the alimentary canal. The foregut is divided into the pharynx, esophagus, crop, proventriculus, and foregut valve. The foregut is primarily a storage organ, but a limited amount of grinding, mixing, and digestion also occur. The midgut is composed of the gastric caeca and the ventriculus (stomach). Gastric caeca, which are fingerlike outgrowths located in the anterior portion of the midgut, produce digestive juices. The rest of the midgut consists of the ventriculus, an elongated uniform sac that digests and absorbs food. The hindgut is divided into the Malpighian tubules, small and large intestine, and rectum. *Malpighian tubules* are long slender excretory tubes that orig-

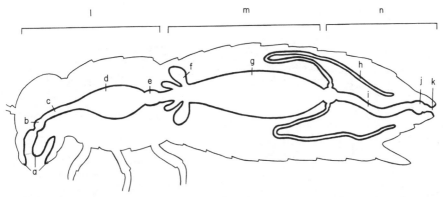

Figure 2.8 Diagrammatic view of the insect's digestive system: a = mouthparts, b = pharynx, c = esophagus, d = crop, e = proventriculus, f = gastric ceca, g = stomach (ventriculus), h = Malpighian tubules, i = large intestine, j = small intestine, k = rectum, l = foregut, m = midgut, n = hindgut.

inate at the hindgut and branch out in many directions from the alimentary canal. The *small* and *large intestines* digest and absorb food that passed from the midgut. The *rectum* is an enlarged sac that accumulates and compresses undigested food that is then excreted through the anus. Insect droppings are called *frass*. The rectum also serves an important function in reabsorbing water, amino acids, and salt. Microorganisms are present in the digestive system of all insects. Those in the hindgut of termites and some cockroaches are extremely important for the digestion of cellulose.

Circulatory System

The circulatory system in insects is an open system while the circulatory system of human beings and other vertebrates is completely closed. In human beings, blood travels only through special vessels such as arteries, capillaries, and veins. The *dorsal vessel,* consisting of the *heart* and *dorsal aorta,* is the only blood vessel in insects (Figure 2.9). Blood enters the heart through slitlike openings and is pumped forward through the dorsal aorta to the head by peristaltic movements of the heart. From the anterior portion of the head, the blood moves freely and slowly through the head, thorax, and abdomen irrigating and nourishing all body tissues. The principal function of insect blood is to transport food, waste products, and hormones from one part of the body to another. Other functions of the blood are (1) lubrication of internal structures; (2) to act as a hydraulic medium (e.g., expansion of wings of emerging adult insects is accomplished in part by forcing blood into the wings); (3) protection through phagocytosis (blood cells ingest small foreign material), encapsulation (blood cells actually surround foreign object), coagulation, or wound healing; and (4) to serve as a simple storehouse for metabolic waste products in many small insects.

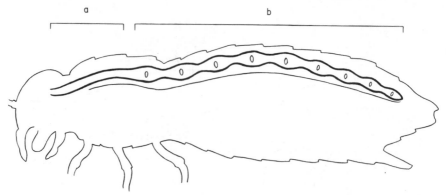

Figure 2.9 Diagrammatic view of the insect's circulatory system: a = dorsal aorta, b = heart.

A *fat body* is an aggregation of cells variously distributed within the insect's blood depending on the species. Fat body cells function as a food storage reservoir for materials such as fat and protein and as an important site of intermediate metabolism. Large food reserves accumulate in fat body cells during the late nymphal or larval instars, especially in insects with complete metamorphosis. These materials provide nutrients and raw materials during the nonfeeding pupal stage. Some insects, which do not feed as adults, retain their fat body cells in the adult stage and obtain nutrients from these fat bodies.

Respiratory System

The intake of oxygen, its transportation to the tissues, and the removal of carbon dioxide are accomplished in most insects by spiracles and tracheae (Figure 2.10). This system is also called the *breathing system, tracheal system,* or *ventilatory system* by some entomologists. The *spiracles* are external open-

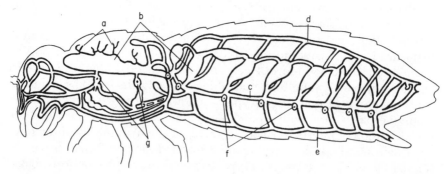

Figure 2.10 Diagrammatic view of the insect's respiratory system: a = tracheole, b = air sac, c = lateral tracheal trunk, d = dorsal tracheal trunk, e = ventral tracheal trunk, f = abdominal spiracles, g = thoracic spiracles. (Redrawn from Romoser 1973. Reprinted with permission from Macmillan Publishing Company, from *The Science of Entomology* by W. S. Romoser. © 1973 by W. S. Romoser.)

ings of the respiratory system. A typical insect has a pair on the meso- and metathorax and a pair on the first eight abdominal segments. The spiracles on each side of an insect are connected to a *trachea* (air tube) that lies longitudinally just inside the exoskeleton.

From the two major tracheal trunks, additional tracheae branch in many directions becoming smaller and more numerous until all tissues in the body of the insect are reached. The very fine terminal branches of the tracheae are called *tracheoles*. Lateral tracheae in some insects are dilated in places to form large air sacs. *Air sacs* serve as air storage pockets to aid in respiration.

Excretory System

The major excretory organs for most insects are the *Malpighian tubules.* Metabolic waste materials, primarily sodium and potassium salts of uric acid, are absorbed from the blood by these tubules, transported, and then passed out through the hindgut and anus. The major function of the excretory system is to maintain a constant internal environment by eliminating waste materials from the blood and by regulating the salt and water balance.

Nervous System

The generalized central nervous system (Figure 2.11) of insects consists of a *brain,* located dorsally in the head, a pair of *connectives* passing around the alimentary canal, and ventrally placed *ganglia* that are interconnected to form the ventral nerve cord. Nerves extend from the brain and ventral nerve cord to various body parts. Nerves conduct information from sense

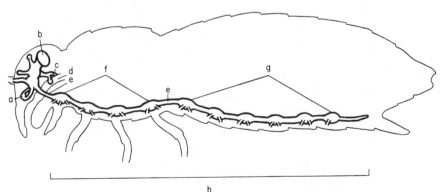

Figure 2.11   Diagrammatic view of the insect's central nervous system: a = frontal ganglion, b = brain, c = hypocerebral ganglion, d = alimentary canal, e = connective, f = thoracic ganglia, g = abdominal ganglia, h = ventral nerve cord. (Redrawn with slight modifications from Romoser 1973. Reprinted with permission from Macmillan Publishing Company, from *The Science of Entomology* by W. S. Romoser. © 1973 by W. S. Romoser.)

organs located on the exoskeleton to the ganglia that generate the motor impulses that flow to the appropriate muscles. These sense organs are extremely sophisticated and usually are excited by only one specific type of stimuli such as mechanical, chemical, auditory, or visual. Chapter 6 of Romoser (1981) gives detailed information on the various types of sense organs.

Reproductive System

Most insects reproduce bisexually, but some insects reproduce by *parthenogenesis* in which the egg develops without fertilization. The generalized male reproductive system (Figure 2.12) is located at the posterior end of the abdomen and usually consists of a pair of *testes,* a number of tubes, and *accessory glands.* The functions of the male system are production, storage, and delivery of the sperm. The generalized female reproductive system (Figure 2.12) is also located at the posterior end of the abdomen and usually consists of a pair of *ovaries,* a number of *tubes,* and the *vagina.* The female reproductive system functions in the production of eggs, storage of eggs and sperm, as the fertilization site, and in the oviposition of the fertilized egg. There are considerable differences in the reproductive system of some insects. Davey (1965) and Romoser (1981) provide detailed information on the reproductive systems of insects.

Endocrine System

The nervous system and endocrine system coordinate the activities of various organs of the insect. As previously described, the nervous system of the insect is mainly involved with rapid adjustments to environmental change

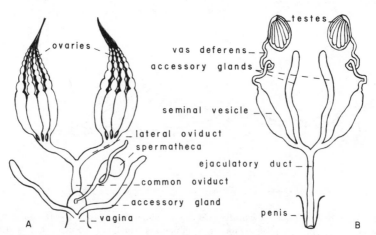

Figure 2.12 Diagrammatic view of the insect's reproductive system: (A) female insect, (B) male insect. (Redrawn with slight modifications from Snodgrass 1935.)

while the endocrine system regulates slower and longer-lasting processes such as growth, development, and reproduction. The endocrine system contains various glands that produce and secrete hormones or pheromones.

Hormones

A basic understanding of insect hormones is important because one hormone, the juvenile hormone, may be a potential tool in insect pest management. Hormones are chemical substances secreted into the blood of an insect from a specific organ. These hormones are transported by the blood into all body regions of an insect; they influence or activate other specific organs or physiological processes.

A brief description of the processes regulating the growth and development of insects is presented by summarizing material from Gilbert (1976), Wigglesworth (1970), and Slama et al. (1974). Three hormones (i.e., *brain hormone, molting hormone,* and the *juvenile hormone*) control the growth and development of insects (Figure 2.13). *Neurosecretory cells* in the insect brain secrete brain hormone that accumulates in the *corpus cardiaca*. When released into the blood, the *brain hormone* activates the *prothoracic glands,* which then secrete the molting hormone called *ecdysone*. Ecdysone initiates growth, development, and molting in an insect. The *corpora allata* secretes the *juvenile hormone* (JH), which works along with ecdysone to regulate the proper growth and development of an insect. The major function of ecdysone is

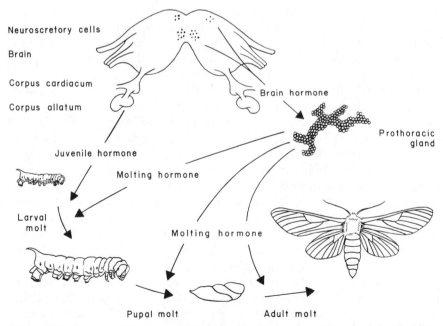

Figure 2.13   Diagram of the hormonal control of molting and metamorphosis in a lepidopterous insect, showing the principal endocrine organs and hormones.

to periodically predispose molting, whereas JH mainly determines the type of molt. A nymphal or larval molt occurs if the concentration of JH in the blood is high. However, when JH levels in the blood are low or absent, insects with no, incomplete, or gradual metamorphosis molt to the adult stage and insects with complete metamorphosis molt to the pupal stage and then to the adult stage. Besides influencing the type of molt, JH also regulates the type of insect diapause and is essential for various reproductive processes (e.g., ovarian development, yolk formation in the egg, maturation of eggs in female).

Pheromones

Pheromones are chemical substances secreted into the environment by one individual that influence the behavior of other individuals of the same species. Pheromones are involved with many behavioral functions such as sexual behavior, oviposition, alarm and defense roles, assembling and formation of aggregations, and trail marking and other types of communication within social insects. Sex pheromones are briefly covered below and aggregation pheromones are discussed in the section on bark beetles in Chapter 15.

Sex pheromones are usually produced in specialized glands by one sex of a species and emitted to elicit a behavioral response from the opposite sex for mating purposes. They are biologically active in very small quantities (as low as 10^{-14} mg) and may consist of a single compound or a mixture of compounds. Sex pheromones can be released by the female, male, or by both the female and male, and varies by species. However, sex pheromones produced by the female generally act as sex attractants, whereas those produced by males usually function as aphrodisiacs. These sex pheromones are generally very species specific.

The females of most species in the orders Lepidoptera and Coleoptera emit the sex pheromone. Release of the sex pheromone is a complex process involving the sexual maturity and age of the virgin female, time of day of the mating period, photoperiod, temperature, air velocity, and light intensity. Shorey (1973) described the sequence of behavioral steps that occurs when the female in many species of lepidopterous and coleopterous insects releases the sex pheromone. These are (1) activation of a resting male of the same species; (2) orientation of male toward the pheromone source; and (3) various short-range behavioral relationships, often called *courtship*, which stimulate the female to mate. The female's sex pheromone is normally produced in glands located on the abdomen, released by the female into the air, and transported by wind currents to a prospective mate. A male downwind from the female perceives the odor with chemoreceptors on his antennae, becomes active, and then flies in a zigzag pattern against the direction of the wind toward the pheromone source. This flying pattern occurs because the male turns left and right to remain in the odor gradient. The male stops its forward flight pattern and uses other senses such as sight to locate the female as he reaches the area of high pheromone concentration close to the female. Courtship and mating are normally governed by short-range communication signals such as visual, tactile, or auditory mechanisms along with or without the long-range sex pheromone communication signals. Birch (1974) and Mitchell (1981) present detailed information on insect pheromone systems and pest management programs utilizing pheromones as a survey or control technique.

INSECT GROWTH AND DEVELOPMENT

Egg

The form of the egg(s) and favorable oviposition sites can vary considerably from one insect species to another. Certain insects lay their eggs singly, whereas others such as many tussock moths, tent caterpillars, and preying mantids lay egg masses that contain hundreds of eggs. Many weevils, sawflies, and bark beetles deposit their eggs within plant tissues. May beetles and grasshoppers lay their eggs in the ground. Aquatic insects normally deposit their eggs in the water, but the eggs are often attached to some type of substrate. Parasitic insects, such as ichneumon wasps and some tachinid flies, normally lay their eggs in or on suitable hosts, whereas other tachinid flies attach their eggs to foliage normally consumed by their host. Females of most insect species lay eggs, but those of flesh flies and many aphids give birth to live immatures.

The majority of species reproduce male and female individuals by the fertilization of the eggs in an adult female by one or more adult males. This is bisexual reproduction. Individuals of some species develop from unfertilized eggs. This is parthenogenetic reproduction. The unfertilized eggs from one adult female may produce entirely male or female offspring or young of both sexes. Many parasitic wasps produce all males from unfertilized eggs and all females from fertilized eggs. Certain aphids, weevils, and sawflies with exclusively female populations always reproduce parthenogenetically. The selective advantage of parthenogenesis is that offspring can be produced immediately when environmental conditions are favorable for the growth and development of the immature stage. However, the offspring are genetically identical to the parent and less capable of change. Certain species of aphids have the advantages of both types of reproduction by alternating generations of fertilized and nonfertilized offspring.

Growth

After hatching, the small immature insects feed and grow in size within the limitations of the exoskeleton. The exoskeleton is a hardened, relatively inelastic, nonliving tissue that does not grow. The immature insect sheds the obstructive exoskeleton and develops another exoskeleton that allows the insect to increase in size. This process is called *molting*. Most insects molt four to eight times.

Each stage between molts is called an *instar*.* For instance, the first instar is between hatching and the first molt, the second instar is between the first and second molt, and so on. Instar numbers vary by species but are usually the same within species. Temperature, humidity, quality and quantity of food, population density, and sex can affect the number of instars. Leonard (1970) showed that the gypsy moth male and female normally have six or seven instars, respectively, but crowding and starvation can cause the number of instars to vary from five to nine. Most insect species do not molt after reaching the adult stage.

Metamorphosis

There are significant changes in the size, form, and habitat between the immature and adult stages of most insects. The term "metamorphosis" refers to change in form during development. Some groups of insects do not undergo metamorphosis. Other groups develop through incomplete, gradual, or complete metamorphosis. These four types of metamorphosis are not accepted by all entomologists. A number of authors refer to only two types: simple (covering the first three types) and complete metamorphosis.

No Metamorphosis

"No metamorphosis" includes the species in which there is no or very little change in the form of the individual after hatching. Springtails, thysanurans, proturans, and diplurans are examples. These insects lack wings and wingpads. Most are small and found in soil or organic debris. Less than 1% of all described insect species have no metamorphosis.

Incomplete Metamorphosis

Insects with incomplete metamorphosis emerge from the egg as immature naiads that develop into adults. Some entomologists use the term "nymph" for all immatures with incomplete or gradual metamorphosis. *Naiads* are aquatic and have gills. The naiads differ considerably from the adults, which are aerial insects without gills. The mayflies, dragonflies, damselflies, and stoneflies are examples of insect species with incomplete metamorphosis. Less than 1% of all described insect species are in this category.

Gradual Metamorphosis

Insects with gradual metamorphosis are primarily terrestrial. The immature nymphs and adults occupy the same habitats and feed on the same

---

*We are using the terms "instar" and "stage" as synonyms [see Jones (1978)].

food. There is a gradual change in size and body proportions and a gradual development of wings and genital structures from one molt to the next. Grasshoppers, termites, psocids, chewing and sucking lice, thrips, true bugs, aphids, and scales are examples of insect species that undergo this type of development. Less than 10% of all described insect species have gradual metamorphosis.

Complete Metamorphosis

Complete metamorphosis occurs in the more advanced orders of insects. Insects with complete metamorphosis develop from an egg to larva, from larva to pupa, and finally from pupa to an adult. All real growth and development results from larval feeding. The pupal stage is a nonfeeding, transformation stage. The adults feed, reproduce, and disperse in the environment.

In some species with complete metamorphosis, the adults feed on the same host as the larvae, others feed on different hosts, and some survive on nutrients stored in the fat body during the larval stage. Complete metamorphosis reduces the competition for food between larvae and adults of some species because habitats favorable to the larval stage of development may not be suitable for the adult stage, and vice versa. For example, May beetle larvae are found in the soil and feed on the roots of many different kinds of plants. These insects pupate in the soil. The adults feed on tree leaves to maintain a reasonably static metabolism and also to provide additional food for maturation of eggs or sperm. The adult May beetles mate and disperse, and the females lay eggs.

ADAPTIVE FEATURES OF INSECTS

Insects are the most numerous organisms in the animal kingdom. They often occur in large numbers and are found in almost all conceivable habitats. Some of the most important adaptive features of insects are (1) exoskeleton, (2) complete metamorphosis, (3) functional wings, (4) small size, (5) adaptability of structures, (6) diverse feeding habits, (7) quiescence and diapause, (8) dispersal and migration, (9) high reproductive potential, and (10) defensive mechanisms to avoid natural enemies. The adaptive features of the exoskeleton and complete metamorphosis have already been discussed. Brief presentations of the other adaptive features follow.

Functional Wings

The adaptive value of functional wings is a major factor contributing to the dominance of insects in so many diverse habitats. Flight generally increases the insect's chances of survival and dispersal. It allows the insect to increase its feeding and breeding ranges and to leave habitats that become unsuitable and provides an important mechanism for eluding natural enemies.

Small Size

The exoskeleton limits the size of insects. Insects must molt to grow and the exoskeleton is quite soft immediately after molting. Terrestrial insects maintain their shape during and immediately after molting by the strength of the soft tissues and/or by inflation of air spaces in some larger insects. These techniques are suitable for small organisms, but larger organisms would collapse during the molting process.

Most insects are less than 50 mm in total length, and a majority are under 5 mm. Small size permits shorter life cycles because less time is required to reach maturity. The small size of insects has allowed them to feed on many additional types of food and also increased the number of available habitats and shelters. In many cases, these food sources and habitats may be small and scattered. Availability of many small, scattered habitats increases the chances of the individual escaping from its natural enemies. The major disadvantage of small size is the significant increase in proportion of total body surface to the body volume, which might seem to make terrestrial life impossible for thin-skinned animals because of the high evaporation quotient. However, the exoskeleton helps to retard desiccation.

Adaptability of Structures

During the evolution of the insects, many structures have become adapted for different functions and habitats. Modification of mouthparts, antennae, legs, wings, and respiratory systems are important examples of adaptability of structures. These have been discussed earlier in this chapter.

Diverse Feeding Habits

Modified mouthparts have evolved in insects that prepare them for survival on diverse food substances. The diverse feeding habits of insects are often used to group them under general terms such as "herbivores," "phytophagous feeders," "scavengers," "omnivores," "predators," and "parasites." These terms are used to describe other animals also. A *herbivore* and a *phytophagous feeder* are animals that feed on plants. A *scavenger* is an animal that feeds on dead plants or animals, decaying vegetation, or animal excrement. The term *"omnivore"* refers to an animal that feeds on two or more types of food, including animal and plant material. *Predators* attack and feed on other animals, usually killing them quickly. A *parasite* is an organism that lives a part of its life cycle on or in the body of another living organism. Specialized terms relating to the feeding habits of forest and ornamental insects, such as "leaf mining," "phloem boring," and "wood boring," will be described in Chapter 4.

Quiescence and Diapause

Many insects survive adverse conditions, such as periods of low or high temperature and water or food shortages, by entering dormancy. Quiescence is the simplest type of dormancy. It is simply a temporary response to immediate adverse conditions (i.e., low temperatures). The insect continues development as soon as favorable conditions (i.e., warm temperatures) resume. Diapause is arrested development induced by certain factors in advance of adverse conditions; the arrested development persists for some time after the adverse conditions pass. There are two types of diapause: obligatory and facultative. *Obligatory diapause* is genetically controlled and affects every individual of every generation within a species regardless of environmental conditions. Insects with one generation per year and most insects living in temperate regions have developed obligatory diapause. *Facultative diapause* may or may not occur within a given individual or population of a species and depends entirely on the environmental conditions prevailing during critical stages of development. For example, many aphids have cycles with several continuous parthenogenetic generations, followed by a sexual generation, and an overwintering diapausing egg stage induced by temperature and photoperiod conditions.

The most common factors inducing diapause in insects are photoperiod, temperature, maternal physiology, and the quality of host food. Diapause is normally terminated by temperature, humidity, and photoperiod. Although insect diapause occurs in all stages of development, each species has one characteristic diapause stage, and most species enter diapause in the egg or pupa stage. Diapause has allowed insects to live in areas that are unsuitable for them during certain periods of the year. Diapause is adaptive in the sense that (1) it ensures that active stages are present only during periods most favorable for development and survival, (2) it synchronizes the life cycles with the seasonal rhythms of the environment, (3) it synchronizes adult emergence, which in turn increases the chance of finding a mate, and (4) it increases the geographic distribution (Andrewartha and Birch 1954).

Dispersal and Migration

Random or directed movements of insects vary by species. Mobility is important to the establishment and survival of forest and shade tree insects in new environments. Insect movements can be divided into three categories: spread, dispersal, and migration (Clark et al. 1967). *Spread* is local movements within a favorable area. *Dispersal* is movement of individuals away from a normally favorable area to other areas that may or may not be favorable for survival. *Migration* is a directed movement from one favorable area to another favorable area. Movement is a regular and adaptive part of the biology of most individuals within an individual species. All insects move by spread and dispersal sometime during their life cycle, but migration occurs in fewer insect species. Many examples of insect spread and dispersal are presented in this text (e.g., bagworms, hairy caterpillars, aphids, scales). Some examples of insects that migrate are the monarch butterfly, *Danaus plexippus* (Linnaeus), desert locusts, female mosquito; and convergent lady beetle, *Hippodamia convergens* Guérin-Méneville. The migration of the convergent lady beetle is described below. During May and June the young adults of the convergent lady beetle migrate from their feeding sites in the Central Valley of California to overwintering sites in the Sierra Nevada mountains. The beetles return the following February and March to reproduction and feeding sites in the Central Valley. The major adaptive features of insect dispersal and migration are (1) a mechanism for escape from environments that become unfavorable, (2) dispersal into other habitats, and (3) colonization of favorable habitats (Johnson 1969, Dingle 1972).

High Reproductive Potential

The reproductive potential of insects depends on (1) fertility, which is number of eggs laid by the female, (2) length of life cycle, and (3) sex ratio. A high reproductive potential alone does not lead to large populations of the species, but only indicates the potential rate of increase when environmental conditions are favorable for the species. Under favorable environmental conditions, one or more of the above factors can result in large numbers of individuals of one species. The time required to complete one generation varies considerably with insects. Most insects in the United States and Canada produce one generation per year. Some of the larger beetles, dragonflies, and moths in the northern part of the United States and in Canada may require 2–3 years to complete their life cycles. Periodical cicadas require 13–17 years to complete their life cycle depending on the location. Other insects such as many bark beetles in the southern regions of the United States may produce six to eight generations per year. Certain insects such as fruit flies, some stored product insects, and house flies may complete their life cycle in less than 2 weeks and produce up to 25 generations per year. The sex ratio of most insects approximates a 1:1 ratio. However, some insects have a sex ratio that favors one sex.

Defensive Mechanisms to Avoid Natural Enemies

Every insect species encounters various natural enemies. The defensive mechanisms evolved by insects for survival are numerous and extremely interesting. Some important types of common defense mechanisms are (1) behavioral, (2) morphological, (3) chemical, (4) use of shelters, and (5) protective color patterns. Individual species may use one, a few, or all of these defensive mechanisms to avoid natural enemies.

Behavioral Defenses

Often insects will escape natural enemies by crawling, flying, jumping, or dropping. Leafhoppers often crawl quickly to the opposite side of the branch and hide. A mosquito or house fly simply flies away from a natural enemy. Many noctuid and geometrid moths detect ultrasonic impulses released by insectivorous bats to locate nocturnal flying insects and escape by making evasive maneuvers such as zigzag movements and power dives. Grasshoppers jump away from natural enemies, whereas many weevils and caterpillars escape by dropping. Some insects such as loopers and other caterpillars fake death and remain motionless when disturbed; they often resemble a twig. A few katydids and mantids adopt a threatening position when encountering an enemy.

Morphological Defenses

Many structures have been described in this chapter. Examples of structures serving dual purposes, including defense of the insect, are chewing mouthparts, hard exoskeleton of many insects, grasping legs of preying mantids, stingers of bees and wasps, and the forceplike cerci of earwigs. However, structures such as spines, spurs, and setae (hairs) are primarily defensive structures. Spines and hairs of many lepidopterous defoliators are often unpalatable or irritating to natural enemies.

Chemical Defenses

Chemical defenses are often grouped into nonvenomous repellent secretions and venoms injected into the attacker. Insects using chemical defense strategies normally rely on (1) the previous unpleasant experience of the natural enemy with intended victim; (2) mechanisms such as distasteful chemicals within its body, release of repugnant odor, or injection of a poison into the natural enemy by means of a stinger, spines, or setae; (3) the natural enemy recognizing the insect in the future so that unpleasant experiences are reduced; and (4) bright coloration that is easily recognized by its natural enemies. Most ladybird beetles and monarch butterflies are seldom attacked by natural enemies because their body fluids are distasteful. A classic example involves the monarch butterfly larva obtaining cardiac glycosides from feeding on milkweed plants. The cardiac glycosides are concentrated in the adult wings. Birds that feed on the monarch butterfly do not die, but vomit because of the distasteful chemical. They quickly learn to avoid the monarch butterfly and other butterflies like the viceroy, *Basilarchia archippus* (Cramer), that resemble them. Certain beetles and stink bugs emit repugnant odors when disturbed. Other insects discharge irritating liquids or discharge oily secretions that are deterrents to many natural enemies.

Use of Shelters

Plant parts, leaf litter, soil, rocks, and cases and tents constructed by insects offer shelter to many insects. Many common forest and shade tree insects are found inside plant parts such as leaf epidermis, stem, bud, seed, or wood. Most rove beetles and many springtails are found in the soil or leaf litter. Other insects hide under rocks. Bagworms and larch casebearers build a bag or case out of various plant materials. Most tent caterpillars, webworms, and many tortricid caterpillars build shelters such as tents, web-enclosed foliage, or rolled leaves. Social insects, such as ants, bees, and termites, build elaborate nests which often are found in the soil. These different types of shelters provide various amounts of protection from natural enemies.

Protective Color Patterns

Protective color patterns of insects are often grouped into cryptic coloration, warning coloration, deceptive coloration, and mimicry. Insects with cryptic coloration, often called *concealing coloration* or *camouflage*, blend into their environment or resemble a particular object in their environment that is not normally eaten. Examples of insects that blend well into the forest environment are caterpillars resembling foliage, walkingsticks resembling twigs, moths resembling tree bark, and mating moths resembling dead foliage. Treehoppers that resemble thorns and lepidopterous caterpillars resembling bird droppings are examples of insects resembling inedible objects. Insects with warning coloration are often brightly colored and distasteful or poisonous to natural enemies. These insects, such as bees and distasteful caterpillars, are normally diurnal, found in exposed places, and frequently occur in aggregations. Some deceptively colored insects have large eyespots (e.g., certain moths) that look like a pair of vertebrate eyes; others have eyespots or antennalike extensions near the end of the wings or at the posterior end of the abdomen. Large eyespots or projections frighten natural enemies or draw their attention to a more protected or less vital portion of the insect body.

Batesian and Mullerian mimicry are two common types of mimicry. In *Batesian mimicry*, an unpalatable protected species (model) is imitated by one or more unprotected palatable insects (mimics). A classic example of Batesian mimicry is the monarch butterfly, as the unpalatable model, and the viceroy butterfly, as the palatable mimic. Other common examples are clear-winged moths, syrphid flies, and reduviid bugs that mimic certain wasps. In *Mullerian mimicry*, several unrelated, unpalatable species occurring in the same area gain additional protection by resembling each other. A natural enemy learns after a few bad experiences to avoid all insects with certain patterns. Many butterflies, bees, and wasps are examples of Mullerian mimicry. Wickler (1968) and Rettenmeyer (1970) present detailed information on insect mimicry.

No one of the described adaptive features of insects can be proved to be the most important factor in the evolution of so many species and such numerous populations of many species. Many combinations of the above features and other factors produced today's situation. Some insects do not make use of certain adaptive features. For example, complete metamorphosis does not occur in two-thirds of the orders. Entire orders of insects such as fleas, chewing lice, and sucking lice had ancestors with wings but have evolved into wingless forms. Further description of adaptive features are presented in the case histories of important individual species of forest and shade tree insects in Chapters 11–17.

REFERENCES

Andrewartha, H. G. and L. C. Birch. 1954. *The Distribution and Abundance of Animals*. University of Chicago Press, Chicago.

Atkins, M. D. 1978. *Insects in Perspective*. Macmillan, New York.

Birch, M. C. (Ed.). 1974. *Pheromones*. North-Holland, Amsterdam.

Borror, D. J., D. M. DeLong, and C. A. Triplehorn. 1981. *An Introduction to the Study of Insects*. Holt, Rinehart & Winston, New York.

Chapman, R. F. 1982. *The Insects: Structure and Function*. American Elsevier, New York.

Clark, L. R., P. W. Geier, R. D. Hughes, and R. F. Morris. 1967. *The Ecology of Insect Populations in Theory and Practice*. Methuen, London.

Daly, H. V., J. T. Doyen, and P. R. Ehrlich. 1978. *Introduction to Insect Biology and Diversity*. McGraw-Hill, New York.

Davey, K. G. 1965. *Reproduction in the Insects*. Freeman, San Francisco.

Dingle, H. 1972. Migration strategies of insects. *Science* **175**:1327–1335.

Essig, E. O. 1942. *College Entomology*. Macmillan, New York.

Gilbert, L. I. 1976. *The Juvenile Hormones*. Plenum Press, New York.

Gillott, C. 1980. *Entomology*. Plenum Press, New York.

Johnson, C. G. 1969. *Migration and Dispersal of Insects by Flight*. Methuen, London.

Jones, J. C. 1978. A note on the use of the terms instar and stage. *Ann. Entomol. Soc. Amer.* **71**:491–492.

Leonard, D. E. 1970. Effect of starvation on behavior, number of larval instars, and development rate of *Porthetria dispar*. *J. Insect Physiol.* **16**:25–31.

Metcalf, C. L., W. P. Flint, and R. L. Metcalf. 1962. *Destructive and Useful Insects*. McGraw-Hill, New York.

Mitchell, E. R. (Ed.). 1981. *Management of Insect Pests with Semiochemicals: Concepts and Practice*. Plenum Press, New York.

Rettenmeyer, C. W. 1970. Insect mimicry. *Annu. Rev. Entomol.* **15**:43–74.

Richards, O. W. and R. G. Davies. 1977. *Imms' General Textbook of Entomology*, Vols. 1 and 2. Chapman and Hall, London.

Rockstein, M. (Ed.). 1973–1974. *The Physiology of Insecta*, 6 vols. Academic Press, New York.

Romoser, W. S. 1973. *The Science of Entomology*, 1st ed., Macmillan, New York.

Romoser, W. S. 1981. *The Science of Entomology*, 2nd ed., Macmillan, New York.

Ross, H. H., C. A. Ross, and J. R. P. Ross. 1982. *A Textbook of Entomology*. Wiley, New York.

Shorey, H. H. 1973. Behavioral responses to insect pheromones. *Annu. Rev. Entomol.* **18**:349–380.

Slama, K., M. Romanuk, and F. Sorm. 1974. *Insect Hormones and Bioanalogues*. Springer-Verlag, New York.

Snodgrass, R. E. 1935. *Principles of Insect Morphology*. McGraw-Hill, New York.

Wickler, W. 1968. *Mimicry in Plants and Animals*. McGraw-Hill, New York.

Wigglesworth, V. B. 1970. *Insect Hormones*. Oliver S. Boyd, Edinburgh.

Wigglesworth, V. B. 1972. *The Principles of Insect Physiology*. Methuen, London.

3 | INSECT CLASSIFICATION

INTRODUCTION

The objectives of this chapter are to provide (1) an understanding of insect classification, (2) a description of the phylum Arthropoda, including a brief survey of the important classes, and (3) a survey of the insect orders.

CLASSIFICATION SYSTEM

There are approximately 1.25 million described species belonging to the animal kingdom. It is difficult to estimate the number that are yet to be described and named. Animals are classified into different groups with members of each group sharing some common characteristics. The classification of the animal kingdom starts with 14 major groups called *phyla* and continues to the species level. The classification system is illustrated for the spruce budworm, *Choristoneura fumiferana* (Clemens):

Kingdom	Animalia
Phylum	Arthropoda
Class	Insecta
Order	Lepidoptera
Family	Tortricidae
Genus	*Choristoneura*
Species	*fumiferana*

Different authors use classification systems that may vary with respect to the taxonomic placement of orders, families, or genera.

Species

The basic category in this classification system is the species. A *species* is a group of interbreeding populations that is reproductively isolated from other populations. It is usually difficult or impossible to determine whether two species will interbreed. We thus rely primarily on morphological characters to identify a species although fully aware that some "verifiable" species groups (*sibling species*) cannot be distinguished by morphological characters (Borror et al. 1981).

Types of Names

Animals have two types of names: common and scientific. In the past, *common names* have been used by anyone who chose to apply them without any rules or regulations. For example, forest tent caterpillar, armyworm, and forest tentless caterpillar are all common names for *Malacosoma disstria*

Hübner, a lepidopteran species in the family Lasiocampidae that defoliates aspen and other hardwoods. When many different common names are applied to one species, they are called *synonyms*. The opposite situation, known as *homonyms*, is when the same common name is used for several species. For example, armyworm is a common name for both *M. disstria* and *Pseudaletia unipuncta* (Haworth), a lepidopteran species in the family Noctuidae that feeds on grasses, wheat, and corn. Official rules have been developed for common names of insects; a list of over 1500 common names of species has been approved by the Entomological Society of America (Werner 1982). Scientists are beginning to use approved common names for the most economically important insects. However, official common names are available for less than 0.1% of all described species.

Common names of insects often refer to groups such as order or families rather than to one species. For example, the name "beetle" refers to approximately 300,000 species worldwide and 30,000 North American species (Borror et al. 1981). The name "bark beetle" refers to all species in the family Scolytidae; there are about 600 species in the United States. A majority of the orders and families have well-established common names. Most common names of insects consisting of one word refer to entire orders, whereas common names of two or more words normally refer to a family or a single species. Two very common names are "fly" and "bug." When the "fly" or "bug" part of an insect name is written separately (i.e., house fly, stink bug), it belongs to the order Diptera (true flies) or Hemiptera (true bugs), respectively. If "fly" or "bug" is combined with a descriptive word, (i.e., sawfly, ladybug), the insect belongs in some other order.

Every species has a *scientific name*, as prescribed by the rules on scientific names published in the *International Code of Zoological Nomenclature* (International Commission on Zoological Nomenclature 1964). This code is followed consistently by zoologists throughout the world. The names are written in Latin and provide a common language for the biological sciences. The system of binomial nomenclature gives every species a scientific name consisting of two parts, the genus and the species. Genus and species names are always underlined or printed in italics. The name of the species is followed by the name of the author who described the species. Parentheses around the author's name signifies that the species is now placed in a different genus than when it was originally described. *Musca domestica* Linnaeus and *Choristoneura fumiferana* (Clemens), respectively, are the scientific names of the house fly and the spruce budworm.

PHYLUM ARTHROPODA

The phylum Arthropoda, or "jointed-legged" animals, contains 80% of the known animal species and includes such diverse creatures as spiders, centipedes, shrimp, and insects. The most important characteristics of the phylum Arthropoda are (1) segmented body with two or three distinct body regions, (2) paired segmented appendages, (3) chitinous exoskeleton, (4) ventral nervous system, (5) open circulatory system, (6) respiration through gills or spiracles and tracheae, (7) excretion by means of Malpighian tubules, (8) bilateral symmetry, and (9) striated skeletal muscles.

Annelida (earthworms) and Onychophora (i.e., genus *Peripatus*) are the phyla most closely related to the Arthropoda. The origin of the phylum Arthropoda and the evolution of the class Insecta are presented in Ross et al. (1982) and Romoser (1981). The phylum Arthropoda is often divided into the following three subphyla and nine classes (Meglitsch 1967):

Subphylum	Trilobita–trilobites: fossils only
Subphylum	Chelicerata
Class	Xiphosura—horseshoe crabs: marine and intertidal zones
Class	Merostomata—sea spiders: marine; euryterids: fossils only
Class	*Arachnida—spiders, mites, ticks, scorpions, pseudoscorpions, daddy longlegs: terrestrial and diverse
Subphylum	Mandibulata
Class	*Crustacea–crustaceans: mostly aquatic, marine
Class	*Diplopoda—millipedes: terrestrial
Class	*Chilopoda–centipedes: terrestrial
Class	Pauropoda–pauropods: terrestrial
Class	Symphyla—symphlans: terrestrial
Class	*Insecta–insects: all ecosystems, diverse

Members of the subphylum Chelicerata are characterized by usually having (1) two body regions: cephalothorax (fused head and thorax) and an abdomen, (2) no antennae, and (3) six pairs of appendages with the anterior pair being jawlike feeding structures called *chelicerae*. The second pair, called *pedipalps*, are leglike in appearance and variable in function. The remaining four pairs of appendages are called "legs" and are normally used for locomotion.

Members of the subphylum Mandibulata are characterized by normally having (1) one or two pairs of antennae, (2) a pair of mandibles and maxillae as head appendages that operate from side to side, (3) two or three body regions, and (4) 3 to 60 or more pairs of legs.

*The starred (*) classes in the above list are the classes in the phylum Arthropoda, whose members are most often encountered, recognized, or of more economic importance in forestry and arboriculture. Since this book concentrates on insects and not all arthropods, the brief coverage of the other arthropod classes is not indicative of the economic or biological importance of some species in the other classes.

Class Arachnida

The Arachnida is the largest, commonest, and most diverse class in the subphylum Chelicerata. The arachnids are recognized by their two body regions, six pairs of appendages, and no antennae. This class is usually divided into 11 orders, of which the following are the most common: Araneida (spiders), Acari (mites, ticks), Phalangida (daddy longlegs), Scorpionida (scorpions), and Pseudoscorpionida (pseudoscorpions).

The spiders are a very large, common, and diverse group. Many people fear spiders, but they very rarely bite human beings; a few (i.e., black widow spider, brown recluse spider) can be dangerous to human beings. Most spiders are predators of insects and other small organisms. Spiders are important in keeping many forest insects at endemic population levels.

Mites are minute animals with little or no differentiation between the two body regions and four pairs of legs. Mites exhibit very diverse life histories; some such as the spruce spider mite, *Oligonychus ununguis* (Jacobi), are important phytophagous pests on trees and shrubs, whereas others are important predators of small insects and phytophagous mites. Many species of mites feed on detritus, fungi, and bacteria; a number of eriophyid mites produce galls on the leaves of many tree species. Some species of mites are also parasitic on human beings and animals. Mite densities often range from 60,000 to over 200,000/m^2 in forest soils (Wallwork 1970).

Ticks usually can be distinguished from mites by their larger size and leathery skin. They are parasitic on mammals, birds, and reptiles. Ticks are annoying pests to humans and can transmit serious diseases such as Rocky Mountain spotted fever and tularemia (see Chapter 18 for additional information on ticks).

The scorpions occur primarily in the southern and western United States. They are nocturnal predators of many types of arthropods, primarily insects and spiders. The sting of a scorpion is very painful to humans. However, only one species in the United States (Arizona) has a sting that may be fatal.

Harvestmen (daddy longlegs) are common and well-known arthropods that occur in leaf litter and outbuildings. They are general feeders, with most species feeding on dead plant and animal matter or on plant juices; some are predators of insects.

Class Crustacea

The crustaceans are a very diverse group with most members found in marine or fresh-water habitats. Commonly found crustaceans include fairy shrimp, water fleas, copepods, barnacles, amphipods, sowbugs, lobsters, crayfish, crabs, and shrimp. Most small fresh-water crustaceans play an important role in the food chains of aquatic systems. The crustaceans are recognized by the following characteristics: (1) two body regions: cephal-

othorax and abdomen, (2) two pairs of antennae, and (3) a pair of appendages on each segment of the cephalothorax.

Sowbugs, often called *pillbugs* because of their habit of rolling into a ball
when disturbed, are the only common terrestrial crustaceans. They are
small, dorsoventrally flattened crustaceans that have seven pairs of legs.
Sowbugs are nocturnal and are found in damp habitats such as soil, bark,
leaf litter, and basements. Sowbugs are primarily scavengers that feed on
decaying plant and animal material, but some eat living plants and are
occasionally pests in greenhouses or flower gardens.

Gribbles, sometimes called *wood lice*, are closely related and similar in
appearance to sowbugs but are found in marine habitats. They attack most
wooden structures placed in the sea or brackish waters. Gribbles often cause
damage to wood piling by honeycombing them with bored galleries, especially on portions between mean and low tide levels.

Class Diplopoda

Millipedes are elongate, wormlike animals with most body segments containing two pairs of legs. Most millipedes are slow moving, have 30 or more
pairs of legs, and vary greatly in size (2–100 mm). They are usually found
in damp places, under bark, and in soil, leaves, and rotting wood. Most
are scavengers and feed on decaying vegetation, a few are predators, and
a few attack living plants, occasionally causing serious damage in gardens
or greenhouses.

Class Chilopoda

Centipedes are wormlike, flattened, elongate animals with one pair of legs
per body segment. They have 15 or more pairs of legs with the last two
pairs directed backward. The first pair of appendages behind the head are
modified, clawlike, and function as poison jaws. Most centipedes are 25–
50 mm long, but some species in the southern United States are 125 mm
long. The smaller species are harmless to human beings, but the larger
species can inflict a painful bite. Centipedes are fast-moving animals that
are found in the soil, rotten logs, and under bark. They are predators of
insects, spiders, mites, nematodes, and mollusks.

Class Insecta

Insects are the most ubiquitous animals, numbering close to 800,000 described species. Based on recent work in the tropics, Erwin (1983) predicted
that there may be as many as 30 million species of insects in the world.
The distinguishing characteristics of the class Insecta are (1) a segmented
body divided into three distinct regions—head, thorax, and abdomen, (2)
three pairs of legs, (3) usually one or two pairs of wings, and (4) one pair

of antennae. There are many different opinions among entomologists regarding the division of insects into orders and families. No particular classification system is uniformly used by entomologists. We have followed the
orders and families listed in Borror et al. (1981), which is the most widely
used classification system in the United States. The class Insecta is divided
into 27 orders; these groupings are based primarily on differences in (1)
mouthparts, (2) wings, (3) metamorphosis, (4) size and shape of insect, (5)
antennae, and (6) other structures such as cerci and elytra.

The insects are divided into two subclasses: Apterygota and Pterygota.
The Apterygota are small, primitive, wingless insects with no metamorphosis; the Pterygota are winged insects with incomplete, gradual, or complete metamorphosis. Certain Pterygota such as the Mallophaga and Anoplura have evolved from winged ancestors into present wingless forms.

The class Insecta is divided into the following two subclasses and 27
orders:

Class Insecta
    Subclass Apterygota—primarily wingless insects
        Order   Protura—proturans
               Diplura—diplurans
               *Collembola—springtails, snowfleas
               *Thysanura—bristletails, silverfish, firebrats
    Subclass Pterygota—winged and secondarily wingless insects
        Order   *Ephemeroptera—mayflies
               *Odonata—dragonflies, damselflies
               *Plecoptera—stoneflies
               *Orthoptera—grasshoppers, katydids, crickets, walkingsticks,
               mantids, cockroaches
               *Dermaptera—earwigs
               *Isoptera—termites
               Embioptra—webspinners
               Zoraptera—zorapterans
               *Psocoptera—psocids, barklice, booklice
               *Mallophaga—chewing lice, bird lice
               *Anoplura—sucking lice
               *Thysanoptera—thrips
               *Hemiptera—true bugs
               *Homoptera—aphids, scales, leafhoppers, planthoppers,
               spittlebugs, cicadas
               *Neuroptera—lacewings, antlions, alderflies, dobsonflies
               *Coleoptera—beetles, weevils

Strepsiptera—twisted-winged parasites
*Mecoptera—scorpionflies
*Trichoptera—caddisflies
*Lepidoptera—butterflies, moths
*Diptera—true flies
*Siphonaptera—fleas
*Hymenoptera—wasps, bees, ants, sawflies

The following descriptions of the starred (*) 22 orders are brief. The five orders deleted from coverage are minute, very seldom collected, and of little importance in forestry and arboriculture. Additional information on insect orders and families can be obtained from Ross et al. (1982), Borror et al. (1981), Gillott (1980), Merritt and Cummins (1978), Richards and Davies (1977), Borror and White (1970), CSIRO (1970), Usinger (1965), Essig (1958), and Brues et al. (1954).

INSECT ORDERS

Collembola

This order includes springtails (Figure 3.1) and snowfleas. Derivation: coll = glue, embola = bolt or wedge (refers to the collophore).

Characteristics
Collembola characteristics are: (1) no wings, (2) chewing mouthparts somewhat concealed, (3) no metamorphosis, (4) quite small, under 6 mm, (5)

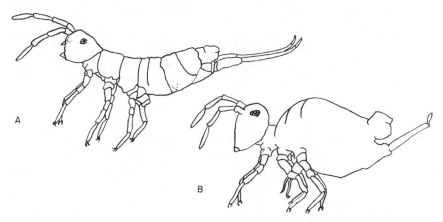

Figure 3.1 Collembola, springtails: (A) elongated body, (B) globular body. (Redrawn from Maynard 1951.)

filiform antennae, usually four segmented, (6) six abdominal segments, and (7) a furcula and its associated tenaculum.

The name "springtail" is derived from the forked jumping structure, the *furcula*, which arises from the ventral side of the fourth abdominal segment. When the insect is at rest, the furcula is folded under the abdomen and held in place by the *tenaculum*, a clasperlike structure located on the third abdominal segment. The insect jumps by extending the furcula downward and backward. The springtails are generally under 6 mm in length, and may jump 70–100 mm.

Ecology

The majority of species live in soil, leaf mold, under bark, and decaying logs. Most springtails feed on decaying plant material, but some feed on algae, fungi, and pollen. A few such as the garden springtail, *Bourletiella hortensis* (Fitch), feed on living plants and may cause some damage. The snowflea is a dark-colored species commonly found in the winter on the snow's surface.

Springtails are very helpful in the breakdown of forest litter. They are widely distributed and among the most abundant insects. Springtails are found in many types of moist sites but seldom are observed because of their size and occupation of secluded microhabitats. Populations often reach five million insects per hectare.

Thysanura

This order includes bristletails (Figure 3.2), silverfish, and firebrats. Derivation: thysan = bristle or fringe, ura = tail.

Characteristics

Thysanura characteristically have (1) no wings, (2) chewing mouthparts somewhat concealed, (3) no metamorphosis, (4) small–medium size (5–20 mm), (5) many segmented, filiform antennae, (6) three tail-like appendages at posterior end of abdomen, (7) body elongated and normally flattened, and (8) stylelike lateral appendages on some abdominal segments.

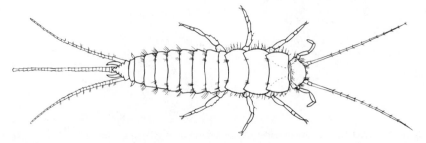

Figure 3.2   Thysanura, bristletail.

The best known and most often seen thysanurans are the two domesticated species: silverfish and firebrat. The silverfish is gray, about 12 mm long, and found in cool, damp surroundings within buildings. The firebrat is tan or brown, about 12 mm long, and usually found in warm habitats such as around furnaces and steampipes.

Ecology
Most thysanurans are outdoor species and occur in organic debris (i.e., decaying bark, leaves). They feed on damp or dry plant material or plant products and usually prefer damp areas. The bristletails play a very helpful part in the breakdown of forest litter. Organic debris, starch in bookbindings, and starch paste in wallpaper are common foods for the two domesticated species.

Ephemeroptera

This order consists of mayflies (Figure 3.3). Derivation: ephemera = short lived, ptera = wings (refers to the short life of the adult stage).

Characteristics
Characteristics of Ephemeroptera are: (1) four net-veined, membranous wings held together above body when at rest, (2) front wings large and triangular, hind wings small and rounded, (3) adults with vestigial mouthparts, naiads with chewing mouthparts, (4) incomplete metamorphosis, (5) variable size (4–50 mm), (6) small, bristlelike antennae, and (7) two or three long threadlike tails.

Mayfly naiads are identified by the leaflike or plumose gills located on the sides of the abdomen and by three (occasionally two) long threadlike tails. The naiad follows the usual type of incomplete metamorphosis with wings developing as external pads. When immature development is complete, the mayfly naiad emerges from the water, molts to the winged form that flies to shore, and lands on nearby vegetation. This stage is not sexually mature and is called a *subimago*. They usually molt to the adult stage 1–2 days later. Mayflies are the only insects to molt after the wings become functional. Adults mate, lay eggs, and die.

Ecology
The mayfly naiads are very diverse in habitat and food preference selection. Some species have very restricted habitat requirements, which makes them useful as indicator species of environmental change (i.e., degree of pollution in streams). Some species are found in swift streams, whereas other species live under stones or among debris on the bottoms of lakes and streams. The naiads have chewing mouthparts and feed on dead plant material, algae, and diatoms. Mayfly naiads are an important food source for fish. Artificial flies modeled after mayfly adults are often used in fishing. Mayfly

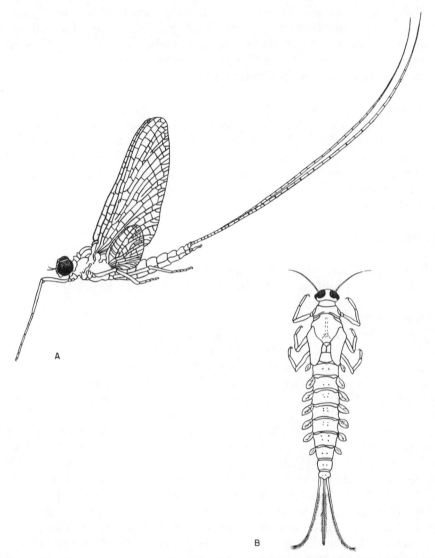

Figure 3.3 Ephemeroptera, mayflies: (A) adult male, (B) naiad. (Redrawn from Leonard and Leonard 1962, by permission of Cranbrook Institute of Science.)

adults commonly emerge in large numbers from streams and lakes. In towns near large nonpolluted lakes, piles of dead bodies of mayfly adults may create a nuisance on streets, sidewalks, and parking lots.

Odonata

This order includes dragonflies (Figure 3.4) and, damselflies (Figure 3.5). Derivation: odonata = tooth (refers to teeth on mandibles).

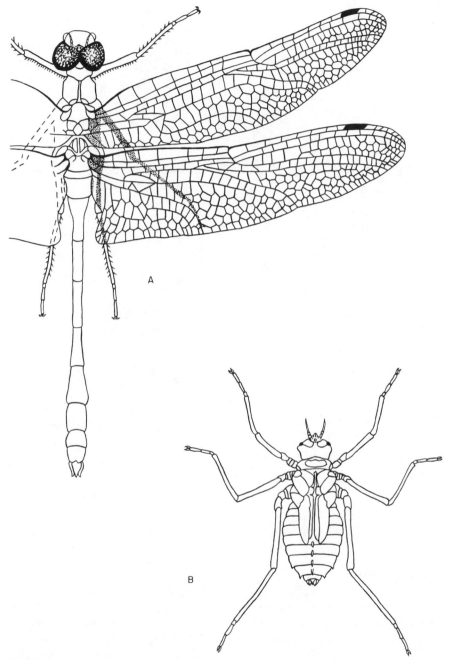

Figure 3.4 Odonata, dragonflies: (A) adult, (B) naiad. (Redrawn with modifications from Kennedy 1915.)

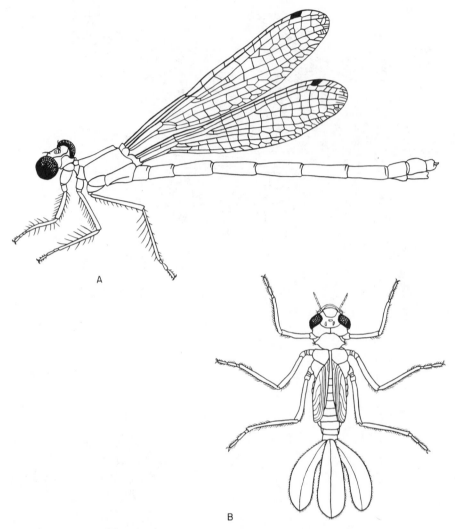

Figure 3.5   Odonata, damselflies: (A) adult, (B) naiad.

Characteristics

Odonata characteristically have (1) four elongated, net-veined membranous wings of approximately equal size; (2) chewing mouthparts; (3) incomplete metamorphosis; (4) moderately large size (20–120 mm), (5) small, bristlelike antennae, (6) large compound eyes, and (7) long, slender abdomen.

Two suborders are present in the United States: Anisoptera, the dragonflies, and Zygoptera, the damselflies. The dragonflies hold their wings in a horizontal position when at rest and are strong, agile fliers. The damselflies are weak fliers and hold their wings back and above the abdomen when at rest. Dragonfly naiads have internal rectal gills, and damselfly naiads are recognized by the three leaflike gills at the end of the abdomen.

Ecology

Immature Odonata are aquatic, whereas the adults are terrestrial and can be far-ranging, but are more common and conspicuous near water. The naiads are predators of various aquatic organisms (i.e., mayfly naiads, mosquito larvae). The naiads are also an important food source for fish. Adults are aerial predators of mosquitos, midges, small moths, horse flies, mayflies, other dragonflies, and other flying insects.

Plecoptera

This order includes stoneflies (Figure 3.6). Derivation: pleco = folded, ptera = wings.

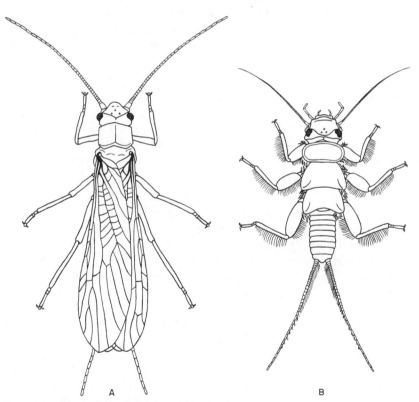

Figure 3.6 Plecoptera, stoneflies: (A) adult, (B) naiad. (Redrawn with slight modifications: A from Frison 1935, B from Claassen 1931.)

Characteristics

Plecoptera characteristics are as follows: (1) most have four net-veined, membranous wings; (2) wings held flat over abdomen when at rest; (3) front wings long, narrow, and elongate whereas hind wings are pleated, fanlike, and often shorter and wider than front wings; (4) chewing mouthparts in naiads that are often reduced in adults; (5) incomplete metamorphosis; (6) variable size (6–64 mm); (7) long, slender antennae; and (8) cerci always present, often large and conspicuous.

Stonefly naiads are similar to mayfly naiads but are distinguished by having only two long posterior tails and usually having branched gills on the thorax and around the base of the legs.

Ecology

Stonefly naiads are aquatic and generally found around or under stones in fast-moving streams. Most naiads feed on plant matter, but several genera are predaceous or omnivorous. Stonefly naiads are generally an important component of aquatic systems (i.e., fish food). Stoneflies are used as indicator species of environmental quality. Stonefly adults are terrestrial but normally are found in the vicinity of fast-moving streams. Adults with vestigial mouthparts do not feed at all, whereas adults with chewing mouthparts feed primarily on algae.

Orthoptera

This order includes grasshoppers, katydids, crickets, walkingsticks, mantids, and cockroaches (Figures 2.2 and 3.7). Derivation: ortho = straight, ptera = wings.

Characteristics

Orthoptera characteristics are: (1) both winged (four wings) and wingless forms; (2) front wings generally long, narrow, multiveined, and leathery or parchmentlike whereas hind wings are broad, multiveined, and membranous; (3) hind wings when at rest are usually folded fanlike beneath front wings; (4) chewing mouthparts; (5) gradual metamorphosis; (6) size and form variable, but many are large insects (5–230 mm); and (7) often with large, conspicuous antennae.

The Orthoptera is a very diverse group. There are many differing opinions concerning the taxonomic classification of insects in this order. We have used the broadest interpretation available. All entomologists place the grasshoppers in the order Orthoptera, but some entomologists place the walkingsticks, mantids, and cockroaches in one order (Dictyoptera or Cursoria), two orders (Cursoria, the cockroaches, mantids; Phasmida, the walkingsticks), or three orders (Phasmida, the walkingsticks; Mantodea, the mantids; and Blattodea, the cockroaches).

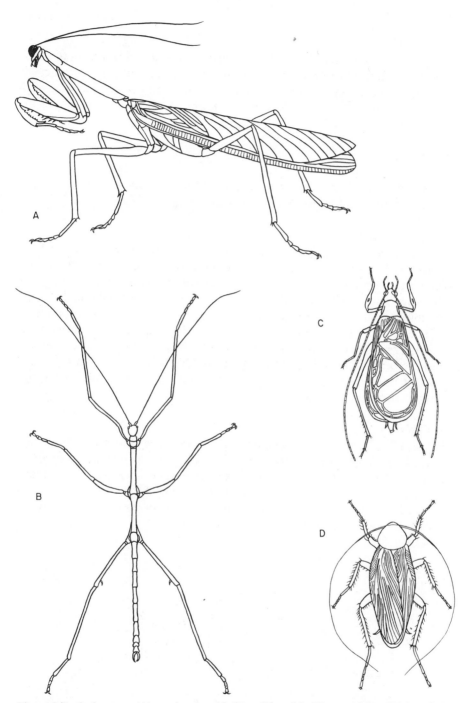

Figure 3.7 Orthoptera: (A) praying mantid, (B) walkingstick, (C) tree cricket, (D) American cockroach. (Redrawn with slight modifications: A, B, and C from Essig 1942; D from Daly et al. 1978. (A), (B), (C) reprinted with permission from Macmillan Publishing Company, from *College Entomology* by E. O. Essig. © by Macmillan Publishing Company.)

Ecology

Orthoptera are terrestrial, with most species found on trees, shrubs, and other vegetation; a few burrow into the ground and others exist in caves. Most species are phytophagous, but the preying mantids and many katydids are predaceous. The cockroaches are omnivorous, and some species are major household pests.

Dermaptera

This order consists of earwigs (Figure 3.8). Derivation: derma = skin, ptera = wings (refers to texture of front wings).

Characteristics

Dermaptera characteristics are: (1) four wings, some wingless; (2) front wings short, leathery, and veinless with most of abdomen exposed; (3) hind wings membranous, semicircular in shape, with radially arranged veins; (4) chewing mouthparts; (5) gradual metamorphosis; (6) small–medium size (4–26 mm); (7) large forcepslike cerci; and (8) long, slender antennae.

The name "earwig" is apparently derived from a superstition that these insects crawl into the ears of sleeping persons and slowly work their way into the brain. There is no foundation for this belief. The common name may have developed from the term "earwing" relating to the hind wing's resemblance to a human ear.

Ecology

Earwigs are primarily nocturnal in habit and hide under soil, bark, leaf litter, boards, or stones during the day. They are primarily omnivorous and feed on dead, decaying plant and animal material as well as live plants and animals. The cosmopolitan European earwig, *Forficula auricularia* Linnaeus, is common in some communities and becomes a problem when it chews off the petals of roses and other flowers.

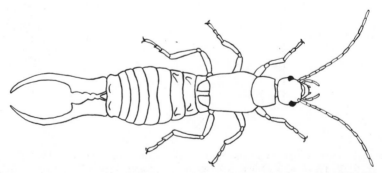

Figure 3.8 Dermaptera, earwig. (Redrawn with modifications from Essig 1942. Reprinted with permission from Macmillan Publishing Company from *College Entomology* by E. O. Essig. © by Macmillan Publishing Company.)

Isoptera

This order consists of termites (see Figure 16.19). Derivation: iso = equal, ptera = wings.

Characteristics

Isoptera characteristics are (1) winged and wingless forms, wings often absent; (2) if winged, four net-veined, equal-size, membranous wings; (3) wings held flat over body when at rest; (4) chewing mouthparts; (5) gradual metamorphosis; (6) small size (2–15 mm) except queen (up to 75 mm); (7) antlike in form, but soft and light bodied; (8) thorax and abdomen broadly joined; and (9) antennae moniliform.

All termites are social insects. Their caste system, biology, ecology, and damage is discussed in detail in Chapter 16.

Ecology

Termites occur primarily in the tropical and subtropical latitudes, but they also occur in the temperate regions. They are largely beneficial in forested areas because of their assistance in the decomposition of deadwood, the reincorporation of this material into the soil, and the aeration of the soil. However, they are often very destructive to buildings, fence posts, and other wood products.

Psocoptera

This order includes psocids, barklice, and booklice (Figure 3.9). Derivation: psoco = rub small, ptera = wings (refers to gnawing habits of these insects).

Characteristics

Psocoptera characteristics are: (1) wings present on most barklice and absent on most booklice; (2) four membranous wings with reduced venation; (3)

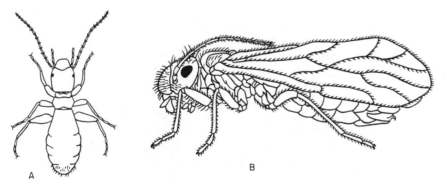

Figure 3.9 Psocoptera: (A) booklice, (B) barklice. (Redrawn with modifications: A from Essig 1942, B from Sommerman 1943. A reprinted with permission from Macmillan Publishing Company, from *College Entomology* by E. O. Essig. © Macmillan Publishing Company.)

front wings larger than hind wings and wings held rooflike over abdomen when at rest; (4) chewing mouthparts; (5) gradual metamorphosis; (6) quite small (under 6 mm); and (7) long, filiform antennae.

The term "lice" in the names barklice and booklice is an unfortunate misnomer because none of these insects are parasitic and only a few appear louselike.

Ecology

Most psocids, often called *barklice*, are found under stones, bark, or on foliage of trees and other vegetation. They are general feeders and consume organic material such as fungi, algae, pollen, or dead insect fragments. There are several wingless species of psocids that inhabit buildings and feed on grain, starch, and mold. Most people see only one species, the booklice, *Liposcelis divinatorious* (Müller). This species is often found among books and papers; it may cause some damage in libraries by eating starch from bookbindings.

Mallophaga

This order includes chewing lice (Figure 3.10) and bird lice. Derivation: mallo = wool, phaga = eat.

Characteristics

Mallophaga characteristics are: (1) no wings, (2) chewing mouthparts, (3) gradual metamorphosis, (4) quite small (under 5 mm), (5) triangular head as wide or wider than thorax, and (6) body flattened dorsoventrally.

Ecology

Chewing lice are minute, external parasites, primarily of birds, but some species have mammalian hosts (excluding humans). Both nymphs and adults feed on feathers, hair, or skin of their hosts. Most species are very host

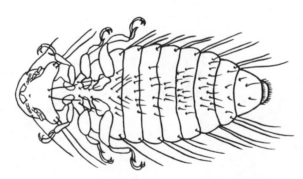

Figure 3.10 Mallophaga, chewing lice. (Redrawn with slight modifications from Borror et al. 1981.)

specific; transmission of chewing lice between two birds of the same species usually occurs only in the nest or when the birds mate. Each species usually infests a particular portion of the host's body. No chewing lice attack human beings, but people handling infested animals may occasionally find a chewing louse on them. Chewing lice die shortly after separation from an acceptable host. Most domesticated animals are attacked by one or more species of chewing lice, but they seldom become a problem except on poultry. Control of chewing lice usually involves treating an infested animal and its living quarters with a chemical insecticide in a dust formulation.

Anoplura

This order consists of sucking lice (Figure 3.11). Derivation: anopl = unarmed, ura = tail.

Characteristics

Anoplura characteristics are: (1) no wings, (2) piercing–sucking mouthparts, (3) gradual metamorphosis, (4) quite small (under 5 mm), (5) head narrower than thorax, and (6) body flattened dorsoventrally.

Ecology

Sucking lice are minute external parasites of mammals, including human beings. They feed by sucking blood from their mammalian hosts, on which they spend their entire life cycle. Like the Mallophaga, Anoplura are very

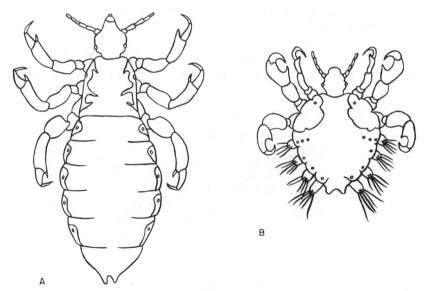

Figure 3.11 Anoplura, sucking lice. A and B are human lice: (A) body louse, female; (B) crab louse, female. (Redrawn with slight modifications from Borror et al. 1981.)

host specific. Some species of this order cause serious problems on domesticated livestock (i.e., hogs).

Two species of sucking lice attack humans: human louse and crab louse. The human louse, *Pediculus humanus* Linnaeus, infests humans and is divided into two subspecies, *P. humanus capitis* DeGeer, head louse, and *P. humanus humanus* Linnaeus, body louse. Feeding by the human louse causes skin irritations, and while feeding, it may transmit typhus fever, relapsing fever, or trench fever. These louse-borne diseases are a major problem during wars or famines when people are crowded in unsanitary, bathless conditions. People who bathe and change clothes regularly seldom become infested with human lice.

The other species of sucking lice found on humans is the crab louse, *Pthirus pubis* (Linnaeus), which generally infests hairy areas around the genitals and armpits and causes intense itching. An infestation may result from contact with an infested person through sexual intercourse or infested clothing and blankets. Sucking lice attacking humans are easily eliminated by using insecticide-impregnated soap.

Thysanoptera

This order includes thrips (Figure 3.12). Derivation: thysano = fringe, ptera = wings.

Characteristics
Thysanoptera characteristics are: (1) winged and wingless species; (2) if winged, four long narrow fringed wings; (3) piercing–sucking mouthparts, (4) gradual metamorphosis; (5) quite small (<6 mm); and (6) long, slender body.

Metamorphosis is somewhat intermediate between gradual and complete. The first two instars, called *larvae*, are active and the wings develop

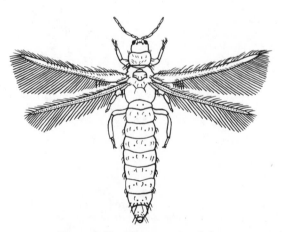

Figure 3.12 Thysanoptera, thrip.

internally; the subsequent two instars are inactive, with external wing pads, and are called *prepupae* and *pupae*. The mature adult is active and often winged.

Ecology

Most thrips are plant feeders. They often feed on plant sap and are found in large numbers on flowers (i.e., daisies), leaves, buds, bark, fruit, and fungi. Several species cause economic damage to pine cones; some are pests on citrus, gladiolus, and tobacco, and a few transmit plant diseases.

Hemiptera

This order consists of true bugs (Figure 3.13). Derivation: hemi = half, ptera = wings (refers to front wings).

Characteristics

Hemiptera characteristics are: (1) *hemelytra* front wings (basal part thickened and leathery and apical part membranous) in most; (2) membranous hind wings and hemelytra front wings held flat over abdomen when at rest; (3) piercing–sucking mouthparts in the form of a prominent beak that arises from front of head; (4) gradual metamorphosis; and (5) variable size (1–100 mm).

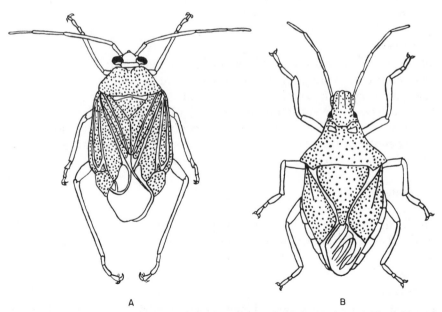

A   B

Figure 3.13 Hemiptera, true bugs: (A) plant bug, (B) stink bug. (Redrawn with slight modifications: A from Britton 1923, B from Essig 1942. A reprinted with permission from Macmillan Publishing Company, from *College Entomology* by E. O. Essig. © by Macmillan Publishing Company.)

Ecology

The true bugs form a large diverse order, the majority of which are terrestrial. There are many common aquatic species such as the giant water bugs, backswimmers, water boatmen, and water striders. Many of the terrestrial forms are phytophagous and feed on plant sap; a number are serious agricultural pests, but few are serious tree pests. A number of species, such as many assassin bugs and stink bugs, are predators and benefit pest managers as natural control agents.

Homoptera

This order includes aphids, scales, leafhoppers, planthoppers, spittlebugs, and cicadas (Figure 3.14). Derivation: homo = alike, ptera = wings.

Characteristics

Homoptera characteristics are: (1) usually winged, but also many wingless species; (2) if winged, both pairs uniform in texture and usually held rooflike over body; (3) piercing–sucking mouthparts with beak arising from back of head; (4) gradual metamorphosis; and (5) small size (1–13 mm) except cicadas (25–50 mm).

The order Homoptera is large, diverse, and closely related to the Hemiptera. Homopterans can be distinguished from Hemiptera (true bugs) by their uniformly textured wings, position of wings at rest, and the position of beak on head.

Ecology

All species are terrestrial and phytophagous. They feed by inserting the beak into plant tissues and sucking the sap. Each species usually feeds on a particular part of a plant and is often specific to one or a few plant species. These insects cause considerable economic damage to agricultural crops and forest and shade trees by their sap feeding habits. Several species act as vectors of plant diseases on agricultural crops. Some groups (i.e., cicadas) cause damage to trees by ovipositing on twigs.

Neuroptera

This order consists of lacewings (Figure 3.15), antlions, alderflies, and dobsonflies. Derivation: neuro = nerve, ptera = wings (refers to wing veins).

Characteristics

Neuroptera characteristics are: (1) net-veined membranous wings with many cross veins, (2) wings held rooflike over abdomen, (3) adults with chewing mouthparts and larvae with biting–sucking mouthparts, (4) complete met-

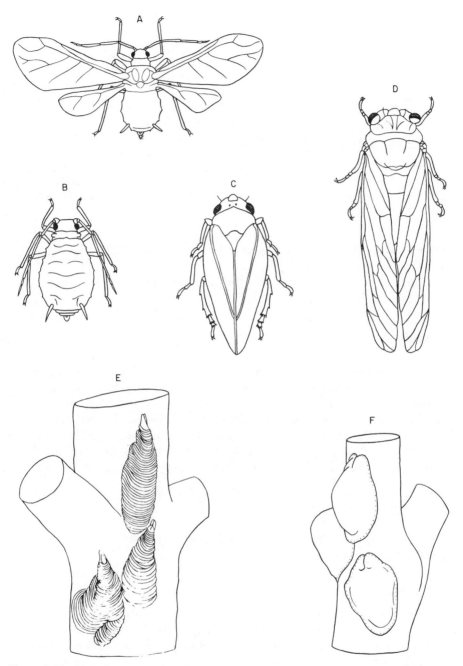

Figure 3.14 Homoptera: (A) winged aphid, (B) wingless aphid, (C) spittlebug, (D) cicada, (E) oystershell scale, (F) magnolia scale. (Redrawn with slight modifications: A and B from Romoser 1981, C and D from Britton 1923. A and B reprinted with permission from Macmillan Publishing Company, from *The Science of Entomology* by W. S. Romoser. © 1981 by W. S. Romoser.)

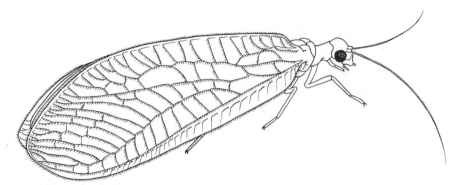

Figure 3.15   Neuroptera, green lacewing. (Redrawn from slight modifications from Ross et al. 1982.)

amorphosis, (5) medium size (most 10–30 mm), and (6) antennae usually long and conspicuous.

Some authorities place the alderflies and dobsonflies in a separate order, Megaloptera.

Ecology
Alderfly and dobsonfly larvae are aquatic and predaceous, whereas the adults are terrestrial and normally found near streams. The mature dobsonfly larvae are known as *hellgrammites* and are excellent fish bait. The antlion larvae are terrestrial and predators of ants and other insects that fall into their conical pits, which are often built in sand. Lacewing larvae are terrestrial; very common; and important predators of aphids, scales, and small caterpillars. Most adults in this order live for only a short time; some species feed as adults whereas others do not feed in the adult stage.

Coleoptera

This order includes beetles and weevils (Figure 3.16). Derivation: coleo = sheath, ptera = wings (refers to elytra).

Characteristics
Coleoptera characteristics are: (1) two thickened, leathery, or horny hard front wings, (elytra) which meet in a straight line down back of insect; (2) chewing mouthparts; (3) complete metamorphosis; and (4) size variable (1–150 mm).

Elytra (singular elytron) are the modified front wings of beetles. They form a hard protective armor over the hind wings. The evolution of the elytra is responsible, in part, for the diversity of the beetles.

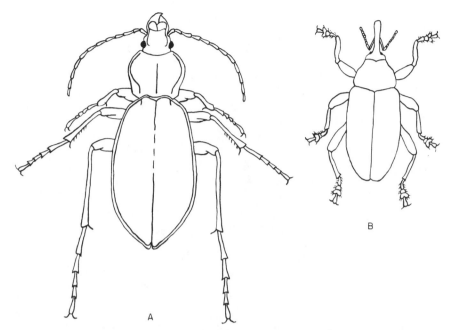

Figure 3.16 Coleoptera, beetles: (A) ground beetle, (B) weevil.

Ecology

This is the largest order of insects in the world; it contains approximately 40% of all species in the class Insecta. The beetles are very diverse in size, behavior, and feeding habits. A majority are phytophagous or predaceous, but others are phloem borers, phloem–wood borers, scavengers, or feed on fungi, pollen, and mushrooms. They are found in all habitats, with a majority occurring in terrestrial habitats. Many species are found in semi-aquatic and aquatic habitats. Certain species of bark beetles and weevils cause serious damage to trees. Insects in the order Coleoptera cause more damage to forest trees in the United States than do any other order; it is the second most important order causing damage to forest trees in Canada.

Mecoptera

This order consists of scorpionflies (Figure 3.17). Derivation: meco = long, ptera = wings.

Characteristics

Mecoptera characteristics are: (1) four long, narrow membranous, often patterned wings; (2) chewing mouthparts that are prolonged ventrally into a beak; (3) complete metamorphosis; (4) medium size (15–25 mm); and (5) peculiar long-faced head.

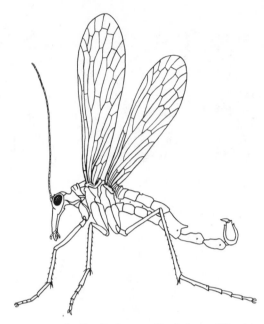

Figure 3.17 Mecoptera, scorpionfly. (Redrawn with slight modifications from Borror et al. 1981.)

The name "scorpionfly" is derived from the appearance of the male genitalia of some species; the tail is large and carried curved upward over the back like the sting of a scorpion.

Ecology

The scorpionflies are usually found in dense vegetation and cool, shaded woods. The larvae are chiefly scavengers living in or on the surface of the soil. The adults are terrestrial, some are scavengers (i.e., common scorpionflies), and others are predators (i.e., hanging scorpionflies).

Trichoptera

This order includes caddisflies (Figure 3.18). Derivation: tricho = hair, ptera = wings.

Characteristics

Trichoptera characteristics are: (1) usually four hairy, membranous wings that are held rooflike over abdomen when at rest; (2) larvae with chewing mouthparts, adults with vestigial mouthparts; (3) complete metamorphosis; (4) small–moderate size (3–25 mm); (5) mothlike in appearance; and (6) long, slender antennae.

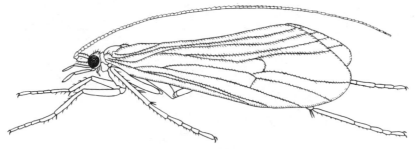

Figure 3.18 Trichoptera, caddisfly.

Ecology

All larvae are aquatic and common inhabitants of streams, ponds, and lakes. Some are very specific in habitat requirements and are used as indicators of environmental quality. The casemaking caddisfly larvae are plant and detritus feeders, whereas the free-living caddisfly larvae are generally predators. The adults are terrestrial, are often attracted to lights, and are usually found near aquatic habitats. The larvae and adults are an important food source for fish and other aquatic organisms.

Many caddisfly larvae are casebearers using a variety of materials such as pebbles, sand, leaves, and twigs, to build cases. The size and shape of the case often is used as one important characteristic in identifying the larva at the genus or species level.

Lepidoptera

This order includes butterflies and moths (Figure 3.19). Derivation: lepido = scale, ptera = wings.

Characteristics

Lepidoptera characteristics are: (1) four scale-covered wings (rarely wingless); (2) larvae with chewing mouthparts, adults mouthparts primarily for sucking, some vestigial; (3) complete metamorphosis; (4) size variable (wingspread 9–250 mm); and (5) antennae variable, but normally conspicuous.

Butterflies differ from moths by: (1) thin antennae with knob on tips versus threadlike or feathery antennae with no knob on tips; (2) wings generally held vertically over body when at rest versus wings generally held flat, either out at sides or over the back; (3) usually diurnal fliers rather than ordinarily nocturnal fliers; (4) brightly colored instead of generally dull colored; and (5) pupa in naked chrysalis versus pupa enclosed in cocoon or concealed under debris, wood, or rocks.

Lepidopterous larvae are generally cylindrical in shape with a well-developed head, body composed of 13 segments (3 thoracic and 10 abdominal), and three pairs of thoracic legs. Abdominal segments 3–6 and 10

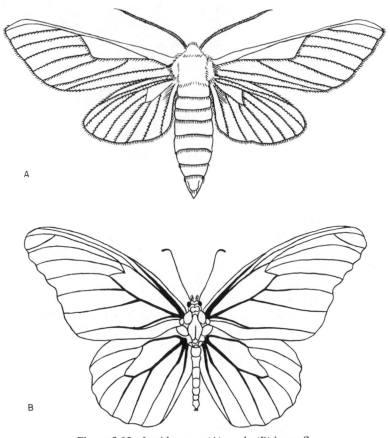

Figure 3.19   Lepidoptera: (A) moth, (B) butterfly.

usually bear a pair of *prolegs*, which are fleshy abdominal "false legs." The prolegs contain hooks called *crochets* (pronounced "croshays").

Ecology

Lepidoptera is the second largest order of insects and is composed of primarily terrestrial species. Economic damage is caused by the larval stages. The larvae are primarily defoliators, but some are phloem borers; phloem–wood borers; stem borers; or seed, grain, and fabric feeders. Insects in the order Lepidoptera cause more damage to forest trees in Canada than does any other order; it is the second most important order causing damage to forest trees in the United States.

Diptera

This order includes true flies (Figure 3.20). Derivation: di = two, ptera = wings.

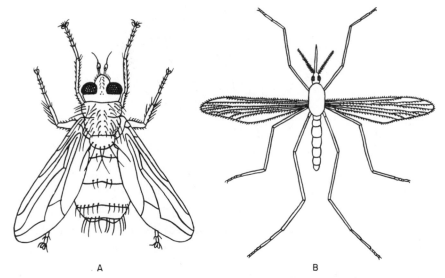

Figure 3.20 Diptera, true flies: (A) tachinid fly, (B) mosquito.

Characteristics

Diptera characteristics are: (1) one pair of membranous wings; (2) hind wings reduced to small knobbed structures called *halteres* that function as balancing organs; (3) variable mouthparts adapted for many different feeding habits such as sucking, piercing, sponging, and lapping; (4) complete metamorphosis; (5) size variable (1–50 mm); (6) antennae variable but usually inconspicuous; and (7) large compound eyes.

Ecology

This order is the fourth largest order of insects and an extremely diverse group. True flies are found in almost all habitats and feed in many different ways. Many are bloodsucking (i.e., mosquitoes, black flies, stable flies, and horse flies) and are serious pests to human beings and animals. Mosquitos, tsetse flies, house flies, black flies, and blow flies are also important disease vectors. Other flies are important as scavengers (i.e., blow flies), parasites (i.e., tachinid flies), predators (i.e., robber flies), and pollinators; cause galls, or act as forest and shade tree pests (i.e., gall midges, leaf mining flies).

Siphonaptera

This order consists of fleas (Figure 3.21). Derivation: siphon = tube, aptera = no wings.

Characteristics

Siphonaptera characteristics are (1) no wings, (2) adults having piercing–sucking mouthparts, larvae having chewing mouthparts, (3) complete met-

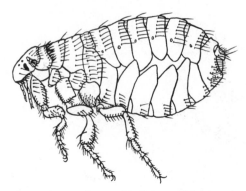

Figure 3.21   Siphonaptera, flea. (Redrawn with slight modifications from Borror et al. 1981.)

amorphosis, (4) quite small (<5 mm), (5) body usually dark and laterally flattened, and (6) legs relatively long with coxae greatly enlarged for jumping.

Ecology
Fleas are external parasites of birds and mammals. The larvae feed on organic debris, their own cast skins, and on the feces of adult fleas. The adults feed on the blood of birds and mammals. Fleas are not as host specific as lice, and some species will feed on many different hosts. Fleas are annoying pests of human beings and domesticated and wild animals. Fleas are vectors of disease and transmitters of bubonic plague from rats to human beings.

Hymenoptera

This order includes wasps, bees, ants, and sawflies (Figure 3.22). Derivation: hymeno = membrane, ptera = wings.

Characteristics
Hymenoptera characteristics are: (1) usually four membranous wings, (2) front wings usually larger than hind wings, (3) chewing or chewing–sucking mouthparts, (4) complete metamorphosis, (5) size variable (1–38 mm), (6) many species having a petiole (narrow connection) between thorax and abdomen, and (7) females of many species having a well-developed ovipositor.

Ecology
The Hymenoptera are primarily terrestrial and are found in many different habitats. Social organization and behavior are well developed in ants, vespid wasps, and bees.

This order contains many species that are economically beneficial and other species that are serious pests or household nuisances. Ants and vespid wasps are valuable predators; ichneumon wasps are important parasites;

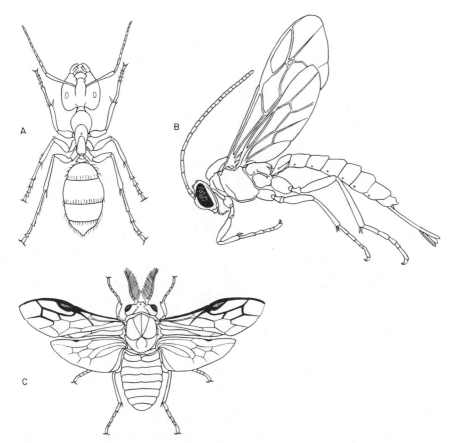

Figure 3.22 Hymenoptera: (A) ant, (B) ichneumon wasp, (C) sawfly. (Part (A) redrawn with slight modifications from Essig 1942. (A) reprinted with permission from Macmillan Publishing Company, from *College Entomology* by E. O. Essig. © by Macmillian Publishing Company.)

bees are important pollinators of plants; sawfly larvae are serious defoliators of ornamental and forest trees; a number of bee and wasp species inflict painful stings to humans; and some ants feed on plants, stored products, and also can be a nuisance in kitchens.

REFERENCES

Askew, R. W. 1971. *Parasitic Insects*. William Heinemann Ltd., London.

Borror, D. J. and R. E. White. 1970. *A Field Guide to the Insects of America North of Mexico*. Houghton Mifflin, Boston.

Borror, D. J., D. M. DeLong, and C. A. Triplehorn. 1981. *An Introduction to the Study of Insects*. Holt, Rinehart & Winston, New York.

Britton, W. E. 1923. The Hemiptera or sucking insects of Connecticut. *Conn. State Geol. Nat. Hist. Surv. Bull.* **34**:1–807.

Brues, C. T., A. L. Melander, and F. M. Carpenter. 1954. Classification of insects. *Harvard Univ. Mus. Comp. Zool. Bull.* **73**.

CSIRO 1970. *The Insects of Australia.* Melbourne University Press, Melbourne.

Claassen, P. W. 1931. Plecoptera nymphs of America north of Mexico. Thomas Say Foundation, *Entomol. Soc. Am.* **3**:1–199.

Daly, H. V., J. T. Doyen, and P. R. Ehrlich. 1978. *Introduction to Insect Biology and Diversity.* McGraw-Hill, New York.

Erwin, T. L. 1983. Tropical forest canopies: The last biotic frontier. *Bull. Entomol. Soc. Am.* **29**:14–19.

Essig, E. O. 1942. *College Entomology.* Macmillan, New York.

Essig, E. O. 1958. *Insects and Mites of Western North America.* Macmillan, New York.

Frison, T. H. 1935. The stoneflies, or Plecoptera, of Illinois. *Ill. Nat. Hist. Surv. Bull.* **20**:281–471.

Gillott, C. 1980. *Entomology.* Plenum Press, New York.

International Commission on Zoological Nomenclature. 1964. International Code of Zoological Nomenclature. International Trust for Zoological Nomenclature, London.

Kennedy, C. H. 1915. Notes on the life history and ecology of the dragonflies of central California and Nevada. *U.S. Nat. Mus. Bull.* **52**:183–635.

Leonard, J. W. and F. A. Leonard. 1962. *Mayflies of Michigan Trout Streams.* Cranbrook Institute of Science, Bloomfield Hills, MI.

Maynard, E. A. 1951. *The Collembola of New York.* Comstock, Ithaca, N. Y.

Meglitsch, R. A. 1967. *Invertebrate Zoology.* Oxford University Press, Oxford.

Merritt, R. W. and K. W. Cummins (Eds.), 1978. *An Introduction to the Aquatic Insects of North America.* Kendall/Hunt, Dubuque, Iowa.

Richards, O. W. and R. G. Davies. 1977. *Imms' General Textbook of Entomology, Vols. 1 and 2.* Chapman and Hall, London.

Romoser, W. S. 1981. *The Science of Entomology.* Macmillan, New York.

Ross, H. H., C. A. Ross, and J. R. P. Ross. 1982. *A Textbook of Entomology.* Wiley, New York.

Sommerman, K. M. 1943. Bionomics of *Ectopsocus pumilis* (Banks) (Corrodentia: Caeciliidae). *Psyche* **50**:55–63.

Usinger, R. L. (Ed.). 1965. *Aquatic Insects of California with Keys to North American Genera and California Species.* University of California Press, Berkeley.

Wallwork, J. A. 1970. *Ecology of Soil Animals.* McGraw-Hill, New York.

Werner, F. G. (Chairman). 1982. Common names of insects and related organisms. Entomology Society of America. Special Publication.

4 | INSECT DAMAGE AND SIGN CATEGORIES

Insects causing damage to forest and shade trees may be difficult to detect. They may be present on the trees for only a short time period, present only during evening hours, or difficult to capture. Fortunately, damage or insect signs are often available, helping foresters, arborists, and entomologists to determine the causal agent(s) without seeing the insect. Sometimes specific types of damage such as shape of leaf mine or leaf gall along with host identification allows the diagnostician to determine the causal agents to species. When damage symptoms are more general, probable causal agents may be determined only to a specific group of insects or a major type of damage such as lepidopterous defoliator or phloem boring. Insect signs, such as silk shelter, bagworm case, scale covering, egg shells, or shed larval skins, also are extremely helpful in determining the causal agent.

The ability to recognize insect damage and insect signs is an important skill that foresters, arborists, and naturalists should develop. The objective of this chapter is to introduce common insect damage categories and insect signs that are found on trees. Insect damage and signs are often divided into four major categories: (1) leaf damage; (2) seed and cone damage; (3) shoot, twig, trunk, and root damage; and (4) insect signs.

The insect damage and sign categories presented in this chapter are general ones. Some examples of insect damage found in the field will not exactly fit into any one category. Also, categories are not always mutually exclusive. Some insects, such as the California oakworm, *Phryganidia californica* Packard, are window feeders when they first emerge from the egg but progress to skeletonizers or free feeders as they grow larger. However, the system presented in this chapter will enable the beginning student to quickly learn to recognize most insect damage and insect signs found on forest and shade trees. Table 4.1 provides a written and pictorial coverage of the types of insect damage and insect signs.

Table 4.1   Common Insect Damage Categories and Insect Signs Associated with Forest and Shade Trees[a]

I. LEAF DAMAGE

A. ***Leaf and Needle Mines***—insect feeding on the inside of leaf or needle between the upper and lower epidermis. Some leaf miners do not feed in the same manner throughout their life cycle. For example, some species are serpentine miners as small larvae and blotch miners as large larvae. This is the reason for category A5, which covers various combinations of categories A1–A4. In other words, it is not uncommon to find a serpentine–blotch mine.

A1. *Linear mine.*

A2. *Serpentine mine.*

For example, aspen leafminer.

A3. *Blotch mine.*

For example, birch leafminer.

A4. *Digitate mine.*

For example, locust leafminer.

A5. *Any combination of A1–A4.*

For example, serpentine–blotch miner.

A6. *Needle mine.*

For example, lodgepole needle-miner.

Table 4.1 *(Continued)*

B. ***External Leaf or Needle Damage***—insect feeding on the external part of leaf or needle.

    B1. *Free feeding*—insect feeding on part or all of leaf or needle except largest leaf veins, which are often left uneaten.

    For example, many lepidopterous caterpillars (forest tent caterpillar, eastern tent caterpillar, western tent caterpillar, gypsy moth, elm spanworm, hemlock looper, late instar larvae of the California oakworm, variable oakleaf caterpillar, red humped oakworm, and saddled prominent).

    B2. *Hole feeding*—insect feeding in small patches through all layers of a leaf, creating many small holes in a leaf.

    For example, fall cankerworm, spring cankerworm, many leaf beetle adults, many June beetle adults, Japanese beetle adults.

    B3. *Skeletonizing*—insect feeding on the soft material between the veins leaving the veins as a "skeleton" of the leaf.

    For example, Japanese beetle adults, many large larval and adult leaf beetles.

    B4. *Window feeding*—insect feeding on only one surface of leaf that allows the light to penetrate through the remaining leaf layer. Common names of insects sometimes are misleading. In the past, window feeding was included under the damage category of skeletonizing. This has led to

Table 4.1   (Continued)

common names in which insects are called skeletonizers when, in fact, they are primarily window feeders. The birch leaf skeletonizer and oak leaf skeletonizer are two examples of misleading common names. Most forest entomologists now differentiate between window feeders and skeletonizers.

For example, birch leaf skeletonizer, oak leaf skeletonizer, early instars of many caterpillars, many leaf beetles, slug sawflies.

C. Shelter Feeding—insects make a shelter out of the leaves or needles and then feed on the foliage. Or abnormal plant growth occurs in reaction to insect feeding, resulting in plants forming a "shelter" around the insect.

   C1. *Web-enclosed foliage*—shelter made when several or many caterpillars web foliage together, live within enclosure, and feed on the enclosed foliage as window feeders, skeletonizers, or free feeders.

For example, fall webworm.

   C2. *Leaf tying or needle tying*—shelter made by caterpillar(s) tying two to six leaves or needles together with silk and feeding primarily as window feeders or skeletonizers on enclosed leaves or feeding on the apex of the needles.

Leaf tying	Needle tying
For example, cherry scallop shell moth.	For example, pine tube moth.

Table 4.1 *(Continued)*

C3. *Leaf folding or leaf rolling*—shelter made by caterpillar(s) that folds or rolls an individual leaf, fastens it together with silk, and feeds as a skeletonizer or window feeder within the shelter (e.g., many caterpillars in the families Tortricidae and Olethreutidae fold or roll leaves).

For example, leaf fold.   For example, leaf roll.

C4. *Crinkled leaves*—feeding by mites and certain insects with piercing–sucking mouthparts (e.g., aphids, thrips), which causes leaves to curl and crinkle.

C5. *Leaf and petiole galls*—feeding by mites and certain insects on actively growing plant tissue causes abnormal growth of a plant around the mite or insect in reaction to its feeding. This abnormal growth of the plant is called a *gall*.

For example, leaf gall.   For example, petiole gall.

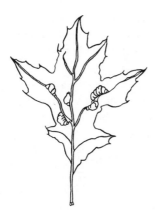

Table 4.1 *(Continued)*

D. *Stippling Damage*—feeding by mites and insects with piercing–sucking mouthparts, causing small dead spots on the leaves. Saliva is injected into the plant to partly predigest the sap before it is sucked up into the food canal. The small dead spot (toxemia) is due to the loss of sap and the toxic effect of the saliva on the leaf tissue.

For example, lace bugs, plant bugs.

II. SEED AND CONE DAMAGE

A. *Cone, Acorn, or Seed Boring*—insect feeding on the inside of the cone, acorn, or seed.

A1. *Cone boring.*	A2. *Acorn boring.*	A3. *Seed boring.*
For example, pine coneworms.	For example, acorn weevil.	For example, pine seedworms.

B. *Cone Scoring*—insect feeding on the surface of the cone.

C. *Shriveled Cones*—feeding on the cone scales by insects with piercing–sucking mouthparts or by some dipterous larvae that causes the cone to shrivel.

D. *Galls Present on Inside or Outside of Acorns and Other Seeds.*

III. SHOOT, TWIG, TRUNK, AND ROOT DAMAGE

A. *External Bark Damage*—insect feeding or ovipositing on the bark of twig or trunk.

   A1. *Bark scoring*—insect feeding on the bark of twig or trunk leaving small holes or irregular surface wounds, for example, larvae of many defoliators, adult weevils, and adult wood boring beetles.

   A2. *Oviposition damage*—slits in twig made during the egg laying process by female ovipositor of cicada, treehoppers, and larch sawfly or small pits chewed out for egg deposition spots by adult buprestids and cerambycids.

For example, cicada.

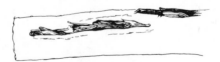

Table 4.1 *(Continued)*

A3. *Feeding punctures*—insects with piercing–sucking mouthparts causing damage similar to stippling damage on twigs that leave scars or cause twigs to wilt (e.g., spittlebug, tarnished plant bug).

B. *Internal Bark Feeding*—insect feeding in the phloem or adjacent surface of the wood.

B1. *Phloem boring*—galleries in the phloem and adjacent surface of the wood caused only by larval feeding.

For example, bronze birch borer.

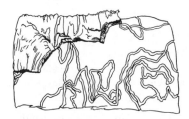

B2. *Bark beetle damage*—galleries in the phloem and adjacent surface of the wood caused by larval and adult bark beetles. Adults construct a gallery in which eggs are laid (egg gallery) and when eggs hatch, the larvae make larval galleries radiating out from the egg gallery. Bark beetle damage is a type of phloem boring. It is separated into a distinct category because of the importance of bark beetles on forest and shade trees and because there are two types of galleries (egg, larval) instead of the usual one type of gallery (larval).

For example, smaller European elm bark beetle.

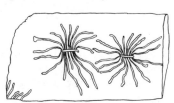

C. *Wood Boring*—insect feeding or boring into the phloem and wood, only wood, only the growing shoot.

C1. *Phloem*—wood boring—identical with phloem boring damage except that when larvae are larger and they bore into the wood (e.g., cerambycid larva).

For example, locust borer.

Table 4.1   (Continued)

C2. *Shoot boring*—phloem-wood boring that occurs only in growing shoots (e.g., Nantucket pine tip moth, European pine shoot moth).

For example, cut open shoot showing damage by a shoot borer.

C3. *Terminal boring*—shoot boring that occurs only on the terminal shoots (e.g., white pine weevil).

C4. *Ambrosia beetle damage*—adults bore small round holes (1–3 mm) directly into the wood of green logs, dying trees, stumps, and moist, freshly sawn lumber without making wandering galleries in the phloem. The galleries are kept free of boring dust and are often stained by fungus.

For example, ambrosia beetle.

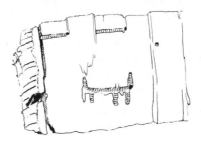

C5. *Powderpost beetle damage*—wood boring that produces very fine dustlike wood powder in dead trees and wood products (e.g., powderpost beetles in the families Bostrichidae, Lyctidae, Anobiidae, and Cerambycidae).

C6. *Honeycomb-type wood boring*—irregular interconnecting galleries in the heartwood or other dead parts of tree made by termites and carpenter ants.

For example, carpenter ants.

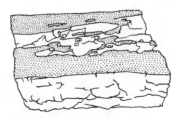

Table 4.1 *(Continued)*

D. ***Damage and Signs Caused by Tree Reactions to Insect Wounds***—see individual descriptions.

   D1. *Pitch, gum, and sap flows on outside of trees*—feeding by borers and bark beetles.

   D2. *Pitch streaks and gum streaks*—excessive production of these "normal" wound covering materials inside the tree in reaction to insect damage (e.g., cambium mining flies, peach tree bark beetle, spittlebugs).

   D3. *Twig galls*—feeding by certain insects in actively growing twigs causes a gall to form around the twig (e.g., spruce gall aphid).

   D4. *Wound tissue*—wound tissue covers the wounds but does not enclose the causal insect (e.g., bark beetles, borers).

   D5. *Abnormal wood grain inside the tree*—most commonly parenchyma wound tissue caused by phloem borers or "redwood" from piercing–sucking insects feeding on live bark.

IV. INSECT SIGNS

A. *Silk Shelters*—made entirely from silk (e.g., eastern tent caterpillar).

B. *Larval Cases*—made of silk, debris, or frass (e.g., bagworm, larch casebearer).

C. *Spittle Masses*—made of many small bubbles that enclose the nymph(s) (i.e., spittlebug).

D. *Scale and Aphid Coverings*—all scales and many aphids excrete a covering.

E. *Honeydew/Black Sooty Mold*—a sticky liquid sugar is excreted by scales and aphids. A black sooty mold often grows on this honeydew.

F. *Insect Remains*—egg shells, shed larval skins, pupal cases, cocoons, frass, and trails of silk.

---

[a]Table 4.1, excluding the drawings, was modified from an unpublished handout on damage categories developed by Dr. H. M. Kulman, Entomology Department, University of Minnesota, St. Paul.

PRINCIPLES AND TECHNIQUES OF INTEGRATED PEST MANAGEMENT

II

Section II is devoted to an examination of the principles and techniques of integrated pest management (IPM) in forests. This section contains six chapters. Chapter 5 is an overview of general principles and components of the concept of IPM. This chapter is the focal point for the remaining chapters in the section, which treat in detail the various components of IPM. Chapter 6 is a review of basic principles of population dynamics of forest insects. Chapter 7 considers the interaction of forest insects on population dynamics of forest trees. Chapter 8 examines the various tactics and strategies used to modify or regulate forest insect population size. Chapter 9 examines the ways that insects impact on forests. Chapter 10 reviews the ways that information on forest stands and insect populations is collected and used in IPM decision-making.

5 | CONCEPTS OF INTEGRATED PEST MANAGEMENT

INTRODUCTION

The economic, ecological, and social values that we associate with forests have increased dramatically in recent years. Efficient utilization of our forest resources requires that we manage depredation caused by destructive insects and diseases. Integrated pest management (IPM) is a philosophy, concept, and methodology for dealing with destructive insect and disease species in forests. Although considerable advancements in defining principles of IPM were achieved during the decade 1970–1980, application of the approach is still in the beginning stage. There are a number of reviews that trace the development and evolution of principles of IPM in forests: Apple and Smith (1976), Baumgartner (1975), NAS 1975, Berryman et al. (1978), Campbell and McFadden (1977), Coulson (1981), Coulson and Stark (1982), Gale (1979), Stark (1976, 1977, 1979a,b, 1980), Stark and Gittens (1973), and Waters and Stark (1980).

The basic issues that IPM addresses are not new. Foresters have recognized the following fundamental relationships between destructive agents and forest resource management for many years: (1) forest insects and diseases are integral components of forest ecosystems, (2) activities of these agents can have major effects on forest stand growth and productivity, and (3) the destructive agents can be disruptive to forest management objectives and schedules (Waters 1978). Basic research on the principles of IPM and the availability of new technologies, such as high-speed computers, have greatly advanced our understanding of IPM. However, we emphasize that implementation of IPM systems for forest insects and diseases is just beginning to be a reality.

The philosophy, concepts, and practice of IPM in forests are the topics of this chapter. We have four specific objectives: (1) we review basic concepts of IPM with regard to forest management practices, (2) we define and examine the conditions where forest insects are considered to be pests, (3) we define the basic components of an IPM system for a forest, and (4) we examine how IPM practices are implemented.

INTEGRATED PEST MANAGEMENT AS A COMPONENT OF FOREST MANAGEMENT

The term "pest" is an anthropocentric designation given to certain forest insects (and other organisms) when they adversely affect ecological, economic, and social values that we associate with forest and shade trees. The term has no basis in the principles of ecology. However, we will see that basic ecological principles are the foundation of IPM. It is important to recognize that most insects that occur in forests are not pests or are so on an infrequent basis.

Before we consider the relationship between IPM and forest management it is necessary to examine a definition of IPM. The philosophy, concept, and methodology of IPM evolved over a period of years and, therefore, so has the definition. Most comprehensive definitions contain four key points. First, the foundation of IPM is based on the principles of ecology. Second, the methodology involves a combination of tactics, that is, discrete techniques aimed at suppression or prevention of population growth. Several tactics together constitute a strategy for regulating population distribution and abundance. In some instances more than one strategy can be applied. Third, the functional goal is to reduce or maintain pest populations at tolerable levels. Economic, ecological, and social values are used in judging what "tolerable levels" are. Fourth, IPM is a component of total forest resource management (Stark 1980, Coulson 1981). These four messages are embodied in the definition of IPM provided by Waters (1974):

> . . . *integrated pest management* is the maintenance of destructive agents, including insects, at tolerable levels by the planned use of a variety of preventive, suppressive, or regulatory tactics and strategies that are ecologically and economically efficient and socially acceptable. It is implicit that the actions taken are fully integrated into the total resource management process—in both planning and operation. Pest management, therefore, must be geared to the life span of the tree crop as a minimum and to a longer time span where the resource planning horizon so requires.

Much of the complexity associated with definitions of IPM results from the need to convey information about the methodologies used in application of the approach. If we remove methodological implications from our definition and focus attention to the "pest" organism, pest management becomes synonomous with population management. In general, a population of insects becomes a problem if it is numerous enough to cause significant damage. Note that it is necessary to retain social and economic values associated with a particular ecosystem, because these values determine whether we classify an insect as a pest. In our discussion of population dynamics (Chapter 6) we will learn that populations become more numerous by reproduction and immigration and less numerous by mortality and emigration (Figure 6.2). Therefore, pest management (population management) is directed to maintenance of pest populations at tolerable levels by either lowering reproduction or immigration or increasing mortality or emigration. How these ends are accomplished is the methodology of IPM. Manipulating reproduction, mortality, immigration, and emigration to manage population distribution and abundance is by no means a simple task.

Now that we have defined the concept of IPM we are in a position to consider how it relates to forestry, forest management, and forest protection. However, we need to consider several additional definitions. *Forestry* is defined as the "scientific management of forests for the continuous production of goods and services" (Society of American Foresters 1958). A component of forestry practice is *forest management*, which is defined as "the application of business methods and technical forestry principles to the operation of a forest property" (ibid.). Forests are (or can be) managed for the multiple values of timber and fiber production, recreation, fish and wildlife, grazing, and hydrology. Insects, as well as other agents, can disrupt our planned uses of forests by affecting one or more of these values. *Forest protection* is, therefore, the component of forest management that is concerned with minimizing losses or other negative effects caused by harmful agents. Traditionally, forest protection has included consideration of insects, disease, weeds, and fire. IPM is the conceptual methodology for accomplishing forest protection goals in light of multiple forest values. The concept of IPM that we provided above is applicable to insects, diseases, and weeds. However, the principles are different for fire. Stark (1979b) suggested that the goals and concepts of forest management, forest protection, and IPM could be incorporated by using the expression "integrated forest protection against pests" (IFPAP).

CONDITIONS WHERE FOREST INSECTS ARE CONSIDERED TO BE PESTS

There are three general circumstances where insects are considered pests of forest trees: (1) in forest ecosystems; (2) in specialized forestry settings such as seed orchards, nurseries, turpentine plantations (gum naval stores), and so on; and (3) in urban forests. In addition, insects are also serious pests of manufactured wood products and structures. The degree of application of the concepts of IPM is dictated in large part by the type of forest situation where a pest occurs. This circumstance exists because there is a wide range of interest in forest resource management between the different forest situations. Therefore, we will examine each of the forest situations in some detail.

Forest Ecosystems

Principles of IPM in forests were developed for application at the ecosystem level of organization. Our interest in managing forests for the multiple values of timber and fiber production, hydrology, recreation, wildlife and fish, and grazing lead to the classification of certain insect species as pests. Forest ecosystems are not uniformly managed for each of the values identified above. One or two values may be emphasized more than the others. Depending on the degree of involvement by forest managers and the values being managed for, therefore, a forest ecosystem can be classified as *intensively* or *extensively* managed. A coastal plain pine forest managed primarily for timber and fiber production in the southern United States is an example of an intensively managed forest. A coniferous–hardwood forest in the Southern Appalachian Mountains managed for recreation, fish and wild-life, and hydrology is an example of an extensively managed forest (Figures 5.1 and 5.2).

Greatest emphasis in IPM has traditionally been directed to the phyto-phagous insects that affect timber and fiber production, because of the paramount importance of these values in forest management planning. In this discussion, therefore, we will focus our attention primarily on phyto-phagous insects that occur in forest ecosystems and affect timber and fiber production values. The concepts of IPM are closely tied to a number of fundamental relationships between phytophagous insects, their host plants, characteristics of the site on which the plant is growing, and forest stand management practices.

Insect–Plant Relationships

A tree species or genus will normally have a characteristic phytophagous insect fauna. For example, the insects that feed on pines will be different from those species that feed on oaks. Throughout the various stages of growth of a particular tree species, the insect fauna changes in composition and number. For example, the insects associated with sapling pines will be different from those species found on mature trees. Furthermore, most phytophagous insects have restricted feeding habits, specifically, phloem feeding, xylem feeding, seed and cone feeding, foliage feeding, and so forth (see Chapter 4). Therefore, in a forest ecosystem we can expect that

Figure 5.1   Intensively managed loblolly pine stand in the southeastern United States.

Figure 5.2 Extensively managed coniferous–hardwood forest in the Appalachian Mountains of western North Carolina.

there will be a characteristic and usually small number of insect species associated with (1) a particular host tree species, (2) a certain age–class of the host, and (3) specific anatomical parts (modules) of the host.

Phytophagous insects can affect a host tree in a number of different ways: (1) directly kill it, (2) impair or slow growth, (3) destroy certain plant parts such as cones or buds, (4) physiologically weaken it and thereby make it susceptible to other tree-killing agents such as plant diseases, and (5) directly inoculate the tree with a plant disease. In addition, feeding by phytophagous insects can structurally weaken trees or cause cosmetic defects (such as wood staining). These latter two types of damage are often of greatest consequence after a tree has been harvested and manufactured into a product. Whether an insect is considered a pest will depend on the degree and extent that one or more of the effects outlined above occur and the value that we place on the particular tree species affected.

Insect–Plant–Site Relationships

A *site* can be considered as a localized area within a forest ecosystem where a particular tree species, along with associated vegetation, grows. The site consists of both abiotic (nonliving) and biotic (living) components. The definition of site provided by the Society of American Foresters (1958) is as follows: "an area considered as to its ecological factors with reference to capacity to produce forests or other vegetation; the combination of biotic, climatic, and soil conditions of an area." Since different tree species have different requirements for growth, the condition of the site has a major influence on productivity of a forest as well as the plant species composition present. Site conditions within an ecosystem vary in two important ways: (1) a forest ecosystem consists of a mosaic of different site conditions, and (2) site condition changes throughout the life cycle (or rotation time) of a tree species.

There are many factors that contribute to variation in site quality within a forest ecosystem. Among the important abiotic factors are (1) soil type and texture, (2) terrain elevation and slope, and (3) watershed drainage patterns. Biotic factors that infuence site quality change with the various stages of ecological succession. Among the important variables are the density and diversity of (1) herbaceous and woody plants, (2) soil microorganisms, (3) soil arthropods, and (4) phytophagous insects. It is important to recognize that there is a dynamic interaction between the abiotic and biotic components of a particular site.

Site condition is an important consideration in IPM for two general reasons. First, the site contains the host material (tree species in various stages of growth) that pest species utilize for food and habitat. The availability of suitable preferred and alternate hosts is a primary requisite for the development of insect populations. Different sites vary in plant species composition, density, and age classes. Therefore, the opportunity for insect populations to grow in size varies on different sites. Second, site condition, in combination with weather, determines the rate of growth and general vigor of the host trees present. Many forest insects exploit trees that are physiologically weakened as a result of stress created by nutrient deficiencies, drought, flooding, overcrowding, and other variables.

Insect–Forest Management Relationships

The basic unit of forest management is the forest stand. A *stand* is a somewhat arbitrary subdivision of a forest ecosystem. It is an aggregation of trees and other vegetation occupying a specific area. It is sufficiently homogeneous in species composition, age, size structure, and condition so as to be distinguishable from the forest and associated vegetation on adjoining areas (Waters and Stark 1980). Because of variations in site conditions, which we discussed above, forest stands differ in species composition, size structure, rate of growth, and mortality.

Many of the activities that distinguish insects as pests, such as defoliating or killing host trees, were beneficial functions, before we became interested in managing forest stand composition, growth, and productivity. For example, grazing by herbivorous defoliating insects likely served as a form of natural forest fertilization. Foliage was utilized for growth and development of the herbivore, and nutrients were made available, primarily in the form of frass, to the ecosystem. Today, defoliation is generally viewed as harmful in managed forest stands because tree mortality or growth reduction can occur in commercially valuable trees. Likewise, mortality to mature and overmature trees resulting from the activities of bark beetles serves as a means of truncating plant community development prior to senescence. Successional openings within the ecosystem are created, and new forests are naturally regenerated. These functional roles of forest insects are often in conflict with our planned uses of forests today (Schowalter et al. 1981). Insects and other arthropods are integral components of forest ecosystems that are normally involved in basic ecological processes such as nutrient cycling and succession. These processes greatly affect site quality and stand characteristics (Figure 5.3).

Certain activities involved in the cultivation of forests create conditions that enhance the likelihood that phytophagous insects will become pests. The two basic activities center on the structure of forest stands and disturbances resulting from cultivation practices.

In circumstances where we are attempting to maximize wood or fiber production, forest structure is tailored in a number of specified ways: (1) there will generally be only one or two tree species in which we are interested; (2) within a particular stand, these trees will all be planted at or

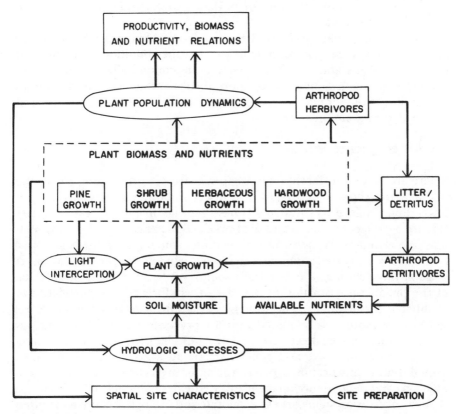

Figure 5.3 Conceptual model illustrating roles of arthropod consumers in forest ecosystems. (Courtesy of T. D. Schowalter.)

about the same time—that is, the stand will be even aged; (3) there will generally be an attempt made at controlling unwanted tree species, such as hardwood species in pine plantations; and (4) density of the trees will be prescribed. Each of these conditions is conducive to the buildup of large population numbers of insects that are associated with a particular tree species, age–class, or plant anatomical structure. Variations in site quality, that is, poor site quality, and stand conditions within a forest ecosystem often create the opportunity for pest species to develop in stressed or weakened trees and later spread throughout a stand.

In a similar manner, many of the management practices necessary for the cultivation of forests create or contribute to potential pest problems. For example, harvesting, site preparation, planting, and thinning forests involve the use of heavy machinery. These activities alter the physical characteristics of the forest and can affect sites by compacting soil, causing soil erosion and nutrient loss, disrupting litter decomposition needed for nutrient recycling, physically damaging nonharvested trees, and so on. Such disturbances can create pest problems associated with trees growing on poor sites (in the next rotation) or in damaged or weakened trees in the current or remaining stand.

Forest managers are aware of these problems and much of the challenge in IPM in forests centers on how to prevent the conditions that can lead to pest problems and yet productively and economically manage forest properties. The challenge is even more difficult when we consider values in addition to timber and fiber production, that is, recreation, wildlife and fish, hydrology, and grazing.

Specialized Forestry Settings

There are several different types of specialized forestry setting where the tolerable threshold to depredation by insect and other arthropods is much lower than in forest ecosystems. These settings include forest nurseries (Figure 5.4); seed orchards and seed production areas (Figure 5.5); Christmas tree plantations (Figure 5.6); turpentine plantations (gum naval stores) (Figure 5.7); and arboretums, research plots, wind breaks; and so on. Insect pests in these settings are extremely important because of the high value of the product (or function in the case of windbreaks) sought relative to traditional forest values. The strategies taken in managing pests in these settings are more closely aligned with the practices used in traditional agriculture than in forest ecosystems. For example, pest management practices are more intensive and generally warrant a greater expenditure of capital than is practical in a forest over an entire rotation. There is also a much greater dependence on the use of pesticides in the specialized settings than in forest ecosystems, where economic and ecological constraints often limit widespread application.

Figure 5.4   Forest nursery illustrating cultivation of pine seedlings. (Courtesy of Texas Forest Service.)

Figure 5.5   Seed orchard containing genetically selected pine trees. (Courtesy of Texas Forest Service.)

Figure 5.6 Christmas tree plantation in western North Carolina. (Courtesy of F. P. Hain.)

The management practices employed in the specialized forest settings are conductive to the implementation of IPM principles for several reasons: (1) the land area set aside for the specialized setting is small relative to most forest management units; (2) the management goal is specific, including production of seed, turpentine, seedlings, and so on; (3) the value of the crop or product is large, and it is thus possible to justify and provide intensive management; and (4) custodial care is usually the responsibility

Figure 5.7 Slash pine stand in northern Florida managed for turpentine production. (U.S. Forest Service photograph.)

of a single organization that has been provided with personnel and financial resources necessary for managing the special setting.

The insect–plant–site relationships in the specialized settings are also conducive to application of IPM. Since the resource we are interested in protecting is discrete (one or two tree species, a single age–class, and specific plant anatomic parts), the number of pest species that we must contend with, at any one time, is generally small. Furthermore, most of the insect pests have been identified, and usually their life histories have been described. Procedures for survey and detection of the pest species are available, and suppression tactics have often been developed. It is, therefore, possible to tailor suppression tactics to specific insects, which can be implemented when the resource is sufficiently threatened to warrant action. Considerable emphasis is also placed on site maintenance and avoidance of cultural disturbances in the specialized setting; the major exception is in turpentine plantations, where trees are purposefully damaged in the turpentine extraction process (Figure 5.7).

Urban Forests

The urban forest can be defined to include trees growing in residential areas at the interface between managed forests and centers of commerce, in yards at residences, along city streets, in city parks, in recreational areas, and in other areas. Some specialists distinguish between urban and suburban forests. In this discussion we combine the two categories. Conceptually, the problems of insect management in urban forests are similar to those in forest ecosystems or the specialized forest settings. The main difference is that trees in urban areas are cultured primarily for aesthetic purposes and because of their usefulness in buffering the effects of weather.

Although the basic relationships betwen insects and their host trees are the same as defined for forest ecosystems and the specialized forestry settings, there are several unique features of pest problems in urban forests. Following are several examples: (1) diversity of valued host species and associated insects is generally greater in urban forests; (2) host trees consist of both native and exotic species; (3) there is usually a greater range in age–classes of host trees in urban forests; and (4) mature, and thus often senescent, hosts are particularly valued.

The opportunity for widespread outbreaks of insect pests in urban forests is minimized somewhat because the number of host species in a vulnerable age–class is usually small. There are several noteworthy exceptions to this generalization. For example, American elm, a dominant landscape tree in the northeastern and midwestern United States, has been ravaged by Dutch elm disease, *Ceratocystis ulmi* (Buisum.) C. Moreau, vectored by the smaller European elm bark beetle, *Scolytus multistriatus* (Marsham), and the native elm bark beetle, *Hylurgopinus rufipes* (Eichhoff). Likewise, urban areas in the southeastern United States, where various pine species are common ornamental trees, have periodically had outbreaks of the southern pine beetle, *Dendroctonus frontalis* Zimmermann. Severe defoliation of a variety of hardwood species by the gypsy moth, *Lymantria dispar* (Linnaeus), has also been a serious problem of urban forests in the northeastern United States.

Cultural disturbances to sites and trees are as important in urban forests as they were in forest ecosystems. The specific types of disturbance are often quite different, however. Examples of cultural disturbance in urban forests are as follows: road construction; power transmission line clearing; photochemical oxidation injury; building construction, including site clearance and dressing, placement of sidewalks, driveways, and conduits; and modification of water drainage patterns.

Manufactured Wood Products and Structures

Insect pests of wood products and structures represent a management problem altogether different from what we have defined for pests of living trees in forest ecosystems, specialized forest settings, and urban forests. The insects responsible for damage to wood products and structures are traditionally discussed in forest entomology because the various species involved are indigenous to forests. However, the economic damage caused by the insects usually occurs outside the forest after trees have been harvested and utilized for a specific purpose. Management of the pest species is usually done by the structural pest control industry. The procedures used rely on preventive wood treatment, pesticides, and sanitation. We will not consider management of insects of wood products and structures in any further detail in this chapter.

It is noteworthy that many of the most injurious insect pest species of wood products and structures are extremely beneficial when confined to forest ecosystems. For example, termites (Isoptera), ants (Hymenoptera), and some wood boring beetles (Coleoptera) are largely responsible for degradation of dead trees and thus are important in recycling of nutrients and preparing the way for ecological succession in forest ecosystems.

COMPONENTS OF INTEGRATED PEST MANAGEMENT IN FORESTS

Multidisciplinary research and application programs on major forest insect pest problems were largely responsible for the solidification of concepts of IPM in forests. In particular, during the decade 1970–1980 there were programs directed to IPM of the gypsy moth, bark beetles of the genus *Dendroctonus*, the Douglas-fir tussock moth [*Orgyia pseudotsugata* (Mc-Dunnough)], and the spruce budworms [*Choristoneura fumiferana* (Clemens) and *C. occidentalis* Freeman]. Although different insect species and forest ecosystems were studied, certain unifying principles and concepts emerged.

One major accomplishment of these projects was the development of an organizational framework, or system structure, that (1) defined the major research and development components of IPM in forests, (2) identified the pathways for interaction between the components, and (3) related IPM to forest resource management at the ecosystem level of organization. Basic elements of the system structure are illustrated in Figure 5.8. This diagram was developed initially for IPM research and applications programs on *Dendroctonus* spp. bark beetles. Basic features of the concept have been discussed in detail by Waters (1974), Waters and Cowling (1976), Stark (1976, 1977), and Waters and Stark (1980). Alternative structures, incorporating essentially the same elements, have been provided by Campbell (1973), Campbell and McFadden (1977), and Brookes et al. (1978).

Since Figure 5.8 represents a concise overview of the concepts of IPM in forests, we will examine the elements contained in it in some detail. Our main focus in this section deals with the research and development components that are represented in the core of Figure 5.8. These components include (1) pest population dynamics and epidemiology, (2) forest stand dynamics, (3) treatment tactics, (4) impact on resource values, and (5) benefit–cost integration. Each of these components is a complex subsystem and ideally consists of detailed information that is usually abstracted in the form of a predictive mathematical model (see Chapter 6 for a discussion

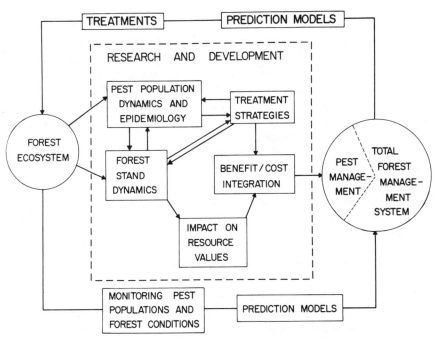

Figure 5.8 General conceptual model structure of a forest pest management system. (From Waters and Cowling 1976.)

of mathematical modeling). The components in the core are linked together as indicated by the arrows. The arrows indicate both the primary direction of information flow, that is, the flow of information needed for analyses, simulation experiments, pest management decisions, and feedback relationships between components (Waters and Stark 1980). We also consider the activities associated with monitoring pest populations and forest stands. This component is represented at the periphery of Figure 5.8. Later in this chapter we will discuss the factors involved in implementation of principles of IPM in forests. The components involved in this phase are also illustrated at the periphery of Figure 5.8.

There are seven fundamental principles of IPM in forests that are conveyed in Figure 5.8.

1. The basic premise of IPM is that there is a resource in need of protection from pests. Knowledge of the resource is abstracted as the "forest stand dynamics" component of Figure 5.8.

2. Insect species are periodically pests because they become sufficiently numerous to damage the resource in some way. Knowledge of fluctuations in pest population numbers is abstracted as the "pest population dynamics and epidemiology" component of Figure 5.8.

3. The actual or potential importance of a pest species is judged by evaluating its effects on values that we associate with the resource, that is, on timber and fiber production, recreation, fish and wildlife, grazing, and hydrology. The process of evaluating the effects of insects on the resource is represented as the "impact on resource values" component of Figure 5.8.

4. It is often possible to employ certain techniques, termed *treatment tactics,* to suppress populations of insects. The judgment to attempt treatments to reduce or suppress insects is based on knowledge of pest population dynamics, stand dynamics, an appraisal of impacts on resource values, and costs of application. These inputs to the "treatment component" of IPM are illustrated in Figure 5.8.

5. The final judgments in IPM decision-making are based on benefit–cost analyses, which, in turn, are based on evaluation of impacts and available treatment tactics. Benefit–cost integration (Figure 5.8) is thus the link of IPM to forest management practice.

6. Pest management is a component of forest resource management (Figure 5.8).

7. Data for monitoring pest populations and stand conditions are obtained from various types of forest surveys.

Ideally, we would have detailed information on stand dynamics, pest population dynamics, treatment tactics, impacts, and benefit–cost analysis routines for all forest insect pests. In reality we have such information on only a few species. Nevertheless, the components identified in Figure 5.8 and the principles outlined above serve as the basis for IPM in forests. Often we are required to make judgments based on imperfect understanding of a pest–host system. Continuing research in IPM is the key to increasing our knowledge and understanding of pest–host problems and eventually being able to predict accurately the outcome of management decisions. It is also worthwhile to point out that even though the components and principles of IPM outlined above were developed for use at the forest ecosystem level, they are also applicable to IPM decision-making in the specialized forestry settings and urban forests.

Since the components of pest population dynamics and epidemiology, forest stand dynamics, treatments, impact on resources, and monitoring pest populations and forest stand conditions play a central role in IPM, we will elaborate on these subjects.

Pest Population Dynamics and Epidemiology

Pest population dynamics (Chapter 6) is the study of change in the distribution and abundance of an organism through space and time. The spatial framework for pest species encompasses a range of square centimeters to hectares and the temporal framework may vary from minutes to years. Within this spatial–temporal framework, it is possible to focus attention on populations within a unit of habitat, within a stand, or within a forest (Coulson 1979).

Pests are of major importance in forest management because they are the agents that detract from resource values and disrupt management objectives. Our interest in managing pests includes immediate short-term response to outbreak conditions involving current population levels and damage as well as long-term planning to anticipate and prevent population levels that lead to outbreaks. Obviously, the approaches used in population management under these two circumstances are quite different.

When one considers all the variables that affect birth, death, immigration, and emigration in a population of forest insects, it is not surprising to find that mathematical models of population systems are utilized to abstract key elements. We note in Chapter 6 that accuracy and precision of predictive models of population dynamics are related to space–time resolution. Both accuracy and precision diminish as the space–time framework is enlarged, primarily because of the difficulties in forecasting weather over long periods of time. Therefore, best results in modeling populations have been obtained at the stand level of organization and in a period of time ranging from several weeks to several months. In management planning for potential pest problems, variables such as stand age, species composition and density, localized site conditions, physiographic conditions, and climatic zones within the range of a particular pest species are used in predicting the likelihood of pest problems occurring at various age intervals of forest growth.

Forest Stand Dynamics

The forest stand is the focal point of IPM because it is the basic unit used by foresters for inventory, planning, and operations. Stand dynamics includes consideration of causes for changes in the distribution, abundance, and size of a host tree species through space and time (see Chapter 7 for further information).

In the context of IPM, we may be interested in either (1) the role of pests (insects, diseases, etc.) in the population dynamics of the host tree species or (2) the role of the host in the population dynamics of the pest. The interaction between pest population dynamics and stand dynamics is illustrated in Figure 5.8.

In the first case, where interest is in the role of pests in the population dynamics of the host, the temporal framework spans the rotation time for a particular tree species, which can range from 6 to 200 years. The spatial framework will normally be in hectares. We emphasized earlier that specific pests are associated with a particular tree species, age–class, and plant anatomic parts. Therefore, during the period from seed to mature tree, many pest species, as well as other biotic and abiotic agents, have the opportunity to affect tree growth rate and survival.

In the second case, where we are interested in the role of the host in the population dynamics of the pest, the spatial framework can range from single trees, to stands, and to forests comprised of stands in different age classes. The temporal framework can span from hours to several years. Host trees vary in susceptibility to colonization by insects and suitability as food and habitat. Tree species, age, and general vigor are variables that influence both susceptibility and suitability. Furthermore, many tree species possess defensive mechanisms that deter insects; for instance, the resin system of pines is considered to be a primary defense against certain bark beetle species.

Foresters have developed mathematical models to predict forest stand growth and yield for many of the commercially important tree species. Data for these models are collected as part of the normal forest inventory conducted on federal, state, and corporate lands. Growth and yield models have proved to be useful in IPM, particularly when we are interested in defining costs associated with tree mortality or growth reduction resulting from the activities of pest species (Stage 1973, 1975).

Treatment Tactics

Treatment tactics are planned procedures that are used to modify or regulate the distribution and abundance of a pest species. As with the other elements of IPM, treatments have time and space components. That is, we are interested in ways and means of *suppression* of existing pest populations and in *prevention* of potential pest population outbreaks. In the case of suppression the time frame may range from several weeks to months and the space framework from single trees to stands. However, more than one stand within a forest ecosystem can be affected. In the case of prevention our time framework may span the rotation period for a tree species and the space framework includes stands within forest ecosystems. Obviously the procedures used in suppression and prevention are quite different.

Historically, a great deal of attention has been given to development of treatments for specific pest problems. Conceptually, these tactics affect reproduction, mortality, immigration, and/or emigration. There are numerous ways to manipulate these population system components. The specific procedure is often referred to as a *control procedure* or *control tactic*. It is not our intention here to review all the procedures used against forest insects. Following are several examples that illustrate various tactics used in suppression and prevention. A detailed examination of ways and means of population modification and regulation using natural and artificial methods is presented in Chapter 8.

Suppression tactics are directed to existing pest problems. Examples of tactics include: (1) biological control, including augmentation of insect parasites, insect predators, avain predators, and diseases; (2) chemicals, including various pesticides and herbicides; (3) behavioral chemicals, including compounds that result in attraction and dispersal; (4) utilization, which involves harvesting of infested host materials; and (5) various mechanical procedures, including felling infested hosts and burning infested hosts.

Techniques used in prevention of insect outbreaks include: (1) regulatory controls, which are designed to prevent introduction of pests into uninfested forests or contain them (through quarantine) in localized areas and (2) cultural or silvicultural controls that include management of stand characteristics such as species composition, age, and density; site maintenance; and avoidance of disturbances to both stands and sites.

The concept of IPM stresses that a variety of tactics can be used simultaneously to manage pest populations. These tactics collectively constitute a *strategy*. It is possible to develop strategies for both suppression or prevention goals. For a particular treatment tactic to be included as part of a strategy, it must be efficacious, safe, and cost-effective. Reference to Figure 5.8 indicates that treatment strategies are directly linked to the pest population dynamics, forest stand dynamics, and benefit–cost integration components and indirectly to the impact component.

Impact on Resource Values

The concept of pest impact on resource values (Chapter 9) is a central issue in IPM. Definitions of the concept and meaning of impact evolved during the decade 1970–1980. Waters and Stark (1980) define the term as follows: "Impact may be . . . explicitly defined as the cumulative net effect(s) of a given pest or pest complex on the realized value of a tree species, forest type, or management unit with respect to different resource uses and management objectives." In determining "realizable values" impact assessment includes consideration of economic, ecological, and aesthetic components (Stark 1979b). Furthermore, these three criteria must be applied to the multiple values of wood and fiber production, hydrology, recreation, wildlife and fish, and grazing.

Evaluating impacts can be extremely complicated. A particular insect can have both negative or positive impacts depending on the criteria used in judgment and the particular forest management goal. For example, a defoliating insect could, at the same time, reduce incremental growth of a host tree species, provide nutrient enrichment to the forest, and serve as food for fish. The first impact would usually be considered negative, whereas the second two would be positive. Because of the difficulties involved in assessing impacts, it is not surprising to find, again, that mathematical models are used for interpretative as well as predictive purposes. Fundamental econometric principles serve as the basis for structuring models of impacts.

Monitoring Pest Populations and Forest Stands

In the preceding sections we have indicated that IPM includes components dealing with population dynamics, stand dynamics, treatment tactics and strategies, impact assessment, and cost–benefit analysis. Information needed for the components of IPM is obtained by monitoring pest populations and forest stands (Chapter 10). In general, monitoring forest stand conditions is undertaken separately from monitoring pest populations, but both activities are essential for providing the information needed for IPM decision-making. The ways and means for collecting the information is accomplished through forest surveys.

There are several different types of insect surveys that can be applied in forest ecosystems, specialized forestry settings, and in urban forests. Forest surveys can be quantitative or qualitative with regard to the type of data collected. Surveys can also be classed according to their purpose in the following way: (1) detection surveys, (2) biological evaluations, (3) loss or damage surveys, and (4) pest control evaluations. The specific procedures used depend on the type of forest situation being sampled, the type of survey being conducted, and the intended use of data being collected.

Monitoring pest populations and forest conditions is represented at the periphery of Figure 5.8 linking activities taking place in the forest ecosystem to predictive models, and finally to forest resource management. Because of the importance of correct information for use in IPM decision-making and the high costs associated with obtaining the information, forest surveys involve use of advanced technologies. Remote sensing techniques, specialized statistical analyses, and high-speed computers are common tools used in forest survey activities.

IMPLEMENTATION OF IPM PRACTICES

At the outset of this chapter we indicated that implementation of the concept, philosophy, and IPM methodology was in the beginning stages. We have reviewed the basic components of an IPM system and are now in a position to consider how pest management decisions can be made. Conceptually, IPM decision-making results from an evaluation of treatment options available and analysis of impacts (Figure 5.8). These two subjects are examined in further detail in Chapters 8 and 9. Information needed for these two components is based on knowledge of pest population dynamics and forest stand dynamics as indicated by the direction of information flow in Figure 5.8. Benefit–cost integration, which is the final component in the IPM system structure, is based on an *interpretation* of information by a forest manager. The final decisions regarding IPM are in large part judgmental. Certainly as our knowledge and understanding of a pest–host plant system increases, so does our ability to predict the likely outcome of a management decision.

There is a great deal of variation in the amount of information we have available for different forest insect pests. In the case of pests such as the gypsy moth, certain *Dendroctonus* spp. bark beetles, the Douglas-fir tussock moth, and the spruce budworms, a great deal of information is available. This information has been abstracted in the form of mathematical models. However, with most forest insects we do not have such models for each of the IPM components identified in Figure 5.8. This fact adds greatly to the uncertainty the forest management specialists face in decision-making about pests.

Where detailed information on pest–host interactions is available, pest management specialists envision the development of computer-based systems that will be suitable for use by forest managers in facilitating judgment of the consequences of pests in forests. These computer-based systems are termed *decision–support systems*. This approach has been used in decision-making in industry for several years and is just beginning to be applied as a tool in IPM. Construction of decision–support systems is an activity that involves operations research engineers, computer scientists, pest management specialists, and foresters. Figure 10.11 illustrates the general components of a decision–support system, and Figure 10.12 illustrates the functions performed by the system. Figure 5.9 is an example of a flow diagram that includes the logic involved in incorporating a forest stand model, pest outbreak model, and treatment strategy model(s). We emphasize that a decision–support system provides information only to the forest

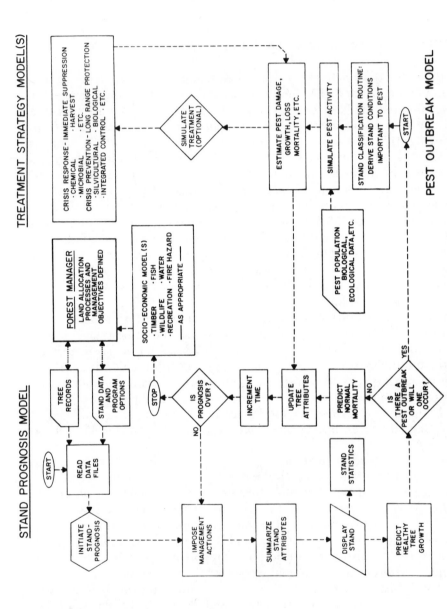

Figure 5.9 Information flow diagram illustrating the logic involved in incorporating a forest stand model, pest outbreak model, and treatment strategy model(s). From Waters and Stark 1980.)

118

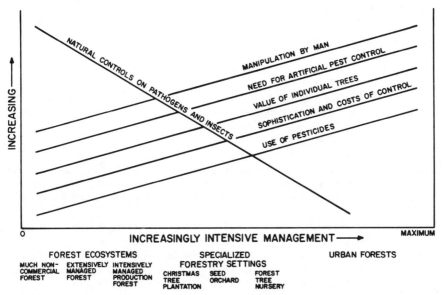

Figure 5.10 General characteristics of variables involved in integrated pest management for forest ecosystems, specialized forestry settings, and urban forests. (Modified from NAS 1975.)

manager. The analysis of benefits and costs and final decision-making is done by the forest manager. It is also noteworthy that, although highly desirable, a computer-based decision–support system is not necessary in order to utilize the philosophy and concepts of IPM.

The degree of implementation or the need to implement principles of IPM varies with different forest circumstances. Figure 5.10 defines some of the characteristics of various forest management situations in regard to IPM. In each circumstance, where insects and other organisms were identified to be pests (forest ecosystems, specialized forestry settings, and urban forests), unique problems for implementing IPM are presented. For example, there is a wide range in interest in managing pests that stems from forest ownership patterns in a particular region. Management goals, if they even exist, vary greatly among different owners. Furthermore, accessibility to the pest may be difficult, which greatly limits our ability to respond to problems once identified.

The principles and concepts identified in this chapter provide the forest manager the option to include IPM as a component of forest resource management. Traditionally, forest pests became important to the manager once a crisis existed. We now have much better tools available for evaluation of the costs and benefits of prevention as well as suppression alternatives. The immediate challenges to implementing IPM principles in forests center on overcoming problems in (1) attitudes of forest managers and (2) existing policy of organizations. As the value of forests and forest products continues to increase, so will the application of the principles of IPM.

REFERENCES

Apple, J. D. and R. F. Smith (Eds.). 1976. *Integrated Pest Management*. Plenum Press, New York.

Baumgartner, D. M. (Ed.). 1975. Management of lodgepole pine ecosystems. Washington State University, Pullman, Cooperative Extension Service.

Berryman, A. A., G. D. Amman, R. W. Stark, and D. L. Kibbee (Eds.). 1978. Theory and practice of mountain pine beetle management in lodgepole pine forests. Proceedings of Symposium, April 25–27, 1978. University of Idaho, Moscow.

Brookes, M. H., R. W. Stark, and R. W. Campbell (Eds.). 1978. *The Douglas-fir Tussock Moth: A Synthesis*. USDA Forest Service Technical Bulletin 1585.

Campbell, R. W. 1973. The conceptual organization of research and development necessary for future pest managememt. In Stark, R. W. and A. R. Gittins (Eds.), *Pest Management in the 21st Century*. Proceedings Idaho Research Foundation, Inc., Natural Resource Series No. 2. Moscow.

Campbell, R. W. and M. W. McFadden. 1977. Design of a pest management research and development program. *Bull. Entomol. Soc. Am.* **23**:216–220.

Coulson, R. N. 1979. Population dynamics of bark beetles. *Annu. Rev. Entomol.* **24**:417–447.

Coulson, R. N. 1981. Evolution of concepts of integrated pest management in forest. *J. Georgia Entomol. Soc.* **16**:301–316.

Coulson, R. N. and R. W. Stark. 1982. Integrated pest management of bark beetles. In Mitton, J. B. and K. B. Sturgeon (Eds.). *Bark Beetles in North American Conifers: A System for the Study of Evolutionary Biology*. University of Texas Press, Austin.

Gale, R. D. 1979. Integrated pest management colloquium. Proceedings of Symposium, October 17–18, 1978. Millford, PA. USDA Forest Service General Technical Report WO-14.

National Academy of Sciences. 1975. Pest control: An assessment of present and alternative technologies. In *Forest Pest Control*, Vol. 4. National Academy of Science, Washington, DC.

Schowalter, T. D., R. N. Coulson, and D. A. Crossley, Jr. 1981. The role of southern pine beetle and fire in maintenance of structure and function of the southeastern coniferous forest. *Environ. Entomol.* **10**:821–825.

Society of American Foresters. 1958. *Forest Terminology*. Society of American Foresters, Washington, DC.

Stage, A. R. 1973. Prognosis model for stand development. USDA Forest Service Research Paper INT-137.

Stage, A. R. 1975. Forest stand prognosis in the presence of pests: Developing the expectations. In Baumgartner, D. M. (Ed.). *Management of Lodgepole Pine Ecosystems*. Washington State University, Pullman, Cooperative Extension Service.

Stark, R. W. 1976. Forest insect pest management. In Metcalf, R. L. and W. H. Luckmann (Eds.). *Introduction to Insect Pest Management*. Wiley, New York.

Stark, R. W. 1977. Integrated pest management in forest practice. *J. For.* **75**:251–254.

Stark, R. W. 1979a. The concept of impact in integrated pest management. In Waters, W. E. (Ed.). *Current Topics in Forest Entomology*. USDA Forest Service General Technical Report WO-8.

Stark, R. W. 1979b. Forest management and integrated pest management. In Gale, R. D. (Ed.), *Integrated Pest Management Colloquium*. USDA Forest Service General Technical Report WO-14: 34–42.

Stark, R. W. 1980. Integrated forest protection: A successful marriage of technology and ecology. Weyerhaeuser Lecture Series, November 1980.

Stark, R. W. and A. R. Gittins. 1973. Pest Management in the 21st Century. Idaho Research Foundation, Inc., Natural Resource Series No. 2. Moscow.

Waters, W. E. 1974. Systems approach to managing pine bark beetles. In Payne, T. L., R. N. Coulson, and R. C. Thatcher (Eds.), *Southern Pine Beetle Symposium*. Proceedings of Symposium, Texas Agriculture Experiment Station, College Station.

Waters, W. E. and E. B. Cowling. 1976. Integrated forest pest management: A silvicultural necessity. In Apple, J. L. and R. F. Smith (Eds.), *Integrated Pest Management*. Plenum Press, New York.

Waters, W. E. 1978. Forest pest management: An overview and perspective. Proceedings Joint Technical Session, Convention of Society American Foresters and Canadian Institute of Forestry. St. Louis.

Waters, W. E. and R. W. Stark. 1980. Forest pest management: Concept and reality. *Annu. Rev. Entomol.* **25**:479–509.

6

POPULATION DYNAMICS OF FOREST INSECTS

INTRODUCTION

Phytophagous insects are common ubiquitous elements of forests. Much of the focus of forest entomology is directed to activities associated with populations of insects. In particular, we are often interested in understanding causes for changes in the distribution and abundance of insects through space and time, which is the study of population dynamics and the topic of this chapter.

Populations of many forest insect species have been studied extensively. There are essentially three reasons for this circumstance: (1) insects have many important functional roles in forest ecosystems, (2) insects can cause significant disruption to our planned use(s) of forests, and (3) forest insects often serve as excellent experimental subjects for studying basic ecological principles and theories.

Generally, insects have beneficial roles in forest ecosystems. Research at the ecosystem level has identified a number of significant roles of forest insects. There is good evidence to suggest that grazing by phytophagous insects influences forest ecosystem structure and function by (1) regulating certain aspects of primary production, that is, the production of green plants by means of photosynthesis; (2) regulating the cycling of important nutrients; (3) preparing the way for orderly forest development through ecological succession; and (4) regulating the size, distribution, and abundance of host trees (Kulman 1971, Mattson and Addy 1975, Mattson 1977, Amman 1977, Peterman 1978, Coulson 1980, Schowalter 1981).

However, some insect species periodically become so abundant that they threaten ecological, economic, or aesthetic values that we associate with forests. These insects are termed "outbreak" or "pest" species. Forest managers and pest management specialists (who are often forest entomologists) are particularly interested in pest species because of their disruptive effects on our planned use of forest resources. Reference to Figure 5.8 indicates that information on pest population dynamics is a main source of input to the stand dynamics (Chapter 7) and treatment tactics (Chapter 8) components of integrated pest management (IPM).

Forest insects often make excellent subjects for studies of population dynamics because of the extensive background of information available for many species. Much of the theory of population dynamics of animals was developed by use of highly simplified laboratory conditions. Application of existing theory, under the complex experimental conditions that exist in forests, permits examination of basic theoretical assumptions, modification of concepts, and development of new theory.

Regardless of whether one is interested in elucidating ecological functions of forest insects, managing pests, or contributing new knowledge to theoretical population ecology, it is necessary to have a basic understanding of concepts and principles of population dynamics. Accordingly, our objectives in this chapter are fourfold: (1) to provide a general overview of the subject of population dynamics, using a method of organization termed the "population system"; (2) to examine components of the population system; (3) to examine factors responsible for changes in the distribution and abundance of insects; and (4) to illustrate how information on population dynamics is applied in forest entomology.

There are a number of excellent general and advanced textbooks in population ecology that treat the subjects covered in this chapter in detail. The following references are particularly useful: Allee et al. (1948), Clark et al. (1967), Odum (1971), Varley et al. (1974), Pielou (1969, 1974), Poole (1974), Price (1975), Southwood (1978), Hutchinson (1978), and Berryman (1981).

PRINCIPLES RELATING TO ORGANIZATION AND STRUCTURE OF INSECT POPULATIONS

To understand how and why insect distribution and abundance change through space and time, it is necessary to consider a population as a system of interacting components. We can then employ a systematic structure to organize principles and concepts relative to the components. We use a method of organization that defines a population system to consist of the following components: (1) properties associated with individuals, (2) properties associated with the environment, (3) population processes, and (4) population states or conditions. This method of organization represents a blend of the approaches for structuring information on population dynamics given by Clark et al. (1967) and Berryman (1981, 1982). In the following sections we provide an overview of the general operation of the population system and then examine each of the components.

The Population System

A *population* is a collective group of individuals of one species that inhabits an area sufficiently small to enable interbreeding. *Population dynamics* is the study of change in the distribution and abundance of the population through space and time. The variables and processes that determine the distribution and abundance of a population can be organized into what is termed a *life system* (Clark et al. 1967) or a *population system* (Berryman 1981, 1982) (Figure 6.1). The basic elements of the system are the individuals who form the population, the environment, population-level processes, and population states or conditions.

There are several different states or conditions used to characterize populations. The most commonly used state is the number or density of individuals in the population. However, a population can also be described by its pattern of distribution (dispersion), growth form, age distribution,

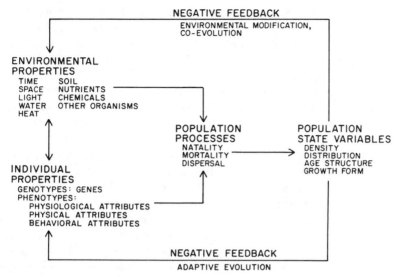

Figure 6.1 The basic components of a population system. (Modified from Berryman 1981, 1982.)

and gene frequency. Because these conditions or states of the population change in time and space, they can be termed *state variables* (Figure 6.1).

The values of the state variables change in time and space because of the operation of three *population processes*. These processes are natality (birth rate), mortality (death rate), and dispersal (movement of individuals into and out of an area of concentration) (Figure 6.1). Historically, the relationship between the state variables and population processes has been described by the *demographic equation*. This fundamental statement of population biology can be expressed as follows:

$$N_{t+1} = N_t + \text{births} - \text{deaths} + \text{immigrants} - \text{emigrants}$$

The term N usually refers to population size, but can just as easily be one of the other state variables.

The population processes are governed by properties associated with individual organisms forming the population (*population properties* in Figure 6.1) and properties associated with the environment in which the population lives (*environmental properties* in Figure 6.1). Individual properties are determined by the particular combination of genes present in the cells of the organism (i.e., the *genotype*). Not all characteristics of the genes are expressed in the development of the individual, so the outward expression of this combination of genes in the individual is its *phenotype*. Phenotypic properties of individuals can be classed as physiological (birth, death, growth, differentiation, maintenance, reproductive potential, locomotion, etc.), physical (structure, form, color, etc.), or behavioral (feeding behavior, mating behavior, defense behavior, etc.). The actual expression of individual properties is determined by interaction of the genotype with components of the environment such as space, food, weather, other organisms (e.g., predators, competitors), chemicals, etc. Clark et al. (1967) used the term "effective environment" to include everything that can influence the chance of an individual to survive and multiply. The effective environment includes all available resources as well as agents causing mortality. Properties of the environment are often segregated as abiotic (nonliving) and biotic (living). It is important to recognize that the subject species is an environmental factor just as are competitors, predators, host plants, and so on.

   Properties of individuals (genotypes and phenotypes) and of the environment change continually in space and time. These changes can occur as a result of the population through a process termed *negative feedback. Negative feedback* is defined as the process by which a control mechanism is regulated through the effects it brings about. In Figure 6.1 we illustrate two pathways for negative feedbacks. The first leads from the population state variables to properties of individuals, through the population processes, back to the state variables. The second leads from the state variables to the environmental properties, through the population processes back to the state variables. The following two examples illustrate how negative feedback works. First, when population size (a state variable) becomes very large, some individuals in the population may die from starvation, some may disperse, whereas others may have reduced reproductive capacity. These conditions directly influence the population processes natality, mortality, and dispersal, which, in turn affect the population state variable, such as population size. Negative feedback can influence phenotypic characteristics of the individuals or result in genetic changes. Changes in genotypes by natural selection or mutation lead to *adaptive evolution* of the species. Second, negative feedback can also operate through alteration of certain environmental properties. In this case both the environment and the population states are affected in important ways. For example, an increase in population size (the state variable) can result in depletion of food resources, reduction of habitat space, and increase in numbers of natural enemies because of the abundance of host insects. These changes in environmental properties, again, affect the processes of natality, mortality, and dispersal, which leads to a change in the state variables. When feedback involves changes in the genetic properties of environmental components such as host plants, food organisms, predators, and competitors, these organisms are said to co-evolve with the population in question (Figure 6.1). The term "co-evolution" was coined by Ehrlich and Raven (1965) and is used to describe those interactions between organisms in which the evolution of one member of an interacting pair elicits an evolutionary response from the other member. Mitten and Sturgeon (1982) provide a comprehensive examination of co-evolution of bark beetles and their coniferous hosts.

This general overview of the population system is intended to provide a framework for the discussion of population dynamics of forest insects. In the following sections we consider the components of the population system in more detail. In Chapter 7 we examine interrelationships between host plant population dynamics and insect population dynamics.

COMPONENTS OF THE POPULATION SYSTEM

In this section we examine the four basic components of a population system. The components in their order of discussion include (1) properties of individuals, (2) properties of the environment, (3) population processes, and (4) population states or conditions. In the previous section, where we described how a population system functions, the starting point for the discussion emphasized the population states first, the population processes second, the individuals third, and environment fourth. Here we begin with the basic elements of the population system, the individuals and the environment, move to the population processes that determine the states, and finally discuss the population states.

Properties of Individuals

Individual insects have unique properties or characteristics (phenotypes) that result from the interaction of their genetic makeup (genotype) with the environment. Specific individual properties can be classed as physiological, physical, or behavioral. These classes of characteristics are the subject matter for courses in insect physiology, morphology and systematics, and behavior. A general overview of these subjects is provided in Chapter 2. We are interested in individual characteristics in this chapter because, together, they define the life history strategy for a particular species of insect.

In chapter 2 we described the different types of development that insects undergo (i.e., no metamorphosis, incomplete metamorphosis, gradual metamorphosis, and complete metamorphosis). The *life cycle* or natural history of an insect can be defined as the events associated with the developmental stages of a particular species. Life cycles are usually expressed in terms of *generation time,* which is the time interval between the production of eggs in one generation to the production of eggs in the next generation. However, it is not uncommon to see generation time expressed as the interval for another life stage, for example, adults to adults. Generation time is distinct from *development time,* which is the length of time required for an insect to develop from an egg to an adult.

The physiological, physical, and behavioral properties or characteristics of individuals provide a remarkable number of adaptations that enhance the likelihood that a particular insect species will persist. These adaptations operate at different stages in the life cycle of the insect. Collectively, the adaptations represent the *life history strategy* for the insect. Examples of specific adaptations include cryptic coloration, polymorphism (the condition of having several forms in the adult), neoteny (precocious reproduction by immatures), parthenogenesis (production of offspring without fertilization), production of defensive compounds and pheromones, ability to perceive pheromones and other behavioral chemicals, ability to detoxify plant secondary compounds, specialized morphological structures (e.g., wings, mouthparts, etc.), utilization of different food sources and/or habitats by immatures and adults, utilization of multiple hosts, and ability to withstand extremes in temperature and moisture. A particular insect species will normally utilize several different adaptations throughout the course of its life cycle. These adaptations are specialized expression of attributes of individuals that have evolved as a result of natural selection.

Generalized life cycles for many forest insect species have been described in the literature. Many of the pest species have been studied in great detail. In the succeeding chapters dealing with the insect feeding groups, we present very brief life cycles that include information on preferred hosts, habits of adults, habits of immatures, number of generations per year, and geographic range. To appreciate the complexity of the life history strategies for the pest species, it will be necessary to refer to the primary literature, which is cited for the major pest species. The significant issue regarding insect life cycles is that the starting point for any study of population dynamics is a thorough examination and description of the life history of the subject species. Furthermore, all treatment tactics and strategies used to suppress populations of forest insects are directed to specific life stages of the target pest. Since all insect species are exposed to a variety of natural mortality agents, the life history strategy utilized by a particular insect can accommodate substantial mortality while still permitting the insect to persist. Most forest insects normally have mortality rates of approximately 80–99% for a particular generation.

Properties of the Environment

Properties of the environment can be organized in a number of different ways but generally include the following components: time, space, light, water, heat, soil, nutrients, chemicals, and other organisms. These components are often simply organized as *biotic* (living) and *abiotic* (nonliving), with nonliving organic matter occupying an intermediate position. Components of the environment interact to produce the conditions in which the forest insect and its host plant(s) live and die. The study of individuals in relation to the environment is treated in the branch of ecology known as *autecology*. A detailed examination of the effects of environmental properties on insect populations is beyond the scope of this chapter. However, we are concerned with several fundamental issues regarding (1) time and space, (2) climate and weather, (3) food, and (4) interactions among organisms.

Time and Space

The distribution and abundance of forest insects and their host plants vary in time and space. Although we can view time and space over long periods (geologic time) and broad areas (regions of the world), in forest entomology we are generally concerned with a time–space framework that is relatively short and small. In the case of insect populations our time frame can involve yearly fluctuations in abundance, seasonal patterns of abundance, or the generation time for a particular species. Our space framework can include the area occupied by a forest biome, forest ecosystem, stand, or a particular habitat. In the case of the host plant, our time frame normally spans the rotation period for a particular species of tree. This period can be partitioned according to time intervals that the tree spends in various stages of growth, such as the sapling stage. We may also be interested in the time intervals associated with periodic phenomena such as flowering or cone production. Our space framework can range from the forest biome, to the forest ecosystem, to the stand, and finally to the area occupied by a particular tree and its structural modules (stem, roots, leaves, etc.). Fluctuations in populations of forest insects in space and time are closely associated with fluctuations in populations of host trees or plant modules. Populations of trees and plant modules also change in space and time in response to the activities of phytophagous insects and other variables such as fire, disease, and so on.

Climate and Weather

Climate and weather represent a composite of environmental components (e.g., heat, light, and water) that greatly affect insect populations. These components interact to directly influence basic physiological processes (e.g., developmental rate, water regulation, diapause), and behavior (e.g., photoperiodic responses, perception of pheromones, host finding). Although somewhat dated, the classic work of Uvarov (1931) provides a detailed examination of insects and climate. Insects have many specific adaptations for dealing with variation of climate and weather.

The general climatic regime of a region determines, in part, the types of plant species and phytophagous insects that live there. Yearly and seasonal variations in weather patterns in a local area within a climatic region result in fluctuations in insect populations. Often, the most violent fluctuations occur at the edges of climatic regions where local variations in weather are acute.

Food

Both the quantity (availability) and quality (nutritional value) of food supplies are important issues for forest insects. We can make a number of generalizations about utilization of food by phytophagous insects: (1) most forest insects are capable of utilizing a number of different species of host plants for food; (2) most forest insects are adapted for feeding on specific plant modules [e.g., phloem, wood, foliage, terminals, cones—this circumstance is the basis for segregating forest insects into various feeding groups (Chapters 11–17); however, with some insects, adults may utilize one type of plant module while immatures another type]; (3) insects generally exhibit a preference for a particular host species, although, as we indicated above, they are capable of subsisting on a number of different plants; and (4) insects also exhibit preferences within a particular class of plant module (e.g., juvenile foliage as opposed to mature foliage).

There are a number of well-documented cases of the effects of food quantity and quality on forest insect populations. For example, very high (epidemic) population levels of the mountain pine beetle, *Dendroctonus ponderosae* Hopkins, are often associated with the occurrence of the insect in lodgepole pines that are more than 80 years old, 20–30 cm in diameter, and with a phloem thickness of 0.25 cm. This insect can infest other pine species as well as lodgepole pines of younger age with smaller diameter and phloem thickness. However, epidemic population levels rarely occur under these circumstances (Amman 1978). Similarly, reduced reproductive performance for the Douglas-fir tussock moth, *Orgyia pseudotsugata* (McDunnough); the fall webworm, *Hyphantria cunea* (Drury); spruce budworm, *Choristoneura fumiferana* (Clemens); and the gypsy moth, *Lymantria dispar* (Linnaeus), all defoliating insects, has also been demonstrated to be associated with different host species, host age, foliage age, previous host defoliation, phase or length of infestation, crown position, and stand composition (Beckwith 1978, Morris and Fulton 1970, Morris 1963, Doane and McManus 1981). Each of these factors is related to food quality and/or quantity.

Obviously the quantity (availability) of food has an important direct effect on populations of insects. However, food quality also has been demonstrated to affect general fitness of insect populations, which is reflected in variables such as reduced reproductive potential and dispersal behavior (Wellington 1977, 1979).

Interactions among Organisms

The organisms that occupy a given area are a component of the environment. Activities of individuals within a particular species and interactions of individuals of different species can have a pronounced influence on the environment. In this section we identify the basic types of insect interaction (and other animal interactions). In Chapter 7 we consider interactions between insects and their host plants.

A particular phytophagous insect species directly alters the environment through its feeding activities. Insects of the same species also compete with one another for food supplies and habitat space. Competition among members of the same species for needed resources is termed *intraspecific competition*.

Populations of different species also interact to modify the environment. Several categories of interaction between two species have been identified (Odum 1971). These categories include the following: (1) *neutralism*, where neither population is affected by the association with the other; (2) *interference competition*, in which both populations actively inhibit each other; (3) *exploitation competition*, where each population adversely affects the other by reducing supply of common resources; (4) *amensalism*, where one population is inhibited and the other is not affected; (5) *parasitism*; (6) *predation*, where one population adversely affects the other by direct attack but is nevertheless dependent on the other; (7) *commensalism*, where one population is benefited while the other is not affected; (8) *protocooperation*, in which both populations benefit by the association but relations are not obligatory; and (9) *mutualism*, growth and survival of both populations is benefited and neither can survive without the other. The significant point with regard to insects and other organisms in the environment is that they interact in many different ways and play a number of functional roles that result in modification of the forest environment in space and time.

Population Processes

Natality (birth rate), *mortality* (death rate) and *dispersal* are processes that determine the values of state variables such as density, age structure, and growth form. Populations increase in size through reproduction (births), and dispersal into an area (immigration) and decrease in size through mortality and dispersal out of an area (emigration) (Figure 6.2). Therefore, knowledge of the processes of natality, mortality, and dispersal are of fundamental importance to understanding population dynamics.

Natality

Natality is defined as birth rate or the production of new individuals in a population in relation to time. Natality has a positive influence on insect population growth. There are two components of the concept of natality: (1) potential and (2) realized natality.

Potential natality is the theoretical production of new individuals under ideal environmental conditions. It is the potential level of reproductive performance and a theoretical constant for a given population. Potential natality is calculated as the number of new individuals produced per unit population per unit time. This quantity can be approximated only under controlled experimental conditions. Calculated estimates of potential natality are of value in comparing potential with observed reproductive performance under field conditions.

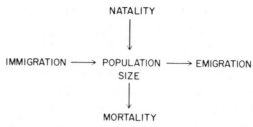

Figure 6.2 Schematic illustrating the effects of natality, mortality, emigration, and immigration on population size.

Realized natality is the actual production of new individuals under a given set of environmental conditions. It is the observed level of reproductive performance and not a constant for a population. Realized natality is calculated as the number of new individuals per unit of time per unit population. Calculated values will vary as a function of the size and composition of a population and particular conditions of the environment.

Realized natality is influenced by properties of the environment such as temperature, food quality and quantity, other organisms, and so on and properties of individual organisms. Individual insects have a maximum theoretical reproductive capacity that is referred to as *fecundity*. Actual or observed reproductive performance of an individual is known as *fertility*.

Mortality

Mortality or *death rate* for a population is the number of individuals that die per unit population per unit time. Mortality has a negative effect on population growth. As with natality, there are two components to the concept of mortality that are generally expressed in terms of longevity or expected length of life: (1) physiological or maximum longevity and (2) realized longevity.

Physiological longevity is the average length of life for individuals of a population living under optimum environmental conditions. Theoretically, it is a constant for a population. Death is a result of senescence and is not caused by mortality agents in the environment. Physiological longevity likely is never attained in nature.

Realized longevity is the observed or empirical length of life of individuals of a population under a given set of environmental conditions. It is not a constant and varies primarily as a result of different environmental conditions.

In studies of population dynamics it is often more convenient to consider survival rate rather than mortality rate. *Survival rate* is simply the number of individuals surviving in a population in relation to time. Survival rate is generally expressed in the form of a *survivorship curve*, which is a plot of the number (or percent) of living individuals in a population versus time. The survivorship curve is the simplest type of budget or record of events that affect a population. It represents the net result of all mortality agents that affect a population during a period of time. Figures 6.3 and 6.4 illustrate survivorship for the Douglas-fir tussock moth (Mason and Luck 1978) and the southern pine beetle (Coulson et al. 1977).

Survivorship curves are useful for identifying (1) where mortality occurs in the life cycle of an insect, (2) how much mortality one can expect during certain time intervals, and (3) how much mortality one can expect for specific life stages. Survivorship curves have a number of specialized applications. In Figure 6.3 the survivorship curves for the Douglas-fir tussock moth serve to inform the pest management specialist of conditions that favor endemic (low) and epidemic (high) population levels. The survivorship curves for the southern pine beetle illustrate that mortality within the tree is uniform at different heights (Figure 6.4). However, specialists in bark beetle ecology recognize that the agents responsible for the mortality along the tree bole are not the same.

Detailed vital statistics about mortality or survival in a population are often recorded in a life table. For our purpose, a *life table* is defined as an age-specific summary of the mortality agents operating on a population. Life tables have been used extensively in studies of forest insects. Table 6.1 is an example of a partial life table for the gypsy moth (Campbell 1981). There are several basic entries or columns associated with life tables. These entries are symbolized by letters that are used in ecology and forest entomology for describing populations. The most common entries in a life table include the following: x, age interval; l_x, the number of survivors at the start of age interval x; d_x, the number dying during the age interval x to $x + 1$; q_x, the rate of mortality during the age interval x to $x + 1$; and e_x, mean expectation of life for organisms alive at the start of age x.

Southwood (1978) provides a detailed discussion of methodologies used in constructing life tables and calculating the various entries in the tables.

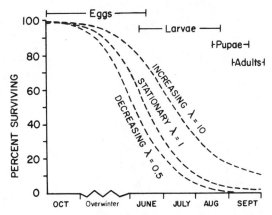

Figure 6.3 Schematic curves for generation survivorship of the Douglas-fir tussock moth illustrating increasing, stationary, and decreasing populations; λ = the annual coefficient of increase. (From Mason and Luck 1978.)

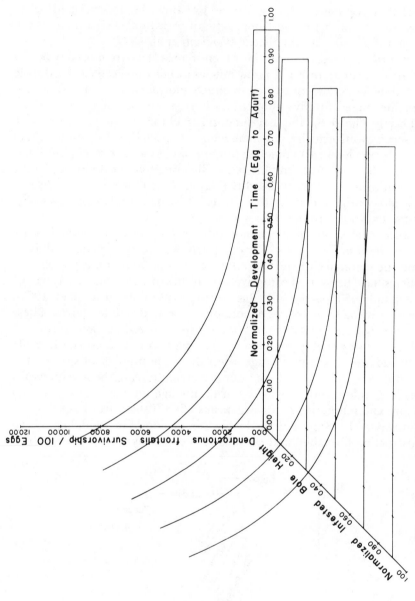

Figure 6.4 Survivorship of the southern pine beetle at several heights along the infested portion of host trees. (From Coulson et al. 1977.)

Table 6.1   Life Table Typical of Sparse Gypsy Moth Subpopulation in an Areawide Outbreak (Glenville Data)

Age Interval (x)	Number Alive at Beginning of x (1x)	Factor Responsible for dx (dfx)	Number Dying during x (dx)	dx as Percent of 1x (100qx)
Eggs	450[a]	Parasites	67.5	15
		Other	67.5	15
		Total	135.0	30
Instars 1–3	315	Dispersion, etc.	157.5	50
Instars 4–6	157.5	Parasites	7.9	5
		Disease	7.9	5
		Other	118.1	75
		Total	133.9	85
Prepupae	23.6	Desiccation, etc.	0.7	3
Pupae	22.9	Vertebrate predators	4.6	20
		Other	2.3	10
		Total	6.9	30
Adults	16.0	Sex (SR = 65 : 35)	5.6	35
Adult females	10.4	—		
Generation	—	—	439.6	97.69

Source: Campbell 1969 (from Doane and McManus 1981).

[a]Number of eggs in an average egg mass.

Life tables of forest insects are particularly useful in studying population dynamics. Ideally, the researcher would construct a series of life tables over a time frame that encompasses a number of generations of the target insect. There are several alternative procedures for analyzing life tables, and Southwood (1978) has provided an excellent review of the options.

In practice, life tables are only partially completed. It is very difficult to account quantitatively for all the mortality caused by a large number of different agents. Various types of mortality agents important in regulating or reducing populations will be discussed later in this chapter and also in Chapters 11–17.

Dispersal

For our purposes we will define "dispersal" to be movement of individuals of a population into or out of an area of concentration. The direction of movement is further specified by the terms "immigration" (movement into an area) and "emigration" (movement out of an area). Insect populations may increase (immigration) or decrease (emigration) as a result of dispersal. Specialists in population ecology often use more rigid definitions of the term, and there are a number of review articles that consider the nomenclature associated with the concept of dispersal (e.g., Delucchi and Baltensweiler 1979; Berryman and Safranyik 1979; Dingle 1972; Edmonds and Benninghoff 1974; Schneider 1962; Southwood 1962, 1977a, 1978; Taylor and Taylor 1976; Williams 1957).

Dispersal has several important functional roles in population dynamics that can either aid or hinder the persistence of a species. Dispersal enhances persistence in three important ways: (1) it permits colonization of new habitats, (2) it allows for exploitation on new food resources, and (3) it may contribute to the likelihood of mate finding. Dispersal can also hinder population persistence. Mortality can occur (1) as a result of deposition of the insect on unsuitable hosts or sites, (2) by exposure of the insect to natural enemies, (3) by exposure to unfavorable weather conditions, and (4) by dilution of population density to a level that reduces the likelihood of finding a mate.

Dispersal can be accomplished by active or passive means. The insect life stage involved in dispersal determines which means is used. *Active dispersal* is accomplished primarily by either flying or walking. Short-distance dispersal of bark beetles is an example of active dispersal. Adults fly from host to host. *Passive dispersal* is generally accomplished by wind carrying or aiding movement of a life stage. Windborne transport of early stage larvae of the gypsy moth is an example of passive dispersal (Cameron et al. 1979). In certain circumstances, an insect utilizes both forms of dispersal. Larvae and adult spruce budworms are passively dispersed. In addition, adults are capable of active dispersal by flight (Morris 1963).

Most habitats and food resources are suitable for use by insects for only a brief period. These resources, like insect populations, have clumped distributions (dispersion patterns) within forests. Their availability to insect populations varies in space and time. As there is an element of chance (stochasticity) involved in dispersal between habitat and food resource centers, insects have evolved a number of behavioral mechanisms that aid survival under ephemeral conditions: (1) although insects have preferences for a certain quality of habitat and food, they also are able to tolerate a wide range of conditions; (2) insects reproduce in large numbers, which increases the likelihood that at least some individuals will locate suitable habitats and food supplies; and (3) many insects have advanced capability to communicate using visual and olfactory cues from the environment. The widespread occurrence and use of pheromones (a chemical secreted by one organism that influences the behavior or physiology of other organisms of the same species) and plant attractants for mate finding, aggregation, and host identification by forest insects have been well documented (Birch 1974, Borden 1974, 1977).

Measurement of dispersal of insects in forests has proved to be a difficult task. We are interested in the number of insects involved, the distance traveled, and the time taken. In general, crude population estimates have been used to describe dispersal. Problems in studying dispersal are related to resolution of space and time. Most of our knowledge on dispersal of forest insects can be classed into one of three categories based on space and time resolution. The first class considers dispersal over a small area in a short time frame. For example, it has been possible to measure dispersal of the southern pine beetle in forest stands over a period of several months (Figure 6.5a,b) (Coulson 1980). Localized dispersal patterns have also been studied for the gypsy moth (Cameron et al. 1979). Micrometeorological conditions within the forest stand (temperature, wind speed, wind direction, wind duration), terrain features, and stand structure (species composition, density, and age) all contribute to the observed dispersal pattern (Cameron et al. 1979, Fares et al. 1980). The second class considers dispersal over a large area in a short time period. For example, long-distance dispersal of the spruce budworm has been well documented (Morris 1963, Clark 1979). Radar has been used in conjunction with information on general meteorological conditions (prevailing winds, presence of weather fronts, etc.) to study long-distance dispersal of this insect (Rainey 1979). The third class considers dispersal over large areas and a long time frame. Generally, these studies are based on historical records developed from various population indices. Perhaps the best documented case is that of the spread of the introduced pest, the gypsy moth, from a localized point in Massachusetts in 1869. This insect increased its range over a large part of the northeastern United States. It has subsequently been detected in various regions throughout the United States. It has been possible to trace the spread of the gypsy moth with the use of historical forest inventory and insect survey records.

Another approach used in studying dispersal is to use mathematical techniques to describe the various components that researchers have identified to be associated with the process, such as stand conditions, weather, and insect longevity. With the use of this approach, it is possible to develop a model that can simulate likely dispersal patterns for the insect. Clark (1979) described such a model of dispersal for the spruce budworm (Figure 6.6). This approach permits prediction of dispersal patterns and is useful in projecting potential losses resulting from the activity of the insect.

Population States or Conditions

As we have seen, properties of individuals and properties of the environment influence the population processes of natality, mortality, and dispersal. The population processes determine the various states or conditions that a population can assume. These states are unique attributes of populations and are generally represented as statistical functions. In this section we examine three basic population states: (1) population size and distribution, (2) population age distribution, and (3) population growth form.

Population Size

In forest entomology we are often interested in measuring or describing population size, or change in population size, through time and space. Therefore, it is necessary to examine basic concepts of density and dis-

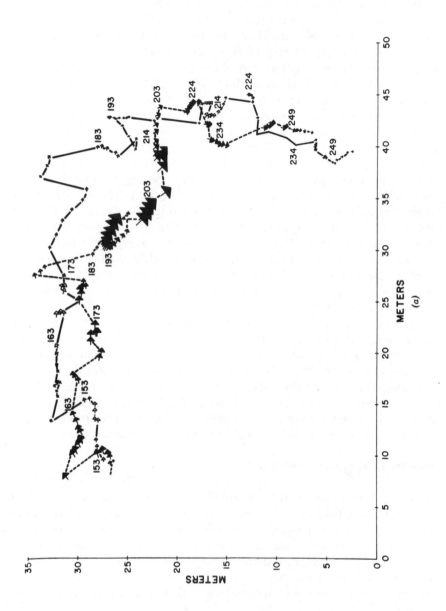

METERS

(a)

140

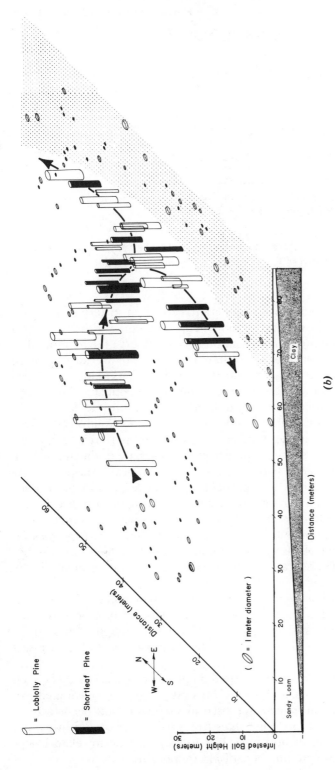

Figure 6.5 (*a*) Dispersal pattern followed by southern pine beetle adults over a 3-month period in an infestation. The arrows are proportional in size to the number of beetles that reemerged (adult beetles that colonized a host, oviposited, and exited) and emerged (adult beetles that developed within the host and then exited). Reemerged beetles = solid line, emerged beetles = dashed line. (From Coulson 1980.) (*b*) Scale reproduction of an infestation of the southern pine beetle illustrating spatial pattern of dispersal. In this case the record of dispersal is represented by the sequence of pines killed by the insect over a period of several months, that is, the cylinders represent trees killed by the insect. The ellipses represent unattacked host pines. (From Coulson 1979.)

141

DISPERSAL MODEL

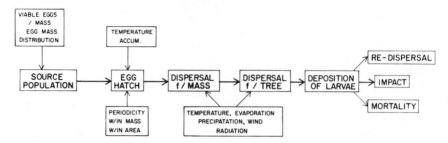

Figure 6.6 Conceptual model illustrating the components identified to be involved in dispersal of the gypsy moth. (From Cameron et al. 1979.)

persion of populations. After considering these topics, we examine some of the general procedures for preparing graphs of population size.

Density

Population size or abundance is generally expressed in terms of *density*, which is defined as the number of individuals (or biomass = living weight) per unit area or volume. It is seldom possible to observe the total number of insects occupying an area or volume of habitat, or we may be more interested in insect activity rather than the actual numbers of insects. Therefore, various types of samples are used to estimate population size. Population estimates can be classed into three general groups as follows: absolute estimates, relative estimates, and population indices (Southwood 1978).

An *absolute estimate* is the number of insects per unit area or volume, such as the number of southern pine beetles per square decimeter of bark area or cubic decimeter of bark volume. Evaluation of the various factors that influence populations of a particular species (e.g., mortality agents, dispersal, reproduction) generally requires that population size be expressed in absolute figures. It is rarely possible to obtain an absolute estimate directly, and population size is expressed as intensity. *Population intensity* is the number of insects per unit area of habitat (e.g., the number of aphids per leaf) and can be converted to an absolute estimate if the number of habitat units per area is known.

A *relative estimate* is a population measurement based on units other than area or volume and is usually expressed as catch per unit of effort, for example, the number of flying gypsy moth adults caught on a "sticky trap" in a 2-hour period. Relative estimates are often used in studies of insect dispersal.

A *population index* is an estimate based on products of insect activity, such as webs, dead trees, frass, and exuviae. Insects per se are not counted. An example of population index often used in surveying bark beetle activity is the number of "red top" pine trees (trees with discolored crowns) observed per 1000 acres of host type. It is usually difficult to relate a population index to absolute numbers of insects per unit area.

Dispersion

Closely associated with insect abundance and the expression of population size are concepts relating to dispersion. The term "dispersion" refers to the internal distribution or pattern of occurrence of individuals in a population. This term should not be confused with insect dispersal (movement), which was discussed earlier. Individuals in a population may be distributed or dispersed according to three basic patterns (Figure 6.7): (1) random, (2) uniform, and (3) clumped. Forest insect populations rarely occur at random because this distribution would require a homogeneous environment and no tendencies for aggregation or antagonism. These conditions normally do not occur in nature. Populations also rarely are uniformly distributed, although this dispersion pattern is approached at high population levels when habitat or food resources are limiting and competition between individuals promotes even spacing. Clumped distribution is by far the most common dispersion pattern. Various degrees of clumping can occur as a result of many factors. The most common reasons for clumped distribution of insect populations are (1) susceptible and suitable host plants or plant modules (food and habitats) have clumped distributions within forests; and (2) insects have communication systems that promote aggregation, host identification, and mate finding.

The importance of dispersion patterns in understanding populations of insects cannot be overemphasized. Dispersion and density are inseparably interrelated. Dispersion patterns dictate in large part how population density can be measured.

Description of Population Size

With our understanding of the distribution (dispersion) and abundance (density), we are in a position to consider ways of numerically describing populations. The starting point in any study of population dynamics is the natural history or life cycle of the subject species. Life cycles can be conveniently partitioned according to developmental stages of the insect and generation time. For example, a holometabolous (complete metamorphosis) insect has four developmental stages: adult, egg, larva, and pupa. As we mentioned previously, generation time is usually expressed as the time

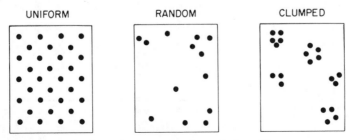

Figure 6.7 Three basic dispersion patterns of populations. These patterns can refer to individuals in a population or some other unit, such as population centers distributed within a forest.

interval between production of eggs in one generation to production of eggs in the next generation.

As an example of the type of census information that one can collect about a population, consider the generalized life cycle of a bark beetle (Coleoptera: Scolytidae). Adults colonize, mate, and females oviposit a complement of eggs within a host. Thereafter, the colonizing adults leave the host or die. From the eggs hatch larvae, which pass through four stages during which time they feed and grow. Pupation follows larval development. Brood adults subsequently emerge and colonize a new host to begin the next generation. We will assume that a procedure is available that permits collection of field data and calculation of absolute population estimates.

The first step in numerically describing this population is to plot density of the life stages in relation to time. The description can be based on either density or cumulative density (Figure 6.8). This plot is referred to as a *partial population curve* (Varley et al. 1974). A series of partial population curves, representing each life stage, provides a numerical description of the population for one life cycle (Figure 6.9). Note that there is overlap

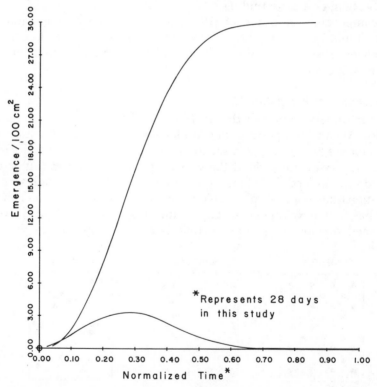

Figure 6.8 Partial population curve for an insect illustrating density and cumulative density of emerging southern pine beetles in relation to time. (From Coulson 1980.)

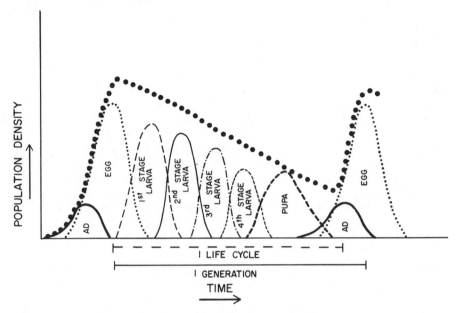

Figure 6.9 A series of partial population curves for a hypothetical insect illustrating the density of adults, eggs, four larval stages, and pupae in relation to time. The cumulative number of insects in all life stages in relation to time represents a total population curve. Generation time is the interval between production of eggs in one generation to the production of eggs in the next. The development time for a life cycle is the length of time it takes for an insect to develop from egg to adult. (After Varley et al. 1974.)

between the successive life stages. Also, the density of successive life stages diminishes because of the action of mortality agents. We discuss the interaction of mortality agents on population size later in this chapter.

From the information in Figure 6.9, it is possible to prepare a *total population curve* that represents the total number of individuals in all stages, or their population density, plotted against time. A series of total population curves, representing successive generations, provides a description of population changes through time (Figure 6.10). In this figure, generation time is defined as the interval between the midpoint of adult colonization in one generation to the midpoint of adult colonization in the next.

Several factors can complicate development of population curves, namely: (1) the occurrence of overlapping generations, (2) differences in generation time due to variations in insect development rate that result from changing weather conditions, (3) influences of dispersal (immigration and emigration), and (4) action of mortality agents. Each of these factors alters the shapes of the curves describing population density.

In practice, detailed population curves for forest insects occurring under field conditions are extremely difficult to obtain, partly for the reasons mentioned above. Under most circumstances, it is not possible to obtain a

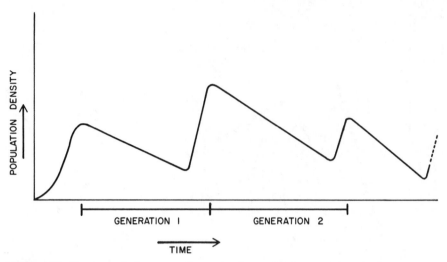

Figure 6.10   Total population curves illustrating fluctuation in population size for successive generations of a hypothetical insect.

budget representing absolute estimates of the total population of all life stages for several successive generations. However, a particular life stage may be relatively easy to sample, and this stage can often be used to demonstrate changes in population trend through time. Campbell and Sloan (1978) used the egg stage to describe numerical change in populations of the gypsy moth. Population trend (Figure 6.11) was followed over a 20-year period by using the number of eggs per acre occurring in the fall of the year. Four distinct features or phases of population abundance were

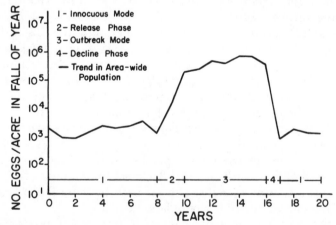

Figure 6.11   Trend in area-wide egg populations of the gypsy moth over a 20-year period illustrating innocuous, release, outbreak, and decline phases. (From Campbell and Sloan 1978.)

identified: innocuous, release, outbreak, and decline. This type of population information is valuable to the forester or pest management specialist in anticipating when significant damage resulting from defoliation will occur.

Population trends for most forest insects can be summarized in a manner similar to the example. The types of graph utilized vary depending on the specific relationships one wishes to describe and the ability of the researcher to obtain measurements of density or numbers of the subject species.

Population–Age Distribution

Population–age distribution is the proportion (or percent) of individuals in a population occurring in specified age classes. Theoretically, a population would develop a *stable age distribution,* that is, a constant proportion of individuals of different ages, if natality and mortality were constant and if population growth was not inhibited by the environment (Lotka 1925). As with the other theoretical constants we have considered, the stable age distribution does not occur in nature, at least for any extended period of time.

Age distribution for a population is often expresed as an age pyramid (Figure 6.12). The idealized patterns illustrated in Fig. 6.12 include cases where population size is (1) declining (a small proportion of individuals in the young age classes), (2) stable (constant proportion of individuals in all age classes), and (3) increasing (large proportion of individuals in the young age classes). It is not uncommon for insect populations to be represented by only one age class. For example, this circumstance would occur in a species such as the Douglas-fir tussock moth, where only eggs survive the winter. At other times of the year, an insect could be represented by all life stages (and hence age classes), particularly when generations overlap.

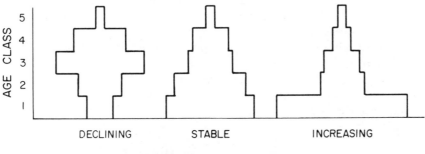

Figure 6.12 Idealized age pyramids illustrating cases where population size is declining (a small proportion of individuals in the young age classes), stable (constant proportion of individuals in all age classes), and increasing (large proportion of individuals in the young age classes).

Age distributions of forest insects occurring in nature are extremely difficult to measure. However, partial information on age distribution can be obtained and is of value to the forest manager or pest management specialist. For example, information on egg mass density is used to predict the likelihood and severity of outbreaks of the gypsy moth (Campbell 1973). In this case only the base of the age pyramid, which includes the youngest members of the population, is known. Experience, based on historical evidence, permits the information on egg mass density to be used in judging the likelihood of an outbreak of the gypsy moth.

Population Growth Form

Population growth form is the group attribute that expresses the manner in which the population size increases or decreases through time. Much of the theory of animal population dynamics is founded on concepts relating to growth form. We will consider two basic types of population growth, exponential and logistic, and several important relationships between the two forms. It is important to have a grasp of the basic principles of population growth in order to understand how various agents in the environment influence the distribution and abundance of forest insects.

Exponential and logistic growth are generally described by use of elementary calculus. We are interested in defining the instantaneous change (denoted by the symbol d, for derivative) in population number N in relation to time t.

Exponential growth, in which populations increase by a constant factor per unit of time (Figure 6.13), can be described by the following equation:

$$\frac{dN}{dt} = rN$$

where N represents the population size, t is time, and r is a constant describing the rate of change per individual (i.e., the instantaneous rate of population increase).

The rate of population growth per unit of time dN/dt is simply a constant r multiplied against the number of individuals already present N. The constant r is the difference between the rate at which new individuals are being born per individual b and the rate at which previously existing individuals are dying per individual d:

$$r = b - d$$

Theoretically, there is an optimum environment for a particular population where r would reach the maximum possible value. This value is termed the *intrinsic rate of increase*, r_{max}, or *biotic potential*. However, the value of r for particular species will vary as a function of environmental conditions. We have already discussed how natality, mortality, and dispersal are

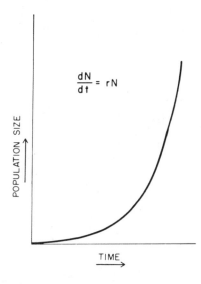

$$\frac{dN}{dt} = rN$$

POPULATION SIZE

TIME

Figure 6.13 Idealized pattern of exponential growth of a population by a constant factor per unit of time.

related and affected by different environmental conditions. These population processes determine the value of r observed for a particular set of environmental conditions. The difference between the intrinsic rate of increase and r observed under field conditions serves as a measure of *environmental resistance*, which Odum (1971) defines as the sum total of environmental limiting factors that prevent the intrinsic rate of increase from being realized.

Populations of forest insects can increase exponentially only for brief periods of time. The "release phase" of population growth, which generally precedes an outbreak of a pest species, undoubtedly involves exponential growth. In Figure 6.11 the change in population size between years 8 and 10 exemplifies the exponential growth of the gypsy moth.

However, it should be recognized that populations cannot continue to grow at an exponential rate indefinitely because food and space become limiting. In order to accommodate this fact, it is necessary to modify the exponential growth equation to include a term that expresses the idea that as population size N increases, the rate of population growth dN/dt decreases and eventually becomes zero or negative. The new function is known as the *logistic growth equation* or *Verhulst–Pearl* equation. It has the following form:

$$\frac{dN}{dt} = rN \frac{K - N}{K}$$

This expression describes an S-shaped or sigmoid curve (Figure 6.14). This expression suggests that population growth proceeds in the following way: when the population is small its overall growth rate (the slope of the

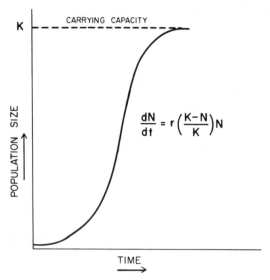

$$\frac{dN}{dt} = r\left(\frac{K-N}{K}\right)N$$

Figure 6.14 Idealized pattern illustrating population growth as described by the logistic equation.

growth curve) increases as the population grows. After the population reaches a certain value, that depends on the *carrying capacity* of the environment K, the growth rate begins to decrease as a result of environmental resistance. The rate of growth ultimately reaches zero. At this point the population has reached its saturation density or carrying capacity and no further growth takes place (Pielou 1974).

Although the logistic equation is a highly simplified model, it has proven to be a useful concept for describing population growth form. There are many factors besides food and space that prevent populations from reaching the carrying capacity of the environment. Forest entomologists and pest management specialists are often concerned with identifying conditions that permit exponential growth of pest species and in defining conditions that limit or regulate population size. Therefore, the concepts of carrying capacity, biotic potential, and environmental resistance are of more than just academic interest.

The two parameters of the logistic equation (the intrinsic rate of increase, r and the carrying capacity, K) are used to describe phases of growth in a population, as we have indicated above. The two parameters are also used to characterize development strategies for animal and plant (see Chapter 7) populations. There are a number of different attributes associated with insect (and other animal) species designated as r or K strategists (Pianka 1970, 1972, Southwood 1976, 1977b, Southwood and Comins 1976). In general, r species are opportunists and exploit ephemeral habitats where emphasis is placed on obtaining maximum food intake. The r species have the following characteristics: (1) rapid development, (2) high intrinsic rate of increase, (3) early reproduction, (4) semiparity (single reproduction), (5) short life cycle, and (6) small size. Populations of r species usually occur at densities well below the carrying capacity of the environment. Population size is influenced by mortality acting in a density-independent manner (see next section). The K species are specialists in resource-limited and stable habitats where emphasis is placed on harvesting food efficiently in crowded environments. The K species have the following characteristics, relative to the r species: (1) slow development, (2) low intrinsic rate of increase, (3) late reproduction, (4) iteroparity (repeated reproduction), (5) long life cycles, and (6) large size. Populations of K species usually operate at the carrying capacity of the environment. Population size is influenced by mortality acting in a density-dependent manner (see next section).

The concepts of r and K strategies for insects (and other animals) are meaningful only in a comparative sense. A given organism is more or less of an r strategist only in comparison with another organism. For example, vertebrates are much more K strategists than insects, which would be considered r strategists. Within the insects, a bark beetle would be considered an r species relative to a 17-year cicada. Southwood (1977b) emphasizes that there is a r–K continuum and that this continuum is related to duration stability of the habitat. One extreme of the continuum is represented by ephemeral habitats (e.g., early successional stages in forest establishment) and characterized by r strategists. The other extreme is represented by relatively stable habitats (e.g., a mature forest) and is characterized by K strategists.

FACTORS RESPONSIBLE FOR CHANGES IN DISTRIBUTION AND ABUNDANCE OF POPULATIONS

Classification of Factors Affecting Population Size

Forest insect populations, when observed over a period of years, characteristically fluctuate in size. Natural populations rarely, if ever, reach their biotic potential or the carrying capacity of the environment because of the intervention of a wide variety of actual or potential mortality factors. Under certain circumstances the saturation density of a particular species can be reached, but this occurrence is usually of short duration.

Mortality factors that affect population density have been classified in several ways. Generally population size is limited by one or more of the following factors: (1) climate and weather, (2) food quality and quantity, (3) host susceptibility and habitat suitability, (4) predation, (5) parasitization, (6) disease, (7) competition among individuals of the same species (intraspecific competition), (8) competition between members of different species (interspecific competition), and (9) genetic defects.

The relative importance of these mortality factors will vary for a particular population. Therefore, it is often useful to classify the factors in terms of how they affect a population. With the use of this functional classification system it is possible to define two general types of interaction: (1) factors that *modify* population size and (2) factors that *regulate* population size. We will examine population modifying and population regulating factors in some detail because much of the theory of population dynamics centers on an understanding of the concepts.

Population Modifying Factors (Density-Independent Factors)

Population modifying factors are also known as *density-independent* or *density-legislative* factors (Clark et al. 1967). These terms simply imply that the effect of a factor on the birth rate or death rate per individual in a population is independent of population size (Figure 6.15). The term "density-independent factor" is used more frequently in the ecological literature than either population modifying or density legislative factor. Also, most references to density-independent factors are expressed in terms of the effect of the factor on mortality (death rate) to a population rather than natality (birth rate). Technically, a density-independent factor could affect population size by acting to increase or decrease mortality or natality.

There are several circumstances where density-independent factors commonly operate to reduce forest insect population size. Catastrophic weather conditions are often associated with direct mortality to certain insect life stages. Harvesting of a forest, or a forest fire, can reduce population size by either causing direct mortality or removing needed food or habitat. Pesticides applied in forests serve as density-independent mortality agents and result in direct mortality. In each of these examples the *effect* of the factor on the population is not influenced by population size.

Adverse or extreme weather conditions are the density-independent factors most often associated with major changes in forest insect population abundance. These factors are consistently important at the outside range

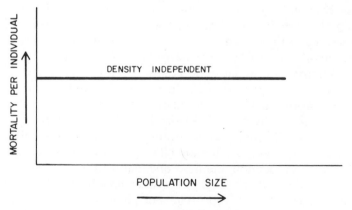

Figure 6.15 Effect of a density-independent factor on population size.

of a particular species, which can be defined in terms of latitude, longitude, and/or elevation. There are many examples that illustrate the effects of climate (or weather) on forest insect populations. One of the better documented cases is the mountain pine beetle. Safranyik (1978) reported that climate at high elevations and at northern latitudes was the dominant factor controlling the distribution and abundance of this bark beetle. Relationships between climatic variables and beetle populations were so strong that Safranyik et al. (1974) developed a procedure for defining outbreak hazards for western Canada.

Density-independent mortality agents have historically been utilized by foresters and forest managers to suppress populations of forest insects. Direct control procedures, such as the application of pesticides and salvaging of infested host material, are examples of the use of density-independent mortality agents to suppress population numbers. It is interesting to note that these tactics rarely are successful for any extended period of time.

Population Regulating Factors (Density-Dependent Factors)

Population regulating factors are also known as *density-dependent* or *density-governing* factors (Clark et al. 1967). These terms indicate that the effect of a factor on the birth rate or death rate per individual in a population is a function of population size (Figure 6.16). The term "regulating factor" implies the presence of some type of control mechanism. Regulating factors, hereafter referred to as *density-dependent factors*, operate through what is termed *negative feedback*, which is defined as the process by which a control mechanism is regulated through the effects it brings about.

As with density-independent factors, most references to density-dependent factors are expressed in terms of the effect of the factor on mortality rather than natality, for example, density-dependent mortality factors.

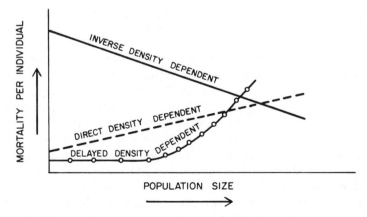

Figure 6.16 Effect of direct, delayed, and inverse density-dependent factors on population size.

Again, a density-dependent factor can affect either mortality or natality in a population.

Density-dependent factors can be further specified as *direct density-dependent*, in which the effect of the factor (on birth rate or death rate per individual) increases as population size increases; *delayed density-dependent*, in which there is a lag time before the effect of the factor is seen as population size increases; and *inverse density-dependent*, in which the effect of the factor declines with incresing population size (Figure 6.16).

At the beginning of this section we listed nine categories of factors that limit population size. With the exception of climate and weather, all these factors can operate in a density-dependent manner. There are many excellent case histories of density-dependent factors influencing populations of forest insects. In Chapter 8 we provide several examples of the density-dependent effects of natural enemies on populations of forest insect pests.

APPLICATION OF INFORMATION ON POPULATION DYNAMICS OF FOREST INSECTS

At the onset of this chapter we indicated that an understanding of principles of population dynamics was of practical importance. We have also seen that the population system of insects is complicated. To use information about populations of insects in IPM, this system must be organized and interpreted. In this section we examine a research strategy termed "systems analysis" and one approach used in the strategy termed "modeling." Systems analysis and the use of models provide a means for utilization information about populations for IPM purposes.

Systems Analysis and Modeling Population Systems

The population systems of several of the most significant forest insect pests of North America have been studied extensively. There is a wealth of information available on *Dendroctonus* bark beetles (Stark and Dahlsten 1970, Berryman et al. 1978, Coulson 1979, Thatcher et al. 1980), gypsy moth (Campbell 1981, Doane and McManus 1981), Douglas-fir tussock moth (Brookes et al. 1978, Overton and Colbert 1978), and spruce budworm (Morris 1963, Holling et al. 1976, Jones 1976, Regniére 1982). Comprehensive investigations of these insects were accomplished by using multidisciplinary teams of researchers consisting of various academic specialities, including entomologists, foresters, plant scientists, statisticians, engineers, and computer scientists. Each population system was found to be extremely complicated. The problem that we are faced with in dealing with these population systems is to synthesize the complex information so that it is usable by forest managers, pest management specialists, or population ecologists. Our goal is to structure the information so that we can describe how a particular population system functions in nature and be able to predict how the system will operate under different conditions. The research approach used to accomplish this goal is termed *systems analysis*. The principal methodology used in systems analysis is modeling. These terms have specialized meanings and can be defined as follows. A *system* is a set of facts, principles, or rules classified or arranged in an orderly form so as to show a logical plan linking the various parts. A *model* is an abstracted or simplified representation of a system. *Systems analysis* is the orderly and logical organization of data and information into models, followed by rigorous testing and exploration necessary for their testing (Jeffers 1978). *Modeling* is simply the activity of constructing models, which may involve use of mathematical techniques and procedures. This methodology has found wide application in ecology (Berryman and Pienaar 1974, Coulman et al. 1972, Garfinkel et al. 1964, Watt 1966, Holling et al. 1976) as well as other areas of science. Rykiel (1984) identified four general purposes of models relative to understanding the structure and organization of systems: exploration, explanation, projection, and prediction (Table 6.2).

Table 6.2   General Purposes of a Model[a]

Exploration	Objectives are very often general or intuitive, usually with no specific criteria for meeting them; main aims are insight, clarification, and understanding of factors that contribute significantly to system behavior
Explanation	General objective is to understand the structural and functional relationships among components and subsystems that explain the pattern of interconnections within the system and generate system behavior; specific objectives are related to level of resolution and the level of the study: system, subsystem, and component levels
Projection	Objective is to examine the dynamic behavior of system variables at any level (i.e., component, subsystem, or system), and the effects of changes in the values of parameters or variables and their variability; the patterns of behavior represented in the dynamic relations among variables are more important than actual values of the variables
Prediction	Specific objective is to estimate future values of particular system variables and/or the nature and timing of events and decisions; emphasis is on the accuracy and utility of the prediction and the reasonableness of the explanation of the prediction

Source: From Rykiel (1984).

[a]Acceptable error can be specified only on the basis of the fitness of results to fulfill objectives of the model and/or meet the needs of practical application; criteria should be given to permit a judgment of how closely a model meets its objectives.

A *mathematical model* of population dynamics can be viewed as a catalog of the best available quantitative statements about a population system. The application of mathematics to describe a population system allows us to abstract key features of the system in an efficient manner. A model is based on an understanding of how components of the system are related. It should be recognized that a model, by definition, is an incomplete representation of a complex system and is, therefore, to some degree incorrect. The usefulness of a particular model will depend in large part on how closely it approximates or simulates a population system as it exists in nature. In general, accuracy and precision of population dynamics models are related to space–time resolution. Detailed models of population systems occurring in forest stands over periods of time ranging from weeks to several months have proved to be most useful. Both accuracy and precision of models diminish as the space–time framework is enlarged. These results occur primarily because of problems in forecasting weather over long periods of time.

There are a number of specific benefits derived from using mathematical modeling as an approach to studying insect population systems: (1) the methodology forces us to clearly define the key components of the system (exploration); (2) this definition of components requires us to utilize existing knowledge about the system and serves to identify missing and needed new information (explanation); (3) the methodology provides a way to interpret the simultaneous interaction of many variables (projection) (counterintuitive results can often be identified); and (4) we can examine certain aspects of the life system, through simulation experiments, that may be impossible or extremely difficult to study experimentally in the forest (prediction).

The southern pine beetle is an example of a forest insect pest for which there is a complex model of population dynamics (Feldman et al. 1981a,b, Turnbow et al. 1982). Although the mathematical formulations used in development of the model are beyond the scope of this chapter, the biological elements treated are of interest to us. The model incorporates information on natality, mortality, dispersal, age distribution of life stages, developmental rates, pheromone communication, stand geometry, host susceptibility, and habitat suitability (Figure 6.18). We mention these components because they represent consideration of the attributes of individuals, attributes of the environment, basic population processes, and population states that were discussed earlier in the chapter. Population dynamics models are also available for the Douglas-fir tussock moth, spruce budworms, and mountain pine beetle.

Simulation Experiments Involving Insect Population Systems

With the aid of a high-speed computer, a mathematical model can be used to simulate growth of a population under conditions that occur in nature or that we specify. Regardless of which circumstance is chosen, we must provide certain basic information about the population and environment to initiate or define the simulation experiments. For example, if our model predicts population growth in a stand for a period of several months, we may need to supply information on population density at the beginning of the experiment, weather conditions, age or density of the host tree, and so forth. This information can be obtained directly from the field by use of survey techniques, or we can simply select "reasonable" starting values based on personal judgment. The significant point is that we must provide information to initiate the model. Thereafter, the model will simulate population growth for whatever period of time we may select, within the limits of resolution of the model. We may also be able to change conditions such as stand density or weather at some point during the simulation trial.

Once we have obtained the necessary starting values to initiate the model and defined the conditions of the simulation trial, we can observe and record the growth of a population for a period of weeks to months in a matter of a few seconds or minutes by using a high-speed computer. Furthermore, it is possible to record as output many different components of the population system, such as survival rate of within-tree life stages, mortality of adults during dispersal between hosts, rate of oviposition, rate of colonization of new hosts, and so on. For these reasons, the simulation model is a powerful tool for the pest management specialist or the population ecologist. Later we will describe how outputs of such models can be used in stand growth prediction (Chapter 7).

To illustrate some of the applications of computer-based models in forest entomology, we will use the population dynamics model of southern pine beetle as an example. The basic components of this model are illustrated in Figure 6.17. The model simulates population growth in a stand for a period of time that can range from a few weeks to several months [see Turnbow et al. (1982) for a detailed description of the interactive version of the TAMBEETLE model of population dynamics of the southern pine beetle].

Suppose that we were interested in investigating the relationship between stand density and tree mortality resulting from an infestation of the southern pine beetle for a period of 2 months. This relationship could be investigated in the field but would be extremely complicated to measure quantitatively and would require at least several months to complete. The cost would be very high. Another approach to the problem is to conduct a simulation experiment by using the model of southern pine beetle population dynamics. In the experiment we would utilize the same set of starting values for each simulation; specifically, the initial infestation size, beetle density, host size, weather conditions, and so on would be the same. The only variable that we would change is the density of the stand. Figure 6.18 illustrates the pattern of tree mortality that would be expected to occur over a period of 56 days in stands with 50, 100, and 150 ft^2 basal area per

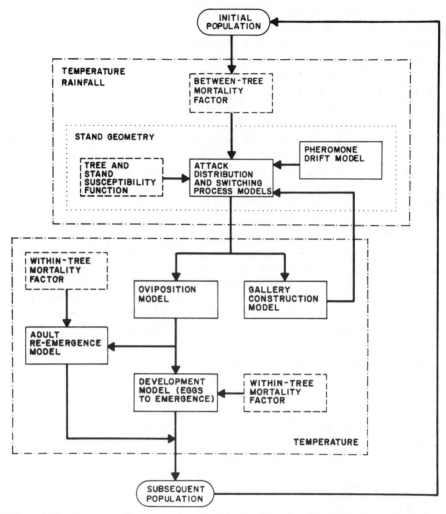

Figure 6.17   A conceptual structure for a model of bark beetle and host population dynamics. (From Turnbow 1982.)

acre. Clearly tree mortality in the stand with basal area of 150 ft² per acre is greatest. The information obtained from the simulation experiment is of value to the pest management specialist in setting priorities for a population suppression project and in determining the value of the loss resulting from the infestation.

The ecologist might be more interested in some aspect of the population per se rather than the amount of tree mortality that occurred. For example, since tree mortality results from colonization by adult southern pine beetles, we may be concerned with the patterns of abundance of this life stage in

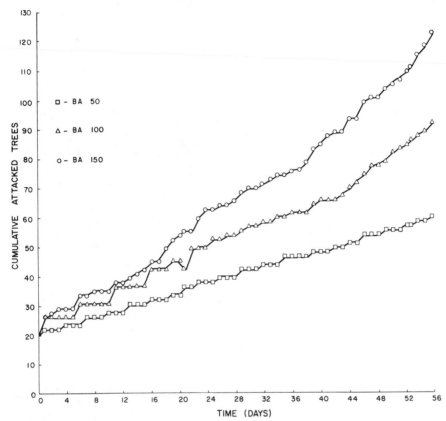

Figure 6.18 Pattern of tree mortality resulting from a simulation experiment utilizing a model of southern pine beetle population dynamics. The experiment was conducted for a period of 56 days in stands where host density was 50, 100, and 150 ft² basal area per acre. This simulation trial indicates that tree mortality is greatest in stands with high basal area. (From Coulson et al. 1979.)

the three simulated infestations (Figure 6.19). In this case, we could "output" the daily patterns of reemerging adults (adults that colonized a host, oviposited, and exited a host), and emerging adults (brood adults that developed in the host and exited). It is possible to examine many other population variables such as survival rate of adults between host trees, attack density, and so on. Analysis of the output could be used to explain the reason(s) why we observed different levels of tree mortality in the three stands.

Another application of the simulation methodology is in evaluating potential efficacy (efficiency) of treatment tactics applied to suppress population size. It is often difficult to determine in the field whether a treatment tactic actually is efficacious, because of intervention of many other variables

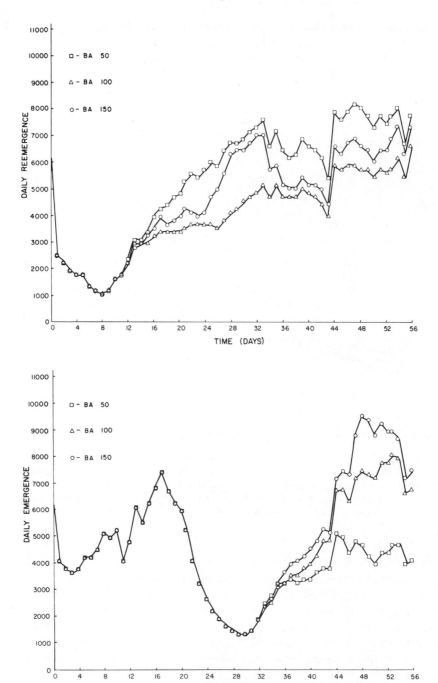

Figure 6.19 Pattern of population abundance for emerging adults (brood that developed within host trees and exited) and reemerged adults (beetles that colonized the host, oviposited, and exited the host) resulting from a simulation experiment utilizing a model of southern pine beetle population dynamics. These patterns reflect the numbers of beetles available to colonize new hosts through time. (From Coulson et al. 1979.)

such as weather conditions, parasites, predators, and other variables. There is no way to control these variables in the field. Again, the costs associated with quantitively measuring treatment efficacy are often sizeable.

It is possible to simulate the proposed mode of action of a treatment tactic by using a mathematical model. For example, with the southern pine beetle, we could propose a tactic that increased mortality of within-tree life stages over what is normally observed. This tactic might involve application of an insecticide to infested trees. We could propose another tactic that increased mortality of adults flying between hosts. This tactic might involve capturing flying adults by using pheromone-baited traps deployed in a stand. As a first measure of efficacy of these two potential tactics, we could observe the pattern of tree mortality that occurred over a specified period of time in relation to a "control" simulation where the treatment tactics

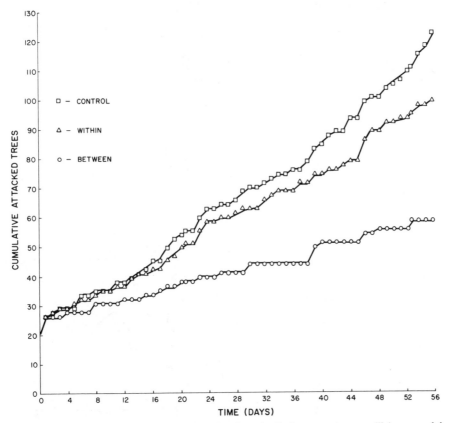

Figure 6.20 Pattern of tree mortality resulting in a simulation experiment utilizing a model of population dynamics of the southern pine beetle. The experiment was designed to test the efficacy of two hypothetical treatments to reduce populations within host trees and flying populations between host trees. Both treatments reduced tree mortality relative to the control. Increased mortality to populations flying between trees had a greater effect than did increased mortality of life stages in the tree in this experiment. (From Coulson et al. 1979.)

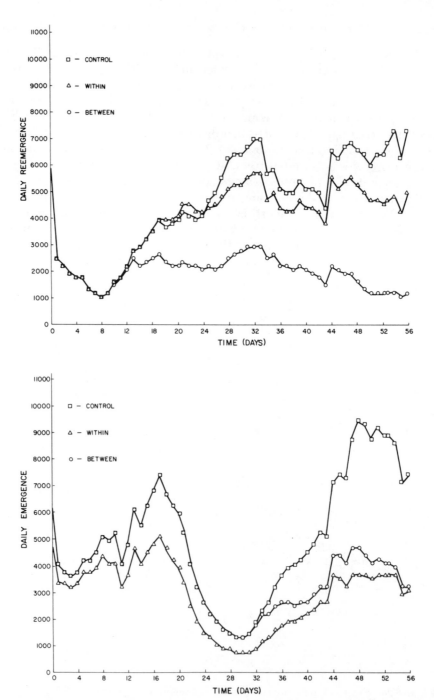

Figure 6.21 Pattern of population abundance for emerging and reemerging southern pine beetles (see Figure 6.20) in a simulation experiment designed to test efficacy of two hypothetical treatments applied to reduce populations within host trees and flying populations between host trees. The pattern of abundance of the beetle populations helps to explain how the treatments are effective in reducing tree mortality. (From Coulson et al. 1979.)

were omitted. In this case, we would standardize the initial conditions of the simulation, such as weather, stand density, and population size. The only variables that we would change relate to the treatment tactic. For example, in the "within-tree" treatment we might stipulate that mortality is 50% greater than the control. Likewise, for the "between-tree treatment" we could stipulate 50% more mortality to flying adults than for the control. Using these conditions, we can perform several simulations and record the pattern of tree mortality observed (Figure 6.20) or some measures of population performance such as daily emergence patterns (Figure 6.21) (Coulson et al. 1979).

In the preceding examples we have indicated some of the uses of a mathematical model of population dynamics. There are many more potential applications. We will see in Chapters 7 and 9 that mathematical models are also used in projecting forest growth and evaluating impact of forest insects.

REFERENCES

Allee, W. C., A. E. Emerson, O. Park, T. Park, and K. P. Schmidt. 1948. *Principles of Animal Ecology.* Saunders, Philadelphia.

Amman, G. D. 1977. The role of the mountain pine beetle in lodgepole pine ecosystems: Impact on succession. In Mattson, W. J. (Ed.), *The Role of Arthropods In Forest Ecosystems.* Proceedings in the Life Sciences. Springer-Verlag, New York.

Amman, G. D. 1978. Biology, ecology, and causes of outbreaks of the mountain pine beetle in lodgepole pine forests. In Berryman, A. A., G. D. Amman, R. W. Stark, and D. L. Kibbee (Eds.), *Theory and Practice of Mountain Pine Beetle Management in Lodgepole Pine Forests.* Symposium Proceedings. University of Idaho, Moscow.

Beckwith, R. C. 1978. Biology of the insect (the Douglas-fir tussock moth). In Brookes, M. H., R. W. Stark, and R. W. Campbell (Eds.), *The Douglas-fir Tussock Moth: A Synthesis.* U.S. Department of Agriculture Forest Service Technical Bulletin 1585.

Berryman, A. A. 1981. *Population Systems, A General Introduction.* Plenum Press, New York.

Berryman, A. A. 1982. Population dynamics of bark beetles. In Mitten, J. B. and K. B. Sturgeon (Eds.), *Bark Beetles in North American Conifers: A System for the Study of Evolutionary Biology.* University of Texas Press, Austin.

Berryman, A. A. and L. V. Pienaar. 1974. Simulation: A powerful method of investigating the dynamics and management of insect populations. *Environ. Entomol.* **3**:199–207.

Berryman, A. A., G. D. Amman, R. W. Stark, and D. L. Kibbee (Eds.). 1978. *Theory and Practice of Mountain Pine Beetle Management in Lodgepole Pine Forests.* Symposium Proceedings. University of Idaho, Moscow.

Berryman, A. A. and L. Safranyik (Eds.). 1979. Dispersal of forest insects: Evaluation, theory, and management implications. Proceedings IUFRO Conference, Sandpoint, Idaho.

Birch, M. C. (Ed.). 1974. *Pheromones.* North-Holland, Amsterdam.

Borden, J. H. 1974. Aggregation pheromones in the Scolytidae. In Birch, M. C. (Ed.), *Pheromones.* North-Holland, Amsterdam.

Borden, J. H. 1977. Behavioral responses of Coleoptera to pheromones, allomones, and kairomones. In Shorey, H. H. and J. J. McKelvey, Jr. (Eds.), *Insect Behavior.* Wiley, New York.

Brookes, M. H., R. W. Stark, and R. W. Campbell (Eds.). 1978. *The Douglas-fir Tussock Moth: A Synthesis.* U.S. Department of Agriculture Forest Service Technical Bulletin 1585.

Cameron, E. E., M. L. McManus, and C. J. Mason. 1979. Dispersal and its impact on the population dynamics of the gypsy moth in the United States of America. *Bull. Soc. Entomol. Suisse* **52**:169–179.

Campbell, R. W. 1973. Numerical behavior of a gypsy moth population system. *For. Sci.* **19**:162–167.

Campbell, R. W. 1981. Population dynamics: Historical review. In Doane, C. C. and M. L. McManus (Eds.), *The Gypsy Moth: Research Towards Integrated Pest Management.* U.S. Department of Agriculture Technical Bulletin 1584.

Campbell, R. W. and R. J. Sloan. 1978. Numerical bimodality among North American gypsy moth populations. *Environ. Entomol.* **7**:641–646.

Clark, L. R., P. W. Geier, R. D. Hughes, and R. F. Morris. 1967. *The Ecology of Insect Populations in Theory and Practice.* Methuen, London.

Clark, W. C. 1979. Spatial structure relationship in a forest insect system: Simulation models and analysis. *Bull. Soc. Entomol. Suisse* **52**:235–257.

Coulman, G. A., S. A. Reice, and R. L. Tummala. 1972. Population modeling: A systems approach. *Science* **175**:518–521.

Coulson, R. N. 1979. Population dynamics of bark beetles. *Annu. Rev. Entomol.* **24**:417–447.

Coulson, R. N. 1980. Population dynamics of the southern pine beetle. In Thatcher, R. C., J. L. Searcy, J. E. Coster, and G. D. Hertel (Eds.), *The Southern Pine Beetle.* U.S. Department of Agriculture Forest Service Technical Bulletin 1631.

Coulson, R. N., P. E. Pulley, J. L. Foltz, W. C. Martin, and C. L. Kelley. 1977. Generation survival models for within-tree populations of *Dendroctonus frontalis* (Coleoptera: Scolytidae). *Can. Entomol.* **109**:1071–1077.

Coulson, R. N., R. M. Feldman, W. S. Fargo, P. J. H. Sharpe, G. L. Curry, and P. E. Pulley. 1979. Evaluating suppression tactics of *Dendroctonus frontalis* in infestations. In Coster, J. E. and J. L. Searcy (Eds.), *Evaluating Control Tactics for the Southern Pine Beetle.* U.S. Department of Agriculture Forest Service Technical Bulletin 1613.

Delucchi, V. and W. Baltensweiler (Eds.). 1979. Dispersal of forest insects: Evaluation, theory, and management implications. *Bull. Soc. Entomol. Suisse* **52**:125–342.

Dingle, H. 1972. Migration strategies of insects. *Science* **175**:1327–1335.

Doane, C. C. and M. L. McManus (Eds.). 1981. *The Gypsy Moth: Research Towards Integrated Pest Management.* U.S. Department of Agriculture Forest Service Technical Bulletin 1584.

Edmonds, R. L. and W. S. Benninghoff (Eds.). 1974. Proceedings of Workshop/Conference III, Ecological Systems Approaches to Aerobiology. III. Further model development. *US/IBP Aerobiology Handbook,* No. 4. University of Michigan, Ann Arbor.

Ehrlich, P. R. and P. H. Raven. 1965. Butterflies and plants: A study in coevolution. *Evolution* **18**:586–608.

Fares, Y., P. J. H. Sharpe, and C. E. Magnuson. 1980. Pheromone dispersion in forests. *J. Theor. Biol.* **84**:335–359.

Feldman, R. M., T. L. Wagner, J. A. Gagne, P. J. H. Sharpe, and R. N. Coulson. 1981a. Within-tree life process models of the southern pine beetle. *Ecol. Modeling* **13**:247–259.

Feldman, R. M., G. L. Curry, and R. N. Coulson. 1981b. A mathematical model of field population dynamics of southern pine beetle, *Dendroctonus frontalis. Ecol. Modeling* **13**:261–281.

Garfinkel, D., R. H. MacArthur, and R. Sach. 1964. Computer simulation and analysis of simple ecological systems. *Ann. NY Acad. Sci.* **115**:943–951.

Holling, C. S., D. D. Jones, and W. C. Clark. 1976. Ecological policy design: A case study of forest and pest management. In Norton, G. A. and C. S. Holling (Eds.), *Pest Management.* Pergamon Press, New York.

Hutchinson, G. E. 1978. *An Introduction to Population Ecology*. Yale University Press, New Haven.

Jeffers, J. N. R. 1978. *An Introduction to Systems Analysis: With ecological applications:* University Park Press, Baltimore.

Jones, D. D. 1976. The budworm site model. In Norton, G. A. and C. S. Hollings (Eds.), *Pest Management*. Pergamon Press, New York.

Kulman, H. M. 1971. Effects of insect defoliation on growth and mortality of trees. *Annu. Rev. Entomol.* **16**:289–324.

Lotka, A. J. 1925. *Elements of Physical Biology*. William & Wilkins, Baltimore.

Mason, R. M. and R. F. Luck. 1978. Population growth and regulation (of the Douglas-fir tussock moth). In Brookes, M. H., R. W. Stark, and R. W. Campbell (Eds.), *The Douglas-Fir Tussock Moth: A Synthesis*. U.S. Department of Agriculture Forest Service Technical Bulletin 1585.

Mattson, W. J. (Ed.). 1977. *The Role of Arthropods In Forest Ecosystems*. Proceedings in the Life Sciences. Springer-Verlag, New York.

Mattson, W. J. and N. D. Addy. 1975. Phytophagous insects as regulators of primary production. *Science* **190**:515–522.

Mitten, J. B. and K. B. Sturgeon (Eds.). 1982. *Bark Beetles in North American Conifers: A System for the Study of Evolutionary Biology*. University of Texas Press, Austin.

Morris, R. F. 1963. (Ed.) The Dynamics of Epidemic Spruce Budworm Populations. *Memoirs, Entomol. Soc. Can.* **31**:1–332.

Morris, R. F. and W. C. Fulton. 1970. Models for the development and survival of *Hyphantria cunea* in relation to temperature and humidity. *Memoirs, Entomol. Soc. Can.* **70**:1–60.

Odum, E. P. 1971. *Fundamentals of Ecology*. Saunders, Philadelphia.

Overton, W. S. and J. J. Colbert. 1978. Population modeling (the Douglas-fir tussock moth). In Brookes, M. H., R. W. Stark, and R. W. Campbell (Eds.), *The Douglas-Fir Tussock Moth: A Synthesis*. U.S. Department of Agriculture Forest Service Technical Bulletin 1585.

Peterman, R. M. 1978. The ecological role of mountain pine beetle in lodgepole pine forests. In Berryman, A. A., G. D. Amman, R. W. Stark, and D. L. Kibbee (Eds.), *Theory and Practice of Mountain Pine Beetle Management in Lodgepole Pine Forests*. Symposium Proceedings. University of Idaho, Moscow.

Pianka, E. R. 1970. On *r*- or *K*-selection. *Am. Nat.* **104**:592–597.

Pianka, E. R. 1972. *r* and *K* selection or *b* and *d* selection? *Am. Nat.* **106**:581–588.

Pielou, E. C. 1969. *An Introduction to Mathematical Ecology*. Wiley, New York.

Pielou, E. C. 1974. *Population and Community Ecology, Principles and Methods*. Gorden and Beach Science Publishers, New York.

Poole, R. W. 1974. *An Introduction to Quantitative Ecology*. McGraw-Hill, New York.

Price, P. W. 1975. *Insect Ecology*. Wiley, New York.

Rainey, R. C. 1979. Dispersal and redistribution of some Orthoptera and Lepidoptera by flight. *Bull. Soc. Entomol. Suisse* **52**:125–132.

Regniére, J. 1982. A process-oriented model of spruce budworm phenology (Lepidoptera: Tortricidae). *Can. Entomol.* **114**:811–825.

Rykiel, E. J. 1984. Modeling agroecosystems: Lessons from ecology. In Stinner, B., G. House, and R. Lowarance (Eds.), *Agricultural Ecosystems: Unifying Concepts*. Wiley, New York, in press.

Safranyik, L. 1978. Effects of weather on mountain pine beetle populations. In Berryman, A. A., G. D. Amman, R. W. Stark, and D. L. Kibbee (Eds.), *Theory and Practice of Mountain Pine Beetle Management in Lodgepole Pine Forests*. Symposium Proceedings. University of Idaho, Moscow.

Safranyik, L., D. M. Schrimpton, and H. S. Whitney. 1974. *Management of Lodgepole Pine to Reduce Losses from the Mountain Pine Beetle*. Environment Canada, Canadian Forestry Service, Technical Report 1. Victoria, B.C.

Schneider, F. 1962. Dispersal and migration. *Annu. Rev. Entomol.* **7**:223–242.

Schowalter, T. D. 1981. Insect herbivore relationship to the state of the host plant: Biotic regulation of ecosystem nutrient cycling through ecological succession. *Oikos* **37**:126–130.

Southwood, T. R. E. 1962. Migration of terrestrial arthropods in relation to habitat. *Biol. Rev.* **37**:171–214.

Southwood, T. R. E. 1976. Bionomic strategies and population parameters. In May, R. M. (Ed.), *Theoretical Ecology: Principles and Applications*. Blackwell, Oxford.

Southwood, T. R. E. 1977a. Habitat, the template for ecological strategies? *J. Anim. Ecol.* **46**:337–366.

Southwood, T. R. E. 1977b. The relevance of population dynamics theory to pest status. In Cherret, J. M. and G. R. Sager (Eds.), *Origins of Pest, Parasitic, Disease, and Weed Problems*. Blackwell, Oxford.

Southwood, T. R. E. 1978. *Ecological Methods*. Wiley, New York.

Southwood T. R. E. and H. N. Comins. 1976. A synoptic population model. *J. Anim. Ecol.* **45**:949–965.

Stark, R. W. and D. L. Dahlsten (Eds.). 1970. Studies on the Population Dynamics of the Western Pine Beetle, *Dendroctonus frontalis* LeConte. University of California, Division of Agricultural Science, Berkley.

Taylor, L. R. and R. A. J. Taylor. 1976. Aggregation, migration, and population mechanics. *Nature* **265**:415–421.

Thatcher, R. C., J. L. Searcy, J. E. Coster, and G. D. Hertel (Eds.). 1980. *The Southern Pine Beetle*. U.S. Department of Agriculture Forest Service Technical Bulletin No. 1631.

Turnbow, R. H., R. N. Coulson, L. C. Hu, and R. F. Billings. 1982. *Procedural Guide for Using the Interactive Version of the TAMBEETLE Model of Southern Pine Beetle Population and Spot Dynamics*. Texas Agricultural Experiment Station Miscellaneous Publication 1518.

Uvarov, B. P. 1931. Insects and climate. *Trans. Entomol. Soc. Lond.* **79**:1–247.

Varley, G. C., G. R. Gradwell, and M. P. Hassell. 1974. *Insect Population Ecology, An Analytical Approach*. University of California Press, Berkeley.

Watt, K. E. F. 1966. The nature of systems analysis. In Watt, K. E. F. (Ed.), *Systems Analysis in Ecology*. Academic Press, New York.

Wellington, W. G. 1977. Returning the insect to insect ecology: Some consequences for pest management. *Environ. Entomol.* **6**:1–8.

Wellington, W. G. 1979. Dispersal and population change. In Berryman, A. A. and L. Safranyik (Eds.), *Dispersal of Forest Insects: Evaluation, Theory, and Management Implication*. Proceedings of IUFRO Conference, Sandpoint, Idaho.

Williams, C. B. 1957. Insect Migration. *Annu. Rev. Entomol.* **2**:163–179.

7

POPULATION DYNAMICS OF FOREST TREES IN RELATION TO PHYTOPHAGOUS INSECTS

INTRODUCTION

Forest stand dynamics is a fundamental issue in forest management. In Chapter 5 we indicated that it was also a basic component of IPM (Figure 5.8). The subject of forest stand dynamics is founded on principles of plant ecology dealing with population dynamics. In commercial forestry the primary interest in stand dynamics may simply be prediction of growth and yield of a particular tree species at various times during a rotation. In integrated pest management (IPM) our interest is in the interactions between populations of forest trees and phytophagous insects. In this chapter we consider basic relationships between forest trees and phytophagous insects. Our objectives are to examine (1) basic principles of forest tree population dynamics, (2) the types of interaction that occur between forest trees and phytophagous insects, (3) the responses of forest trees to phytophagous insects, and (4) the effects of phytophagous insects on trees. We will see that phytophagous insects influence forest tree growth and form, community (stand) development, and ecosystem structure and function.

There are a number of sources for additional information on the subjects treated in this chapter: plant ecology—Harper (1977, 1981), Harper and White (1974), Miles (1979), Barbour et al. (1980), Hallé et al. (1981); forest ecology—Spurr and Barnes (1980), Barrett (1962), Bormann and Likens (1979), West et al. (1981), Horn et al. (1979), Cairns (1980); insect plant interactions—Mattson (1977), Mattson and Addy (1975), Van Emden and Way (1973), Rosenthal and Janzen (1979), and Zlotin and Khodashova (1980). In addition to these references, the *Annual Review of Ecology and Systematics* and the *Annual Review of Entomology* contain many papers dealing with specific aspects of the topics covered in this chapter.

BASIC PRINCIPLES OF FOREST TREE POPULATION DYNAMICS

Basic theory on population dynamics was developed largely from contributions by animal ecologists. Although there are many parallels between principles of population dynamics of animals and plants, there are also a number of fundamental differences. Harper (1977) provides a comprehensive examination of principles of population dynamics as they relate to plants in general, and Spurr and Barnes (1980) provide a similar perspective directed to forestry in particular. In this section we will examine two issues of population dynamics of forest trees: (1) the organization and structure of forest tree populations and (2) models of forest tree populations.

Organization and Structure of Forest Tree Populations

In our discussion of insect population dynamics (Chapter 6) we had no difficulty in defining the basic element of a population, the individual. The individual insect is a discrete unit with a determinate number of parts; that is, it has unitary structure. The size of a population of insects was expressed using the symbol N, which represented the number of individuals present.

By contrast to insects, the definition of an individual tree in a population of forest trees is somewhat more complicated. There are a variety of different definitions applied to forest trees. Most definitions include reference to size and physiognomy (existence of a major axis or trunk) (Hallé et al. 1981). Because of the importance of trees as a merchantable commodity, foresters often use a rigid definition. One such definition, provided by Little (1953), illustrates this point: a tree is a woody plant having one erect woody stem or trunk at least three inches (7.5 cm) in diameter at breast height, a more or less definitely formed crown of foliage, and a height of at least 12 ft (4.0 m). This definition is not particularly useful for describing the interactions that occur between forest trees and insects.

An alternative way of defining the individual in a population of forest trees that is useful for describing plant–insect interactions is to employ the concept of a tree as a modular organism. This approach has been described in detail by Harper (1977, 1981) and Harper and White (1974). A *modular organism* is one that develops from a zygote (fertilized egg cell) by the repeated sequential iteration (repetition) of units of construction. The product of the zygote is called a *genet*. The units of construction of the organism are called *modules* (Figure 7.1). A module is defined as a repeated unit of multicellular structure normally arranged in a branched system, as is the case with a forest tree. Modules constitute clearly recognizable units of construction that compose the genetic individual (genet). A forest tree consists of several kinds of modules, including a main stem or stem system, foliage (leaves, needles), meristems, reproductive structures (flowers, cones),

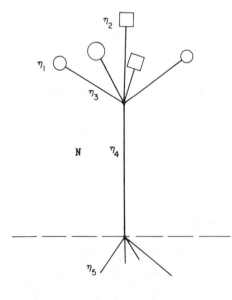

Figure 7.1 Diagrammatic representation of a forest tree genet (N) composed of five types of structural modules (η_{1-5}).

roots, or a root system. In summary, an *individual* forest tree consists of a genet (the product of a zygote) and is composed of a number of recognizable modules of construction that are arranged in a branched system.

The importances of the concept of modular organization of trees becomes more apparent when we begin to consider *populations* of trees. It will become even more evident when we consider interactions between forest trees and phytophagous insects. One immediate consequence of modular organization is that, unlike most insect populations, there are two levels of organization, instead of one, for a population of forest trees: (1) the number of individual trees (genets) and (2) the number of individual modular units forming each individual tree.

With the foregoing discussion in mind we can define forest tree *population dynamics* to consist of two levels of structure. The first level deals with changes in the distribution and abundance of forest tree genets through space and time. This definition is similar to that given for insect (animal) population dynamics. Populations of genets are denoted by the symbol N, and Harper (1977) refers to population events at this level as N *demography*. The second level deals with changes in the distribution and abundance of tree modules through space and time, which determines the growth rates of genets. There is not an equivalent level of structure for most insect populations.* Populations of modules are denoted by the symbol η, and Harper (1977) refers to population events at the modular level as η *demography*.

Forestry is concerned with both levels of forest tree population structure, that is, with numbers of trees (N demography) and with growth rates of trees (η demography). Because phytophagous insects also influence both the numbers and growth rates of forest trees, we examine the two levels of structure of forest tree populations in further detail.

Populations of Forest Tree Genets

The first level of organization in a population of forest trees is the genet, which is the genetically homogeneous unit on which natural selection acts. It may or may not be possible to identify and count genets easily. In many cases the genet is simply the tree as we commonly view it; thus the oak tree that we see in the forest (whether an immature or mature tree) is easily identified as an individual and it is also a genet. In this case all the modules that form the genet are held together on a common trunk or stem. In Figure 7.2 the population size N of species A is 4. In other cases, however, the tree that we view may have developed by vegetative growth of a genet that expanded laterally. Aspen, which develops by suckering, is an example. In this case the genet is the entire clone and each stem is a complex module

---

*It is possible to envision populations of social insects (some Hymenoptera and Isoptera) as having two levels of organization. For example, in the case of the honeybee, *Apis mellifera* Linnaeus, the queens could be considered analogous to genets and the castes analogous to modules.

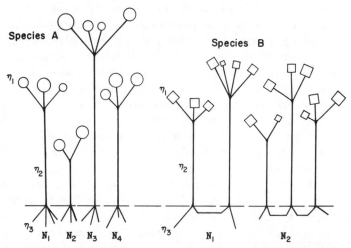

Figure 7.2 Diagrammatic representation of two populations of forest trees. Species A consists of four genets (N_{1-4}), and we are interested in populations of three types of module (η_{1-3}). The population size of $\eta_1 = 12$, $\eta_2 = 4$, and $\eta_3 = 13$. Species B consists of two genets (N_{1-2}), and we are interested in populations of three types of module (η_{1-3}). The population size of $\eta_1 = 15$ and $\eta_2 = 5$. In this case the number of main stems (η_2) does not equal the number of genets (as was the case with species A) because the stems developed by lateral growth. The population size of η_3 would likely be expressed in terms of biomass rather than number of units.

(Figure 7.2). In Figure 7.2 the population size N of species B is 2, although there are five main stems. Collectively, the number of genets in a population is equivalent to N (population size) in equations describing insect (animal) population dynamics. Therefore, the demographic equation, presented in Chapter 6, is applicable for describing changes in *numbers* of genets in a population of forest trees:

$$N_{t+1} = N_t + \text{births} - \text{deaths} + \text{immigrants} - \text{emigrants}$$

In Chapter 6 we used a format for organization of concepts about insect (animal) populations termed a *population system* (Figure 6.1). This system is also suitable for describing population dynamics of forest tree genets. There are four basic interconnected elements in the population system: (1) properties of individuals, (2) properties of the environment, (3) population processes, and (4) population states or conditions. Inherited properties associated with individual genets and properties of the environment interact to influence the population processes of natality, mortality, and dispersal. These processes determine various states or conditions of the forest tree population, including density, dispersion, age structure, and growth form. The population states influence properties of individuals and properties of the environment through negative feedback. Co-evolution of insects and their hosts and adaptive evolution of forest tree genets occur as a result of negative feedback (Figure 6.1).

It is beyond the scope of this chapter to examine each component of the population system for forest trees, as we did for insects in Chapter 6. Most of the definitions and concepts presented in Chapter 6 are applicable, in a general way, to forest trees. There are several unique features of the system that are noteworthy, and we briefly discuss the aspects pertinent to our interest in insect–host interactions.

The most obvious difference in the population systems of forest trees and insects centers on the interaction of individual genets with the environment. Since forest trees are spatially fixed, the interaction of genets with the environment takes place through various types of adaptation in structure and form. In particular, we are interested in the number, types, and arrangement of structural modules of a forest tree through space and time. In addition to structural diversity, interaction of genets with insects and other biotic agents of the environment is also mediated through production of secondary chemicals by the tree. These chemicals, which are not essential for maintenance of fundamental metabolic processes of the tree, are termed *allelochemicals* or *allelopathic* chemicals.

The population processes (natality, mortality, and dispersal) conceptually operate in the manner described for insects. Dispersal, of course, is accomplished by passive means. Again, specific morphological adaptations of seed (e.g., wings, plumes, spines) aid in dispersal, and some seeds can remain dormant for many years (Gadgil 1971).

The population states or conditions can be described by using the same nomenclature as applied to insects: density, dispersion, growth form, and age structure. Many of the principles relating to the population states of insect populations are also applicable for forest tree populations. For example, the logistic equation is suitable for describing changes in numbers of genets through time. The parameters of the equation, r and K, are interpreted in the same way as for insects. Furthermore, we can segregate plant species as r and K strategists, as we did for insects.

Phytophagous insects enter into the population system of forest tree genets as one of the important components of the environment that interacts with individual genets to influence the population processes and subsequently the population states. The forest entomologist is often concerned with the effects of insects on natality, mortality, and dispersal (the population processes) of genets. The forester is usually more concerned with the effects of insects on density, dispersion, age structure, and growth form (the population states) of genets. Individual forest tree genets have many adaptations that have, in some cases, co-evolved in response to the pressures exerted by insects or because of their presence (e.g., the availability of insects to pollinate flowers). Among the important adaptations that we will examine later in our discussion of insect–host interactions are structural diversity, chemical defense mechanisms, seasonal phenology, and reproductive strategies.

Populations of Forest Tree Modules

The second level of organization in a population refers to the asexually derived modules of construction of each genet, including meristems, leaves, flowers, and roots. In other words, each individual tree (genet) consists of a collection or subpopulation of connected parts or modules, which are displayed in the form of a branched system. The number of a particular type of module per tree is designated as η (Figure 7.1). In Figure 7.1 there is one genet with five different types of module designated as η_{1-5}: $\eta_1 = 3$, $\eta_2 = 2$, $\eta_3 = 4$, $\eta_4 = 1$, $\eta_5 = 4$. The total number of a particular type of module in an entire population of trees (genets) is designated as N_η (Figure 7.2). For example, in Figure 7.2 the population size N of species A = 4. The population size of the three modules η is: $\eta_1 = 12$, $\eta_2 = 4$, $\eta_3 = 13$. The population size N of species B = 2 because the main stems of the two genets developed following lateral growth. The population size of module $\eta_1 = 15$ and $\eta_2 = 5$. The population size of module η_3, which represents the roots of the genets, would likely be expressed in terms of biomass rather than numbers. In practice, it would also be extremely difficult to distinguish between individual genets in a field population of a tree species that developed as a clone.

An individual genet grows as a function of the birth and death rates of modules. Therefore, the *growth* of a genet can be represented by the following equation (Harper 1981):

$$\eta_{t+1} = \eta_t + \text{module births} - \text{module deaths}$$

where η can be expressed in terms of numbers or biomass ($=$ living weight). Discrete modules, such as flowers or the main stems of trees, are conveniently represented by numbers. Modules such as roots or leaves may be easier to describe in terms of biomass.

The *form* that a forest tree takes is also determined in part by the birth and death rates of modules. There are certain specific characteristics that influence the particular architecture of an array of modules. Among the important ones are branch angles, internode length, and the probability that a bud will die, remain dormant, or develop to produce daughter buds (Harper 1981). Because forest trees are spatially fixed, certain aspects of tree form play a major role in activities such as nutrient acquisition (e.g., growth pattern of the root system), avoidance of competition (e.g., number and types of leaves), defense from predators (e.g., presence of thorns), and reproduction (e.g., numbers and locations of flowers). Insects and other animals accomplish these same activities through behavioral mechanisms that often involve movement.

In the previous section we indicated that phytophagous insects were involved in influencing natality, mortality, and dispersal of genets. They are also important in influencing birth and death rates of plant modules, which affect both the growth rate and growth form of a tree.

There is a distinct relationship between the number, types, and arrangement of structural modules of a tree and the diversity of insects associated with it. In general, the greater the diversity in plant architecture, the greater the insect diversity (Lawton 1983, Coulson et al. 1971). In Chapters 11–17 we examine the major forest insect pests. These insects are organized into categories based on the type of plant module(s) infested. The amount of damage associated with a particular insect pest is often related to the availability of a preferred plant module. Certainly insects influence the birth and death rates of plant modules and are, therefore, extremely important in determining genet growth rate.

Models of Forest Tree Populations

There are a number of different models of forest trees. Some models are appropriate for organizing information about forest tree populations, whereas others are suitable for describing or predicting populations of genets or modules through space and time. Since we are interested in both the fundamental interactions of insects with forest trees and the effects of insects on growth and yield of forests, two different types of models are needed. In the following sections we present (1) a conceptual model, developed by Harper (1977), of the life cycle of a population of forest trees and (2) a review of models used in predicting growth and yield of forest trees.

Life Cycle Model for Populations of Forest Trees

The events that lead to changes in the population processes (birth rate, death rate, and dispersal) of forest trees, which affect the various state variables (density, growth rate, etc.), take place at different stages of development of the population. With insects, we found that the life cycle was a convenient way to organize information about a particular species. The life cycle could be partitioned according to the various developmental stages of the insect. Harper (1977) developed a diagrammatic model that describes the various life history events or phases of development of a population of forest trees (Figure 7.3). This model represents a forest tree population as a series of repeating modular units (the shoots) and provides a particularly useful way or organizing information about both forest tree population dynamics and the interaction of insects with trees. The model separates the life cycle of a forest tree into four distinct phases. The first phase (I) considers the bank of seeds of a particular tree species stored in the forest soil or on the forest floor (Figure 7.3). Many factors influence dispersal and dispersion patterns of forest trees and insect predation of seeds is clearly among the important ones. The second phase (II) considers recruitment and establishment of individuals of the population from the seed

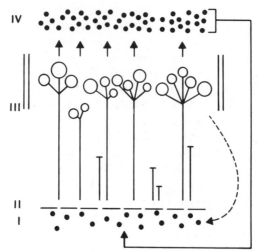

Figure 7.3 Diagrammatic representation of the plant life cycle, illustrating a tree as a series of repeating modular units (the shoots). There are four basic components in the life cycle: (I) the seed bank, (II) recruitment and establishment of individuals of the population from the seed bank, (III) growth of individuals, and (IV) reproduction and dispersal. (Modified from Harper 1977.)

bank. The third phase (III) considers growth in size (height and volume). This phase requires space, nutrients, water, and so on. These requisite resources are not uniformly available to all trees, and some individuals may die (represented by unbranched stems T in Figure 7.3), others may be suppressed, and still others may grow vigorously (the branched units). Eventually, the carrying capacity for a particular site is approached and the growth rate of a population declines. The intervention of environmental constraints and limited resources are indicated by the vertical parallel lines in Figure 7.3. Growth and development of the population results in changes to the environment of the understory and forest floor, which influences recruitment from the seed bank. This negative feedback process is indicated by the dashed arrow in Figure 7.3. The fourth phase (IV) involves reproduction and dispersal of seeds to the forest floor.

Although Harper (1977) developed the conceptual model of a plant life cycle primarily for use in organizing and describing plant population dynamics, the model is also very useful for defining or evaluating the impact of phytophagous insects. In studying the effects of insects on trees, forest entomologists have traditionally organized their efforts around the various feeding groups, with primary emphasis on plant modules. In considering the interactions between population dynamics of forest trees in relation to population dynamics of phytophagous insects, an alternative approach is to organize around the phases of the tree life cycle. Such an approach would consider insect effects on (1) the seed bank, (2) recruitment and establishment of trees, (3) growth and development of trees, and (4) seed production and dispersal. Insect life cycles linked to forest tree life cycles through the common attributes associated with the population systems of both components (e.g., birth rate, death rate, dispersal, density, growth rate) offers a challenging approach to the study of reciprocal interactions between insect and host tree population dynamics (Figure 6.1).

Mathematical Models of Forest Trees

As with population dynamics of insects, mathematical models have been developed for forest trees. However, because of the long time frame associated with forest tree growth, computer simulation models are structured differently from models of insect population dynamics. The primary use of simulation models of forest trees is in prediction of stand growth and yield. The models have been employed to aid forest managers in making decisions regarding harvesting schedules and projected resource availability for forest products. The models are an important component of IPM because they provide essential information needed for evaluation of impact of pest insects on forest resources.

There are essentially three types of models available: (1) whole stand models, (2) diameter distribution models, and (3) individual tree models. The *whole stand models* were developed from basic information (measurements) on stand growth and yield. Under the whole stand approach, some specified aggregate stand volume is predicted from stand level variables such as age, site index, and basal area or number of trees per acre. No information on volume distribution by size class is provided. *Diameter distribution models* provide information on the number of trees per acre in each diameter class present. Mean total tree heights are predicted for trees of given diameters growing under given stand conditions. Volume per diameter class is calculated by using the predicted mean tree heights and the midpoints of the diameter class intervals. This information is substituted into tree volume equations. Yield on a per acre basis is estimated by summing diameter classes of interest. The information needed for the diameter distribution models includes stand measurements such as age, site index, and number of trees per acre. Detailed information on stand distribution can be obtained from the models. *Individual tree models* predict stand yield from information on individual trees. The components of tree growth in these models are commonly linked together through a computer program that simulates the growth of each tree and then aggregates these to provide estimates of stand growth and yield (Burkhart et al. 1981).

With most forest trees, the main stem, which is a module of construction, is numerically equivalent to the genet. That is, the number of main stems is equivalent to the number of genets ($\eta = N$). The various types of models take into account both the number of trees present (survivorship) and their size throughout a rotation period. However, the type of information actually provided to the user by the different kinds of models varies as we have indicated above.

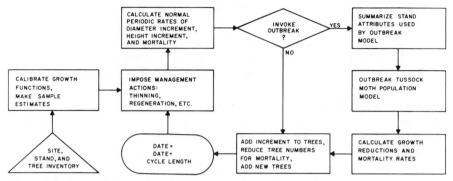

Figure 7.4   Logic of the combined stand prognosis model of forest tree growth and a model of population dynamics of the Douglas-fir tussock moth. (From Stage 1978.)

Stand growth and yield models have been used as a tool in forestry for a number of years. In IPM these models are an essential link to evaluating impact(s) of forest pests. The stand growth and yield models can be used in conjunction with insect population dynamics models (Wykoff et al. 1982, Monserud and Crookston 1982). Figure 7.4 illustrates the logic involved in interfacing the two types of models. In this case the stand prognosis model is linked to an outbreak model of the Douglas-fir tussock moth, *Orgyia pseudotsugata* (McDunnough) (Stage 1978). There are many different applications of the combined pest insect–stand prognosis models. For example, it is possible to examine the expected long-term volume yields of Douglas-fir when subjected to single or multiple outbreaks of the Douglas-fir tussock moth (see Figure 7.5). In this example, basing harvest schedules on yields anticipated from the "no outbreak curve" in Figure 7.5 would

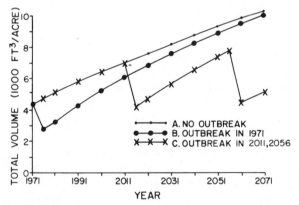

Figure 7.5   An example of predicted total volume (ft³/acre) versus time for three Douglas-fir tussock moth outbreak scenarios: A = no outbreak, B = outbreak in 1971 only, C = outbreaks in years 2011 and 2056. Simulations were conducted by use of the combined stand prognosis model and Douglas-fir tussock population dynamics model (see Figure 7.4). (From Monserud and Crookston 1982.)

result in suboptimal long-range plans, if the stand were subjected to one or more Douglas-fir tussock moth outbreaks (Monserud and Crookston 1982).

TYPES OF INTERACTIONS BETWEEN FOREST TREES AND PHYTOPHAGOUS INSECTS

Insect–plant interactions have been classified in a number of different ways. Southwood (1973) summarized basic interactions under three broad categories: food, shelter, and transport. Gilbert (1979) defined insect–plant interactions according to ecological relationships and identified seven types (Table 7.1). For our purposes, where we are concerned primarily with phytophagous insects on forest trees, there are three important classes of interactions: (1) insects acting as predators, (2) insects acting as parasites, and (3) insects acting as mutualists with forest trees. We do not suggest that the other relationships are unimportant. However, forest entomology and IPM in forests generally deal with the first two categories (predators and parasites) and to a lesser degree to the third category (mutualists).

Insects as Predators of Forest Trees or Plant Modules

In this first type of interaction, the insect serves as the predator and the forest tree (genet) or module serves as the prey. By definition, the predator kills the genet or plant module on which it feeds.

In the case of predation of forest tree genets, several groups of insects are important throughout the different stages of growth of a particular tree species. Typically, greatest mortality to genets occurs as a result of predation of seeds (see Chapter 14). In some cases insects are capable of killing seedlings (e.g., reproduction weevils—see Chapter 13) and mature trees (e.g., bark beetles—see Chapter 15; spruce budworms—see Chapter 11).

Table 7.1 Categories of Insect–Plant Interactions

Insects	Plants
Predators, parasitoids	Prey
Parasites	Host
Pollinators, seed dispersal agents	Provide a reward
Allelopathic agents, antiherbivore defense force	Provide food reward and a domicile
Nutrient gatherers	Provide domicile
Host	Parasite
Prey	Predator

Source: Gilbert (1979).

Insect predation of tree modules, where the module is killed but the genet survives, is a much more common phenomenon. There are several groups of insects that occur in this category (e.g., some defoliators—see Chapter 11; and tip moths feeding on buds and terminals—see Chapter 13). In this case, the insect is a predator on the plant module but a parasite on the genet. Under some circumstances, however, predation of plant modules can also result in mortality to genets; for instance, severe and/or repeated defoliation by insects can result in mortality to the genet as well as the modules.

Insects as Parasites on Forest Trees or Plant Modules

In the second type of interaction, insects serve as parasites and the tree or module serves as the host. By definition, the host is normally not killed. There are a large number of different insects that fit into this category (e.g., most sapsucking insects—see Chapter 12; some phloem-feeding insects—see Chapter 15; wood boring insects—see Chapter 16; and gall forming insects—see Chapter 17). This category includes the largest number and greatest diversity of insect–tree interactions.

As was the case with insect predation of plants, in some cases mortality to genets or modules occurs as a result of excessive levels of herbivory. Furthermore, mortality can also occur from secondary factors such as innoculation of the tree with diseases vectored by the insect.

Insects as Mutualists with Forest Trees

In the third type of interaction, both the insect and tree derive benefit from the association. There are a number of different expressions of mutualism between forest insects and trees. The most obvious and important association involves pollination of trees by insects. In this case the tree benefits through efficient transfer of gametocytes while the insect benefits by obtaining food. Another type of mutualism involves defense of trees by herbivores. Some trees produce extrafloral nectar which results in attraction of predacious ants that serve to limit activity by other herbivores (Stephenson 1982). Production of honeydew as a result of feeding by aphids produces the same type of response from predacious hymenoptera (Gilbert 1979). In these associations the insects benefit by obtaining food, either directly from the tree or as a result of predation of other herbivores visiting the plant. The tree benefits by obtaining protection from extensive grazing by other herbivores. A further example of mutualism involves feeding by defoliating insects. In some cases grazing by defoliators can result in increased foliar output from the host and thereby increased net primary production.

These examples simply illustrate that there are a wide variety of different types of mutualism between insects and trees. The benefits accruing to the insects or trees may not be readily apparent simply by observing the interactions, as in the defoliator example above. Owen (1980) and Owen and Weigert (1976) discuss in detail the various benefits derived by plants from consumers.

RESPONSE OF FOREST TREES TO INSECTS: PLANT DEFENSE MECHANISMS

Forest trees employ a number of different natural mechanisms that serve to mollify the effects of herbivory by insects and other animals. The mechanisms can be classed as follows (Harris 1979): (1) spatial escape, (2) temporal escape, (3) biological associations, (4) accommodation, and (5) confrontation. These mechanisms benefit plants by (1) repelling insect predators or parasites, (2) allowing the plant to escape damage by insect enemies, (3) providing tolerance to feeding by insect enemies, or (4) attracting beneficial insects. The particular defense mechanism (or combination of mechanisms) used by a plant is influenced by the susceptibility of the plant to discovery by its enemies. Variables such as tree size, growth form, persistence, and abundance are involved in determining susceptibility to discovery. To denote the interaction of abundance, persistence, and other plant characteristics that influence the likelihood of discovery, Feeney (1976) described plants according to their "apparency," that is, susceptibility to discovery by enemies. Plants that are easy for herbivores to find are termed *apparent*. For example, a tree's size, longevity, and abundance may make it more or less apparent to herbivores. On the other hand, plants that are difficult for herbivores to find by their enemies are termed *unapparent*. The concept is heuristic but difficult to use because it is not known how herbivores find their host plants. Feeney (1976) nevertheless hypothesized that the types of plant defense utilized by apparent and unapparent plants are different as are the types of enemy defended against. Regardless of the particular type of mechanism employed, plant defenses theoretically operate to influence populations by affecting birth rate, death rate, immigration, or emigration. It is important to recognize that plant defense strategies are closely linked to foraging strategies of phytophagous insects. When we attempt to interpret the relative significance of a particular type of plant defense, we must also consider the type of foraging strategy used by the particular insect being defended against (Rhodes 1979). This concept is illustrated in Figure 7.6.

Spatial Escape

Spatial escape as a defense mechanism against phytophagous insects involves dispersion patterns and dispersal characteristics of host trees. Dis-

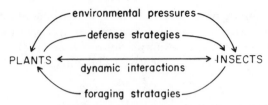

Figure 7.6 Interpretation of the dynamic interactions between populations of plants and phytophagous insects involves consideration of both the defense strategies of the plants and the foraging strategies of the insects. The intereactions are mediated by environmental pressures.

persion patterns (the distribution patterns) of host trees within a forest can influence their accessibility to phytophagous insects. Dispersion patterns can refer to plant modules on individual trees, individual trees within a population, or population of different tree species. There are a wide variety of dispersion strategies utilized by plant species to escape phytophagous insects. For example, in tropical forests, mahogany trees are distributed at a low density. Under this circumstance, damage to young trees by the mahogany shoot borer, *Hypsiphyla grandella* Zeller, is minimal. When mahogany is grown in plantations (uniform distribution and high density), however, the tree is ravaged by the shoot borer. Many of the instances of outbreak conditions of pest insects in plantation settings are attributable, in part, to disruption of the spatial escape defense mechanism of the host tree. In effect, a large food resource is conveniently provided to the insect pest, which is one of the negative consequences of attempting to maximize growth, yield, and density of our commercially valuable tree species.

Temporal Escape

Temporal escape as a defense mechanism against phytophagous insects generally involves variations in phenology of trees or modules (i.e., the timing of plant development) relative to development of phytophagous insects. There are several different strategies possible: early phenology, late phenology, accelerated phenology, prolonged phenology, and irregular phenology. In each instance the strategy of the plant is to avoid synchrony of plant development with that of the injurious insect. Insect life cycles are often closely related to their host plants. For example, the *Dioryctria* coneworms develop primarily in second-year cones of various pine species, although several other alternate plant modules are utilized. Therefore, the prosperity of the coneworm populations is tied rather closely to development of second-year cones. Pines characteristically have cyclic periods of cone production, which tends to limit insect population size in forests. In seed orchards emphasis is placed on continuous cone production as well as large populations of cones. These circumstances tend to diminsh temporal escape as a mechanism of cone protection in seed orchards.

Biological Associations

There are several different types of biological association utilized in plant defense from phytophagous insects. The mutualistic associations, described above, represent examples where extrafloral nectars attract predators that protect the host plant from extensive grazing by phytophagous insects. A particular host can also benefit from the presence of companion plant species, which can serve to increase activity and numbers of beneficial insect parasites or predators and thereby reduce the effects of a pest insect. Companion plant species can also serve as alternate hosts for pest species, which can decrease the effects of the pest on the principal host.

Accommodation

Accommodation as a plant defense mechanism can operate in two ways: satiation and tolerance. In the case of satiation, the host plant produces sufficient plant modules (buds, foliage, flowers, roots, etc.) to survive parasitization or predation by phytophagous insects. In other words, the plant produces an excess of the module fed on by the insect pest. In the case of tolerance, the host withstands attack by predators and parasites, because the insects can only remove surplus modules, modules that can be replaced, or modules not needed for continued survival of the plants. Most forest trees utilize these two mechanisms extensively and are capable of satiating or tolerating considerable activity by phytophagous insects without being killed. However, since birth and rates of modules influence the growth rate of the genet, considerable growth reduction can take place as a consequence of the plant defense strategies.

Confrontation

Confrontation as a plant defense mechanism can take two forms: physical and chemical. In the case of physical defense, the plant possesses specialized structures that act to deter herbivory. Examples of specialized structures include texture and thickness of bark, foliage, or seed coats and thorns. In the case of chemical defense, there are three basic ways that plants interact with phytophagous insects: nutrient deficiency, nutrient surplus, and toxins and repellants. In the first instance (nutrient deficiency), the plant is lacking in one or more primary plant compounds (compounds essential for plant growth and development) that are needed for insect development; in other words, the concentration of the essential compound(s) is sufficient for plant growth but insufficient for insect development. In the second instance (nutrient surplus) the host has an overabundance of one or more primary plant compounds that may be harmful to the insect so that damage to the plant or module is minimized. In the third instance (toxins and repellants), the host produces secondary plant compounds (compounds not essential for plant growth and development) that adversely affect the insect.

Plant chemical defenses (toxins and repellants) against insects have been studied extensively [see Harborne (1982), Feeney (1975, 1976), Rhoades (1979), Rhoades and Cates (1976), Cates and Rhoades (1977), Cates and Alexander (1982), Dethier (1970), Gilbert (1979), Gilbert and Raven (1975), and Whittaker (1970) for a thorough review of the subject]. In general, plant chemical defenses can be classed as quantitative or qualitative according to their effect on insects. Collectively these compounds are often referred to as *allelochemicals*.

Quantitative defenses are chemicals produced by plants that act in a dosage-dependent manner; in other words, the more of the chemical compound consumed, the greater the effect on the insect. An example of a quantitative defense chemical is tannin produced in the leaves of many woody plants. Tannins normally do not kill defoliators but act to reduce the digestability of leaves, which limits consumption by insects. Forest trees (which are apparent plants) typically have quantitative defense chemicals that serve as feeding deterrents to phytophagous insects.

Qualitative defenses or toxins are chemicals produced by the plant that act in a dosage-independent manner; thus consumption of low concentrations of the chemicals is lethal to insects. Alkaloids are an example of a qualitative defense chemical. Qualitative defenses are usually associated with early successional plants (i.e., unapparent plants).

Within a particular species of tree, there is often considerable variation in the effectiveness of a chemical defense system to protect the host from phytophagous insects. It has been observed that trees under stress from various factors (e.g., root diseases, flooding, drought, defoliation) are more

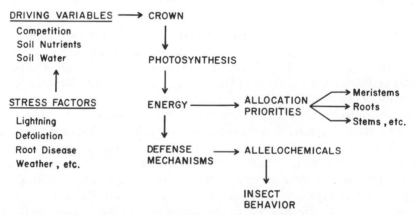

Figure 7.7 Conceptual model of the effects of stress factors on trees relative to the defense systems used for protection against insect herbivores. The diagram suggests that under stress conditions energy is preferentially allocated to basic physiological processes involved in maintaining the life of the plant at the expense of secondary plant defense systems.

vulnerable to insect attack than are healthy, vigorously growing trees. The causes for the variation in the effectiveness of the defense systems are not well understood. One explanation is that when the tree is under stress, most available energy is allocated to basic physiological processes involved in maintaining the life of the tree. Hence defense mechanisms decline in effectiveness because they are considered secondary. The general concept is illustrated in Figure 7.7.

EFFECTS OF INSECTS IN FORESTS

The consequences of phytophagous insects on populations of forest trees or plant modules, forest stands (plant communities), and forests (ecosystems) can be considered both harmful and beneficial. Forest entomologists traditionally have dealt with insect interactions on populations of trees or modules, whereas foresters have been concerned with the effects of insects on stands, and resource managers have focused on insect effects in ecosystems. It is not our intent here to attempt to catalog all the beneficial and harmful effects of insects at each of the three levels. We are, however, interested in defining some of the basic consequences of insect–tree interactions. In particular, we are concerned with the effects of insect predators and/or parasites on their host trees.

Effects of Phytophagous Insects on Trees and Modules

Phytophagous insects have a number of different direct effects on individuals within populations of forest trees and on plant modules.

1. Some feeding groups kill their hosts. As we have indicated earlier, very few forest insects directly kill their hosts. Colonization by bark beetles, severe and repeated defoliation, and girdling by reproduction weevils represent exceptions to this generalization.

2. Feeding by phytophagous insects can result in mortality to plant modules, such as cones, seeds, leaves, and branches. These types of activity alter growth rate, influence the form of the tree, and in some cases kill the tree.

3. Insects are responsible for the introduction of various plant pathogenic diseases of forest trees. Introduction can occur through direct inoculation of the tree by the insect, or the disease can be transported by the wind and enter the tree through wounds caused by insect feeding.

4. Excessive feeding by phytophagous insects can physiologically weaken the tree. Under this circumstance the tree may become susceptible to attack by other insects that would normally be defended against through one or more of the mechanisms discussed previously. Physiologically, weakened trees are also more susceptible to infection by plant pathogens.

5. Feeding by phytophagous insects can structurally weaken host trees. This effect can accentuate damage resulting from wind, snow, or ice storms.

6. Phytophagous insects play a dominant role in pollination of flowering plants.

7. Feeding and boring activities of phytophagous insects in dead or dying trees provide inoculum of wood-rotting fungi. These combined activities (boring, feeding, and inoculation) provide the initial conditions that result in subsequent decomposition of dead trees.

When the above effects of phytophagous insects are evaluated in terms of tree populations, they act by changing the distribution and abundance of forest trees or modules by altering birth rate, death rate, and dispersal, which, in turn, affect tree density, growth rate, and growth form of the trees or modules. Since the effects of insect populations on plant populations are primarily density-dependent, insect populations tend to regulate (through negative feedback) rather than modify plant populations (see Chapter 6 for the distinction between regulating vs. modifying agents). A major portion of Chapters 11–17 is devoted to detailing the various interactions that occur between forest insects and their hosts. In Chapter 9 we interpret the significance of the interactions in terms of impact on the values for which forests are managed.

Effects of Phytophagous Insects on Genets in Forest Stands

Within a stand containing mixed species of trees and other vegetation, phytophagous insects influence the pattern of differential establishment of populations of plant species and the pattern of differential growth of populations of plant species within the community. The direct effects of insects occur at the various stages in the life cycles of the resident plant species. Therefore, activities such as insect consumption, pollination, and decomposition are involved in regulating the size and composition of the seed bank, the composition and rate of recruitment from the seed bank, the rate of growth and development of trees, and reproduction and dispersal of propagules (see Figure 7.3). It is important to recognize that insects are only one component involved in plant community development. The degree to which insects are involved in regulating the pattern of establishment and growth of forest trees is poorly understood.

Effects of Phytophagous Insects in Forest Ecosystems

Phytophagous insects are involved in a number of different aspects of forest ecosystem development. We are particularly interested in their involvement in the processes of ecological succession and nutrient dynamics.

The development of forest ecosystems through space and time can be characterized by patterns of differential establishment of plant communities and patterns of differential growth of the communities. These two components are the central issues in the concept of ecological succession in forests. There is an extensive literature dealing with principles relating to succession in forests which is reviewed by West et al. (1981), McIntosh (1980), Bazzaz (1979), Bazzaz and Pickett (1980), White (1979), Horn (1981), and Drury and Nisbet (1973).

Succession can be defined as the process of ecosystem organization through which a relatively stable community ultimately develops on the newly exposed or disturbed site. In forest ecosystems this process is typically an orderly sequence of community types beginning with an annual plant community and progressing sequentially through communities dominated by perennial grasses, shrubs, and finally trees (Connel and Slayter, 1977, Bazzaz 1979, Schowalter 1981). The entire sequence of communities that replace one another in a given area is termed the *sere*. The transition communities are termed *seral stages*. The final established community is termed the *climax*.

One can further describe succession as *autogenic* or *allogenic*. These two terms are used to characterize the causes for observed patterns of succession. *Autogenic succession* refers to succession brought about as a result of activities of the organisms (plants and animals) present, i.e., biotic processes operating within an ecosystem. For example, growth of forest trees creates a number of conditions that influence community and hence ecosystem development: shading, litter accumulation, temperature dampening, increased humidity, soil nutrient depletion, and so on. These conditions create changes in the physical environment that favor growth of some plant species and deter growth of others. *Allogenic succession* refers to succession brought about by disturbance that is extrinsic or from outside of the ecosystem. Such disturbances are abiotic and can be of a long-term nature, such as a change in the geophysical nature of an ecosystem or a gradual change in the climate, or of a short-term nature, such as a forest fire.

In this section we are interested in forest succession because of the involvement of insects (and other animals) in regulating certain aspects of the process. In the context of integrated pest management, insects are important in forest succession because they can alter the patterns of establishment and/or growth of plant communities and thereby influence our planned uses of forest ecosystems. Physical disturbances are also common phenomena in forest ecosystems that modify establishment and growth of plant communities.

Within the time frame in which forest management actually operates, it is useful to consider that forest establishment and growth are influenced by a combination of autogenic and allogenic processes. In most cases forest management practices, which may include integrated pest management, are directed to the rotation time of a particular preferred species. In theory, at least, planning horizons may include several rotations.

Activities of phytophagous insects such as defoliation, phloem feeding, and wood boring are expected occurrences in forest ecosystems. In certain cases these activities have a significant influence on establishment and growth of forest trees. For example, mortality to pines resulting from bark beetle attack creates gaps in forests that are subsequently vegetated by plants adapted to the increased light made available by removal of the overstory, that is, gap-phase plant species. The effects of insects on establishment and growth of forest trees are autogenic since the insects are an integral part of the forest ecosystem. Because the effects produced by insect populations on forest trees are often density-dependent, they can serve to regulate (through negative feedback) the rate of establishment and growth of plant communities. Short-term allogenic processes that result in disturbance to a forest modify, rather than regulate, the establishment and growth of plant communities. The effects produced by allogenic processes are generally density-independent. Allogenic processes can create conditions that permit autogenic processes to operate. For example, a plant community dominated by pines can be severely damaged by an ice storm that, in turn, can increase susceptibility of the pines to attack (and subsequent mortality) by bark beetles. Likewise, autogenic processes can influence the allogenic processes. For example, infection of pines by fusiform rust disease, *Cronartium fusiforme* Hedgecock and Hunt, can structurally weaken trees, thus increasing the likelihood that stems will break during wind or ice storms.

Closely associated with succession is the process of nutrient cycling or nutrient dynamics in forest ecosystems. Insects are believed to influence nutrient dynamics in the following ways (Schowalter 1981): (1) stimulating net primary productivity and nutrient uptake by moderately grazed plants; (2) increasing translocation of nutrients from plant reserves to sites of insect grazing; (3) increasing mass and nutrient content of litterfall during the growing season; (4) increasing leaching from chewed leaves; (5) stimulating (through nutrient-rich leachate, litterfall, and insect feces) nitrification, nitrogen fixation, litter decomposition, and/or root growth rates within the litter/soil complex; and (6) altering long- and short-term nutrient cycling pathways through changes in the relative biomass of canopy and subcanopy plant species.

Although the full extent of insect involvement at the forest ecosystem level is not known, there is good evidence that insects are important in biotic regulation of ecosystem nutrient cycling. The effects of the insects are reflected, in part, in the process of ecological succession.

REFERENCES

Barbour, M. G., J. H. Burk, and W. D. Pitts. 1980. *Terrestrial Plant Ecology*. Benjamin/Commings, Menlo Park, CA.

Barrett, J. W. 1962. *Regional Silviculture of the United States*. Wiley, New York.

Bazzaz, F. A. 1979. The physiological ecology of plant succession. *Annu. Rev. Ecol. Syst.* **10**:351–371.

Bazzaz, F. A. and S. T. A. Pickett. 1980. The physiological ecology of tropical succession: a comparative rev. *Annu. Rev. Ecol. Syst.* **11**:287–310.

Bormann, F. H. and G. E. Likens. 1979. *Pattern and Process in a Forested Ecosystem.* Springer-Verlag, New York.

Burkhart, H. E., Q. V. Cad, and K. D. Ware. 1981. *A Comparison of Growth and Yield Prediction Models for Loblolly Pine.* Virginia Polytechnic Institute and State University Publication No. FWS-2-81.

Cairns, J. Jr. (Ed.). 1980. *The Recovery Process in Damaged Ecosystems.* Ann Arbor Science Publ., Inc. Ann Arbor, MI.

Cates, R. G. and D. F. Rhoades. 1977. Patterns in the production of antiherbivore chemical defenses in plant communities. *Biochem. Syst. Ecol.* **5**:185–193.

Cates, R. G. and H. Alexander 1982. Host resistance and susceptability. In Mitten, J. B. and K. B. Sturgeon (Eds.), *Bark Beetles in North American Conifers.* University of Texas Press, Austin.

Connel, J. H. and R. O. Slayter. 1977. Mechanisms of succession in natural communities and their role in community stability and organization. *Am. Nat.* **III**:1119–1144.

Coulson, R. N., D. A. Crossley, Jr., and C. S. Gist. 1971. Patterns of Coleoptera species diversity in contrasting white pine and coppice canopy communities. *Am. Midland Natr.* **86**:145–151.

Dethier, V. G. 1970. Chemical interactions between plants and insects. In Sondheimer, E. and J. B. Simeone (Eds.) *Chemical Ecology.* Academic Press, New York.

Drury, W. H. and I. C. T. Nisbet. 1973. Succession. *J. Arnold Arbor.* **54**:331–368.

Feeney, P. O. 1975. Biochemical coevolution between plants and their insect herbivores. In Gilbert, L. E. and P. R. Raven (Eds.). *Coevolution of Animals and Plants.* University of Texas Press, Austin.

Feeney, P. O. 1976. Plant apparency and chemical defense. In Wallace, J. and R. Mansell (Eds.), *Biochemical Interactions Between Plants and Insects.* (Reprinted in *Rec. Adv. Phytochem.* **10**:1–40.)

Gadgil, M. 1971. Dispersal: Population consequences and evolution. *Ecology* **52**:253–261.

Gilbert, L. E. 1979. Development of theory in the analysis of insect plant interactions. In Horn, D. J., R. D. Mitchell, and G. R. Stairs (Eds.). *Analysis of Ecological Systems.* Ohio State University Press, Columbus.

Gilbert, L. E. and P. R. Raven (Eds.). 1975. *Coevolution of Animals and Plants.* University of Texas Press, Austin.

Hallé, F., R. A. A. Oldeman, and P. B. Tomlinson. 1981. *Tropical Trees and Forests.* Springer-Verlag, New York.

Harborne, J. B. 1982. *Introduction To Ecological Biochemistry.* Academic Press, New York.

Harper, J. L. 1977. *Population of Biology of Plants.* Academic Press, New York.

Harper, J. L. 1981. The concept of population in modular organisms. In May, R. M. (Ed.), *Theoretical Ecology.* Sinauer Associates, Inc., Sunderland, MA.

Harper, J. L. and J. White. 1974. The demography of plants. *Annu. Rev. Ecol. Syst.* **5**:419–463.

Harris, M. K. 1979. Arthropod–plant interactions related to agriculture, emphasizing host plant resistance. In Harris, M. K. (Ed.), *Biology and Breeding for Resistance.* Texas Agricultural Experiment Station Miscellaneous Publication 1451.

Horn, H. S. 1981. Succession. In May, R. M. (Ed.), *Theoretical Ecology.* Sinauer Associates, Inc., Sunderland, MA.

Horn, D. J., R. D. Mitchell, and G. D. Stairs (Eds.). 1979. *Analysis of Ecological Systems*. Ohio State University Press, Columbus.

Lawton, J. H. 1983. Plant architecture and the diversity of phytophagous insects. *Annu. Rev. Entomol.* **28**:23–39.

Little, E. L. 1953. *Check-list of Native and Naturalized Trees in the United States (Including Alaska)*. U.S. Forest Service Handbook 41.

Mattson, W. J. (Ed.). 1977. *The Role of Arthropods in Forest Ecosystems*. Springer-Verlag, New York.

Mattson, W. J. and N. D. Addy 1975. Phytophagous insects as regulators of forest primary production. *Science* **190**:515–522.

McIntosh, R. P. 1980. Succession and Ecological Theory. In West, D. C., H. H. Shugart, and D. B. Botkin (Eds.) *Forest Succession*. Springer-Verlag, New York.

Miles, J. 1979. *Vegetation Dynamics*. Halsted Press, New York.

Monserud, R. A. and N. L. Crookston. 1982. *A User's Guide to Combined Stand Prognosis and Douglas-Fir Tussock Moth Outbreak Model*. USDA Forest Service General Technical Report INT-127.

Owen, D. F. 1980. How plants may benefit from the animals that eat them. *Oikos* **35**:230–235.

Owen, D. F. and R. W. Weigert. 1976. Do consumers maximize plant fitness? *Oikos* **27**:488–492.

Rhoades, D. F. 1979. Evolution of plant chemical defense against herbivores. In Rosenthal, G. A. and D. J. Janzen (Eds.), *Herbivores*. Academic Press, New York.

Rhoades, D. F. and R. G. Cates. 1976. Towards a general theory of plant antiherbivore chemistry. In Wallace, J. and R. Mansell (Eds.), *Biochemical Interactions Between Plants and Insects*. (Reprinted in *Rec. Adv. Phytochem.* **10**:168–213.)

Rosenthal, G. A. and D. H. Janzen (Eds.). 1979. *Herbivores*. Academic Press, New York.

Schowalter, T. D. 1981. Insect herbivore relationship to the state of the host plant: Biotic regulation of ecosystem nutrient cycling through ecological succession. *Oikos* **37**:126–130.

Southwood, T. R. E. 1973. The insect/plant relationship—an evolutionary perspective. In Van Emden, H. F. (Ed.), *Insect/Plant Relationships*. Wiley, New York.

Spurr, S. H. and B. V. Barnes. 1980. *Forest Ecology*. Wiley, New York.

Stage, A. R. 1978. The stand prognosis model. In Brookes, M. H., R. W. Stark, and R. W. Campbell (Eds.), *The Douglas-Fir Tussock Moth: A Synthesis*. USDA Forest Service Technical Bulletin 1585.

Stephenson, A. G. 1982. The role of extrafloral nectaries of *Caltalpa speciosa* in limiting herbivory and increasing fruit production. *Ecology* **63**:663–669.

Van Emden, H. F. and M. J. Way. 1973. Host plants in the population dynamics of insects. In Van Emden, H. F. (Ed.), *Insect/Plant Relationships*. Wiley, New York.

West, D. C., H. H. Shugart, and D. B. Botkin, (Eds.). 1981. *Forest Succession*. Springer-Verlag, New York.

White, P. S. 1979. Pattern, process, and natural disturbance in vegetation. *Bot. Rev.* **45**:229–299.

Whittaker, R. H. 1970. The biochemical ecology of higher plants. In Sondheimer, E. and J. B. Simeone (Eds.), *Chemical Ecology*. Academic Press, New York.

Wykoff, W. R., N. L. Crookston, and A. R. Stage. 1982. *User's Guide to the Stand Prognosis Model*. USDA Forest Service INT-133.

Zlotin, R. I. and K. S. Khodashova. 1980. *The Role of Animals in Biological Cycling of Forest-Steppe Ecosystems*. Dowden, Hutchinson, and Ross, Inc. Stroudsburg, PA.

8 | PRINCIPLES OF POPULATION MODIFICATION AND REGULATION USING ARTIFICIAL AND NATURAL AGENTS

INTRODUCTION

The various procedures used to modify or regulate populations of forest insects are a key element of integrated pest management (IPM). In Figure 5.8 the compartment labeled "treatment tactics" refers to the component of IPM that deals with pest population modification and regulation. In the literature the various tactics are often referred to as "control tactics" or "control procedures" and the subject is designated "pest control."

Reference to Figure 5.8 indicates that there are three major outputs from the treatment compartment: (1) to pest population dynamics, (2) to stand dynamics, and (3) to benefit–cost integration. In Chapter 6 we discussed basic principles of insect population modification and regulation. The interaction of insect populations with trees (and modules), stands, and forests was discussed in Chapter 7. Benefit–cost integration is treated in the next chapter, which deals with impact assessment. The primary inputs to the treatment compartment are from pest population dynamics and stand dynamics.

Our objectives in this chapter are to investigate three aspects of forest pest population modification and regulation. First we consider basic principles involved in population modification and regulation using artificial and natural agents. Then we describe the various procedures (tactics) used to modify or regulate population size, and finally we illustrate how various tactics are combined into a strategy for managing pest populations.

There is a vast literature dealing with many aspects of insect population modification and regulation. Since insects are the largest group of consumers in the animal kingdom, they are our primary competitors for food and fiber. It is not surprising to find that considerable research effort in forestry and agriculture has been devoted to developing ways and means for managing populations of pest species. Following are a number of references that elaborate the subjects discussed in this chapter. Major texts include National Academy of Sciences (1969, 1972, 1975, 1980), Smith (1962), Rabb and Guthrie (1970), Ware (1983), Anderson and Kaya (1976), Apple and Smith (1976), Coppel and Mertins (1977), Frankie and Koehler (1978), Knipling (1979), Dickson et al. (1979), Mitchell (1981), Hamel (1981), Flint and van den Bosch (1981), and Perkins (1982). Recent *Annual Review of Entomology* articles include Stairs (1972), Poinar (1972), Pal and LaChance (1974), Whitten and Foster (1975), David (1975), Croft and Brown (1975), Deck (1975), Falcon (1976), Pschorn-Walcher (1977), Ferron (1978), Tinsley (1979), and Metcalf (1980). Detailed examination of methods and procedures of population suppression of the Douglas-fir tussock moth, *Orgyia pseudotsugata* (McDunnough); southern pine beetle, *Dendroctonus frontalis* Zimmermann; mountain pine beetle, *D. ponderosae* Hopkins; and gypsy moth, *Lymantria dispar* (Linnaeus), are reviewed in Brookes et al. (1978), Thatcher et al. (1980), Berryman et al. (1978), and Doane and McManus (1981).

PRINCIPLES AND DEFINITIONS

There is a unique nomenclature associated with insect pest management. The terms are not new, but they have specific connotations when used in the context of forest protection. The terms described in the following paragraphs are of particular importance.

Nomenclature of Pest Management

Injury and Damage

Traditionally the terms "injury" and "damage" have been used interchangeably. "Injury" is used here to describe an abnormal physical or physiological condition on a host plant resulting from the activity of a phytophagous insect species. For example, feeding by tip moths, *Rhyacionia* spp., results in injury to meristems. The term "damage" is used to interpret the significance of injury through a value system. In Chapter 9 we define impact in terms of ecological, social, and economic values. Therefore, damage occurs when injury to a host affects one or more of these values in a negative manner. In the example above, tip moth injury could result in economic damage if tree growth were retarded.

Pest

In Chapter 5 we define the term "pest" as an anthropocentric designation given to certain forest insects (and other organisms) when they adversely affect ecological, social, or economic values that we associate with forest and shade trees. We can expand this definition by adding that phytophagous insects become pests when they occur in sufficient numbers to cause damage to host trees in specialized forestry settings, forest ecosystems, or urban forests.

Pest Control, Pest Management, and Integrated Pest Management

Much of the literature dealing with the subjects treated in this chapter historically was catalogued under the heading of "pest control." This term implies a degree of domination by humans over insect pests, which we have come to realize is unjustified. The attitude developed as a result of the availability of pesticides following World War II. The term "pest management" is more commonly used today. This term suggests that pest species and their damage can be regulated or modified within tolerable limits. "Integrated pest management" is a philosophy and methodology for achieving pest population modification or regulation by using a variety of procedures. The goal of IPM is to reduce damage caused by pest species to tolerable levels.

Suppression and Prevention

The term "suppression" is used to describe a condition where we wish to regulate or modify populations of an insect species that is currently causing intolerable levels of damage. The time frame for suppression activities is generally short—several weeks to months—and the space framework is usually small—the stand level in a forest (see Chapter 5). However, more than one stand within a forest ecosystem can be affected. Suppression activities are often undertaken in response to a crisis that developed as a result of an insect outbreak.

The term "prevention" is used to describe a condition where we wish to avoid potential damage by pest species through application of management procedures designed to maintain pest populations below levels where significant damage occurs. The time frame for prevention management is usually the rotation period for a particular tree species, and the space framework includes stands within forest ecosystems.

Treatment Tactics and Treatment Strategies
In Chapter 6 we indicated that insect population size was a function of natality minus mortality plus immigration minus emigration. A *treatment tactic* is a planned procedure designed to reduce pest population size. The goal of application of a treatment is to reduce damage caused by a pest species to a tolerable level. A treatment tactic can be directed to one or more of the determinants of population size, specifically, natality, mortality, immigration, and emigration. A treatment tactic can be viewed simply as a mortality agent acting on a population. As such, a treatment tactic can act as a density-independent mortality agent and thereby modify population size or a density-dependent mortality agent and thereby regulate population size (see Chapter 6). Application of an insecticide is an example of a treatment tactic that operates as a density-independent mortality agent. Application of a biocontrol agent such as an insect predator or parasite is an example of a treatment tactic that can operate in a density-dependent manner.

In the literature, treatment tactics are also referred to as *control procedures, control tactics,* and *suppression tactics.* There are many different tactics used to modify or regulate insect population size. The various types of treatment tactics can be classed in several ways. The references in the introduction to this chapter serve as a guide to literature on the various practices and procedures. National Academy of Sciences (1969) and Knipling (1979) provide comprehensive examinations of the various classes of treatment tactics. For our purposes the tactics used in suppression of populations are (1) chemicals, including insecticides, behavioral chemicals, and hormones; (2) biological control; and (3) mechanical control. Treatment tactics used for prevention of insect outbreaks include primarily (1) silvicultural control and (2) regulatory control. In the following sections we consider each of these classes of treatment tactics. Because of the occurrence of pests in forest ecosystems, specialized forestry settings, urban forests, and manufactured wood products, virtually all techniques are potentially useful. However, the cost of application, particularly in forest ecosystems, is a major consideration when evaluating a particular approach. We emphasize that treatment tactics represent a basic element in pest management.

A *treatment strategy* is a combination of treatment tactics applied to regulate or modify populations of a pest species. Treatment strategies can be directed to suppression of outbreak populations or to prevention of potential outbreaks. Treatment strategies are also an important aspect of IPM. It is generally acknowledged that management of insect pests requires a variety of treatment tactics, that is, a treatment strategy. The combination of several tactics into a treatment strategy provides an approach to population modification or regulation that takes into consideration the remarkable adaptability of insects to mortality agents. Table 8.1 illustrates

Table 8.1   Practiced or Potentially Feasible Strategies and Tactics for Ambrosia Beetle Management

Strategy	Tactic
Habitat management	Eliminate potential or occupied habitat by
	Removing vulnerable logs from the forest before they are attacked during the beetle flight season, that is, "hot logging"
	Minimizing storage time in dryland sorts and sawmill yards
	Disposal or burning of logging slash
Protection of product	Deter ambrosia beetle attack by use of
	Insecticides
	Water misting
	Repellents
Suppression of beetle populations	Intercept and kill host seeking beetles by use of
	Unbaited trap logs or lumber piles
	Pheromone-baited trap logs or piles
	Pheromone-baited, insecticide-treated traps, logs, or piles
	Pheromone-baited traps

Source: Borden and McLean (1981).

how specific treatment tactics can be combined to form a strategy for managing ambrosia beetle damage. In this case the strategies include habitat management, protection of the product, and suppression of beetle populations (Borden and McLean 1981). The natural history of ambrosia beetles is examined in Chapter 16.

TACTICS USED TO MODIFY OR REGULATE POPULATION SIZE: CHEMICALS

There are more than 1000 chemical compounds used in various phases of IPM. These compounds are used in insect, disease, vegetation, and animal (vertebrate) damage management. The compounds are known collectively as pesticides, which are (1) any substance or mixture of substances intended to prevent, destroy, repel, or mitigate any pest; (2) any substance or mixture of substances intended for use as a plant regulator, defoliant, or desiccant; or (3) literally, killers of pests. We are interested in a particular category of pesticides, insecticides, which are (1) any substance or mixture of substances intended to prevent, destroy, repel, or mitigate insect pests or (2) literally killers of insects. About 35% of pesticides are insecticides. Insect hormones (growth regulators) and behavioral chemicals can be classed as insecticides, using the first definition presented above. We discuss behavioral chemicals (semiochemicals) and hormones separately from insecticides.

Chemical Insecticides

Insecticides represent a class of treatment tactics that is very important in forest management. Ware (1983) provides a general overview of the subject of pesticides. The *Pesticide Handbook—Entoma,* published by the Entomological Society of America (ESA 1974), is a valuable reference for the use of insecticides. Hamel (1981) has compiled an anthology of insecticides and their use against forest insect pests.

   Although various types of insecticides, principally inorganic compounds and compounds extracted from plants, have been used for several thousands of years, widespread application in both agriculture and forestry can be traced to the years following World War II. Dichlorodiphenyltrichloroethane (DDT) was the first widely used synthetic insecticide commercially available. A large variety of different types of insecticides soon were developed. Increased dependence on insecticides and attendant problems associated with misuse, overuse, unnecessary use, and unsuccessful use created the conditions that fostered development of the concept of integrated pest management during the 1960s and 1970s. Although insecticides have been used in the past and are used presently against forest insects pests, the amount of use in forests (i.e., quantity of insecticides) has never and does not today remotely approach the degree of use found in agriculture.

In this section we consider the following subjects: (1) types of insecticides, (2) formulations of insecticides, (3) delivery systems for insecticides, (4) advantages and disadvantages in using insecticides, and (5) registration and labeling of insecticides.

Types of Insecticides.

Although there are several thousand different insecticides, for discussion purposes they can be categorized into two major groups: organic compounds, namely, insecticides containing carbon; and inorganic compounds, insecticides that do not contain carbon. The organic insecticides can further be distinguished as synthetic organic compounds, which are insecticides that are manufactured commercially; and botanicals, which are compounds made by plants that have insecticidal properties. Of the more than 105 elements, only 21 are used in the construction of insecticides. The most common constituents of insecticides include carbon, hydrogen, oxygen, nitrogen, phosphorus, chlorine, and sulfur. Some may include the metallic and semimetallic elements, iron, copper, mercury, zinc, and arsenic (Ware 1983).

The nomenclature used to describe insecticides is rather complex. For our purposes we will use generic names to describe the general type of insecticide; common names, which are approved by the Entomological Society of America; and trade names, which are assigned by manufacturers. Insecticides are also described by a structural formula, which is a picture of the insecticide molecule; a chemical name; and an empirical or molecular formula, which indicates the various numbers of atoms present in the molecule. We do not use the latter three names in this discussion.

Organic Insecticides

As the name implies, these insecticides contain the element carbon. There are several classes of organic insecticides.

1. Organochlorines.   As the name implies, the molecules of these compounds contain carbon (organo), chlorine, and hydrogen. There are four different categories of organochlorines, and they contain many of the common insecticides used in forests in the past and some presently. These categories include (a) chlorinated hydrocarbons (DDT and related compounds), (b) cyclohexane derivatives (lindane and BHC), (c) cyclodienes (chlordane, aldrin, dieldrin, heptachlor, endrin, mirex), (d) and polychloroterpenes (toxaphene and strobane). Although the mode of action of the organochlorines is not completely understood, it is known that they affect nerve impulse transmission. The chlorinated hydrocarbon insecticides alter the balance between sodium and potassium ions within the neuron, thereby preventing normal transmission of nerve impulses. The others probably act by causing the release of acetylcholine, the major neurotransmitter from presynaptic vesicles. Many of the organochlorines, although effective insecticides, have restricted uses because of their chronic toxicity to other animals including humans (a toxicity expressed mainly through interference with reproduction), persistence in the environment, and accumulation in food chains. Furthermore, many of the target pest insects have developed resistance to various organochlorines.

The compound DDT is of particular importance because it initiated the era of synthetic insecticide use. It was the most commonly used insecticide in the United States between 1945 and 1965. More than four billion pounds of DDT have been used throughout the world since the 1940s. The DDT compound was used against many different types of insects such as flies, mosquitoes, and lepidopterous defoliators. It was often used in forest situations because of its effectiveness and low cost. The use of DDT was banned in the United States by the Environmental Protection Agency (EPA) on January 1, 1973. There was a "special use" permit allowed so that DDT could be used against the Douglas-fir tussock moth, *Orgyia pseudotsugata* (McDunnough), during the summer of 1974 when 160,000 hectares of Douglas-fir forest in Oregon, Washington, and Idaho were treated with DDT.

2. Organophosphates.   Insecticides in this group are also known as organic phosphates, phosphorous insecticides, nerve gas relatives, and so on. All are derived from phosphoric acid. The organophosphates have two distinctive features: many are much more toxic to vertebrates than the organochlorines, and they are environmentally nonpersistent (Ware 1983). The organophosphates are a large class of insecticides. There are three general groups: (a) aliphatic derivatives (TEPP, MALATHION, MONO-CROTOPHOS-Azodrin®, DICHLORVOS-Vapona®), (b) phenyl derivatives (ETHYL PARATHION and METHYL PARATHION), and (c) heterocyclic derivatives (DIAZINON, AZINPHOSMETHYL-Guthion®, CHLORPYRIFOS-Dursban®). The aliphatic derivatives contain some insecticides that are termed plant *systemics*. These insecticides are taken into the roots and translocated to plant modules where they are toxic to grazing phytophagous insects and sapsucking insects. The mode of action of organophosphate insecticides involves inhibition of acetylcholinesterase, the enzyme associated with ending transmission of nerve signals between nerves and from nerves to muscles. This inhibition results in rapid twitching of voluntary muscles and finally in paralysis. This condition is particularly important in the proper functioning of the respiratory system (Ware 1983). The organophosphate insecticides have a wide variety of uses in agriculture and forestry; however, their application has been somewhat restricted because of high toxicity to vertebrates.

3. Organosulfurs.   The organosulfurs are constructed around sulfur. Although not highly toxic to insects, the organosulfurs are effective against mites; that is, they are acaricides (kill mites). Sulfur alone is often used by foresters and field biologists as a means of protection against chiggers and ticks. The organosulfurs are much more toxic than sulfur alone.

4. Carbamates. The carbamate insecticides are derived from carbamic acid. The mode of action of carbamates is similar to the organophosphates in that they inhibit acetylcholinesterase. There are a number of commonly used carbamate insecticides: CARBARYL-Sevin®, METHOMYL-Lannate®, ALDICARB-Timik®, CARBOFURAN-Furadan®, PROPOXUR-Baygon®, and MEXACARBATE-Zectran®. Some of the carbamates serve as plant systemics, for example, METHOMYL, ALDICARB, and CARBOFURAN. In general, the carbamates are narrow-spectrum insecticides; that is, they are effective against a specific range of pests.

5. Thiocyanates. The thiocyanate insecticides have molecular structures containing —SCN, or thiocyanate endings. Their mode of action is complex and involves interference with cellular respiration and metabolism. Insecticides in this group are effective against certain flying insects.

6. Other Groups of Synthetic Organic Insecticides. There are three additional groups of synthetic organic compounds that have a variety of uses as insecticides, herbicides, fungicides, and acaricides. These groups include compounds known as formamidines, dinitrophenols, and organotins.

7. Botanicals. Botanical insecticides are toxicants derived from plants. Nicotine, pyrethrum, and rotenone are examples of botanical insecticides. *Nicotine* is an alkaloid that occurs in tobacco. Nicotine acts on the ganglia of the central nervous system of insects which results in twitching, convulsions, and death. *Pyrethrins* are toxicants extracted from the flower heads of chrysanthemum plants. *Pyrethrums,* which are insecticides made from pyrethrin, are among the safest insecticides and are common ingredients in household sprays. The mode of action is probably identical to that of DDT. These insecticides are characterized by having an extremely rapid knockdown. However, the insects can recover; therefore, compounds that enhance the activity of insecticides, termed *synergists,* are used with pyrethrins to increase their effectiveness. Pyrethrums have a low degree of toxicity to mammals and break down rapidly, but they are expensive. *Rotenone* or the rotenoids represent one of the oldest known insecticides. Rotenone is prepared from the roots of tropical plants in the legume (bean) family belonging to the genera *Derris* and *Lonchocarpus.* It is highly toxic to insects and fish but has a low degree of toxicity to mammals. The mode of action is through interference with energy production; that is, it blocks oxidative phosphoralation. Rotenone is also very useful for reclaiming lakes for game fishing because it degrades rapidly and is toxic to fish and relatively nontoxic to fish food organisms. After treatment the lake can be restocked with desired species.

8. Synthetic Pyrethroids. These compounds are related to the natural pyrethrins but are synthesized from petroleum-based chemicals. They are slightly toxic to mammals and highly toxic to insects and often have a quick knockdown. Some of the pyrethroid insecticides, such as RESMETHRIN, appear to have some advantages over botanical insecticides such as the pyrethrins. For instance, the synthetic pyrethroids may be less toxic to mammals and more toxic to insects, have a greater residual activity, are lower priced, and do not require the addition of synergists.

9. Fumigants. The term "fumigant" describes both a type of delivery system and a group of insecticides. Fumigants are insecticides that are gases at temperatures above 5°C. These insecticides are usually small, volatile, organic molecules containing one or more of the halogens (chlorine, fluorine, or bromine). In general, fumigants act as narcotics, with a mode of action that is more physical than chemical. However, the mode of action of some fumigants is unknown but more involved than narcotic. Examples of fumigants include methyl bromide [sometimes used to destroy town ant, *Atta texana* (Buckley), nests], hydrogen cyanide (used in insect "collecting bottles"), and naphthalene (often used to protect insect collections and prevent moth damage to clothing). Fumigants are particularly well suited for use in enclosures such as warehouses, greenhouses, and grain elevators.

10. Oils. Oils have been used to protect fruit and shade trees from insect damage for many years. One problem in using oils is that some are highly phytotoxic. There are two types of oil commonly used: (1) "summer oils," consisting of highly refined mixtures of hydrocarbons, which can be applied to trees with foliage present; and (2) "dormant" or "winter" oils, consisting of less highly refined mixtures of hydrocarbons. Dormant oils are phytotoxic and cannot be applied to trees with foliage present. The mode of action of oils is interference with gaseous exchange of organisms during respiration. There are two advantages of oils relative to other insecticides: (1) oils are very low in mammalian toxicity, and (2) pests apparently are not able to develop resistance to oils.

Inorganic Insecticides

Inorganic insecticides, which are distinguishable from organic insecticides by the absence of carbon in their molecules, are seldom frequently used today. A number of different materials have been used as inorganic insecticides, including compounds containing mercury, boron, thallium, arsenic, antimony, selenium, and fluoride. Arsenic is the only material used commonly today. There are two principal forms: arsenites, salts of arsenious acid, and arsenates, salts of arsenic acid. "Paris green" is an arsenite that was one of the first insecticides used extensively on vegetables. The arsenical insecticides must be ingested and are thus termed "stomach poisons." These compounds have multiple modes of action: (1) interference with energy production in cells, (2) inhibition of enzymes that contain sulfhydryl (—SH) groups, and (3) coagulation of protein.

Silicates, formulated as gels or aerogels, are a type of inorganic insecticide often used against household pests. These insecticides kill insects by absorbing waxes from the insect cuticle. This action results in desiccation and death from dehydration.

Formulation of Insecticides

Once an insecticide has been synthesized it must be provided in a form that can be used by an applicator. *Formulation* is the task of processing an insecticide by any method that will improve its properties of storage, handling, application, effectiveness, or safety (Ware 1983). Furthermore, the method of formulation also influences the cost of using insecticides. The formulation step is necessary because the product provided by the manufacturer, termed *technical-grade* or raw insecticide, may not be suitable for use by applicators, because of a number of factors such as lack of stability in sunlight, volatilization characteristics, and solubility in oil or water. The final formulated product must satisfy federal and state regulations and still meet the needs of the user.

There are a number of common insecticide formulations in use in forest ecosystems, the specialized forestry settings, and urban forests. The most common formulations are (1) sprays, (2) dusts, (3) granulars, (4) impregnating materials, (5) baits, (6) fumigants, (7) aerosols, and (8) encapsulation. The specific application (i.e., forest ecosystem, specialized setting, or urban forest) and insect pest determine the most suitable insecticide and formulation. The process of formulation, as discussed here, does not include the final dilution procedures used in application equipment.

Methods of Delivery of Insecticides

The *delivery system*, or method of application, of an insecticide, is determined by the type of forest situation to be treated (e.g., forest ecosystem, specialized forestry setting, or urban forest), the natural history of the specific target insect, and the formulation requirements for the approved insecticide. The goal of using an insecticide is to modify population size to a desired level using the least amount of chemical necessary. Achievement of this goal requires efficient application procedures. Efficiency involves cost of application, accuracy in delivering the insecticide to the desired target, and safety.

There are many different types of delivery systems for insecticides. Most of the technology centers around various types of spraying equipment. Much of this equipment was developed for use in agriculture and has been adapted for use in forestry. Among the common types of spraying equipment are the following (the name of the equipment is descriptive of how the device works):

1. Hydraulic sprayers. These devices utilize a liquid mixture of insecticide and usually water forced through a spraying system at a specified pressure to provide a desired rate of application. There are several categories of hydraulic sprayers: multipurpose sprayers, low-pressure–low-volume sprayers, and high-pressure–high-volume sprayers. There are a wide variety of uses for hydraulic sprayers in the specialized forestry settings and urban forests (Figure 8.1).

2. Air-blast sprayers. This type of sprayer utilizes air instead of large volumes of water to propel sprays. Air-blast sprayers are designed to inject small droplets of spray material through nozzles into an airstream produced by a powerful fan that carries the spray to the target. A "mist blower," which is used in seed orchard management, is an example of the air-blast sprayer (Figure 8.2a,b).

3. Dusters. This device is similar to the air-blast sprayer in that it utilizes air to propel the insecticide. However, the insecticide is impregnated on a suitable carrier (e.g., talc, calcite, clay, silica gel, calcium silicate or diatomaceous earth) and then introduced into the airstream.

4. Granular-insecticide applicators. This device is designated to dispense insecticides impregnated onto a carrier such as clay or vermiculite. Granular-insecticide applicators are mechanical devices consisting of a hopper (for the insecticide), an agitator at the base of the hopper, and a metering device to govern the flow of insecticide (Figure 8.3).

Figure 8.1 Application of insecticide in a pine seed orchard by use of a hydraulic sprayer. (U.S. Forest Service.)

Figure 8.2 (*a*) One type of air-blast sprayer, a "mist blower" often used in insect suppression in orchards (U.S. Forest Service); (*b*) Application of a "mist blower" in a pine seed orchard (U.S. Forest Service).

Figure 8.3 Example of a granular insecticide applicator used in protection of a young white pine seed orchard. (U.S. Forest Service.)

5. Aerosol generators. This device is also known as a "fogger." Aerosol generators dispense extremely fine particles of insecticide into the air. The particles remain airborne for a considerable period of time. Aerosol generators are commonly used in mosquito and fly control programs, and applications are generally carried out at night when air movement is minimal and air inversion conditions prevail.

6. Aircraft application. Aircraft, either fixed-wing or helicopters, are used primarily in forest ecosystems where large areas must be treated. There are a variety of specific devices used to dispense the insecticides. The efficiency of delivery of insecticides has received considerable attention, and it is possible to control spray droplet patterns by using various nozzle designs and adjustments (Figure 8.4).

7. Hand-application equipment. There are a number of different devices suitable for hand application of insecticides. These devices include aerosol bombs, compressed air sprayers, knapsack sprayers, and hose sprayers. All the hand-application equipment is designed for portability and for use over small areas and confined spaces (NAS 1969).

Advantages and Disadvantages of Using Insecticides

The use of pesticides in general, and insecticides in particular, has been a subject of considerable controversy for a number of years. Public attention

Figure 8.4 Aircraft application of insecticide to protect newly established pine plantation from tip moth damage. (U.S. Forest Service.)

to the subject was focused by the publication of *Silent Spring* by Rachael Carson in 1962. Further, less emotional, commentary was provided by Rudd (1964). Van den Bosch (1978), one of the notable early architects of the concept of IPM, added an interesting perspective on the subject in his book entitled *The Pesticide Conspiracy*. Clearly, there are various views on how insecticides can be used safely and effectively in forestry and agriculture. Some of the advantages and disadvantages to using insecticides are discussed below (Knipling 1979, Perkins 1982).

Advantages of Using Insecticides

1. Chemical insecticides provide an effective means of *modifying* population size of pest insects.

2. The effects of insecticides on insect populations are dramatic. Population size and damage can be reduced in a short period of time.

3. Certain insecticides are effective against a broad spectrum of pest insects whereas other insecticides are effective against a narrow spectrum of pests. Within limits, it is possible to select an insecticide or combination of insecticides for a specific pest insect or pest complex.

4. Because of the availability of insecticides through commercial markets, individual property owners can take unilateral action needed to protect commodities.

5. Suitable materials, formulations, and equipment are readily available through commercial markets.

6. When new pest problems develop, it is likely that an existing insecticide is available that can be used to modify population size.

Disadvantages of Using Insecticides

1. The broad-spectrum action of many insecticides creates hazards or risks of hazard to nontarget organisms in the environment. The hazards may involve immediate harm to operators who must handle or apply the insecticides or may involve immediate or long-range hazards to various nontarget organisms in the treated environment. The fate of insecticides in the environment is an issue of considerable importances. For example, it is known that certain insecticides persist in the environment for considerable periods of time and are concentrated in food chains (Table 8.2). The long-range effects of insecticides on public health and nontarget organisms are not well understood.

2. Insecticides *modify* populations of natural control agents as well as the pest species. This nonselective action largely nullifies the action of natural agents in *regulating* pest population size. The broad-spectrum action of many insecticides can cause an upsurge of certain pests when treatments are discontinued or elevate minor or secondary pests to major pest status.

3. Insecticides provide only a temporary solution to a pest problem.

4. Dependence on chemical insecticides is costly on a long-term basis.

5. Insects can develop resistance to insecticides (Georghiou 1972, Plapp 1976). When resistance does develop, populations of natural control agents often have been reduced to levels where pest outbreaks can occur.

Registration of Insecticides

Registration is the process of certifying that an insecticide is effective for the purpose intended and that the proposed handling and use of the chemical do not present intolerable hazards to humans or the environment. Only a small number of insecticides are registered for use in forests. The Federal Insecticide, Fungicide, and Rodenticide Act of 1947 as amended (FIFRA) is the main statute that deals with pesticide regulatory programs in the United States. There are a number of significant aspects to FIFRA, but perhaps the most important is that it places the burden of proof of acceptability of a product on the manufacturer prior to its being marketed.

Table 8.2   Concentration of DDT in a Lake Michigan Food Chain

	DDT in ppm	Biomagnification
Water	0.000002	1
Bottom mud	0.014	7000
Fairy shrimp	0.410	205,000
Coho salmon, lake trout	3–6	$1.5–2.0 \times 10^6$
Herring gull	99	5×10^7

Source: Modified from Harrison et al. (1970).

The manufacturer (or registrant) is required to submit scientific proof of the efficacy (i.e., effectiveness) and safety of the chemical relative to specific intended uses. The U.S. Environmental Protection Agency (EPA), created in 1970, is charged with the responsibility for enforcement of FIFRA. However, monitoring the use of pesticides involves several additional agencies (e.g., Food and Drug Administration, Department of Agriculture, Federal Aviation Administration) as well as cooperation with State agencies (Deck 1975).

Semiochemicals (Behavioral Chemicals)

The term "semiochemicals" is used to describe all chemicals that act as messengers between organisms (Law and Regnier 1971). Insects use semiochemicals to communicate a variety of different types of messages or information. In the context of insect treatment tactics and strategies, we are particularly interested in two categories of semiochemicals: pheromones and kairomones. A *pheromone* is a chemical emitted by an organism that induces a behavioral or physiological response in another organism of the same species. Examples of behavioral responses to pheromones include searching for mates (e.g., sex attractants or sex pheromones), aggregation at specific host plants (e.g., aggregation pheromones), and dispersal from specific sites (antiaggregation pheromones). A *kairomone* is a chemical emitted by an organism that induces in an organism of another species a behavioral or physiological response of adaptive benefit to the perceiver but not the emitter (Borden 1977), for instance, a natural enemy perceiving and responding to a chemical signal produced by its host. It is possible for a chemical to act as both a pheromone and a kairomone. For example, an insect species might produce an aggregation pheromone that is perceived by individuals of that species as well as a predator or parasite. This circumstance occurs with the southern pine beetle and a clerid predator, *Thanasimus dubius* (Fabricius).

There is a vast literature on the subject of semiochemicals and their use in population management and monitoring: Birch (1974), Beroza (1970, 1976), Nordlund et al. (1976), Mitchell (1981), and Wood (1982). Many different semiochemicals have been identified from insects, and some have been synthesized. Ultimately we would like to use semiochemicals to manipulate populations of pest species in ways beneficial to humans. The use of semiochemicals in treatment tactics and strategies is contingent on (1) knowledge of the function of the chemical, (2) availability of sufficient quantities of the chemical for deployment, and (3) availability of suitable deployment devices. Semiochemicals offer a particularly useful approach to population management because they have been demonstrated to have pronounced influences on insect behavior (mating, oviposition, host finding, feeding, etc). Insects respond to minute quantities of the chemicals, and the chemicals differ in their mode of action from organic and inorganic insecticides.

There are several different ways that semiochemicals can be used in insect management. We discuss three of the common approaches: (1) bio-monitoring, (2) mass trapping, and (3) mating disruption. Because semi-ochemicals are being used in insect management, that is, deployed in the environment, they are subject to governmental regulation, and this topic is also discussed. We emphasize that, although there is a great deal known about semiochemicals of some forest insects, there are few operational insect management programs using these chemicals.

Biomonitoring

Biomonitoring refers to the use of pheromones for the purpose of survey and detection of pest species. In this type of application pheromones are used to attract target insects to some type of trap. Biomonitoring was one of the first applications of pheromones in pest management. It can be used to detect the presence of pest species, monitor the distribution and relative abundance of a pest, and monitor seasonal activity of a pest. Traps, baited with synthetic pheromones, have been used to monitor population levels and distribution of gypsy moth (Elkington and Carde 1981) and spruce budworm (Sanders 1981) for a number of years (Figure 8.5).

Figure 8.5 Trap baited with pheromones. Pheromone-baited traps are particularly useful for monitoring activities of forest insects and can be used to detect the presence and relative abundance of pest insects. These types of traps can provide information useful in timing insecticide applications for pests such as tip moths or certain seed and cone insects (Texas Forest Service).

Mass Trapping

Mass trapping involves use of synthetic pheromones in combination with some type of trap to capture a significant portion of individuals from a population. This approach has received a great deal of attention in forest pest management, with programs designed to evaluate the procedure for bark beetles: Bedard and Wood (1981)—western pine beetle, *Dendroctonus brevicomis* LeConte; Lanier (1981) and Peacock et al. (1981)—smaller European elm bark beetle, *Scolytus multistriatus* (Marsham); Lie and Bakke (1981) and Bakke et al. (1983)—*Ips typographus* (Linnaeus); and Borden and McLean (1981)—ambrosia beetles. The first operational use of the mass trapping technique in forest pest management was for ambrosia beetles infesting hosts in log sorting areas and at sawmills (Borden and McLean 1981).

Mating Disruption

The objective of *mating disruption* is to use pheromones for interfering with sexual communication between males and females of a pest species. The most obvious application of this technique is through inundation of an area where the pest occurs with synthetic attractant, thereby confusing the mate responding to the attractant; that is, the mates cannot find each other. Another approach, potentially useful for bark beetles, is the use of inhibitor or antiaggregation pheromones that disrupt the colonization process that occurs prior to mating (Payne 1981). Sower et al. (1981) discuss the use of the technique for several lepidopterous insects of western forests: Douglas-fir tussock moth; western spruce budworm, *Choristoneura occidentalis* Freeman; and western pine shoot borer, *Eucosma sonomana* Kearfott (Figure 8.6 a,b).

Registration of Semiochemicals

As with the organic and inorganic insecticides, in the United States the EPA is responsible for registration of semiochemicals used in pest management. A new classification of compounds termed "biorational pesticides" was established because it was recognized that certain naturally occurring biochemicals differ in their mode of action from most inorganic and organic insecticides. *Biorational pesticides* include compounds such as microbial pesticides, synthetically produced biochemicals that occur naturally, and analogs of such biochemicals. Clearly, many of the semiochemicals come under this classification. Basic policy of EPA toward registration of biorational pesticides was formulated in 1979, and there are several semiochemicals registered for use in pest management (Plimmer 1981, Dover 1981).

Insect Hormones

In Chapter 2 we discussed the roles of hormones in regulating insect development, reproduction, and diapause. Three types of hormones were

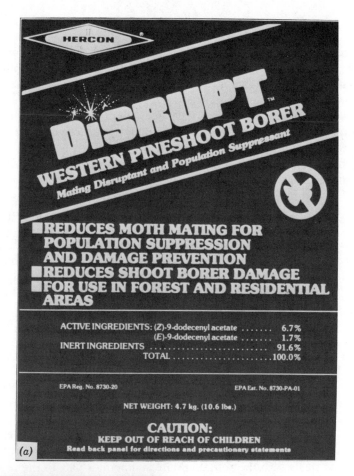

Figure 8.6 (*a*) Registration label for Hercon® (Health Chemicals Corp.) controlled-release formulation for the western pine shoot borer, *Eucosma sonomana*, pheromone used in mating disruption (U.S. Forest Service photograph); (*b*) Hercon® "flake" lodged in crown of young pine. The pheromone for the western pine shoot borer, *Eucosma sonomana*, is contained in the flake and is emitted slowly over a period of time (U.S. Forest Service photograph).

discussed: the brain hormones, the molting hormones (ecdysones), and juvenile hormones. Of these three types of hormones, the molting hormones and juvenile hormones offer potentially useful means of insect suppression. The chemical structures for these types of hormones, and chemicals with similar structures, have been identified. The brain hormone is a complex protein molecule and thus much less practical for use in insect suppression.

The basic rationale for using insect hormones in insect suppression is to administer the chemicals in excessive quantities, relative to their normal quantity in the insect pest, or at an inappropriate time in insect development. Under these circumstances normal development is disrupted and death or sterility of the pest occurs.

The use of insect hormones in insect suppression potentially offers some advantages over traditional insecticides in that (1) hormones have been demonstrated to be effective in small quantities, (2) some are highly specific, and (3) they have low vertebrate toxicity. Registration of insect hormones is being dealt with in a manner similar to the semiochemicals.

TACTICS USED TO MODIFY OR REGULATE POPULATION SIZE: BIOLOGICAL CONTROL—NATURAL ENEMIES

The term "biological control" was coined by Smith (1919) and refers to the use of natural enemies, either native or exotic, to regulate insect pest populations. Natural enemies include all predators, parasites, and pathogens of insects. Wilson and Huffaker (1976) defined biological control as "the science that deals with the role that natural enemies play in the regulation of the numbers of their host." Using this definition biological control covers two major areas: (1) natural biological control, which is the work of the natural enemies without human involvement; and (2) applied biological control, which is the manipulation of natural enemies by humans for pest suppression.

However, some entomologists prefer a broader definition of biological control that includes "any method of pest control that utilizes living organisms or their natural (nontoxic) products" (Price 1975). Coppel and Mertins (1977) used a very similar definition but chose the term "biological insect pest suppression" because of semantic problems with the term "control." The broader definition used by Price, Coppel, Mertins, and others includes the following areas under biological control: natural enemies, pheromones, hormones, sterilization techniques, genetic manipulations, and plant resistance. We use the narrower, traditional definition of biological control.

This section, which deals with natural enemies, is divided into six parts: (1) scope of studies on natural enemies; (2) attributes of an effective natural enemy; (3) predators; (4) parasites; (5) pathogens; and (6) successes, failures, and future importance of natural enemies in integrated pest management. Additional information on natural enemies is provided by Sweetman (1958), DeBach (1964, 1974), Askew (1971), Burges and Hussey (1971), Huffaker (1971), Cantwell (1974), Huffaker and Messenger (1976), Coppel and Mertins (1977), Clausen (1978), and van den Bosch et al. (1982).

Scope of Studies on Natural Enemies

The information available on natural enemies is divided into four areas: (1) basic research, (2) importation and colonization, (3) augmentation, and (4) conservation and enhancement.

Basic Research

Basic research on natural enemies is divided into two major categories: (1) biology, ecology, taxonomy, physiology, genetics, behavior, nutrition, and rearing methods of natural enemies and (2) ecological aspects of pest management with emphasis on the relationship of natural enemies to other factors (i.e., environmental factors, management tactics) that regulate host population densities.

Many of the past failures in the importation and colonization of natural enemies were due to (1) incorrect identification of the pest and/or natural enemy, (2) no or insufficient information on the biological and ecological requirements of the natural enemy, and (3) poor collecting and rearing techniques for the natural enemy. Townes (1972) reported that at least 70% of parasitic hymenoptera were undescribed and that no biological information was available on 97% of the described species. Correct identification of the pest and natural enemy is necessary so that entomologists can consult the available literature to determine the probable origin and previous distribution of the pest and natural enemy, ecological conditions essential for survival of the pest and natural enemy, potential range of the pest and natural enemy in a new location, and management procedures applicable for each pest and natural enemy. Many basic studies have provided important information that has led to the successful use of natural enemies in pest management.

Ecological studies on the interaction of the natural enemies and the pest are necessary for deciding whether the native natural enemies can normally exert regulation over the pest, whether there are vacancies in the system that can be filled with an introduced natural enemy, and whether any important requirement of the natural enemies can be enhanced by managing for them. The importance of native predators, parasites, and pathogens in the reduction of populations of potential forest pests and the successful production of various forest crops cannot be overemphasized. Approximately 99% of the potential forest pests never cause serious economic damage and/or reach epidemic population levels (Coppel and Mertins 1977). Often endemic pest populations are kept in check primarily by natural enemies.

The extreme importance of natural enemies began to surface with the use of chemical insecticides and quantitative studies on the population dynamics of insect pests. Natural enemies were greatly reduced after spraying with chemical insecticides, and secondary insects became pests. This phenomenon was first commonly observed in cotton fields and apple orchards where numerous treatments of chemical insecticides were applied each year (Ripper 1956). In apple orchards the chemical insecticides quickly eliminated most of the general predators such as thrips, predaceous mites, ladybird beetles, syrphid flies, and lacewings. Outbreaks of formerly endemic pest insects such as the European red mite, *Panonychus ulmi* (Koch), and codling moth, *Cydia pomonella* (Linnaeus), became a problem. Excellent examples of the importance of native predators and parasites have been reported for a pine forest in a residential area of California and for fir–spruce forests in eastern Canada. Scale insect populations increased to epidemic population levels after the natural enemies of the scale insects had been inadvertently killed by chemical spraying against biting insects. Luck and Dahlsten (1975) showed that pine needle scale, *Chionaspis pinifoliae* (Fitch), populations declined following the reduction of spraying for mosquitoes as the result of an increase in the populations of the predators and parasites of this scale. Neilson et al. (1971) reported that European spruce sawfly, *Gilpinia hercyniae* (Hartig), populations reached outbreak levels after 3 consecutive years of spraying fir–spruce forests to reduce spruce budworm populations. Populations of sawfly parasites, a virus, and the sawflies were reduced to very low numbers. The sawfly population increased to high levels for one year before the parasites and virus were able to increase their populations and again become effective natural enemies.

Quantitative studies on the population dynamics of forest insects, such as Varley and Gradwell's (1968) long-term study on defoliators and natural enemies in an oak forest in England, have demonstrated the importance of natural enemies in reducing forest pest populations. Miller's (1966) study on the eastern blackheaded budworm, *Acleris variana* (Fernald) in eastern Canada and a review by Hagen et al. (1971) on the importance of natural enemies in coniferous and hardwood forests, chaparral biome, and grasslands of the western United States, contain additional information that supports the importance of natural enemies in reducing pest populations.

Importation and Colonization

The importation and colonization of natural enemies became an extremely viable method to reduce exotic pest populations in 1889 with the successful introduction of an Australian ladybird beetle, called the vedalia beetle, *Rodolia cardinalis* (Mulsant). The vedalia beetle is a predator of the cottonycushion scale, *Icerya purchasi* Maskell. This accidentally introduced scale insect was first discovered in California in 1872. By 1887 the entire citrus industry of southern California was threatened by the scale insect that sucks the sap from the twigs and leaves of citrus trees. In 1888 the USDA sent an entomologist to Australia, the original site of this pest, to collect its natural enemies. Two insect species, the vedalia beetle and a tachinid parasite, *Cryptochaetum iceryae* (Williston), were collected and imported to California in late 1888 and early 1889. The vedalia beetle virtually eliminated the scale insect from the citrus orchards in California within 1 year after its release. Both species of natural enemies became established and have kept the cottonycushion scale at endemic levels since 1889. The vedalia beetle remains the dominant natural enemy in all interior and desert citrus areas of California, whereas the tachinid fly remains the most important natural enemy of the scale insect in the coastal areas. The cost of this biological pest suppression program including salaries was less than $5000.

The Canadian government has been a strong supporter of biological control program against forest insects for many years, whereas support from the USDA has fluctuated over the years. Some of the most successful biological programs against forest and shade tree pests were: (1) introduction of an ichneumon wasp and tachinid fly from Europe to control the winter moth, *Operophtera brumata* (Linnaeus), in North America, (2) accidental introduction of the nuclear polyhedrosis virus (NPV) and planned introduction of several species of ichneumon wasps from Europe to control the European spruce sawfly in North America, (3) introduction of several species of ichneumon wasps from Europe to control the larch sawfly, *Pristiphora erichsonii* (Hartig), in North America, (4) introduction of a braconid wasp and chalcidoid wasp from Europe to control the larch casebearer, *Coleophora laricella* (Hübner), in North America (Figure 8.7), and (5) introduction of a scelionid wasp, an egg parasite of the fall cankerworm, *Alsophila pometaria* (Harris), from the United States to control a geometrid forest pest, *Osydia trychiata* (Guenée), in Columbia, South America.

In the case of importation and colonization of insects against weeds, the plant is the pest and the natural enemy is the introduced phytophagous insect. An excellent example of a natural enemy reducing weeds in range lands occurred in Australia. The prickly pear cacti, primarily *Opuntia stricta* Haworth, was introduced into Australia from the western hemisphere as an ornamental plant. By 1900 it had become a major pest in northeast Australia. Twenty-four million hectares of range land were heavily infested by 1925. The prickly pear cacti were reduced to endemic levels in 1932 following the 1925–1927 introduction of the cactus moth, *Cactoblastis cactorum* (Berg), from Argentina. The larvae of this insect feed on cacti leaves and continues to keep prickly pear cacti at endemic levels in Australia (Debach 1964). In range management in the western United States introduced natural enemies have reduced the Klamath weed (also called *St.*

Figure 8.7 A chalcidoid wasp, *Chrysocharis laricinellae,* an introduced parasite of the larch casebearer, *Coleophora laricella.* (U.S. Forest Service photograph, courtesy of R. Ryan.)

John's wort) from a major rangeland weed pest in California, Oregon, and Washington to a roadside weed. Two species of chrysomelid beetles introduced from Australia in 1945 are responsible for this success story.

Basic studies on natural enemies and the importation and colonization of natural enemies were the major areas studied until the 1960s. Coppel and Mertins (1977) present detailed coverage of the procedures involved in the importation and colonization of natural enemies.

Augmentation

Augmentation is the manipulation of the natural enemies to make them more efficient. Techniques that improve the efficiency of natural enemies may develop from basic ecological studies on a particular natural enemy. Many species of natural enemies such as ladybird beetles, green lacewings, and chalcidoid wasps may be reduced to very low numbers by extremely hot or cold temperatures. Entomologists have experimented with two approaches to solving this problem: (1) mass culture and periodic release of natural enemies and (2) development of new strains of natural enemies through breeding. There are very few good examples of these techniques in forestry today. Mass culture and periodic releases of egg parasites have been made in Germany, Poland, and Russia against the European pine shoot moth, *Rhyacionia buoliana* (Denis and Schiffermüller) and in Russia against lepidopterous and sawfly defoliators (Turnock et al. 1976). By selective breeding Wilkes (1947) was able to develop a better laboratory strain of the chalcidoid wasp, *Dahlbominus fuscipennis* (Zetterstedt), an introduced parasite of the European spruce sawfly.

Conservation and Enhancement

Conservation is the use of management techniques that reduce harmful effects on natural enemies, whereas *enhancement* refers to the use of management techniques that increase the longevity and reproduction of natural enemies or increase the attractiveness of an area for natural enemies (Stehr 1982). Most of the studies on conservation and enhancement of natural enemies have occurred since 1960. Commonly used techniques are:

1. Reducing the number of chemical insecticide treatments in a specific area.
2. Reducing the concentration of the chemical insecticide.
3. Modifying the timing of the chemical insecticide treatment to reduce its effect on natural enemies.
4. Providing nesting sites for natural enemies (i.e., nesting boxes for birds in German forests; U.S. Forest Service policy of leaving snags to insure homes for cavity nesting birds such as woodpeckers).
5. Providing certain types of food for adult parasites and predators to increase the fecundity and longevity of natural enemies. Leius (1967) found much higher parasitism of tent caterpillar eggs and pupae and of codling moth larvae in unsprayed apple orchards in Ontario that contained abundant nectar-producing flowers and lower parasitism in unsprayed orchards containing few such flowers. Adults of several species of hymenopterous parasites of the European pine shoot moth are dependent on the presence of wild carrots or other nectar producing plants for maximum effectiveness (Syme 1975). Growers in Ontario are encouraged to plant wild carrot or other nectar producing plants in their pine plantations to increase the effectiveness of natural enemies (Corbet 1974).
6. Providing maximum diversification of flora and fauna. Synchronization of life cycles of the alternative host and the natural enemy is extremely important for the success of many introduced parasites. Many of the failures in introducing natural enemies have been attributed to the lack of alternate hosts. Diversification of flora and fauna is generally much greater in forests than in agricultural systems. Mixed forest stands and stand edges around forest plantations increase the availability of alternate hosts.

Attributes of an Effective Natural Enemy

It is very difficult to predict accurately which imported natural enemies will be most effective in a new habitat. Some important characteristics of an effective natural enemy, whether native or imported, are: (1) ecological compatibility, (2) synchronization of life cycles, (3) high searching ability, (4) high dispersal ability, (5) no hyperparasites or other secondary enemies, and (6) easy culturability. No predator, parasite, or disease will meet all the criteria of an effective natural enemy. *Rodalia cardinalis,* the Australian ladybird beetle introduced against the cottonycushion scale is an example of an insect that fulfills the requirements of an effective natural enemy.

Ecological Compatability

The natural enemy must become established in all or most of the habitats utilized by the host. Ideally the two organisms will have equivalent distributions. Usually natural enemies survive better in some habitats than others.

Synchronization of Life Cycles

Synchronization of life cycles between the natural enemy and its host is often very vital for a successful importation program. Many biotic and abiotic factors affect the synchronization of life cycles. A temporal asynchrony between the emergence of the adult parasite and a suitable stage of the host may thwart the establishment of the parasite in a new area. Timing of the release of certain natural enemies is critical, especially for parasites that only oviposit in a host larva of a certain age (e.g., second instar larva).

High Searching Ability

A successful natural enemy must be able to find a host when pest populations are low. In selecting natural enemies for an importation program, many habitats in the country of origin, including areas of both endemic and epidemic host populations, must be searched for all possible natural enemies. The most easily found or most abundant natural enemy in a particular habitat may attack many different species but may not be primarily responsible for keeping a certain host at fairly stable low population levels.

High Dispersal Ability

Dispersal ability of a natural enemy should be equal to or greater than the host. A lag in the dispersal of natural enemies always occurs when pest populations disperse into new areas. Natural enemies increase in the new area after the host species becomes established and increases in population.

No Hyperparasites or Other Secondary Enemies

Introduced natural enemies are inspected and studied before releases are made in another country. Hyperparasitism and parasitism of predators or the phytophagous agent are carefully observed during introductions of natural enemies to prevent the introduction of hyperparasites and other secondary enemies. Hyperparasites and other secondary agents can reduce the effectiveness of a natural enemy. Entomologists normally release the predators and parasites in the adult stage to reduce the possibility of introducing hyperparasites and other secondary enemies into the new environment.

Culturability

In many cases only small numbers of a potential natural enemy can be collected from its native habitat because the natural enemy and host population may have stabilized at very low densities. Some natural enemies often must be reared in the laboratory or greenhouse for one generation to eliminate the hyperparasites. It is important to have a natural enemy that can be reared easily and in large numbers because of the high cost of labor.

Other Considerations

The reproductive potential of the natural enemy needs to be considered when selecting natural enemies for introduction purposes. The potential rate of increase of a natural enemy should be approximately the same as the host.

Host specificity of the natural enemy may or may not be an important attribute for a potential natural enemy. Literature shows that both monophagous and polyphagous natural enemies have been effective as introduced biotic agents. A monophagous natural enemy is more attuned to the host species and responds more quickly to changes in host density. A polyphagous natural enemy changes to another host when the population of one host is reduced to low numbers. Usually the life cycle of a polyphagous natural enemy is not as well synchronzied with one host species as a monophagous natural enemy. However, a polyphagous natural enemy may counteract the lack of synchronization with overlapping generations, more generations per year, and the use of alternative hosts.

Predators

Predators kill their host, normally consume more than one individual host to reach maturity, and are free-living organisms throughout their life cycle. Most are predaceous in both the immature and adult stages, but others such as syrphid flies and some lacewings are predaceous only as larvae. Predators of forest and shade tree insects are often divided into predatory insect arthropods, predatory noninsect arthropods, and insectivorous vertebrates.

Predatory Insect Arthropods

Predaceous insect species belong to 16 orders and over 200 families (Sweetman 1958). The most common predators in forest and urban ecosystems belong in the orders Coleoptera, Neuroptera, Hymenoptera, Hemiptera, Diptera, Orthoptera, and Odonata (see Chapter 3). A brief description of the characteristics and ecology of the common predaceous members of these seven orders is presented.

Coleoptera

For foresters and arborists, the most important predators in this order are found in three families: Coccinellidae, Carabidae, and Cleridae.

Ladybird beetles (Coccinellidae) are very common, small (usually <6 mm), oval, convex insects that are often recognized by their red, yellow, or pink bodies with black spots or their black bodies with white, red, or yellow spots. Most ladybird beetles overwinter as adults. All members of this family are predaceous except for two phytophagous species, the Mexican bean beetle, *Epilachna varivestis* Mulsant, and squash beetle, *Epilachna borealis* (Fabricius). Ladybird beetle larvae and adults usually feed on aphids, scales, small sawflies, and lepidopterous caterpillars. They also feed on mites and other small organisms. Many species consume large numbers of hosts. For example, *Hippodamia convergens* Guérin-Méneville, a common native predator in western North America, consumes 200–500 aphids during its larval stage and approximately 3000–6000 aphids during its adult life span of 1–2 months (Sweetman 1958).

Carabidae (ground beetles) is the second largest family of beetles in the United States. Most ground beetles are dark, shiny, somewhat flattened beetles that vary in size from 2 to 30 mm. Larval and adult ground beetles are commonly found under leaves, logs, stones, or running on the ground. Many species hide during the day and are active only at night. Most ground beetles are predaceous as larvae and adults; they feed on many types of arthropod and other ground-inhabiting organisms. Ground beetles in the genus *Calosoma* (Figure 8.8) are very important predators of lepidopterous larvae such as gypsy moth, elm spanworm, *Ennomos subsignarius* (Hübner), and forest tent caterpillar, *Malacosoma disstria* Hübner (Kulman 1974). Some ground beetles such as *Calosoma calidum* (*Fabricius*) climb trees as larvae and adults and feed on tree inhabiting lepidopterous larvae.

Checkered beetles (Cleridae) are elongated, pubescent beetles 7–12 mm long; most are brightly colored and predaceous both as larvae and adults. Many checkered beetles are very common predators of bark beetles and other wood boring insects.

Neuroptera

Green lacewing (Chrysopidae) adults are usually green slender bodied insects, about 12 mm in length, with long slender antennae and delicate

Figure 8.8   The ground beetle *Calosoma scrutator,* feeding on a mature elm spanworm, *Ennomos subsignarius.* (U.S. Forest Service photograph.)

multiveined membranous wings (Figure 3.15). The larvae, often called *aphidlions,* are active, voracious, elongated, and somewhat flattened insects with powerful sickle-shaped sucking mandibles. Green lacewing larvae and adults are common on grasses, weeds, and foliage of trees and shrubs. Adults are often seen in flight and are commonly collected at lights. All green lacewing larvae and adults of some species are important predators of aphids and scales. They also feed on mites, small caterpillars, and other small insects. The adult female lays eggs in groups usually on foliage; each egg is placed on the tip of a silken stalklike structure. This egg-laying habit probably evolved as a defense mechanism against the cannibalistic habit of lacewing larvae, especially when host material is scarce.

Hymenoptera

About 25% of the families in this order are strictly predaceous; most of the families with predaceous habits are social insects and live in colonies. Ants (Formicidae) are the most important predators in this order, but the predatory wasps such as vespid wasps (Vespidae) and sphecid wasps (Sphecidae) are also very common predators.

Ants are easily recognized by the narrow pedicel at the base of the abdomen, which attaches the swollen part of the abdomen to the thorax (Figure 3.22). Ants are as successful as any insect group and occur in extremely large numbers in most terrestrial habitats. Their feeding habits are extremely variable. Some are carnivores, other scavengers, or predators, whereas other species feed on nectar, sap, and honeydew. Adult ants of many species are predaceous on lepidopterous and sawfly caterpillars and bark beetle larvae and are effective predators of many ground inhabiting insects. Red wood ants, about eight species in the *Formica rufa* group, are extremely important predators in maintaining many forest insect populations (e.g., lepidoptera and sawfly larvae and pupae) at endemic levels in Germany, Italy, and Russia (Finnegan 1974). These red wood ants are quite abundant, develop many large populations (nests), forage over large areas, and can survive on honeydew from aphids when insects become scarce. Coppel and Mertins (1977) described studies in Europe where entomologists had successfully moved ants in the *F. rufa* group from one location to another in Italy and Germany to reduce outbreak populations of the pine sawfly, *Pristiphora abietina* Christ, and the pine processionary caterpillar, *Thaumetopoea pityocampa* (Denis and Schiffermüller). Ants as predators of forest insects have not been as widely studied in North America (Campbell and Torgersen 1982).

Predatory wasps (e.g., vespid wasps, sphecid wasps) provision their nests with lepidopterous and sawfly caterpillars, aphids, cicadas, beetles, other insects, and spiders. The solitary vespid wasps (e.g., potter wasps) construct small juglike nests of mud and provision them with paralyzed lepidopterous caterpillars or beetles. Eggs are then laid on the inside of the nest. Social vespid wasps (e.g., yellowjackets, hornets, and paper wasps) provision their paper nests primarily with insects and spiders that are fed to the young. Sphecid wasps (e.g., mud daubers) are primarily solitary wasps that provision their nests with various types of insects. Each group (subfamily and/or species) of sphecid wasps usually feeds a specific type of food (usually insects) to their young.

Hemiptera

Most true bugs are plant feeders, but several familes [e.g., stink bugs, Pentatomidae (Figure 3.13); assassin bugs, Reduviidae; and plant bugs, Miridae (Figure 3.13)] contain a number of species that are predaceous throughout all or part of the life cycle. These predaceous hemipterans commonly feed on lepidopterous and sawfly larvae, aphids, scales, leafhoppers, and other small insects.

Diptera

The most commonly observed predaceous insects in this order belong in the families Syrphidae (syrphid flies) and Asilidae (robber flies). The adult syrphid flies, often called flower flies, are common around flowers and feed on pollen and nectar. Many species mimic bees, wasps, or honeybees, but they do not sting. The adult flies are often brightly colored with black bodies and yellow bands. The larvae vary in habit and appearance, but many are predaceous on aphids and other small insects.

Robber flies are 5–30 mm long and often have a stout thorax, a long slender abdomen, and long, strong, legs. The head has a bearded appearance and is hollowed out between the eyes. Robber flies are very fast fliers and feed on beneficial and harmful insects such as wasps, bees, beetles, flies, grasshoppers, and dragonflies. The larvae occur in the soil and decaying wood and feed on white grubs and other insects in the egg and larval stages found in these habitats.

Orthoptera

Preying or praying mantids are easily recognized by their characteristic position of waiting for prey with the enlarged grasping front legs in an upright position (Figure 3.7). These insects are primarily southern and tropical in distribution, but several species have been introduced and are now found throughout most of the United States. Preying mantids are predaceous on many different species of beneficial and harmful insects. They are cannibalistic and readily devour each other, especially in the early instars. Preying mantids lay their eggs in paper-machélike cases that are attached to grass stems or twigs of shrubs. They overwinter in the egg stage and usually there is one generation per year in the United States.

Odonata

All species of dragonflies (Figure 3.4) and damselflies (Figure 3.5) are predaceous both as naiads and adults. The naiads feed on many different species of aquatic immature insects, especially mayflies. The adults normally capture only moving prey and feed on many flying insects such as midges, mosquitoes, and moths, but the larger species of Odonata also prey on bees, mayflies, butterflies, and other dragonflies.

Predatory Noninsect Arthropods

Many arachnids (e.g., spiders, mites, scorpions, pseudoscorpions, daddy longlegs), centipedes, and a few millipedes prey on insects found in the forests and urban settings. Unfortunately, these groups have never been adequately studied to determine their effectiveness as natural enemies. Spiders and mites are the most important predatory noninsect arthropods of forest and shade tree pests. Dahlsten et al. (1977) and Morris (1963) provide information on spiders feeding on Douglas-fir tussock moth larvae and spruce budworm larvae, respectively.

Insectivorous Vertebrates

The following classes in the phylum Chordata contain species that commonly feed on insects during all or part of the life cycle: Aves (birds), Mammalia (moles, shrews, voles, mice, skunks, raccoons, and fox), Amphibia (frogs, toads, salamanders), Reptilia (snakes, lizards), and Pisces (fish). With some minor exceptions, very little quantitative information is available on the effect of insectivorous vertebrates on the population dynamics of insects. Birds and mammals are the two most important classes of vertebrates that regularly consume large numbers of forest and shade tree pests.

Sweetman (1958) reported that 50–67% of all food consumed by birds are insects. Feeding habits of birds vary with the season. Many species of birds feed on insects primarily during the spring and summer. Nesting birds are fed large quantitities of insects. Birds feed on all stages of insects. Predation by birds is generally most effective when insect populations are at endemic levels. However, during the winter months, woodpeckers will concentrate in areas where there are small bark beetle outbreaks. Knight (1958) demonstrated that up to 75% of the spruce beetle, *Dendroctonus rufipennis* (Kirby), population in small localized outbreaks was destroyed by woodpeckers.

European and Russian scientists have expended much effort in studying bird predation and methods to increase bird populations in forested areas. Franz (1961) reported that the provision of nesting boxes in some parts of Germany has increased the number of insectivorous birds by five- to tenfold. We presume that birds are beneficial in reducing pest populations, but data documenting their effectivenesss are meager at best. Dickson et al. (1979) consider some of the roles of insectivorous birds in forest ecosystems.

Several orders of mammals are important insectivores. The most noteworthy are Insectivora (moles and shrews), Rodentia (some mice and moles), and Chiroptera (bats). The Insectivora and Rodentia contain a number of species that are predators of forest insects. Most of the species are terrestrial and thus feed on larvae and pupae in the soil and litter. Coppel and Mertins (1977) report one successful case of introduction of a mammalian predator (Figure 8.9) for suppression of larch sawfly in Newfoundland, Canada. The introduced species, the masked shrew, *Sorex cinereus* Kerr, was a common mainland inhabitant, known to be an effective predator, that did not occur

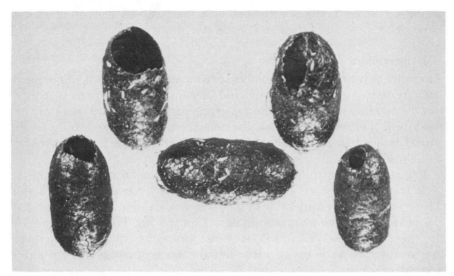

Figure 8.9 Larch sawfly, *Pristiphora erichsonii*, cocoons attacked by predators. (U.S. Forest Service photograph.)

on the island province of Newfoundland. The shrew became established and is judged to be an effective predator of the larch sawfly and the yellowheaded spruce sawfly, *Pikonema alaskensis* (Rohwer) (Warren 1971). Bats are beneficial predators of crepuscular and nocturnal flying insects. Their effectiveness in suppression of insect populations has not been evaluated.

Parasites

Parasites of vertebrates or invertebrates live in or on the host during part or all of the life cycle of the parasite and may or may not kill its hosts. Parasites of vertebrates are usually in a taxonomic class different from that of their host, are smaller than the host, and a single parasite seldom kills its host. A parasite of a vertebrate may complete its life cycle on a single host (e.g., lice), may be free living and nonparasitic during part of its life cycle (e.g., mosquitoes, fleas), or may have a complicated life cycle involving several host species (e.g., tapeworms). Parasites of vertebrates are normally considered pests and are not covered in this chapter.

Parasites of insects are called parasites or *parasitoids*. We use the more common term "parasite." A parasite is approximately the same size as the host, in the same taxonomic class as the host, usually kills the host, and requires only one host to complete its life cycle. Insect parasites are parasitic in the larval stage and free living as adults.

There are parasitic insect species belonging to five orders and over 80 families (Sweetman 1958). However, only two orders, Hymenoptera and

Diptera, contain families with members that play an important role as parasites of potential forest and shade tree pests.

Hymenoptera

There are approximately 40 families of hymenopterous insects whose members are strictly parasites. Coppel and Mertins (1977) reported that there may be 500,000 species of hymenopterous parasites that are currently undescribed. The most important hymenopterous parasites belong in the superfamilies Ichneumonoidea (families Ichneumonidae and Braconidae) and Chalcidoidea (20 families).

Ichneumonidae (ichneumon wasps) is one of the largest families in the class Insecta, with over 4000 species described from the United States. These wasps vary considerably in size, shape, and color, but most are slender wasps with an elongated abdomen (Figure 8.10). The female's ovipositor may be extremely conspicuous or inconspicuous. All ichneumon wasps are parasitic; occur in many different habitats, most commonly in natural and urban forests; and attack a wide variety of hosts. Certain species, such as *Itoplectus conquisitor* (Say), have been reared from 200 different host species, but most species attack only one or a few host species. The majority of the ichneumon wasps are internal parasites of larval or pupal stages of the hosts. Insects in the orders Lepidoptera, Hymenoptera (e.g., sawflies),

Figure 8.10 Adult ichneumon wasp, *Glypta fumiferanae,* ovipositing into an overwintering western spruce budworm, *Choristoneura occidentalis,* larva concealed in a twig scar. (U.S. Forest Service photograph.)

Coleoptera, and Diptera are the most common hosts. Certain species of ichneumons are common parasites of spiders. Both native and introduced species of ichneumon wasps are important natural enemies of many destructive or potentially damaging lepidopterous and sawfly defoliators of forests and shade trees (Figure 8.11). Biological control programs using ichneumon wasps as one of the introduced species of natural enemies have been extremely effective against the larch sawfly, European spruce sawfly, and the winter moth.

Adults feed on various plant materials such as pollen, nectar, honeydew, and on the body fluid of their hosts. Sweetman (1958), Askew (1971), and Townes (1972) provide additional information on ichneumon wasps.

Braconid wasps (Braconidae) are similar taxonomically to the ichneumon wasps but usually much smaller (i.e., rarely over 15 mm in length), more stout bodied, and not as brightly colored. The major taxonomic charac-

Figure 8.11   Full-grown larva of the ichneumon parasite, *Phytodietus fumiferanae,* killing its host, a mature larva of the western spruce budworm, *Choristoneura occidentalis.* (U.S. Forest Service photograph.)

teristic that separates the two families is wing venation with braconid wasps usually having one recurrent vein and ichneumon wasps having two recurrent veins. Braconid wasps are common parasites of lepidopterous and coleopterous larvae. They also parasitize the larvae of some dipterous, hymenopterous (e.g., sawfly), and homopterous (e.g., aphids) insects. Many species of braconids pupate in silken cocoons on the outside of the host, whereas ichneumon wasps normally pupate in cocoons within the host. Matthews (1974) presents a thorough review of the biology of this important insect family.

Chalcidoid wasps, superfamily Chalcidoidea, include approximately 20 families. They are easily recognized at the superfamily level because of their small size (i.e., 2–3 mm with a few reaching 10–15 mm), reduced wing venation, and dark coloration, with many being metallic green or blue. Taxonomic identification at the family level is rather difficult. Chalcidoid wasps are very important parasites of the egg or larval stages of many insects in the orders Lepidoptera (Figure 8.12), Coleoptera, Diptera, and Homoptera. Most of the important egg parasites of forest and shade tree pests belong to this superfamily. *Trichogramma* species, common egg parasites of many forest, shade, and orchard tree pests are also in this

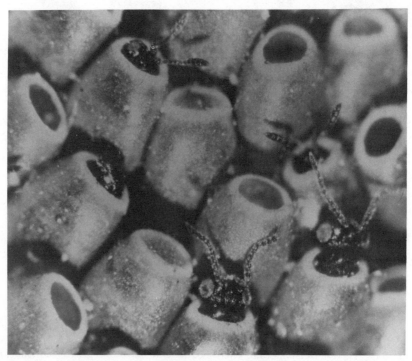

Figure 8.12 Egg parasites of a chalcidoid wasp, *Telenomus droozi*, emerging from an elm spanworm, *Ennomus subsignarius*. (U.S. Forest Service photograph.)

superfamily. Anderson (1976) reviews the importance of egg parasites in reducing populations of lepidopterous defoliators such as the elm span-worm and cankerworms.

Diptera

There are only seven families in this order that are exclusively parasitic. However, all members of the Tachinidae (tachinid flies) are parasitic; over 1300 species are found in North America (Arnaud 1978). Tachinid flies resemble house flies and flesh flies but usually have large bristles near the end of the abdomen that easily distinguish them from other flies (Figure 3.20). Many species of tachinid flies are important native parasites of lep-idopterous and sawfly defoliators. *Cyzenis albicans* (Fallén), an introduced tachinid fly, has been extremely effective in reducing population size of the winter moth in eastern Canada. Some tachinid species only attack one host species, whereas others such as *Compsilura concinnata* (Meigen), an introduced parasite of the gypsy moth, has been reared from over 200 hosts (Figure 8.13). Tachinid flies normally oviposit in one of the following four ways: (1) lay eggs on host larva, (2) deposit eggs into host larva, (3) deposit eggs on foliage, or (4) deposit live maggots onto host larva.

Flesh flies are in the family Sarcophagidae. Some members of this family act as parasites and/or scavengers of lepidopterous pupae. *Sarcophaga ald-richi* (Parker) is one of the most common sarcophagids associated with outbreak populations of forest defoliators such as the forest tent caterpillar,

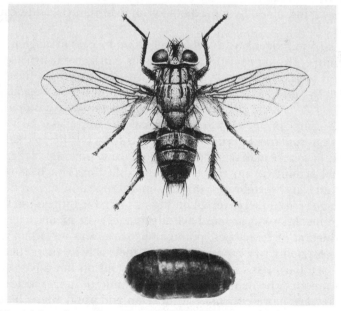

Figure 8.13 Adult and puparium of a tachinid parasite, *Compsilura concinnata*, a parasite of the gypsy moth larva, *Lymantria dispar*, and other defoliators. (U.S. Forest Service photograph.)

gypsy moth, and spruce budworm. *Sarchophaga aldrichi* is a very important pupal parasite of the forest tent caterpillar. In the Great Lake states and adjacent Canadian provinces, the percentage of parasitism by *S. aldrichi* normally increases with the age of the forest tent caterpillar outbreak and often reached 75% in the third or fourth year of an outbreak. This fly overwinters in a puparium in the soil; the adult flies emerge in late May and mate. The females are ready to lay live maggots by the time the forest tent caterpillar cocoons are formed. *Sarchophaga aldrichi* larvae attack normal prepupae, pupae, parasitized, and diseased forest tent caterpillars, carrion, mashed caterpillars, and other organic material (Hodson 1939). Campbell (1963) found that *S. aldrichi* always attacked dead or dying gypsy moth pupae, especially pupae stung by ichneumonids.

Pathogens

A *pathogen* is any microorganism capable of producing a disease. Microorganisms associated with insects are the same general types common to vertebrates. The most important types of insect pathogens occurring in forest and shade tree systems are bacteria, viruses, fungi, and protozoa. Most viruses, bacteria, and protozoa are consumed orally by the host insect along with its food. Fungi invade the insect through the intact integument. Viruses and protozoa are also often transferred by "transovum passage" of the pathogen from the adult to the offspring (i.e., in the egg or on the egg covering). All pathogens can invade the insect through a wound such as a biting wound made by a predator or an ovipositing wound caused by a parasite.

The use of pathogens as a viable technique in pest management is attracting more public attention. Pathogens can accomplish long-term suppression [e.g., nuclear polyhedrosis virus (NPV) on sawflies, *Bacillus popilliae* Dutky and *B. lentimorbus* Dutky on Japanese beetle, *Popillia japonica* Newman] or short-term suppression as microbial insecticides (e.g., *B. thuringiensis* Berliner on lepidopterous and sawfly caterpillars, NPV on lepidopterous caterpillars). Specific requirements for a reliable microorganism to be used in a pest management program are as follows: (1) reasonably quick lethal action; (2) no risk to all other life forms such as beneficial insects, plants, and vertebrates; (3) economical to produce; and (4) resting stage or stage resistant to adverse conditions so that pathogen can be stored for a long time. Microorganisms have advantages over chemical insecticides in the reduction of insect pest populations because: they occur naturally in many ecosystems, are more selective in their activity than chemical insecticides, are harmless to beneficial insects, and do not adversely affect the environment. The major disadvantage of microbial insecticides is economics; they are more expensive to develop and apply then chemical insecticides. Production costs cannot be spread over as many crops since microbial insecticides generally are narrow spectrum in activity and at most kill only a few species of insects. It is difficult for a company to make a profit on the production and sale of microbial insecticides because of the small demand for the products. The exception to this principle would be a microorganism that is effective on a major pest or on an extremely important crop such as the spruce budworm in the boreal forests of North America. The U.S. Forest Service is developing the Douglas-fir tussock moth virus for use in the mid-1980s.

Additional detailed information on insect pathogens is presented in Burges and Hussey (1971), Cantwell (1974), Coppel and Mertins (1977), and Maddox (1982).

Bacteria

Bacteria are minute, unicellular plantlike organisms that lack chlorophyll and organelles. Bacterial pathogens of insects are often classified as non-spore-forming and spore-forming bacteria. Most insects contain many non-spore-forming bacteria within their digestive systems. Non-spore-forming bacteria are often called "potential pathogens" since these bacteria are relatively nonpathogenic as long as they remain in the midgut. Non-spore-forming bacteria can be very pathogenic if they enter the insect's blood. Certain stress factors such as temperature extremes, other pathogens, parasites, and poor food quality may cause conditions that allow these non-spore-forming bacteria to enter into the insect's blood. These bacteria are probably important mortality factors in some situations, but they have not been studied in detail. They have little potential as microbial insecticides because of their cosmopolitan distribution, poor invasion power, storage problems, and rapid loss of viability in the field, and some are very pathogenic to vertebrates.

Spore-forming bacteria, especially members of the genus *Bacillus*, are promising potential microbial agents. All spore-forming bacteria produce endospores that persist inside or outside the dead host in a dormant stage for a long time. The two most promising *Bacillus* pathogens are *B. thuringiensis* and *B. popillae*.

Bacillus thuringiensis Berliner, often called *B.t.*, is a highly pathogenic bacteria of many species of lepidopterous caterpillars. It has been field tested on over 20 species of lepidopterous forest defoliators (Harper 1974). Many strains of *B.t.* have been isolated from natural insect populations, but naturally occurring epizootics are rare (Maddox 1982). However, this species of bacteria can easily be produced on artificial media. Commerical preparations have been available since the 1960s. Currently, commercial preparations such as Biotrol®, Dipel®, and Thuricide® can be purchased from most nurseries and hardware stores. Unlike most spore-forming bacteria, *B.t.* produces a protein crystal in addition to forming an endospore. It primarily affects lepidopterous larvae with a high pH (9.0–10.5) in the midgut and enzyme systems that dissolve the protein crystal and release the toxin. Susceptible lepidopterous larvae may be killed by the toxic protein crystal alone, or by the combined action of the toxic crystals and endospores. A few species are only affected by the endospores.

B.t. is commonly recommended by city foresters and entomologists to reduce high populations of common shade tree pests such as gypsy moth (Figure 8.14), tent caterpillars, bagworms, oakworms, elm spanworms, and cankerworms. Many cities in California have used *B.t.* regularly since 1971 as part of their pest management program against the California oakworm, *Phryganidia californica* Packard, and the redhumped caterpillar, *Schizura concinna* (J. E. Smith) (Olkowski et al. 1978).

B. popillae and *B. lentimorbus,* spore-forming bacteria, which cause milky disease in white grubs, have been used to reduce pest populations of the Japanese beetle in turf on golf courses and city grass strips in the northeastern United States since 1939. It can be purchased under the trade names of Japidemic® and Doom®. The Japanese beetle, an exotic pest, was first discovered in 1916 in New Jersey. The origin of the milky disease pathogen is unknown but is believed to be a native pathogen on scarab beetle larvae in North America. When present in an area, the spores of *B. popillae* and *B. lentimorbus* are extremely common in the upper 95 mm of the soil. Once ingested by the Japanese beetle larvae, the endospsores

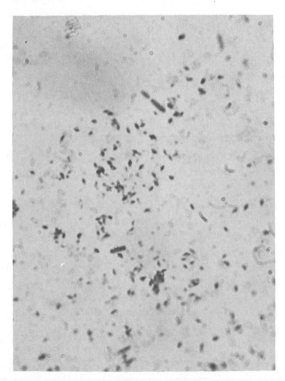

Figure 8.14 Spores, crystals, and vegetative cells of *Bacillus thuringiensis.* (U.S. Forest Service photograph, courtesy of N. Dubois.)

develop in the gut, produce vegetative bacterial cells, enter the blood, multiply rapidly in the blood, and destroy certain tissues, and the refractile endospores are formed just before the host dies (Coppel and Mertins 1977). The name milky disease originated from the abnormally white milky color of the blood of diseased larvae; this color is due to the presence of the highly refractile endospores.

Viruses

Insect viruses are common natural insect pathogens that have considerable promise as microbial insecticides. Over 450 insect viruses have been described from insects and mites (Coppel and Mertins 1977). Most insect viruses presently identified are included within a large protein crystal and are called *inclusion viruses*. Virus inoculum can persist in the soil for several years. Sunlight can rapidly kill virus particles present on foliage, but rain has very little effect on removing virus particles from plant surfaces.

Nuclear polyhedrosis viruses (NPV) are the most common inclusion viruses. These viruses account for over 40% of the described insect viruses. The NPV consist of a core of nucleic acid enclosed in a protein coat. These NPV are normally host specific, often self-perpetuating in the environment, and commonly infect many species of lepidopterous and sawfly larvae.

The NPV are either ingested by the insect host or contact the host by transovum passage of the microorganism in or on the host's eggs. Once ingestion occurs, the polyhedra (Figure 8.15) dissolves and releases virus rods (virions) into the midgut. The virions soon pass through the midgut and enter susceptible cells such as fat bodies, blood cells, and epidermis tissue. Little is known about how these viruses invade susceptible cells. The length of time from ingestion of the polyhedra to death of larvae varies from 4 days to 3 weeks. Factors responsible for these variations are different NPV, different hosts, number of polyhedra ingested, age of larva at the time polyhedra are ingested, and the environmental temperature (Maddox 1982).

Larvae infected with NPV show few external symptoms until a few days before dying. Then the larval skin often darkens and becomes fragile, and the larva often climbs to the top of the leaf. Dead larvae are found hanging by the prolegs (Figure 8.16). The insect's integument often ruptures after death, releasing millions of polyhedra into the environment (i.e., on adjacent foliage and the soil surface). Natural epizootics of NPV often spread through the host population very rapidly at high host population densities.

Some NPV are extremely common in the environment and often are a major factor responsible for the collapse of outbreak populations of forest defoliators such as the Douglas-fir tussock moth, gypsy moth, and European spruce sawfly. The NPV of the Douglas-fir tussock moth and gypsy moth are now registered and available in the United States for use in suppression of these two pests.

The best documented and most successful case of a pathogen reducing

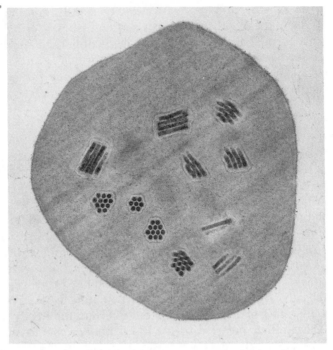

Figure 8.15 Scanning electron micrograph of polyhedral inclusion body from a Douglas-fir tussock moth, *Orgyia pseudotsugata*, larva. (Electron micrograph by K. M. Hughes, Forestry Science Laboratory USDA, Forest Service, Corvallis, Oregon.)

Figure 8.16 A mature Douglas-fir tussock moth, *Orgyia pseudotsugata*, larva killed by a nuclear polyhedrosis virus. (Courtesy of P. J. Iwai, Corvallis, Oregon.)

a forest pest population developed with the accidental colonization of the NPV of the European spruce sawfly in eastern Canada in the 1930s. The European spruce sawfly was first recorded in North America near Ottawa in 1922. By 1934, a major outbreak was reported on white spruce in the Gaspé Peninsula of Quebec. European spruce sawfly populations were found in many areas in Ontario, Quebec, New Brunswick, and adjacent areas of the United States by 1936. The Canadian government started a large scale parasite introduction program in 1933 and introduced 27 species of parasites into eastern Canada between 1933 and 1951 (McGugan and Coppel 1962). An NPV of the European spruce sawfly was first observed in the field in 1938. By 1945 the European spruce sawfly populations had collapsed, primarily due to the NPV. The origin of this virus is unknown, but it is generally accepted that the virus was introduced fortuitously while making parasite releases in the 1930s. The virus and two introduced parasites, a tachinid fly, *Drino bohemica* Mesnil, and an ichneumon wasp, *Exenterus vellicatus* Cushman, have maintained very low population levels of the European spruce sawfly in North America since 1945 (Bird and Elgee 1957, Neilson and Morris 1964). The economic savings due to this fortuitous introduction of the virus and planned introductions of the parasites have been enormous. For example, the European spruce sawfly had killed over 11 million cords of spruce in the Gaspé Peninsula alone during 1930–1945 (Reeks and Barter 1951).

However, European spruce sawfly populations increased significantly in the early 1960s in some spruce–fir stands in New Brunswick, which had been sprayed with DDT for three consecutive years to control the spruce budworm. The spraying operations reduced the sawfly population densities to the lowest levels ever recorded; the NPV and the parasites were reduced to nondetectable numbers. Population levels of the European spruce sawfly increased to pre-1945 levels during 1965, but the virus and the two parasite populations increased in 1966 and reduced the sawfly populations to very low endemic levels (Neilson et al. 1971). The European spruce sawfly is presently not a problem in North America and is not likely to become one in the near future unless large-scale forest spraying to reduce spruce budworm populations in New Brunswick and Quebec disrupts the European spruce sawfly–virus–parasite interaction, which now appears to be in a relatively stable state.

Fungi

Fungi are lower forms of plant life that lack chlorophyll and are unable to manufacture carbohydrates in the presence of sunlight. There are at least 35 genera of fungi that contain species that cause diseases in insects (Coppel and Mertins 1977). Numerous species of fungi in the genera *Beauveria, Metarrhizium, Entomophthora,* and *Coelomomyces* often kill large numbers of insects under natural conditions.

Insect mortality due to pathogenic fungi is highly dependent on favorable environmental conditions. Natural epizootics of fungi can occur only under conditions of high humidity. These humid conditions are needed for the transmission and germination of the fungi spores. Fungi are important natural enemies of many forest pests but probably will not be used as microbial insecticides because of the very specific environmental conditions needed for the occurrence of germination.

Unlike most other pathogens, fungi infect their host directly through its integument. An infection begins when a spore lands on a host and under proper moisture conditions, the spore germinates and forms a special structure that penetrates the insect's integument. Once within the integument, the fungi proliferates, invades the various insect tissues, and fills the insect body with hyphae. The insect dies at this point. Under favorable weather conditions, the fungus continues to grow, produces structures that erupt through the integument and then forms spores.

Protozoa

The taxonomy of this group is difficult because there are few distinct morphological characters available. Protozoa affecting insects are found in several classes, but protozoa in the order Microsporidia are the most important group found infecting forest and shade tree insects, especially lepidopterous defoliators. These pathogens are very common and important natural microorganisms. They will not be an integral part of any forest pest management program until more basic information is obtained on their biology and effectiveness as a microbial agent, and until more safety tests are conducted on them because a few members in the order Microsporidia cause diseases in fish and mammals.

Most common protozoa, including the microsporidia, enter the insect as a resistant spore through the digestive system or by transovum transmission from an infected female to her progeny through the eggs. Most microsporidia act rather slowly on their hosts and seldom kill them but reduce the host's vitality. Infected hosts suffer other symptoms such as lower fecundity, reduced movement, and diminished size of larvae and adults. The host's life cycle is lengthened, which increases its vulnerability to attack by other natural enemies.

Microsporidia populations appear to increase in an area during the latter years of an insect outbreak. There is little information available on natural microsporidia affecting forest pest populations. Wilson (1977), Nordin (1975), and Stairs (1972) present information on the effect of microsporidia infestations of spruce budworm, tent caterpillars, and fall webworm populations.

Successes, Failures, and Future Importance of Natural Enemies in Pest Management

Importation and colonization of natural enemies of forest and shade tree insects in North America has been quite successful. The best summary of the classical biological control attempts on forest and shade tree pests in North America was presented by Munroe (1971) and covers only the Canadian programs. From an examination of Munroe's report, we would rate at least 6 of the 23 serious attempts in using biological control in Canada against forest and shade tree insects as very successful. Cost–benefit analyses are not available for the early importation programs. In 1965 the President's Science Advisory Committee estimated that 30 dollars were returned in accrued benefits for every dollar invested in biological control during 1923–1959 (Coppel and Mertins 1977).

Fortunately, the field of forest and shade tree entomology has several good examples of pest populations reduced to low levels along with simultaneous quantitative studies on the population dynamics of the pest insect. Biological control of the winter moth, *Operophtera brumata* (Linnaeus), in eastern Canada by two introduced parasites is an excellent example of the potential use of predators and parasites against this forest and shade tree pest. This geometrid moth was accidently introduced into Nova Scotia from Europe in the 1930s. The winter moth was first reported in 1949 and was only considered a nuisance pest of shade trees in the early 1950s. This insect dispersed slowly into eastern Canada, but by the early 1960s it was present in Nova Scotia, New Brunswick, and Prince Edward Island. Entomologists predicted in the early 1950s that the winter moth, whose common hosts are red oak, apple, elm and basswood, was capable of spreading through most of North America.

A tachinid fly, *Cyzenis albicans* (Fallén), and an ichneumon wasp, *Agrypon flaveolatum* (Gravely), were primarily responsible for the collapse of epidemic populations of the winter moth in Nova Scotia in 1961. The two species of parasites are compatible and complementary; *C. albicans* is more effective at low host population densities (Embree 1965, 1966). Embree analyzed the information gathered from 37 life tables, built a population model, and showed that parasitism by the introduced parasites was the key factor in reducing most winter moth populations in Nova Scotia to endemic levels.

The economic benefits of these parasite introductions were enormous, but it is difficult to place an accurate economic value on the success of this program. This entire biological control program, including the detailed population studies, cost about $500,000. During the 10 years prior to the success of the natural enemies in 1961, about 26,000 cords of wood per year were destroyed in the center of the outbreak, valued at 2 million dollars (DeBach 1974).

Some biological control programs against forest and shade tree pests have not been successful. An enormous amount of time, effort, and money has been and is being spent on the introduction and establishment of natural enemies against the gypsy moth and the balsam woolly adelgid, *Adelges piceae* (Ratzeburg), in North America. However, establishment of these natural enemies did not significantly reduce the outbreak populations of these two pests. The factors that have led to failures in past biological control attempts are discussed earlier in this chapter.

Continued research on the complex plant–pest–parasite and plant–pest–parasite–hyperparasite interactions will lead to the development of more efficient management plans for the common pests during the next several decades. Information developed since 1965 has enabled us to better use, conserve, and enhance the natural enemies that are now present in the various ecosystems. Computer modeling of insect populations has increased our understanding of the role of natural enemies in a particular crop system. Recent accelerated research on microorganisms and the registration of NPV against the gypsy moth and Douglas-fir tussock moth by the EPA indicate greater use of pathogens in future insect pest management programs. Natural enemies, including predators, parasites, and diseases, will be one major tool used in integrated pest management systems developed for forest and shade tree pests in the future.

TACTICS USED TO MODIFY OR REGULATE POPULATION SIZE: MECHANICAL OR PHYSICAL METHODS

Prior to the widespread availability of chemical insecticides, mechanical or physical methods were the main approaches used in direct insect suppression. There are several tactics that have been used, the most common of which include (1) trapping insects, (2) habitat destruction, (3) habitat modification, and (4) collecting insects. Obviously, the applicability of a particular method depends on the type of forest situation with which one is dealing, that is, forest ecosystem, specialized forestry setting, or urban forest and the particular insect pest.

Trapping

There are a number of different approaches to insect suppression using traps. The objective of all trapping procedures is to concentrate populations of a pest species to prescribed locations, where they can be destroyed. Trapping techniques are based on knowledge of specific behavioral characteristics of insects.

Perhaps the oldest application of the trapping technique in forestry is the "trap tree" procedure for bark beetles and some wood borers. This technique, which has been used in European forests for many years, involves felling healthy trees that serve to attract and concentrate the bark beetles and wood borers. The infested trees are destroyed prior to beetle emergence.

Flight traps are another common method. The most common type is the light trap. In this case insects are attracted to a light (usually ultraviolet light) and are concentrated in a canister or bag attached to the trap. Pheromone-baited traps provide still another approach. In this case the trap often consists of a panel, or several panels, coated with an adhesive substance such as Stickem Special® or Tangle Foot® (Figure 8.17). Insects are attracted to the pheromones and captured in the adhesive. This approach has been utilized for bark beetles and defoliators (Mitchell 1981). Traps baited with food or food extracts work in the same ways as described above.

The various types of trap have applicability in forest ecosystems, the specialized forestry settings, and urban forests. Traps and baits are generally safe to use and usually are not prohibitively expensive to operate.

Habitat Destruction

Habitat destruction is a tactic that can be used in suppression of existing populations or in prevention of a population buildup. In the case of suppression we are simply interested in destroying the habitat while the damaging insects are present. Examples of this type of tactic include salvaging infested host material or burning infested hosts. Both approaches have been used against bark beetles. Harvesting a cone crop in a seed orchard prior to emergence of pest insects is another example. In this case the pest insects are removed with the cones, that is, the habitat, and damage to the next cone crop or terminals is prevented. Sanitation, following logging operations, is a commonly used tactic to prevent the buildup of bark beetle populations in slash and tree crowns.

Figure 8.17 Interception trap used to capture flying insects. In this example insects are attracted to the trap by pheromones deployed at the base of the interception panel. The panel can be coated with a sticky substance such as Stickem Special®. Flying insects can be trapped on the panel or collected in the jar that contains an insecticide. (Texas Forest Service.)

Habitat Modification

Habitat modification involves changing the condition of the habitat so that it is no longer suitable for insect development or colonization and utilization. This type of activity generally involves changing the temperature or moisture conditions of the habitat (Figure 8.18). An example of this type of tactic is the practice of storing harvested logs in water at mill sites. This practice prevents colonization by bark beetles or ambrosia beetles and also results in mortality to insects infesting the logs.

Collecting

This tactic simply involves collecting or removing insects from hosts. Obviously, the tactic has only limited applicability, but it may be all that is necessary for insects infesting an ornamental tree.

TACTICS USED TO MODIFY OR REGULATE POPULATION SIZE: SILVICULTURAL PRACTICES

Silviculture is the theory and practice of controlling forest establishment, composition, and growth (Spurr and Barnes 1980). The theory of silviculture is based on principles of plant population dynamics, plant community dynamics, and forest ecosystem dynamics (see Chapter 7). The

Figure 8.18 Storage deck of pondersa pine sprayed with water to prevent damage by bark beetles. The habitat of the bark beetles is modified by soaking the logs; thus, the habitat is unsuitable for colonization.

practice of silviculture includes consideration of both ecological and economic principles. The subject matter of silviculture includes the various types of treatment that can be applied to forest stands to maintain or enhance their productivity (Smith 1962). Because phytophagous insects can reduce stand productivity and, in some cases, kill trees in stands, silvicultural practice includes treatments or tactics directed to pest species.

Silvicultural tactics are generally concerned with prevention of insect-caused losses in stands rather than suppression of populations. Although we have seen that there are numerous ways to modify or regulate populations of pest insects, it is generally acknowledged that, where possible, pest management is best achieved through practices that prevent outbreaks from occurring, rather than through attempts to suppress populations once they have reached outbreak proportions. However, the goal of prevention is difficult to achieve for several reasons, First, there is a great deal of variation in the degree of management applied to forests. In some cases the forests are intensively managed; for example, pine forests in the southern United States and in other cases the forests are extensively managed (a euphemism for little or no management), as, for instance, are aspen forests in the Great Lake states. Second, the goal of management in a particular forest type may create conditions where the likelihood of an insect outbreak is high, and this fact is recognized but does not override the management goal. For example, a company in the southeastern United States interested in growing pines for use in pulp mills recognizes that the likelihood of southern pine beetle occurring in densely stocked stands is high. However, if the management goal is to optimize for production of the maximum number of pulp wood-size stems per hectare, the manager may be willing to gamble that an insect outbreak will not occur before harvest at 25–30 years. The manager also recognized that the likelihood of a southern pine beetle outbreak could be substantially reduced if stands were thinned at 20 years. The thinning treatment represents an additional cost to the manager as does an outbreak of southern pine beetle. Third, it does not always follow that well-managed stands prevent outbreaks of phytophagous insects. Fourth, the relationships between insect population dynamics and host tree population dynamics are not fully understood. We have indicated (Chapter 7) that insect–host interactions are complex and often beneficial. Fifth, the costs associated with some silvicultural practices directed to pest management may be greater than the benefits received from the treatment (Figure 8.19).

In the following sections we consider silvicultural tactics involved in forest establishment, forest composition, and forest growth. In each of the chapters dealing with insect feeding groups (Chapters 11–18) we have identified conditions where insect damage occurs as a result of forest management practices and indicated some of the silvicultural treatments used for specific pests. Furthermore, in Chapter 7 we discuss in some detail plant population dynamics and the interaction of insects with host trees

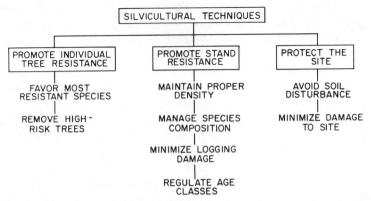

Figure 8.19 Silvicultural techniques identified to be useful for prevention of outbreaks of the southern pine beetle, *Dendroctonus frontalis* (Belanger 1980).

and plant modules, communities (stands), and ecosystems. The technical information presented in Chapter 7 is the foundation for silvicultural tactics. In discussing silvicultural practices it is given that we are dealing with managed stands.

Forest Establishment

The issues dealing with forest establishment begin with the harvesting procedures used for the previous stand. Harvesting tends to be a destructive operation that requires site preparation before a new stand is established. Essential minerals and other plant nutrients are removed from the site; soil is often compacted as a result of the use of harvesting machines; soil erosion can occur; road beds are often damaged; and there is an accumulation of debris from unused tree crowns, roots, and slash. Site preparation practices are used to minimize effects of these, and other, conditions on the next stand. Ideally we would like our harvesting practices to enhance or at least conserve soil moisture, soil organic matter, decomposition and nutrient cycling processes, and soil nutrients. Whereas these goals may not always be possible to achieve, several actions can be taken to enhance the likelihood: (1) using equipment that causes minimum soil compaction, displacement of topsoil, or erosion; (2) using slash disposal practices that do not further decrease soil nutrient capital; (3) fostering conditions conducive to increasing the rate of decomposition of organic matter and nutrient cycling; and (4) avoiding damage of the residual stand that would increase vulnerability to insect attack (Coulson and Stark 1982).

An example of a silvicultural practice associated with forest establishment is sanitation relative to logging debris. A number of important pests breed in logging debris. In pine forests, reproduction weevils, seedling debarking weevils, and turpentine beetles are attracted to harvested sites. In the case of reproduction and seedling debarking weevils, large brood populations build up in the roots of harvested trees and can decimate seedlings if planting follows directly behind harvest. One silvicultural control for the weevils is to delay planting until populations become less concentrated (6 months to 1 year after harvest). However, this practice means that the site is out of production for a period of time. An alternative approach is to protect the seedlings with insecticides. A number of bark beetles commonly utilize logging slash as breeding sites, which can lead to outbreaks of these insects in surrounding stands. The important point is that logging debris can be managed as part of the site preparation procedure and prevent potential pest insect outbreaks for a number of species.

Forest Composition

The initial activities of forest establishment are highly related to several issues associated with forest composition. In particular we are interested in species of trees selected for replanting and diversity of the replanted stands.

Selection of Tree Species for Use in Reforestation

In cases where sites are planted with seeds or seedlings, selection of tree species is an important consideration. One clear trend in reforestation is the use of genetically superior stock that has been selected for characters such as growth rate, form class, and disease resistance. Breeding plants for insect resistance has been practiced in agriculture for a number of years. This approach may be practical for forest trees as well (Hanover 1975). Within a particular genus of trees there is often a gradation of susceptibility or resistance to insects. For example, longleaf pine is much less susceptible to southern pine beetle than is loblolly or shortleaf pine.

In addition to the quality of the tree selected for reforestation, variables such as geographic location, specific site characteristics, and potential insect and disease problems are important considerations. For example, there are sections of southeastern Texas where southern pine beetle infestation in pines has been a chronic problem for many years. Although this area produces rapid growth in pines, the problems associated with the southern pine beetle have resulted in land managers substituting tree species, such as cottonwood, for pines on certain sites. In this example the silvicultural control is to replace the tree species susceptible to significant insect damage with one that is not and thereby avoid the problem. In many cases it is possible to anticipate that specific insect problems will be associated with the selection of a tree species on particular sites.

Species Diversity

In forestry, as in agriculture, intensive management favors a cropping system with a single species (monocultures) and even age distribution. The advantages to this type of cropping system are numerous: replanting, maintenance, and harvest are simplified; wood and fiber yield can be predicted using mathematical models or yield tables; management costs are minimized; it is possible to coordinate resource availability or supply with mill demand; and so forth. However, there are a number of problems created by even-aged monocultures. For example, these forests provide food and habitat conditions that favor the buildup of outbreak population levels for virtually all the insect feeding groups. Naturally regenerated forests are generally represented by a variety of tree species and/or multiple-age classes. Forests characterized by high species and age–class diversity are less prone to violent fluctuations in phytophagous insect populations.

One obvious silvicultural tactic, useful in prevention of insect outbreaks, is to increase tree species diversity and vary age–class distribution within stands. However, both of these practices represent additional costs, when considered from the viewpoint of wood and fiber production.

Forest Growth

Once the stand has been established with a tree species composition that is suited for specific intended uses (e.g., pines to be used for the manufacture of paper), the final goal of silviculture deals with stand growth and yield. The annual increment (radial increase in size) for a specific age–class of tree growing on a certain type of site is one way of assessing growth of a particular tree species in a stand. There are many different variables that influence stand growth such as site quality; competition between trees for nutrients, water, and sun light; diseases; foraging by phytophagous insects; and so on.

A great deal of empirical evidence has been accumulated over the years that suggests that the vulnerability of forest stands to damage by phytophagous insect pests is related to the vigor of stands. Of course, the components discussed above, relative to species and age–class diversity, are also important. In some cases it is possible to rate a stand according to vulnerability to damage. The terms risk and hazard are used to describe susceptibility and vulnerability, respectively. *Risk* refers to insect activity in space and time, that is, the likelihood that a pest species will occur in a stand. *Hazard* refers to the degree of vulnerability of a stand to a particular pest, given that the insect is present. Stand risk or hazard rating systems have been developed for a number of major pest species (e.g., see Hedden et al. 1981). The stand risk or hazard rating systems use information such as stand density, radial growth rate for a period of years, terrain features, tree species present, geographic location, and so on to predict the probable occurrence and likely severity of an insect outbreak.

The significant point with regard to silvicultural treatment is that it is possible to alter conditions in a stand that favor insect outbreaks. For example, radial growth (and stand vigor) in a dense, stagnated, 25-year-old loblolly pine stand can be increased by thinning the stand. This activity decreases the susceptibility (hazard) of the stand to damage by bark beetles. There are many other techniques that can be used to promote stand vigor such as modification of drainage patterns, suppression of undesirable plant species, and fertilization. Many of the treatments used for forest insect pests are directed to the forest growth aspect of silviculture, and we provide specific examples in the chapters dealing with insect feeding groups. General guidelines for silvicultural practices relative to the southern pine beetle are illustrated in Figure 8.19.

TACTICS USED TO MODIFY OR REGULATE POPULATION SIZE: REGULATORY PRACTICES

Regulatory practices are legal procedures used to prevent the transport, entry, and establishment of plant and animal pests into a country, state, or locality. Regulatory practices also deal with legal aspects associated with containment or suppression of pests species. There are a number of important forest insect pests that were introduced into North America, such as the gypsy moth, the European pine shoot moth, the smaller European elm bark beetle, the elm leaf beetle, *Pyrrhalta luteola* (Müller), the European spruce sawfly, the larch casebearer, and the balsam woolly adelgid. Most of those pests became established in North America before 1912, when the first legislation was enacted to prevent such introductions.

There are two basic aspects associated with regulatory practices: the first is concerned with prevention of establishment of pests in new localities, and the second is concerned with containment and suppression of introduced pests.

Quarantines

Quarantines are regulatory programs designed to prevent the introduction and spread of pest species into new localities. Because individual actions are not adequate for this purpose, adoption and enforcement of quarantines is accomplished by governments. In the United States the Department of Agriculture (USDA) has the authority and responsibility to enforce quarantine regulations. However, this work is accomplished through cooperation with state and local governments, other organizations, and individuals.

Infested commodities or host materials can be transported by commercial carriers or by individuals. The rapid expansion of the range of the gypsy moth is thought to be a result of transportation of egg masses on privately owned automobiles. The first line of defense against introduction of pests is at ports of entry into a locality.

The simplest way to prevent the introduction and spread of pest species is through treatment and certification at the point of origin of potentially infested commodities or host material. For example, nursery stock, seeds, milled lumber, and so on can be inspected for the presence of pest species prior to shipment. These products can be treated to destroy pests and/or certified to be free of pests.

Containment and Suppression

Containment and suppression programs are designed to prevent reinfestation of spread of pests into new areas. These programs involve the use of direct tactics such as application of insecticides to suppress existing populations, silvicultural practices to prevent population buildup, or a combination of suppression and prevention tactics (NAS 1969).

STRATEGIES FOR MANAGING PEST POPULATIONS

In the preceeding sections we have discussed various tactics that are available for suppression of insect populations and prevention of damage. These tactics are applicable to insects in general. There are some cases where a single procedure is adequate for protection of a host tree from a specific type of damage. However, the protection is usually only temporary. Management of insect populations, or the damage they cause, requires a combination of tactics, that is, a strategy. Management strategies are specific to individual pest species.

Throughout the chapters dealing with insect feeding groups (Chapters 11–18) we have identified tactics and strategies used for various pest species. The strategies are developed from a synthesis of information about the pest species. The basic considerations include (1) knowledge of the population dynamics of the insect in relation to trees (or plant modules), stand, or forest ecosystem; (2) knowledge of the impact of the insect on forest resource values; (3) examination of the potential tactics suitable for application; and (4) the goal of management, that is, prevention of damage or suppression of populations.

The strategies used for specific forest insects change as new knowledge and technology is acquired. In some cases tactics become obsolete or are discontinued because of expense or legal regulation (e.g., some insecticides). In the United States contemporary strategies for a specific pest can be obtained through consultation with the U.S. Forest Service, Forest Pest Management, or the state forestry organizations.

REFERENCES

Anderson, J. F. 1976. Egg parasitoids of forest defoliating lepidoptera. In Anderson, J. F. and H. K. Kaya (Eds.), *Perspectives in Forest Entomology.* Academic Press, New York.

Anderson, J. F. and H. K. Kaya (Eds.). 1976. *Perspectives in Forest Entomology.* Academic Press, New York.

Apple, J. L. and R. F. Smith (Eds.). 1976. *Integrated Pest Management*. Plenum Press, New York.

Arnaud, Jr., P. H. 1978. *A Host Parasite Catalog of North American Tachinidae*. USDA SEA Miscellaneous Publication 1319.

Askew, R. R. 1971. *Parasitic Insects*. American Elsevier, New York.

Bakke, A., T. Saether, and T. Kvamme. 1983. Mass trapping of the spruce bark beetle, *Ips typographus*. Pheromone and trap technology. Reports for Norwegian Forestry Research Institute 38.3.

Bedard, W. D. and D. L. Wood. 1981. Suppression of *Dendroctonus brevicomis* by using a mass trapping tactic. In Mitchel, E. R. (Ed), *Management of Insect Pests with Semiochemicals: Concepts and Practice*. Plenum Press, New York.

Belanger, R. P. 1980. Silvicultural guidelines for reducing losses to the southern pine beetle. In Thatcher, R. C., J. L. Searcy, J. E. Coster, and J. H. Hertel (Eds.), *The Southern Pine Beetle*. U.S. Department of Agriculture Technical Bulletin 1613.

Beroza, M. (Ed.). 1970. *Chemicals Controlling Insect Behavior*. Academic Press. New York.

Beroza, M. (Ed.). 1976. *Pest Management with Insect Sex Attractants and Other Behavior Controlling Chemicals*. American Chemical Society Symposium Series 23, American Chemical Society, Washington, DC.

Berryman, A. A., G. D. Amman, R. W. Stark, and D. L. Kibbee (Eds.). 1978. Theory and practice of mountain pine beetle management in lodgepole pine forests. University of Idaho Forest Wildlife Range Experiment Station, Moscow.

Birch, M. C. (Ed.). 1974. *Pheromones*. North-Holland, New York.

Bird, F. T. and D. E. Elgee. 1957. A virus disease and introduced parasites as factors controlling the European spruce sawfly, *Diprion hercyniae* (Htg.), in central New Brunswick, *Can. Entomol.* **89**:371–378.

Borden, J. H. 1977. Behavioral responses of Coleoptera to pheromones, allomones, and kairomones. In Shorey, H. H. and J. J. McKelvey, Jr. (Eds.), *Chemical Control of Insect Behavior: Theory and Application*. Wiley, New York.

Borden, J. H. and J. A. McLean. 1981. Pheromone-based suppression of ambrosia beetles in industrial timber processing areas. In Mitchell, E. I. (Ed.), *Management of Insect Pests with Semiochemicals: Concepts and Practice*. Plenum Press, New York.

Brookes, M. H., R. W. Stark, and R. W. Campbell (Eds.). 1978. *The Douglas-Fir Tussock Moth: A Synthesis*. U.S. Department of Agriculture Technical Bulletin 1585.

Burges, H. D. and N. W. Hussey. 1971. *Microbial Control of Insects and Mites*. Academic Press, London.

Campell, R. W. 1963. Some ichneumonid–sarcophagid interactions in the gypsy moth. *Can. Entomol.* **95**:337–345.

Campbell, R. W. and T. R. Torgersen. 1982. Some effects of predacious ants on western spruce budworm pupae in north central Washington. *Environ. Entomol.* **11**:111–114.

Cantwell, G. E. (Ed.). 1974. *Insect Diseases*, Vols. I and II. Marcel Dekker, New York.

Carson, R. 1962. *Silent Spring*. Houghton Mifflin, Boston.

Clausen, C. R. 1978. *Introduced Parasites and Predators of Arthropod Pests in Weeds: A World Review*. USDA Agriculture Handbook 480.

Coppel, H. C. and J. W. Mertins. 1977. *Biological Insect Pest Suppression*. Springer-Verlag, Berlin.

Corbet, P. S. 1974. Habitat manipulation in the control of insects in Canada. *Proc. Tall Timbers Conf. Ecol. Animal Contr. Habitat Manage.* **5**:141–174.

Coulson, R. N. and R. W. Stark. 1982. Integrated management of bark beetles. In Mitten, J. B. and K. B. Strugeon (Eds.). *Bark beetles in North American Conifers: A System for the Study for Evolutionary Biology*. University of Texas Press, Austin.

Croft, B. F. and A. W. A. Brown. 1975. Responses of arthropod natural enemies to insecticides. *Annu. Rev. Entomol.* **20**:285–335.

Dahlsten, D. L., R. F. Luck, E. I. Schlinger, J. M. Wenz, and W. A. Copper. 1977. Evaluation of parasitoids, predators, spiders and defoliator associates of the Douglas-fir tussock moth, *Orgyia pseudotsugata* (McD.) (Lepdoptera: Lymantriidae), at low to moderate levels in central California. *Can. Entomol.* **107**:727–746.

David, W. A. L. 1975. The status of viruses pathogenic for insects and mites. *Annu. Rev. Entomol.* **20**:97–117.

DeBach, P. (Ed.) 1964. *Biological Control of Insect Pests and Weeds.* Reinhold, New York.

DeBach, P. 1974. *Biological Control by Natural Enemies.* Cambridge University Press, London.

Deck, E. 1975. Federal and state pesticide regulation and legislation. *Annu. Rev. Entomol.* **20**:119–131.

Dickson, J. G., R. N. Connor, R. R. Fleet, J. A. Jackson, and J. C. Knoll (Eds.). 1979. *The Role of Insectivorous Birds in Forest Ecosystems.* Academic Press, New York.

Doane, C. C. and M. L. McManus. 1981. *The Gypsy Moth: Research Towards Integrated Pest Management.* U.S. Department of Agriculture Forest Service Technical Bulletin 1584.

Dover, M. J. 1981. Position of the U.S. Environmental Protection Agency on registration of biorational pesticides. In Mitchell, E. I. (Ed.), *Management of Insect Pests With Semiochemicals: Concepts and Practice.* Plenum Press, New York.

Elkington, J. S. and R. T. Carde. 1981. The use of pheromone traps to monitor distribution and population trends of the gypsy moth. In Mitchell, E. R. (Ed.), *Management of Insect Pests with Semiochemicals: Concepts and Practices.* Plenum Press, New York.

Embree, D. G. 1965. The population dynamics of the winter moth in Nova Scotia, 1954–1962. *Mem. Entomol. Soc. Can.* **46**.

Embree, D. G. 1966. The role of introduced parasites in the control of winter moth in Nova Scotia. *Can. Entomol.* **98**:1159–1168.

Entomological Society of America. 1974. *Pesticide Handbook—Entoma.* Entomology Society of America, College Park, MD.

Falcon, L. A. 1976. Problems associated with the use of arthropod viruses in pest control. *Annu. Rev. Entomol.* **21**:305–323.

Ferron, P. 1978. Biological control of insect pests by entomogenous fungi. *Annu. Rev. Entomol.* **23**:409–442.

Finnegan, R. J. 1974. Ants as predators of forest pests. *Entomophaga Mem. Hors-Ser.* **7**:53–59.

Flint, M. L. and R. van den Bosch. 1981. *Introduction to Integrated Pest Management.* Plenum Press, New York.

Frankie, G. W. and C. S. Koehler. 1978. *Perspectives in Urban Entomology.* Academic Press, New York.

Franz, J. M. 1961. Biological control of pest insects in Europe. *Annu. Rev. Entomol.* **6**:183–200.

Georghiou, G. P. 1972. The evolution of resistance to pesticides. *Annu. Rev. Ecol. Syst.* **3**:133–168.

Hagen, K. S., R. van den Bosch, and D. L. Dahlsten. 1971. The importance of naturally-occurring biological control in the western United States. In Huffaker, C. B. (Ed.), *Biological Control.* Plenum Press, New York.

Hamel, D. R. 1981. *Forest Management Chemicals.* U.S. Department of Agriculture Forest Service Agriculture Handbook 585.

Hanover, J. W. 1975. Physiology of tree resistance to insects. *Annu. Rev. Entomol.* **20**:75–95.

Harper, J. D. 1974. *Forest Insect Control with Bacillus thuringiensis: Survey of Current Knowledge.* Auburn University Press, Auburn, AL.

Harrison, H. L., O. L. Loucks, J. W. Mitchell, D. F. Parkhust, C. R. Tracy, D. C. Watts, and V. J. Yannacone, Jr. 1970. Systems studies of DDT transport. *Science* **170**:503.

Hedden, R. L., S. J. Barras, J. E. Coster (Eds.) 1981. Hazard-rating systems in forest insect pest management. U.S. Department of Agriculture Forest Service General Technical Report WO-27.

Hodson, A. C. 1939. *Sacophaga aldrichi* Parker as a parasite of *Malacosoma disstria* Hbn. *J. Econ. Entomol.* **32**:396–401.

Huffaker, C. B. (Ed.). 1971. *Biological Control.* Plenum Press, New York.

Huffaker, C. B. and P. S. Messenger. (Eds.). 1976. *Theory and Practice of Biological Control.* Academic Press, New York.

Knight, F. B. 1958. The effects of woodpeckers on populations of the Engelmann spruce beetle. *J. Econ. Entomol.* **51**:603–607.

Knipling, E. F. 1979. *The Basic Principles of Insect Population Suppression and Management.* U.S. Department of Agriculture Handbook 512.

Kulman, H. M. 1974. Comparative ecology of North American Carabidae with special reference to biological control. *Entomophaga Mem.* **7**:61–70.

Lanier, G. N. 1981. Pheromone-baited traps and trap trees in the integrated management of bark beetles in urban areas. In Mitchell, E. R. (Ed.), *Management of Insect Pests with Semiochemicals: Concepts and Practice.* Plenum Press, New York.

Law, J. H. and F. E. Regnier. 1971. Pheromones. *Annu. Rev. Biochem.* **40**:533–548.

Leius, K. 1967. Influence of wild flowers on parasitism of tent caterpillar. *Can. Entomol.* **99**:444–446.

Lie, R. and A. Bakke. 1981. Practical results from the mass-trapping of *Ips typographus* in Scandinavia. In Mitchell, E. I. (Ed.), *Management of Insect Pests with Semiochemicals: Concepts and Practice.* Plenum Press, New York.

Luck, R. F. and D. L. Dahlsten. 1975. Natural decline of a pine needle scale (*Chionaspis pinifoliae* [Fitch]), outbreak at South Lake Tahoe, California, following cessation of adult mosquito control with malathion. *Ecology* **56**:893–904.

Maddox, J. V. 1982. Use of disease in pest management. In Metcalf, R. L. and W. H. Luckmann (Eds.), *Introduction to Insect Pest Management.* Wiley, New York.

Matthews, R. W. 1974. Biology of Braconidae. *Annu. Rev. Entomol.* **19**:15–32.

McGugan, B. M. and H. C. Coppel. 1962. Biological control of forest insects 1910–1958. In *A Review of the Biological Control Attempts Against Insects and Weeds in Canada.* Commonwealth Institute Biol. Contr. Tech. Commun. 2.

Metcalf, R. L. 1980. Changing role of insecticides in crop protection. *Annu. Rev. Entomol.* **25**:219–256.

Miller, C. A. 1966. The black-headed budworm in eastern Canada. *Can. Entomol.* **98**:592–613.

Mitchell, E. R. (Ed.) 1981. *Management of Insect Pests with Semiochemicals: Concepts and Practice.* Plenum Press, New York.

Morris, R. F. 1963. The dynamics of epidemic spruce budworm populations. *Entomol. Soc. Can. Mem.* **31**.

Munroe, E. G. 1971. Status and potential of biological control in Canada. In *Biological Control Programs Against Insect and Weeds in Canada 1959–1968.* Commonwealth Institute Biol. Contr. Tech. Commun. 4.

National Academy of Sciences. 1980. *Urban Pest Management.* National Academy of Sciences, Washington, DC.

National Academy of Sciences. 1975. *Pest Control. An Assessment of Present and Alternative Technologies.* Vol. 4. *Forest Pest Control.* National Academy of Sciences, Washington, DC.

National Academy of Sciences. 1972. *Pest Control Strategies of the Future.* National Academy of Sciences, Washington, DC.

National Academy of Sciences. 1969. *Principles of Plant and Animal Pest Control*. Vol. 3. *Insect Pest Management and Control*. National Academy of Sciences, Washington, DC.

Neilson, M. M. and R. F. Morris. 1964. The regulation of European spruce sawfly numbers in the Maritime Provinces of Canada from 1937 to 1963. *Can. Entomol.* **96**:773–784.

Neilson, M. M., R. Martineau, and A. H. Rose. 1971. *Diprion hercyniae* (Hartig), European spruce sawfly (Hymenoptera: Diprionidae). In *Biological Control Programs Against Insects and Weeds in Canada 1959–1968*. Commonwealth Institute Biol. Contr. Tech. Commun. 4.

Nordin, G. L. 1975. Transovarial transmission of a *Nosema* sp. infecting *Malacosoma americanum*. *J. Invertebr. Pathol.* **25**:221–228.

Nordlund, D. A., W. J. Lewis, R. L. Jones, H. R. Gross, Jr. 1976. Kairomones and their use for management of entomaphagous insects. IV. Effect of kairomones on productivity and longevity of *Trichogramma pretiosum* Riley (Hymenoptera: Trichogrammatidae). *J. Chem. Ecol.* **2**:67–72.

Olkowski, W., H. Olkowski, A. I. Kaplan, and R. Van den Bosch. 1978. The potential for biological control in urban areas: Shade tree insect pests. In Frankie, G. W. and C. S. Koehler (Eds.). *Perspectives in Urban Entomology*. Academic Press, New York.

Pal, R. and L. E. LaChance. 1974. The operational feasibility of genetic methods for control of insects of medical and veterinary importance. *Annu. Rev. Entomol.* **19**:269–291.

Payne, T. L. 1981. Disruption of southern pine beetle infestations with attractants and inhibitors. In Mitchell, E. I. (Ed.), *Management of Insect Pests with Semiochemicals: Concepts and Practice*. Plenum Press, New York.

Peacock, J. W., R. A. Cuthbert, and G. N. Lanier. 1981. Deployment of traps in a strategy to reduce populations of the European elm bark beetle, and the incidence of Dutch elm disease. In Mitchell, E. I. (Ed.), *Management of Insect Pests with Semiochemicals: Concepts and Practice*. Plenum Press, New York.

Perkins, J. H. 1982. *Insects, Experts, and the Insecticide Crisis*. Plenum Press, New York.

Plapp, F. W. 1976. Biochemical genetics of insecticide resistance. *Annu. Rev. Entomol.* **21**:179–197.

Plimmer, J. R. 1981. Formulation and regulation: Constraints on the development of semiochemicals for insect pest management. In Mitchell, E. I. (Ed.), *Management of Insect Pests with Semiochemicals: Concepts and Practice*. Plenum Press, New York.

Poinar, G. O., Jr. 1972. Nematodes as faculative parasites of insects. *Annu. Rev. Entomol.* **17**:103–122.

Prebble, M. L. (Ed.). 1975. *Aerial Control of Forest Insects in Canada*. Department of Environment, Ottawa.

Price, P. W. 1975. *Insect Ecology*. Wiley, New York.

Pschorn-Walcher, H. 1977. Biological Control of forest insects. *Annu. Rev. Entomol.* **22**:1–22.

Rabb, R. L. and F. E. Guthrie (Eds.). 1970. *Concepts of Pest Management*. North Carolina State University Press, Raleigh.

Reeks, W. A. and G. W. Barter. 1951. Growth reduction and mortality of spruce caused by the European spruce sawfly, *Gilpinia hercyniae* (Htg.) (Hymenoptera: Diprionidae). *For. Chron.* **27**:140–156.

Ripper, W. E. 1956. Effects of pesticides on balance of arthropod populations. *Annu. Rev. Entomol.* **1**:403–438.

Rudd, R. L. 1964. *Pesticides and the Living Landscape*. University of Wisconsin Press, Madison.

Sanders, C. J. 1981. Sex attractant traps: Their role in the management of spruce budworm. In Mitchell, E. R. (Ed.), *Management of Insect Pests with Semiochemicals: Concepts and Practice*. Plenum Press, New York.

Smith, D. M. 1962. *The Practice of Silviculture*, 7th ed. Wiley, New York.

Smith, H. S. 1919. On some phases of insect control by the biological method. *J. Econ. Entomol.* **34**:1–13.

Sower, L. L., G. E. Daterman, and C. Sartwell. 1981. Control of moth pests by mating disruption in forests of the western U.S. In Mitchell, E. I. (Ed.), *Management of Insect Pests with Semiochemicals: Concepts and Practice*, Plenum Press, New York.

Spurr, S. H. and B. V. Barnes. 1980. *Forest Ecology.* Wiley, New York.

Stairs, G. R. 1972. Pathogenic microorganisms in the regulation of forest insect populations. *Annu. Rev. Entomol.* **17**:355–372.

Stehr, F. W. 1982. Parasitoids and predators in pest management. In Metcalf, R. L. and W. H. Luckmann (Eds.), *Introduction to Insect Pest Management.* Wiley, New York.

Sweetman, H. L. 1958. *The Principles of Biological Control.* Brown, Dubuque.

Syme, P. D. 1975. The effects of flowers on the longevity and fecundity of two native parasites of the European pine shoot moth in Ontario. *Environ. Entomol.* **4**:337–346.

Thatcher, R. C., J. L. Searcy, J. E. Coster, and G. H. Hertel (Eds.). 1980. *The Southern Pine Beetle.* U. S. Department of Agriculture Technical Bulletin 1613.

Tinsley, T. W. 1979. The potential of insect pathogenic viruses as pesticidal agents. *Annu. Rev. Entomol.* **24**:63–87.

Townes, H. 1972. Ichneumonidae as biological control agents. *Proc. Tall Timers Conf. Ecol. Animal Contr. Habitat Manage.* **3**:235–248.

Turnock, W. J., K. L. Taylor, D. Schroder, and D. L. Dahlsten. 1976. Biological control of pests of coniferous forests. In Huffaker, C. B. and P. S. Messenger (Eds.), *Theory and Practice of Biological Control.* Academic Press, New York.

van den Bosch, R. 1978. *The Pesticide Conspiracy.* Doubleday, Garden City, NY.

van den Bosch, R., P. S. Messenger, and A. P. Gutierrez. 1982. *An Introduction to Biological Control.* Plenum Press, New York.

Varley, G. C. and G. R. Gradwell. 1968. Population models for the wintermoth. In Southwood, T. R. E. (Ed.), *Insect Abundance.* Proceedings of Royal Entomological Society, London 4. Blackwell, Oxford.

Ware, W. W. 1983. *Pesticides, Theory and Application.* Freeman, San Francisco.

Warren, G. L. 1971. Introduction of the masked shrew to improve control of forest insects in Newfoundland. *Proc. Tall Timbers Conf. Ecol. Animal Control Habitat Manage.* **2**:185–202.

Whitten, M. C. and G. G. Foster. 1975. Genetical methods of pest control. *Annu. Rev. Entomol.* **20**:461–476.

Wilkes, A. 1947. The effects of selective breeding on the laboratory propagation of insect parasites. *Proc. Roy. Soc. Lond.* **134B**:227–245.

Wilson, F. and C. B. Huffaker. 1976. The philosophy, scope, and importance of biological control. In Huffaker, C. B. and P. S. Messenger (Eds.), *Theory and Practice of Biological Control.* Academic Press, New York.

Wilson, G. G. 1977. Observations on the incidence rates of *Nosema fumiferanae* (Miscrosporidia) in a spruce budworm, *Choristoneura fumiferana* (Lepidoptera: Tortricidae) population. *Proc. Entomol. Soc. Ont.* **108**:144–145.

Wood, D. L. 1982. The role of pheromones, kairomones, and allomones in the host selection and colonization behavior of bark beetles. *Annu. Rev. Entomol.* **27**:411–446.

9 | IMPACT ASSESSMENT

INTRODUCTION

Assessment of impact of insects on forest ecosystems, the specialized forestry settings, and urban forests is one of the fundamental elements of IPM. Reference to Figure 5.8 indicates that information on impact of insects on forest resource values is one of the two main sources of input to benefit–cost integration, which is the methodology used in IPM planning and decision making.

As with the other components in the conceptual model of IPM (Figure 5.8), principles relating to impact assessment have been advanced as a result of the large multidisciplinary research and development programs on a small number of key pest species. Forest economists, and to some degree social scientists, participated with foresters, entomologists, and ecologists in formulating and applying principals of impact assessment. Much of the literature on impact has been summarized by Leuschner (1980) for the southern pine beetle, *Dendroctonus frontalis* Zimmermann; White and Schneeberger (1981) for the gypsy moth, *Lymantria dispar* (Linnaeus); Schreuder (1978) for the Douglas-fir tussock moth, *Orygia pseudotsugata* (McDunnough); and Walters (1978) for dwarf mistletoe, *Arceuthobium* spp.. General principles are reviewed by Stark (1979), Leuschner (1979), Leuschner and Newton (1974), and Waters and Stark (1980).

In this chapter we consider several aspects of the concept. In particular, our objectives are to (1) define the concept of impact, (2) examine categories of impact, (3) investigate various types of impact on resource values, and (4) illustrate how information on impact is used in IPM decision making.

DEFINITION OF IMPACT

There are several different and yet acceptable definitions of the term "impact." This circumstance occurs for two reasons. First, the term can be used to describe the effects of insects on the multiple values associated with forest property. Typical values include timber and fiber production, fish and wildlife, hydrology, grazing, recreation, real estate, and aesthetic enjoyment. Second, the effects of insects on these values can be interpreted from ecological, economic, or social perspectives. We discuss both these points below.

Following are examples of definitions given for impact:

1. Impact is simply any change brought about in the forest by an insect population. It may be positive or negative, affecting either flora or fauna. This definition, which is broad in scope, was provided by Leuschner (1980) and served as a guide in impact assessment for the southern pine beetle.

2. Pest impact is the net effect by pests on any forest resource that requires a management action change now or in the future. This (action change) implies that management objectives are previously set for forest resources (especially timber), and this is the standard against which impact is measured. This definition was provided in White and Schneeberger (1981) and was developed for impact assessment for the Douglas-fir tussock moth.

3. Impact is the cumulative net effects of insects and diseases, which results in modifications of management activities for specialized forest resource uses and values. This general definition was developed by participants in a USDA Forest Service workshop devoted to impact assessment held in 1972 and known as the "Marana Workshop."

4. Impact occurs when effects of insects and diseases result in response by people. This definition was developed specifically in reference to impact of gypsy moth infesting hardwood species in the eastern United States. The definition illustrates the fact that gypsy moth is perceived by the general public to be a serious pest in urban settings.

There are a number of additional definitions reported in the literature: Stark (1979), Waters and Stark (1980), and Johnson (1972), but those presented above represent the spectrum of sentiment on the subject. Although there is some difference between these definitions, there are several commonalities among them: (1) in the context of IPM, impact assessment is directed to species of insects considered to be *pests*—as we have previously indicated, most forest insects are not pests; (2) impact occurs when an insect causes some type of change in forest growth, productivity, or use; (3) this change is in conflict with planned or projected uses of the forest; (4) the conflict created by the change requires alteration of forest management plans, schedules, or uses; and (5) the change created by the insect can be measured and evaluated through some type of value system; thus some unit of value is affected.

CATEGORIES OF IMPACT

In general, impact of insects can be classed under three categories: ecological impacts, economic impact, and sociological impact. These three categories are not mutually exclusive (Stark 1979). The methods and procedures used to measure and evaluate impact differ with each category.

Ecological Impact

Ecological impact can be viewed from two different perspectives. The first perspective considers the functional roles of populations of phytophagous insects on forest trees, plant communities (stands), and forest ecosystems. No judgment is made regarding positive or negative effects of the roles played by the insects or the effects resulting from the interaction of insects and their hosts. In Chapter 7 we reviewed basic types of insect interaction at the different levels of ecological organization (individual trees, communities, and ecosystems). Examples of documented effects (impacts) resulting from grazing by phytophagous insects include the following: increased light penetration through the forest canopy, reduced competition among plants, altered plant species composition, altered plant biomass, increased rates of water runoff and nutrient leaching, increased rates of litter decomposition, and redistribution of nutrients (Stark 1979). Taken together, these effects (impacts), as well as many others, influence processes such as ecological succession and mineral cycling in forests.

The second perspective considers the various functional roles of phytophagous insects and the effects resulting from insect–host interaction in terms of a value system. A particular forest may be managed for a primary goal, such as timber production, and for several secondary goals such as grazing, wildlife and fish, and recreation. In other words, forest property is generally managed for particular purposes. The activities of phytophagous insects may be in conflict with management objectives. For example, one ecological effect of bark beetle infestation in pine forests is to truncate community development by killing mature hosts. This impact is known to influence a number of other ecological processes such as nutrient redistribution, development of early successional plants, and alteration of wildlife habitat. These effects (impacts) may be judged as beneficial (positive) or harmful (negative) depending on the planned use(s) of the forest. If the primary use of the forest was timber production, the ecological impact would clearly be judged harmful, and some attempt (e.g., application of an insect suppression technique) might be made to reduce or eliminate the impact. If the primary use of the forest was as a wilderness area, infestation by bark beetles would be considered as an expected ecological event and would likely be judged as a positive impact.

There are several significant issues regarding ecological impact, when viewed in the context of IPM, that is, the second perspective discussed above. First, the various functional roles (impacts) of phytophagous insects in forests are not well understood. Research at the ecosystem level of organization will eventually provide much better information on the roles of insects in forests, which, in turn, will permit better evaluation of the consequences of management decisions, such as insect suppression projects. Second, ecological impact resulting from forest management actions is now examined through formal documentation procedures. Environmental impact statements are required for many types of proposed manipulation of state, private, and federal forest lands. The main problem with environmental statements at present is the lack of fundamental knowledge regarding measuring and interpreting the results of manipulations performed on forest property. Munn (1975) provides a comprehensive review of the status of environmental impact assessment. Third, preparation of environmental impact statements is costly and requires input from a number of different academic specialists including foresters, economists, ecologists, and pest managers.

Economic Impact

Historically, greatest emphasis has been placed on economic impact, relative to the other two categories. Economic impact can be simply defined as the effect of phytophagous insects, diseases, and other injurious agencies on the monetary receipts from the production of goods and services from forest lands (Stark 1979).

An economic impact is any change in (1) a socially useful forest product; (2) socially useful items needed to produce a fixed level of forest products; or (3) the distribution of forest products, the income derived from them, or the cost of production (Leuschner 1980). Therefore, economic impact has three elements: production level, inputs for production, and the distribution of production and costs. In the context of IPM primary emphasis is generally placed on measuring the effects of pests species on the first element, production level (Leuschner 1980).

Economic impacts can be classified as primary or secondary. A *primary impact* is caused by the direct action of the insect, such as killing trees or defoliation. A *secondary impact* occurs as a result of the primary impact, such as changes in water yield caused by canopy reduction from the dead or defoliated tree, reduced number of visitor days to a campground because of the presence of dead trees, and so on.

The impact of insects on production levels has received considerable attention in agricultural crops. The terms "economic threshold" and "economic injury level" are used to describe the lowest insect population density that will cause economic damage. A pest has reached the economic threshold when the population is sufficient to cause damage valued at the cost of practical control (Stern et al. 1959, Stark 1979) (Figure 9.1). The concept of economic injury level has not been used as widely in forestry as agriculture because of the long-term nature of "crop" production in forestry and because of the multiple values placed on forest trees. The concept of economic injury level is clearly applicable in the specialized forestry settings such as seed orchards, nurseries, and Christmas tree plantations where the value of the crop with and without insect damage can be estimated. In forest ecosystems the value of the loss (impact on production) is more difficult to estimate. For example, Kanamitsu (1979) reported on a study of the rate of natural tree mortality in an intensively managed stand of Japanese cedar. In this stand the annual rate of tree mortality was approximately 3% a year:

Age of tree	10	20	30	40	50
Trees per hectare	3000	1900	1300	900	700

This percentage decrease was not considered as a real loss to the forest, but a necessary sacrifice for the remaining trees to attain better growth. The noxious level of pest density, for this example, was defined to be more than 30% tree mortality in 10 years, if stands were normally stocked. Economic loss to the forest was defined as the reduced value of dead trees that exceeds normal decreases in tree density (Kanamitsu 1979).

Parameters of the Economic Impact

There are a number of different parameters that influence economic impact of insects in forests. The more important parameters include those described in the following paragraphs (Stark 1979).

Ownership or User Group

Forests are owned, operated, and used by a broad spectrum of interested parties. The value of trees in forest ecosystems, the specialized forestry settings, and urban forests varies greatly. Furthermore, within a particular category of forest, the value placed on trees is often difficult to determine. For example, it is fairly simple to calculate the value of a stand of mature trees destined for harvest. However, this same stand would be valued differently if it occurred in an area designated as a wilderness.

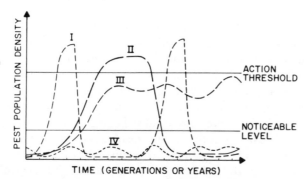

Figure 9.1 Hypothetical types of forest insect pest population gradation relative to the economic injury level (Waters 1979): (I) violent oscillations, very rapid increase to very high densities, sharp dropoff or collapse of populations in 1–3 years (or generations), variable time between epidemic increase (e.g., Douglas-fir tussock moth, southern pine beetle, some pine engraver beetles); (II) more or less regular oscillations, less rapid increase to high densities but longer duration at those levels, rapid decline in 4–8 years, time between epidemic increases more or less the same (e.g., gypsy moth, spruce budworm); (III) initial rise in densities following establishment in new areas gradual, population densities maintained at relatively high levels with only weak oscillations over extended period (>10 years), densities never reaching levels of types I and II (e.g., European pine shoot moth, white pine weevil, balsam woolly adelgid); (IV) oscillations of very low amplitude, average densities very low (rarely noticeable even at "peak" densities) [e.g., oak leaf tier(s), red turpentine beetle, some pine sawflies].

Vagaries Associated with the Marketplace

In the context of wood and fiber production, forest trees are a commodity with a market value that fluctuates in response to many variables. Severe insect outbreaks and natural disasters such as hurricanes, ice storms, and wind storms can temporarily influence supply of wood and fiber. Excesses or deficits relative to demand can cause fluctuations in the value of trees, which are difficult or impossible to predict.

Regulatory or Tax Laws

Under some circumstances federal and state laws make provisions for natural disasters, including outbreaks by insects and resulting damage. These laws and regulations may result in positive economic benefit being derived by the landowner as a result of insect outbreaks.

Objectives and Flexibility of Landowners and Managers

Both the timing and location of insect outbreaks have a major influence on the economic impact of insect outbreaks. For example, an outbreak occurring in a stand scheduled for harvest may be extremely consequential and require major alteration in management plans in order to meet demands from mills. In contrast to this circumstance, insect outbreaks in residual stands, that is, stands not immediately needed for the production of goods, may have little immediate consequence to the owner or manager.

Effects on Residual Stands Under Management

A management unit in which an outbreak has occurred can be influenced in both positive and negative ways. For example, productivity of stands may be increased following an insect outbreak as a result of reduced competition between trees, nutrient enrichment, increased sunlight, and other factors. Furthermore, the quality of wildlife habitat may be increased thereby improving hunting. To some degree these benefits offset losses attributable to the insect outbreak. By contrast, the residual stands may require extensive site preparation and replanting to bring them back into production. These activities are costly and disruptive to management schedules and are impacts in addition to the actual insect-caused losses.

Investment Consideration

An insect outbreak can result in direct and measurable losses. Part of the cost associated with the loss includes expenditures for suppression, site preparation, replanting, and other measures. These costs can be estimated at the time of the event but also must be discounted over time. The following simplified example illustrates the issue. Suppose that the interest rate on a dollar today is 8%. One could invest the dollar at 8% and have $1.08 in one year ($1.00 × $1.08) or $1.17 in 2 years ($1.00 × $1.08 × $1.08). Therefore, a dollar received 2 years from now is worth less than a dollar received today because the dollar received today would have grown to $1.17

in 2 years. Similarly, $0.9259 invested today is worth $1.00 in a year ($0.9259 × $1.08), and $0.8571 is worth $1.00 in 2 years ($0.8571 × $1.08 × $1.08). Therefore, economists say that a dollar received 1 year in the future is worth only 93¢ today (present value) and one received 2 years in the future is worth only 86¢ today, at 8% interest. This circumstance occurs because the opportunity cost of investing the money at 8% for 1 year or 2 years has been lost. *Costs* are treated in the same way. A dollar spent a year in the future is valued at only 93¢ because one had the opportunity to invest that dollar at 8% interest for the year. Similarly, a dollar spent 2 years in the future is valued at only 86¢. Therefore, there are two major problems in evaluating the impact of losses plus expenses, that is, costs incurred as a result of an insect outbreak: (1) determining the appropriate interest or discount rate and (2) determining the value of the "crop" at the end of the projected rotation (Leuschner and Lewis 1979). The losses can, of course, be valued beyond a single rotation.

Costs of Contemplated Action

Forest protection, which includes consideration of fire, diseases, and insects, requires considerable organization and planning. There are direct costs associated with these activities. Therefore, managerial costs should be included in impact analyses in the same manner as costs associated with suppression and prevention projects and estimates of losses.

In summary, economic impact of insects on forest ecosystems, on the specialized forestry settings, and in urban forests is extremely difficult to measure and evaluate. Forest economists utilize mathematical models to aid in determining the economic impact of insects as well as the costs and benefits of suppression tactics and strategies used to reduce impacts.

Social Impact

We use the term "social impact" to refer to the effects of insects on aesthetic values associated with forests. Stark (1979) used the term "axiological impact." The latter expression is derived from the branch of philosophy, axiology, which deals with matters of morals, aesthetics, and metaphysics. Social impacts are difficult to express in quantitative terms but nevertheless represent a category of impact important to a large number of forest users.

Economists, working with social scientists, have attempted to define social impacts in a precise manner by examining patterns of use of forests. In general, aesthetic values stem from recreational uses of forests; that is, aesthetic values usually occur in conjunction with other primary activities such as hunting, fishing, and backpacking. To some degree, which may be very difficult to define, insect outbreaks can influence the primary activities in both positive and negative ways. For example, severe defoliation may be unpleasant to a hiker, inconsequential to a hunter, and beneficial to a fisherman.

One technique employed by economists in defining social impacts is to measure patterns of recreational use of forests. During or after an insect outbreak, a recreationist might continue to use a particular site, substitute another site, or no longer recreate. Of course, the type of recreation and degree of distraction created by the insect outbreak enter into the use pattern (Leuschner and Young 1978).

To this point we have emphasized social impacts as they relate to individuals physically in the forest and involved in some type of primary activity. Social impacts are also perceived by those individuals who view the forest from a distance and obtain a scenic vista. The importance of scenic vistas is a function of the physiography of the area. For example, in the coastal plain of the southeastern United States there is no vista relative to mountainous regions of the country.

In summary, social or aesthetic impacts resulting from insects, although difficult to define in quantitative terms, are an important component in the concept of impact. In some cases it is possible to define social impacts in terms of economic values. This definition is usually based on primary recreational uses of forests.

IMPACT OF INSECTS ON RESOURCE VALUES

Forests are managed primarily for the following purposes: timber and fiber production, hydrology, fish and wildlife, recreation, and grazing. Impact of insects on these resource values, as we have seen, can be viewed from economic, ecological, and social perspectives. The exact nature of the impact is determined by (1) the type of activity of the insect (e.g., defoliation, tree killing, etc.), (2) the distribution and abundance of the insect, (3) the particular resource value of concern, and (4) the particular perspective of the individual or organization involved in making the impact assessment with regard to the category of impact (economic, ecological, or social). Most emphasis in impact assessment in forests has been directed to insects that directly affect the economics of timber and fiber production. Furthermore, the assessments have been made when the damaging insects were abundant and widespread. Often the motivation behind impact assessment is to determine the various costs and benefits associated with suppression or prevention projects.

In the following sections we examine some of the major types of insect impact on the primary forest values. It is important to recognize that each of the feeding groups affects forests in different ways. Specific impacts for the feeding groups were covered in the section on categories of impact.

Timber Production

We have discussed in some detail the various types of interaction of insects with trees (and plant modules), communities (stands), and forest ecosystems

(Figure 9.2). If our interest is simply evaluating the effects of insects on forest productivity, specifically the rate of production of wood and fiber, the significant interactions at the tree and stand level are illustrated in Figure 9.3 (Waters 1979). The various changes in the stand parameters, caused by insects, influence the value of the stand. In our discussion of economic impact we emphasized that there is a direct and immediate loss attributable to insect damage, but that this loss must be discounted through to at least the end of the rotation.

Specific insect pests exert different primary economic impacts. For example, bark beetles that kill their host, e.g., *Dendroctonus* spp., influence the stand parameter *mortality rate* (Figure 9.3) first. This impact directly and immediately influences timber and fiber production and would likely be of greatest concern to the forest manager. The other stand parameters

Figure 9.2 Longleaf pine plantation in south Georgia intensively managed for timber production. (U.S. Forest Service.)

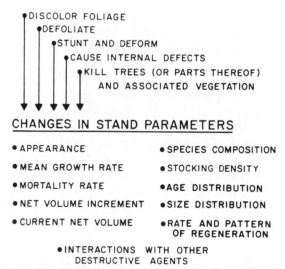

Figure 9.3 Pest effects on individual trees and consequent changes in stand parameters. (From Waters 1979.)

are, of course, also affected (Leuschner et al. 1978, Leuschner 1980). By contrast, the most significant direct impact of a defoliator may be on the stand parameters *mean growth rate* and *net volume increment*. In an urban forest the primary stand parameter affected would likely be appearance (Schreuder 1978, White and Schneeberger 1981).

Hydrology

Hydrologic impacts of insects on forests are measured in terms of water quantity (yield), timing and duration of high and low flows (regimen), and water quality. Most hydrologic studies are conducted in gauged watersheds where these three variables can be monitored (Figure 9.4). In general, water yield increases as precipitation increases and as vegetation decreases. Regimen is determined by the timing of precipitation, soil permeability, soil water deficits, and soil depth. In general, water stays in the watershed longer and flow is attenuated in response to the amount of vegetation present. There are several aspects of water quality. The most critical components are sediment, dissolved nutrients, and water temperature (Leuschner et al. 1979). Only a few studies deal directly with impacts of insects on hydrology (Bethlahmy 1975, Corbett and Heilman 1975, Leuschner et al. 1979, Leuschner 1980, Schreuder 1978, White and Schneeberger 1981). Howell et al. (1975) provide a comprehensive treatment of mineral cycling in southeastern forest ecosystems, which includes consideration of the roles played by arthropods.

Figure 9.4 Notch-type weir used to monitor hydrological events on a mountainous watershed in Arizona (Burro Mt. Watershed, Apache National Forest). (U.S. Forest Service.)

In general, insect outbreaks in forests increase water yield and decrease water retention time on watersheds. These circumstances occur because reduced vegetation levels, resulting from insect consumption, decrease the rate of evapotranspiration and increase the rate of runoff. Water quality is influenced in several ways: increased nutrient content of streams (primarily phosphorous and nitrogen) and organic debris, increased turbidity, and slightly increased temperature. The nutrient loading of streams and increased turbidity occur as a result of increased levels of frass production and increased rates of transport out of the watershed. The amount of runoff (retention time) is a function of duration and intensity of storm events, steepness of terrain (percent slope), permeability of the soil, and previous soil moisture conditions. Increases in stream temperature occur because of reduced shading resulting from tree mortality or defoliation.

Although insects have been demonstrated to exert measurable impacts on water quality and quantity, in general these impacts are not of economic importance. Leuschner (1979) concluded that for southern pine beetle, there is no economic impact because the supply of water at the watershed is so large that people will not pay for it and because the impact on water quality is too small to make any practical difference. However, local conditions of water shortage, insect infestation characteristics, or other unique factors could cause economic impacts (Leuschner 1979).

Fish and Wildlife

Phytophagous insects impact on fish and wildlife populations primarily through influences on habitat structure and food resources (Figure 9.5). Insects and other arthropods are also involved in vectoring diseases of wildlife, but we do not consider this type of impact.

We have previously discussed (Chapter 7) the various ways that phytophagous insects influence individual trees and plant modules, communities (stands), and forest ecosystems. The activities of phytophagous insects alter the distribution and abundance of plant species that are used as food and habitat by wildlife. Changes in the pattern of vegetation also influence fish populations through modifications of water quality and quantity (see previous section). Of course, insects serve as a primary or secondary food source for insectivorous birds, mammals, and fish. The major effect of outbreaks of insects on wildlife in forests is to change stand parameters such as density, species composition, and age distribution. Of course, the high population density of the insects during outbreaks is exploited by the insectivores.

There have been few studies directed specifically to defining quantitatively the effects of insect outbreaks on populations of fish and wildlife. Most of the information available has been inferred. The probable effects of activities of insects on fish and wildlife have been deduced by examining

Figure 9.5 Wildlife openings and fringe planting of pine to enhance cover, habitat, and food (Monongahela National Forest, West Virginia). (U.S. Forest Service.)

natural history, food requirements, preferred habitats, and so on in terms of the altered forest conditions created by the insects. These studies have been qualitative because of difficulties associated with measuring fish and wildlife populations and because the other forest values (e.g., timber and fiber production) generally receive more attention during insect outbreaks. Maine et al. (1980) conducted a qualitative study on the impact of southern pine beetle infestations on wildlife. In this study six different areas of impact were examined (Figure 9.6): increase in food supply for insectivores resulting from high population levels of secondary insects, increase in stream temperature and sedimentation, increase edge effect (i.e., increase in plant species diversity created by gaps produced as a result of infestations), change in availability of nesting sites for birds, change in shelter and cover, and change in amount and kinds of food available. The wildlife species considered included woodpeckers, turkey, quail, other birds, squirrels, rabbits, deer, small mammals, fish, and other mammals (opossum, foxes, skunks, etc.). This study concluded that southern pine beetle infestation had a positive impact on the species studied, principally because of increased food and habitat diversity.

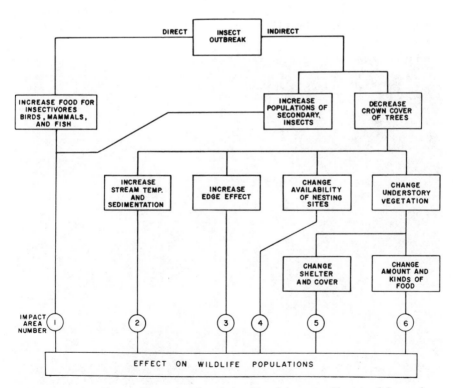

Figure 9.6 Flow diagram illustrating the relationship of six areas of impact of the southern pine beetle on fish and wildlife populations. (From Maine et al 1980.)

Recreation

Forests are used for many different types of recreation. The most common activities include camping, hiking, fishing, boating, hunting, and observing (Figure 9.7). To define the potential or actual impacts of insects on outdoor recreation, it is necessary to consider the basic elements associated with the activity. Clawson and Knetsch (1974) identified five distinctly different phases of outdoor recreation: anticipation, travel, on-site experience, travel back, and recollection. The net effect generated to the recreationist of a single recreation experience is a composite of these phases (Schreuder 1978). Insects can have an impact on recreation by intervening into one or more of the phases. Negative or positive impacts influence not only the individual(s) involved directly in the recreation activity, but the service industries that provide the facilities and means for recreation.

Several studies have been conducted on the impact of insect outbreaks on recreation (e.g., Downing et al. 1977, Downing and Williams 1978 for the Douglas-fir tussock moth; Leuschner and Young 1978 for the southern pine beetle; and Michalson and Findeis 1976 for mountain pine beetle, *D. ponderosae* Hopkins). In general, *phytophagous insects* had little impact on recreation. In Chapter 18 we discuss recreational insects (and other arthropods) in detail. The insects catalogued as "recreational insects" are

Figure 9.7 Recreational use of forested land. Fishermen float by old bridge pilings on Beaver Dam Creek, Mississippi. (U.S. Forest Service.)

generally better known because of their medical importance. These insects and other arthropods have a distinct impact on the pattern and use of forests for recreation.

Grazing

Phytophagous insects can have an impact on domesticated herbivores by increasing grazing capacity of the forest. This circumstance occurs when activities of the insects (e.g., defoliation, tree mortality) create conditions that support greater forage production. This benefit also accrues to grazing wildlife species (Figure 9.8).

Evaluation of the effects of insects on grazing involves several steps. First, the change produced by the insects on crown cover or density must be estimated. This change is related to amount of forage (herbage) that is produced. The change in herbage is then translated to grazing capacity change. Finally, the change in grazing capacity can be extrapolated to a region, based on an estimate of the distribution and size of infestations producing the change (Leuschner 1980).

In general, although grazing may benefit by insect outbreaks, the value of the benefits, in terms of cash receipts for livestock, is negligible. Furthermore, other values, such as timber and fiber production, are affected to a greater degree by insect outbreaks.

Figure 9.8 Example of type of forage available to domesticated and wild herbivores in a forest (Snoqualmie National Forest, Washington). (U.S. Forest Service.)

Other Forest Values

In the preceding sections we have emphasized insect impact as it relates to timber and fiber production, hydrology, fish and wildlife, recreation, and grazing. There are other areas of impact that we have not addressed. For example, residential property and risk of fire are both influenced by insect outbreaks. Furthermore, we have not emphasized the considerable importance of insects and other arthropods in transmission of disease. Populations of these insects are as subject to outbreaks as the phytophagous species and are capable of causing severe impacts on forest use and wildlife.

BENEFIT–COST ANALYSIS

In the generalized model of IPM (Figure 5.8) the last component in the research and development section is benefit–cost integration. There are two inputs to this component: (1) treatment strategies and (2) impact on resource values. Both of these subjects have been covered in some detail. The results obtained from benefit–cost integration lead directly to the forest resource management component. If a forest manager perceives that there is a problem resulting from an insect outbreak, judgments on what action to take or not to take become an issue of considerable importance. The decision-making process involves consideration of the probable impacts of the infestation on forest resource values and on evaluation of the treatment tactics or strategies available. The usual procedure for making these judgments is based on what is termed a *cost–benefit analysis*.

Cost–benefit analysis (CBA = BCA = B/C analysis = B–C analysis) is an investment analysis procedure. The procedure was developed in the early 1900s, but its application in assessing forest pest management programs occurred in the 1970s as part of the research and development work conducted on the gypsy moth, southern pine beetle, mountain pine beetle, Douglas-fir tussock moth, and spruce budworms, *Choristoneura fumiferana* (Clemens) and *C. occidentalis* Freeman. CBA is a loosely defined set of techniques and principles used to evaluate alternatives for achieving defined public goals (Sassone and Shaffer 1978). The public goals usually require a financial investment. Achieving the public goal is the return on that investment. CBA can be applied to either public or private investment analysis, but common usage implies only public investment analysis. The procedure compares costs to public benefits to indicate whether public investment is worthwhile. The procedures for CBA analysis are loosely defined because public projects are very different and no one unique procedure can be written to cover all cases. This circumstance is certainly true for forest pest management projects (Leuschner and Lewis 1979).

Within the framework of IPM, the *benefits* of a suppression or prevention program are the damages that the program prevents from occurring. In estimating benefits it is usually necessary to estimate the level of damage that would occur without the program and then estimate the proportion of these damages that the program will eliminate. The multiple uses (discussed above) associated with forests makes valuing damage very difficult. Along with the benefits of a prevention or suppression project, it is necessary to estimate the *costs* of the project. Cost analysis is generally easier than benefit analysis because most costs are labor or materials for which estimates are readily available.

Interpretation of the estimated benefits and costs is straightforward. One simply adopts the tactic or strategy which has the greatest positive difference between benefits and costs. A program is not undertaken if the benefits are less than the costs (Leuschner 1979). This "with-without" criterion is one general principle that is useful in all CBA analysis.

Leuschner and Lewis (1979) provide a simple example of the use of CBA. The manager of a seed orchard, stocked with trees that produce superior seed, has an infestation of seed and cone insects. The problem that the manager faces is whether a suppression project, using insecticides, is needed. Suppose that the suppression project prevents seed and cone insects from destroying a crop of superior seed, which can provide enough seed to plant 10,000 acres in a year. Superior trees yield 50 cords when harvested at age 25, whereas the regular seed source trees yield 30 cords. With the suppression project, 500,000 cords will be harvested. Without the project, 300,000 cords will be harvested. The benefits derived from the project are 200,000 cords occurring 25 years in the future. The costs include labor and materials for the suppression project. In this example we consider only one value, fiber production. In most forest insect prevention or suppression projects, the other values (recreation, hydrology, fish and wildlife, and grazing) must be included.

The basic criterion for policy decisions on initiating, increasing, or decreasing forest insect management programs is that the benefits resulting from the action exceed the costs. Actual determination of whether this criterion has been met is a complicated task. Each of the forest values must be examined. In some cases, it is possible to identify benefits through straightforward analysis. For example, Leuschner and Newton (1974) defined the timber production benefits that arise from preventing insect attack (Figure 9.9). It is possible to place a value on each of these benefits. However, the social or aesthetic benefits that do or do not occur as a result of suppression or prevention projects are much more difficult to value. Therefore, inclusion of aesthetic benefits into a CBA is a difficult task.

It should be obvious that one of the major issues in conducting CBA is obtaining the information needed for the analysis. Interpretation of the significance of the information is another major issue. Actual data collection is a normal activity of monitoring forests (see next chapter). Interpretation of the information requires individual judgment. Decision making in IPM is characteristically done under conditions of uncertainty. Enhanced de-

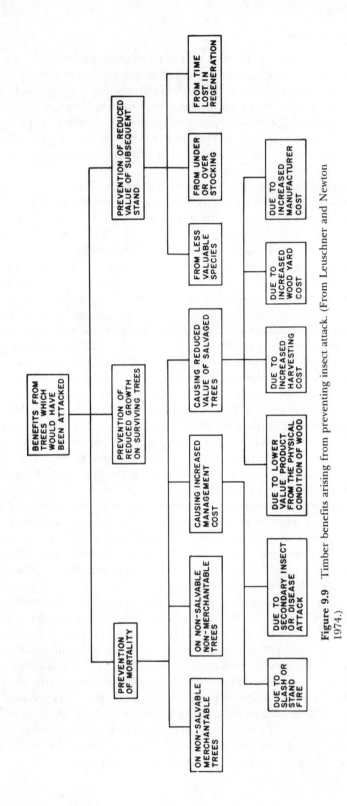

Figure 9.9 Timber benefits arising from preventing insect attack. (From Leuschner and Newton 1974.)

cision making by forest managers is aided by the use of mathematical models of pest population dynamics, stand dynamics, and impact. Information obtained from mathematical models can be organized by using decision support systems (see Chapter 10). However, the final judgments in IPM generally require CBA.

REFERENCES

Bethlahmy, N. 1975. A Colorado episode: Beetle epidemic, ghost forests, more streamflow. *Northwest Sci.* **49**:95–105.

Clawson, M. and J. L. Knetsch. 1974. *Economics of Outdoor Recreation.* Resources for the Future, Inc., Johns Hopkins Press, Baltimore.

Corbett, E. S. and J. M. Heilman. 1975. Effects of management practices on water quality and quantity: The Newark, N.J. Municipal Watersheds. In *Municipal Watershed Management.* USDA Forest Service General Technical Report NE-13.

Downing, K. B. and W. R. Williams. 1978. Douglas-fir tussock moth: Did it affect private recreational business in Northeastern Oregon. *J. For.* **76**:29–30.

Downing, K. B., P. B. Delucchi, and W. R. Williams. 1977. Impact of the Douglas-fir tussock moth on forest recreation in the Blue Mountains. USDA Forest Service Research Paper PNW-224.

Howell, F. G., J. B. Gentry, and M. H. Smith (Eds.). 1975. *Mineral Cycling in Southeastern Ecosystems.* ERDA Symposium Series. CONF-740513.

Johnson, N. E. 1972. The assessment of social and economic impact of pests. In Stark, R. W. and A. R. Gittins (Eds.), *Pest Management for the 21st Century.* Idaho Research Foundation. Natural Resources Series 2.

Kanamitsu, K. 1979. One aspect of damage to the forest caused by insects. In Waters, W. E. (Ed.), *Current Topics in Forest Entomology.* USDA Forest Service General Technical Report WO-8.

Leuschner, W. A. 1979. Impact analysis, interpretation, and modeling. In Waters, W. E. (Ed.), *Current Topics in Forest Entomology.* USDA Forest Service General Technical Report WO-8.

Leuschner, W. A. 1980. Impacts of the southern pine beetle. In Thatcher, R. C., J. L. Searcy, J. E. Coster, and G. D. Hertel (Eds.), *The Southern Pine Beetle.* USDA Forest Service Technical Bulletin 1631.

Leuschner, W. A. and J. Lewis. 1979. From notes taken by the senior author at a workshop on benefit/cost analysis at the Southern Forest Insect Work Conference, August 1979, Lexington, KY.

Leuschner, W. A. and C. M. Newton. 1974. Benefits of forest insect control. *Bull. Entomol. Soc. Am.* **20**:223–227.

Leuschner, W. A. and R. L. Young. 1978. Estimating southern pine beetle's impact on reservoir recreation. *For. Sci.* **24**:527–537.

Leuschner, W. A., T. A. Max, G. D. Spittle, and H. W. Wilson. 1978. Estimating southern pine beetle's timber damages. *Bull. Entomol. Soc. Am.* **24**:29–34.

Leuschner, W. A., D. G. Shore, and D. W. Smith. 1979. Estimating the southern pine beetle's hydrologic impact. *Bull. Entomol. Soc. Am.* **25**:147–149.

Maine, J. D., W. A. Leuschner, and A. R. Tipton. 1980. A qualitative analysis of the southern pine beetle's wildlife impact. Publication FWS-1-80, School of Forest and Wildlife Resources, VPI and SU, Blacksburg.

Michalson, E. L. and J. Findeis. 1979. Economic impact of mountain pine beetle on outdoor recreation. In Waters, W. E. (Ed.), *Current Topics in Forest Entomology.* USDA Forest Service General Technical Report WO-8.

Munn, R. E. 1975. (Ed.). *Environmental Impact Assessment, Principles and Procedures.* United Nations Environmental Program (UNEP), Environment Canada, and UNESCO. SCOPE Report 5. Toronto.

Sassone, P. G. and W. A. Schaffer. 1978. *Cost–Benefit Analysis: A Handbook.* Academic Press, New York.

Schreuder, G. F. 1978. Socioeconomic impact. In Brookes, M. H., R. W. Stark, and R. W. Campbell, (Eds.), *The Douglas-Fir Tussock Moth: A Synthesis.* USDA Forest Service Technical Bulletin 1585.

Stark, R. W. 1979. The concept of impact in integrated pest management. In Waters, W. E. (Ed.), *Current Topics in Forest Entomology.* USDA Forest Service General Technical Report WO-8.

Stern, V. M., R. F. Smith, R. van den Bosch, and K. S. Hagen. 1959. The integrated control concept. *Hilgardia* **29**:81–101.

Walters, J. W. 1978. Impact evaluation for dwarf mistletoe-infested ponderosa pine in the Southwest. In Scharpf, R. F. and J. R. Parmeter (Eds.), *Symposium on Dwarf Mistletoe Control Through Forest Management.* USDA Forest Service General Technical Report PSW-31.

Waters, W. E. 1979. Biomonitoring, assessment, and prediction in forest pest management systems. In Cairns, J., G. P. Patil, and W. E. Waters (Eds.), *Environmental Biomonitoring, Assessment, Prediction, and Management—Certain Case Studies and Related Quantitative Issues.* International Co-operative Publishing House, Fairland, MD.

Waters, W. E. and R. W. Stark. 1980. Forest pest management: Concept and reality. *Annu. Rev. Entomol.* **25**:479–509.

White, W. E. and N. F. Schneeberger. 1981. Socioeconomic impacts. In Doane, C. C. and M. L. McManus (Eds.), *The Gypsy Moth: Research Towards Intregrated Pest Management.* USDA Forest Service Technical Bulletin 1584.

10 MONITORING PEST POPULATIONS AND FOREST STANDS

INTRODUCTION

The forest insect survey is the operational component of integrated pest management aimed at monitoring the distribution and abundance of forest insects or the damage they cause. Surveys are a central issue in forest resource management because they provide the data (in the form of measurements and estimates of populations and population artifacts) that are used in IPM decision-making (see Figure 5.8). Although surveys are an applied component of IPM, the methodologies used are founded on (1) basic principles of population dynamics in relation to host trees (2) sampling techniques developed to collect data on specific insects and insect groups, and (3) statistical and computational procedures for analysis and interpretation of sample data.

In this chapter we examine a number of different aspects of forest insect surveys: (1) we consider different types of survey and their appropriate uses, (2) we review basic procedures used in collection and analysis of survey data, (3) we discuss applications of advanced technology in forest survey, and (4) we define the organizations responsible for conducting surveys.

A number of reviews treat forest insect surveys. Following are general references that cover specific aspects of the subject: Morris (1960), Knight (1967), NAS (1969), Ruesink and Kogan (1975), Southwood (1978), Coster and Searcy (1979), and the U.S. Forest Service Manual.

TYPES OF FOREST INSECT SURVEYS

There are several basic guidelines that determine the various kinds of insect surveys and define their appropriate uses: (1) surveys are conducted for a number of different purposes; (2) surveys are directed to different forest situations including forest ecosystems, specialized forestry settings (seed orchards, nurseries, Christmas tree plantations, etc.), and urban forests; and (3) the procedures used will vary according to the goal of the survey, the type of forest situation being surveyed, the availability of needed sampling and analytical technology, and the resources available for the survey.

Several different systems have been used to classify surveys. One common method is to distinguish surveys according to the type of data collected. With the use of this approach, a survey may be classed as qualitative or quantitative. A second approach is to segregate surveys according to function. Surveys classed in this manner include (1) detection surveys, (2) biological evaluations, (3) loss or damage surveys, and (4) pest control evaluations. This second system is used to the U.S. Forest Service in classifying both insect and disease surveys. A third approach is to define survey activities in the context of providing information for IPM. We will discuss the latter two systems of classification separately and identify which types of survey utilize or require qualitative or quantitative data.

Functional Classification of Forest Insect Surveys

Detection Surveys

The detection survey, as the name implies, is oriented to identification of insects, insect-caused damage, or products resulting from insect activity. Detection surveys, which are the most common type, are founded on basic principles of insect and plant taxonomy (Chapter 3) and recognition of signs or damage that result from insect activity (Chapter 4).

Detection surveys are generally qualitative in that we are interested in identifying the presence and kinds of species rather than estimating population size. The procedures used in detection surveys involve basic entomological techniques for collecting, preserving, and identifying insects. Most detection surveys are based on direct observation by a trained individual but can involve application of remote sensing techniques using cameras.

Detection surveys are conducted in forest ecosystems, specialized forestry settings, and urban forests. Examples of detection surveys include (1) exploration and/or inventory of insects associated with a specific ecosystem, geographic region, and so on; (2) exploration for candidate biological control agents; and (3) identification of specific or potential pest species. It is also noteworthy that systematic insect collections are developed from detection surveys.

Biological Evaluations

Biological evaluations are surveys directed at appraising some attribute of existing populations of a particular species. For example, we might be interested in defining population size and distribution of a pest species. Furthermore, we might also want to make a prognosis about the growth or decline of a population over a period of time.

Biological evaluations are most useful if they are quantitative. Many different procedures have been developed for sampling insect populations. Southwood (1978) provides a comprehensive review of the various methodologies. Specific sampling procedures exist for most of the serious forest insect pests. Often the result of insect activity is measured rather than populations per se. For example, it is easier to count webs of the fall webworm, *Hyphantria cunea* (Drury), rather than webworms. Likewise, bark beetle activity at certain times of the year is easily identified by the presence of faded tree crowns. The important point is that it is necessary to relate the sample information to actual population size. This step is by no means a simple one. In practice, most biological evaluations utilize the best sampling procedures available with interpretations of the meaning of the information based on professional experience and historical records.

Biological evaluations can be conducted in forest ecosystems, specialized forestry settings, and urban forests. An example of a biological evaluation is the annual survey of southern pine beetle, *Dendroctonus frontalis* Zimmermann, conducted in the spring of each year by most Southern state forestry services and the U.S. Forest Service. These surveys are designed to detect the location, number, and approximate size of infestations of the insect. The infestations, which are termed "spots," are visible from aircraft because the crowns of attacked trees are discolored. These surveys are used as the basis for predicting population levels for the summer months and in evaluating the need for suppression projects.

Loss or Damage Surveys

Loss or damage surveys are conducted in order to evaluate the impact of pests on forest resource values. These surveys are generally conducted in the aftermath of an outbreak of a particular pest. Information from the surveys can be used simply to calculate loss or damage estimates or in making judgments regarding utilization of damaged or killed trees. Furthermore, these surveys (along with biological evaluations) can be conducted on values other than timber and fiber production. For example, it is possible to evaluate the effects of insect depredation on recreational uses of a forest.

Loss or damage surveys are, again, most useful if they are quantitative. The procedures used in loss or damage surveys are based on detecting and estimating the amount of depredation resulting from insect activity. Insect population levels are not of particular importance unless we are interested in forecasting further loss.

Loss or damage surveys are a vital part of forest resource management. Impact assessments can be made in response to immediate or existing pest situations. However, you will recall that IPM is concerned, in part, with evaluating impact over a period of time that spans the rotation period of a forest (see Chapter 9).

Loss or damage surveys can be conducted in forest ecosystems, specialized forestry settings, and urban forests. An example of a loss survey in a specialized forestry setting is evaluation of the impact of seed and cone insects in seed orchards. Cone and seed production in an orchard can be estimated. It is possible to calculate potential production during winter months and later evaluate the impact of pest insects by comparing actual yield realized in the fall when cones are harvested.

Pest Control Evaluations

Pest control evaluations are surveys conducted to appraise the efficacy and/ or safety of a treatment tactic or strategy (referred to hereafter as a *treatment*) applied to suppress populations of an insect. This type of survey can also be used to evaluate treatments aimed at prevention of insect-caused damage. The ultimate goal of a treatment is to protect one or more of the resource values that we associate with a forest. Therefore, the standard used for evaluating a treatment is usually based on an appraisal of the degree of protection realized from the treatment relative to conditions that would have resulted if no treatment had been applied.

There are four basic types of information needed for a pest control evaluation. We need to know (1) what effect the treatment had on populations of the target insect, (2) how efficacious the treatment was in reducing impact of the target species on the resource value in question, (3) what the cost of the treatment was relative to the benefits attained by application, and (4) whether the treatment was safely applied. We may also be interested in the effect of the treatment on nontarget organisms such as natural enemies, wildlife, and fish.

Pest control evaluations are quantitative and are based on procedures for measuring insect population abundance and distribution; resource size and value; ecological, economic, and social impacts; costs and benefits of treatments; and safety. Mathematical models of pest population dynamics, forest stand growth and yield, impact, and cost–benefit analysis routines are valuable tools in pest control evaluations. These tools can be used in simulation experiments before a treatment is actually applied in the field (Coulson et al. 1979b). The technologies needed to accomplish a pest control evaluation are available for only a few of the most important pest species. However, the concepts for conducting the surveys are generally applicable for all forest insect pests. Often the pest management specialist is required to make professional judgments on treatment efficacy, costs, benefits, and other variables.

Pest control evaluations can be conducted in forest ecosystems, specialized forestry settings, and urban forests. Often pest control evaluations and damage or loss surveys are carried out simultaneously. In the previous example of a loss or damage survey conducted in a seed orchard, we might also be interested in evaluating a treatment such as an insecticide application. In addition to simply defining loss in seed yield, we could appraise the efficacy of the treatment on populations of target and nontarget insects and the various costs and benefits associated with the treatment.

Forest Surveys as the Source of Information for Integrated Pest Management

Application of IPM as a component of forest resource management and planning is predicated on the availability of certain basic information about forest stands and insect populations. Most of the information is obtained from surveys of various kinds. The information is used as an aid in solving forest management problems that occur as a result of the presence and activity of pest insects in forests. Surveys also provide inventory information that is needed to monitor forest growth and productivity. The general activity of forest surveillance and inventory is, therefore, more involved than indicated by our discussion of the four kinds of functional surveys.

There are many problems that forest resource managers and pest management specialists face that these surveys do not directly address.

Another approach to organization is to classify surveys in terms of general needs for information to solve forest management problems that occur because of pest insects. Survey information needs for the purpose of problem solving can be placed into the following categories: *detection, prevention, prediction, evaluation, suppression,* and *utilization.* The interrelationships between these components and the type of specific information associated with each is illustrated in Figure 10.1, which is a *problem analysis decision tree.*

This decision tree was developed to classify survey information needs for bark beetle management. However, it is applicable to forest insect pests in general. There are several noteworthy features of Figure 10.1. The *surveillance–inventory* compartment has two main branches; one branch to *prevention* and the other to *detection.* The prevention compartment is included to emphasize that forest stands are managed in the absence of pest problems. Monitoring stand growth, yield, and structure often allows us to identify potential pest problems before they occur. As we learned in Chapter 5, many pest problems result from disturbances to stands and sites. The detection compartment implies that there is an existing pest problem or outbreak and that we are interested in obtaining information for use in management decision-making. We may wish to (1) make an *evaluation* or *prediction* about the pest problem, (2) initiate a *suppression* project, or (3) consider *utilization* or infested or damaged trees. In the case of an evaluation or prediction we can focus attention to the host trees or stands, insect populations, and/or economics. Each of these activities is represented as a separate compartment in Figure 10.1. There are specific types of information associated with the various compartments.

The problem analysis decision tree is useful for selecting the types(s) of survey information needed to solve a particular problem. For example, consider the problem that a pest management specialist faces when deciding whether to initiate a suppression project for an insect outbreak. This problem deals with an existing infestation; therefore, we would go to the detection compartment of Figure 10.1. The first consideration would be to evaluate the severity of the problem. We could consider severity in terms of trees and/or economics. There are several different types of information associated with each of these compartments (Figure 10.1). Next, we might wish to predict the likelihood of further expansion of the outbreak. In this case we could examine a number of different attributes of the pest population. If we judged that the outbreak was likely to increase in severity and that a suppression project was warranted, we could consider the various treatment options available and the economic consequences of the treatment(s) selected. Finally, it might be important to consider utilization of infested or damaged host material.

In the preceding example we have analyzed or evaluated information

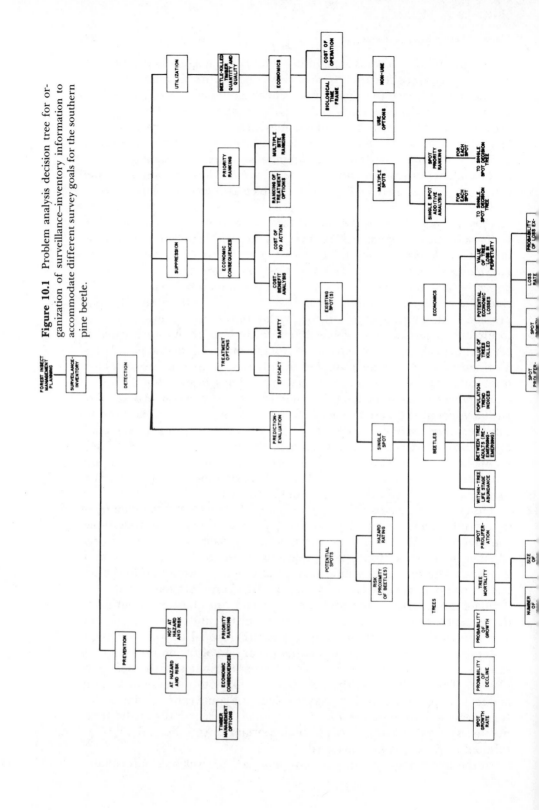

Figure 10.1 Problem analysis decision tree for organization of surveillance–inventory information to accommodate different survey goals for the southern pine beetle.

needs relative to a pest problem by using the problem analysis decision tree (Figure 10.1). The forest manager or pest management specialist must evaluate information needs for each specific pest problem. The actual steps involved in the evaluation can be summarized as illustrated in Figure 10.2, which is a *problem analysis information tree.* The information tree, which was developed from the decision tree, guides the user in defining the exact nature of the information needed for a particular problem. The information (data and models) available to aid in problem solving is associated with the terminal branches (nodes) of the information tree. This base of information varies with each insect pest. The pertinent data and models must be assembled by the pest management specialist for the user, which is a research and development task. In the case of the southern pine beetle there are more than 30 models that are useful in IPM decision-making. See Turnbow et al. 1983 for a detailed explanation of the use of a computerized version of the problem analysis decision and information keys. Once the information needs are defined, the next step is to identify how the information is to be collected. Forest surveys are generally used for this purpose.

The main point of the previous discussion was to illustrate that pest management decisions are often quite complicated and require a great deal of information. The information is collected as part of the activity of forest survey and inventory. This activity involves consideration of many different, but often related, problems.

SURVEY PROCEDURES

As we have seen from our review of different types of surveys, the information needs are many and varied. In the simplest types of detection surveys we need only qualitative information on insect species present, host infested, or recognition of damage or activity. The procedures used in these surveys, as we emphasized above, are based on principles of insect and plant taxonomy and recognition of damage categories. In virtually all other surveys, we are required to make estimates that are based on measurements of insect populations or the result of population activity. These quantitative surveys require that we have substantial basic knowledge of the insect population system in question. Furthermore, quantitative surveys must be carefully organized if they are to provide meaningful information for the forest managers. In this section we will consider three activities involved in conducting quantitative surveys. These three activities include (1) sampling plan design, (2) data collection procedures, and (3) analysis and interpretation of data.

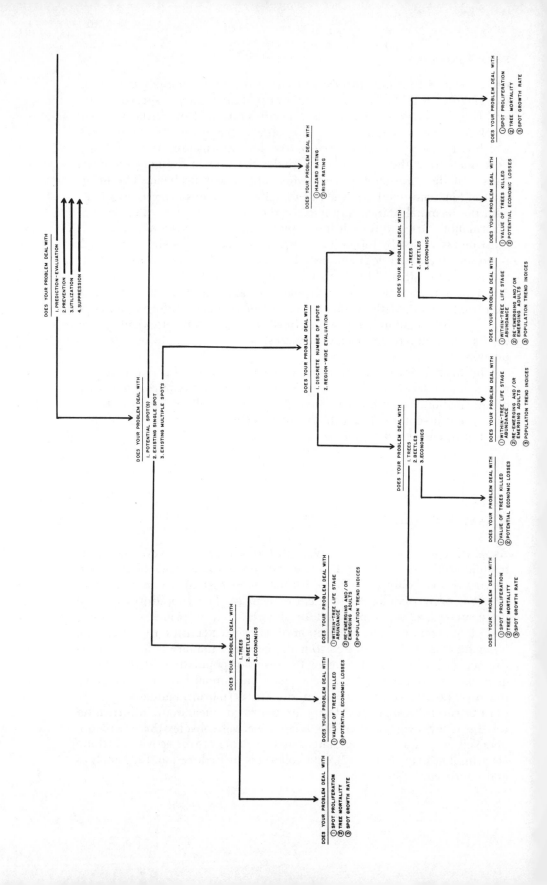

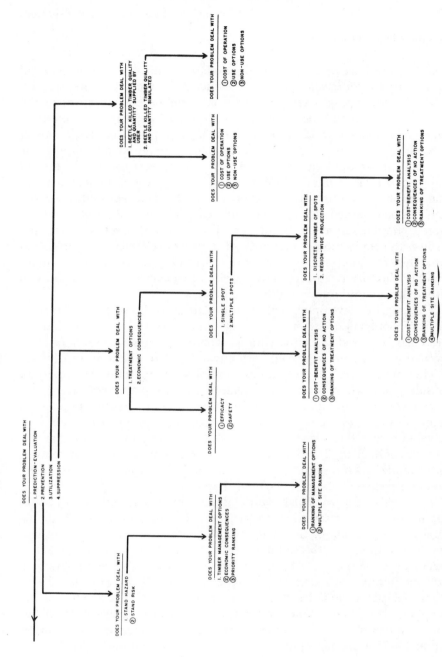

Figure 10.2 Problem analysis information tree for defining the technology available to aid in IPM of the southern pine beetle.

Sampling Plan Design

Sampling plans are designed to accommodate specific survey objectives and the financial resources available to conduct the survey. The first step involved in developing a sampling plan is to define the objectives of the survey. For example, the information required for a sampling plan designed to evaluate efficacy of a treatment tactic applied to a specific insect in a forest stand is quite different from that required to appraise the potential for an outbreak of an insect in a forest ecosystem. The second major consideration in sampling plan design is the cost of implementation. The sampling plan must be designed so that the data required to use the plan can be obtained economically and efficiently. Actual development of survey sampling procedures for a particular forest insect is a task that involves the application of principles of statistics to characterize population size. The term "population size" here can refer to an actual insect population or the forest resource, such as, size of cone crop damaged, amount of defoliation, and number of infested trees.

The goal of developing a sampling plan is to devise a procedure to estimate population size by collecting samples from the population. In particular, we need to estimate the population attribute *density* and its associated component, *dispersion*; both attributes were discussed in Chapter 6. The number, size, and spatial location of sampling units are important considerations when developing a plan to measure population size.

You will recall also that we identified three general ways that population density could be expressed: (1) absolute estimate = number per unit area or volume, and the related measure population intensity = number per unit area of habitat; (2) relative estimate = units other than area or volume, for example, catch per unit of effort; and (3) population index = estimate based on products of insect activity (Chapter 6).

The utility of a particular sampling plan for making inferences about population size is determined in large part by our knowledge of the accuracy and precision of the plan. "Accuracy" refers to the degree of bias that is introduced by the sampling plan. For example, it is important to know how close the population estimate is relative to the true population size; for instance, whether the estimate is within 10–15% or 30–40% of the actual population size. "Precision" refers to the repeatability of the sampling plan. For example, under repeated use of the procedure, will we obtain estimates that are consistently within a particular range, for example, within 10–15% of the population size 80–90% of the time?

In general, sampling plans that result in high levels of accuracy and precision require absolute population estimation procedures and are expensive to implement. In some cases it is possible to convert measures of population intensity, relative estimates, or population indices to absolute estimate. Such conversions require substantial knowledge of the population system of the insect being sampled (see Schowalter et al. 1982 for an example of the use of information on host tree size as a means for estimating populations of the southern pine beetle). In most instances the costs associated with obtaining absolute estimates prohibit their use in survey sampling. In certain types of surveys where a high degree of accuracy and precision is mandatory, the added expense of obtaining the information needed is justified. For example, in establishing efficacy standards for a treatment tactic we need accurate and precise information about the treatment relative to target and nontarget organisms. Substantial expense will be associated with the application of any treatment; therefore, it is essential that we know how effective it is before its use is recommended.

Data Collection Procedures

Designing a sampling plan and selecting or developing a data collection procedure are highly related activities. The utility of a particular sampling plan will be determined in large part by the ease with which we can collect needed information. There are numerous procedures that have been developed to measure population size. Southwood (1978) and Ruesink and Kogan (1975) provide comprehensive treatment of procedures used in sampling insect populations.

Although there are many different ways to catalog sampling procedures, most forest insect surveys involve making estimates of (1) insects associated with plants or plant habitats, (2) damage caused to plants by insects, (3) insects that are flying, and (4) insects that are in the soil or litter. Specific data collection procedures have been developed for surveying many of the major forest insect pests occurring in these four circumstances. Details relating to methodologies for particular species are in some cases documented in the entomological literature [e.g., see Coulson et al. (1975, 1979a) for the southern pine beetle], the U.S. Forest Service Manual, or the state forestry organizations.

Selection of specific data collection procedures is guided by a number of different variables, including the goal of the survey, the financial resources available, the size of the area being surveyed, the frequency of the survey, and the level of accuracy and precision desired. Following are several examples that illustrate the variety of data collection options available.

Sampling Insects Associated with Plants or Plant Habitats

Procedures for sampling insects occurring on plants or infested plant modules such as buds or tips, cones and seed, branches, bark, and foliage can range from simple to complex. For example, common implements used in sampling insects include insect nets, hand and pole pruners, saws, various types of traps and cages, hand- or power-assisted aspirating devices, and so on (Figure 10.3). In some habitats, where the insect or damage is difficult

Figure 10.3 Aspiration device used to sample insects associated with foliage.

to observe directly, it may be necessary to use more sophisticated techniques. For example, techniques employing X-ray technology have been used extensively in forest entomology. Wood boring insects, bark beetles, and seed insects are routinely sampled by using techniques termed "radiography" (Figures 14.27 and 15.5).

Sampling Damage Caused to Plants By Insects

Damage caused by specific insects can be observed and tallied by systematically inspecting a forest or stand. The techniques used can range from observation of the damage categories (described in Chapter 4) by a trained individual to the application of advanced procedures of remote sensing (Figure 10.4). We will review basic principles of the application of remote sensing of insect damage because this procedure has been widely applied in forest survey.

Remote sensing is a survey technique where information is obtained from a vantage point that is distant from the phenomenon being observed. The basic goals of remote sensing in forest surveys are to locate, identify, and evaluate the severity of insect outbreaks. There are a number of different methodologies involved in remote sensing that vary substantially in their degree of complexity.

The simplest type of remote sensing survey utilizes an aircraft, an observer, and a map of the area to be surveyed. The forested area is flown in some systematic manner, and the observer records the location and suspected causal agent of damage observed. This type of survey is generally

Figure 10.4 Remote sensing using a camera installed in a fixed-wing aircraft.

followed by an inspection (ground check) of the infested area by a field crew to verify the causal agent, that is, to obtain "ground truth." Aerial surveys are commonly used by the U.S. Forest Service, the state forestry agencies, and private industry for inventory of loss or damage and in establishing priorities for control projects.

The great utility of aerial surveys fostered adaptation of advanced navigational guidance and camera systems to aircraft. With the use of these techniques it is possible to survey large areas and obtain photographs that can be interpreted in great detail. A wide variety of different types of information can be obtained from aerial surveys by specifying variables such as the altitude of the aircraft, the lens system of the camera, the film type (e.g., black and white, color, infrared), the photographic scale, the frequency with which photographs are taken, and so on. The different types of aerial surveys provide an immense amount of information regarding the incidence, location, and severity of insect outbreaks. In addition, it is possible to define topographic features of the area surveyed and vital inventory statistics about forests such as stand type, age distribution, density, timber volume, and insect-caused loss.

Aerial photographic surveys require efficient procedures for collecting and processing information contained on the photographs. The photographs must be interpreted and the data catalogued in a manner that permits convenient access. High-speed computers are used in storage and retrieval of survey information. The information can be taken directly from the photographs, coded, and stored. These data can be analyzed, interpreted, and displayed in many different ways that are useful to the forest manager. Klein et al. (1980) provide an example of the use of aerial photographic surveys in measuring annual mortality of lodgepole pine, caused by the mountain pine beetle, *Dendroctonus ponderosae* Hopkins, and Hain (1980) reviews procedures used for the southern pine beetle.

Sampling Flying Insects

Sampling flying insects is often a vital part of detection surveys. The simplest tool for collecting flying insects is a net. There are also a wide variety of interception traps where insects fly into a barrier and fall into a preservative, are entrapped on a sticky surface, or are captured in a cage. The most novel procedure for surveying flying insects involves the use of baits of various kinds. Pheromones and host attractants have been identified for many forest insects. These chemical compounds can often be used with traps and cages to detect the presence of various species (Figure 10.5). Pheromone-baited traps are particularly useful in surveys connected with monitoring quarantines and in pest management programs where it is important to know the periods of adult insect activity.

Sampling Insects in the Litter and Soil

Many important forest insects spend a portion of their life cycle in the litter or soil. Sampling insects in the litter and soil is accomplished in two principal ways. First, small arthropods are generally collected using a device designed

Figure 10.5 Pheromone-baited trap for surveying flying insects. (Texas Forest Service photograph.)

to remove a core of soil and litter (Figure 10.6). The insects contained in the core can be extracted by using a Berlese funnel, by flotation procedures, or by soil washing. Second, larger arthropods are often sampled using pitfall traps. These traps can be constructed in various sizes and shapes.

Data Analysis Procedures

The final consideration in forest surveys is summary, analysis, and interpretation of the information collected. The meaningfulness of data collected in a survey depends on the care given to the design of the sampling plan and the execution of the plan to collect the needed and specified information. In a properly designed survey, the sampling plan, data collection procedures, and analytical routines are developed concurrently.

It is not our intent here to review specific procedures for analysis and interpretation of data. This subject is rather complex and involves application of principles of statistics. The analytical procedures that are appropriate for a specific type of survey are often defined by consultation and collaboration with authorities in statistics and computing science. This activity is conducted as part of the research and development phase of survey design and should be well defined before implementation of a survey. That is, the survey entomologist should not have to design analytical procedures after a survey is completed.

The requirements for analyses vary according to the type of survey being conducted and the intended use of the information being collected. In the

Figure 10.6 Core sampling device for surveying insects in the soil and litter.

case of detection surveys, we may be interested only in preparing maps that define the distribution of a particular pest or the damage caused by the pest. In more complicated surveys, for example, a pest control evaluation, detailed statistical analysis may be required. There are several computer-based systems available to aid in statistical analysis and data file management, such as the Statistical Analysis System (SAS). Furthermore, most state university data processing centers maintain files of computer programs to aid in statistical analysis.

Regardless of how simple or complicated the analysis of survey information, the survey entomologist will be required to make judgmental interpretation of the meaning and significance of the data. Statistical or graphic analyses of survey information simply aid or enhance the judgments. It is important to recognize that few surveys provide highly accurate or precise information. This circumstance occurs because of the high cost associated with conducting surveys.

APPLICATION OF ADVANCED TECHNOLOGY IN FOREST SURVEY

Tremendous advancements in technology for gathering survey information have been made recently. The need for reliable information for use in forest resource management and IPM fostered development of automated survey procedures. Aerial surveys using remote sensing techniques have been particularly well developed. Many different organizations in private, state, and federal sectors are recipients and users of the information gained through the various types of surveys. Furthermore, survey information is applied at local, regional, and national levels.

Advanced techniques for conducting forest surveys have necessitated concurrent development of systems for information or data base management. *Information management* is an activity that involves the use of high-speed computers for the purpose of data capture or collection, storage, retrieval, analysis, summary, and display. There are three general types of computer-based systems used for forest survey information management: transaction processing systems, management information systems, and decision support systems.

Transaction Processing Systems (TPS)

A transaction processing system (TPS) is a computer-based system consisting of programs for gathering, updating, and posting information according to predefined procedures. A TPS is frequently devoted to routine data processing involving a high degree of formality, timeliness, accuracy, and efficiency. A TPS is usually used for processing large volumes of data.

Transaction processing is an important aspect of aerial photographic surveys. Specific information contained on aerial photographs must be identified (interpreted) and coded in a manner that can be used by a computer. The PISYS (photographic interpretation system) developed by DeMars (see Hain 1980) is an automated system for acquiring, comparing, locating, and filing sets of point locations that represent infestations of bark beetles (or other insects) contained on aerial photographs. To use PISYS, an operator views aerial photographs with a scanning stereoscope (Figure 10.7). Points on the photograph are digitized (i.e., coded by coordinates) by using a graphics calculator interfaced to a desk-top microcomputer. Once digitized, the points representing infestations can be stored and recalled from computer memory and used for various types of specified analysis and summary. One common summary procedure is to prepare scale maps defining the intensity and extent of an insect outbreak. The entire process of photointerpretation and information storage, retrieval, analysis, summary, and display can be expedited by using PISYS.

Management Information Systems (MIS)

A management information system (MIS) is a computer-based system that has predefined aggregation and reporting capabilities. An MIS is often "report oriented" in the sense that data are extracted and summarized into predefined formats, usually on a periodic basis. This type of system commonly is used for the purpose of managerial review in reporting exceptions, deviations from standards, and historical trends. There are several excellent examples of the application of MIS in forest survey.

Figure 10.7 Examination of aerial photograph for bark beetle infestations. Data are stored in a computer for later reference. (U.S. Forest Service photograph.)

Geographic Data Base Management

In the U.S. Forest Service, State and Private Forestry, Forest Pest Management is the agency responsible for management of damage and losses caused by insects and diseases on forest lands. The National Forest Management Act (NFMA) of 1976 specified that insect and disease management should be accomplished through application of principles of integrated pest management (IPM). Since Forest Pest Management has responsibility for planning and operation at forest, regional, and national levels, the problems of obtaining and effectively utilizing necessary data for IPM decision-making are substantial. Data that are sound, timely, and comparable are required on the current status and trend of major forest insect and disease pests. One way to effectively utilize the existing forest insect and disease reporting system is through application of a geographic data base system. Simply stated, a *geographic data base system* is a form of computerized mapping that can be used for inputing, storing, retrieving, analyzing, and reporting resource information in a timely and efficient manner. The geographic data base system, which is a specialized type of MIS, can perform the following functions:

1. Summarize data at the forest, regional, or national levels.
2. Provide for data comparability between regions.
3. Inhance compatibility with other resource data elements (e.g., soil types, vegetation, access, land-use classification).
4. Provide for reporting of insect and disease status.
5. Provide graphic and tabular outputs (Young 1979).

Operational Pest Management Information Reporting

Certain insect pests annually cause serious damage and are, therefore, often the targets of intensive detection and evaluation surveys. These surveys provide information on the location of outbreaks and an index of severity, land ownership, access, and so on. The information is used for establishing priorities for suppression projects, evaluating the efficacy of suppression activities, and inventory of loss or damage resulting from the pest.

The southern pine beetle is an example of a pest that annually requires intensive as well as extensive survey activity throughout the southern United States. The state of Texas has had a history of severe outbreaks of the southern pine beetle dating back to 1957. Management activities for the southern pine beetle in Texas require a high degree of coordination as land ownership is divided between a number of different industrial landowners, many private owners, and national and state forests. The potential infestation area is approximately 12 million acres and thus requires the use of aerial survey techniques. The Texas Forest Service, Forest Pest Control Section is the agency responsible for conducting and coordinating survey activities in Texas. This organization provides information to the various landowners on the location and approximate size of southern pine beetle

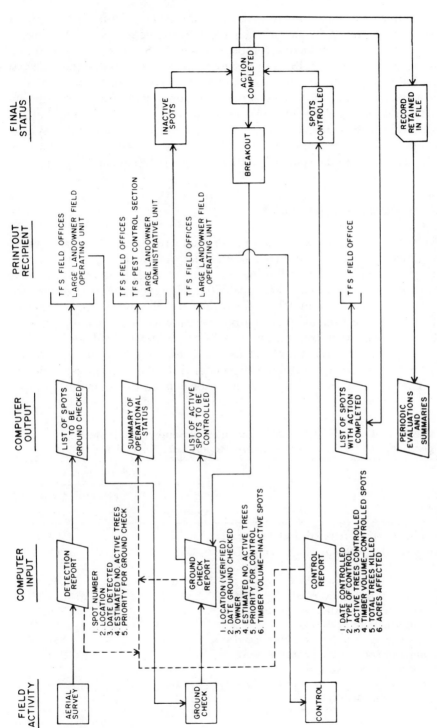

Figure 10.8 Flowchart illustrating the Texas Forest Service operational information system.

infestations and maintains records on suppression activities. These survey activities require an efficient data file management system. The Texas Forest Service developed a computer-based MIS called the "operations information system" (OIS). The system (Figure 10.8) was designed to assist the field professional or technician in actually conducting the survey and providing notification to landowners regarding southern pine beetle infestations and simultaneously provide capsuled summaries for middle- and top-level forest managers. There are many different types of survey data summary available from the OIS, which are provided to the various cooperators that use the system (Tables 10.1 and 10.2) (Pace and Fagala 1978).

Decision Support Systems (DSS)

A decision support system (DSS) is an interactive computer-based system designed to help decision-makers utilize data and models to solve unstructured problems. A DSS subsumes portions of a MIS, especially the data summarization and extraction capabilities. However, the procedures used in the DSS are more loosely defined than in MIS and, therefore, permit the user to select on an ad hoc basis the frequency and content of reports. The key factor that distinguishes a DSS from a MIS is the degree to which the information processing task can be prespecified by the user of the system: an MIS is by definition prespecified; a DSS is not prespecified.

The DSS is an important tool that uses data and mathematical models

Table 10.1   Example of Biweekly Summary of Southern Pine Beetle Operations for XYZ Timber Company (Report Date November 3, 1977)

	Texas Forest Service	
	Cooperator	TFS Owner Code 30 State Totals
Number of spots detected since January 1	336	4504
Number of spots on which action is complete	258	3903
Total SPB spots controlled	166	2042
Total SPB trees controlled	13341	151807
Number of spots with incomplete information	0	0
Number of spots to be ground checked	4	337
Number of spots lacking control—have been ground checked	104	264
Number of spots lacking control—30 + days since detection	105	596

Table 10.2   Example of Biweekly Summary of Southern Pine Beetle Operations for Texas Forest Service Administrative Area 4 (Report Date July 13, 1977)

	Texas Forest Service			
	Cooperators	TFS	Area Totals	State Totals
Number of spots detected since January 1	1510	240	1750	3561
Number of spots on which action is complete	1007	80	1087	1963
Total SPB spots controlled	903	10	913	1301
Total SPB trees controlled	60847	1039	61886	94639
Number of spots with incomplete information	0	0	0	0
Number of spots to be ground checked	372	78	450	1008
Number of spots lacking control	131	82	213	590
Number of spots lacking control—30+ days since detection	0	0	0	0

to aid managers in decision-making relative to forest insect pests. The necessity of ad hoc problem solving and flexibility in content of reports in IPM decision-making is clearly evident when we consider that, for a particular insect pest, we may wish to have information regarding some aspect of detection, prediction, evaluation, suppression, prevention, or utilization. It is not possible for a pest management specialist to anticipate which functions or problems will be presented or when they will be presented. The problem analysis information tree (Figure 10.1) is a useful means of identifying the types of information needed and available for aiding in assessing alternative solutions to a particular problem. A DSS does not solve problems per se. Rather, DSS provides information that is used by an individual in making judgments regarding the consequences of various optional courses of action. Survey information provides data that are used by the various types of models available, for example, pest population dynamics, stand dynamics, and impacts. The DSS provides a computer-based structure for the models (Figure 10.9). The actual functions performed by the DSS are illustrated in Figure 10.10.

Because of the widespread use of mathematical models in science and industry there is considerable interest in development of DSS. Although mathematical models have been developed for a number of specific components of IPM (e.g., population dynamics, stand growth and yield, impact), they have not been generally accessible to the pest management specialists. One goal of a DSS is to take available models and make them accessible to the user community. There are a number of comprehensive texts that deal with principles relating to DSS: for example, see Keen and Morton 1978, Fick and Sprague 1980, and Bonczek et al. 1981.

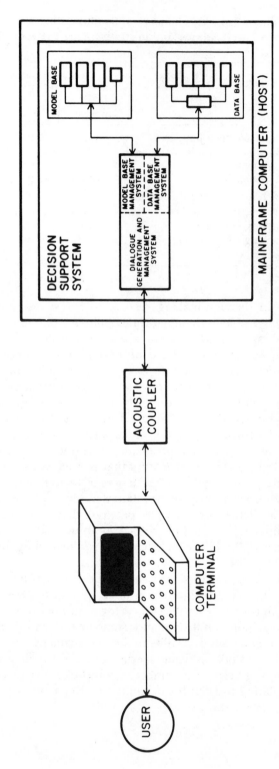

Figure 10.9 Flowchart illustrating a simplified conceptual framework for a decision-support system.

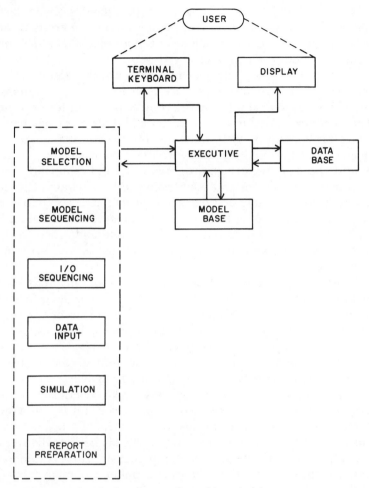

Figure 10.10 The functions performed by a decision–support system.

ORGANIZATIONS RESPONSIBLE FOR CONDUCTING FOREST SURVEYS

In the United States the primary agencies involved in conducting forest surveys include the U.S. Forest Service, the state forestry organizations, and the private forest industry. The survey activities of these organizations are interrelated and often highly coordinated.

The U.S. Forest Service has responsibilities that include conducting research, providing assistance to state and private forestry, and management of the National Forest System under multiple use-sustained yield principles. Within the Forest Service, the agency responsible for survey and detection activities is State and Private Forestry, Forest Pest Management. This organization is charged with survey, detection, and pest management responsibility on all federal land. In addition, the agency provides technical and financial assistance to state and private forestry interests through a variety of programs aimed at prevention or suppression of pests that threaten trees, forests, wood products, and stored wood.

Survey, detection, and management activities at the state level are the responsibility of the state forestry service. State forestry organizations were developed initially to deal with the fire control aspects of forest protection and later were expanded to include insect and disease management. The states work cooperatively with State and Private Forestry in conducting forest surveys and in implementing forest pest management practices. In some cases, the state forestry services are involved in conducting research in forest pest management and pilot testing and evaluation of promising treatment tactics. The state pest management specialists also participate in protection activities relating to forest nurseries and seed orchards. In addition, the states provide technical council to private landowners (both rural and urban) on matters relating to insects and diseases of forest and ornamental trees.

Many of the forest industrial corporations are also involved in survey and detection activities on their forest properties. The state forestry organizations and State and Private Forestry often work cooperatively with industry in their survey, detection, and management activities.

In recent years many of the large cities in the United States have employed "city foresters" to assist in management of urban forests. Insect and disease management in parks, recreational areas, residences, and along city streets is a major concern. Urban foresters work cooperatively with local arborists, the state forestry organizations, and State and Private Forestry.

In Canada survey and detection and management of forest insects is the responsibility of the Forest Protection Branch of the Canadian Forestry Service. This organization performs comprehensive surveys to obtain information on the status of distribution and abundance of many forest insect species.

REFERENCES

Bonczek, R. H., C. W. Holsapple, and A. B. Whinston. 1981. *Fundamentals of Decision Support Systems*. Academic Press, New York.

Coster, J. E. and J. L. Searcy, (Eds.). 1979. *Evaluating Control Tactics for Southern Pine Beetle*. U.S. Department of Agriculture Forest Service, Technical Bulletin 1613.

Coulson, R. N., F. P. Hain, J. L. Foltz, and A. M. Mayyasi. 1975. *Techniques for Sampling the Dynamics of Southern Pine Beetle Populations*. Texas Agricultural Experiment Station Miscellaneous Publication 1184.

Coulson, R. N., W. S. Fargo, L. J. Edson, P. E. Pulley, and A. M. Bunting. 1979a. *Procedural Guide for Conducting Field Investigations on the Population Dynamics of the Southern Pine Beetle*. Texas Agricultural Experiment Station Miscellaneous Publication 1427.

Coulson, R. N., R. M. Feldman, W. S. Fargo, P. J. H. Sharpe, G. L. Curry, and P. E. Pulley. 1979b. Evaluating suppression tactics for *Dendroctonus frontalis* in infestations. In Coster, J. E. and J. L. Searcy (Eds.), *Evaluating Control Tactics for Southern Pine Beetle*. U.S. Department of Agriculture Forest Service, Technical Bulletin 1613.

Fick, G. and R. H. Sprague, Jr. (Eds.). 1980. *Decision Support Systems: Issues and Challenges*. Pergamon Press. New York.

Hain, F. P. 1980. Sampling and predicting population trends. In Thatcher, R. C., J. L. Searcy, J. E. Coster, and G. D. Hertel, (Eds.), *The Southern Pine Beetle*. U.S. Department of Agriculture Forest Service Technical Bulletin 1631.

Keen, P. G. W. and M. S. S. Morton. 1978. *Decision Support System: An Organizational Perspective*. Addison-Wesley, Philippines.

Klein, W. H., D. D. Bennett, and Robert W. Young. 1980. Evaluation of panoramic reconnaisance aerial photography for measuring annual mortality of lodgepole pine caused by the mountain pine beetle. U.S. Department of Agriculture Forest Service Report 80-2.

Knight, F. B. 1967. Evaluation of forest insect infestations. *Annu. Rev. Entomol.* **12**:207–228.

Morris, R. F. 1960. Sampling insect populations. *Annu. Rev. Entomol.* **5**:243–264.

National Academy of Sciences. 1969. *Insect Pest Management and Control*. Vol. 3, *Principles of Plant and Animal Pest Control*. National Academy of Sciences, Washington, DC.

Pace, H. A. and E. P. Fagala. 1978. *A Computer Based Information System to Aid Southern Pine Beetle Control Operations*. Texas Forest Service Publication 120.

Poole, R. W. 1974. *An Introduction to Quantitative Ecology*. McGraw-Hill, New York.

Ruesink, W. G. and M. Kogan. 1975. The quantitative basis of pest management: Sampling and measuring. In Metcalf, R. L. and W. H. Luckmann (Eds.), *Introduction to Insect Pest Management*. Wiley, New York.

SAS. 1979. *User's Guide*. Helwid, J. T. and K. A. Council (Eds.). SAS Institute, Inc., Raleigh, NC.

Schowalter, T. D., R. N. Coulson, R. H. Turnbow, Jr., and W. S. Fargo. 1982. Accuracy and precision of procedures for estimating populations of the southern pine beetle (Coleoptera: Scolytidae) by using host correlates. *J. Econ. Entomol.* **75**:1009–1016.

Southwood, T. R. E. 1978. *Ecological Methods, with Particular Reference to the Study of Insect Populations*. Halsted Press, Wiley, New York.

Turnbow, R. H., Jr., L. C. Hu, E. J. Rykiel, R. N. Coulson, and D. Loh. 1983. *Procedural Guide to FERRET, the Question Analysis Routine of the Decision Support System for Southern Pine Beetle Management*. Texas Agricultural Experiment Station Miscellaneous Publication 1533.

Young, R. W. 1979. Evaluation of a commercial geographic data base system for storage and retrieval of forest insect and disease information. U.S. Department of Agriculture Forest Service Report 79-4.

III | INSECT FEEDING GROUPS

Section III consists of eight chapters dealing with the principal forest insect feeding groups. In this section we examine ecological functions of forest insects, case histories of important species, and treatment tactics and strategies used in regulating and modifying populations of the pest species. The feeding groups discussed include defoliators (Chapter 11); sapsucking (Chapter 12), terminal, shoot, twig, and root (Chapter 13); seed and cone (Chapter 14); phloem boring (Chapter 15); wood boring (Chapter 16); gall forming (Chapter 17); and arthropod pests in recreational areas (Chapter 18).

11 DEFOLIATING INSECTS

INTRODUCTION

Leaf-eating insects are found in five orders: Lepidoptera (e.g., moths and butterflies), Hymenoptera (e.g., sawflies, leafcutting ants), Coleoptera (e.g., leaf beetles, scarab beetles), Orthoptera (e.g., walkingsticks, grasshoppers), and Diptera (e.g., leaf mining flies) (Table 11.1). Leaf-eating insects in the orders Lepidoptera, Hymenoptera (i.e., sawflies), and Diptera are leaf feeders during the larval stage, whereas leaf-eating insects in the orders Coleoptera and Orthoptera feed on foliage in both the larval and adult stages. Adult leafcutting ants and leafcutting bees also feed on foliage.

The effect of insect defoliators on forest and shade trees can be very conspicuous and dramatic. Outbreaks often appear to develop suddenly over very large areas. The gypsy moth, *Lymantria dispar* (Linnaeus); forest tent caterpillar, *Malacosoma disstria* Hübner; spruce budworm, *Choristoneura fumiferana* (Clemens); Douglas-fir tussock moth, *Orgyia pseudotsugata* (McDunnough); pine sawflies in the genus *Neodiprion*; and larch sawfly, *Pristiphora erichsonii* (Hartig), are examples of common defoliators that can increase to epidemic populations. Many insect defoliators cause major impacts in forest stands. Tree and stand mortality, changes in stand composition, growth loss, weakening of trees so that they become more susceptible to other insects and diseases, and aesthetic and nuisance problems are commonly caused by defoliating insects.

Forest entomologists rank Lepidoptera as the second most damaging order to forest stands in the United States. Destruction of balsam fir and spruce by the spruce budworm in the boreal forests of Canada causes Canadian forest entomologists to rank Lepidoptera as the most damaging order. Lepidopterous defoliators are also serious pests of shade trees. The gypsy moth is an outstanding example of the damage to shade trees and nuisance to homeowners caused by lepidopterous insects. Diprionid and tenthredinid sawflies are major pests of forest stands and Christmas tree plantations. Leaf beetles are often major pests on shade trees, whereas leaf mining insects cause problems on both forest and shade trees. Information on defoliating insects that damage trees and shrubs, and the various management approaches used to control these pests are presented in this chapter.

Symptoms and Damage

Trees attacked by leaf-eating insects can often be recognized easily by missing foliage and uneaten leaf parts such as petioles and veins. Insects that feed between the upper and lower epidermis of the leaf are called "leaf miners." The shape of the leaf mining distinguishes the type of mine (e.g., blotch mine, serpentine mine) (see Chapter 4). Common symptoms or signs of heavily defoliated trees are (1) large amounts of missing foliage; (2) browning of foliage, often associated with leaf miners, leaf folders, leaf rollers, and leaf tiers, (3) silk shelters and web-enclosed foliage, associated

Table 11.1   Insect Orders That Contain Leaf-Eating Insects, the Most Important Types of Insect in Each Order, and an Example of Each

Order	Type	Example
Lepidoptera	Case and bag makers	Bagworm
	Tent makers and webworms	Fall webworm
	Leaf rollers, folders, leaf and needle tiers	Spruce budworm
	Loopers	Elm spanworm
	Naked caterpillars	Variable oakleaf caterpillar
	Hairy caterpillars	Gypsy moth
	Spiny caterpillars	Pandora moth
	Slug caterpillars	Hag moth
Hymenoptera	Diprionid sawflies	Redheaded pine sawfly
	Tenthredinid sawflies	Larch sawfly
	Cimbicid sawflies	Elm sawfly
	Slug sawflies	Pin oak sawfly
	Leafcutting ants	Texas leafcutting ant
	Leafcutting bees	Leafcutting bees
Coleoptera	Leaf beetles	Cottonwood leaf beetle
	Weevils	Adult weevils
	Scarab beetles	Japanese beetle
Orthoptera	Walkingsticks	Walkingstick
	Grasshoppers	Post oak grasshopper
Leaf Miners		
Lepidoptera		Lodgepole needleminer
Hymenoptera		Birch leafminer
Coleoptera		Locust leafminer
Diptera		Holly leafminer

with tent makers and webworms; (4) insect remains such as egg shells, shed larval skins, pupal cases, cocoons, frass, and trails of silk; (5) branch mortality and top-kill; and (6) tree mortality.

Insect defoliation affects the tree by reducing photosynthesis, interfering with transpiration, and interfering with the processes of translocation of food within a tree. Effects of insect defoliation on forest and shade trees will vary considerably depending on tree species, age of tree, site, prior stresses on the tree, insect population density, weather conditions, and secondary insects and diseases (Mattson and Addy 1975, Kulman 1971). General comments on the effects of insect defoliation on an individual tree are presented in the following paragraphs. Individual situations may not always follow these general statements.

Light defoliation (i.e., <20% defoliation) normally has very little effect on the tree, but moderate to severe defoliation reduces tree growth. Reduction in radial growth of 70–100% often occurs with 2 or more consecutive years of moderate or heavy defoliation. Rootlet mortality normally begins after 1 or 2 years of heavy defoliation. If the insect population collapses after 1 or 2 years of feeding, growth reductions of at least 10–50% often occur the following year with growth returning to predefoliation levels during the second year after the collapse of the insect population. Heavy defoliation for 1–2 years may not kill the tree but may weaken it enough to increase its susceptibility to secondary insects and disease. Tree mortality usually begins after more than 2 or 3 years of moderate to heavy defoliation. An example of the succession of events associated with a spruce budworm outbreak is presented in Table 11.2.

Site and weather conditions are important factors in the overall effect of insect defoliation on individual trees and stands. Trees on very poor sites may show major effects from defoliation much sooner than trees on good sites. Unusual weather conditions such as droughts or floods increase the effects of defoliation on individual trees and forest stands. Trees planted in cities (e.g., which often are planted off-site, out of their natural range, and on highly disturbed sites) may show the effect of defoliation much sooner than individuals of the same species would under more normal forest conditions.

Susceptibility to defoliation varies considerably in different tree species. Evergreen conifers, such as spruce or hemlock, will die as a result of one single complete defoliation if it occurs before midsummer. It will take 2 years to kill conifer trees if complete defoliation occurs after midsummer since the buds are already formed for next year. Some defoliators such as the spruce budworm and some diprionid sawflies prefer to feed on new needles. Other insects such as the jack pine sawfly, *Neodiprion pratti bank-*

Table 11.2 Succession of Events Associated with a Spruce Budworm Outbreak on Balsam Fir

Number of Years of Heavy to Severe Defoliation	Impact
1	Flowers and cone crops die; radial growth loss occurs in the upper crown
2–3	Rootlets begin to die; radial growth loss occurs over the entire stem; height growth ceases; some tree tops die
4–6	Suppressed trees in the understory and mature and overmature trees in overstory die; tree growth and wood production nearly cease
7–15	Budworm populations begin to collapse; more trees die, especially balsam fir; some seedlings and saplings die; dead tops break; dead trees begin to deteriorate as a result of disease, secondary insect attack, and wind breakage; protective cover in deer yards is diminished

Source: After Montgomery et al. 1982a.

sianae Rohwer, feed only on old needles. Many conifers such as balsam fir, spruce, and jack pine hold their needles for several years. Conifers such as balsam fir and white spruce often are heavily defoliated by the spruce budworm for 3–5 years before the trees begin to die. Deciduous conifers, such as larch, often show great resistance to injury from defoliation. Larch trees often endure 7 or more years of defoliation by the larch sawfly before tree mortality occurs.

Under normal conditions, hardwood trees are relatively resilient to defoliation for 3 or more years because of their relatively large supply of stored food and their ability to produce a second set of foliage following heavy defoliation. Time of defoliation on hardwoods is a critical factor since defoliation by early or midseason defoliators normally has more effect on the tree than does defoliation by a late season defoliator. Heavy defoliations in the same year by two different insect species (e.g., early- and late-season defoliators) can cause tree mortality on hardwoods.

Effects of heavy defoliation can vary considerably between individual trees of the same tree species. Fast-growing dominant trees without competition are usually less affected by defoliation than are slow-growing suppressed and intermediate trees that are growing under less favorable conditions. Fast-growing trees have more stored food reserves and usually are better able to withstand both the effect of defoliation and secondary insect and disease attacks.

Population Dynamics

Extensive information is available on the population dynamics of approximately 20 forest insect defoliators. Little detailed information is available on the population dynamics of most other insect defoliators found on forest and shade trees. Numerous predators and parasites such as birds, spiders, rodents, ants, ladybird beetles, stink bugs, lacewings, ground beetles, tachinid flies, ichneumon wasps, and chalcidoid wasps are important regulators of many insect defoliators.

Most insect defoliators never reach outbreak numbers because natural enemies and weather factors keep them at fairly low levels. Other insect defoliators occasionally reach outbreak numbers (e.g., once every 40 years), whereas some defoliators are much more cyclic and occur about once every 10 years. Some insect defoliators appear to be fairly common every year but seldom are present in epidemic numbers over large areas.

Insect defoliators are often present in very low numbers between outbreaks. Several years of inconspicuous increase occurs in the insect population before it reaches the release phase of an outbreak. During the release phase, the defoliating larval population may show a five- to twentyfold increase in population numbers during 1 year. Most defoliation occurs when the defoliator is in the outbreak phase; this phase normally lasts 1–7 years depending on the species of defoliator and many complex interactions between the defoliator, natural enemy, and the physical environment. The decline phase is reached when conditions become unfavorable for a high survival rate and the population levels of the defoliator drops quickly. This decline may be rapid or may take several years. Many different factors such as weather, natural enemies, and changes in quantity and quality of food have been responsible for the decline of outbreaks of insect defoliators. For additional information on factors affecting the population dynamics of insects, see Chapters 6 and 7 and Ives (1981). Information on factors affecting the population dynamics of specific insect defoliators is presented throughout the remainder of this chapter.

ORGANISMS INVOLVED

Defoliating insects that commonly damage forest and shade trees are present in the orders Lepidoptera, Hymenoptera, Coleoptera, Orthoptera, and Diptera.

Lepidopterous Insects

Leaf-eating insects in the order Lepidoptera cause damage only in the larval stages. Many larvae are free feeders, but some are window feeders and skeletonizers during the early instars and later become free feeders. Others are window feeders and skeletonizers during all larval stages. A few are leaf or needle miners. Adult moths and butterflies have either vestigial mouthparts or siphoning mouthparts adapted for feeding on nectar. Most lepidopterous insects generally have five or six instars, overwinter in the egg or pupal stage, and have one generation per year.

Lepidopterous insects generally have three major seasonal development patterns: early, long, and late. Early season defoliators generally overwinter as eggs or small larvae and emerge from the eggs or hibernating locations when new foliage appears in early spring. Larval development is completed in 4–8 weeks. Pupation lasts for about 2 weeks and occurs inside cocoons, in webbing above ground, among remaining leaves, or on bark of branches and trunks. Adults emerge and mate, and the females lay eggs for the next generation. Normally, males and females live for only a few days. Most of the major lepidopterous forest pests have this early season development pattern.

The long season development pattern for insect defoliators is similar to the early season pattern. The major differrence is that the larvae take longer to complete development; often they feed for 2–4 months.

Late-season defoliators represent the third type of development pattern. They usually overwinter as prepupae or pupae in the soil. Adults emerge in late spring or early summer. Mating, egg laying, and emergence from eggs occur in June or July. Larval development takes 4–8 weeks and occurs during late summer and early fall.

The most important lepidopterous defoliators of forest and shade trees are divided into the following types for discussion purposes (Table 11.3): (1) case and bag makers; (2) tent makers and webworms; (3) leaf rollers, leaf folders, and leaf and needle tiers; (4) leaf and needle miners; (5)

Table 11.3 Common Types of Defoliating Lepidopterous Caterpillar

Type and Examples	Characteristics
Associated with Enclosures	
Case and bag makers Larch casebearer, bagworm	Caterpillars have five pairs of prolegs; build and inhabit an individual movable case or bag constructed from silk and foliage parts
Tent makers and webworms Eastern tent caterpillar, fall webworm	Caterpillars have five pairs of prolegs; usually build and inhabit conspicuous silken tent or web; colonial inhabitant
Leaf rollers, leaf folders, leaf and needle tiers Oak leaf roller, spruce budworms, pine tube moth	Caterpillars have five pairs of prolegs; fold or roll individual leaves or needles, or parts of leaves or needles, or ties several leaves, shoots, or needles together
Leaf and needle miners Lodgepole needleminer, aspen leafminer	Caterpillars bore inside epidermis of leaf or needle; prolegs are very short or absent, but five pairs of crochets visible
No Enclosures	
Loopers Fall and spring cankerworms, elm spanworm	Caterpillars have two or three pairs of prolegs; body relatively free of hair; usually live exposed on foliage
Naked caterpillars California oakworm, variable oakleaf caterpillar	Caterpillars have five pairs of prolegs; live exposed on foliage; body relatively free of hair, tubercles, or spines
Hairy caterpillars Gypsy moth, Douglas-fir tussock moth	Caterpillars have five pairs of prolegs; live exposed on foliage; body covered with short or long hairs
Spiny caterpillars Cercropia moth, mourningcloak butterfly	Caterpillars have five pairs of prolegs; live exposed on foliage; body covered with numerous spines, enlarged tubercles, or body covered, with only one to three spines
Slug caterpillars Hag moth, saddleback caterpillar	Caterpillars have no prolegs; prolegs replaced by five pairs of sucking disks with crochets; sluglike in appearance; always are window feeders and skeletonizers on hardwood tree species

loopers; (6) naked caterpillars; (7) hairy caterpillars; (8) spiny caterpillars; and (9) slug caterpillars.

Case and Bag Makers

Four families contain caterpillars that construct a case or bag from silk and foliage, but only casebearers (Coleophoridae) and bagworms (Psychidae) are common in the United States on urban and forest trees. Most casebearer larvae are leaf miners during the early instars and construct cases as larger larvae. Only bagworms construct bags immediately after emerging from the egg. One caterpillar is present per case or bag; this shelter provides protection from natural enemies and environmental conditions. The anterior part of the larva is exposed to the environment only when it is moving, feeding, or enlarging the case or bag.

Case and bag makers occur on conifers and hardwoods but are more common on conifers. Approximately 100 species of casebearers are found in North America. The elm casebearer, *Coleophora ulmifoliella* McDunnough, and the birch casebearer, *C. fuscedinella* Zeller, are common but minor pests of forest and shade trees in eastern North America. The birch casebearer is considered an important pest of birch in Newfoundland (Raske and Bryant 1977). The larch casebearer, *C. laricella* (Hübner), is a major pest of larch throughout the range of larch in North America.

Twenty-two species of bagworms belonging to the family Psychidae are present in the United States (Davis 1964). However, only the bagworm, *Thyridopteryx ephemeraeformis* (Haworth), is extremely common on both shade and forest trees. The larch casebearer and the bagworm are described.

Larch Casebearer, Coleophora laricella (Hübner)

The larch casebearer, an accidently introduced pest from Europe, was first recorded in Massachusetts in 1886. It is now found throughout most of the eastern larch range in the eastern United States, Atlantic Provinces of Canada, and as far north as 49–50°N latitude in Quebec and Ontario. This insect was discovered on western larch in Idaho in 1957. The larch casebearer is now found throughout most of the western larch forests in the northwestern United States and southeastern British Columbia (Denton 1979, Denton and Tunnock 1972).

The larch casebearer has one generation per year and overwinters as a third instar larva in a case fastened to the end of a twig (Figure 11.1). In the spring, the larva molts to the fourth instar, detaches its case from the overwintering site, and moves to newly developing foliage, where it attaches the case to a needle. The larch casebearer larva proceeds to chew into the needle and mines the needle in both directions, stretching as far as possible without entirely leaving the case.

After feeding on one needle, the larva frees its case and moves onto another needle. It enlarges its case as the larva grows in the spring. Mature larvae are about 6 mm long. Pupation occurs during early May to mid-

Figure 11.1 Overwintering cases of the larch casebearer, *Coleophora laricella*. (U.S. Forest Service photograph, courtesy of R. Ryan.)

June depending on the location and yearly weather conditions. Cocoons are found at various locations on the tree. At low and high population densities, the pupae are found in the center of a fascicle of needles or in bunches at the end of the branch, respectively. Adults emerge during May and June and mate 1–2 days later. A female lays about 50–100 eggs separately on individual needles. Most eggs hatch in 2 weeks. A newly emerged larva chews directly into a needle and feeds as a needle miner during the first two instars. Late in the summer, a late second instar larva constructs a case out of mined needles, molts to the third instar, and continues mining needles from its case until shortly before the needles drop. In October the larva moves to the base of a bud and attaches its case to a twig, where it overwinters.

The most serious damage to larch trees is caused by the fourth instar larvae feeding on new foliage in early spring. Heavily damaged trees appear scorched because of the redness of dead foliage. A needle cast disease on larch also gives the trees a scorched appearance, so entomologists and pathologists must examine the damage close up to confirm the mining damage caused by the larch casebearer and to actually see the larvae. Later in the season, the tree produces a second set of foliage. Defoliation over

Figure 11.2 A braconid wasp, *Agathis pumila*, an important introduced parasite of the larch casebearer, *Coleophora laricella*. (U.S. Forest Service photograph, courtesy of R. Ryan.)

several years leads to reduction of tree growth, branch mortality, and occasionally tree mortality (Tunnock et al. 1969).

The behavior of epidemic larch casebearer populations tends to change with the duration of the casebearer populations in an area. The initial outbreaks of the exotic larch casebearer on eastern larch in eastern North America and on western larch in the western United States had similar patterns. The first outbreak persisted over wide areas for 10 or more years and caused serious damage. In new areas, the larch casebearer outbreaks finally collapsed as a result of starvation of larvae. Additional outbreaks in the same area tend to be sporadic, short lived, and occur at 7–8-year intervals. These outbreaks are usually regulated by natural enemies.

During the 1930s, several species of parasites from England were released into the eastern United States and Canada to control an outbreak that began in the early 1900s. Two parasites, *Agathis pumila* (Ratzeburg), a braconid wasp (Figure 11.2), and *Chrysocharis laricinellae* (Ratzeburg), an eulophid wasp, readily became established in Canada and the United States. These two parasites have been very successful in reducing larch casebearer populations in eastern North America (Quednau 1970a,b, 1967). A similar biological control program is currently being conducted in western North America.

Bagworm, *Thyridopteryx ephemeraeformis* (Haworth)

The bagworm (Figure 11.3) is a very important shade tree, ornamental, and nursery pest that also is commonly found along the edges of forest stands. This insect, sometimes called the *evergreen bagworm*, feeds on over 128 plant species. It is found throughout the United States east of the Rocky Mountains but is uncommon in the states bordering Canada (Davis

Figure 11.3 Case of the bagworm, *Thyridopteryx ephemeraeformis*. (North Carolina Agriculture Experiment Station photograph.)

1964). Common hosts of the bagworm are junipers, cedars, arborvitae, white pine, cypress, sycamore, black locust, maple, oaks, willows, and poplars.

Generally the bagworm is a late spring–late summer defoliator, but the exact time of its feeding activity depends on the location and yearly weather conditions. The bagworm has one generation per year and overwinters in the egg stage inside the old female bag. Eggs hatch in May in the extreme south and during late May and early June throughout the rest of its range. Immediately after emerging from the old female bag and before feeding, the small larva weaves leaf and twig fragments together with silk to form a new baglike shelter (Kaufmann 1968). The larva feeds, moves, and enlarges its shelter through an opening at the anterior end of the bag. During the early instars, the larva is a window and hole feeder on hardwood foliage and nibbles on the edges of coniferous foliage. As its size increases the larva becomes a free feeder. The position of the bag, as the larva carries it around, changes from an upright position during the early larval instars to a downward position in the late instars. When resting, preparing to molt, or hiding from natural enemies, the bagworm larva withdraws its head and thorax into the bag through the anterior opening and closes the opening. The larva pushes frass and cast skins out of its bag through a small opening at the posterior end of the bag.

Larva feeding lasts for 12–14 weeks. The body of a mature larva is dark brown, and the head and thoracic plates are yellow with dark brown spots.

After a mature larva attaches the anterior end of the bag to a twig, it turns around inside the bag so that its head is near the original posterior opening and then molts to the pupal stage. This process allows the male pupa and female adult easy exit through the posterior opening.

The male bagworm pupa and adult are typical lepidopterous forms; the female pupa and adult are specifically adapted to the bag and are not typical lepidopterous forms. An adult male is a hairy, slender wasplike black moth with clear wings and a wingspread of 25 mm. These male moths are strong fliers and often mate with more than one female. The adult female is wingless, legless, wormlike, soft, yellowish white, and remains inside the bag after emerging from the pupal case. Almost immeditely after splitting the pupal case, she becomes receptive to mating and releases a pheromone to attract males. During copulation, the female remains inside the bag; the male perches near the opening of the bag and inserts his abdomen through the opening until he reaches the female genitalia. After mating, the male withdraws his abdomen and flies away. The female lays 500–1500 eggs within her pupal case and then slips down to the bottom of the bag, wriggles out of it, falls to the ground, and dies shortly afterward.

High bagworm populations have completely defoliated and killed arborvitae and junipers. Less severe defoliation leads to reduced radial growth, topkilling, branch mortality, weakened shrubs and trees, and unsightly ornamentals.

Bagworm populations appear to fluctuate considerably from year to year in some locations, with extremely high populations occurring during certain years. Parasitism, predation, diseases, low winter tempertures, starvation, and chemical or microbial insecticides are the primary factors causing bagworm mortality (Berisford and Tsao 1975, Barrows 1974, Kulman 1965a). Low winter temperatures cause high mortality of the overwintering eggs. Consequently, bagworm populations are low or not present in most of the northern states bordering Canada.

Dispersal of bagworms occur through (1) accidental shipment of infested nursery stock from one area to another; (2) winds transporting newly emerged larvae, before bag construction, from one location to another; (3) crawling of larvae from tree to tree; (4) transportation of larvae by birds and mammals; and (5) floods dislodging old female bags containing fertilized eggs from host trees. Bagworms appear biologically adapted to survive in a wide range of habitats. Biological factors influencing their survival and dispersal successes are polyphagous feeding habit, ability of larvae to resist starvation for long time periods, habit of mature larva firmly attaching the bag to almost any support for pupation purposes, and high reproductive potential.

The following procedures are recommended for reducing bagworm populations: (1) continued inspection and/or fumigation of ornamentals before making intra- and interstate plant shipment; (2) manually picking all bags from small shade trees and ornamentals and destroying them in late fall, winter, or early spring before the eggs hatch; and (3) in heavy infestations, spraying of infested plants with *Bacillus thuringiensis* Berliner, a microbial insecticide, or with a chemical insecticide in late spring or early summer just after egg hatch. Larger larvae are very difficult to control with chemicals.

Tent Makers and Webworms

Caterpillars in nine different lepidopterous families build tentlike or weblike structures from silk, or silk and foliage, or frass and foliage. These insects occur on hardwoods and conifers but are more common and cause more damage on hardwoods. Most tent caterpillars in the family Lasiocampidae build a characteristic tent out of silk. No foliage is enclosed in the tent which is used only as a shelter. A few insects, such as the poplar tentmaker, *Ichthyura inclusa* (Hübner), in the family Notodontidae, web several leaves together and use this enclosure only as a shelter.

All of the six species of tent caterpillars that occur in North America belong to the genus *Malacosoma*. Except for the forest tent caterpillar, they all construct some type of silk shelter. Individual variation for each species, especially in relation to egg laying differences, appearance of egg mass and cocoon, tent construction, and preferred food hosts, are presented by Stehr and Cook (1968). Information on three commonly encountered *Malacosoma* species are presented.

Most caterpillars of the webworm type construct weblike enclosures of silk and foliage in which they feed and rest. These caterpillars are often called *web-enclosed foliage feeders*. Size and shape of the enclosure usually varies by species. Examples of common webworm caterpillars are the fall webworm, *Hyphantria cunea* (Drury)—Arctiidae; uglynest caterpillar, *Archips cerasivorana* (Fitch), and oak webworm, *Archips fervidana* (Clemens)—Tortricidae; mimosa webworm, *Homadaula anisocentra* Meyrick—Glyphipterygidae; and juniper webworm, *Dichomeris marginella* (Fabricius)—Gelechiidae. Some species, like the pine webworm, *Tetralopha robustella* Zeller—Pyralidae, build shelters of frass and silk and feed on foliage outside the shelter. The fall webworm is presented as a representative insect for this type.

Eastern Tent Caterpillar, Malacosoma americanum (Fabricius)

The eastern tent caterpillar, found throughout the United States east of the Great Plains and in the southern part of eastern Canada, is usually considered a nuisance pest of open-grown trees in the family Rosaceae, especially black cherry, crabapple, and apple trees in unkept orchards (Kulman 1965b). Defoliation by the eastern tent caterpillar normally does not cause tree mortality, but reduces the aesthetic value of trees in urban–suburban areas. Crawling tent caterpillars, large silk tents, and defoliated trees are the major problems local residents mention when discussing the eastern tent caterpillar.

The eastern tent caterpillar has one generation per year and overwinters in the egg stage. Eggs hatch in the spring at about the same time that the buds begin to open on host trees. The small caterpillars cluster on or near the egg mass and feed on expanding leaf buds. They build temporary resting pads (i.e., silk pads) on the egg mass or on nearby branches. Some colonies build their tents 1–2 days after hatching, whereas other colonies wait about a week before beginning construction of a silk tent. As the caterpillars grow, they enlarge the tent by laying more silk on the surface of the tent (Figure 11.4). Soon the tent becomes a beautiful object that is often pyramidal in shape. During the first four instars tent caterpillars normally leave the tent shelter to feed three times each day. Late fourth and fifth instar larvae feed at night and rest inside the tent during the daytime. The mature larva is a hairy caterpillar about 50 mm long with a black head and a dark body with a stripe down the back (Figure 11.5). When full-grown, the mature larvae leave the tent and wander in search of places to spin their cocoons. They spin yellow silken cocoons 18–35 mm long in rolled leaves, under fallen branches, in hollow logs, in old tents, on fences, and on other natural and artificial objects. Adult moths emerge in 2–3 weeks and mate. Each fertilized female lays a cylindrical egg mass 12–25 mm long on a twig of the host tree. Egg masses are generally laid near the tips of twigs located 1–5 m above the ground. However, egg masses may also be laid on twigs 20 m above the ground or on the trunks of small trees about 1.5 m above the ground.

During most years, the eastern tent caterpillar is reduced to low numbers by its natural enemies such as ichneumon wasps; tachinid flies; spiders; ants; birds; and virus, bacterial, and fungus diseases (Witter and Kulman 1972). However, populations periodically reach outbreak numbers.

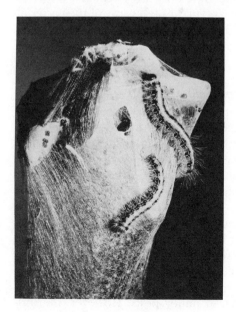

Figure 11.4 Silk tent of the eastern tent caterpillar *Malacosoma americanum*. (Texas Forest Service photograph.)

Figure 11.5 Comparison of the larvae of the eastern tent caterpillar, *Malacosoma americanum* (solid stripe down the back) with the forest tent caterpillar, *M. disstria* (keyhole-shaped spots on its back). (Texas Forest Service photograph.)

The following pest management techniques are recommended for the eastern tent caterpillar: (1) prune off and burn twigs containing egg masses; (2) destroy the small tent when the tent is first noticed (be sure that caterpillars are in the tent and not out feeding on nearby foliage); (3) use a strong water spray from garden hose; and (4) apply a spray of the bacterial disease, *B. thuringiensis*, or a registered chemical insecticide to the tents and surrounding foliage if the tents are extremely numerous or impossible to remove.

Western tent caterpillar, Malacosoma californicum (Packard)

In North America the western tent caterpillar consists of six subspecies that occupy fairly well defined geographic areas (Stehr and Cook 1968). The subspecies *M.c. pluviale* (Dyar) has the largest geographic range and is found in areas of moderate rainfall from the Pacific Northwest eastward through Canada and the northern United States to Quebec. The subspecies *M.c. fragile* (Stretch) inhabits the southwestern states and eastern California. The subspecies *M.c. lutescens* (Neumoegen and Dyar) occur in the Great Plains. Three other subspecies have localized populations in California. All subspecies of the western tent caterpillar build large conspicuous tents (Figure 11.6). Their life cycles are similar to the eastern tent caterpillar. Preferred hosts varies with subspecies and location. Common hosts are oak, willow, cherry, aspen, rose, serviceberry, currant, and bitterbrush. Although conspicuous, most are generally considered minor pests. However, the sub-

Figure 11.6 Western tent caterpillar, *Malacosoma californicum fragile,* on aspen. Note the large silk tents and complete defoliation. (U.S. Forest Service photograph.)

species *M.c. fragile* is considered an important pest of aspen in the southern Rocky Mountains and of bitterbrush in the western United States (Hewitt et al. 1974, Stelzer 1968). This subspecies can reduce growth and kill aspen and bitterbrush, an important browse plant for big game in mountainous areas of the western United States.

Forest Tent Caterpillar, Malacosoma disstria Hübner

The forest tent caterpillar is found throughout the United States and adjacent Canadian provinces on a wide variety of hardwoods. Common hosts are aspen, oaks, sugar maple, water tupelo, black gum, red alder, and willow (Batzer and Morris 1978).

This insect has one generation per year, is a spring–early summer defoliator, and the exact time of defoliation depends on location and yearly weather conditions. Mating and egg laying occur in May in the South and in late June to mid-July in the North. A female moth usually lays a single egg mass, approximately 200 eggs, in a cylindrical band around a small twig (<8 mm in diameter) (Figure 11.7). Egg masses are found predominantly on branches in the upper two-thirds of the crown. Embryo development begins immediately after the egg is laid and the young caterpillar (pharate larva) is fully formed within the egg in 3 weeks. It overwinters as a pharate larva within the egg. Eggs hatch from late February to mid-

(a)

(b)

Figure 11.7 Forest tent caterpillar, *Malacosoma disstria:* (*a*) eggs, (*b*) larvae (*a*—U.S. Forest Service photograph, *b*—The University of Michigan photograph).

March in the South and in late April to late May in the North. The caterpillars are gregarious during the first three larval instars. Although more independent in their feeding habits, the late larval instars are still gregarious and normally rest, feed, or molt in groups until late in the last larval instar or until depletion of their food source. Forest tent caterpillars normally spend 5–8 weeks in the larval stage. The mature larva is 50 mm long and bluish-gray with a row of white keyhole-shaped spots on its back (Figure 11.5). A cocoon is constructed inside a leaf or leaves rolled up by the caterpillar. Cocoons are found on ground vegetation, shrubs, and trees. The location of the cocoons varies with tent caterpillar population density. When light and moderate defoliation occurs, the cocoons are found primarily on leaves of the host tree. If heavy or complete defoliation occurs the majority of cocoons are on ground and shrub vegetation and on nonhost tree species. Adults emerge from the cocoons in 2–3 weeks. The adult moth is 12–18 mm long and light to dark chocolate brown with two darker oblique lines near the middle of the front wings.

The forest tent caterpillar has defoliated aspen and other broad-leaved tree species covering areas as large as 39,000 km^2. In Minnesota and throughout much of the aspen range, the forest caterpillar has greatly reduced tree growth. However, in most studies tree mortality was negligible except for small suppressed trees (Kulman 1971). Tree stem densities and basal areas were reduced per plot by 41 and 27%, respectively, during the 1964–1972 northern Minnesota outbreak (Witter et al. 1975). Tree mortality was most severe on plots with high water tables. Heavy defoliation occurred in the same area for 5–7 consecutive years during this outbreak instead of the 3–4 consecutive years that is characteristic of most outbreaks on aspen. Reduction in radial growth of 70–100% often occurs with 2 or more consecutive years of moderate or heavy defoliation (Duncan and Hodson 1958). They also reported 16–22% growth reductions 1 year beyond cessation of defoliation. Growth returned to predefoliation averages during the second year following the collapse of an outbreak.

Although the forest tent caterpillar is present at endemic levels throughout most of the southern hardwood forests, epidemic population levels seldom occur in the South. The only major exception is the nearly continuous epidemic population of the forest tent caterpillar in the water tupelo and black gum forests of Alabama and Louisiana (Stark and Harper 1982).

Annual flooding of the water tupelo forests during late spring and early summer drowns the pupal stage of many tachinid and sarcophagid flies and prevents the buildup of these parasite populations, which overwinter on the forest floor.

The most important factors affecting the collapse of most forest tent caterpillar outbreaks, acting by themselves or in combination, appear to be (1) high pharate larval mortality due to low winter temperature, (2) high early larval mortality due to harsh weather conditions during the first weeks after hatch, (3) high late larval mortality from starvation, and (4) high pupal parasitism by *Sarcophaga aldrichi* (Parker) (Witter 1979). Witter et al. (1975)

showed a significant relationship and an exponential rise in pharate larval mortality during 1964–1972 with the coldest winter temperature. During this outbreak in northern Minnesota, all observations showed a precipitous rise in pharate larval mortality occurred at -40.6 to -41.7°C. Hanec (1966) reported that the lowest limit of cooling which pharate larva could tolerate before freezing was -40.6 to -41.4°C.

Early spring weather conditions after egg hatch have been responsible for the collapse of several outbreaks. Hodson (1941) and Blais et al. (1955) have shown that the combined action of one or more weather factors (i.e., cold temperature, rain, wind, snow, and absence of foliage due to frost damage) on small larvae have been responsible for the collapse of several outbreaks.

It is difficult to obtain quantitative information on the various mortality factors affecting outbreak populations of fourth and fifth instar larvae because of the wandering larval behavioral patterns. Parasitism, primarily by tachinid flies, ranged from 3 to 23% during 1967 to 1972 (Witter and Kulman 1979). Starvation can lead to extremely high mortality of fourth and fifth instar larvae in areas where egg densities are high, egg hatch is high, and survival during the first 30 days is high because of favorable weather conditions (Hodson 1977). A nuclear polyhedrosis virus can kill large numbers of late instar larvae while the fungus *Entomophthora* often kills large numbers of fifth instar larvae in sites or years with high humidity (Stairs 1972).

Pupal parasitism of the forest tent caterpillar normally increases with the age of the outbreak. However, for reasons discussed earlier, pupal parasitism seldom exceeds 50% in the water tupelo forests of Alabama and Louisiana. In the Great Lakes states and adjacent Canadian provinces, pupal parasitism often approaches 90% or more during the third or fourth year of an outbreak (Hodson 1941). Sarcophagid and tachinid flies are the most common pupal parasites. *Sarcophaga aldrichi* is the most common pupal parasite in the Great Lakes states and adjacent Canada (Witter et al. 1972). Populations of this flesh fly normally increase with the age of the outbreak and parasitize at least 75% of the forest tent caterpillar during the third or fourth year of an outbreak. Heavy pupal mortality caused by *S. aldrichi* augmented by prior reduction in the caterpillar population due to severe weather conditions or starvation can lead to a population collapse.

Pest management techniques suggested for the forest tent caterpillar in forested areas are an annual aerial survey and/or egg mass survey to determine the current or potential defoliation and inspections by the forest manager of the quality of the mature and overmature hardwood stands affected during the outbreak. In Minnesota, it appears that overmature stands have a tendency to deteriorate faster immediately after an outbreak.

In highly used forest recreation areas or urban parks, public demands may occasionally require the use of *B. thuringiensis*, a microbial insecticide, or a chemical insecticide to reduce forest tent caterpillar populations.

Homeowners can mechanically reduce the population in their yards by cutting the egg masses off the trees in the winter or early spring. After the larvae hatch, homeowners can apply microbial or chemical insecticides.

Fall Webworm, Hyphantria cunea (Drury)

The fall webworm, a native insect that occurs throughout North America, is also a major exotic pest in Europe and Asia, first being found in Hungary in 1940. This insect feeds on almost all trees except for conifers and has been collected from over 200 host species in the United States (Warren and Tadic 1970). However, the fall webworm's favored host plants vary by region and country.

In early literature the fall webworm was divided into two species: H. cunea (black-headed race), and H. textor (red-headed race). Today the fall webworm is considered one species with the black-headed predominant in the northern United States and Canada and the red-headed predominant in the southern United States. Both can occur throughout the geographic range. Numerous differences are found in the two races: color marking of larvae and adults, host preferences, behavioral differences, emergence pattern of adults, variations in nest shape, and oviposition habits (Oliver 1964).

The number of generations per year depends on temperature and race. Both races have one generation per year in Canada and the eastern United States. However, the black-headed race has two generations per year in Arkansas and southeastern Oklahoma and four generations per year are common in Louisiana.

The following life cycle covers areas where the fall webworm has one generation per year. Adults emerge during May through June. Mating occurs and females deposit egg masses on the underside of leaves. As soon as small larvae hatch from the eggs, they begin to feed on foliage and enclose it with a silken web. The larvae enlarge the web to enclose more foliage as they grow larger. The black-headed race builds a flimsy web while the red-headed race builds a larger and more compact enclosure (Figure 11.8). Small larvae are window feeders on the enclosed foliage while the large larvae are free feeders on enclosed foliage. Mature larvae leave the web and wander alone for a few days looking for a pupation site. Cocoons are spun in bark fissures on tree trunks, under soil litter or stones, under artificial objects, or underneath the soil surface.

Natural enemies, such as birds, spiders, assassin bugs, ants, ichneumon wasps, and braconid wasps, and various weather factors normally keep fall webworm populations at low to moderate levels in the United States and Canada. However, populations tend to increase over very large areas in eastern Canada during years of high heat accumulation and to decrease during years of low heat accumulation. Morris and Fulton (1970) developed models that showed the potential rate of increase of fall webworm populations should be the highest in areas where mean temperature is high but

Figure 11.8 Fall webworm, *Hyphantira cunea:* (*a*) mature larva, (*b*) web-enclosed foliage (*a*—U.S. Forest Service photograph, *b*—U.S. Forest Service photograph, courtesy of J. Solomon).

not extreme, and where the daily temperature range is small enough to encourage nocturnal activity of the larvae and to discourage diurnal overheating of the webs. Morris (1971) showed that the fall webworm is a sun-loving species and generally occurs in fairly open areas even though high humidity is very critical for the successful hatch and survival of early larval instars.

The fall webworm generally causes no damage in North American forest stands because it prefers more open-grown trees. But the aesthetic value of roadside edges may be reduced by the large number of webs spun by the fall webworm. It can be a pest on ornamentals and shade trees.

Two available pest management techniques are removing and destroying the nests of all webworms on small ornamentals and spraying the ornamental trees with a registered chemical or microbial insecticide.

Leaf Rollers, Leaf Folders, Leaf and Needle Tiers

Caterpillars that roll, fold, or tie leaves or needles together are present in many families, but the majority are found in the families Tortricidae and Olethreutidae. Both conifers and hardwoods are attacked by these caterpillars but conifers are more seriously damaged. Leaf rollers and leaf folders feed inside the shelter of an individual leaf. Leaf or needle tiers, such as the cherry scallop shell moth, *Calocalpe undulata* (Linnaeus), and pine tube moth, *Argyrotaenia pinatubana* (Kearfott), usually tie two to six leaves or needles together with silk and feed inside the shelter. One or more larvae are found per shelter depending on the insect species. Budworm larvae feed in many different ways, but the third to fifth instar larvae tie needles together and use the tied needles as shelter and a food source. Conifer-feeding *Choristoneura* spp. in the family Tortricidae are the most economically important insects with this feeding behavior. Information is presented on four species of *Choristoneura*: spruce budworm, *C. fumiferana* (Clemens); western spruce budworm, *C. occidentalis* Freeman; jack pine budworm, *C. pinus* Freeman; and large aspen tortrix, *C. conflictana* (Walker).

Spruce Budworm, Choristoneura fumiferana (Clemens)

Spruce budworm, the most important insect in North American fir–spruce forests, is found throughout the range of the northern boreal forest (Powell 1980). The most extensive and destructive outbreaks have occurred in the Maritime Provinces (i.e., New Brunswick, Nova Scotia, Newfoundland), Quebec, Ontario, Maine, and the Great Lakes states. This native defoliator feeds primarily on balsam fir and white, red, and black spruce throughout most of its range. At high population densities, the spruce budworm will also feed on associated conifers such as larch and hemlock.

Moths emerge from the pupae in late June to late July and mate soon after emergence. A female moth normally deposits about 170 eggs over a 1–2-week period. She lays 5–50 eggs in each of 5–10 egg clusters with an average cluster containing about 20 eggs (Figure 11.9). Egg clusters are

Figure 11.9 Spruce budworm, *Choristoneura fumiferana:* (*a*) egg, (*b*) larva, (*c*) pupa, (*d*) moth, (*e*) top-kill and severe defoliation on balsam fir. (*a,d*—Canusa Spruce Budworms Program photograph; *b,c,e*-Canadian Forestry Service Photograph, courtesy of I. Otvos.)

found on fir and spruce needles on peripheral shoots in all crown levels, but most eggs occur in the upper half of the crown. Eggs hatch in 10–14 days.

First instar larvae are photopositive and move toward the distal end of branches. This movement can be interrupted by high temperatures, which cause the larvae to settle down and spin a silk shelter called a hibernaculum or by turbulent winds that cause the larvae to drop from the branch on silken threads. Newly hatched larvae do not feed, but disperse within the forest stands, spin hibernaculae on both host and nonhost trees, and then molt to the second instar, which overwinter inside the hibernaculum. Hibernaculae are commonly found in bark fissures, staminate flower bracts, and on lichen mats on branches of host trees (Miller 1958). In late April to mid-May, second instar larvae emerge from the hibernacula and move toward feeding sites. Wind dispersal of small larvae on silk threads also occurs at this time. Second instar larvae mine old needles, unopened vegetative buds, or feed on staminate flowers of host trees. As the buds open and shoots expand, the caterpillars begin feeding on succulent new foliage. A half-grown larva generally constructs a small web-enclosed shelter on one twig and feeds inside this shelter. Larger larvae also prefer current year's foliage but may be forced to "backfeed" and consume old foliage when spruce budworm populations reach high densities. Most feeding damage is caused by fifth and sixth instars. Mature larvae are 20–30 mm long, brown, black, and green with light areas on each side, and with brownish-black prothoracic shield, head, and thoracic legs (Figure 11.9). Pupation occurs in mid-June to early July. After 10–14 days, the adult moth (Figure 11.9) emerges from the pupal case and the spruce budworm has completed its 1-year life cycle.

For centuries the North American boreal forest has experienced periodic spruce budworm outbreaks. Although the spruce budworm is an integral component of the fir–spruce forests in North America, it normally does not prevent the continuity of fir–spruce forests. Fir and spruce usually regenerate after a spruce budworm outbreak, reaching a merchantable size in 40–60 years. The impact of the spruce budworm on forests depends on the intensity and duration of the outbreak and on the value of the affected stands. Defoliation by the spruce budworm results in growth loss, top-kill, tree mortality, stand mortality, changes in stand composition, and economic losses (Table 11.2). Studies on growth loss in North America have shown a 30–90% reduction in radial growth in spruce–fir stands heavily defoliated by the spruce budworm for 2–6 years (Kulman 1971). Minnesota surveys reported as much as 78% of the balsam fir had 183 cm or more of top-kill after 3 years of complete defoliation of new growth (Schmiege 1961). Three or more years of heavy defoliation by the spruce budworm will usually kill the tree. In general, mature fir stands suffered mortality of 70–100% during an outbreak while mortality in immature stands ranges from 30–

70% (MacLean 1980). Economic impact can be severe with losses from the latest outbreak in North America estimated at 283 million m³.

The following factors and conditions usually make a stand more susceptible to outbreaks, more vulnerable to damage, and more favorable to high budworm survival: (1) 50% or more of stand is composed of preferred host species–balsam fir, red spruce, white spruce; (2) the stand has a small percentage of nonhost species; (3) the stand is greater than 50 years old with host trees that are overmature, slow-growing, and producing flowers; (4) an open stand in which spike tops of host species protrude from the forest canopy; (5) a stand with a relatively large number of host trees that have their upper crown needles in direct sunlight; (6) a high stand density of preferred host trees; and (7) a stand under water stress such as a site that is very dry or very wet.

The latest spruce budworm infestation area in North America covers approximately 810,000 ha (Irland 1977, 1980). Active infestations are found in all the Canadian provinces from Ontario eastward, the Great Lake states and in Maine, Vermont, and New Hampshire. Seven major outbreaks, lasting 7–16 years, have been recorded in North America during the last 200 years. Major outbreaks were separated by 30–60 years of very low populations held in check by adverse weather conditions, parasites, and predators. It is difficult to find any larvae between outbreaks, but adults are occasionally collected in light traps. At endemic population levels, the cumulative mortality of each generation of the spruce budworm is 98.8% or greater. Approximately one male and one female moth survive from the complement of eggs ($\bar{X} = 170$) laid by a female moth. However, spruce budworm populations have the potential to increase 300-fold or more during a 4-year period when 3–4 consecutive years of dry, sunny weather occurs during the late spring and early summer in extensive continuous areas of mature and overmature balsam fir (Morris 1963). Under these conditions the spruce budworm mortality rate may drop to 95% or less. Population numbers actually change within an area due to increased local survival and/or immigration of ovipositing females.

A study of the population dynamics of the spruce budworm in northern New Brunswick was conducted from 1945–1959. This classical study produced the first field insect life tables, the first field insect survivorship curves, and the first detailed statistical analysis on the survival and reproduction of a forest insect (Morris and Miller 1954, Morris 1963). These studies showed that mortality occurred in all life cycle stages, but population losses were the most variable during four stages of development: (1) dispersing first instar larvae after hatching in late July or early August, (2) dispersing second instar larvae after emerging from the hibernaculum in the spring, (3) large fourth to sixth instar larvae starving following complete defoliation, and (4) dispersal losses during the adult stage.

Mortality losses of 60–80% usually take place during the early larval stages and are caused primarily by dispersal losses of the newly hatched larvae in late summer and of second instar larvae emerging from hibernaculae and seeking a feeding site in the spring. Weather conditions (e.g., temperature, wind) while the small larvae are dispersing and the characteristics of the forest stand (e.g., density, composition) are the most important factors affecting survival of early instar larvae. Kemp and Simmons (1978) found that open crowns and nonhost tree densities significantly increased mortality of dispersing first and second instar spruce budworm larvae during the late summer and early spring dispersal periods. However, analyses showed that extreme variation in percent survival (10–60%) of large larvae (fourth to sixth instar) had the greatest correlation with population increase or decrease in the next generation, in the absence of moth dispersal. Warm and dry weather conditions in May and June greatly enhance large larvae survival.

Another critical period of population fluctuation is during the adult stage. The newly emerged female is not an active flier, but becomes capable of active flight during the second or third day after laying a few egg clusters. Female moths which have laid about half of their eggs are active fliers and have flight patterns that appear well adapted for long range dispersal (Greenbank et al. 1980). Dispersing females begin their flight by ascending from the trees to heights of 150–300 m above the canopy, and terminate flight with a wind directed dispersal away from the stand. Females make several flights on separate evenings with each flight covering about 80 km, occasionally extending to 250 km.

In the absence of any management technique, spruce budworm outbreaks normally collapse after 7–10 (occasionally 16) years of heavy defoliation. The collapse of outbreaks appears to be related to unfavorable weather conditions in May and June along with a decreased number of favorite host trees and very little available new foliage. As spruce budworm populations decline, predators, parasites, and diseases help to further reduce its populations to endemic levels.

The status of the spruce budworm as a forest management problem depends primarily on the current social and economic conditions, and the management objectives of the landowner. Great regional variations are present in the objectives and strategies for managing the spruce budworm–fir–spruce forest system. In eastern Canada and Maine, the spruce budworm was not considered a major problem until the 1930s, when development of the pulp and paper industry created an economic demand for fir and spruce fiber. By 1950 New Brunswick's economy depended, to a great extent, on six pulp and paper mills. Major economic, social, and political considerations in New Brunswick led to the use of insecticides for foliage protection as the major control technique when the latest spruce budworm outbreak started in the early 1950s. The situation in Quebec and Maine is similar to New Brunswick, except these regions have not used insecticides quite as intensively. In Ontario, the management objectives emphasized protecting forested areas with high recreational value and harvesting susceptible and heavily infested stands when markets were available for the fir and spruce. Management objectives in Minnesota, Wisconsin, and Michigan were primarily "do nothing" except for harvesting susceptible and heavily infested stands if markets were available for the fiber. The economies and forests of the Great Lakes states and Ontario are more diversified than in New Brunswick, Quebec, and Maine. Forest industries in the Great Lakes states are not primarily dependent on fiber from fir and spruce, but also use other tree species such as aspen, red pine, jack pine, sugar maple, and white oak.

Simulation models are extremely useful in evaluating the consequences of alternative management options. There are a number of similar spruce budworm–forest simulation models (Holling 1978, Stedinger 1977, Jones 1976). Using a slight modification of Jones's (1976) model, the Task-Force for Evaluation of Budworm Control Alternatives in New Brunswick considered the impact of several management techniques and policies on New Brunswick's fir-spruce forests and the economic activities of the Canadian forest industry (Baskerville 1976). These and many other analyses showed that the persistence of spruce budworm outbreaks relates to forest structure and is not related to any one budworm control procedure. The Task Force reports that the spruce budworm problem is a lasting one as long as humans continue to have nearly equal annual harvests and "As long as man systematically converts the forest to a balanced age–class structure (the goal of management) the budworm as a competitor to man is here to stay." Some type of forest protection program will continue to be necessary if New Brunswick wants to maintain a forest industry based on fir–spruce forests. Two pest management techniques, which have considerable potential in reducing the impact of spruce budworm outbreaks, are insecticides and forest management–silviculture procedures.

The only technique frequently used to reduce spruce budworm populations has been the application of chemical or microbial insecticides. Programs for spraying forests with insecticides to protect foliage and/or suppress populations have been conducted in New Brunswick, Quebec, Ontario, Manitoba, Nova Scotia, Maine, and Minnesota. Most Canadian spray programs stress foliage protection while the early Maine program (1954 to early 1960s) emphasized population control. The objectives of the Maine programs from the mid-1960s to present has been foliage protection. Prebble (1975) and Irland (1977) provide excellent coverage of the aerial control programs in Canada and Maine, respectively.

The size of these aerial control projects is unique in entomology. They are the largest control projects in the world. The level of specialization of aerial spraying technology for the spruce budworm is unsurpassed by any other insect pest program. These boreal forests of eastern North America are the only extensively managed forests that receive such intensive insect control. The major reasons for the long-term intensive use of chemical insecticides against the spruce budworm in eastern North America are:

regional outbreaks of the spruce budworm that often kill most mature and overmature fir–spruce stands in a reasonably short time period (7–10 years); the dependence of New Brunswick, Quebec, and Maine on forest industry; lack of diversity in forest composition; the availability of an effective insecticide, DDT, during the outbreak of the early 1950s; and the potential economic losses that could occur if insecticides were not used during major regional outbreaks.

Pest managers often must limit the areas receiving insecticides to forest stands and shade trees with the greatest amount of damage (e.g., high hazard) and/or with the highest economic value. Many different sampling techniques can be used to rank damage and/or estimate insect population densities. The spruce budworm biological evaluation program and the general planning procedures for a forest insect spray program in fir–spruce forests in Maine and New Brunswick are used as examples to illustrate (1) a technique for determining high hazard areas and (2) general planning procedures followed in most spray programs involving forest insects. A chronological account of these examples is presented in the following paragraphs and is based on information from Maine and New Brunswick.

In July aerial surveys of the entire fir–spruce types are conducted within the region (i.e., state, province). The amount of defoliation is recorded on a defoliation map for the entire area.

Egg mass surveys are conducted at 1000 sampling locations throughout the region during August and/or September. The number of new egg masses/10.75 m² of foliage is determined by sampling one branch from each of four dominant or codominant fir trees at each location. After estimates of egg mass density, current defoliation, previous defoliation, and tree vigor are obtained, a hazard rating is assigned to each location (Table 11.4). With this information, an egg mass density map and a hazard map are prepared for the region. Finally, a composite hazard map is developed from the hazard map, egg density map, and defoliation map.

Federal, state/province, local and private timber owners meet during the fall and study the data gathered by forest entomologists. The group makes a preliminary decision for or against insecticide spraying in the different areas on the composite map. If their decision recommends spraying, funding is obtained, environmental impact statements are prepared, and other federal and state/provincial regulations are met before the spray program becomes a reality. The final selection of spray areas is determined by the composite hazard map; economic situation (i.e., economic values of timber, dollars available for spraying); management plans; and environmental, social, and political conditions. For example, areas with high environmental hazards, such as beehives, fish hatcheries, poultry houses, major highways, and residential areas are deleted from the spray program and buffer zones are established around them. Recently cutover lands and stands scheduled for cutting within a year are often not included in the spray progam.

Table 11.4   Hazard-Rating System Used in Maine During 1982 (Trial, Unpublished Information)

Current Defoliation, %	Value	Previous Defoliation,[a] %	Value[b]
Trace (0–5)	0	Trace (0–9)	0
Light (6–20)	1	Light (10–49)	3
Moderate (21–50)	2		
Heavy (51–80)	3	Moderate (50–129)	6
Severe (81+)	4	Severe (130+)	9

Egg Mass and Overwintering Larval Deposit

Category	Egg Mass[c]	Second-Instar Larvae[d]	Value
Light	0–99	0–175	1
Moderate	100–239	176–500	2
High	240–399	501–1099	3
Very high	400–999	1100+	5
Extreme	1000+	1100+	5

Tree Vigor	Value	Total Hazard Rating	
		Category	Hazard Value
Good (current foliage healthy)	0	Low	0–6
Fair (shoot production moderate)	1	Moderate	7–16
Poor (some growth capacity)	2	High	16–22
Very poor (nil)	3	Severe	23–26

[a]The 2 previous years' needles.
[b]Add 3 points if there are trees with dead tops in the area (10–20% of the trees).
[c]Number of budworm egg masses/100 ft^2 of foliage.
[d]Number of second-instar budworm larvae/100 ft^2 of foliage.

By mid-winter, insecticides are purchased, contracts for aircraft are obtained, and the final organization plan for the spray program is ready for implementation. The public is kept informed throughout the entire planning and operational stages of the program. Maximum foliage protection and spruce budworm population reduction is obtained by spraying from late May to mid-June when the caterpillars are in the third and fourth instars. Environmental monitoring and evaluation of the spray programs occurs in May through July.

No pest management technique, by itself, will give consistent protection from the spruce budworm. Forest management techniques, which are clearly outbreak prevention strategies, must be integrated with other techniques (i.e., chemical insecticides, microbial insecticides, pheromones) for the development of a more effective pest management program.

All the forest management tactics (Table 11.5) used against the spruce budworm are operational but have developed without the opportunity to be tested effectively. Any recommended forest management techniques are

Table 11.5 Summary of Forest Management Techniques Available for Spruce Budworm/Spruce–fir Management[a]

Method	Use Strategy	Status	Limitations Research and Development	Limitations Use	Potential
Salvage cutting	5	6	Application efficiency	12,14	Low–high
Presalvage cutting	1,2,4	6	Risk-rating systems; application efficiency	14	High
40-year rotation	1	6	Application efficiency	14	High
Changes in stand composition	1	6	Application efficiency cost	10,14	Medium–high
Harvest by "block cutting" in checkerboard pattern	1	6	Application efficiency	14	Medium–high
Maintaining a species mix	1	6	Application efficiency; production methods cost	14	Medium
Clearcut on a 40-year rotation	1	6	Application efficiency	11,14	Medium–high
Developing improved road systems	1,2,3,4	6	Cost	14,15	Medium
Operate harvest cut following a risk-rating system	1,2,4	6	Application efficiency	13	High

Source: After Montgomery et al. 1982b.

[a]Codes:
1 = outbreak prevention	10 = inconsistent
2 = accelerate collapse	11 = public sentiment
3 = foliage preservation during outbreak	12 = application
4 = outbreak suppression	13 = undeveloped
5 = salvaging timber	14 = institutional problems and time requirements
6 = operational	15 = economic costs

based primarily on retrospective analysis of spruce budworm outbreaks. No management techniques have been applied over a long period of time (i.e., 50–100 years) or a sufficient area to predict their effectiveness. The major problems related to their increased use are institutional ones, time requirements, and lack of opportunity to practice intensive forest management instead of extensive forest management in the boreal forests of eastern North America.

The silvicultural tactics for the spruce budworm in the future will include some combination of the following techniques: (1) salvage cut in areas of tree mortality where demand for spruce–fir is high; (2) shorten rotation age to 50 years or less; (3) modify the stand composition to reduce preferred host species by preferential cutting that favors spruce or planting spruce on cutover areas; (4) harvest by strip or patch clearcuts to break up the continuity of large acres of susceptible mature forests (once this pattern is established, higher dispersal losses of both small larvae and adult moths should occur); (5) maintain a mixed species composition whenever possible; (6) presalvage areas identified as vulnerable; (7) develop road systems to permit flexibility in harvesting schedules; and (8) operate the harvest cutting cycle for each year with the following priorities; (a) cut forests that are potential sources of infestation to reduce future risks, (b) presalvage (i.e., cut stands that are severely defoliated), and (c) cut stands that are secondary sources of infestation.

These forest management techniques cannot be practiced at maximum efficiency without an overall management plan for the region, cooperation between landowners, hazard rating systems for each region, yield tables for unmanaged and managed forests so that productivity can be determined, and more information on the stand structure–age class distribution of forests.

Additional information on the spruce budworm can be found in Flexner et al. (1983), Montgomery et al. (1982b), Hudak and Raske (1981), Jennings et al. (1979), Prebble (1975), and McKnight (1968).

Western Spruce Budworm, Choristoneura occidentalis Freeman

The western spruce budworm is an extremely important pest of Douglas-fir, grand fir, subalpine fir, Engelmann spruce, and western larch in British Columbia, Pacific Coast states, and the Rocky Mountain states (Fellin and Dewey 1982, Johnson and Denton 1975, McKnight 1968). The biology and impact of the western spruce budworm are fairly similar to the spruce budworm. Major biological differences of the western spruce budworm are (1) dispersal and feeding of second-instar larvae is extended about 1 month to late June; (2) mature larvae are present to mid-July, and adults are present into early August (Figure 11.10); (3) egg masses contain 25–40 eggs instead of about 20 eggs (Figure 11.10); and (4) overwintering sites for the hibernating larvae includes the boles of host and nonhost trees.

No typical pattern has been apparent in western spruce bedworm outbreaks. Outbreaks in the early twentieth century usually lasted for a few years. The most recent outbreak in the northern Rocky Mountains has persisted since 1949. The extent, tenacity, and stability of the western spruce budworm in the northern Rocky Mountains have been strongly influenced by past fire management practices and partial selective cutting practices. Before colonial settlers entered the area, frequent light ground fires burned through the ponderosa pine-Douglas-fir forests and prevented the establishment of understory thickets of Douglas-fir (Fellin et al. 1983). The recent absence of fire in the Douglas-fir, spruce, and subalpine fir forests has resulted in an increasing proportion of shade-tolerate, bud-worm-vulnerable host species such as true firs and Douglas-fir and has produced a much higher proportion of climax multistoried stands domi-nated by shade-tolerant species. Also, 50 years of uneven-aged stand man-agement has discriminated against intolerant species such as ponderosa pine; this has given the more shade tolerant species such as Douglas-fir and true firs a distinct advantage over intolerant species over large areas.

The greatest impact of the western spruce budworm in mature stands is reduced tree growth. However, repeated defoliation results in top-killing and tree mortality, especially in the suppressed and intermediate trees. Severely defoliated and top-killed Douglas-fir are often attacked and killed by the Douglas-fir beetle, *Dendroctonus pseudotsugae* Hopkins. Budworm larvae also feed on the staminate flowers and developing cones of host trees, causing a serious reduction in the amount of viable seeds. In some Douglas-fir stands, nearly all cones are destroyed when budworm popu-lation densities are high. The western budworm also can affect regenera-tion, especially young trees growing beneath healthy trees; this often occurs in multistoried stands. In young western larch stands, sustained larval feed-ing and severance of new shoots causes top deformity, reduces height growth, and can predispose young trees to secondary insects and wood-decaying fungi (Schmidt and Fellin 1973).

The impact of the budworm on the stand varies considerably, depending on the species composition, stand density, stand age, and site characteristics. Dense, mature, pure stands of host species are highly prone to damage. Defoliation increases in Douglas-fir stands as crown closure increases. Stands composed of mixed species are less vulnerable than pure stands of host species. Losses of volume are greater in shade-tolerant than in shade-in-tolerant species. The budworm does not appear to be a problem in young managed stands under 20 years of age. Growth loss is highest in dry Doug-las-fir habitat types at low elevations on steep slopes, whereas forests in cooler, wetter habitats substain less injury. Also, more defoliation of Doug-las-fir occurs on sites with shallow and dry soils.

Recent pest management approaches in the west have concentrated on silvicultural techniques. Current recommendations are (Schmidt et al. 1983): (1) use the regeneration cutting system most appropriate for the site, (2) use even-aged silvicultural system whenever possible, (3) encourage species

(a)

(b)

Figure 11.10   Western spruce budworm, *Choristoneura occidentalis:* (a) egg masses, (b) feeding shelter and mature larva, (c) adult. (U.S. Forest Service photograph.)

diversity through regeneration and cultural techniques, but always maintain at least two-thirds of stand in seral species, (4) when using the shelterwood system, favor seral species and minimize the number of budworm host species, and (5) enhance the vigor of immature stands by thinnings.

Jack Pine Budworm, *Choristoneura pinus* Freeman

The jack pine budworm is a serious pest of jack pine and occasionally red pine in the Great Lakes states and adjacent Canadian provinces. The life cycle is very similar to the spruce budworms. Jack pine budworm populations are more dependent on male staminate flowers to increase their population numbers. Outbreaks of the jack pine budworm tend to occur at fairly short intervals (i.e., 10–15 years) in an area and generally persist for 3–5 years (Foltz et al. 1972). Outbreaks result from climatic release of endemic populations in susceptible stands (Clancy et al. 1980). Conditions causing the collapse of jack pine budworm populations are poorly understood. Reduced quality of food supply and unfavorable weather conditions, during times when early larval and adult stages disperse, probably cause the collapse (Batzer and Jennings 1980).

Extensive top-killing is common during jack pine budworm outbreaks, but tree and stand mortality is usually less severe than that associated with spruce budworm outbreaks. Tree mortality has been as high as one-third of the merchantable volume and 90% of suppressed and intermediate trees (Kulman et al. 1963). Tree mortality occurs much faster and to a much greater extent when jack pine budworm outbreaks coincide with drought conditions or with outbreaks of the jack pine sawfly, *Neodiprion pratti bank-sianae* Rohwer, or pine tussock moth, *Dasychira pinicola* (Dyar). Usually the most severe damage is found in understocked or overstocked, overmature stands or in stands growing on poor sites.

Chemical or microbial insecticides applied on high-valued stands and good silvicultural practices are the two major techniques used against the jack pine budworm. Commonly recommended silvicultural techniques for the jack pine budworm are planting jack pine and red pine on proper sites, maintaining fully stocked vigorous jack pine and red pine stands, eliminating old "orchard-type" jack pine that have large numbers of male staminate flowers, and utilizing the trees before they become overmature.

Large Aspen Tortrix, Choristoneura conflictana (Walker)

The large aspen tortrix periodically causes heavy defoliation of trembling aspen throughout Canada, northeastern United States, and the Rocky Mountain region (Beckwith 1968, Prentice 1955). Extensive outbreaks have occurred in Manitoba, Saskatchewan, and Alaska. Outbreaks generally last 2–3 years. Starvation of larvae is considered the major cause of the collapse of outbreaks.

The major impact of a large aspen tortrix outbreak is reduced tree growth and occasionally branch and some tree mortality on poor sites. Defoliation also can effect recreational and aesthetic values of host stands located in high-use areas.

Adults of the large aspen tortrix emerge in late June and July. Eggs are laid in flat clusters primarily on the upper surface of trembling aspen leaves located in the upper half of the crown. Eggs begin to hatch in early July. First-instar larvae are found from early July to August. Small larvae are gregarious, appear to web flat leaf surfaces together, and window feed within this closed habitat. The first-instar larvae then move to hibernation sites, such as bark crevices or under a layer of moss at the base of the tree trunk, on the bole of the tree during August. The larvae then molt to the second instar and spin hibernaculae (silken cases) in which they overwinter. Second-instar larvae emerge from the hibernaculae and crawl up the tree during early to mid-May. Dispersal losses can occur at this time. The larvae are sometimes exposed to unfavorable weather such as cold or wet conditions or find tight buds (Witter and Waisanen 1978). Larvae then mine the aspen buds shortly after the buds begin to swell. The second and third-instar larvae remain in the mined buds and developing shoots and leaves for 10–14 days. The fourth- and fifth-instar larvae roll leaves and feed within the enclosures. Pupation normally occurs in June within rolled leaves.

Pest management techniques are usually not required against the large aspen tortrix because the population collapses in 2–3 years, before tree mortality occurs. Occasionally, a registered chemical or microbial insecticide may be used to reduce larval populations in high-use areas such as campgrounds.

Leaf and Needle Miners

Lepidopterous caterpillars that bore inside the epidermis of a leaf or needle are identified by their feeding damage and by bodies with five pairs of visible crochets and prolegs that are very short or absent. All leaf and needle miners, regardless of insect order are described together later in this chapter.

Loopers

All looper caterpillars belong to the family Geometridae; over 1200 species occur in the United States and Canada. All members of this family are free feeders, most inhabit urban and forest trees, and they occur on both hardwoods and conifers. Looper caterpillars are distinguished from all other lepidopterous caterpillars by having two or three pairs of prolegs that are located on the posterior abdominal segments instead of the normal five pairs that are located on the middle abdominal segments. Without prolegs on the middle abdominal segments, these looper caterpillars crawl in a looping motion, bringing the rear end up to the thoracic legs, forming a loop of the body, and then it extends the whole body forward. This characteristic looping motion was responsible for many common names for this family such as inchworms, measuring worms, geometers, and spanworms. Another behavioral trait of loopers is cryptic coloration. When disturbed, these naked drab-colored caterpillars remain motionless and resemble small twigs or spurs. Information is presented on cankerworms, elm spanworm, and hemlock loopers.

Cankerworms

The fall cankerworm, *Alsophila pometaria* (Harris), and the spring cankerworm, *Paleacrita vernata* (Peck), occur throughout the eastern United States, eastern Canada, Prairie states, and westward to Alberta, Montana, and Colorado (Johnson and Lyon 1976). The spring cankerworm is also found in Texas, Colorado, Utah, New Mexico, and California. These two species of cankerworms often occur together, feed at the same time of year, cause similar damage, and appear similar in the adult stage. Cankerworms feed on many different hardwood trees, including elm, apple, maple, hickory, hackberry, oak, boxelder, and basswood.

These insects average about 4 years of high population levels in the same area followed by 12–18 years of low population levels. Fall and spring cankerworm populations are usually regulated by numerous species of natural enemies. It appears that mortality in the egg stage due to egg parasites and unfavorable weather conditions are often responsible for the collapse of cankerworm outbreaks. Cool, wet weather during early larval development and food shortages during large larval development have also led to population collapse.

Cankerworms have one generation per year. Eggs hatch in early spring. Small larvae are hole feeders; large larvae are free feeders. Cankerworm larvae spin silk thread while feeding, which allows them to drop from the foliage if disturbed, to escape predators. The silk threads also enhance wind dispersal from tree to tree and stand to stand. Cankerworm larvae vary considerably in color from green to black, but the fall cankerworm larvae can be distinguished from the spring cankerworm by the number of pairs of prolegs. Fall cankerworms have three pairs of prolegs, whereas spring cankerworms have two pairs of prolegs. Larval development is completed in 5–6 weeks. During June, the mature larvae normally drop to the ground, burrow through the litter layer, and spend the pupal period in a cocoon (e.g., fall cankerworm) or as mature larvae in earthen cells in the soil (e.g., spring cankerworm).

Fall cankerworm adults emerge from the soil during late October to December after some heavy freezes. Male cankerworms are winged moths, whereas female cankerworm moths are wingless and somewhat spiderlike. Mating occurs while the wingless females crawl up tree trunks searching for places on small twigs to deposit their eggs. Fall cankerworm females each lay about 100 eggs in a compact mass with uniform rows of single layers on smaller twigs and branches (Figure 11.11). The fall cankerworm overwinters in the egg stage.

The spring cankerworm spends June to late winter as a mature larva in an earthen cell in the soil. During late winter, the spring cankerworm

Figure 11.11 Larva of fall cankerworm, *Alsophila pometaria*, emerging from an egg mass. Dark spots on egg mass are individual eggs from which larvae have emerged. (U.S. Forest Service photograph.)

pupates in the soil. Adults emerge in very early spring and mate. The wingless female moths crawl up the tree and deposit loose clusters of about 100 eggs in bark cracks and under bark scales. Eggs of both species hatch in early spring, and both species of cankerworms feed as larvae on foliage during May and June.

Cankerworm infestations usually are very localized on shade trees, but cankerworm outbreaks have also occurred over large areas of shelterbelt plantings and forests. Damage by cankerworm feeding has caused reduced tree growth, branch dieback, and general weakening of trees so that secondary insects and diseases may kill the tree. However, tree mortality seldom occurs strictly as a result of cankerworm feeding. The major impact of large numbers of cankerworms on shade and park trees is the nuisance they cause humans.

Control programs for cankerworm infestations in cities and farm shelterbelts have involved (1) the application of chemical and microbial insecticides to kill small larvae and (2) banding of tree trunks 1 m above ground to prevent the wingless females from crawling up the tree to lay eggs. This technique of banding trees to prevent wingless females from laying eggs is fine in theory, but it normally does not control cankerworms because (1) young cankerworms readily blow from tree to tree on silk threads and can avoid bands, (2) people do not clean the bands and apply new sticky material when they become crowded with moths, and (3) people forget or fail to recognize that there are two species and only band for one species—either the fall or spring cankerworm.

Elm Spanworm, Ennomos subsignarius (Hübner)

The elm spanworm is a major forest and shade tree pest in the eastern United States and southeastern and southcentral Canada (Drooz 1980). Outbreaks normally appear at infrequent intervals within a particular locality. The name "elm spanworm" was applied to this insect in the late 1800s when a prolonged outbreak developed in the elm-shaded cities of the northeastern United States. Its name is misleading because the elm spanworm is a polyphagous feeder, preferring hickories, black walnut, white ash, and oaks as hosts. During outbreaks it feeds on most hardwood tree species except for tulip-poplar.

This insect is an early spring to summer defoliator, has one generation per year, and overwinters in the egg stage. Egg masses are predominately found on the trunk and branches of host trees. The compact egg mass (Figure 11.12) contains a few to 150 eggs, with most masses having 50–80 eggs. Eggs hatch from late April to late May in the South and mid-May to early June in the Northeast. Newly hatched larvae often drop from branches on silk strands. Large numbers of first-instar larvae, that are suspended on silk strands, are transported up mountain slopes by winds. Early-instar larvae are hole feeders, whereas the later-instar larvae are free feeders. Elm spanworm larvae usually develop through five instars over a 6–week period. Mature caterpillars (Figure 11.12) are naked, twiglike, slightly greater than 50 mm long and normally dull slate black at epidemic population levels and a lighter color at endemic population levels. White elm spanworm moths (Figure 11.12) with a wingspread of 30–37 mm emerge from the pupal stage during the evening hours in late June and early July. Mating and egg laying takes place within 1–2 days after emergence. Very often

Figure 11.12 Elm spanworm, *Ennomos subsignarius:* (*a*) egg mass, (*b*) larva, (*c*) pupae, (*d*) adults. (U.S. Forest Service photograph.)

spectacular swarms of primarily male moths are attracted to the lights of nearby cities during elm spanworm outbreaks.

The elm spanworm is a sporadic pest of shade and forest trees in the Northeast and of forest trees in the southern Appalachians. Elm spanworm populations were extremely abundant in the northeastern urban areas such as New York and Philadelphia during 1836–1870. The last extensive outbreak in the Northeast was in southeastern New York and Connecticut from 1971 to 1973. Outbreaks of over 0.6 million ha have occurred in the oak–chestnut and oak–hickory forests of the southern Appalachians. The factors responsible for the release of elm spanworm populations to outbreak levels are unknown. Entomologists have observed that egg parasites and a late spring frost are the major factors causing the collapse of an outbreak. Fedde (1964) reported that 2 or more consecutive years of defoliation caused 50% radial growth loss and stem dieback. He also stated that tree mortality losses were estimated at greater than 800 thousand cubic meters for Georgia and Tennessee during the 1954–1964 outbreak. The upper slopes and ridgetops of the southern Appalachians were afflicted with the most severe defoliation and heaviest tree mortality. The factors responsible for this have not been proved conclusively, but it may be due to (1) increased population levels at these locations due to wind dispersal of larvae and adults, (2) increased larval survival due to abundance of preferred hosts, and (3) poorer site conditions leading to trees being under more stress. Trees, especially oaks, weakened from elm spanworm defoliation are often killed by the twolined chestnut borer, *Agrilus bilineatus* (Weber), a secondary invader.

The oviposition location of elm spanworm females varies by region and probably evolved through differential survival of eggs laid in shady locations. In the South egg masses are deposited on the underside of branches with 60% of the masses laid on sections of branches 1.0–1.5 cm in diameter and 75% of the masses located 1.0–1.5 m from branch tip (Drooz and Solomon 1961). Later field experiments determined that mortality within the egg mass from solarization increased clockwise from north through west with 100% mortality in masses directed toward zenith and normal survival for masses exposed toward nadir (Drooz and Solomon 1964). Most egg masses in Connecticut are found on the tree trunks with only 21% on the branches (Kaya and Anderson 1973). They also reported that egg masses were deposited primarily on the southeastern side of the tree bole 5–12 m above the ground.

Egg parasitism is the most common cause of egg mortality. Egg parasitism was the primary factor responsible for the collapse of the 1954–1964 and 1971–1973 outbreaks (Ciesla 1964, Kaya and Anderson 1974). Egg parasites were not identified correctly until 1978. A scelionid wasp, *Telenomus droozi* Muesebeck (formerly called *T. alsophilae* Viereck), is the important egg parasite found in the Southeast. An encyrtid wasp, *Ooencyrtus ennomophagus* Yoshimoto [formerly most often called *O. clisiocampae* (Ashmead)], and *T. droozi* are the major egg parasites reared from elm spanworm eggs in the Northeast. Both parasites, either separately or in combination, are often responsible for elm spanworm population collapses in the Northeast. The biologies of the egg parasites, including percentage of egg parasitism, are presented by Ciesla (1965) and Kaya and Anderson (1976).

A second important factor leading to collapse of elm spanworm outbreaks is weather. Late spring frosts can cause the collapse of elm spanworm populations in the Appalachian Mountains from Pennsylvania to Georgia. For example, a late spring frost in 1977 killed the newly flushed foliage and led to the starvation of the early larvae during an outbreak in Pennsylvania.

The quality and quantity of foliage can affect the survival, length of developmental times, and fecundity of the elm spanworm. In laboratory studies, Drooz (1970) showed that larvae reared on juvenile foliage from red oak or pignut hickory had significantly greater fecundity and larval weight than did elm spanworms reared on more developed foliage from the same hosts. Elm spanworms reared on hickory matured faster and had greater fecundity than did those reared on oaks. A diet of foliage from previously defoliated mockernut hickory and red oak caused no known effects on the development of elm spanworms. Observations indicated that the major effect of an outbreak on the diet of elm spanworm was the scant, erratic, or late foliation of the host tree species.

Several pest management techniques can be used with the elm spanworm: (1) annual aerial surveys of damage and/or egg mass surveys of the elm spanworm are suggested in forested areas (Drooz and Solomon 1961, Kaya and Anderson 1973), (2) salvage operations are appropriate for high-valued forest lands if mortality begins to occur, and (3) public demands may occasionally require the use of a microbial or chemical insecticide to reduce elm spanworm populations in heavily used forest recreation areas or urban parks.

Hemlock Loopers

Two subspecies of the hemlock looper are major pest problems in the coniferous forests of North America. The hemlock looper, *Lambdina fiscellaria fiscellaria* (Guenée), is found in the eastern United States and in Canada from Newfoundland to Alberta. Its preferred hosts are balsam fir, white spruce, black spruce, and eastern hemlock. The western hemlock looper, *Lambdina fiscellaria lugubrosa* (Hulst), occasionally is an extremely destructive pest in the coastal forests of Oregon, Washington, and British Columbia. It is also found in Alaska and in the interior mountainous areas of south-central British Columbia, northern Idaho, western Montana, and northeastern Oregon. The western hemlock looper usually feeds on western hemlock; Sitka, Engelmann, and white spruce; Douglas-fir; western red cedar; and true firs.

The life cycles of both subspecies are similar. The hemlock loopers have one generation per year and overwinter in the egg stage. Eggs hatch in late May, June, or early July. Young larvae feed on new foliage, whereas older larvae feed on new and old foliage. They are wasteful feeders and seldom consume the entire needle. The damaged needles begin to turn brown in July. During heavy infestations, caterpillar feeding causes the stands to have a brown scorched appearance from July to October. The mature larvae, about 30 mm long, complete feeding in late summer. Pupation sites include bark crevices, moss on bark, and debris on the ground. Adults are present in early to middle fall. Eggs are laid on moss, lichens, and bark of tree trunks and limbs and on moss on understory shrubs and downed logs.

The hemlock looper is primarily a major pest on mature balsam fir and eastern hemlock from southern Ontario to Newfoundland and in the northeastern United States (Carroll 1956). During a recent outbreak in Newfoundland, about 1 million hectares of balsam fir were sprayed to protect host trees from hemlock looper (Prebble 1975). Also, about 700,000 cunits of balsam fir were salvaged during the 1966–1971 outbreak, about 16% of the timber volume killed by the hemlock looper.

The western hemlock looper has caused the most damage in mature and overmature western hemlock stands. However, recent outbreaks have also occurred in vigorous 80–100-year-old hemlock stands.

Periodic outbreaks of both subspecies occur in North America. Hemlock loopers usually persist in outbreak numbers for 2–3 years before the insect population collapses as the result of predators, parasites, diseases such as a polyhedrosis virus and *Entomophthora* fungi, food shortage, and unusually wet cool weather.

The major pest management techniques used against hemlock loopers in the past have been chemical insecticides and salvaging of dead timber.

Naked Caterpillars

These caterpillars have five pairs of prolegs and generally live exposed on foliage, and the body is relatively free of hairs, tubercles, or spines. Naked caterpillars meeting the above criteria usually are found in the families Notodontidae, Dioptidae, Noctuidae, and Lyonetiidae. However, all species in each of these four families do not meet the above requirements, and some are not leaf feeders. Examples of naked caterpillars belonging to the four families are presented.

Notodontids, Notodontidae

This family contains over 100 species of caterpillars that feed on the leaves of deciduous trees and shrubs. Notodontid larvae vary from having very few hairs, tubercles, or spines to having many hairs, striking protuberances, or being humpbacked in appearance. The examples covered in this type represents members of the family that have few hairs, tubercles, or spines.

The redhumped oakworm, *Symmerista canicosta* Franclemont, is primarily a pest in the northern oak forests of the eastern United States and southern Canada. Outbreaks develop in predominantly mature white oak forests, occur at 10–15-year intervals, and last for 1–3 years (Miller and Wallner 1975). This insect seldom causes tree mortality, but its major impact is on humans using the infested areas for recreation during August through October. People are extremely annoyed by the large number of mature caterpillars crawling about in outbreak areas during August and September. Also, the tourist industry in Michigan reported a business decline in outbreak areas during September and October of the early 1970s because there were few leaves remaining on the trees, thus reducing the amount of fall colors. Most outbreaks collapse as a result of starvation and diseases affecting mature larvae.

The redhumped oakworm produces one generation per year and overwinters as a pupa in the duff, usually as a cocoon spun among leaves or pieces of litter. Moths emerge in June or July, mate, and lay egg masses on the underside of oak leaves. Small caterpillars hatch from the eggs in July and August. This late season defoliator feeds, as a window feeder, in a colony on the upper surface of the leaf. Larger larvae are less gregarious than smaller larvae and consume entire leaves except for major veins. A mature larva has a smooth, hairless body with four longitudinal yellow stripes on the body separated by five black lines along the back and three black lines along each side (Figure 11.13). It is also about 40 mm long and has an orange–red head and an enlarged orange–red hump on the eighth abdominal segment.

The orangehumped mapleworm, *Symmerista leucitys* Franclemont, is very similar to the redhumped oakworm except that mature larvae have three black lines along the back instead of five. It prefers to feed on sugar maple, basswood, and elm, but also may feed on oak. The life cycle, range, and habits are approximately the same as the redhumped oakworm (Allen 1979).

The variable oakleaf caterpillar, *Heterocampa manteo* (Doubleday), a very common pest of white oaks, is found throughout most of the United States and Canada east of a line drawn from western Ontario to eastern Texas (Wilson 1971a). It is often found on oak but also causes damage to other hardwood trees such as beech, basswood, paper birch, and elm. Outbreaks normally last for 2–3 years before collapsing. Infestations are normally more severe in the South, where some tree mortality occasionally occurs. However, the major impacts are reduced tree growth, nuisance effect of mature caterpillars on homeowners and recreationists, and the aesthetic effects of bare trees on humans.

This insect produces one generation per year in the northern part of its range, and two generations per year occur south of a line extending from Virginia to Missouri. Its life cycle in the North is very similar to the life cycle just described for the redhumped oakworm. In the South, the variable oakleaf caterpillar moths emerge and lay eggs in April, larvae hatch

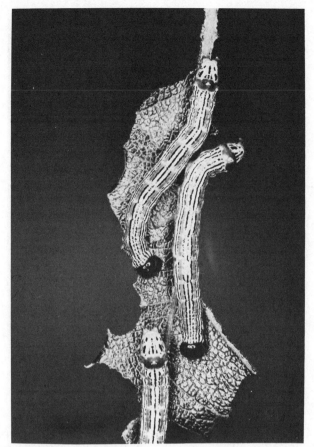

Figure 11.13 An oak leaf with feeding larvae of the redhumped oakworm, *Symmerista canicosta*. (U.S. Forest Service photograph.)

in May, and feeding occurs during May and June. Pupation takes place in the soil during late June. Adults emerge, mate, and lay eggs in July. Second-generation larvae feed during August, September, and early October. Mature larvae spin cocoons in the ground litter. This insect overwinters as a prepupa in a cocoon and pupates the following spring.

The variable oakleaf caterpillar is a window feeder in the early instars, whereas the larger larvae are free feeders. Mature larvae are about 40 mm long, vary considerably in color, but generally have a yellow–green body with a pale line running along the dorsal midline (Figure 11.14). These larvae may have a very striking reddish-brown color pattern on the dorsal side of the body; this color pattern is highly variable and irregular in size and shape.

The saddled prominent, *Heterocampa guttivitta* (Walker), is a pest of sugar maple, beech, and paper birch throughout the eastern United States and

Figure 11.14   Variable oak leaf caterpillar, *Heterocampa manteo*. (U.S. Forest Service photograph, courtesy of J. Solomon.)

southern Canada (Allen and Grimble 1970). Mature larvae are about 30 mm long and are usually green with purple, gold, and brown markings on the back. Life cycle, habits, and impact of this insect are similar to the variable oakleaf caterpillar.

No pest management actions are normally recommended for any of the late-season notodontids that attack forest stands. The outbreaks generally collapse before any serious tree mortality occurs. Homeowners can use a registered microbial or chemical insecticide to kill the notodontid larvae if these insects become a problem on shade trees in cities.

California Oakworm, Phryganidia californica Packard

The California oakworm is the only species in the family Dioptidae. It has not been found outside of California except for feeding on golden chinkapin in Oregon. The California oakworm normally does not cause any major problems, but at irregular intervals it reaches outbreak numbers and becomes an important ornamental pest of primarily live oak and California oak in the coastal valleys of California. The oakworm seldom causes tree mortality, but reduces tree growth, makes the trees unsightly, and reduces the shade-producing value of affected trees. The small larvae are window feeders while the older larvae are free feeders. Outbreaks usually last for 2–3 years with starvation, parasites, predators, and a virus disease responsible for the collapse of the population (Wickman 1971, Harville 1955).

There are two generations per year throughout California except in southern California where three generations per year with overlapping broods are found. In most of California, there is a 3-month summer brood and a 9-month winter brood. Eggs are laid in October and November with the small larvae emerging in November and December. The larvae from the winter brood can survive only on evergreen live oak and they pupate in May and June. Adults lay eggs in June and July; the summer brood feeds on live or diciduous oaks during July, August, and early September. Pupation occurs in September and early October.

The best pest management strategy is to do nothing unless the California oakworm larvae reaches high population levels and becomes a major nuisance factor. Then, a bacterial insecticide, *B. thuringiensis*, can be used on third instar larvae to reduce populations (Pinnock and Milstead 1971).

Cutworms, Noctuidae

The Noctuidae is the largest family of Lepidoptera in North America (Crumb 1956). Adult noctuids are commonly attracted to night lights, are heavy bodied, and dull colored with wings folded tentlike when at rest. The larvae, often referred to as cutworms, are naked, dull colored, sluggish caterpillars that feed at night, and often cut off the stem of young succulent plants. Other species of noctuid larvae feed on the foliage of many different forest and shade trees and ornamental plants. Cutworms can be serious problems on agricultural crops, but seldom cause major problems to forest and shade trees. However, they can occasionally cause serious problems in nurseries, in young conifer plantations, and on young ornamental plantings. Clean cultural techniques and the use of chemical insecticides are the two major techniques used against cutworms.

Bucculatrix Leaf Skeletonizers

The *Bucculatrix* leaf skeletonizers are in the family Lyonetiidae. Most species of *Bucculatrix* are leaf miners during the early larval stages and window feeders when the larvae become older (Figure 11.15). The two most common species are the birch skeletonizer, *B. canadensisella* Chambers (Friend 1927), and the oak skeletonizer, *B. ainsliella* Murtfeldt (Gibbons and Butcher 1961).

The birch skeletonizer is found throughout the United States and Canada wherever birch grows. The tiny moths appear in late June and July; they mate and the females lay eggs singly on birch leaves. Young larvae (first through third instars) feed as serpentine miners for 2–4 weeks. They emerge through the lower surface of the leaf and then spin a small, flat web in which they molt to the next instar. The last two instars (about 6 mm long) feed as window feeders on the underside of birch leaves. Pupation

Figure 11.15   Window feeding on red oak leaves by the oak skeletonizer, *Bucculatrix ainsliella*. When this insect was named, both window feeding damage and skeletonizing damage were lumped together and called leaf skeletonizers. (U.S. Forest Service photograph.)

occurs in September and they overwinter as cocoons on the underside of fallen leaves. The birch skeletonizer tend to occur in outbreaks at about 10-year intervals with the duration of outbreak lasting 2–3 years. Heavy defoliation can occur, but the birch skeletonizer alone seldom causes tree mortality. However, the birch skeletonizer alone or along with another defoliator such as the birch leafminer, *Fenusa pusilla* (Lepeletier), may seriously weaken the tree. The tree then often is attacked and killed by the bronze birch borer, *Agrilus anxius* Gory.

Hairy Caterpillars
This group includes caterpillars that live exposed on the foliage, has a body that is covered with short or long hairs, enlarged tubercles, or lobelike extensions of the exoskeleton. These hairy caterpillars (Figure 11.16) are found on both hardwood and conifers. They belong to the families Lymantriidae, Arctiidae, Notodontidae, and Pieridae. Not all species in the Notodontidae and Pieridae meet the above requirements. The forest tent caterpillar, *M. disstria*, meets the requirements of a hairy caterpillar, but it was covered under the tent makers and webworms type since all other species in the genus *Malacosoma* build tents. Detailed information is now presented on three species of hairy caterpillars.

Figure 11.16 White marked tussock moth larvae, *Hemerocampa leucostigma,* an example of a hairy caterpillar in the family Lymantriidae that is commonly found on shade trees in eastern North America. (U.S. Forest Service photograph.)

Gypsy Moth, Lymantria dispar (Linnaeus)

The gypsy moth is native to temperate regions of Europe, southern Asia, and Africa. Over much of its native range, it occasionally reaches outbreak numbers. It was accidentally introduced from Europe into North America in 1869 at Medford, Massachusetts, by a French naturalist who had intended to cross it with the silkworm, *Bombyx mori* (Linnaeus). In North America, the initial spread was to the north and east reflecting the prevailing winds during dispersal of first instar larvae. The gyspy moth slowly expanded its range to cover all of the New England states. It is now found in New Jersey, New York, Pennsylvania, Delaware, Maryland, and Virginia. The gypsy moth is also found in southern Canada. Isolated populations have been found in numerous areas throughout the United States including the South, Midwest, and Far West. Because of the severity and scope of the gypsy moth problem in the United States during the early 1970s, the insect was selected by the USDA for accelerated research work during 1971 through 1978. A true state-of-the-art compendium, covering this work, entitled "The Gypsy Moth: Research Toward Integrated Pest Management" (Doane and McManus 1981) was published in 1981. Most of the material presented in this section on the gypsy moth was taken from the compendium.

The gypsy moth overwinters in the egg stage. The majority of the egg masses are laid on trunks, boles, and branches of trees, but many egg masses also are found on rocks, fallen logs, and stumps. Survival of egg masses may increase in colder regions by behavioral adaptations, with females depositing eggs nearer the ground, where they are more likely to be protected by insulation from snow. Leonard (1972) showed that 81% of the egg masses from a gypsy moth population in northern Maine were laid below 1.5 m whereas only 30% of the egg masses in most areas of New England were found below 1.5 m. In northern Maine, less than 1% of the masses above 1.5 m survived whereas 74% of the egg masses below 0.3 m survived. The effect of snow as an insulation factor is clearly seen. Temperatures of $-29°C$ are lethal to overwintering eggs, but factors such as duration of low temperature, winter conditioning of eggs to low temperature, and population quality can have additional effects on overwintering survival of eggs.

An average egg mass contains about 750 eggs when conditions are optimum and about 300 eggs per egg mass when populations start to decline near the end of an outbreak. The newly hatched larvae are morphologically and behaviorally well adapted for dispersal. Most larvae disperse short distances by air currents, usually less than 1 km from point or origin. This distance is probably covered through a series of short hops or by several dispersal episodes.

Larvae feed from early May to late June. Young larvae are restricted to feeding on tree species such as oaks, birches, aspen, and basswood. Older larvae can survive on most tree species; over 300 different tree species have been recorded as hosts for gypsy moths. The feeding rhythm differs between small and large larvae (Leonard 1970). The first three larval stages feed in the daytime, after sunrise and at lesser amounts before sunset. The older larvae (fourth through sixth instars) begin feeding just before sunset and feed until midnight, with smaller feeding peaks occurring from midnight to 6 A.M. The older larvae then descend the tree to darkened, sheltered areas on the lower tree bole such as crevices in the trunk, under loose bark, or on the underside of the scaffold limbs near the trunk. If no suitable sites are located on the tree, larvae will seek shelter in nearby leaf litter, in rocky areas, or in nearby human-provided shelters such as firewood and abandoned trash. During heavy infestations, larvae remain on the foliage and are active continuously.

Mature larvae (Figure 11.17) seek sheltered places to pupate with pupation generally occurring in early July. They pupate almost anywhere, for example, on limbs and trunks of standing trees, stones, and fallen branches; in woodpiles; under lumber; and on automobiles and campers. We immediately see another important means of dispersal—long-range dispersal of pupae and egg masses by means of recreational vehicles, building materials, lumber, and firewood. Adults emerge and mate in late July or early August. Females cannot fly but crawl a short distance, up to 1 m, from the empty pupal case and mate. Females immediately lay oval egg masses that are covered with buff-colored hair from their abdomens.

Male gypsy moths can fly and are dark brown with blackish bands across

Figure 11.17 Gypsy moth, *Lymantria dispar:* (*a*) adult male, (*b*) adult female, (*c*) larva, (*d*) pupa. (U.S. Forest Service photograph.)

the forewings (Figure 11.17). Females are almost white (Figure 11.17), are larger than the males, and they cannot fly.

In summation, the following factors have contributed to the success of the gypsy moth in North America: (1) high reproductive potential, (2) its polyphagous feeding habits, (3) large acreages of its preferred host plant, oaks, (4) short-range dispersal power of first instar larvae, (5) behavioral adaptations of larvae and adults, (6) spread of pupae and egg masses into new areas by way of recreational vehicles, (7) large outbreaks of gypsy moth in the northeastern United States during the 1970s and 1980s, (8) lack of predators and parasites of gypsy moth in new areas of infestation, and (9) a reduction in acreage being treated with insecticides.

Numerous studies have been conducted on the population dynamics of the gypsy moth (Doane and McManus 1981, pp. 65–214, Campbell et al. 1978, Campbell 1967). In North America, the gypsy moth operates in a bimodal fashion with stable modes (innocuous and outbreak) and transient modes (release and decline) (Campbell and Sloan 1978a,b). In contrast, the gypsy moth populations in Europe are cyclic and tend to increase from innocuous to outbreak levels every 7–9 years.

In North America the gypsy moth population may remain in the innocuous mode (i.e., range of 2–25,000 larvae per hectare) indefinitely, although factors that result in stability at low levels have the least effect along the advancing front of the generally infested area. Vertebrate and invertebrate predators, such as black-capped chickadees, blue jays, white-footed mice, shorttail shrews, spiders, harvestmen, and ground beetles, exert the most general regulating effect on sparse gypsy moth populations (Campbell and Sloan 1977b, Campbell 1974). However, predation plays a minor role in regulating population numbers once the gypsy moth reaches outbreak numbers. Under favorable weather conditions, adequate plant numbers, and appropriate plant quality, gypsy moths may exceed the limit of predatory influence, and the insect population enters the release phase. Gypsy moth populations in the release phase are characterized by large egg masses, a high percentage of female pupae, and healthy and vigorous caterpillars (Campbell 1978b). Under these condition, gypsy moth populations enter the outbreak phase, with population densities ranging from 250,000 to 12,500,000 per hectare. Area-wide outbreaks can occur for up to 10 years, but generally population densities in localized areas remain high for 2–3 years. At this time, the impact of defoliation on the host tree changes the nutritive quality of the host tree foliage, which affects the quality of the gypsy moth population. Gypsy moth populations at this point are characterized by reduced pupal weights, high mortality, and physiological stress. Decline of the population from the outbreak phase to innocuous phase occurs due to adverse weather conditons, such as low winter temperatures or abundant precipitation during larval development, or nucleopolyhedrosis virus.

The gypsy moth has killed large numbers of oaks, gray birch, and lesser amounts of white pine and red maple throughout New England, New Jersey, and Pennsylvania (Campbell and Sloan 1977a). Reanalysis of defoliation records in New England between 1911 and 1922 by Campbell and Valentine (1972) of 121 plots showed that after 12 years, including 2 consecutive years of heavy defoliation, tree losses averaged 58% for white oak, 55% for gray birch, 46% for black and scarlet oak, 27% for red oak, 26% for white pine, and 25% for red maple. Mortality was the highest in trees suppressed and in poor condition before defoliation. Heavy to severe defoliation by the gypsy moth for longer than 2 consecutive years can have devastating effects. Coniferous trees die after one severe defoliation, but deciduous trees can usually withstand several defoliations. Little tree growth occurs during these outbreaks. Understory trees and trees suffering from drought conditions or poor site conditions are the first to die (Houston and Valentine 1977). Defoliation by the gypsy moth predisposes trees to attack by the shoestring fungus, *Armillariella mellea* (Vahl. ex. Fr.) Karst and the twolined chestnut borer, *Agrilus bilineatus* (Weber). Houston (1973, 1974) and Wargo (1977, 1978) suggest that both the gypsy moth and secondary organisms are involved with oak mortality. On some trees, shoestring root-rot was the most important secondary organisms; on other trees it was the two-lined chestnut borer, and on other trees both organisms were equally involved. Therefore, both secondary organisms can be involved. Trees die because photosynthesis, growth regulators, and water and nutrition relations are affected in the crown by the defoliator and the borer, in the main stem by the borer, and in the roots by the fungus (Wargo 1977).

Currently, the gypsy moth is a notorious nuisance pest in Europe and much of the New England states. It often kills a large number of trees as it first moves into a new area as indicated by historical records for New England (Campbell 1978a, Campbell and Valentine 1972). More recently this sequence has occurred in parts of New Jersey and Pennsylvania (Kregg 1973, Nichols 1968).

Tree mortality has been less of a concern in the Northeast than the loss of the use of recreational areas. Moeller et al. (1977) showed that home-owners considered the effects of nuisance and defoliation by the gypsy moth on backyard recreation and on the enjoyment of natural beauty as the major impacts with tree mortality a distance third. If and when the gypsy moth reaches high populations on hardwood trees in the southern Appalachians, timber impacts will be of greatest interest because these forests are heavily utilized for sawlog production.

The larvae can be a considerable nuisance during an outbreak since larvae crawling around homes, backyards, and recreational areas reduces the value of these areas to serve their purposes during late May, June, and early July. For example, people do not react too well to frass (i.e., insect droppings) in their hamburgers. Reduced attendance in recreational areas and resorts are common during outbreaks. The reduced value of residential homelots with defoliated and dead trees and replacement and removal costs of dead oak trees are other factors that concern homeowners. In other words, the experience of living with gypsy moths is distasteful for persons who cannot avoid coexisting with gypsy moth outbreaks.

For the above reasons, many states have been strongly encouraged by individuals and certain groups that gypsy moth populations must be treated with insecticides. Motives and reasons for desiring treatment varies somewhat but the desire to suppress gypsy moth populations and to prevent the resultant damage to urban, suburban, and forested areas is very strong. Likewise, another portion of the public is opposed to insecticidal treatment under existing conditions. Their reasons vary, but one objection is frequently voiced. They are concerned as to whether the gypsy moth is causing sufficient damage to warrant the introduction of an insecticide into the environment. Both types of human responses are complex and must be viewed as only two points of a broad spectrum of public responses. There is still much to learn about human interest in and their response to the gypsy moth and various suppression programs.

Common management techniques currently being used are: (1) enforcement of a Federal Domestic Quarantine has slowed down the artificial spread of the insect. Tactics include the following: (a) accidentally introduced infestations (Figure 11.18) in remote areas are eliminated or suppressed to low levels with insecticides; (b) interstate movement of articles, such as nursery stock, firewood, or timber products, that often harbor gypsy moth eggs or pupae, is restricted; and (c) infested camp grounds and parks are sprayed with insecticides to reduce the risk of gypsy moths being transported on recreational vehicles and camping equipment; (2) educating the public about the gypsy moth through various mass media presentations is essential during an outbreak since it helps to reduce public hysteria; (3) several chemical insecticides, a bacterial insecticide, *B. thuringiensis*, and Gypcheck®, a product containing the natural nucleopolyhedrosis virus of the gypsy moth, are registered and can be used to reduce nuisance insects, protect foliage, and prevent tree mortality in forested residential communities and on high value and heavily used recreational lands; and (4)

Figure 11.18 Gypsy moth egg masses on a recreational vehicle. (USDA, Animal Plant Health Inspection Service photograph.)

homeowners might help to alleviate the gypsy moth problem when insect populations are sparse by maintaining healthy, vigorously growing trees, by removing objects around the yard that provide shelter for larvae and pupae (e.g., dead branches, boxes, old tires), and by destroying egg masses that are found in their yards.

Douglas-Fir Tussock Moth, Orgyia pseudotsugata (McDunnough)

The Douglas-fir tussock moth periodically causes serious damage to Douglas-fir, grand fir, and white fir in western North America. Preferred host species vary by geographic location: Douglas-fir in British Columbia, white fir in California and southern Oregon, and Douglas-fir and white fir in the southwestern United States. Douglas-fir and white fir are both defoliated in the Blue Mountains of the Pacific Northwest. Because of the severity of the Douglas-fir tussock moth outbreak in the early 1970s, the Douglas-fir tussock moth was selected by the USDA for accelerated research work during 1974 through 1978. A comprehensive compendium on this work, "The Douglas-Fir Tussock Moth: A Synthesis" (Brookes et al. 1978) was published in 1978. Most of the material in this section on the Douglas-fir tussock moth can be found in the compendium.

The Douglas-fir tussock moth has one generation per year that overwinters in the egg stage (Figure 11.19). Caterpillars hatch in the spring shortly after bud burst of host tree species (Wickman 1976). Newly emerged larvae usually crawl to the upper crown of the tree, where there is the greatest percentage of new foliage. Since Douglas-fir tussock moth females are wingless, dispersal by wind occurs during the first and second instars and is usually limited to short distances of 150–300 m. First and second instar larvae require new needles to survive, but old larvae feed on both new and old needles. Larvae feed from late May to early September. Mature larvae are 25–30 mm long and have a gray or brown body, shiny black head, and brightly colored tufts of hair on the body (Figure 11.19). Pupation occurs from late August to October. Under light to moderate population densities, mature larvae spin their cocoons on the underside of old foliage in the upper part of the tree. At heavy to severe population densities, larvae are forced to pupate on branches in the lower part of the tree, on the tree bole, or on understory vegetation. Peak adult emergence and mating occurs in September. Each female lays all her eggs, usually 150–200, in one mass on her own cocoon.

Douglas-fir tussock moth outbreaks have been shown to occur at 7–10-year intervals in western North America. Outbreaks usually last 3–4 years, develop mostly in place from nonmigrating low residual populations, and have a consistent pattern. This pattern is divided into four phases: release, peak, decline, and postdecline. Each phase generally lasts about 1 year and is represented by a specific pattern of population density, defoliation intensity, and within-generation survival. Population densities of 2–20 larvae/ 6450 cm² foliage are considered suboutbreak levels. In the release phase,

Figure 11.19 Douglas-fir tussock moth, *Orgyia pseudotsugata:* (*a*) egg mass covered with body hairs, (*b*) mature larva, (*c*) adult female, (*d*) adult male. (U.S. Forest Service photograph.)

insect numbers rapidly increase to levels that cause visible defoliation. Several years of inconspicuous buildup are often required before the population reaches this quick release phase. The peak phase occurs when maximum population densities cause heavy defoliation. The decline phase is comprised of a rapid reduction in population density as a result of depleted food supply and an increased effectiveness of diseases, predators, and parasites. The virus is primarily responsible for this rapid reduction in tussock moth populations. Nuclear polyhedrosis virus is rare at low insect densities but common at high population densities, Nuclear polyhedrosis virus, starvation, predators, parasites, and dispersal losses, acting separately or jointly, have been implicated in the collapse of most outbreaks (Mason 1981, Dahlsten et al. 1977). The postdecline phase is characterized by a complete collapse of the population.

Douglas-fir tussock moth outbreaks develop very rapidly and can occur over large areas. The 1971–1973 outbreak in Oregon, Washington, and northern Idaho covered 320,000 ha. Accumulated timber and growth losses were estimated at one billion board feet of timber (Furniss and Carolin 1977). The needles turn brown, especially the needles covering the outer edge, after young larvae eat the mesophyll along the midrib of new needles. Stands of infested trees are readily noticeable during midsummer as a result of the scorched appearance of the foliage. The percent of growth reduction is directly proportional to the defoliation in the crown area. Top-kill starts when 40% of the top is defoliated, but the long-term impact of top-kill appears to be negligible in larger trees (Wickman and Schnarpf 1972). Tree mortality occurs primarily when defoliation is higher than 90%. Most mortality in small trees is caused by defoliation, whereas mortality in most larger trees is achieved by secondary insects. Bark beetles, such as the fir engraver, *Scolytus ventralis* LeConte, and the Douglas-fir beetle, *Dendroctonus pseudotsugae* Hopkins, and roundheaded borers are associated with 75% of the total merchantable volume killed during and immediately after a Douglas-fir tussock moth outbreak. Growth recovery of affected trees usually begins during the second year after collapse of an outbreak. The effect of tussock moth and bark beetles may not be as great on the long-term productivity of the stand as previously thought. Stands recover somewhat through increased radial growth and ingrowth during the 10-year postoutbreak period (Wickman 1978a,b).

Studies in northern Idaho showed that the following relationships occurred between Douglas-fir tussock moth defoliation and site and stand characteristics (Stoszek et al. 1981): (1) stands on ridge tops and upper slopes sustained the heaviest defoliation, (2) stands on sites with a deep mantle of volcanic ash were less defoliated than those on sites with little or no ash, (3) defoliation in the stand increased with an increase in the average age of grand fir and Douglas-fir, (4) defoliation increased as the proportion of total foliage biomass of grand fir increased in the stand, and (5) defoliation was greater in stands with a large range of tree heights.

An IPM program for the Douglas-fir tussock moth has been developed (Brookes et al. 1978). First, the susceptibility of the various stands to the tussock moth is determined by using a site and stand classification system. Also, a pheromone sampling system for adults and a sequential sampling system for small larvae in the lower tree crowns are used to determine suboutbreaks and incipient outbreaks. After sampling the tussock moth population, it is evaluated using a stand–outbreak model. The probable effects of an uncontrolled outbreak are estimated with a stand-prognosis model. The probable effects of selected treatments, such as a registered chemical or microbial insecticide or salvage logging, are reviewed by use of stand–prognosis model. The above data are used to predict the probable socioeconomic impacts.

Pine butterfly, Neophasia menapia (Felder and Felder)

The pine butterfly, belonging to the family Pieridae, is a serious pest of ponderosa pine in Washington, Oregon, Idaho, and British Columbia (Cole 1971). It occurs throughout the pine forests of the western United States. Occasionally, the pine butterfly causes mortality of large numbers of mature trees as evident by an extensive even-aged ponderosa forest that developed in southern Washington after a 1921–1923 outbreak (Weaver 1961). The species has one generation per year and overwinters in the egg stage. Eggs are deposited in single rows, 5–20 per row, primarily on new needles in the upper crown of ponderosa pine. After hatching in June, small larvae cluster together in small groups and feed on old needles. Larger larvae feed singly on both old and new needles. Mature larvae are covered with fine, closely set hairs; are about 30 mm long; and have dark green bodies with dull green heads. Pupation occurs during July and August; adults emerge during August through October.

Outbreaks usually last for 2–3 years. Populations collapse as a result of natural enemies and adverse weather conditions. Pest management techniques for the pine butterfly has been limited to salvage operations and the use of chemical insecticides on highly valued ponderosa pine stands after the appearance of damage.

Spiny Caterpillars

Caterpillars in at least seven families have bodies covered with spines or enlarged tubercles and live exposed on the foliage of both hardwoods and conifers. Examples from the families Nymphalidae, Saturniidae, and Sphingidae are presented in the following paragraphs.

Nymphalids, Nymphalidae

This family contains some of our most common butterflies such as the mourningcloak butterfly, *Nymphalis antiopa* (Linnaeus), crescent-spots, admirals, and the viceroy, *Basilarchia archippus* (Cramer). None of these insects cause serious damage to shade or forest trees, but they are often very abundant.

The mourningcloak butterfly is found on elm, willow, poplar, hackberry, and other hardwoods throughout the United States and most of Canada (Johnson and Lyon 1976). It causes no serious damage in forests, but occasionally is abundant on shade trees and shelterbelt plantings. Depending on the location, this butterfly has one or two generations per year. Adults hibernate in secluded places such as hollow trees, old stumps, and buildings. It is often the first butterfly seen flying in woodlands and cities during early spring. The female lays a single egg mass of 300–450 eggs on a limb or twig of a newly flushed tree. After hatching, the caterpillars, commonly referred to as *spiny elm caterpillars*, feed gregariously, Mature larvae are about 50 mm long; heads are covered with tubercles; bodies have many large formidable, branched spines; and larvae are black with a single row of conspicuous red spots on back and red abdominal legs. After a larva completes development, a chrysalis is formed. Adult butterflies emerge a week later. Pest management techniques on shade trees are limited to removing and destroying the branches containing caterpillars or applying a registered chemical insecticide.

Saturniids, Saturniidae

The family Saturniidae contains three subfamilies: Saturniinae, giant silkworm moth; Hemileucinae, consisting of the pandora moth, *Coloradia pandora* Blake, several species of buck moths, and the io moth, *Automeris io* (Fabricius); and Citheroniinae, royal moths (Ferguson 1972). Larvae of most saturniids contain conspicuous tubercles or spines. Spring saturniids feed on many different plants but seldom cause major damage since they occur singly and at relatively low population densities. Many members of this family are called *giant silkworm moths* because the Saturniinae larvae spin large, dense silk cocoons. Some of the large, colorful Saturniinae moths are easily identifiable. Examples of giant silkworm moths commonly collected in the United States are the cecropia moth, *Hyalophora cecropia* (Linnaeus); luna moth, *Actias luna* (Linnaeus) (Figure 11.20); polyphemus moth,

Figure 11.20   Luna moth, *Actias luna*, resting on a lichen-covered rock. (U.S. Forest Service photograph.)

Antheraea polyphemus (Cramer); and the promethea moth, *Callosamia promethea* (Drury). The only spiny saturniid that causes serious damage to forest and shade trees is the pandora moth.

The pandora moth is a pest of western pines, primarily ponderosa, lodgepole, and Jeffrey (Schmid et al. 1982, Carolin and Knopf 1968, Wygant 1941, Patterson 1929). This insect is found in the United States west of the Rocky Mountains. The pandora moth generally requires 2 years to complete its life cycle, but some individuals take up to 6 years. Depending on the location, adults are present from late June to August. Eggs are laid in clusters of 2–70 eggs, usually on the bole of the tree or on needles, with the highest concentration of eggs found on needles located in the lower or middle crown levels. It is not unusual for the female moth to deposit the first cluster of eggs on the trunk of the tree. She then crawls or flies to the foliage and deposits the remaining eggs. Small larvae feed gregariously on new foliage. In late October or November, the small larvae cluster and hibernate at the base of needles. Larvae resume feeding the following spring and consume numerous needles, both new and old needles. Most visible defoliation occurs during April through June. Mature larvae are 60–70 mm long, yellowish green to brown, and each segment supports a few stout branched spines (Figure 11.21). In June and early July these larvae crawl down the trees and pupate in the litter or in the first few centimeters of soil. Unlike many saturniids, the pupae of the pandora moth are not enclosed in a cocoon. This insect usually remains in the pupal stage

Figure 11.21 Mature larva of pandora moth, *Coloradia pandora*. (U.S. Forest Service photograph.)

for 1 year, but some pupae remain in diapause for as long as 5 years (Carolin 1971).

Outbreaks occur at intervals of 20–30 years and last for 6–8 years. These outbreaks are found primarily in areas where the soil is loose enough for the larvae to bury themselves in the soil just before pupation. Such areas are the pumice soils of the Pacific Coast states and the decomposed granite soils of the Rocky Mountain states (Furniss and Carolin 1977). The population dynamics of pandora moth outbreaks is poorly understood. Some factors that appear to be responsible for the collapse of outbreaks are nuclear polyhedrosis virus; mortality of second instar larvae due to very cold winter temperatures; predation of pupae by ground squirrels, chipmunks, and bears; and high soil temperature during the time that the matue larvae are seeking pupation sites and are entering the litter or soil.

Pandora moth outbreaks can lead to reduced tree growth and tree mortality. Since the terminal buds are not eaten, feeding can be fairly heavy without a great deal of impact. The trees have an opportunity to recover somewhat before receiving the next serious defoliation since the pandora moth has a 2-year life cycle and feeds primarily during alternate years. In some instances, trees weakened from defoliation by the pandora moth are further damaged by outbreaks of bark beetles.

Sphinx Moths, Sphingidae

The sphinx moths, also known as hawk moths or hummingbird moths, are medium to large moths with heavy, spindle-shaped bodies and long narrow wings. The beaks in most species are very long and are held coiled beneath the head when not in use. Moths feed similarly to hummingbirds, hovering in front of the flower and extending their beaks into the flower. Sphinx moths are strong fliers, and most are active at dusk or twilight, but some feed during the daytime.

Most larvae are easily recognized by a single conspicuous hornlike or spinelike projection located at the dorsal side of the eighth abdominal segment. Larvae such as the tomato hornworm, *Manduca quinquemaculata* (Haworth), and the tobacco hornworm, *M. sexta* (Linnaeus), are important agricultural pests. A number of species of sphinx moth larvae feed on hardwood trees and shrubs. Four species of sphinx moths that are common but usually insignificant forest and shade tree pests in the United States are elm sphinx, *Ceratomia amyntor* (Geyer); catalpa sphinx, *Ceratomia catalpae* (Boisduval); great ash sphinx, *Sphinx chersis* (Hübner); and the walnut sphinx, *Cressonia juglandis* (J. E. Smith).

Slug Caterpillars, Limacodidae

These caterpillars are sluglike in appearance and have no prolegs, and the prolegs are replaced by five pairs of sucking disks with crochets. Slug caterpillars are window feeders and skeletonizers on hardwood tree species. They cause no significant damage as defoliators. However, slug caterpillars are often noticed because some of them, such as the hag moth, *Phobetron pithecium* (J. E. Smith); saddleback caterpillar, *Sibine stimulea* (Clemens); and the oriental moth, *Cnidocampa flavescens* (Walker), cause severe burning and a skin rash when people come into contact with their poisonous spines or hairs.

Hymenopterous Insects

Sawflies and leaf miners cause damage only in the larval stages, whereas leafcutting ants and leafcutting bees only cause damage as adults. Most sawfly larvae are free feeders, but some are leaf miners. Leafcutting ants and leafcutting bees remove a portion of the leaf and carry it back to the nest.

Table 11.6   Common Types of Defoliating Hymenopterous Caterpillar and Adults

Type and Examples	Characteristics

Diprionid sawflies
  Redheaded pine sawfly,
  Swaine jack pine sawfly,
  hemlock sawfly
	Adults have antennae with 13 or more segments; caterpillars have six to eight pairs of prolegs without crochets; normally found on conifers, primarily pine

Tenthredinid sawflies
  Larch sawfly, yellowheaded
  spruce sawfly, mountain
  ash sawfly
	Adults have antennae with 7–10 segments; caterpillars have six to eight pairs of prolegs with crochets; normally found on both conifers and hardwoods, but not found on pine

Cimbicid sawflies Elm sawfly	Adults are robust, large sawflies with a short-knobbed antennae; full-grown larvae have large heads and body tapers at rear
Slug sawflies Pear slug, pin oak sawfly	Caterpillars lack prolegs, but instead have seven pairs of small, flat, suctionlike areas; no crochets; sluglike; about 12 mm long; window feeders as large larvae
Leafcutting ants Texas leafcutting ant	Adult ants are red–brown insects with body constricted between thorax and abdomen in shape of a petiole; adult ants remove a portion of needle or leaf and carry it to their nest
Leafcutting bees	Adult bees are dark moderate size stout-bodied bees that cut circular or oval pieces of leaves from various trees or shrubs and use the leaf parts to line their nests
Leaf miners Birch leafminer	Small (<6 mm), flat, primarily white caterpillars with six to eight pairs of prolegs; no crochets; leaf miners on hardwoods

The most important hymenopterous defoliators of forest and shade trees are divided into the following types for discussion purposes (Table 11.6): (1) sawflies, which include (a) diprionid sawflies, (b) tenthredinid sawflies, (c) cimbicid sawflies, (d) slug sawflies; (2) leafcutting ants; (3) leafcutting bees; and (4) leaf miners.

Sawflies

Sawflies, belonging to the superfamily Tenthredinoidea, received their name from the sawlike ovipositor of the female. The ovipositor is used to cut slits into needles or shoots and to insert the eggs into the slits (Figure 11.22). Eggs may be laid singly or in rows. Larvae, feeding in colonies or singly, cause damage by removing the foliage (Figure 11.23). Sawfly larvae are similar to lepidopterous larvae. They are normally naked, but a few species are covered with a gummy or waxy material. Sawfly larvae can be identified from lepidopterous larvae by the number of pairs of simple eyes. Sawfly larvae have one pair of simple eyes, whereas lepidopterous larvae have six pairs. Sawfly larvae usually have six or more pairs of prolegs with no crochets, whereas lepidopterous larvae have five or fewer pairs of prolegs with crochets. Slug sawfly larvae have no prolegs but instead have seven pairs of small, flattened, suctionlike areas.

Sawflies are found in eight families with most of the destructive sawflies belonging to the families Diprionidae and Tenthredinidae. Diprionid adults have antennae with 13 or more segments, whereas tenthredinid sawflies have antennae with 7–10 segments.

The symptoms of feeding by various species of sawflies are very similar. Very young larvae only feed on a portion of the needle. Damaged foliage

Figure 11.22 Egg nitches and ovipositing adult of a conifer sawfly in the genus *Neodiprion*. (From the Southern Forest Insect Work Conference Slide Series.)

Figure 11.23   Larvae of a conifer sawfly in the genus *Neodiprion* feeding on ponderosa pine foliage. (U.S. Forest Service photograph.)

appears as brown, dried-up tufts of needles. As the larvae become older and larger, they feed on parts of needles or consume entire needles (Figure 11.24). Sawflies feed on both coniferous and hardwood tree species. Diprionid sawflies feed primarily on pines, whereas tenthredinid sawflies feed on spruce, fir, larch, and hardwoods. Most sawflies feed as free feeders, but some are window feeders or leaf miners.

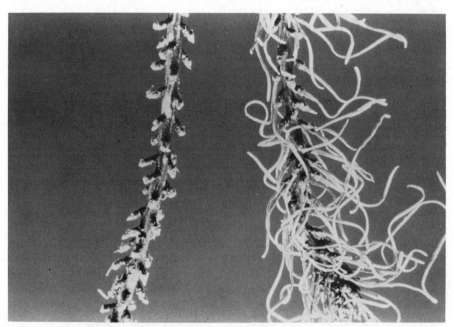

Figure 11.24   Feeding damage caused by sawfly larvae. (From the Southern Forest Insect Work Conference Slide Series.)

Sawflies are often divided into two groups: spring sawflies and summer sawflies. Spring sawflies feed in early spring, primarily on old foliage, have one generation per year, and rarely kill trees directly because they feed early in the spring before the new foliage has fully appeared. Most of the less destructive sawflies are spring sawflies. The summer sawflies feed during the spring and summer, feed on both new and old needles, and have more than one generation per year. Most of the more destructive sawflies are summer sawflies.

The larvae of many species of sawflies are very similar in appearance, but distinctive markings are usually present on the larger instars. Information on color and markings of large larvae, host plant, and larval feeding period are important factors in identifying the larvae as to species. Additional information on the biology and ecology of sawflies can be obtained from Wilson (1977), Smith (1974), Krerer and Atwood (1973), Rose and Lindquist (1973), and Coppel and Benjamin (1965).

Diprionid Sawflies, Diprionidae

All diprionid sawflies are considered pest insects, but the greatest damage in North America is caused by exotic species, accidentally introduced into North America from Europe. Native diprionid sawflies often reach outbreak populations in localized areas. These outbreaks normally last for only a few years. Natural enemies such as predators, parasites, and diseases are normally responsible for the collapse of most outbreaks. Seven species of diprionid sawflies are discussed.

The redheaded pine sawfly, *Neodiprion lecontei* (Fitch), is found throughout southeastern Canada and the eastern United States (Benjamin 1955). It generally prefers pine trees in the small-sized classes, 1–5 m high, and is most often found on jack, red, Scots, shortleaf, loblolly, longleaf, slash, and pitch pine. Severe outbreaks of the redheaded pine sawfly did not occur until after extensive plantings of pure pine stands during the early 1930s. Young pine trees are often completely defoliated and killed during an outbreak.

The number of generations per year varies from one in Canada and the northern United States to three or more generations per year in the southeastern United States. The redheaded pine sawfly overwinters as a prepupa within a cocoon in the soil or litter. Pupation occurs in the spring and adults emerge in a few weeks. Some prepupae may remain in diapause for several years before transforming to adults. Females deposit about 120 eggs in slits of adjacent needles on current or the previous year's needles. Larvae hatch in 3–5 weeks. They feed gregariously in colonies on both new and old foliage for about a month. Mature larvae are about 25 mm long, have a shiny red head, and six rows of black spots and a black tail patch (Figure 11.25). The mature larvae drop from the host tree to the ground, where they spin their cocoons. The life cycle is repeated several times per year in the southern part of its range.

Figure 11.25 Redheaded pine sawfly larvae, *Neodiprion lecontei.* (Courtesy of L. Thompson, University of Arkansas at Monticello.)

The initiation of outbreaks of the redheaded pine sawfly is poorly understood. Averill et al. (1982) reported that for Michigan, moist periods tended to be associated with endemic sawfly populations, normal years with local sawfly outbreaks, and drier years with widespread outbreaks. Natural control factors such as a nuclear polyhedrosis virus disease, bird and rodent predation, wasp parasitism, and temperature extremes during the larval stage normally causes the collapse of redheaded pine sawfly outbreaks after about 3 years from the onset of the outbreak. Inclement weather can adversely affect larval population numbers. Heavy rains may knock young larvae off of the trees. Unseasonal snowfalls in northern Michigan and southern Canada may cause the collapse of populations. Large larvae searching for food may encounter high soil temperatures on sandy soils and die before reaching new host plants.

The redheaded pine sawfly often kills and deforms young pine trees. Averill et al. (1982) reported that tree mortality and deformity on good sites appear to be insufficient to affect future sawlog harvest. Sawflies kill and deform young red pine trees on high stress areas such as sites that support dense growth of bracken fern or sod, zones adjacent to hardwoods, fields with a high water table, frost pockets, or areas with soils excessively poor in nutrients. These high-risk areas make excellent wildlife openings if identified prior to planting. They can be left unplanted to trees and managed exclusively for wildlife.

Pest management practices for the redheaded pine sawfly are dependent on site conditions. No specific treatment is usually needed on sites where risk for the sawfly is low. In moderate- or high-risk sites, a chemical or microbial (e.g., NPV) insecticide may be necessary for very young trees during an outbreak. A cultural preventative treatment such as destroying the bracken fern by plowing or using herbicides will improve site conditions if the soil has adequate nutrients and water-holding capacity.

The Swaine jack pine sawfly, *Neodiprion swainei* Middleton, is a serious pest on maturing and mature jack pine stands growing on flat outwash plains in the vicinity of bodies of waters in Quebec and northeastern Ontario (McLeod 1970, 1972). It also occurs and occasionally causes damage to jack pine stands in the Great Lakes states (Becker and Benjamin 1964). There is one generation per year, and the life cycle is similar to the redheaded pine sawfly. Outbreaks tend to occur at intervals of 8–10 years. These outbreaks often are synchronized over large areas but are patchy and localized rather than continuous. Low temperatures during the larval development period, July through October, can prevent most larvae from completing development. Parasites, bird predation, and small mammals such as rodents and shrews feeding on cocoons are additional important natural control factors. If control is needed, a registered microbial or chemical insecticide can be used.

The introduced pine sawfly, *Diprion similis* (Hartig), was accidentally introduced in North America in 1914. It is now found throughout most of eastern North America wherever its preferred host, eastern white pine, occurs. The introduced pine sawfly also is commonly found on Scots, jack, red, and mugho pine. It attacks trees of all sizes but is generally more common on ornamental, nursery, and plantation trees. Heavily infested trees may be completely defoliated in 1 year. Tree mortality occasionally occurs under these circumstances.

The life cycle of the introduced pine sawfly is similar to the redheaded pine sawfly. There are two generations per year in most of its range. A third generation is found in some years in the southernmost part of its range. The mature larvae are easily distinguished from other sawflies found on pine because the yellow–green body has a black double stripe above, numerous yellow and white spots on the sides, and a shiny black head. Cocoons of the introduced pine sawfly are found on trees, ground vegetation, or in the duff. The location of the cocoons varies by generation and area. Populations of the introduced pine sawfly are often maintained at relatively low levels as a result of natural control factors such as parasitism by introduced hymenopterous wasps on sawfly cocoons, bird predation on sawfly cocoons, and mortality of exposed cocoons caused by low winter temperatures (Coopel et al. 1974).

The European spruce sawfly, *Gilpinia hercyniae* (Hartig), an accidentally introduced sawfly, was first found in North America near Ottawa, Canada in 1922. This sawfly soon became a major pest of white spruce in Ontario, Quebec, and New Brunswick. Over 11 million cords of spruce were killed by the European spruce sawfly in the Gaspé Peninsula of Quebec alone from 1930 to 1945 (Reeks and Barter 1951). Its life cycle is similar to the redheaded pine sawfly. A large scale biological control program was conducted for this sawfly in Canada from 1933 to 1951 (see Chapter 8 for details). By 1945, the European spruce sawfly populations had collapsed primarily due to a nuclear polyhedrosis virus disease that was fortuitously introduced while making parasite releases in the 1930s. The virus and two introduced parasites have maintained very low population levels of the European spruce sawfly in North America since 1945 (Bird and Elgee 1957, Neilson and Morris 1964). The European spruce sawfly is no longer considered a pest insect in North America.

The European pine sawfly, *Neodiprion sertifer* (Geoffroy), accidentally introduced into North America in 1925, is now widely found throughout Ontario and from New England to parts of Ohio, Michigan, Illinois, and Iowa. It has caused damage primarily to Scots, red, and jack pine. Trees are seldom killed by the European pine sawfly since it feeds only on old foliage. The most damage is found in Christmas tree plantations in southern Ontario.

The life cycle of the European pine sawfly is different from the redheaded pine sawfly and other sawflies previously covered. The European pine sawfly overwinters as eggs in the current year's needles. Generally, 6–8 eggs are laid per needle, with 10–12 needles in a single cluster usually infested. Eggs hatch in May. Larvae feed gregariously on last year's foliage. Mature larvae have a black head and the body is gray–green with several light and dark green stripes that tend to break up into spots. The full-

(a)

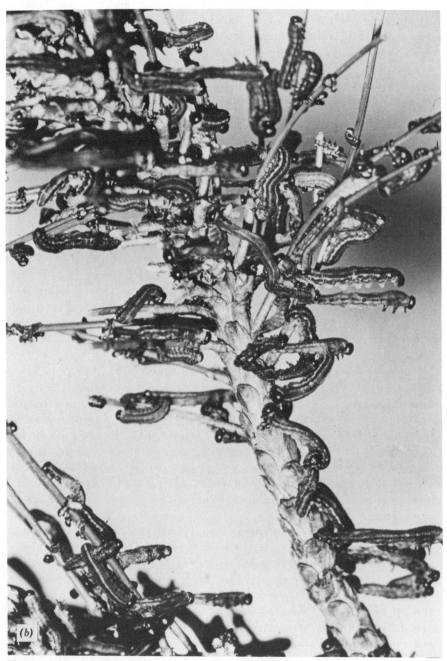

(b)

Figure 11.26 Colonies of the European pine sawfly, *Neodiprion sertifer:* (a) healthy colony, (b) dead colony killed by the nuclear polyhedrosis virus (a—courtesy of L. Thompson, University of Arkansas at Monticello; b—U.S. Forest Service photograph).

grown larvae drop to the forest floor in July. Golden brown cocoons are spun in the duff. Adults emerge from the cocoons in September and October. Mating and egg laying occurs at this time. There is one generation per year.

In southern Ontario, most outbreaks of the European pine sawfly are unsynchronized, independent events that start in a young, previously uninfested pine forest containing few natural enemies. Sawfly populations increase rapidly for 4–6 years before declining to low levels. Factors responsible for the reduction of population levels during a typical outbreak were late larval mortality as a result of starvation, parasitism of prespinning larvae by an introduced ichneumon wasp, and cocoon mortality due to an introduced ichneumon wasp and small rodent populations such as shrews and mice (Lyons 1964, 1977). A registered microbial or chemical insecticide can be used, if needed, to reduce pest population levels (Figure 11.26).

The hemlock sawfly, *Neodiprion tsugae* Middleton, is an important pest of western hemlock in the coastal forests of Oregon, Washington, British Columbia, and Alaska. It is also found in the interior forests of Montana, Idaho, and British Columbia. Impact is primarily limited to top-killing and reduced radial growth since this sawfly prefers old needles and most outbreaks collapse after 2 or 3 years. Tree mortality usually only occurs when the hemlock sawfly and the western blackheaded budworm, *Acleris gloverana* (Walsingham), are found feeding on the same trees.

The life cycle is similar to the European pine sawfly. The population dynamics of the hemlock sawfly is poorly understood over most of its range. In southeastern Alaska, adverse weather conditions, a fungus disease, and parasites are the factors responsible for the collapse of most outbreaks (Hard 1976, Hard et al. 1976). Colder than normal temperatures during the summer and fall causes reduced larval survival and reduced fecundity and inhibits egg laying. Starvation and poor nutrition caused by depletion of host foliage also affects sawfly fecundity. Frequent rainfall promotes the spread of fungus disease, *Entomophthora sphaerosperma* Fres., in larval populations.

The balsam fir sawfly, *Neodiprion abietis* (Harris), attacks primarily balsam fir, but also spruce in the eastern United States and throughout southern Canada. There are several forms or a species similar to the balsam fir sawfly that is found on true firs, spruce, Douglas-fir, and hemlock in the western regions of the United States. A widely scattered outbreak, covering thousands of hectares of a western form of the balsam fir sawfly occurred on white fir in California from 1951 to 1955. The outbreak in California was believed to have collapsed due to a nuclear polyhedrosis virus (Struble 1957).

Tenthredinid Sawflies, Tenthredinidae

The tenthredinid sawflies are diverse in appearance and habits, but all are leaf feeders. Some are free feeders, whereas others are leaf miners. In this section we cover the tenthredinid sawflies that are free feeders. They are found on conifers and hardwoods, but they do not occur on pines. Three species of tenthredinid sawflies are covered.

The larch sawfly, *Pristiphora erichsonii* (Hartig), is found in North America, Europe, and Asia. There are four strains of the larch sawfly present in North America. Two strains are native to North America, and two strains were accidentally introduced from Europe into Canada between 1910 and 1913 among sawfly cocoons shipped for release of the ichneumon wasp parasite, *Mesoleius tenthredinis* Morley (Wong 1974, Turnock 1972). Early infestations in North America consisted of North American strains, whereas the recent outbreaks in North America were caused by the introduced European strains of the sawfly.

The larch sawfly is a major pest of larches, especialy tamarack, in North America. Severe outbreaks occurred in the late nineteenth and early twentieth centuries, killing most of the mature larch in the Great Lakes states and eastern Canada. It commonly is found on western larch in Washington, Oregon, Idaho, Montana, and British Columbia, but usually causes only reduced tree growth on western larch.

The larch sawfly has one generation per year, but some individuals have prolonged diapause and remain as prepupae in cocoons for 2–3 years. Pupation occurs in the spring. Adults emerge from late May to mid-August depending on climatic and site conditions. Females are parthenogenetic and make up about 98% of the population. An individual female lays about 75 eggs, depositing 10–30 eggs in a current developing long shoot. Using her ovipositor, the female cuts a double row of alternating slits into the underside of a long shoot. She then deposits a single translucent egg into each slit (Figure 11.27). This oviposition damage inhibits growth on the damaged side of the long shoot, but the undamaged side of the long shoot continues to grow, leading to the characteristic curling of the shoots.

Eggs hatch in about 10 days. The tiny emerging larvae cut notches into the side of single needles on long shoots. The larvae then move to the tufts of needles that arise from buds on short shoots 1 or more years old. They feed gregariously on these needles, consuming all the foliage. Feeding is completed in about 3 weeks. Fully grown larvae are about 15 mm long, gray to green on top side, white on bottom side, and have dark black heads (Figure 11.27). The last instar larvae tend to wander and may feed singly or in small groups. Mature larvae drop from the trees to the ground and then spin tough leathery brown cocoons in the duff or sphagnum moss. The larch sawfly overwinters as prepupae within the cocoon (Drooz 1960).

A study on the population dynamics of the larch sawfly in southeastern Manitoba was conducted from 1956 to 1972 (Ives 1976). This study showed that mortality of the larch sawfly in the cocoon and adult stages is largely responsible for determining population trends. Important factors contributing to mortality of cocoons and adults are effects of high water tables during larval drop period and immediately after cocoon formation; small mammal predation of cocoons; parasitism of cocoons by two ichneumon wasps, *Olesicampe benefactor* Hinz and the Bavarian strain of *M. tenthredinis*;

Figure 11.27   Larch sawfly, *Pristiphora erichsonii*: (*A*) ovipositing adult, (*B*) eggs and oviposition damage, (*C*) mature larvae, (*D*) cocoons. (U.S. Forest Service photographs.)

invertebrate and avian predation of adults; and reduced adult fecundity due to partial starvation of larvae.

High water tables kill larch sawfly larvae when they drop from the trees and also after the cocoons have been spun. Larch sawfly cocoons that are in diapause are highly resistant to flooding (Lejune et al. 1955). There are two critical times during which heavy cocoon mortality can occur with relatively short periods of flooding. Submergence of postdiapause stages in cocoons for as short a time period as a week around early to mid-June can lead to 100% cocoon mortality. The second critical time period is late July and early August, when the new cocoons are being formed. New cocoons are easily killed by flooding and seldom become highly resistant to flooding until mid-September.

Shrews and voles may destroy large numbers of cocoons in late summer and early fall (Buckner 1959). Ichneumon wasps and a tachinid fly, *Bessa harveyi* (Townsend), may kill large numbers of larvae within cocoons. Invertebrate and avian predation of adults also appear to be important, but it is very difficult to estimate mortality of adults due to predation (Buckner and Turnock 1965).

Studies conducted in the early 1900s indicated that the scarcity of larch sawfly parasites might be why the larch sawfly was a much more serious pest in North America than elsewhere. Therefore, *M. tenthredinis* was introduced from England to Manitoba in 1913. This parasite became established and appeared to be an important factor in the termination of the outbreak in 1927. However, parasitism was not as high as expected in many areas during the next outbreak in the early 1940s. Subsequent investigation revealed that a strain of the larch sawfly had developed resistance to *M. tenthredinis* (Muldrew 1953). It now appears that the resistant strain was introduced along with the ichneumon wasp in 1913. The progeny of these resistant females apparently increased slowly in numbers over time.

A new biological control program against the larch sawfly was initiated in Canada in 1957. Several new species were introduced, and two became established. They were *O. benefactor* and the Bavarian strain of *M. tenthredinis*. These two parasites caused additional mortality to larch sawfly cocoons. Ives (1976) predicted that the populations of the larch sawfly in southeastern Manitoba should be controlled in the future by *O. benefactor*. It appears that the improved effectiveness of these ichneumon parasites could change the present population pattern of high sawfly densities with relative low amplitude changes, to one of widely fluctuating densities resulting in periodic outbreaks of short duration (Thompson et al. 1977, Turnock 1972). Forest industry in the Great Lakes states and southern Canada is now considering European larch as a possible plantation species since the risk of injury to the larch sawfly has been reduced.

Larch trees do not die quickly from larch sawfly defoliation because the trees can refoliate again in the same year. Common symptoms of trees in stands with prolonged outbreaks are thin foliage, reduced radial increment, reduced production of new shoots, and branch mortality. Major reductions in radial growth increment appear after 4–6 years of heavy defoliation. Tree mortality begins after 6–9 years of heavy defoliation. Complete stand mortality can occur during severe outbreaks as indicated by the amount of mortality that occurred in Minnesota during the 1910–1926 outbreak (Kulman 1971).

The yellowheaded spruce sawfly, *Pikonema alaskensis* (Rohwer), is found in Alaska, southern Canada, and the northern United States, where it feeds on most species of spruce (Schoenfelder et al. 1978, Houseweart and Kulman 1976). This sawfly causes the most damage to shade and ornamental trees, trees in shelterbelts, nursery stock, and trees in young spruce plantations. Most natural closed stands are fairly free of attack. Open-grown trees are most susceptible to damage. Tree mortality and branch killing from feeding by the sawfly does occur, but in forest plantations most of the economic impact is due to growth loss.

The yellowheaded spruce sawfly has one generaion per year and overwinters as a prepupa in a cocoon. Pupation occurs in the spring. Adults are present in May and June. Eggs are deposited in the current season's needles or sometimes in the tender bark. Young larvae feed on new needles,

Figure 11.28 Yellowheaded spruce sawfly larva, *Pikonema alaskensis*. (Courtesy of L. Thompson, University of Arkansas at Monticello.)

whereas mature larvae feed on old needles (Figure 11.28). Mature larvae drop to the ground and spin cocoons in the duff or topsoil.

The mountain-ash sawfly, *Pristiphora geniculata* (Hartig), is not a forest pest, but it is a common and often serious pest of ornamental mountain ash throughout the northeastern United States and eastern Canada. Its major impact is in reducing the aesthetic value of ornamentals since mountain ash trees usually survive even when completely defoliated. This sawfly overwinters as a prepupa in a cocoon in the soil. Pupation occurs in the spring and adults appear in May and June. Mating occurs, and females deposit the eggs in slits around the edges of leaflets. Eggs hatch in about a week. The young larvae are gregarious and feed from the edge of the leaf inward until the entire leaf except the midrib is consumed. The feeding period is completed in about 3 weeks. Mature larvae then drop to the ground and spin cocoons in the duff and topsoil. A partial second generation occurs in eastern Canada, where about 20% of the mountain-ash sawflies pupate and appear as second-generation adults in July and August (Forbes and Daviault 1964).

Cimbicid Sawflies, Cimbicidae

Cimbicid sawfly adults are large sawflies with clubbed antennae. In the caterpillar stage these sawflies are solitary feeders on broad-leaved trees. None cause any damage in forest stands, but the elm sawfly, *Cimbex americana* Leach, can occasionally be a serious defoliator of elms and willows that serve as shade trees or windbreaks.

The elm sawfly is found in Alaska, from coast to coast in southern Canada, and throughout the northeastern and northcentral United States, and west into Oregon and Washington (Stein 1974). Its preferred hosts are elm and willow, but it also feeds on other hardwoods such as alder, poplar, birch, and apple. Several years of severe defoliation of willows and elms by this sawfly may kill the entire tree or weaken it so that the tree becomes more susceptible to other stresses.

The elm sawfly usually has one generation per year, but extended diapause is common. It overwinters as a prepupa within a cocoon in the debris around the base of host trees. Adults emerge in May and June and mate, and the female then deposits eggs in pocketlike slits on the underside of host leaves. Depending on location, the larvae feeds from June to October. Mature larvae are about 50 mm long, are yellow–green in color, have a wartlike or pebbly skin, and have a black dorsal stripe down the back.

Slug Sawflies, Tenthredinidae

The larvae of slug sawflies, family Tenthredinidae, possess seven pairs of small flat suctionlike areas instead of prolegs on the abdomen. They do not have a pair of suctionlike areas on the last abdominal segment. None of the suctionlike areas contain crochets. These larvae do not resemble most sawfly larvae since the larvae of most slug sawflies are slimy, nonsegmented, and sluglike in appearance. Slug sawflies feed as window feeders on many different hardwood tree species. None are forest pests. Slug sawflies are sometimes a problem on ornamentals, fruit, and shade trees in the family Rosaceae and on ornamental oaks.

The pear sawfly, *Caliroa cerasi* (Linnaeus), an accidentally introduced insect from Europe, now occurs throughout the United States and is most often a pest on ornamentals, shade, and fruit trees. This insect overwinters as a mature larva in the ground within an earthen cell or cocoon. The pear slug pupates in the spring, and the adult emerges in late May and June. Eggs are deposited singly in slits cut into the leaf tissue. The larval stages are window feeders that feed primarily on the upper surface of the leaf for about 4 weeks before becoming mature larvae. They then drop to the ground, form earthen cells, and pupate. Adults emerge in 2–3 weeks. A second generation occurs during August and September.

Leafcutting Ants

Ants are extremely common insects whose feeding habits vary considerably. Some are predators on insects and other small animals. Most ants that live in the temperate regions do not defoliate trees. The Texas leafcutting ant, *Atta texana* (Buckley), is an exception.

Texas Leafcutting Ant, Atta texana (Buckley)

The Texas leafcutting ant is a serious pest of pine seedlings and field crops in Texas and Louisiana. It also removes foliage from hardwood trees and other plants. The major damage occurs to forest reproduction during the fall and early spring when other green vegetation is scarce. Pines with small buds, such as slash pine, can be killed quickly if the ants cut off the needles and buds and remove the bark from the stem.

The Texas leafcutting ants are red to brown in color and have a strongly bilobed head, and the workers are 2–12 mm long. This ant is a soil-inhabiting species that usually constructs their nest in well-drained sandy or loamy soils (Bennett 1967). The nest areas are usually recognized by many crescent-shaped mounds, up to about 350 mm high and 300 mm in diameter. The nest has many galleries and chambers with some galleries penetrating at least 5 m into the soil.

The Texas leafcutting ants may forage away from their nests for at least 200 m in any one direction. During these foraging trips, the ants move in a column along the foraging trails from their nest to the feeding site. Each worker returns to the nest carrying a small fragment of a leaf, bud, or bark that is shaped into the form of a small pellet. These pellets, often twice the size of the ant, are carried upright over the head. The ants do not eat the foliage. They carry these small fragments ino their underground gardens and place them in special chambers called "fungus gardens." The fungus that grows in these fragments is used as food for the colony.

Leafcutting Bees

Leafcutting bees belong to the family Megachilidae and are dark moderate size stout-bodied bees. The female bee cuts circular pieces of leaves from rose and other hardwood leaves. She then uses the circular leaf pieces as a lining and plug for her egg cells, which are normally found in natural cavities such as hollowed-out twigs and rotten wood. These leafcutting bees are found throughout the United States. They seldom cause any damage to ornamentals except in localized small areas.

Leafmining Wasps

Hymenopterous caterpillars that bore inside the epidermis of a leaf are identified by their feeding damage and by their primarily flat, white bodies that have six to eight pairs of prolegs with no crochets. All leaf miners regardless of insect order, are described together later in this chapter.

Coleopterous Insects

The adult stage of some scarab beetles, usually in the genera *Phyllophaga*, *Dichelonyx*, and *Popillia*, in the family Scarabaeidae, and some weevils in the family Curculionidae, feed on hardwood and pine foliage, whereas the larval stages of these same insects feed on roots of plants. The larval and adult stages of many leaf beetles cause considerable damage to many forest and shade trees. Information is presented on the following three groups of coleopterous insects that contain species that eat leaves: leaf beetles, weevils, and scarab beetles.

Leaf Beetles

Leaf beetles, family Chrysomelidae, represent a large family of beetles in which all species feed on foliage as larvae or adults or in both stages. Many species are serious pests on agricultural crops, whereas some species are very abundant and cause damage to forest and shade trees (Wilcox 1954, 1972). Some of the most common leaf beetles that cause damage to shade and forests trees in the United States are the cottonwood leaf beetle, *Chrysomela scripta* Fabricius; elm leaf beetle, *Pyrrhalta luteola* (Müller); alder flea beetle, *Altica ambiens* LeConte; imported willow leaf beetle, *Plagiodera versicolora* (Laicharting); and the pine colaspis, *Colaspis pini* Barber. Information is presented below on the cottonwood leaf beetle and the elm leaf beetle.

Two leaf beetles, *Chrysolina quadrigemina* (Suffrian) and *C. hyperici* (Forester), were introduced into California in 1945 to control the Klamath weed, a major rangeland weed pest. These two natural enemies quickly became established and reduced the Klamath weed to a roadside weed (Huffaker and Kennett 1959).

Cottonwood Leaf Beetle, Chrysomela scripta Fabricius

The cottonwood leaf beetle is found throughout the United States and Canada. Larvae and adults feed on the leaves of cottonwood, other poplars, and on several willows (Figure 11.29). They can also destroy the apical tips, thereby causing severe growth loss and deformed trees. Cottonwood leaf beetles sometimes are serious defoliators of host trees in the southern and western states.

Figure 11.29 Cottonwood leaf beetle, *Chrysomela scripta*, larvae and adults feeding on foliage. (U.S. Forest Service photograph, courtesy of J. Solomon.)

The cottonwood leaf beetle overwinters as adults under bark, litter, and forest debris. Adults become active in early spring, and begin feeding on tender leaves and bark of host trees. The female deposits yellow eggs in clusters of 15–75 eggs on the underside of leaves. Young larvae are gregarious, feed in groups, and are skeletonizers and window feeders. Larger larvae feed singly and consume entire leaves, except for veins. Mature larvae are black and about 12 mm long. The larvae complete development in about 2 weeks and then attaches itself to a surface such as a leaf or bark and pupates. Adults emerge in about 2 weeks, and the cycle is repeated. The number of generations per year varies from two in the North to seven in Mississippi (Burkot and Benjamin 1979, Head et al. 1977).

Elm leaf beetle, *Pyrrhalta luteola* (*Müller*)

The elm leaf beetle was accidentally introduced into the eastern United States in 1834. It is now established wherever elms grow. This insect is a serious pest of ornamental elms but is not considered a significant forest pest (Luck and Scriven 1976, 1979). Its life cycle is similar to the cottonwood leaf beetle. The adults are about 7 mm long and, dull olive–green in color and have a black stripe along the sides of each elytra. Adults overwinter in sheltered locations including inside homes. The elm leaf beetle often becomes a nuisance inside of homes during the fall when they are searching for suitable overwintering sites. In the spring, adults chew holes in the newly emerged foliage, but the majority of damage is caused by larvae feeding as window feeders on the underside of the leaf (Figure 11.30). The

Figure 11.30 Elm leaf beetle, *Purrhalta luteola*, damage. (U.S. Forest Service photograph, courtesy of J. Solomon.)

upper surface of the leaf and the veins are not eaten. The leaves of heavily infested trees soon turn brown and premature leaf drop often occurs. Under heavy population densities, individual limbs or entire trees may be killed. The number of generations per year varies from one in the North to four generations in the warmer parts of the West.

Weevils

The adults of many species of weevils free feed on hardwood or conifer foliage. Generally, they cause little or no damage, but these weevils sometimes can be extremely abundant. The Asiatic oak weevil, *Cyrtepistomus castaneus* (Roelofs), an accidentally introduced pest, is an example of a weevil that is often present in large numbers. It feeds on many different kinds of hardwood trees in the eastern United States. This insect has one generation per year and overwinters primarily as larvae in the soil (Triplehorn 1955). The larvae complete development in the spring, and the adults lay eggs in the soil. Emerging larvae feed on roots. Adults are most commonly found from July to October.

Scarab Beetles

Scarab beetles belong to a large and diverse family called the *Scarabaeidae*. Adults in this family vary considerably in size, but all have a clubbed antennae with the last three to seven segments leaflike. We are interested in the scarab beetles that feed on foliage as adults and on roots of trees as larvae. The larvae of some scarab beetles are called "white grubs." The damage caused by white grubs to trees in forest nurseries and plantations is covered in Chapter 13. Adult scarab beetles, such as May beetles, genus *Phyllophaga*; rose chafer, *Macrodactylus subspinosus* (Fabricius); and the Japanese beetle, *Popillia japonica* Newman, feed on the young leaves of plants, sometimes causing conspicuous defoliation. Information is presented on the Japanese beetle.

Japanese beetle, Popillia japonica Newman

The Japanese beetle, an accidentally introduced pest, was first found in the United States in 1916. It is now present throughout much of the eastern United States (Fleming 1963). Adults of the Japanese beetle feed on the foliage of trees, shrubs, or food crops for about 30–45 days each year. Adults mate, and females then enter the soil and deposit eggs in small groups in the ground at depths of 2–10 cm. Moist loamy soil covered with closely cropped grass appears to be a very favorite site for oviposition. Eggs hatch in about 2 weeks. The young larvae, often called *grubs*, feed on the fine roots until cold weather forces them to overwinter as partially grown larvae in the soil below the frost line. The larvae resume feeding in the spring, primarily on roots of grasses, and then pupate near the soil surface. Mature larvae are about 25 mm long and typically grub shaped. Adults emerge from late May to early July, depending on location. The life cycle is usually completed in 1 year, but some grubs may require 2 years to complete the life cycle in the northern part of its range. It appears that the Japanese beetle will slowly become established in all the southern states along the Gulf of Mexico. The spread of this insect into the northern areas will be limited as a result of cold winter temperatures, whereas the spread into the Plains states may be limited by lack of rainfall during the late summer months and by cold winter temperatures.

Adults of the Japanese beetle have been recorded as feeding on over 300 species of plants. On emerging from the soil, adults normally feed on the foliage and flowers of low growing plants such as grapes, roses, and shrubs. They then move to tree foliage. The type of feeding by the adults varies from total consumption of leaves with delicate veins to skeletonizing on most tree leaves. The rose plant is a favorite host of Japanese beetles. Adults are most active during the warmest part of the day. They prefer to feed on plants that are exposed to the sun. White grubs feed primarily on roots of grasses, but larvae can seriously damage the roots of ornamental nursery stock. In urban areas, white grub populations can be reduced somewhat by using a bacterial insecticide, *Bacillus popilliae* Dutky, or a registered chemical insecticide.

Orthopterous Insects

Common orthopterous insects that defoliate forest and shade trees, ornamentals, and trees in shelterbelts are walkingsticks in the family Phasmatidae, shorthorned grasshoppers in the family Acrididae, and longhorned grasshoppers in the family Tettigoniidae. Some of the shorthorned and longhorned grasshoppers are destructive pests of agricultural crops. None of the insect defoliators in the order Orthoptera are serious forest pests. Some are locally very common and can occasionally cause significant damage in localized areas.

Walkingsticks

Walkingsticks are large, slender, twiglike insects that feed on plants. The walkingstick, *Diapheromera femorata* (Say), is the most abundant species in the eastern United States and adjacent Canada. It has been found widely distributed throughout most states east of the Great Plains and also in parts of Texas, Arizona, and New Mexico. Outbreaks have been observed in the northern tier states from North Dakota to New England and at high elevations in Pennsylvania, Maryland, Virginia, Arkansas, and Oklahoma (Hodson 1972). These outbreaks are usually very localized since walkingsticks do not fly. Three or four generations of walkingsticks causing heavy defoliation on oaks can lead to branch mortality and occasionally some tree mortality.

The walkingstick overwinters in the egg stage in the leaf litter. In the North most eggs remain unhatched throughout the following summer and winter, whereas in the South most of the eggs hatch the year following

Figure 11.31 Adult walkingsticks, *Diapheromera femorata*, on oak foliage. (U.S. Forest Service photograph.)

oviposition. In other words, there is one generation every 2 years in the North and one generation per year in the South. Nymphs hatch in May and June. The young nymphs feed on low-growing plants such as sweet fern, blueberry, beaked hazel, and strawberry until about midsummer. At this time, most nymphs begin feeding on preferred tree species such as black oaks, basswood, and wild cherry. The mature nymphs consume the entire leaf blade except for major veins. Walkingsticks (Figure 11.31) reach the adult stage in July and August, mate, and lay eggs until the onset of cold weather. Eggs are dropped indiscriminately by the female. Additional information is provided by Hodson (1972), Readshaw and Bedford (1971), Wilson (1971b), and Readshaw (1965).

Grasshoppers

The shorthorned grasshoppers, Acrididae, have short antennae, usually much shorter than the body. This family includes most of the common grasshoppers found in rangelands, meadows, and along roadsides. They usually do not cause much damage to trees. However, shorthorned grasshoppers may disperse into forested areas and damage trees when severe outbreaks are present on agricultural lands. Young trees in nurseries, shelterbelts, and plantations are most vulnerable, especially in the western states and the Great Plains. For example, *Bradynotes obesa opima* Scudder, damaged about 1700 ha of pine plantations in northern California in 1968. They killed nearly all the trees on 320 ha and required the use of a chemical

insecticide (Furniss and Carolin 1977). Most species of shorthorned grasshoppers overwinter in the egg stage, but in the South a few species overwinter as nymphs. There is one generation per year and most species
deposit their egg pods 25–75 mm into the soil during late summer or fall.
Eggs hatch as early as February in the South and during May and June in
the North. Nymphs reach maturity after feeding for 40–70 days.

The longhorned grasshoppers and katydids, Tettigoniidae, are identified by the long antennae, usually much longer than the body. These insects
usually overwinter in the egg stage with the eggs being laid singly or in
rows on leaves or twigs. Biology and damage is similar to the shorthorned
grasshoppers. The Mormon cricket, *Anabrus simplex* Haldeman, found primarily in the western United States, is the most common species.

Leaf and Needle Miners

Leaf and needle miners are insects that feed on the inside of the leaf or
needle between the upper and lower epidermis (Table 4.1). Some leaf
miners do not feed in the same manner throughout the larval stage. For
example, some are serpentine miners in the early larval stages and feed as
blotch miners during the later instars. Leaf and needle miners only cause
damage as larvae. Many leaf mining insects are specific to one tree species.
These insects are found in the orders Lepidoptera, Hymenoptera, Coleoptera, and Diptera (Needham et al. 1928).

Lepidopterous Insects

Lepidopterous insects that feed as leaf miners are found in at least four
different families. Many of these leaf miners are very common insects, but
only the lodgepole needleminer, *Coleotechnites milleri* (Busck), is considered
a serious forest pest.

Leaf Blotch Miners in the Family Gracillaridae

The leaf blotch miners in this family contains many species of blotch miners
that are often extremely common on hardwood tree species. They are not
important forest pests, but some cause damage to ornamentals. Some of
the most commonly found species are the solitary oak leafminer, *Cameraria
hamadryadella* (Clemens) (Figure 11.32); gregarious oak leafminer, *C. cin-
cinnatiela* (Chambers); aspen blotchminer, *Phyllonorycter tremuloidiella* (Braun);
and aspen leafminer, *Phyllocnistis populiella* Chambers (Condrashoff 1964).

Arborvitae Leafminer, Argyresthia thuiella (Packard)

Needle miners in the family Yponomeutidae are often common pests of
ornamental conifers. The arborvitae leafminer, one of four species of leaf
miner that attack arborvitae, is the most abundant species and has a much
greater host range than the other known species. It is found on arborvitae

Figure 11.32 Solitary oak leafminer, *Camararia hamadryadella*, damage on white oak. (U.S. Forest Service photograph.)

throughout northeastern North America. The arborvitae leafminer produces one generation per year and overwinters as half-grown larvae inside mined leaves (Bazinet and Sears 1979, Silver 1957). Larvae resume feeding in early spring. Pupation occurs within the mined leaves during May. Adults emerge during June and July and lay eggs in the axils of branches or along leaf edges. Young larvae bore into the leaves and feed as a digitate miner until late fall.

Arborvitae leaves turn brown and die back as a result of the leaf mining damage inflicted by these leafminers. Damage to ornamental trees is often serious. The only available control technique is the use of a registered chemical insecticide. The cypress tipminer, *A. cupressella* Walsingham, has a similar life cycle and causes the same type of damage as the arborvitae leafminer. It is a pest of ornamental cypress, juniper, and arborvitae in the coastal region of the western United States (Brown and Eads 1967).

White Fir Needleminer, Epinotia meritana Heinrich

The white fir needleminer, *E. meritana*, in the family Olethreutidae, mines the needles of white and red fir in Utah, Arizona, and California. Five separate outbreaks have occurred in the western United States during the last 40 years with several outbreaks in the Bryce Canyon National Park area. Repeated defoliation in the National Park caused a noticeable aesthetic impact. Heavy defoliated stands often decline in vigor and become more susceptible to attack and damage by the fir engraver beetle, *Scolytus ventralis* LeConte (Washburn and McGregor 1974).

Lodgepole Needleminer, Coleotechnites milleri (Busck)

The lodgepole needleminer, belonging to the family Gelechiidae, is a serious pest in extensive stands of mature lodgepole pine (Figure 11.33) on the upper slopes of California's central Sierra Nevada. Destructive out-

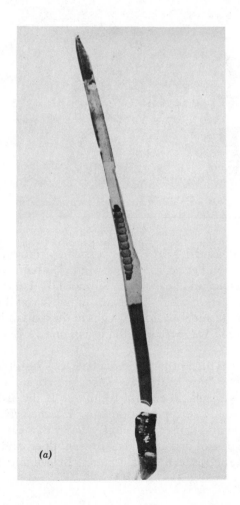

(a)

Figure 11.33 Lodgepole needleminer, *Coleotechniter milleri:* (a) mature larva in mined needle of lodgepole pine, (b) dead lodgepole pine killed in Yosemite National Park by lodgepole needleminer. (U.S. Forest Service photographs.)

breaks of the lodgepole needleminer has occurred in the Yosemite National Park during 1903 to 1921, 1933–1941, and 1947–1963.

The lodgepole needleminer has a 2-year life cycle. Adults, emerge, mate, and oviposit between mid-July and mid-August of odd-numbered years. Eggs are most frequently deposited as a single group in old needle mines, and the eggs hatch by mid-September. First instar larvae normally enter a fresh green needle and mine the needle near the tip, remaining there over the winter. During the next growing season, the larvae develop to the fourth instar, often feeding in several needles. They overwinter during the second winter as fourth-instar larvae. The larvae complete development the following spring, with mature fifth-instar larvae pupating in mined needles during mid-June (Figure 11.33). Adults emerge about 1 month later.

Infested trees may lose nearly 90% of their needles during the first generation of an outbreak. Lodgepole needleminer populations per twig decline somewhat in the second, third, and fourth generations, but impact on host trees often increases. Loss of needles, shortened new growth, and decline in stem and shoot growth can lead to the death of mature and overmature lodgepole pine forests. Entire forest stands, covering at least 2400 ha of lodgepole pine were killed in Yosemite National Park between 1953 and 1963. The trees were weakened by the needle miner and later attacked by the mountain pine beetle, *Dendroctonus ponderosae* Hopkins (Struble 1972).

The northern lodgepole needleminer, *Coleotechnites starki* (Freeman), is similar to the lodgepole needleminer and was at one time considered the same species. The only major difference is that the adults of the northern lodgepole needleminer emerge, mate, and oviposit in even-numbered years. A major outbreak of the northern lodgepole needleminer occurred in the Canadian Rocky Mountain Parks during the 1940s and early 1950s (Stark 1954, 1959). The major impacts of the northern lodgepole needleminer during the last outbreak were aesthetics and radial increment loss.

Hymenopterous Insects

Leaf miners in the family Tenthredinidae are common on both shade and forest trees, especially in eastern North America. The most commonly occurring species are the birch leafminer, *Fenusa pusilla* (Lepeletier), and the elm leafminer, *F. ulmi* Sundevall. Information is presented on the birch leafminer.

Birch Leafminer, Fenusa pusilla (Lepeletier)

The birch leafminer, an accidently introduced pest, was first recorded in North America in Connecticut in 1923. It has spread throughout eastern North America and is now found also in Oregon, Washington, and Alberta. The birch leafminer is found on all species of birch (Friend 1933). Depending on location, there are two to four generations per year. There are three generations per year throughout most of the northeastern United States.

The birch leafminer overwinters as mature larvae in cocoons in earthen cells 25–50 mm below the soil surface. Pupation occurs in the spring, with adults beginning to appear in early to mid-May. Mated females deposit eggs singly in the upper surface of expanding leaves. Eggs hatch in about a week. Young larvae begin feeding singly, but individual mines often come together, creating large hollowed-out brown areas on the leaf (Figure 11.34). Larvae feed for about 2 weeks. Then the mature larvae chew an exit hole in the leaf mine and drop to the ground, where they construct an earthen cell. The life cycle is repeated an additional two to three times per year.

Most damage is caused by the spring generation. Therefore, any registered chemical insecticide used against the birch leafminer to reduce damage on valuable ornamentals should be concentrated on the spring

Figure 11.34   Birch leafminer, *Fenusa pusilla*, damage. (Connecticut Agricultural Experiment Station photograph.)

generation. Tree mortality of ornamental birches from the leaf miner is rare. However, injury from the birch leafminer can weaken the tree and then cause the tree to be more susceptible to attack by the bronze birch borer, *Agrilus anxius* Gory. Outbreaks of the birch leafminer have resulted in the browning of natural stands of birch throughout wide areas of eastern North America. The actual impact of the birch leafminer on natural birch stands is unknown. Some tree mortality occurs, but it is probably caused by other insects and diseases that attack the weakened trees.

Coleopterous Insects

Beetles in three families mine various species of hardwood leaves. The most commonly found species are the locust leafminer, *Odontota dorsalis* (Thunberg), and the basswood leafminer, *Baliosus ruber* (Weber). Information is presented on the locust leafminer.

Locust Leafminer, Odontota dorsalis (Thunberg)

The locust leafminer is found on black locust throughout most of southern Canada and the eastern United States. It overwinters in the adult stage under debris on the ground or in bark crevices on the host tree (Weaver and Dorsey 1965, Dominick 1938). In the spring the adult beetles feed for a short time on the newly developing foliage. The mated female then deposits eggs into the lower surface of leaves in groups of three to five each. Eggs hatch in about 10 days, and the larvae from each group of eggs bore into a leaf and feed in a common mine for several days. They then separate and each larva mines a separate leaf. A single larva may mine several leaves. The insect is in the larval stage for about 2–3 weeks. The mature larva is flat, yellowish-white in color with a black head, legs, and anal shield (Figure 11.35). Pupation occurs within the leaf mine. Adults emerge in July and August and feed as window feeders on the undersurface of leaves. There is one generation per year over most of its range, with two generations per year occurring in southern Ohio and adjacent areas.

Outbreaks of the locust leafminer are extremely common and occur very often throughout large portions of its range, especially throughout the eastern seaboard from Alabama to Canada, and in West Virginia, Ohio, Tennessee, and Kentucky. Heavily defoliated trees are seldom killed. The major impact is aesthetics, because heavily defoliated trees often have a scorched appearance in July and August when the mined foliage turns brown. A registered chemical insecticide is sometimes used on adults in early spring, when they are abundant on ornamental black locust or on park trees.

Dipterous Insects

Leaf miner flies, in the family Agromyzidae, commonly mine leaves of many broad-leaf trees and shrubs (Spencer 1969). These agromyzid flies

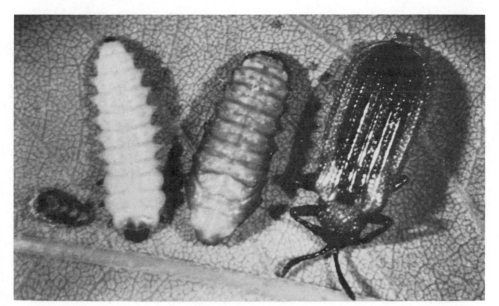

Figure 11.35 Larvae and the adult of the locust leafminer, *Odontota dorsalis*. (From the Southern Forest Insect Work Conference Slide Series.)

often attack only one or a few species of plants. They often can easily be identified to species by using the shape of the mine and the species of host plants. None of the leaf miner flies are important forest pests, but several species cause damage to ornamental trees and shrubs. Information is presented on two common leaf miner flies.

Native Holly Leafminer, Phytomyza ilicicola Loew

The native holly leafminer is a common pest of American holly in the eastern United States (Johnson and Lyon 1976). This insect produces one generation per year and overwinters as a larva in a leaf mine. Pupation occurs in the spring and adults emerge in late spring. Females lay eggs in the undersurface of the leaf. On hatching, the small larvae make narrow, slender, serpentine mines, about 12 mm in length. As the larvae grow, they feed and broaden the mine so that it becomes a long blotch mine. In heavy infestations, premature leaf drop occurs.

The Holly Leafminer, Phytomyza ilicis Curtis

The holly leafminer is an accidentally imported pest from Europe that causes damage to ornamental holly from California to British Columbia. The biology and damage caused by this insect is similar to that of the native holly leafminer.

REFERENCES

Allen, D. C. 1979. Observations on biology and natural control of the orangehumped mapleworm, *Summerista leucitys* (Lepidoptera: Notodontidae), in New York. *Can. Entomol.* **111**:703–708.

Allen, D. C. and D. G. Grimble. 1970. Identification of the larval instars of *Heterocampa guttivitta* with notes on their feeding behavior. *J. Econ. Entomol.* **63**:1201–1203.

Averill, R. D., L. F. Wilson, and R. F. Fowler. 1982. Impact of the redheaded pine sawfly (Hymenoptera: Diprionidae) on young red pine plantations. *Great Lakes Entomol.* **15**:65–91.

Barrows, E. M. 1974. Some factors affecting population size of the bagworm, *Thyridopteryx ephemeraeformis* (Lepidoptera: Psychidae). *Environ. Entomol.* **3**:929–932.

Baskerville, G. L. 1976. (Task-Force Leader). Report of the task-force for evaluation of budworm control alternatives. Prepared for the New Brunswick Cabinet Committee on Economic Development. Department of Natural Resources, Fredericton.

Batzer, H. O. and D. T. Jennings. 1980. Numerical analysis of a jack pine budworm outbreak in various densities of jack pine. *Environ. Entomol.* **9**:514–524.

Batzer, H. O. and R. C. Morris. 1978. Forest tent caterpillar. U.S. Forest Service Forest Pest Leaflet 9.

Bazinet, N. L. and M. K. Sears. 1979. Factors affecting the mortality of leafminers *Argyresthia thuiella* and *Pulicalvaria thujaella* (Lepidoptera: Yponomeutidae and Gelechiidae) on eastern white cedar, in Ontario. *Can. Entomol.* **111**:1299–1306.

Becker, G. C., Jr. and D. M. Benjamin. 1964. Biology of the Swaine jack-pine sawfly in Wisconsin. *Can. Entomol.* **96**:589–599.

Beckwith, R. C. 1968. The large aspen tortrix, *Choristoneura conflictana* (Wallkr.) in interior Alaska. U.S. Forest Service Research Note PNW-81.

Beckwith, R. C. 1976. Influence of host foliage on the Douglas-fir tussock moth. *Environ. Entomol.* **5**:73–77.

Benjamin, D. M. 1955. *The Biology and Ecology of the Redheaded Pine Sawfly.* USDA Technical Bulletin 1118.

Bennett, W. H. 1967. The Texas leaf-cutting ant. U.S. Forest Service Forest Pest Leaflet 23.

Berisford, Y. C. and C. H. Tsao. 1975. Parasitism, predation and disease in the bagworm, *Thyridopteryx ephemeraeformis* (Haworth) (Lepidoptera: Psychidae). *Environ. Entomol.* **4**:549–554.

Bird, F. T. and D. E. Elgee. 1957. A virus disease and introduced parasites as factors controlling the European spruce sawfly, *Diprion hercyniae* (Htg.) in central New Brunswick. *Can. Entomol.* **87**:371–378.

Blais, J. R., R. M. Prentice, W. L. Sippell, and D. R. Wallace. 1955. Effects of weather on the forest tent caterpillar, *Malacosoma disstria* Hbn., in central Canada in the spring of 1953. *Can. Entomol.* **87**:1–8.

Brookes, M. H., R. W. Stark, and R. W. Campbell (Eds.). 1978. *The Douglas-Fir Tussock Moth: A Synthesis.* U.S. Forest Service Science Education Administration Technical Bulletin 1585.

Brown, L. R. and C. O. Eads. 1967. *Insects Affecting Ornamental Conifers in Southern California.* California Agricultural Experiment Station Bulletin 834.

Buckner, C. H. 1959. The assessment of larch sawfly cocoon predation by small mammals. *Can. Entomol.* **91**:275–282.

Buckner, C. H. and W. J. Turnock. 1965. Avian predation on the larch sawfly, *Pristiphora erichsonii* (Htg.) (Hymenoptera: Tenthredinidae). *Ecology* **46**:223–236.

Burkot, T. R. and D. M. Benjamin. 1979. The biology and ecology of the cottonwood leaf beetle, *Chrysomela scripta* (Coleoptera: Chrysomelidae), on tissue cultured hybrid *Aigeiros* (*Populus* X *euramericana*) subclones in Wisconsin. *Can. Entomol.* **111**:551–556.

Campbell, R. W. 1967. The analysis of numerical change in gypsy moth populations. *For. Sci. Monogr.* **15**.

Campbell, R. W. 1974. *The Gypsy Moth and Its Natural Enemies.* USDA Agriculture Information Bulletin 381.

Campbell, R. W. 1978a. *Gypsy Moth: Forest Influence.* USDA Agriculture Information Bulletin 423.

Campbell, R. W. 1978b. Some effects of gypsy moth density on rate of development, pupation time, and fecundity. *Ann. Entomol. Soc. Am.* **71**:442–448.

Campbell, R. W. and R. J. Sloan. 1977a. *Forest Stand Responses to Defoliation by the Gypsy Moth. For. Sci. Monogr.* 19.

Campbell, R. W. and R. J. Sloan. 1977b. Release of gypsy moth populations from innocuous levels. *Environ. Entomol.* **6**:323–330.

Campbell, R. W. and R. J. Sloan. 1978a. Numerical bimodality among North American gypsy moth populations. *Environ. Entomol.* **7**:641–646.

Campbell, R. W. and R. J. Sloan. 1978b. Natural maintenance and decline of gypsy moth outbreaks. *Environ. Entomol.* **7**:389–395.

Campbell, R. W. and H. T. Valentine. 1972. Tree condition and mortality following defoliation by the gypsy moth. U.S. Forest Service Research Paper NE-236.

Campbell, R. W., L. C. Levitan, E. R. Sobecki, and M. F. Tardiff. 1978. *Population Dynamics of the Gypsy Moth: An Annotated Bibliography.* U.S. Forest Service General Technical Report NE-48.

Carroll, W. J. 1956. History of the hemlock looper in *Lambdina fiscellaria fiscellaria* (Guen.) (Lepidoptera: Geometridae) in Newfoundland, and notes on its biology. *Can. Entomol.* **88**:587–599.

Carolin, V. M., Jr. 1971. Extended diapause in *Coloradia pandora* Blake (Lepidoptera: Saturniidae). *Pan.-Pac. Entomol.* **47**:19–23.

Carolin, V. M. and J. A. E. Knopf. 1968. The pandora moth. U.S. Forest Service Forest Pest Leaflet 114.

Ciesla, W. M. 1964. Egg parasites of the elm spanworm in the southern Appalachian Mountains. *J. Econ. Entomol.* **57**:837–838.

Ciesla, W. M. 1965. Observations on the life history of *Telenomus alsophilae*, an egg parasite of the elm spanworm, *Ennomos subsignarius. J. Econ. Entomol.* **58**:702–704.

Clancy, K. M., R. L. Giese, and D. M. Benjamin. 1980. Predicting jack pine budworm infestations in northwestern Wisconsin. *Environ. Entomol.* **9**:743–751.

Cole, W. E. 1971. Pine butterfly. U.S. Forest Service Forest Pest Leaflet 66.

Condrashoff, S. F. 1964. Bionomics of the aspen leaf miner, *Phyllocnistis populiella* Cham. (Lepidoptera: Gracillariidae). *Can. Entomol.* **96**:857–874.

Coppel, H. C. and D. M. Benjamin. 1965. Bionomics of the nearctic pine-feeding disprionidae. *Annu. Rev. Entomol.* **10**:69–96.

Coppel, H. C., J. W. Mertins, and J. W. Harris. 1974. *The Introduced Pine Sawfly, Diprion similis* (*Hartig*) (*Hymenoptera: Diprionidae*)—*A Review with Emphasis on Studies in Wisconsin.* University Wisconsin Research Bulletin R2393.

Crumb, S. E. 1956. *The Larvae of the Phalaenidae.* USDA Technical Bulletin 1135.

Davis, D. R. 1964. Bagworm moths of the Western Hemisphere. U.S. Natural Museum Bulletin 244.

Dahlsten, D. L., R. F. Luck, E. I. Schlinger, J. M. Wenz, and W. A. Copper. 1977. Evaluation of parasitoids, predators, spiders and defoliator associates of the Douglas-fir tussock moth, *Orgyia pseudotsugata* (McD.) (Lepidoptera: Lymantriidae), at low to moderate levels in central California. *Can. Entomol.* **107**:727–746.

Denton, R. E. 1979. Larch casebearer in western larch forests. U.S. Forest Service General Technical Report INT-55.

Denton, R. E. and S. Tunnock. 1972. Larch casebearer in western larch forests. U.S. Forest Service Forest Pest Leaflet 96.

Doane, C. E. and M. L. McManus. (Eds.). 1981. *The Gypsy Moth: Research Toward Integrated Pest Management.* U.S. Forest Service Science Education Administration Service Technical Bulletin 1584.

Dominick, C. B. 1938. Notes on the locust leaf miner, *Chalepus dorsalis* Thumb. *J. Econ. Entomol.* **31**:186–189.

Drooz, A. T. 1960. *The Larch Sawfly—Its Biology and Control.* USDA Technical Bulletin 1212.

Drooz, A. T. 1970. The elm spanworm (Lepidoptera: Geometridae): How several natural diets affect its biology. *Ann. Entomol. Soc. Am.* **68**:391–397.

Drooz, A. T. 1980. A review of the biology of the elm spanworm (Lepidoptera: Geometridae). *Great Lakes Entomol.* **13**:49–53.

Drooz, A. T. and J. D. Solomon. 1961. Elm spanworm egg mass studies. *J. Econ. Entomol.* **54**:1060–1061.

Drooz, A. T. and J. D. Solomon. 1964. Effects of solarization on elm spanworm eggs (Lepidoptera: Geometridae). *Ann. Entomol. Soc. Am.* **57**:95–98.

Duncan, D. P. and A. C. Hodson. 1958. Influence of the forest tent caterpillar upon the aspen forests of Minnesota. *For. Sci.* **4**:72–93.

Fedde, G. F. 1964. Elm spanworm, a pest of hardwood forests in the southern Appalachians. *J. For.* **62**:102–106.

Fellin, D. G. and J. E. Dewey. 1982. Western spruce budworm. U.S. Forest Service Forest Insect Disease Leaflet 53.

Fellin, D. G., R. C. Shearer, and C. E. Carlson. 1983. Western spruce budworm in the northern Rocky Mountains. *West. Wildlands* **9**:2–7.

Ferguson, D. A. 1972. Bombycoidea: Saturniidae. Fascicle 20.2A and 20.2B. In Domminick, R. B. (Ed.), *The Moths of America North of Mexico.* Classey, London.

Fleming, W. E. 1963. *The Japanese Beetle in the United States.* USDA Agriculture Handbook 236.

Flexner, J. L., J. R. Bassett, B. A. Montgomery, G. A. Simmons, and J. A. Witter. 1983. *Spruce–Fir Silviculture and the Spruce Budworm in the Lake States.* Michigan Cooperative Forest Pest Management Program Handbook 83-2.

Foltz, J. L., F. B. Knight, and D. C. Allen. 1972. Numerical analysis of population fluctuations of the jack pine budworm. *Ann. Entomol. Soc. Am.* **65**:82–89.

Forbes, R. S. and L. Daviault. 1964. The biology of the mountain-ash sawfly, *Pristiphora geniculata* (Htg.) (Hymenoptera: Tenthredinidae), in eastern Canada. *Can. Entomol.* **96**:1117–1133.

Friend, R. B. 1927. *The Biology of the Birch Leaf Skeletonizer, Bucculatrix canadensisella Chambers.* Connecticut Agricultural Experiment Station Bulletin 288.

Friend, R. B. 1933. *The Birch Leaf-Mining Sawfly Fenusa pumila Klug.* Connecticut Agricultural Experiment Station Bulletin 348.

Furniss, R. L. and V. M. Carolin. 1977. *Western Forest Insects.* U.S. Forest Service Miscellaneous Publication 1339.

Gibbons, C. F. and J. W. Butcher. 1961. The oak skeletonizer, *Bucculatrix ainsliella*, in a Michigan wood lot. *J. Econ. Entomol.* **54**:681–684.

Greenbank, D. O., G. W. Schaefer, and R. C. Rainey. 1980. Spruce budworms (Lepidoptera: Tortricidae) moth flight and dispersal: New understanding from canopy observations, radar, and aircraft. *Mem. Entomol. Soc. Can.* 110.

Hanec, W. 1966. Cold-hardiness in the forest tent caterpillar, *Malacosoma disstria* Hübner (Lepidoptera: Lasiocampidae). *J. Insect Physiol.* **12**:1443–1449.

Hard, J. S. 1976. Natural control of the hemlock sawfly, *Neodiprion tsugae* (Hymenoptera: Diprionidae), populations in southeast Alaska. *Can. Entomol.* **108**:485–498.

Hard, J. S., T. R. Torgersen, and D. C. Schmiege. 1976. Hemlock Sawfly. U.S. Forest Service Forest Insect Disease Leaflet 31.

Harville, J. P. 1955. Ecology and population dynamics of the California oak moth. *Microentomology* **20**:83–166.

Head, R. B., W. W. Neel, and R. C. Morris. 1977. Seasonal occurrence of the cottonwood leaf beetle *Chrysomela scripta* (Fab.) and its principal insect predators in Mississippi and notes on parasites. *J. Georgia Entomol. Soc.* **12**:154–157.

Hewitt, G. B., E. W. Huddleston, R. J. Lavigne, D. N. Ueckert, and J. G. Watts. 1974. *Rangeland Entomology.* Society of Range Management Range Science Series 2.

Hodson, A. C. 1941. *An Ecological Study of the Forest Tent Caterpillar, Malacosoma disstria Hbn.* Minnesota Agricultural Experiment Station Technical Bulletin 148.

Hodson, A. C. 1972. Distribution and abundance of the northern walkingstick *Diapheromera femorata. Ann. Entomol. Soc. Am.* **65**:876–882.

Hodson, A. C. 1977. Some aspects of forest tent caterpillar population dynamics. In Kulman, H. M. and H. C. Chiang (Eds.), *Insect Ecology: Papers Presented in the A. C. Hodson Ecology Lectures.* Minnesota Agricultural Experiment Station Technical Bulletin 310.

Holling, C. S. (Ed.). 1978. *Adaptive Environmental Assessment and Management.* Wiley, New York.

Houseweart, M. W. and H. M. Kulman. 1976. Life tables of the yellowheaded spruce sawfly, *Pikonema alaskensis* (Rohwer) (Hymenoptera: Tenthredinidae) in Minnesota. *Environ. Entomol.* **5**:859–867.

Houston, D. R. 1973. Diebacks and declines: Diseases initiated by stress, including defoliation. *Proc. Int. Shade Tree Conf.* **49**:73–76.

Houston, D. R. 1974. Diagnosing and preventing diebacks and declines. *Morton Abor. Q.* **10**:55–59.

Houston, D. R. and H. T. Valentine. 1977. Comparing and predicting forest stand susceptibility to gypsy moth. *Can. J. For. Res.* **7**:447–461.

Hudak, J. and A. G. Raske. (Eds.). 1981. *Review of the Spruce Budworm Outbreak in Newfoundland—Its Control and Forest Management Implications.* Canadian Forest Service Information Report N-X-205.

Huffaker, C. B. and C. E. Kennett. 1959. A ten-year study of vegetational changes associated with the biological control of Klamath weed. *J. Range Mgmt.* **12**:69–82.

Irland, L. C. 1977. Maine's spruce budworm program: Moving toward integrated management. *J. For.* **75**:774–777.

Irland, L. C. 1980. Pulpwood, pesticides, and people: Controlling spruce budworm in northeastern North America. *Environ. Mgmt.* **4**:381–389.

Ives, W. G. H. 1976. The dynamics of larch sawfly (Hymenoptera: Tenthredinidae) populations in southeastern Manitoba. *Can. Entomol.* **108**:701–730.

Ives, W. G. H. 1981. *Environmental Factors Affecting 21 Forest Insect Defoliators in Manitoba and Saskatchewan, 1945–1969.* Environment Canada, Canadian Forestry Service, Northern Forest Research Centre Information Report NOR-X-233.

Jennings, D. J., F. B. Knight, S. C. Hacker, and M. E. McKnight. 1979. *Spruce Budworm Bibliography*. Maine Life Science Agriculture Experiment Station Miscellaneous Report 213.

Johnson, P. C. and R. E. Denton. 1975. *Outbreaks of the Western Spruce Budworm in the American Northern Rocky Mountain Area from 1922 Through 1971*. U.S. Forest Service General Technical Report INT-20.

Johnson, W. T. and H. H. Lyon. 1976. *Insects that Feed on Trees and Shrubs*. Cornell University Press, Ithaca.

Jones, D. D. 1976. The budworm site model. Univ. British Columbia, Institute of Resource Ecology Working Paper W-13.

Kaufmann, T. 1968. Observations on the biology of the evergreen bagworm moth, *Thyridopteryx ephemeraeformis* (Lepidoptera: Psychidae). *Ann. Entomol. Soc. Am.* **61**:38–44.

Kaya, H. K. and J. F. Anderson. 1973. Elm spanworm egg distribution in a Connecticut hardwood forest. *Ann. Entomol. Soc. Am.* **66**:825–829.

Kaya, H. K. and J. F. Anderson. 1974. Collapse of the elm spanworm outbreak in Connecticut: Role of *Ooencyrtus* sp. *Environ. Entomol.* **3**:659–663.

Kaya, H. K. and J. F. Anderson. 1976. Alternate hosts of the elm spanworm egg parasitoid, *Ooencyrtus ennomophagus*. *Ann. Entomol. Soc. Am.* **69**:35–37.

Kegg, J. D. 1973. Oak mortality caused by repeated gypsy moth defoliation of oak in New Jersey. *J. Econ. Entomol.* **66**:639–641.

Kemp, W. P. and G. A. Simmons. 1978. The influence of stand factors on parasitism of spruce budworm eggs by *Trichogramma minutum*. *Environ. Entomol.* **7**:685–688.

Krerer, G. and C. E. Atwood. 1973. Diprionid sawflies: Polymorphism and speciation. *Science* **179**:1090–1099.

Kulman, H. M. 1965a. Natural control of the bagworm and notes on its status as a forest pest. *J. Econ. Entomol.* **58**:863–866.

Kulman, H. M. 1965b. Natural control of the eastern tent caterpillar and notes on its status as a forest pest. *J. Econ. Entomol.* **58**:66–70.

Kulman, H. M. 1971. Effect of defoliation on tree growth. *Annu. Rev. Entomol.* **16**:289–324.

Kulman, H. M., A. C. Hodson, and D. P. Duncan. 1963. Distribution and effects of jack pine budworm defoliation. *For. Sci.* **9**:146–157.

Lejeune, R. R., W. H. Fell, and D. P. Burbridge. 1955. The effect of flooding on the development and survival of the larch sawfly, *Pristiphora erichsonii* (Tenthredinidae). *Ecology* **36**:63–77.

Leonard, D. E. 1970. Feeding rhythm in larvae of the gypsy moth. *J. Econ. Entomol.* **63**:1454–1457.

Leonard, D. E. 1972. Survival in a gypsy moth population exposed to low winter temperatures. *Environ. Entomol.* **1**:549–554.

Luck, R. F. and G. T. Scriven. 1976. The elm leaf beetle, *Pyrrhalta luteola* in southern California: Its pattern of increase and its control by introduced parasites. *Environ. Entomol.* **5**:409–416.

Luck, R. F. and G. T. Scriven. 1979. The elm leaf beetle, *Pyrrhalta luteola*, in southern California: Its host preference and host impact. *Environ. Entomol.* **8**:307–313.

Lyons, L. A. 1964. The European pine sawfly, *Neodiprion sertifer* (Geoff.) (Hymenoptera: Diprionidae): A review with emphasis on studies in Ontario. *Proc. Entomol. Soc. Ont.* **94**:5–37.

Lyons, L. A. 1977. On the population dynamics of *Neodiprion* sawflies. In Kulman, H. M. and H. M. Chiang (Eds.), *Insect Ecology—Papers Presented in the A. C. Hodson Lectures*. University of Minnesota Agricultural Experiment Station Technical Bulletin 310.

MacLean, D. A. 1980. Vulnerability of fir–spruce stands during uncontrolled spruce budworm outbreaks: A review and discussion. *For. Chron.* **56**:213–221.

Mason, R. R. 1981. Numerical analysis of the causes of population collapse in a severe outbreak of the Douglas-fir tussock moth. *Ann. Entomol. Soc. Am.* **74**:51–57.

Mattson, W. J. and N. D. Addy. 1975. Phytophagous insects as regulators of forest primary production. *Science* **190**:515–522.

McKnight, M. E. 1968. A literature review of the spruce, western and 2-year cycle budworms. U.S. Forest Service Research Paper RM-44.

McLeod, J. M. 1970. The epidemiology of the Swaine jack pine sawfly, *Neodiprion swainei* Midd. *For. Chron.* **44**:14–20.

McLeod, J. M. 1972. The Swaine jack pine sawfly, *Neodiprion swainei* life system: Evaluating the long-term effects of insecticide applications in Quebec. *Environ. Entomol.* **1**:371–381.

Miller, C. A. 1958. The measurement of spruce budworm populations and mortality during first and second larval instars. *Can. J. Zool.* **36**:409–422.

Miller, I. and W. E. Wallner. 1975. The redhumped oakworm. USDA Forest Service Forest Pest Leaflet 153.

Moeller, G. H., R. L. Marler, R. E. McCay, and W. B. White. 1977. Economic analysis of the gypsy moth problem in the Northeast. 3. Impacts on homeowners and managers of recreation areas. U.S. Forest Service Research Paper NE-360.

Montgomery, B. A., G. A. Simmons, J. A. Witter, and J. L. Flexner. 1982a. *The Spruce Budworm Handbook: A Management Guide for Spruce–Fir Stands in the Lake States.* Michigan Cooperative Forest Pest Management Program Handbook 82-7.

Montgomery, B. A., J. A. Witter, G. A. Simmons, and R. G. Rogan. 1982b. *The Spruce Budworm Manual for the Lake States—1982.* Michigan Cooperative Forest Pest Management Program Manual 82-6.

Morris, R. E. (Ed.). 1963. The dynamics of epidemic spruce budworm populations. *Mem. Entomol. Soc. Can.* 31.

Morris, R. F. 1971. The influence of land use and vegetation on the population density of *Hyphantria cunea. Can. Entomol.* **103**:1525–1536.

Morris, R. F. and W. C. Fulton. 1970. Models for the development and survival of *Hyphantria cunea* in relation to temperature and humidity. *Mem. Entomol. Soc. Can.* 70.

Morris, R. F. and C. A. Miller. 1954. The development of life tables for the spruce budworm. *Can. J. Zool.* **32**:283–301.

Muldrew, J. A. 1953. The natural immunity of the larch sawfly [*Pristiphora erichsonii* (Htg.)] to the introduced parasite, *Mesoleius tenthredinis* Morley, in Manitoba and Saskatchewan. *Can. J. Zool.* **31**:313–332.

Needham, J. G., S. W. Frost, and B. H. Tothill. 1928. *Leaf-Mining Insects.* Williams & Wilkins, Baltimore.

Neilson, M. M. and R. F. Morris. 1964. The regulation of European spruce sawfly numbers in the Maritime Provinces of Canada from 1937 to 1963. *Can. Entomol.* **96**:773–784.

Nichols, J. O. 1968. Oak mortality in Pennsylvania: A ten-year study. *J. For.* **66**:681–694.

Oliver, A. D. 1964. A behavioral study of two races of the fall webworm, *Hyphantria cunea* (Lepidoptera: Arctiidae) in Louisiana. *Ann. Entomol. Soc. Am.* **57**:192–194.

Patterson, J. E. 1929. *The Pandora Moth, a Periodic Pest of Western Pine Forests.* USDA Technical Bulletin 137.

Pinnock, D. and J. Milstead. 1971. Biological control of California oakworm with *Bacillus thuringiensis. Calif. Agric.* **25**:3–5.

Powell, J. A. 1980. *Nomenclature of Nearctic Conifer-Feeding Choristoneura (Lepidoptera: Tortricidae): Historical review and present status.* U.S. Forest Service General Technical Report PNW-100.

Prebble, M. L. (Ed.). 1975. *Aerial Control of Forest Insects in Canada.* Canadian Forestry Service, Department of the Environment, Ottawa, Ontario.

Prentice, R. M. 1955. The life history and some aspects of the ecology of the large aspen tortrix, *Choristoneura confictana* (n. comb.) Lepidoptera: Tortricidae. *Can. Entomol.* **87**:461–473.

Quednau, F. W. 1967. Ecological observations on *Chrysocharis laricinellae* (Hymenoptera: Eulophidae), a parasite of the larch casebearer (*Coleophora laricella*). *Can. Entomol.* **99**:631–641.

Quednau, F. W. 1970a. Competition and cooperation between *Chrysocharis laricinellae* and *Agathis pumila* in larch casebearer populations in Quebec. *Can. Entomol.* **102**:602–612.

Quednau, F. W. 1970b. Notes on life history, fecundity, longevity, and attack patterns of *Agathis pumila* (Hymenoptera: Braconidae), a parasite of the larch casebearer. *Can. Entomol.* **102**:736–745.

Raske, A. G. and D. G. Bryant. 1977. Distribution, survival, and intra-tree movement of late-instar birch casebearer larvae on white birch (Lepidoptera: Coleophoridae). *Can. Entomol.* **109**:1297–1306.

Readshaw, J. L. 1965. A theory of phasmatid outbreak release. *Aust. J. Zool.* **13**:475–490.

Readshaw, J. L. and G. O. Bedford. 1971. Development of the egg of the stick insect *Didymuria violescens* with particular reference to diapause. *Aust. J. Zool.* **19**:141–158.

Reeks, W. A. and G. W. Barter. 1951. Growth reduction and mortality of spruce caused by the European spruce sawfly, *Gilpinia hercynia* (Htg.) (Hymenoptera: Diprionidae). *For. Chron.* **27**:1–16.

Rose, A. H. and O. H. Lindquist. 1973. *Insects of Eastern Pines*. Department of Environment, Canadian Forest Service Publication 1313.

Schmid, J. M., P. A. Farrar, and J. C. Mitchell. 1982. Distribution of pandora egg masses and pupae near Jacob Lake, Arizona. *Environ. Entomol.* **11**:701–704.

Schmidt, W. C., and D. G. Fellin. 1973. Western spruce budworm damage affects form and height growth of western larch. *Can. J. For. Res.* **3**:17–26.

Schmidt, W. C., D. G. Fellin, and C. E. Carlson. 1983. Alternatives to chemical insecticides in budworm-susceptible forests. *West. Wildlands* **9**(1):13–19.

Schmiege, D. C. 1961. *Mortality and Top Killing of Spruce Fir Caused by Repeated Budworm Defoliation*. U.S. Forest Service Lake States Experiment Station Technical Note 597.

Schoenfelder, T. W., M. W. Houseweart, L. C. Thompson, H. M. Kulman, and F. B. Martin. 1978. Insect and mammal predation of yellowheaded spruce sawfly cocoons (Hymenoptera: Tenthredinidae). *Environ. Entomol.* **7**:711–713.

Silver, G. T. 1957. Studies on the arborvitae leaf miners in New Brunswick (Lepidoptera: Yponomeutidae and Gelechiidae). *Can. Entomol.* **89**:171–182.

Smith, D. R. 1974. Conifer sawflies, Diprionidae: Key to North American genera, checklist of world species and new species from Mexico (Hymenoptera). *Proc. Entomol. Soc. Wash.* **76**:409–418.

Spencer, K. A. 1969. The Agromyzidae of Canada and Alaska. *Entomol. Soc. Can. Mem.* 64.

Stairs, G. R. 1972. Pathogenic microorganisms in the regulation of forest insect populations. *Annu. Rev. Entomol.* **17**:355–372.

Stark, E. J. and J. D. Harper. 1982. Pupal mortality in forest tent caterpillar (Lepidoptera: Lasiocampidae): Causes and impact on populations in southwestern Alabama. *Environ. Entomol.* **11**:1071–1077.

Stark, R. W. 1954. Distribution and life history of the lodgepole needle miner (*Recurvaria* sp.) in Canadian Rocky Mountain parks. *Can. Entomol.* **86**:1–12.

Stark, R. W. 1959. Population dynamics of the lodgepole needle miner, *Recurvaria starki* Freeman, in Canadian Rocky Mountain parks. *Can. J. Zool.* **37**:917–943.

Stedinger, J. R. 1977. *Analysis of Spray Policies with the Maine Budworm—Forest Simulation Model*. School of Forest Resources, University of Maine Technical Notes 69.

Stehr, F. W. and E. F. Cook. 1968. *A Revision of the Genus Malacosoma Hübner in North America (Lepidoptera: Lasiocampidae)*: Systematics, Biology, Immatures, and Parasites. U.S. Natural History Museum Bulletin 276.

Stein, J. D. 1974. Elm sawfly. U.S. Forest Service Forest Pest Leaflet 142.

Stelzer, M. J. 1968. The Great Basin tent caterpillar in New Mexico: Life history, parasites, disease, and defoliation. U.S. Forest Service Research Paper RM-39.

Stoszek, K. J., P. G. Mika, J. A. Moore, and H. L. Osborne. 1981. Relationships of Douglas-fir tussock moth defoliation to site and stand characteristics in northern Idaho. *For. Sci.* **27**:431–442.

Struble, G. R. 1957. Biology and control of the white-fir sawfly. *For. Sci.* **3**:306–313.

Struble, G. R. 1972. *Biology, Ecology, and Control of the Lodgepole Needle Miner.* USDA Technical Bulletin 1458.

Thompson, L. C., H. M. Kulman, and J. A. Witter. 1977. Introduction, establishment, and dispersal of exotic parasites of the larch sawfly in Minnesota. *Environ. Entomol.* **5**:649–657.

Triplehorn, C. A. 1955. The Asiatic oak weevil in Delaware. *J. Econ. Entomol.* **48**:289–293.

Tunnock, S., R. E. Denton, C. E. Carlson, and W. W. Janssen. 1969. Larch casebearer and other factors involved with deterioration of western larch stands in northern Idaho. U.S. Forest Service Research Paper INT-68.

Turnock, W. J. 1972. Geographical and historical variability in population patterns and life systems of the larch sawfly (Hymenoptera: Tenthredinidae). *Can. Entomol.* **104**:1883–1900.

Wargo, P. M. 1977. *Armillariella mellea* and *Agrilus bilineatus* and mortality of defoliated oak trees. *For. Sci.* **23**:485–492.

Wargo, P. M. 1978. Insects have defoliated my tree—now what's going to happen? *J. Abor.* **4**:169–175.

Warren, L. O. and M. Tadic. 1970. *The Fall Webworm, Hyphantria cunea (Drury).* Arkansas Agriculture Experiment Station Bulletin 759.

Washburn, R. I., and M. D. McGregor. 1974. *White Fir Needle Miner.* U.S. Forest Service Forest Insect and Disease Leaflet 156.

Weaver, H. 1961. Ecological changes in the ponderosa pine forest of Cedar Valley in southern Washington. *Ecology* **42**:416–420.

Weaver, J. E. and C. K. Dorsey. 1965. Parasites and predators associated with five species of leafmining insects in black locust. *Ann. Entomol. Soc. Am.* **58**:933–934.

Wickman, B. E. 1971. *California Oakworm.* U.S. Forest Service Forest Pest Leaflet 72.

Wickman, B. E. 1976. Phenology of white fir and Douglas-fir tussock moth egg hatch and larval development in Canada. *Environ. Entomol.* **5**:316–322.

Wickman, B. E. 1978a. A case study of a Douglas-fir tussock moth outbreak and stand conditions 10 years later. U.S. Forest Service Research Paper PNW-244.

Wickman, B. E. 1978b. Tree mortality and top-kill related to defoliation by the Douglas-fir tussock moth in the Blue Mountains outbreak. U.S. Forest Service Research Paper PNW-233.

Wickman, B. E. and R. F. Scharpf. 1972. Decay in white fir top-killed by Douglas-fir tussock moth. U.S. Forest Service Research Paper PNW-133.

Wilcox, J. A. 1954. The leaf beetles of Ohio (Chrysomelidae: Coleoptera). *Ohio Biol. Surv. Bull.* **43**(8):353–506.

Wilcox, J. A. 1972. A review of the North American Chrysomeline leaf beetles (Coleoptera: Chrysomelidae). NY State Museum of Science Service Bulletin 400.

Wilson, L. F. 1971a. *Variable Oak Leaf Caterpillar.* U.S. Forest Service Forest Pest Leaflet 67.

Wilson, L. F. 1971b. *Walkingstick*. U.S. Forest Service Forest Pest Leaflet 82.

Wilson, L. F. 1971c. *Yellow-Headed Spruce Sawfly*. U.S. Forest Service Forest Pest Leaflet 69.

Wilson, L. F. 1977. *A Guide to Insect Injury to Conifers in the Lake States*. U.S. Forest Service Agriculture Handbook 501.

Witter, J. A. 1979. The forest tent caterpillar (Lepidoptera: Lasiocampidae) in Minnesota: A case history review. *Great Lakes Entomol.* **12**:191–197.

Witter, J. A. and H. M. Kulman. 1972. *A Review of the Parasites and Predators of Tent Caterpillars (Malacosoma spp.) in North America*. Minnesota Agricultural Experiment Station Technical Bulletin 289.

Witter, J. A. and H. M. Kulman. 1979. The parasite complex of the forest tent caterpillar in northern Minnesota. *Environ. Entomol.* **8**:723–731.

Witter, J. A. and L. A. Waisanen. 1978. The effect of differential flushing times among trembling aspen clones on tortricid caterpillar populations. *Environ. Entomol.* **7**:139–143.

Witter, J. A., H. M. Kulman, and A. C. Hodson. 1972. Life tables for the forest tent caterpillar. *Ann. Entomol. Soc. Am.* **65**:25–31.

Witter, J. A., W. J. Mattson, and H. M. Kulman. 1975. Numerical analysis of a forest tent caterpillar (Lepidoptera: Lasiocampidae) outbreak in northern Minnesota. *Can. Entomol.* **107**:837–854.

Wong, H. R. 1974. The identification and origin of the strains of the larch sawfly, *Pristiphora erichsonii* (Hymenoptera: Tenthredinidae), in North America. *Can. Entomol.* **106**:1121–1131.

Wygant, N. D. 1941. An infestation of the pandora moth, *Coloradia pandora* Blake, in lodgepole pine in Colorado. *J. Econ. Entomol.* **34**:697–702.

12 | SAPSUCKING INSECTS AND MITES

INTRODUCTION

Sapsucking insects and mites are a large group of organisms with piercing–sucking mouthparts that feed on sap by piercing the plant tissue with its beak and sucking the fluid from the plant (Figure 2.5). Sapsucking insects that attack trees and shrubs are found in the orders Homoptera and Hemiptera, whereas the sapsucking mites are in the class Arachnida and order Acari. Generally, the effect of sapsucking insects and mites on forest stands is much less conspicuous and damaging than the effect of many defoliators and bark beetles. Only a few species of sapsucking organisms kill forest trees directly. The balsam woolly adelgid, *Adelges piceae* (Ratzeburg), and the red pine scale, *Matsucoccus resinosae* Bean and Godwin, have killed a large number of mature trees. Also, sapsucking insects and mites can greatly harm or kill individual shade trees and ornamentals. In a recent survey, urban forest managers ranked scales and aphids as the third and fifth most important pest problems in the north central region of the United States (Parks et al. 1982). This chapter provides information on (1) sapsucking insects and mites that damage trees and shrubs and (2) various management approaches used against sapsucking pests.

Symptoms and Damage

Trees attacked by sapsucking insects and mites have numerous symptoms. Common symptoms are: (1) discolored (i.e., yellow) needles or leaves; (2) curled foliage; (3) honeydew and sooty mold on leaves, twigs, branches, and on the ground or sidewalk below the tree; (4) fine silk webbing on the needles and leaves, especially associated with spider mites; (5) premature leaf drop; (6) branch mortality; (7) tree mortality; (8) oviposition scars caused by cicadas and treehoppers; and (9) galls. Exact symptoms seen by the observer will depend on the specific sapsucking organism involved, its population density, time of year the damage is observed, and the observer's experience.

The most common type of damage caused by sapsucking organisms is the discoloration of needles and leaves that occurs when the nymph or adult stage of the insect or mite is feeding on the plant. Saliva is pumped into the plant tissues when the organism is feeding on the host tissue. The saliva is usually toxic to the plant tissue, causing necrotic spots that block translocation. Continued feeding by these organisms interferes with the trees' supply of food and water. Reduced tree growth, branch mortality, and finally tree mortality occurs if large population densities of sapsucking insects or mites feed for an extended time period (i.e., generally 1–7 years depending on the insect species).

Mechanical damage occurs when certain female sapsucking insects oviposit in stems or twigs. Most often oviposition damage is caused by female cicadas and treehoppers that insert eggs into twigs and stems of saplings.

405

Some sapsucking insects are vectors of plant diseases. Many species of leafhoppers transmit plant diseases to vegetable and agriculture crops. The best known disease vector in forests is the whitebanded elm leafhopper, *Scaphoideus luteolus* Van Duzee, which feeds on leaves of a diseased elm tree and transmits the phloem necrosis virus to the leaves of healthy elms where it continues to feed.

Honeydew and sooty mold are often found on trees with large populations of sapsucking organisms such as aphids, scales, and leafhoppers. These sapsucking organisms excrete large quantities of a liquid called "honeydew" that consists of unused portions of plant sap and certain insect waste products. Honeydew is a valuable food source for many species of insects, especially ants. However, honeydew is often very abundant and becomes a nuisance because it is sticky and a fungus disease, called "sooty mold," often develops on the honeydew. Black sooty mold accumulates on ornamental and shade trees and reduces the aesthetic value of the trees.

Population Dynamics

Very little information is available on the population dynamics of sapsucking insects and mites on forest and shade trees except for the balsam woolly adelgid, red pine scale, and the elongate hemlock scale, *Fiorinia externa* Ferris. Numerous predators and parasites, such as ladybird beetles, predaceous mites, lacewings, syrphid flies, and chalcidoid wasps are important population regulators of many sapsucking insects. The two most important sapsucking insect pests in forestry are exotic pests that were accidently introduced into the United States without their natural enemies.

Numerous examples exist of sapsucking insect populations increasing dramatically after their natural enemies were reduced by insecticide sprays or by the accumulation of dust on plants that thwarts the natural enemies (Kennedy and Merritt 1980, McClure 1977b, Luck and Dahlsten 1975, Edmunds 1973, Johnson 1958).

Extremely cold weather and a major decline in the quantity and quality of the host's food supply also have been responsible for the collapse of some sapsucking populations (McClure 1979a, 1980, Miller and Kosztarab 1979, Beardsley and Gonzalez 1975, Greenbank 1970).

Dispersal mechanisms are another critical aspect that affects the population dynamics of scale insects. The most important methods of dispersal for sapsucking organisms are wind, crawling, active flight, and passive transport on infested plant material. A large number of scale insects and aphids are commonly found on an individual branch or tree because wind dispersal and wandering by the crawlers (unfed first-instar nymphs), until they find suitable feeding sites, are the common methods of dispersal for these sapsucking insects. Most of the major sapsucking pests were transported on infested nursery stock from one country to another. Enforcement of plant quarantine and nursery regulations has significantly reduced the spread of sapsucking organisms. Aphids, scales, and mites are the most common pests transported on nursery stock. There small size makes it more difficult to locate on infested nursery stock.

Interactions between sapsucking organisms and host plants are extremely complex but are very important when studying the population dynamics of many sapsucking organisms. Most of the studies involving plant-sucking organism interactions have focused on scale insects. Host plants show major variations in their susceptibility to a specific sapsucking organism. It is not uncommon for this variation to occur on two trees of the same species growing next to each other. One tree has a very heavy infestation of a specific sapsucking organism (i.e., scale, aphid), and the other tree has a very light infestation. A tree species may be heavily infested in one forest stand and lightly infested in another nearby forest stand. Also, a tree species may be very susceptible to a certain sapsucking organism one year and almost immune the next year. McClure (1977a, 1980), Edmunds and Alstad (1978), and Flanders (1970) attempt to explain these variations in susceptibility to attack and the reasons for increased survival of sapsucking organisms in certain situations.

ORGANISMS INVOLVED

Sapsucking organisms that commonly damage forest and shade trees are present in the classes Insecta and Arachnida. Sapsucking insects are found in the orders Homoptera and Hemiptera, whereas arachnid sapsuckers are found in the order Acari.

Homopterous Insects

In the following section we discuss the most common homopterous insects found on forest and shade trees: cicadas, spittlebugs, treehoppers, leafhoppers, psyllids, aphids, gall and woolly adelgids, whiteflies, and scales.

Cicadas, Cicadidae

The characteristic shape, relatively large size, and the distinct song produced by the male during the summer months easily identifies the cicada for many people in North America. An adult cicada (Figure 12.1) has large compound eyes, a stocky body, and two multiveined membranous wings that are held rooflike over the abdomen when at rest. Dog-day cicadas and periodical cicadas are the common names of the two major types of cicadas.

The life cycles are similar for both types of cicadas; the only major difference is the duration of the cycle. Dog-day cicadas have a 2–7-year life cycle. Periodical cicadas have a 13-year life cycle in the South and a 17-year life cycle in the North. The adult female oviposits eggs into the twigs of young trees. Small nymphs emerge from the eggs in about 1 week.

Figure 12.1 Adult periodical cicada, *Magicicada septendecim*. (Connecticut Agricultural Experiment Station photograph, courtesy of C. Maier.)

Figure 12.2 Oviposition damage in branch of tree caused by the adult periodical cicada, *Magicicada septendecim*. (Connecticut Agricultural Experiment Station photograph, courtesy of C. Maier.)

Immediately after dropping to the ground, they burrow into the soil and feed on roots located 8–100 cm below the ground surface. Each nymph hollows out a chamber next to small roots of woody plants and inserts its mouthparts into the roots. They feed on the roots for 2–17 years depending on the species of cicada. Mature nymphs crawl to the surface and transform into adults that can live for 5–6 weeks.

Adult cicadas cause no noticeable feeding damage. The only severe injury to host plants is caused by the female's egg-laying habits. She uses a sawlike ovipositor to cut slits into twigs of trees and shrubs (Figure 12.2). Oviposition damage has been observed on about 100 different plant species. Cicadas generally oviposit on deciduous tree species and usually avoid coniferous species. Cicadas are not serious forests pests, but high populations can kill many twigs and small branches of host trees. Serious damage can occur to young, transplanted trees in nurseries and orchards.

Dog-day cicadas, Tibicen spp.

Dog-day cicadas, large black cicadas with green markings, are found throughout the United States. Very little is known about their life cycle except that it ranges from 2 to 7 years. Adults are found during July and August of every year resulting from the occurrence of overlapping populations; different populations are called *broods*.

Periodical cicadas, Magicicada spp.

Periodical cicadas are extremely common in the eastern United States and have the longest life cycle of any insect in North America. There are at least 5 broods of 13-year cicadas in the South and 13 broods of 17-year cicadas in the North. This does not mean that periodical cicadas are only found at intervals of 13–17 years. They emerge somewhere almost every year. Emergence of the larger broods is very spectacular. All individuals of a brood emerge at about the same time (i.e., late May and early June). The appearance of a brood can be predicted accurately. Most broods are separated geographically and by year of emergence. Dybas and Lloyd (1974) and Alexander and Moore (1962) provide detailed information on the six species of periodical cicadas. Maier (1980, 1982) presents excellent information on the most common species, *Magicicada septendecim* (Linnaeus).

Spittlebugs, Cercopidae

Spittlebugs are most easily recognized under field conditions by the frothy spittle mass that surrounds the nymphs (Figure 12.3). The spittle mass consists of air bubbles and partially digested sap. Immature spittlebugs rest with their heads down on the plant so that the spittle, excreted from the anus and glands on the seventh and eighth abdominal segments, flows down over and covers the insect. A spittle mass provides a moist environment and protects the nymph from predators. Adults do not produce spittle.

Figure 12.3 Nymphal spittle mass of the pine spittlebug, *Aphrophora parallela*. (Courtesy of R. Heyd, Michigan Department of Natural Resources.)

Adult spittlebugs, about 8 mm in length, resemble leafhoppers. The number and form of spines on the hind tibia distinguish spittlebug adults from leafhopper adults. Over 30 species of spittlebugs occur in the United States. Three spittlebug species are described.

Saratoga spittlebug, *Aphrophora saratogensis* (Fitch)

The Saratoga spittlebug is found throughout the eastern United States and southern Canada on numerous species of pines. They can cause serious damage in pine plantations that are 1–5 m high, especially red pine and jack pine plantations in the Great Lakes states. The most obvious signs indicating the presence of the Saratoga spittlebug are: (1) spittlelike masses on the alternate hosts (e.g., herbaceous plants, sweet fern, willow sprouts); (2) reddish-colored branches on host trees; and (3) tan or brown flecks on the surface of the wood of host tree, flecks that are very noticeable when the outer bark is removed from the 2-year-old internodes on the reddish-colored branches. Adult feeding causes the puncture wounds that appear as flecks on the surface of the wood. Numerous puncture wounds interfere with nutrient transport in the branches. Heavy feeding damage causes branch mortality, top-kill, stem deformity, growth loss, and tree mortality (Heyd and Wilson 1981). The greatest impact occurs in young pine plantations that have abundant alternate hosts for the nymphs.

Saratoga spittlebugs have one generation per year and overwinter in the egg stage. Eggs are laid during mid- to late summer under the outer scales of large buds in the upper branches of red pine (1–5 m high) and in the needle sheaths of jack pine. During May, small nymphs emerge from the eggs, drop to the ground, and seek alternate hosts. As soon as a nymph begins to feed, it excretes the spittle mass. These small nymphs feed on herbaceous plants such as raspberry, blackberry, and orange hawkweed, whereas the older nymphs feed on sweet fern and willow sprouts (Wilson 1978). After a 2–3-month feeding period on the alternate hosts, the mature nymphs leave the spittle mass, climb to the upper portion of their alternate host plant, and transform to the adult stage. Adults fly to red pine or jack pine and begin feeding on twigs. Peak adult feeding occurs during July and August, but spittle masses are not formed by the adults on the pine trees.

An excellent pest management program has been developed for the Saratoga spittlebug in Michigan. It is described under the heading "IPM for Saratoga Spittlebug" at the end of this chapter.

Pine spittlebug, *Aphrophora parallela* (Say)

The pine spittlebug is found throughout the eastern United States and southern Canada on pine, spruce, hemlock, and balsam fir. It is often a serious pest in Scots pine Christmas tree plantations. The life cycle and damage symptoms of the pine spittlebug are similar to the Saratoga spittlebug, except that pine spittlebug does not have alternate hosts (Speers 1941). The nymphal stage and accompanying spittle mass are found on coniferous hosts. Young nymphs are found on twigs of the host tree, whereas the older nymphs often feed together under large spittle masses on the main trunk. Full-grown nymphs disperse to the needles and transform to adults that feed on the pine twigs during July and August. Adults do not form spittle masses.

Western pine spittlebug, *Aphrophora permutata* Uhler

Western pine spittlebug is closely related to the pine spittlebug. It is commonly found on pine, hemlock, Douglas-fir, spruce, and fir in the western United States and western Canada. Western pine spittlebug is not considered a serious pest (Kelson 1964).

Treehoppers, Membracidae

Treehoppers are sapsucking insects that often have unusual, variable shapes. They are characterized by a large pronotum that covers the head, extends backward over the abdomen, and in some species extends sideward and upward. Treehoppers, which often resemble thorns, are very common on trees and shrubs. Any disturbance causes them to move very quickly or hop. Normally damage caused by treehoppers is not noticeable on shade or forest trees. Oviposition damage can occur when female leafhoppers deposit eggs into twigs of young trees such as apple, oak, elm, and ash. Small twigs may die from desiccation or from disease-causing fungi entering through the slits cut into the bark by the female's ovipositor.

Buffalo treehopper, Stictocephala bisonia Kopp & Yonke

Buffalo treehoppers are common on many hardwood tree species throughout much of Canada and the United States. After overwintering, eggs hatch in the spring and nymphs immediately drop to the ground and feed on herbaceous material. Adult treehoppers return to the trees and the females deposit their eggs on young twigs. Treehoppers have one or two generations per year.

Oak treehopper, Platycotis vittata (Fabricius)

The oak treehopper is a common species that is found on oaks throughout much of the United States and Canada. Its life cycle is similar to the buffalo treehopper. The only major difference is that the nymphs and adults of the oak treehopper feed on the oak twigs (Brown and Eads 1965).

Leafhoppers, Cicadellidae

Hundreds of species of leafhoppers feed on trees and shrubs, but few are known to cause any serious damage. The only visible effect of feeding by nymph and adult leafhoppers is white stippling damage on the foliage and/ or the browning and curling of some leaves. The leafhopper adults are similar to spittlebugs in size and appearance, except for one or more rows of small spines extending the length of the hind tibia.

Many leafhoppers are vectors of plant diseases, especially mycoplasma and virus diseases. These plant diseases are common to cultivated herbaceous plants but are not common on trees. The only exception in forest and shade trees is the whitebanded elm leafhopper, which is the vector of phloem necrosis, a virus disease of American elm.

Whitebanded elm leafhopper, Scaphoideus luteolus Van Duzee

The whitebanded elm leafhopper is found on American and winged elm throughout the eastern United States. It is the only known vector of phloem necrosis on elms. Adults are very difficult to separate from other closely related species, but the nymphs are easily identified because most are brown and have a transverse white band on the dorsal side that covers the first two and part of the third abdominal segment.

The whitebanded elm leafhopper overwinters in the egg stage and has one generation per year. On hatching in the spring, the young nymphs often cluster into groups of 10 or more and are found feeding on the midribs or larger veins of leaves on the tiny branches growing from the trunk of the tree. Older nymphs are usually found in the tree crowns. Adults transmit the elm phloem necrosis virus by feeding on leaves of diseased trees and then on leaves of healthy trees (Baker 1948, 1949). The female lays its eggs in the cork parenchyma of elm bark.

Psyllids, Psyllidae

Many of the approximately 150 species of psyllids or jumping plant lice in North America are found on trees and shrubs, but most are only an occasional nuisance. Psyllid adults are 1–5 mm long and resemble miniature cicadas, or small aphids, but unlike aphids, they have stout and tough legs and bodies adapted for jumping. Many psyllids are either leaf or woolly gall makers. See Chapter 17 on insects and mites causing galls for more information on psyllids.

Aphids, Aphididae

Aphids are a very large group of small (1–6-mm), soft-bodied, usually gregarious insects that suck sap from leaves, stems, or roots of ornamental plants and trees. Aphids usually have pear-shaped bodies, relatively long antennae, and a pair of tubelike structures called *cornicles* that arise from the top of the fifth or sixth abdominal segment. There are both winged and wingless forms. Aphid wings are delicate, membraneous, practically veinless, and are held vertically above the body when at rest.

Life cycles of aphids are extremely variable, ranging from simple to complex life cycles with alternate hosts, winged and wingless generations, and asexual and sexual generations. Most species overwinter in the egg stage.

Almost every tree or shrub has aphids, but only a few species of aphids are sometimes important shade tree pests. Three common types of aphids are described.

Cinara spp.

A number of the *Cinara* species occur in large colonies on branches, stems, or roots of coniferous trees (Figure 12.4). Three species of *Cinara* aphids cause reduced growth of young Douglas-fir seedlings in Washington (Johnson 1965). White pine aphid, *Cinara strobi* (Fitch), occurs in the eastern United States, where it has killed young trees and branches of large trees, and reduced tree growth. Other species of *Cinara* have caused damage to juniper, cypress, cedar, and pine.

A generalized life cycle for aphids in the genus *Cinara* is presented. After hatching from the eggs in the spring, the nymphs begin feeding, and in time wingless parthenogenetic females give birth to live young, and another generation of wingless parthenogenetic females is produced. Then several generations of parthenogenetic winged females are produced. In the fall, winged males and females mate and the overwintering eggs are laid. Depending on the aphid species, eggs are found on needles or bark.

Spruce aphid, Elatobium abietinum (Walker)

The spruce aphid is a serious pest of Sitka spruce and blue spruce along the Pacific Coast (Holms and Ruth 1968). Outbreaks in the forests are

Figure 12.4   Colony of giant conifer aphids, *Cinara* sp., and an attending carpenter ant, *Camponotus* sp., on Douglas-fir. (U.S. Forest Service photograph.)

sporadic and short-term, but infestations of ornamentals occur more regularly and often for a longer duration. Although there are several generations per year, most damage occurs during late winter and early spring. Spruce aphids feed mostly on old needles in the lower and more shaded portion of trees.

Balsam twig aphid, *Mindarus abietinus* Koch

The balsam twig aphid feeds on new needles and twigs of fir, spruce, and juniper. It is found throughout most of the United States and Canada. Obvious symptoms of heavy infestation are curling and twisting of needles, premature needle drop, distortion of twigs, and the white waxy material that covers the intermediate form of this insect. Balsam twig aphids are not an important forest pest but can damage the appearance of ornamental trees and seriously reduce the value of Christmas trees (Nettleton and Hain 1982, Saunders 1969).

Gall and Woolly Adelgids, Phylloxeridae

Insects in the family Phylloxeridae were formerly placed in the families Chermidae and Adelgidae and had common names such as gall aphids, pine aphids, or woolly aphids. Currently these insects are referred to as *gall adelgids, pine adelgids,* or *woolly adelgids,* and only insects in the family Aphididae are referred to as *aphids.* The gall and woolly adelgids are closely related to aphids but are different because they have no cornicles, only lay eggs, and are only found on conifers. Woolly adelgids are described in this chapter, and the gall adelgids are described in Chapter 17.

Balsam Woolly Adelgid, Adelges piceae (Ratzeburg)

The balsam woolly adelgid was accidentally introduced into the state of Maine around 1900 on imported nursery stock from Europe. It was first reported in the western United States near San Francisco, California in 1928 and in the southeastern United States near Skyland, Virginia in 1956. The balsam woolly adelgid is now a serious pest of balsam fir in the north-eastern United States and eastern Canada, of subalpine fir, Pacific silver fir, and grand fir in the Coast and Cascade Mountains from Oregon into British Columbia, and of Fraser fir in the southeastern United States.

The most obvious signs of the balsam woolly adelgid are the white woolly material that covers the insect (Figure 12.5) and swelling of twigs and buds (Figure 12.5) caused by adelgid feeding. This insect can be found anywhere on the stems, branches, and twigs of host tree. However, adelgid survival on the various parts of the trees varies significantly by area and host species. Stem infestations, also called *bole infestations,* are commonly found on Fraser fir, subalpine fir, and balsam fir (i.e., in the Maritime Provinces only).

There are two to four generations per year, with the variation due primarily to latitudinal and elevational differences (Bryant 1971, Amman 1970, Mitchell et al. 1961, Balch 1952). All stages of this parthenogenetic insect from egg to adult may enter the winter, but only first-instar sessile nymphs can survive winter temperatures greater than $-15°C$. On hatching from the egg, the first-instar nymph is motile (i.e., called a "crawler") and moves about the host tree until it finds a suitable spot to feed. Dispersal within the forest stand is normally by wind during the crawler stage. The first-instar nymph is stationary for the rest of the life cycle once the adelgid inserts its stylet into the parenchyma tissue and starts feeding. Dispersal into new areas has been due primarily to people moving infested nursery stock, Christmas trees, and infested logs from one area to another.

The distribution of adelgid populations within geographic areas and within the tree is regulated by low winter temperatures. Mortality of overwintering first-instar sessile nymphs starts at about $-20°C$ and is complete at about $-37°C$ (Bryant 1975, 1976). Winter temperatures in Newfoundland and the coastal areas of the Maritime Provinces are not sufficiently low to prevent spread or increase of populations on host trees. However, in most of Maine and northwestern New Brunswick, the extreme winter temperatures periodically kill all adelgids above the snow line. In Oregon, Washington, British Columbia, and Newfoundland, differences in balsam woolly adelgid infestation levels occur as a result of altitudinal differences. Severe infestations generally occur on trees at lower elevations, and less

Figure 12.5 Balsam woolly adelgid, *Adelges piceae:* (*a*) gouting of twigs on subalpine fir, (*b*) bole infestation of subalpine fir. (U.S. Forest Service photographs.)

damage occurs on host trees at high elevations (Greenbank 1970, Johnson et al. 1963).

Tree species also affects adelgid population numbers. True firs vary considerably in susceptibility to balsam woolly adelgid attack. The balsam woolly adelgid is considered a secondary pest of true firs in Europe. For example, a plantation of European silver fir in western North Carolina suffered no appreciable damage from the balsam woolly adelgid, whereas all surrounding Fraser fir trees of the same size were killed by the adelgid. In North America, Fraser fir, subalpine fir, and balsam fir are the true firs most susceptible to damage. It is not unusual for these trees species to be killed in less than 5 years when severe population densities are present. Grand fir may survive infestations for up to 15 years before dying, whereas Pacific silver fir is intermediate in susceptibility between the western species, subalpine fir and grand fir. Noble fir, white fir, and Shasta red fir are attacked, and sometimes the twigs and buds swell as a result of adelgid feeding but all appear to be fairly resistant to attack.

The characteristics and condition of the tree affect the survival of adelgid populations. Rough-barked trees with numerous crevices and lenticels are more susceptible to adelgid attack than are smooth-barked trees. Generally,

Figure 12.5   (*Continued*)

small-diameter trees and young dense stands are less susceptible than large-diameter trees and open-grown mature stands. Schooley and Bryant (1978), Page (1975), Amman (1970), and Mitchell (1966) provide additional information on adelgid survival under different stand conditions.

True firs succumb to balsam woolly adelgid attack in two ways. First, heavy bole infestations cause the production of reddish-colored compressionlike wood with poor conduction qualities. The saliva from the adelgid's feeding causes an increase in the number of cells, size of cells, and production of tracheids with thickened cell walls. During the first 2 or 3 years of an outbreak, heavy bole infestations cause accelerated growth manifested by wide annual growth rings. Reduced tree rings occur in subsequent years until death of tree. The tree dies when the food reserves are used up.

Second, heavy infestations in the crowns of trees can also cause tree mortality. The adelgids that settle on the twigs, nodes, and under bud scales normally cause gouting (i.e., swelling) of the twigs and buds, which discourages new shoot growth and eventually can result in the death of the tree.

The impact of the balsam woolly adelgid on true firs in North America has been severe. Complete stand mortality, severe timber losses, reduced tree growth, and reduction in amount of viable seed has occurred in many stands of true firs in North America (Schooley and Bryant 1978, Schooley 1976, Page 1975, Fedde 1973, Amman 1970, Mitchell 1966). Balsam fir regeneration is often gouted or killed, but usually a sufficient amount of regeneration occurs so that the succeeding stand is fir. The balsam woolly adelgid has killed millions of board feet of true fir timber since becoming established in North America around 1900. It continues to be one of our most important forest pests because there are few control techniques available to the land manager that will reduce adelgid damage.

There have been numerous attempts to control the balsam woolly adelgid during the last 50 years. None has been particularly successful, but a few do work under specific circumstances. Over 20 species of predacious insects, primarily beetles from Europe, Asia, and Australia, were released into adelgid-infested areas in Canada and the United States. Six species became established, but neither the introduced nor native predator complex has made any significant impact in reducing adelgid populations (Clark et al. 1971). Insecticides sprayed from the air were ineffective in controlling balsam woolly adelgids in forest stands. However, ground applications of insecticides to protect Christmas trees, seed orchards, and highly valued yard trees and park trees do reduce population levels but are extremely costly.

The province of British Columbia has had success with using voluntary restrictions on moving true fir logs out of the infested area and by placing a province-wide band on growing, moving, and importing true fir nursery stock or ornamentals. All existing true fir nursery stock was destroyed. These restrictions were started in the mid-1960s and have been a main factor in helping to stabilize the infestation boundary since 1967.

A number of silvicultural and management techniques can be used to reduce adelgid damage or reduce the spread of infestations. The harvesting of all fir trees in newly infested areas in Newfoundland has retarded development of the adelgid in nearby stands. Stand fertilization may reduce adelgid numbers and could reduce the risk of attack by shortening the rotation age (Carrow and Betts 1973). Conversion of fir stands to nonsusceptible or less susceptible species by harvesting, site preparation, and planting is a promising technique on some sites. The use of Page's hazard rating system in Newfoundland (Page 1975) as a management tool to minimize the number of high-hazard stands and to eliminate concentrations of high-hazard stands should have long-term beneficial effects.

Whiteflies, Aleyrodidae
Whiteflies are often a serious economic pest on citrus trees and greenhouse crops, including ornamentals, but normally do not cause a major problem

on outdoor ornamentals except in the most southern portions of the United States. Whiteflies are small (1–3-mm) mothlike insects; adults have four wings that are covered with a white powder. The nymphs are scalelike in appearance and have a distinctive waxy fringe around the outside of their bodies. Whiteflies cause damage by removing sap from the plant. A heavily damaged plant often has a yellow mottled appearance, honeydew, and sooty mold. In the United States the most common whiteflies on ornamentals are the rhododendron whitefly, *Dialeurodes chittendeni* Laing, found only on rhododendron; azalea whitefly, *Pealius azaleae* (Baker and Moles), found only on azalea; and the crown whitefly, *Aleuroplatus coronatus* (Quaintance), primarily a pest of live oaks in California.

Scales, Superfamily Coccoidea

Most species of scale insects are small, under 10 mm. Some species are very specialized and found only on certain parts of one plant species, but members of the superfamily are very diverse in form and habit. In fact, it is doubtful that a person unfamiliar with scales would recognize them as insects.

Scale insects are among the most destructive agents on ornamental shrubs and trees. A recent survey of urban forest managers in the north-central United States showed that scale insects were their third major pest problem, with only borers and dutch elm disease ranking as more serious problems (Parks et al. 1982).

Scale insect life cycles vary somewhat by species, but the following generalized life cycle is presented. Most female scales lay eggs, but a few species give birth to live young. The first-instar nymph, often called a "crawler," emerges from underneath the female scale or egg sac. Crawlers have legs, antennae, and usually actively search for an acceptable feeding site on the plant.

After finding a suitable feeding site, the crawler inserts its mouthparts into the plant host. All armored scales and some of the soft scales are immobile during the next one to three instars. When the first-instar nymph starts feeding, a waxy or scalelike covering is secreted that covers the body. Armored scales have a shell-like covering which is often separated from the body of the scale insects. In soft scales, the "shell" or outer covering is the exoskeleton, and it cannot be removed without killing the insect. Wingless females remain under the scale covering when they become adults and produce eggs or live young from under the scale covering. Male development is similar to that of the females, except that the last instar before the adult is quiescent and the wings develop externally during the last nymphal instar. Adult males resemble small gnats but can be recognized by the one pair of membranous wings with two veins, no mouthparts, and the stylelike process at the end of abdomen (Figure 3.14). The number of generations per year varies by species and by location.

There are 16 families of scale insects in the United States. The specific families and species presented in this chapter were chosen to represent the most common groups found on shade and forest trees.

Soft Scales, Coccidae

Soft scales, Coccidae, are generally soft, convex, spherical scales that are commonly found on the twigs and branches of ornamental trees and shrubs (Williams and Kosztarab 1972). They are considered important pests of ornamental and fruit trees, sometimes a problem in Christmas tree plantations, and minor pests of forest stands. Seven examples of soft scales are presented in this chapter.

The cottony maple scale, *Pulvinaria innumerabilis* (Rathvon), occurs throughout the United States and southern Canada. It is an important pest of shade tree maples, but it is also found on apple, ash, linden, locust, willow, aspen, alder, and many other deciduous shade trees. Cottony egg masses on twigs (Figure 12.6), the 6-mm brown, oval female scale, honeydew drippings, and sooty mold are the most obvious signs of the presence of this insect. Heavy population densities cause damage such as yellow leaves, premature leaf drop, and branch and tree mortality. Often cottony maple scale is very abundant for 2–3 years, then numerous natural enemies such as dipterous parasites and ladybird beetles greatly reduces the scale populations.

The cottony maple scale overwinters as a half-grown immature fertilized female on twigs and small branches of host trees. Her development is resumed in the spring. During May and June the female secretes a white, cottony mass and lays 500 or more eggs underneath it. Young light yellow crawlers leave the cottony mass in June and July and crawl to the under-surface of the leaves, insert their mouthparts, and feed on the plant juices. Mating occurs in August and September. One generation is produced annually (Blackman and Ellis 1916).

Lecanium scales, *Lecanium* spp., are 3–12 mm long, dark brown to reddish, oval, convex scales that are located on twigs and branches of host trees (Figure 12.7). At least 10 species of lecanium scales are common pests on fruit and shade trees in the United States and Canada. Identification of lecanium scales is difficult at the species level, but the relative size of the scales and host preferences are helpful characteristics when making identifications in the field.

Lecanium scales usually have one generation per year and overwinter as immature scales on twigs and branches. Most damage to the plant host occurs when immature nymphs feed during spring and early summer. Eggs are laid in early summer and hatch in June or July. After hatching, the crawlers move to the underside of leaves and feed on the leaves until late summer, when the nymphs return to the twigs and branches where they overwinter.

The European fruit lecanium, *Parthenolecanium corni* (Bouché), the most abundant species in the genus, ranges throughout the United States and

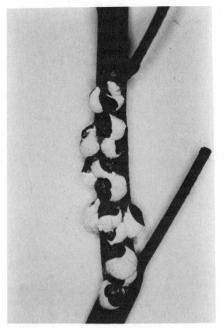

Figure 12.6 Cottony maple scale, *Pulvinaria innumerabilis*. (From Southern Forest Insect Work Conference Slide Series.)

Figure 12.7 Lecanium scales on water oak. (U.S. Forest Service photograph, courtesy of J. Solomon.)

southern Canada and occurs on almost any species of fruit tree and deciduous shade or forest tree.

The Fletcher scale, *Parthenolecanium fletcheri* (Cockerell), another common lecanium scale, sometimes is a pest on yew, juniper, and arborvitae.

Pine tortoise scale, *Toumeyella parvicornis* (Cockerell), is primarily found on Scots, Austrian, jack, and red pine in the eastern United States and southern Canada but also occurs in Nebraska and the Dakotas (Wilson 1971, Rabkin and Lejeune 1954). The most obvious evidence of this scale is the 6-mm oval, brown scale, honeydew, and sooty mold. Severe damage to ornamental trees, especially seedlings and young saplings, and Christmas tree plantations can result from pine tortoise scale infestations. Tree mortality can occur after several years of heavy infestation. The life cycle of the pine tortoise scale is similar to the cottony male scale. The scale overwinters as an immature fertilized female and produces one generation per year. A close relative of the pine tortoise scale is the irregular pine scale, *Toumeyella pinicola* Ferris, which is an important pest or ornamental pines, especially Monterey pine in coastal areas of California (Kattoulas and Koehler 1965).

The tuliptree scale, *Toumeyella liriodendri* (Gmelin), is found east of the Mississippi Valley and in California on yellow poplar and magnolia trees. The most obvious signs of this scale are the large (6–12-mm) dark brown hemispherical female scale (Figure 12.8), honeydew, and sooty mold. Die-back of branches and mortality of trees up to 12-cm DBH often occurs during heavy infestations of the tuliptree scale (Donley and Burns 1971). Tuliptree scale infestations on pioneer yellow poplar in abandoned fields and pastures have resulted in suppression and mortality of trees. Mortality of the terminal shoots of surviving yellow poplar saplings is common and leads to crooks that make the tree worthless for future lumber or veneer (Burns and Donley 1970).

One generation of tuliptree scale is produced annually throughout all the range, except in the extreme southern part of the range, where multiple generations probably occur each year. This scale overwinters as a second-instar nymph, but all stages may be present in the extreme southern pop-ulations. The tuliptree scale actively feeds from spring to late summer. Males emerge in June and mate with half-grown females. Mature females give birth to live young in late August and September. Crawlers find a suitable spot on the woody part of the tree, where they feed and develop to second-instar nymphs before winter.

The magnolia scale, *Neolecanium cornuparvum* (Thro), the largest scale found in the United States, is an ornamental pest of primarily magnolia trees in the eastern United States. The most obvious signs of the magnolia scale are the 13-mm, elliptical, shiny brown females scales and the black sooty mold, which makes heavily infested trees and ground beneath trees unsightly. The life cycle of the Magnolia scale is very similar to the tuliptree

Figure 12.8 Tuliptree scale, *Toumeyella liriodendri*. (North Carolina Agriculture Extension Service photograph.)

scale. Both species overwinter as first instar nymphs on young twigs and produce one generation per year.

The spruce bud scale, *Physokermes piceae* (Schrank), feeds primarily on spruce in the eastern United States, southern Canada, Oregon, and California. Clusters of three to five dusty, reddish brown scales (3 mm long) on lower branches at the base of recent twig growth are the most obvious evidence of an infestation. This is a common scale that produces one generation per year and overwinters as a half-grown fertilized female.

Armored scales, Diaspididae

Over 300 species of armored scales occur in North America. Many are serious pests of ornamentals, shade trees, and Christmas trees, but none are major forest pests. Armored scale adults hide under a scale composed of its own cast skins and waxy secretions. Various species of armored scales have distinct colors and shapes. Eight common species are presented as examples of this group.

The oystershell scale, *Lepidosaphes ulmi* (Linnaeus), a very common pest of ornamentals, shade, and forest trees, is found throughout North America. It has been recorded on more than 100 species of deciduous trees and ornamentals but is commonly found on ash, lilac, willow, aspen, and maple. Heavily attacked trees and shrubs are severely weakened and sometimes killed by this insect. Its most recognizable feature is the resemblance of the scale (3 mm in length) to miniature gray–brown oystershells (Figure 12.9). The two forms of the oystershell scale are the banded or lilac form and

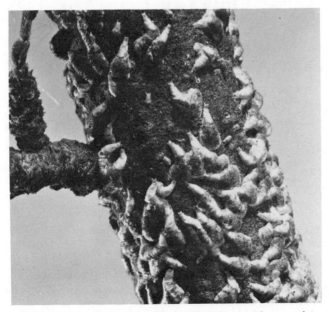

Figure 12.9 Oystershell scale. (U.S. Forest Service photograph.)

the brown or apple form. The banded form is lighter in color, slightly larger, and somewhat slower in development than the brown form. Populations of the oystershell scale often build up and completely cover one branch or a portion of the stem before infesting other parts of the tree.

Oystershell scales overwinter as egg masses beneath the scale coverings of the female (Samarasinghe and Leroux 1966). One generation is produced each year in the North with eggs laid during late summer and early fall. In the South two generations are produced each year with eggs laid during early summer and early fall. After emerging from the egg, the crawler wanders about on the tree for some time before finding a suitable location on the branches or bole and inserts its mouthpart into the host plant to feed on sap. Feeding and secretion occur simultaneously. The scale covering increases as the insect grows, protecting the entire scale except for the head. Oystershell scale nymphs are stationary at their feeding sites for the remainder of their developmental period. Adult females do not leave their scale coverings, but the winged males do leave the scale coverings. Reproduction in most armored scales is bisexual, but the oystershell scale has both bisexual and parthenogenetic races (Beardsley and Gonzalez

(a)

Figure 12.10   (a,b) Pine needle scale, *Chionaspis pinifoliae*. (Connecticut Agricultural Experiment Station, courtesy of M. McClure.)

1975). The mature female scale lays 20–100 eggs under her scale covering and dies shortly afterward.

The pine needle scale, *Chionaspis pinifoliae* (Fitch), primarily a pest on ornamentals, Christmas trees, and shelterbelt trees, occurs widely throughout the United States and Canada. Its primary hosts are pines and spruces in the East and pines, Douglas-fir, spruces, and cedars in the West. The pine needle scale can kill trees but normally only weakens them. The major impacts are reduced tree growth and effects on the aesthetic appearance of the tree. Heavy infestations over several years can change beautiful ornamental trees into sickly looking trees with sparse and gray-colored foliage. Small trees, especially along dusty roads, are often heavily infested with this scale.

The mature female pine needle scale is white, narrow, slender in shape, and 3 mm long (Figure 12.10). Her life cycle is similar to the oystershell scale with the egg stage overwintering under the abandoned female's scale

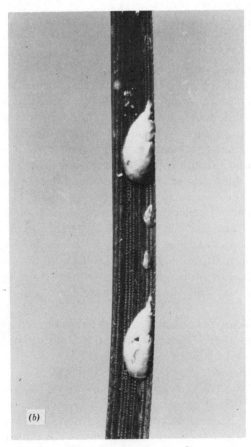

Figure 12.10 *(Continued)*

covering. Depending on location, there are one or two generations per year (Luck and Dahlsten 1974, Nielsen and Johnson 1973).

The black pineleaf scale, *Nuculaspis californica* (Coleman), often found on the same hosts as the pine needle scale, is easily identified by its oval yellowish-brown to black scale covering with a central nipple. Most outbreaks of the black pineleaf needle in the West have been associated with dust or insecticidal spray drift that reduced the population levels of a chalcid parasite that normally keeps the scale population at low levels (Edmunds 1973).

The juniper scale, *Carulaspis juniperi* (Bouché), is an important pest of juniper throughout the United States and southern Canada, but it is also found on arborvitae, incense ceder, and cypress. This insect usually has one generation per year and overwinters as a mature female. The juniper scale feeds on leaves, twigs, branches, and cones. The first indication of damage is often sickly yellow foliage. Heavily infested trees can die from juniper scale feeding. A second obvious sign of infestation is the dirty white female scale with a yellow center.

The euonymus scale, *Unaspis euonymi* (Comstock), is a major pest of deciduous and evergreen euonymus throughout the United States and Canada (Cantelo 1953). This scale may also infest nearby bittersweet, pachysandra, and English ivy. Injury signs are yellow foliage, premature leaf drop, and branch and plant mortality. The most obvious sign of infestation by this scale is the large number of white, elongate males (1–2 mm) that cover the leaves and stems of euonymus. The female scale is brown and oval in shape. Two or three generations occur annually with these scales overwintering as mature females. *Euonymus kiautschovica* is apparently resistant to heavy attack by the euonymus scale and should be substituted for *Euonymus japonica* which is often heavily damaged (Johnson and Lyon 1976).

The elongate hemlock scale, *Fiorinia externa* Ferris, is a serious pest of ornamental and native hemlocks in the northeastern United States (McClure 1978, 1979b, McClure and Fergione 1977). It also occurs on fir, spruce, yew, and other conifers located near heavily infested hemlocks. Yellowing of needles and premature needle drop are the most obvious signs of the elongate hemlock scale on hemlock. Eggs, crawlers, and females are most abundant during May and June, but all stages are found throughout the growing season.

The obscure scale, *Melanaspis obscura* (Comstock), commonly found in the eastern and southern United States and in California, is a pest of shade trees such as oak and willow in Maryland and Pennsylvania and often causes damage to pecan in the South (Stoetzel and Davidson 1971). The scale attacks the stem and larger branches of host trees. The first obvious sign of damage is dieback of branches. Closer observation may reveal clusters of female scales that are circular in shape, 3 mm long, and gray to black.

The San Jose scale, *Quadraspidiotus perniciosus* (Comstock), is a serious pest of apples and other fruit trees throughout the United States and southern Canada. It is commonly found on many decidiuous shade and ornamental trees such as alder, ash, birch, cherry, elm, maple, poplar, and willow (Jorgensen et al. 1981, Gentile and Summers 1958). This scale attacks twigs, branches, and stems of host trees and can cause serious problems on ornamental trees. There may be as many as five overlapping generations per year with this insect overwintering as immature females and males. The most obvious sign of infestation is scale coverings encrusting part of the host tree. Both sexes are gray and approximately 2 mm long. The female scales are nearly round, with a raised nipple in the center; the scale covering of the male is oval with a raised nipple nearer the larger end of the scale.

Eriococcid Scales, Eriococcidae

The beech scale, *Cryptococcus fagisuga* Lindinger, and the European elm scale, *Gossyparia spuria* (Modeer), are two common pests of beech and elm, respectively, throughout most of North America.

The beech scale is easily identified by the white woolly material, secreted by the female, which often covers the bole of the tree (Figure 12.11). One generation occurs annually, overwintering as small nymphs. The nymphs resume feeding in the spring, and parthenogenetic females begin egg laying in June. Crawlers hatch in about 4 weeks and move about until a suitable feeding site is found. After inserting their mouthparts into the bark, the young nymphs excrete a white woolly material and become quiescent until spring.

Figure 12.11 Beech scale, *Cryptococcus fagisuga*, showing white woolly material on bole of tree. (Connecticut Agricultural Experiment Station, courtesy of M. C. McClure.)

Beech scale populations may increase to severe levels in 2 or 3 years. Heavy stem infestations rupture the smooth bark and provide an entry point for fungi, especially *Nectria coccinea faginata*, which have killed numerous shade and forest beech trees in the northeastern United States. Nectria fungus, often referred to as "beech bark disease," penetrates the cambium and sapwood, killing the tissues and interfering with many functions of the tree such as conduction and storage processes. Numerous fungal lesions, caused by the red fruiting bodies of the fungus, coalesce and girdle the tree trunk. The scales do not endanger the beech tree but are indirectly responsible for killing their host because the fungi are completely dependent on beech scales for providing the entry wound and for dispersal of the fungus. Houston (1975) and Shigo (1970, 1972) present detailed information on the beech bark disease situation in the northeastern United States.

The European elm scale, *Gossyparia spuria* (Modeer), is found on ornamental elms throughout much of the United States and southern Canada, especially in the West. It often causes severe injury to young or transplanted elm. European elm scale is easily recognized because the mature females are dark reddish brown with a conspicuous fringe of white wax around the edge of the scale covering (Figure 12.12).

Figure 12.12 European elm scale, *Gossyparia spuria*. (Courtesy of M. Williams, Auburn University.)

Margarodid Scales, Margarodidae

Approximately 20 species of margarodid scales attack forest and shade trees, mostly pines, in the United States. Nymphs and adults of most species attacking forest trees are small (2-mm), oval, yellow–brown insects that are difficult to see because they bury themselves under the sheath of needle fascicles. Often an infestation is not detected until the appearance of discolored foliage and dead tips of branches. Life histories of two margarodid scales are presented.

The red pine scale, *Matsucoccus resinosae* Bean and Godwin, is a serious pest of red pine in Connecticut, New Jersey, and New York. Two generations occur annually. Eggs in the first generation are laid in May and nymphs molt to adults in August; in the second generation, eggs are laid in August and September with nymphs molting to adults the following spring (McClure 1977a, Bean and Godwin 1955). This scale overwinters as a partly grown first-instar nymph at its feeding site under loose bark flakes on red pine branches.

The most obvious signs of the red pine scale are changes in foliage color, swollen and cracked bark on branches and trunks of heavily infested trees, woolly scales in bark crevices, and a patch of dead tissue beneath each feeding scale (Figure 12.13). Brown lesions appear in the phloem of heavily infested trees. These lesions coalesce in time and the branches and tree are killed.

Large numbers of trees in red pine plantations in the northeastern United States have been killed by this insect (Figure 12.13). The spread of the red pine scale into natural stands to the north and west has probably been limited by cold temperatures of $-23°C$, which are fatal to all scales on trees above snow cover.

The pinon needle scale, *Matsucoccus acalyptus* Herbert, another margarodid scale, often causes damage to pinyon and foxtail pines in the southwestern United States (McCambridge 1974). Small trees can be killed directly by the scale, whereas larger trees are only weakened by scale infestations, and then killed by a bark beetle, *Ips confusus* (LeConte).

Pit Scales, Asterolecaniidae

In the United States 15 species of pit scales belong to the genus *Asterolecanium*. Three different species of *Asterolecanium* occur on the twigs of oaks in eastern and western United States. Life histories and food preferences are similar for *A. variolosum* (Ratzeburg), called the *golden oak scale* in the East, *A. minus* Lindinger, and *A. quercicola* (Bouché) (Pritchard and Beer 1950). The three species produce one generation per year and overwinter as adults on twigs. Adults produce live nymphs during the spring and summer. As the crawlers begin to feed, small pits develop on the twigs. The scales appear to be in a depression leading to the common name "pit scales." Both small and large oak trees can be killed by pit scales, especially

Figure 12.13 Red pine scale, *Matsucoccus resinosae:* (*a*) immature scales on a branch, (*b*) red pine trees over 15 m tall killed by the red pine scale (*a*—Connecticut Agriculture Experiment Station, courtesy of M. McClure; *b*—U.S. Forest Service photograph.)

during periods of drought or when the anthracnose fungus disease occurs on an infested tree (Johnson and Lyon 1976).

Mealybugs, Pseudococcidae

Over 300 species of mealybugs are present in North America (McKenzie 1967). Numerous species of mealybugs occur on forest and shade trees, but generally they do not cause severe damage. However, mealybugs can cause severe damage to citrus and greenhouse plants. They are found on all portions of the plant. Mealybugs are recognized by white waxy cottony or mealy secretions that cover the insect. The female's elongate–oval segmented body is 2–10 mm long and has well-developed legs.

Hemipterous Insects

Numerous species of Hemipterous sapsucking insects in three families are commonly found on forest and shade trees, but they do not cause nearly as much damage to their hosts as do sapsucking insects in the order Homoptera. The life history and damage caused by plant bugs, lace bugs, and boxelder bugs are described.

Plant Bugs, Miridae

Approximately 1600 species of plant bugs occur in the United States and Canada. Most plant bugs are phytophagous feeders, but a few are predaceous. Plant bugs can be found on almost any tree, shrub, or ornamental plant. Very few species significantly damage forest trees, but plant bugs may damage ornamentals, shrubs, and nursery seedlings (Wheeler and Miller 1981, Knight 1941, 1968). The tarnished plant bug, *Lygus lineolaris* (Palisot de Beauvois), and the fourlined plant bug, *Poecilocapsus lineatus* (Fabricius), are two extremely common plant bugs that feed on a wide range of host plants throughout the United States. All plant bugs are 2–10 mm in length and easily identified by the presence of a *cuneus* (small triangular section of the hemelytra wing at leading wing margin and next to membranous part of wing) and by only one or two closed cells in membranous part of hemelytra wing (Figure 3.13).

Nymphs and adults of plant bugs insert their piercing-sucking mouthparts into leaf tissue, secrete a toxic salivary substance into the leaf tissue, and remove chlorophyll from the plant. Damage from feeding, called *stippling damage* (Figure 12.14), appears as a dot that ranges in color from white to brownish black. Heavy feeding can result in a large brown area on the leaf or into distortion and curling of leaf. Dead tissue may sometimes drop from stippling damage after several weeks, leaving tiny holes in the leaf.

Figure 12.14 Stippling damage on green ash caused by plant bugs in the family Miridae. (U.S. Forest Service photograph, courtesy of J. Solomon.)

Lace Bugs, Tingidae

There are about 140 species of lace bugs in North America with sycamore, birch, azalea, rhododendron, and shelterbelt plantations of bur oak as favorite hosts. Many species are host specific. Johnson and Lyon (1976) provide a list of common lace bugs and host preferences for each species. Lace bugs cause no significant damage to forest stands but ocasionally damage seedlings in nurseries. However, lace bugs are common pests of ornamental trees and shrubs.

The adult lace bug is about 5 mm long and easily recognized by the sculptured gauzelike or lacelike wings (Figure 12.15). The immature nymphs remotely resemble adults but usually are dark and often covered with spines. Most species of lace bugs feed on the underside of leaves. The upper leaf surface often has heavy stippling damage, where color varies from white to brown. Lace bug damage often appears similar to leafhopper damage but can be distinguished by the cast skins of lace bug nymphs that are attached to the underside of the leaf, the presence of adult lace bugs, and the small spots of black frass and black fungus that appear on the underside of the leaf. Heavily damaged leaves may turn brown and fall off prematurely.

Boxelder Bugs, Rhopalidae

The boxelder bug, *Leptocoris trivittatus* (Say), primarily an eastern North American species, is now found as far west as Alberta, Montana, Utah, and

Figure 12.15 Lacebug adults in the family Tingidae. (From Southern Forest Insect Work Conference Slide Series.)

Arizona (Wollerman 1971, Tinker 1952). The adult is 12 mm long, brown to black on the dorsal side with a narrow red line, and bright red on the ventral side of the abdomen (Figure 12.16). Preferred food of the boxelder bug is seeds of the female boxelder tree, but they also will feed on the flowers and foliage of boxelders, other ornamental trees and shrubs, and on the old boxelder seeds until the new seeds begin to form. Two generations occur annually. Adults become gregarious in the fall of the year and crowd together on the south side of trees, buildings, and rocks. Adults

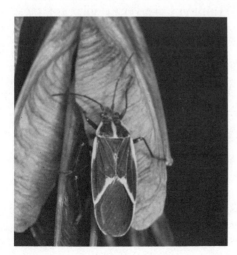

Figure 12.16 Boxelder bug, *Leptocoris trivittatus*. (U.S. Forest Service photograph.)

overwinter inside homes and buildings and in the spring return to the female boxelder trees to lay eggs. The boxelder bug is not a forest pest but is a major nuisance in houses located near boxelder trees. The boxelder tree is dioecious, so the homeowner should eliminate the female boxelder tree and favor the male boxelder trees if there is a choice. The life cycle of the western boxelder bug, *Leptocoris rubrolineatus* Barber, is similar to that of the boxelder bug. However, it is found on boxelder and maple primarily in the states and provinces along the Pacific Ocean.

Arachnid Sapsuckers

Arachnid sapsuckers that damage forest, shade and ornamental trees, and shrubs are found in two families: spider mites, Tetranychidae, and eriophyid mites, Eriophyidae. Spider mites are described in this chapter. Since most eiriophid mites cause galls, delineation of these mites is included in Chapter 17 on insects and mites causing galls.

Spider Mites, Tetranychidae

Spider mites are found throughout most of the United States and Canada. They feed on a wide range of trees and shrubs and are important pests of ornamentals and shade trees. The spruce spider mite, *Oligonychus ununguis* (Jacobi), is the only spider mite that has seriously damaged forest stands. Spider mites are all less than 1 mm long, with green, yellow, and orange–red pigmentation. Major symptoms of spider mite damage are silk webbing, cast skins, active mites, and discolored yellowish brown foliage. The easiest way to confirm spider mite damage in the field is to vigorously shake a branch containing the damaged foliage over a piece of white paper. Spider mites are most likely present if tiny organisms move on the paper and if a red smear results when the organisms are pressed against the paper. Spider mite life cycles and damage symptoms are very similar for most species of Tetranychidae.

Spruce spider mite, Oligonychus ununguis (Jacobi)

The spruce spider mite, a serious pest of conifers throughout the world, is most commonly found in the United States and Canada on spruce, cedar, juniper, fir, Douglas-fir, pine, and hemlock. Spruce spider mite, a common pest of ornamental conifers, has also occurred at outbreak population levels on Douglas-fir. An outbreak of the spruce spider mite was detected on over 320,000 ha of Douglas-fir forests in 1957 following the spraying of forests with DDT to control the western spruce budworm, *Choristoneura occidentalis* Freeman (Johnson 1958).

Spruce spider mites overwinter as eggs, primarily on the twigs, which hatch in early spring. Five to eight generations occur annually. The mites suck sap from the needles and shoots, causing discoloration of the foliage.

These mites also spin very fine silk webbing as they move about on the foliage. Spruce spider mites tend to become extremely numerous during hot dry seasons and after improper use of insecticides on conifers. Insecticides kill off the natural enemies of the mites, causing mite populations to increase substantially. Outbreaks in a forest often develop and subside during the same year.

MANAGEMENT APPROACHES USED AGAINST SAPSUCKING INSECTS AND MITES

No control or educational techniques have been the major management approaches used for most sapsucking pest organisms on forest lands. Insecticides have been the major approach chosen by urban land managers and homeowners when dealing with sapsucking pest organisms. The following management approaches have been used by forest pest managers, urban foresters, and homeowners to control sapsucking insects and mites: (1) no control or very limited educational information; (2) insecticides; (3) natural enemies; (4) cultural, silvicultural, and management tactics; (5) regulations such as quarantines; and (6) integrated pest management.

No Control or Educational Information

In most forest situations, no control has been the management technique used against most sapsucking organisms. There are a few exceptions such as the balsam woolly adelgid on true firs; Saratoga spittlebug in red pine plantations; and scales, aphids, and plant bugs in seed orchards and Christmas tree plantations.

Foresters, urban foresters, forest entomologists, and extension personnel use educational techniques to keep the public aware of major problems dealing with sapsucking organisms. Newspaper articles, do-it-yourself literature, and tree clinics (Witter and Morton 1982) are useful techniques for informing the public about common shade tree and ornamental sapsucking pests.

Insecticides

Insecticides have not been used very often to control sapsucking organisms in natural forest stands because it is difficult to obtain satisfactory control of sapsucking pests by using aerial application of insecticides. Cost of ground application of insecticides is too great in most natural stands. Ground applications of insecticides have been used occasionally to protect high-valued true firs in recreational areas from the balsam woolly adelgid. Insecticides have been the major tool used by Christmas tree growers, urban foresters, and homeowners to control sapsucking organisms affecting Christmas trees, shade trees, and ornamentals. Two main approaches have been used: (1) spraying a dormant oil on twigs and branches to control aphids and scales in the spring before the plant begins to grow, as dormant oil suffocates the pest; and (2) contact or systemic insecticides, used to control the scale and adelgid crawlers or the nymphs and adults of spittlebugs and plant bugs.

Natural Enemies

Natural enemies appear to be very important in keeping most potential native scale populations below levels causing economic damage. However, natural enemies have not successfully controlled exotic pests such as scales and aphids on forest and shade trees. Several biological control programs, spanning many years, were unsuccessful in controlling the balsam woolly adelgid in North Carolina, northeastern and western United States, and adjacent provinces in Canada. Additional research work is needed on the use of exotic natural enemies to reduce exotic pests such as the red pine scale and elongate hemlock scale.

Cultural, Silvicultural, and Management Tactics

Many sapsucking organisms (i.e., scales, aphids) build up large population levels on shade and ornamental trees under stress, planted off-site, or planted out of their natural range. Homeowners should be encouraged to plant the proper tree species and to provide an adequate watering and fertilizing program for young trees. Presalvage and salvage cuts of true firs attacked by the balsam woolly adelgid, of red pine killed by the red pine scale, and beech damaged by the beech bark disease are examples of silvicultural control of sapsucking pests on forest trees. Rating systems that determine what sites should be planted in red pine (i.e., to reduce risk from Saratoga spittlebug) and what balsam fir sites should be harvested (i.e., to reduce hazard from balsam woolly adelgid) are examples of current management of sapsucking pests on forest trees.

Regulations

Quarantines, embargoes, inspections, and certification of plants entering this country have greatly reduced the number of new exotic pests introduced in North America. These regulations are extremely important for reducing the number of sapsucking organisms that enter this country on nursery stock. We all should be very cautious about transferring plant material from one area to another, even within our country, without first checking for pest problems. Also, everyone should check for pests before removing plants from an infested area.

Integrated Pest Management

An IPM approach for sapsucking insects and mites is exemplified by the Saratoga spittlebug.

IPM for Saratoga Spittlebug

This system is currently used for management of red pine in Michigan (Heyd and Wilson 1981) (Figure 12.17). The proposed planting site or an established plantation is risk-rated for Saratoga spittlebug injury. Saratoga spittlebug causes economic damage only when suitable alternate hosts are present. Heavy infestations of the Saratoga spittlebug are normally correlated with density of sweet fern. Risk-rating of proposed planting site or young plantation under 5 m high is conducted between May and September, when alternate hosts can be easily identified. At chosen intervals within the site, the forester or pest management specialist determines the percentage of ground cover occupied by sweet fern. A risk-rating triangle (Figure 12.18) is used to determine whether the area is of low, moderate, of high risk. Low risk indicates that injury from spittlebugs will not occur or will be minor; moderate risk indicates that spittlebugs may cause some growth loss, light flagging injury, and crooked stems on a few trees; and high risk indicates the potential for heavy growth loss, many crooked stems, and numerous top-killed or dead trees. Data for the entire stand are sketched onto a map (Figure 12.19). With this survey information, the land manager can apply preventive, silvicultural, or chemical techniques. Prevention in-

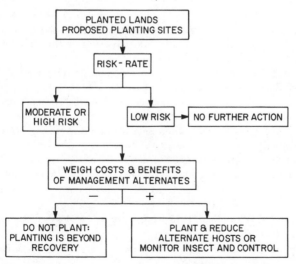

Figure 12.17 Flowchart of steps in determining management strategies for red pine based on potential susceptibility to damage by Saratoga spittlebug, *Aphrophora saratogensis*. (After Heyd and Wilson 1981.)

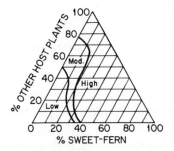

Figure 12.18 Saratoga spittlebug risk-rating triangle. (After Heyd and Wilson 1981.)

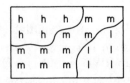

Figure 12.19 Sample plot sketch showing areas of low, moderate, and high risk for Saratoga spittlebug. (After Heyd and Wilson 1981.)

volves restricting red pines to only nonrisk or low-risk areas. Silvicultural techniques that reduce the number of alternate host plants are deep plowing, shallow plowing, or chemical herbicides. Registered insecticides may be used effectively against the adult spittlebug if a spittlebug problem develops on an established plantation. The pest management specialist or land manager uses a net present value analysis for each management strategy before making the final decision on techniques applied to a particular site or plantation.

REFERENCES

Alexander, R. D. and T. E. Moore. 1962. *The Evolutionary Relationship of 17-Year and 13-Year cicadas, and Three New Species (Homoptera, Cicadidae, Magicicada)*. University of Michigan Zoological Miscellaneous Publication 121.

Amman, G. D. 1970. Phenomena of *Adelges piceae* populations (Homoptera: Phylloxeridae) in North Carolina. *Ann. Entomol. Soc. Am.* **63**:1721–1734.

Baker, W. L. 1948. Transmission by leafhoppers of the virus causing phloem necrosis of American elm. *Science* **108**:307–308.

Baker, W. L. 1949. Studies on the transmission of the virus causing phloem necrosis of American elm, with notes on the biology of its vector. *J. Econ. Entomol.* **42**:729–732.

Balch, R. E. 1952. *Studies of the Balsam Woolly Aphid, Adelges piceae (Ratz.) and Its Effect on Balsam Fir, Abies balsamea (L.) Mill*. Canada Department of Agriculture Publication 867.

Bean, J. L. and P. A. Godwin. 1955. Description and bionomics of a new red pine scale, *Matsucoccus resinosae*. *For. Sci* **1**:164–176.

Beardsley, J. W. and R. H. Gonzalez. 1975. The biology and ecology of armored scales. *Annu. Rev. Entomol.* **20**:47–73.

Blackman, M. W. and W. E. Ellis. 1916. Cottony maple-scale. *NY State Coll. For. Bull.* **16**:26–107.

Brown, L. R. and C. O. Eads. 1965. *A Technical Study of Insects Affecting the Oak Tree in Southern California*. California Agriculture Experiment Station Bulletin 810.

Bryant, D. G. 1971. Balsam woolly aphid, *Adelges piceae* (Homoptera: Phylloxeridae), seasonal and spatial development in crowns of balsam fir, *Abies balsamea*. *Can. Entomol.* **103**:1411–1420.

Bryant, D. G. 1975. Balsam woolly aphid. In Prebble, M. L. (Ed.), *Aerial Control of Forest Insects in Canada*. Canada Department of the Environment, Ottawa.

Bryant, D. G. 1976. Distribution, abundance, and survival of the balsam woolly aphid, *Adelges piceae*, on branches of balsam fir. *Can. Entomol.* **108**:1097–1111.

Burns, D. P. and D. E. Donley. 1970. Biology of the tulip tree scale *Toumeyella liriodendri*. *Ann. Entomol. Soc. Am.* **63**:228–235.

Cantelo, W. W. 1953. *Life History and Control of Euonymus Scale in Massachusetts*. Massachusetts Agricultural Experiment Station Bulletin 471.

Carrow, J. R. and R. E. Betts. 1973. Effects of different foliar-applied nitrogen fertilizers on balsam woolly aphid. *Can. J. For. Res.* **3**:122–139.

Clark, R. C., D. O. Greenbank, D. G. Bryant, and J. W. E. Harris. 1971. In *Biological Control Programs Against Insects and Weeds in Canada* 1959–1968. Commonw. Inst. Biol. Cont. Tech. Commun. 4. Commonw. Agric. Bureaux.

Donley, D. E. and D. P. Burns. 1971. The tulip tree scale. USDA Forest Service, Forest Pest Leaflet 92.

Dybas, H. D. and M. L. Lloyd. 1974. The habitats of 17-year periodical cicadas (Homopeta: Cicadidae: *Magicicada* spp.). *Ecol. Monogr.* **44**:279–324.

Edmunds, Jr., G. F. 1973. Ecology of black pineleaf scale (Homoptera: Diaspididae). *Environ. Entomol.* **2**:765–777.

Edmunds, Jr., G. F. and D. N. Alstad. 1978. Coevolution in insect herbivores and conifers. *Science* **199**:941–945.

Fedde, G. F. 1973. Impact of the balsam woolly aphid (Homoptera: Phylloxeridae) on cone and seed produced by Fraser fir. *Can. Entomol.* **105**:673–680.

Flanders, S. E. 1970. Observations on host plant induced behavior of scale insects and their endoparasites. *Can. Entomol.* **102**:913–926.

Gentile, A. G. and F. M. Summers. 1958. The biology of San Jose scale on peaches with special references to the behavior of males and juveniles. *Hilgardia* **27**:269–285.

Greenbank, D. O. 1970. Climate and the ecology of the balsam woolly aphid. *Can. Entomol.* **102**:546–578.

Heyd, R. L. and L. F. Wilson. 1981. Risk-rating red pine plantations to predict losses from saratoga spittlebug for management decisions. In Hedden, R. L., S. J. Barras, and J. E. Coster (Eds.), *Hazard Rating Systems in Forest Insect Pest Management: Symposium Proceedings*. USDA Forest Service General Technical Report WO-27.

Holms, J., and D. S. Ruth. 1968. Spruce aphid in British Columbia. Canada Forest Service Forest Pest Leaflet 16.

Houston, D. R. 1975. Beech bark disease—the aftermath forests are structured for a new outbreak. *J. For.* **73**:660–663.

Johnson, K. 1980. Fraser fir and balsalm woolly aphid: Summary of information. Southern Appalachian Research Resource Management Cooperative Report.

Johnson, N. E. 1965. Reduced growth associated with infestations of Douglas-fir seedlings by *Cinara* species. *Can. Entomol.* **97**:113–119.

Johnson, N. E., P. G. Mitchell, and K. H. Wright. 1963. Mortality and damage to Pacific silver fir by the balsam woolly aphid in southwestern Washington. *J. For.* **61**:854–860.

Johnson, P. C. 1958. Spruce spider mite infestations in northern Rocky Mountain Douglas-fir forests. USDA Forest Service Research Paper INT-55.

Johnson, W. T. and H. H. Lyon. 1976. *Insects that Feed on Trees and Shrubs.* Cornell University Press, Ithaca.

Jorgensen, C. D., R. E. Rice, S. E. Hoyt, and P. H. Westigard. 1981. Phenology of the San Jose scale (Homoptera: Diaspididae). *Can. Entomol.* **113**:149–159.

Kattoulas, M. E. and C. S. Koehler. 1965. Studies on the irregular pine scale. *J. Econ. Entomol.* **58**:727–730.

Kelson, W. E. 1964. The biology of *Aphrophora permutata* and some observations on *Aphorophora canadensis* attacking Monterey pine in California (Homoptera: Cercopidae). *Pan-Pac. Entomol.* **40**:135–146.

Kennedy, M. K. and R. W. Merritt. 1980. Horse and buggy island. *Nat. Hist.* **891**:34–40.

Knight, H. H. 1941. *The Plant Bugs or Miridae of Illinois.* Illinois Natural History Survey Bulletin 22.

Knight, H. H. 1968. Taxonomic review: Miridae of the Nevada test site and the western United States. *Brigham Young Univ. Sci. Bull., Biol. Sci.* **9**:1–282.

Luck, R. F. and D. L. Dahlsten. 1974. Bionomics of the pine needle scale, *Chionaspis pinifoliae*, and its natural enemies at South Lake Tahoe, Calif. *Ann. Entomol. Soc. Am.* **67**:309–316.

Luck, R. F. and D. L. Dahlsten. 1975. Natural decline of a pine needle scale [*Chionaspis pinifoliae* (Fitch)], outbreak at South Lake Tahoe, California following cessation of adult mosquito control with malathion. *Ecology* **56**:893–904.

Maier, C. T. 1980. A mole's-eye view of seventeen-year periodical cicada nymphs, *Magicicada septendecim* (Hemiptera: Homoptera: Cicadidae). *Ann. Entomol. Soc. Am.* **73**:147–152.

Maier, C. T. 1982. Observations on the seventeen-year periodical cicada, *Magicicada septendecim* (Hemiptera: Homoptera: Cicadidae). *Ann. Entomol. Soc. Am.* **75**:14–23.

McCambridge, W. F. 1974. Pinyon needle scale. USDA Forest Service Forest Pest Leaflet 148.

McClure, M. S. 1977a. Population dynamics of the red pine scale, *Matsucoccus resinosae*: The influence of resinosis. *Environ. Entomol.* **6**:789–795.

McClure, M. S. 1977b. Resurgence of the scale, *Fiorinia externa* (Homoptera: Diaspididae), on hemlock following insecticide application. *Environ. Entomol.* **6**:480–484.

McClure, M. S. 1978. Seasonal development of *Fiorinia externa*, *Tsugaspidiotus tsugae* (Homoptera: Diaspididae), and their parasite *Aspidiotiphagus citrinus* (Hymenoptera: Aphelinidae): Importance of parasite–host synchronism to the population dynamics of two scale pests of hemlock. *Environ. Entomol.* **7**:863–870.

McClure, M. S. 1979a. Self-regulation in populations of the elongate hemlock scale, *Fiorinia externa* (Homoptera: Diaspididae). *Oecologia* **39**:25–36.

McClure, M. S. 1979b. Spatial and seasonal distribution of disseminating stages of *Fiorinia externa* (Homoptera: Diaspididae) and natural enemies in a hemlock forest. *Environ. Entomol.* **8**:869–873.

McClure, M. S. 1980. Foliar nitrogen: A basis for host suitability for elongate hemlock scale, *Fiorinia externa* (Homoptera: Diaspididae). *Ecology* **61**:72–79.

McClure, M. S. and M. B. Fergione. 1977. *Fiorinia externa* and *Tsugaspidiotus tsugae* (Homoptera: Diaspididae): Distribution, abundance, and new hosts of two destructive scale insects of eastern hemlock in Connecticut. *Environ. Entomol.* **6**:807–811.

McKenzie, H. L. 1967. *Mealybugs of California, with Taxonomy, Biology and Control of North American Species.* University of California Press, Berkeley.

Miller, D. R. and M. Kosztarab. 1979. Recent advances in the study of scale insects. *Annu. Rev. Entomol.* **24**:1–27.

Mitchell, R. G. 1966. Infestation characteristics of the balsam woolly aphid in the Pacific Northwest. USDA Forest Service Research Paper PNW-35.

Mitchell, R. G., N. E. Johnson, and J. A. Rudinsky. 1961. Seasonal history of the balsam woolly aphid in the Pacific Northwest. *Can. Entomol.* **93**:794–798.

Nettleton, W. A. and F. P. Hain. 1982. The life history, foliage damage, and control of the balsam twig aphid, *Mindarus abietinus* (Homoptera: Aphididae), in Fraser fir Christmas tree plantations of western North Carolina. *Can. Entomol.* **114**:155–165.

Nielsen, D. G. and N. E. Johnson. 1973. Contribution to the life history and dynamics of the pine needle scale, *Phenacaspis spinifoliae*, in central New York, *Ann. Entomol. Soc. Am.* **66**: 34–43.

Nielson, M. W. 1968. *The Leafhopper Vectors of Phytopathogenic Viruses (Homoptera, Cicadellidae): Taxonomy, Biology, and Virus Transmission.* USDA Technical Bulletin 1328.

Page, G. 1975. The impact of balsam woolly aphid damage on balsam fir stands in Newfoundland. *Can. J. For. Res.* **5**:195–209.

Parks, B. O., F. A. Fear, M. T. Lambur, and G. A. Simmons (Eds.). 1982. *Urban and Suburban Trees: Pest Problems, Needs, Prospects, and Solutions.* Symposium Proceedings, Michigan State University, East Lansing.

Pritchard, A. E. and R. E. Beer. 1950. Biology and control of *Asterolecanium* scales on oak in California. *J. Econ. Entomol.* **43**:494–497.

Rabkin, F. B. and R. R. Lejeune. 1954. Some apsects of the biology and dispersal of the pine tortoise scale (*Toumeyella numismaticum*). *Can. Entomol.* **86**:570–575.

Samarasinghe, S., and E. J. Leroux. 1966. The biology and dynamics of the oystershell scale, *Lepidosaphes ulmi* (L.) on apples in Quebec. *Ann. Entomol. Soc. Quebec* **11**:206–259.

Saunders, J. L. 1969. Occurrence and control of the balsam twig aphid on *Abies grandis* and *Abies concolor*. *J. Econ. Entomol.* **62**:1106–1109.

Schooley, H. O. 1976. Effect of balsam woolly aphid on cone and seed production by balsam fir. *For. Chron.* **52**:237–239.

Schooley, H. O. and D. G. Bryant. 1978. *The Balsam Woolly Aphid in Newfoundland.* Canadian Forestry Service, Information Report N-X-160.

Shigo, A. L. 1970. Beech bark disease. USDA Forest Service Pest Leaflet 75.

Shigo, A. L. 1972. The beech bark disease today in the northeastern United States. *J. For.* **70**:286–289.

Speers, C. F. 1941. The pine spittlebug (*Aphrophora parallela* Say). New York State College Forestry Technical Publication 54.

Stoetzel, M. B. and J. A. Davidson. 1971. Biology of the obscure scale, *Melanaspis obscura* (Homoptera: Diaspsidae), on pin oak in Maryland. *Ann. Entomol. Soc. Am.* **64**:45–50.

Tinker, M. E. 1952. The seasonal behavior and ecology of the boxelder bug *Leptocoris trivittatus* in Minnesota. *Ecology* **33**:407–414.

Wheeler, Jr., A. G. and G. L. Miller. 1981. Fourlined plant bug (Hemiptera: Miridae), a reappraisal, life history, host plants, and plant response to feeding. *Great Lakes Entomol.* **14**:23–35.

Williams, M. L. and M. Kosztarab. 1972. *Morphology and Systematics of the Coccidae of Virginia with Notes on Their Biology.* Virginia Polytechnic Institute State University Research Division Bulletin 74.

Wilson, L. F. 1971. Pine tortoise scale. USDA Forest Service Forest Pest Leaflet 57.

Wilson, L. F. 1978. Saratoga spittlebug. USDA Forest Service Forest Pest Leaflet 3.

Witter, J. A. and H. L. Morton. 1982. The role of tree clinics in urban forestry. *Great Lakes Entomol.* **15**:119–121.

Wollerman, E. H. 1971. The boxelder bug. USDA Forest Service Forest Pest Leaflet 95.

13 TERMINAL, SHOOT, TWIG, AND ROOT INSECTS

INTRODUCTION

A large number of insect species infest terminals, shoots, twigs, and roots of living trees. In general, insects included in this group utilize meristematic tissue of host trees for food and habitat for at least a portion of the life cycle. Infestations in juvenile trees are usually more important than in mature hosts.

Some of the insects in this group are important pests in forest ecosystems, specialized forestry settings, and urban forests. A number of species feed on *tips*, *terminal branches*, and *lateral branches* of seedlings and saplings. This feeding influences both the growth form (shape of the tree) and rate of growth of the host. The consequences to forestry are that the normal (or planned) growth schedules are disrupted, wood quality may be adversely affected, and wood volume at the time of harvest may be reduced. Other species feed on the *main stem* of juvenile trees. This activity can kill the host, structurally or physiologically weaken the host, provide a portal for entry of diseases, and detract from the aesthetic appearance of ornamental trees. In forest ecosystems, insects responsible for this type of damage can significantly disrupt stand regeneration practices. Still other species feed on the *roots* or the *root collar* of hosts. These insects also physically weaken host trees and in some cases kill the host.

In this chapter we catalog insect species according to the general anatomical structures that are infested. We discuss three categories of insects: (1) terminal and shoot feeding, (2) twig borers and girdlers, and (3) root feeding. This classification system is simple, albeit somewhat arbitrary. It should be recognized that terminal, shoot, twig, and root insects constitute the second largest group of forest insects, in terms of number of species. Only the defoliators (Chapter 11) have more representatives. Emphasis in this chapter is placed on primary pest insects associated with the plant classifications. Some species of secondary importance are included to illustrate the types of damage they cause.

TERMINAL AND SHOOT INSECTS

Terminal and shoot insects are of particular importance in the initial stages of forest regeneration and early growth of stands. Forest nurseries and ornamental trees are also affected. Two groups of insects are of major concern: (1) tip and shoot moths and (2) terminal and shoot weevils. There are also a large number of secondary species within each of these groups that periodically are pests.

Tip and Shoot Moths

The most important and widespread tip moths belong to the genus *Rhyacionia* (Lepidoptera: Tortricidae). *Rhyacionia* spp. were formerly classified in the family Olethreutidae. Powell and Miller (1978) in their biosystematic review placed the genus in the family Tortricidae. There are 24 known species that occur in North America. The greatest diversity of species occurs in the western and southwestern United States. The few species that occur in the eastern and southeastern United States are among the most important pests in the genus. Powell and Miller (1978) revised the classification of *Rhyacionia* and reviewed the literature on the genus. Although there are many species in the genus *Rhyacionia* that infest pines in North America, only a small number have been studied in detail. We shall examine the species that are considered to be pests of forest and ornamental trees. The following species are treated: *R. frustrana* (Comstock), Nantucket pine tip moth; *R. bushnelli* (Busck), western pine tip moth; *R. rigidana* (Fernald), pitch pine tip moth; *R. subtropica* (Miller), subtropical pine tip moth; *R. buoliana* (Denis and Schiffermüller), European pine shoot moth; and *R. neomexicana* (Dyar), southwestern pine tip moth. In describing the pest species in the genus *Rhyacionia* we emphasize the scientific names of the insects, because several species do not have approved common names and the scientific nomenclature is more frequently used.

Generalized Description and Life Cycle

Adults of most *Rhyacionia* spp. are small (forewing length 4.0–18 mm) and inconspicuous (see Figure 13.1). The moths are cryptically colored in shades of brown, gray, silver, and blue. When at rest, the wings are folded over the abdomen. The adults are crepuscular (active at dusk) or nocturnal.

Figure 13.1 Adult Nantucket pine tip moth, *Rhyacionia frustrana*. This insect is considered to be an allopatric species with the western pine tip moth, *Rhyacionia bushnelli*. The two insects cannot be easily distinguished with the use of morphological characters. (From Hedlin et al. 1980, courtesy of Canadian Forestry Service.)

Eggs, which are elliptical, are placed near the terminal and lateral buds on or between needles, needle sheaths, or bud scales. After egg development, early instar larvae, which are quite small (ca. 1.0–1.5 mm), feed on and in needles and succulent shoot tissue. It is difficult to detect the presence of early larval feeding. Careful inspection often reveals a small silken web in the axil formed by a developing needle and the stem. Feeding by intermediate instar larvae is easily detected by the presence of silken webs and accumulation of frass and resin around the tip (Figure 13.2). Late instar larvae, which are light brown to orange in color and approximately 6–10 mm long, mine into the shoots causing browning of tips and needles, shoot dieback, and destruction of buds. At high population levels it is not uncommon for several larvae to infest a single shoot (Figure 13.3). With some species, a single larva will infest more than one shoot. Most species have

Figure 13.2 Evidence of intermediate instar larval feeding by *Rhyacionia* species: loblolly pine terminal with silken webs and the accumulation of frass and resin. (U.S. Forest Service photograph.)

Figure 13.3 Evidence of late instar larval feeding by *Rhyacionia* species: loblolly pine terminal with several larvae present and accumulation of frass and resin. (U.S. Forest Service photograph.)

three or more larval instars. The site of pupation varies with different species. Pupation occurs in the injured shoot (Figure 13.4), at the base of the tree, or in the litter. The pupae are about 4–8 mm in length. In some species the larva overwinters, whereas in others it is the pupa. Adult flight takes place in the spring of the year. Mate finding is guided by perception of pheromones produced by females. Some species are univoltine (have only one generation per year). Others are multivoltine and have from two to six generations. In the multivoltine species there are several flight periods at intervals throughout the summer (Powell and Miller 1978, Yates 1960, Stephen and Wallis 1981, Miller 1967a, Jennings 1975, Smith et al. 1974).

Damage Characteristics for *Rhyacionia* Tip Moths

Rhyacionia spp. infest pines in several different settings: naturally regenerated and planted forests, nurseries, Christmas tree plantations, and or-

Figure 13.4 Pupation site for some *Rhyacionia* species is in the terminal, whereas other species pupate at the base of the tree or in the soil. (U.S. Forest Service photograph.)

namental plantings. Most infestations occur on small seedling or sapling-size trees less than 3 m in height. Feeding on terminal or lateral buds as well as stems results in discoloration of the tree during the growing season when the insects are actively feeding and deformation of the tree crown, as a result of destruction of terminal and lateral buds and shoots. Host pines are rarely killed by tip moths.

Depending on the degree or intensity of infestation, tip moth activity can alter the host growth form in a number of different ways. Several types of deformity have been defined (Miller 1967b, Telerico and Heikkenen 1962, Lessard and Jennings 1976) (Figure 13.5):

1. *Prune.* One or more lateral buds killed, resulting in fewer branches per whorl; no crook in main stem.

2. *Crook.* A departure from straightness, resulting from complete or partial destruction of the terminal shoot. Lateral shoot generally assumes dominance over damaged terminal; alteration in form depends on degree of crook and number of lateral shoots that continue height growth.

3. *Fork.* Two or more laterals assume dominance. Forking may result in a crook if one lateral branch becomes dominant.

4. *Posthorn.* A severe crook resulting from feeding on only one side of the terminal shoot; feeding stops before the shoot is killed, and the injured leader bends at the point of attack.

5. *Bush.* An increase in the normal number of branches at a whorl; adventitious buds produce multiple shoots after destruction of terminal and lateral shoots.

6. *Spiketop.* Insect attack kills the terminal, but adventitious buds do not develop, resulting in a dead top [descriptions taken from Lessard and Jennings (1976)].

Figure 13.5 Types of damage caused by *Rhyacionia* species: (a = prune, b = crook, c = fork, d = posthorn, e = bush, and f = spiketop. (U.S. Forest Service photograph.)

The various types of deformities that occur while the host trees are infested may not persist in later stages of growth. Once tip moth damage ceases, the tree may resume normal growth and regain typical form class.

Pest Species of *Rhyacionia*

In their systematic review of the genus *Rhyacionia*, Powell and Miller (1978) identified allopatric pairs of species. These species are morphologically very similar but occur in different geographic areas and feed on different host pines. Of the six species discussed here four are included as allopatric pairs: *frustrana–bushnelli* and *rigidana–subtropica*. These pairs are discussed together. The other species, *R. buoliana* and *R. neomexicana*, are treated separately. The allopatric pairs of species cannot be separated by using morphological characteristics. Furthermore, the sympatric species (species with overlapping distributions, e.g., *R. frustrana* and *R. rigidana*) cannot be easily distinguished by simple inspection. Therefore, we have attempted to describe in only a general way the size and appearance of the various species discussed.

Rhyacionia frustrana (Comstock) and *R. bushnelli* (Busck)

The Nantucket pine tip moth, *R. frustrana* (Figure 13.1), and the western pine tip moth, *R. bushnelli*, are considered to be separate species (Powell and Miller 1978). *R. bushnelli* formerly was classified as a variety of *R. frustrana*. Separation of the two species is based on size, geographic distribution, and place of overwintering.

R. frustrana is a widely distributed native species occurring in the eastern, southern, and south-central United States. It infests most native and exotic pines within this geographic range but is a particularly important pest of shortleaf pine and loblolly pine in the South. Longleaf pine, slash pine, and eastern white pine are not reported to be suitable hosts (Yates 1960). However, Miller and Wilson (1964) reported collecting *R. frustrana* from slash pine.

R. frustrana adults are small, with a forewing length of approximately 4.0–7.0 mm. The head, body, and appendages are covered with gray scales, and the forewings are reddish brown with silver–gray markings.

The life cycle follows the general pattern described earlier. The characteristic features are as follows: the pupae overwinter within infested tips; adults may be active as early as February in the extreme South; and, depending on the geographic location, there may be as few as one and as many as six generations per year.

Although *R. frustrana* is a common pest in ornamental trees and nursery stock, its primary importance is in even-aged loblolly or shortleaf pine plantations. Infestations can result in growth loss, excessive branching, multiple terminals, and deformed bushy trees. Damage is most apparent in trees less than 3 m tall (Stephen and Wallis 1981).

The western pine tip moth, *R. bushnelli,* is also widely distributed, having been reported to occur in the north central, northwestern (Montana, the Dakotas, and Nebraska), and southwestern United States. The insect is associated primarily with ponderosa pine, which has been used in shelter belt plantings. However, it infests other pines as well. Aside from infesting different host species, *R. bushnelli* differs from *R. frustrana* by being somewhat larger (adult forewing length 5.0–8.0 mm) and by pupating in the soil, rather than in an infested tip. *R. bushnelli* produces one or two generations per year.

Rhyacionia rigidana (Fernald) and R. subtropica (Miller)

The pitch pine tip moth, *R. rigidana,* and the subtropical pine tip moth, *R. subtropica,* are morphologically indistinguishable native species (Figure 13.6). Their geographic distributions overlap in the deep South and along the Gulf Coast. The two species also share common hosts. However, *R. rigidana* and *R. subtropica* are considered to be an allopatric pair (Powell and Miller 1978).

R. rigidana occurs in the eastern, southern, and south-central United States and infests the same host species as reported for *R. frustrana.* However, *R. rigidana* apparently does not infest slash pines, whereas *R. frustrana* does. It is difficult for the nonspecialist to distinguish between the two species, although the coloration patterns of the wings are slightly different and *R. rigidana* is slightly larger (forewing length 5.5–9.0 mm) than *R. frustrana.*

Figure 13.6 Adult subtropical pine tip moth, *Rhyacionia subtropica.* This insect is morphologically undistinguishable from the pitch pine tip moth, *Rhyacionia rigidana.* (U.S. Forest Service photograph.)

The life history for *R. rigidana* follows the general pattern described above and is very similar to *R. frustrana*. *R. rigidana* pupates in infested tips, adults emerge in early spring, and the insect has multiple generations per year. Damage characteristics are identical to those of *R. frustrana*. Berisford (1974a) reported that development time for *R. rigidana* was longer than for *R. frustrana*, which resulted in fewer generations per year. The two insects often infest the same host, with *R. frustrana* generally being more numerous than *R. rigidana* (Miller and Wilson 1964, Baer and Berisford 1975). In studying the behavior of the two species, Berisford (1974b) found that each insect produced species-specific pheromones, that the pheromones produced by females of one species were inhibitory to males of the other (Berisford and Brady 1974), and that females of each species used pheromones to attract mates at different times during the evening hours. These behavioral mechanisms, plus differences in the genital structures of the two insects, were suggested to be mechanisms for species isolation.

R. subtropica was described by Miller (1960) as a new species found along the Gulf Coast. It infests primarily slash and longleaf pine and has been collected from loblolly pine (Merkel 1963, Miller and Wilson 1964). The insect has been reported to be periodically an important pest in slash pine plantations and to cause serious damage and killing of grafted slash pine scions in tree improvement programs. It has forewing markings similar to *R. rigidana*. The forewing length ranges from 5.0 to 9.0 mm.

Rhyacionia buoliana (Denis and Schiffermüller)

The European pine shoot moth, *R. buoliana*, is a pest species that was introduced into the eastern United States in 1914 from western Europe on imported nursery stock (Miller 1967b). The insect is now distributed throughout the northeastern United States and adjacent Canadian provinces, west through the Great Lakes states, and in the Northwest (Oregon, Washington, and British Columbia). The distribution of *R. buoliana* enlarged rapidly as a result of the movement of infested nursery stock that was used in reforestation and ornamental plantings.

R. buoliana infests many pine species. Red pine, is the most susceptible host. Ponderosa pine (planted in the East), Scots pine, and Austrian pine are also common hosts. Damage caused by *R. buoliana* is most severe in young plantations growing on poor sites. The insect is primarily a pest of ornamental trees in the northwestern United States. Carolin and Daterman (1974) suggested that *R. buoliana* could become an important pest of young even-aged monocultures of ponderosa pine and lodgepole pine in the Northwest. However, cold temperatures were thought to limit distribution of the insect in these tree species.

R. buoliana adults are medium sized, relative to other tip moths, with a forewing length of 9.0–11.0 mm. The forewings are rusty orange-red marked with several irregular silvery white transverse bands. The hindwings are dark brown (Figure 13.7).

Figure 13.7   Adult European pine shoot moth, *Rhyacionia buoliana*. (From Hedlin et al. 1980, courtesy of Canadian Forestry Service.)

The life history of *R. buoliana* follows the general pattern described above. Distinguishing characteristics are as follows: the larval stage over-winters in buds and shoots, larvae leave the overwintering sites during the spring and infest new buds and shoots where pupation takes place. Adults emerge during June and July, and there is only one generation per year. In addition to feedings on needles, buds, and shoots, larvae are found in developing cones (Miller 1967b, Harris and Wood 1967, Coulter 1973, Hedlin et al. 1980).

The pheromone communication system for *R. buoliana* has been inves-tigated in detail (Smith et al. 1974, Daterman et al. 1975). The pheromones involved in mate finding have been identified and synthesized. Daterman (1970, 1974) developed a procedure for surveying the insect using pher-omone-baited "sticky traps." Detection surveys using these traps are very useful in monitoring changes in the distribution of the pest.

R. buoliana damage to forest trees is typical of tip moths in general. Young plantations containing hosts less than 3 m in height growing on poor sites are affected most severely. Ornamental trees and Christmas tree plantations are also infested.

Rhyacionia neomexicana (Dyar)

The southwestern pine tip moth, *R. neomexicana*, is found primarily in the southwestern United States but occurs also in Nebraska, Montana, and North Dakota. The insect is primarily a pest of young ponderosa pine. However, ornamental plantings of Scots pine, jack pine, and Austrian pine are also infested.

Figure 13.8 Adult southwestern pine tip moth, *Rhyacionia neomexicana*. (U.S. Forest Service photograph.)

Adult *R. neomexicana* are among the largest tip moths with a forewing length of 8.0–13.5 mm. The distal area of the forewing is pinkish buff-colored and contains two black horizontal lines (Figure 13.8).

The life history follows the general sequence described above. Distinguishing features include the following: the pupal stage overwinters as a cocoon attached to the root collar of the host and adult emergence occurs in the spring. The insect has one generation per year (Jennings 1975).

Damage is most severe in young ponderosa pines less than 3 m in height. As with the other tip species, repeated attacks retard height and radial growth and cause a bushy deformed tree crown. Lessard and Buffam (1976) and Lessard and Jennings (1976) found that both height and radial growth of ponderosa pine were reduced in seedlings and saplings infested with *R. neomexicana*.

Impact of Tip Moth Infestations

There is little doubt that tip moth infestations during the seedling and sapling stages of pine growth results in reduced radial and height growth and deformation of crown form. This type of damage may be extremely important in commercial nurseries, Christmas tree plantations, and ornamental plantings. The value placed on trees in these circumstances may be significantly reduced. Furthermore, it is generally possible to calculate the loss in value of infested trees relative to uninfested trees.

In forest ecosystems managed for wood and fiber production, evaluation of impact of tip moths is somewhat more complicated. We are primarily interested in (1) the volume or quantity of wood or fiber at the end of a rotation and (2) perhaps the grade or quality of wood.

Intensive forest management practices aimed at optimizing wood and fiber production involve use of genetically superior seed; site preparation; even-aged plantations; monocultures; and site maintenance, which may include fertilization, hardwood control, and thinning. Tip moth infestations flourish as a consequence of intensive forest management. Indeed, tip moths are rarely considered pests in uneven-aged, naturally regenerated forests (Stephen and Wallis 1981, Lashomb and Steinhauer 1974, Hertel and Benjamin 1975, 1977).

There have been several investigations of pine growth following cessation of tip moth attack. In general, on sites that are suitable for pine cultivation, growth resumes a normal rate after tip moth infestation declines. In even-aged plantations of shortleaf pine and loblolly pine, a long-term study of growth and yield in Arkansas indicated that a significant increase in volume could be achieved in trees freed from *R. frustrana* attack during early years of growth. This study was conducted over a period of 11 years. In a similar study Williston and Barras (1977) found that by year 16 there were no substantial differences in height or diameter for loblolly or shortleaf plantations that were treated for tip moths and left untreated. Overall, treatment increased loblolly yield 3.9 cords per acre, and the shortleaf yield was increased 0.4 cords per acre. Given these circumstances, the costs associated with a remedial treatment tactic such as the application of insecticides, using conventional techniques, would not be warranted. However, the conditions reported in these studies may not be typical, and there is little agreement among researchers on the effects of tip moth damage on growth and yield of stands at the end of a rotation.

The effects of previous tip moth infestation on wood quality in sawlog size trees has not been investigated. It is possible that trees are structurally weakened or that grade quality is affected.

Other Tip and Shoot Infesting Insects

In addition to the *Rhyacionia* spp., there are a large number of other insects found infesting tips and shoots of forest and shade trees. In general, these insects are not serious pests although certain species are periodically. For example, the western pine shoot borer, *Eucosma sonomana* Kearfott (Lepidoptera: Tortricidae), occasionally causes serious damage to pines in the western and Great Lakes states (Stevens and Jennings 1977, MacAloney and Schmiege 1962). Certain species of *Dioryctria* (Lepidoptera: Pyralidae) and numerous Coleoptera in the families Scolytidae, Cerambycidae, and Buprestidae are also occasionally important.

Terminal and Shoot Weevils

The terminal and shoot weevils (Coleoptera: Curculionidae) are an important group of insects that often cause serious damage in seedling and sapling size conifers. Some of the insects in the group are extremely important pests in the early stages of forest regeneration, whereas others impact primarily on nurseries and Christmas tree plantations. Unlike the tip moths, activity of some of the terminal and shoot weevils results in death of host trees. Intensive management practices, following harvest of mature forests, contribute to the extent of damage caused by the terminal and shoot weevils. The economically important representatives in this group are commonly classified for discussion purposes as follows: seedling debarking weevils [*Hylobius pales* (Herbst) and *Pachylobius picivorus* (Germar)], reproduction weevils (*Cylindrocopturus eatoni* Buchanan and *C. furnissi* Buchanan), root collar weevils (*Hylobius radicis* Buchanan and *H. warreni* Wood), and terminal weevils (*Pissodes* spp.).

Seedling Debarking Weevils

Pales Weevil, Hylobius pales (Herbst)

The pales weevil is an oblong, robust, black to reddish brown weevil about 6–10 mm in length. The elytra are covered with small scattered patches of yellowish setae (Figure 13.9). The insect infests young coniferous trees, particularly pines. Preferred hosts include white pine, loblolly pine, short-leaf pine, and pitch pine. It is an important pest affecting pine regeneration following harvest. Damage is caused by adults. The insect is distributed throughout the eastern United States from Maine to Florida and westward to Texas and the Great Lake states and in eastern Canada from southern Ontario to Nova Scotia.

Figure 13.9 Adult pales weevil, *Hylobius pales*. U.S. Forest Service photograph.)

Injury caused by the pales weevil is most severe on seedlings. The first evidence of attack is a series of small holes or pits on the stem resulting from feeding by adults. If weevil feeding is light, the holes fill in with oleoresin and eventually the wounds heal. Heavy feeding results in girdling of the stem above and/or below the ground, which often kills the host (Figure 13.10). In some cases, adults feed on terminals, twigs, or buds of sapling-size trees (Speers and Rauschenberger 1971).

The life history of *H. pales* has been studied in several parts of its range (e.g., Pierson 1921 in the Northeast, Finnegan 1959 in eastern Canada, and Taylor and Franklin 1970 in the Southeast). The general life history is as follows: adults emerge in the spring following winter hibernation and are attracted to sites that have been recently harvested or where the hosts have been damaged or disturbed. Presumably the adults are attracted to oleoresin emanating from the host material. Adults are active at night or on cloudy days. After a brief feeding period, the adults mate and the females oviposit in roots of cut pine stumps, weakened trees, or pine slash buried during site preparation. Adult weevils burrow into the soil to find oviposition sites. After the eggs hatch larvae begin to tunnel and feed beneath the bark. Pupation occurs in the sapwood in individual cells, called "chip cocoons." The new adults emerge in the fall to feed on stems of seedlings, terminals, and buds.

Timing for the life history varies with geographic locality. In the northern ranges of the insect there is one generation per year, and in the South there is a partial second generation. The adults can live two seasons and it is common for both parent and brood adults to be present at the same time.

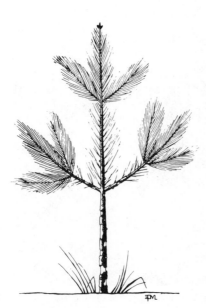

Figure 13.10 Damage to pine seedling caused by seedling debanding weevils (the pales weevil, *Hylobius pales,* and the pitch-eating weevil, *Pachylobius picivorus.* (U.S. Forest Service photograph.)

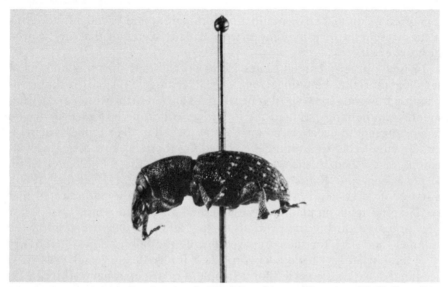

Figure 13.11   Adult pitch-eating weevil, *Pachylobius picivorus*. (Courtesy of P. W. Kovarik.)

Pitch-Eating Weevil, Pachylobius picivorus (Germar)

The pitch eating weevil is very similar in appearance to the pales weevil, being dark brown, robust, and covered with yellow to reddish brown setae (Figure 13.11). The insect is generally distributed throughout the eastern United States and is prevalent in the Southeast, where it commonly occurs with the pales weevil and infests the same pine hosts.

The life history of the pitch eating weevil follows the general pattern described for the pales weevil. Franklin and Taylor (1970) observed two population peaks during the year in the Georgia Piedmont and noted that the adults were long-lived. Thatcher (1960) reported that 6–11 months were required for brood development in east Texas, depending on the season in which the broods were established. Damage by the pitch-eating weevil is indistinguishable from that of the pales weevil.

Impact of Seedling Debarking Weevils

The seedling debarking weevils are rarely considered to be pests in naturally regenerated stands, although their occurrence in these stands is common. The insects are particularly important in the southern United States. The problem centers on seedling mortality following harvest and site preparation. The factors that contribute to the problem are as follows: (1) weevils are attracted to freshly cut areas where there are abundant sites for brood establishment in pine stumps, weakened trees, and in buried slash; (2) the mechanical equipment used in site preparation to remove slash and brush frequently prolongs attractiveness to the harvested area; and (3) the forest owner is usually interested in placing the harvested area back into production by planting seedlings soon after site preparation. These three factors often result in a large number of both parent and brood adult weevils being present at the same time there are many seedlings that are favored host material.

In the southern United States it has been found that the amount of seedling mortality resulting from weevil feeding is related to timing of planting following harvest. In general, areas logged in the winter and spring months can be safely planted the following winter, because weevils are no longer present in great abundance. Areas logged in the summer are moderately vulnerable to attack. Severe seedling mortality can occur in plantations established in the winter after logging in the fall (Doggett et al. 1977, Speers and Rauschenberger 1971, Speers 1974, Thatcher 1960). Surveys of forest land in Arkansas and eastern Oklahoma indicated that seedling mortality on plantations established during the winter was 6% for sites prepared during the previous spring, 20% for sites prepared in the summer, and 58% for sites prepared during the fall (Cade et al. 1981).

Several strategies have been proposed for reducing losses caused by seedling debarking weevils, for example, (1) disperse harvest areas, (2) restrict harvesting to spring months, (3) delay planting after harvest, and (4) use seedling protective treatments. Most emphasis has been placed on use of insecticide treatments to protect seedlings (Cade et al. 1981), because economic constraints and land ownership patterns make the other strategies difficult to justify or implement.

Pine Reproduction Weevils

There are a number of weevils in the genus *Cylindrocopturus* but only two are considered to be pests: *C. eatoni* and *C. furnissi*. Of these two species *C. eatoni* is the most important.

Figure 13.12   Adult pine reproduction weevil, *Cylindrocopturus eatoni*, feeding on ponderosa pine needle. (U.S. Forest Service photograph.)

Pine reproduction weevil, *Cylindrocopturus eatoni Buchanan*

The pine reproduction weevil is a small (ca. 2.5 mm in length) weevil clothed in bronze and silvery scales that together give a gray appearance (Figure 13.12). The insect occurs primarily in northern and central California, where it is a pest of various species of pines. Ponderosa pine is the principal host.

The weevils infest young trees (50 cm to 3.5 m tall) and are pests in plantations. Adults feed on needles (Figure 13.13) and on twigs and stems, which results in crown discoloration and resin exudation but rarely tree death. Larvae excavate galleries in the cambium which generally kills the tree (Figure 13.14). Successful weevil attack is usually accompanied by development of woodstaining fungi.

The life history of *C. eatoni* was described by Eaton (1942) and reviewed by Stevens (1971) and Furniss and Carolin (1977). Adult emergence from infested trees takes place from late May to early July. The adults feed for

Figure 13.13   Feeding punctures by adult pine reproduction weevil, *Cylindrocopturus eatoni,* on needles of Jeffery pine. (U.S. Forest Service photograph.)

Figure 13.14   Natural reproduction of ponderosa pine killed by the pine reproduction weevil, *Cylindrocopturus eatoni.* (U.S. Forest Service photograph.)

2–3 weeks, mate, and the females oviposit eggs singly in feeding punctures on the main stem and twigs of hosts below the current year's growth. After the eggs hatch, the larvae tunnel in the cambium, where they continue feeding between the wood and outer bark until maturity. Larvae complete development in the outer layers of the wood in larger twigs and stems or in the pith of smaller twigs. Pupation occurs in the following spring. There is usually only one generation per year.

Root Collar Weevils

There are two species of root collar weevils that are significant pests of pine plantations: *Hylobius radicis* Buchanan and *Hylobius warreni* Wood. For discussion purposes, these insects are often classified as root feeding insects as well.

Pine Root Collar Weevil, Hylobius radicis Buchanan

The pine root collar weevil is very similar in appearance to the pales weevil, *H. pales,* and, indeed, was originally thought to be the same species. The insect occurs in the Northeast along the Atlantic seaboard south to Virginia and northwestward to Minnesota. In Canada the insect has been reported to occur from Newfoundland westward through the southern parts of all intervening provinces to Manitoba. The pine root collar weevil infests many pine species but is considered to be a primary pest in Scots pine and red pine as these species are planted extensively within the weevils' range. Pitch pine and eastern white pine are rarely attacked.

The pine root collar weevil infests both young and old pines but is considered to be a pest in plantations and windbreaks growing on poor sites. Natural stands are attacked, but damage is seldom heavy unless there are plantations nearby. Damage is caused by larval feeding on the bark and cambium around roots and root collar beneath the soil. This feeding restricts transport of nutrients, weakens the tree, and results in reduced growth rate. Infested trees are prone to breakage as a result of heavy winds or snow. In some cases girdling kills the host. Damage to infested trees is easily recognized by clearing away the duff surrounding the base of the tree, which reveals a swollen trunk and darkened pitch-infiltrated soil. Within an even-aged plantation infested trees will be smaller than noninfested hosts.

The life history of the pine root collar weevil is somewhat complicated as adults, larvae, and sometimes pupae overwinter. The majority of eggs are laid in mid-June and the resulting larvae overwinter, pupate, and become adults the following July or August. The newly emerged adults feed on the lower branches of hosts during the day and move to the bark and branches in the crown at night. These adults do not oviposit until the following season. Eggs are laid in wounds at the root collar or in adjacent soil. Larvae feed on the inner bark and surface of the wood. Pupal chambers are constructed in resin-soaked soil or in the bark. The ecology and management of the pine root collar weevil are reviewed in detail by Wilson and Millers (1983).

Warren's Collar Weevil, *Hylobius warreni* Wood

This insect is the western counterpart of the root collar weevil (Figure 13.15). It occurs in western Canada, southeastern Alaska, and presumably other western states bordering Canada. The insect infests pines, larch, fir, and spruce, causing growth loss as a result of girdling. Wounds serve as a portal for entry of root-rotting fungi. Trees 6–8 years to maturity are infested. The life cycle of the *H. warreni* takes 2 years, and adults may live as long as 4 years (Furniss and Carolin 1977).

Terminal Weevils, *Pissodes* spp.

The genus *Pissodes* contains a number of species that are important pests of forest trees. The adult weevils are similar in appearance and often difficult even for specialists to identify to species. The adults are 4–8 mm in length, ranging in color from light reddish brown to dark brown, and the elytra are marked with patches of white scales.

Figure 13.15   Adult Warren's collar weevil, *Hylobius warreni*. (U.S. Forest Service photograph.)

Hosts, Distribution, and Taxonomy of Pissodes spp.

Terminal feeding weevils in the genus *Pissodes* occur throughout the United States, Canada, and Mexico. Species of the genus feed on and breed in the phloem of conifers in the family Pinaceae. Common hosts include pines, true firs, spruces, larches, hemlocks, Douglas-fir, and true cedars.

Because of the high degree of morphological similarity, it is difficult to distinguish between the various *Pissodes* species. Identification of species is usually based more on collection data such as host, breeding site, and locality rather than on morphological characteristics (Atkinson 1979). Although there have been as many as 31 species included in the genus *Pissodes,* only 13 are now recognized. Of these 13 species several are important forest pests. Along the Eastern Seaboard and into the Midwest the most important species include the white pine weevil, *P. strobi* (Peck), the northern pine weevil, *P. approximatus* Hopkins, and the deodar weevil, *P. nemorensis* Germar. These three sympatric species are indistinguishable using morphological characteristics. In the West the most important species is *P. strobi.* This species is considered to include the forms previously classified as the Englemann spruce weevil, *P. englemanni* Hopkins, and the Sitka spruce weevil, *P. sitchensis* Hopkins (Smith and Sugden 1969). The lodgepole terminal weevil, *P. terminalis* Hopping, is also an important western species.

Generalized Life Cycle of Pissodes spp.

Adults of most *Pissodes* species emerge in the late summer or early fall and overwinter in the litter on the forest floor. In the spring adults resume activity and the terminal damaging species (e.g., *P. strobi* and *P. terminalis*)

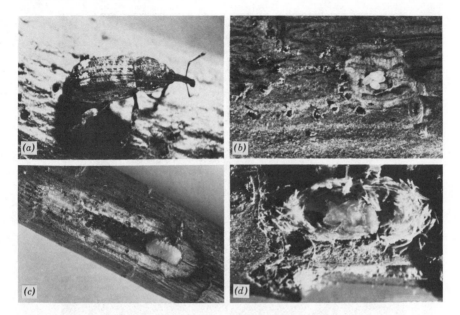

Figure 13.16 Life cycle of the white pine weevil, *Pissodes strobi*, illustrating the general pattern for members of the genus: (*a*) adult insect, (*b*) eggs in terminal, (*c*) larva feeding in terminal, (*d*) pupa in chip cocoon. (U.S. Forest Service photograph.)

feed on and oviposit in terminals. In the case of *P. strobi* eggs are laid in the previous year's growth, whereas *P. terminalis* oviposits in the current year's growth. The eggs hatch and the larvae bore downward through the inner bark. Late instar larvae also feed in the pith of the stem. Larval development takes place throughout the summer. The last larval instar constructs a "chip cocoon" where pupation occurs (Figure 13.16).

The life cycle of *P. nemorensis* differs from the generalized pattern in that oviposition occurs in fall and larvae feed on terminals during the winter. Adults emerge in the spring and remain inactive during the summer (estivate) in the litter. This species is distributed in the deep southern United States.

The generalized life cycle is somewhat simplified for several reasons: oviposition often is extended over a long period, which alters the timing of the life cycle presented above, adults often live for more than one season, and the life cycle of some species takes 2 or more years.

Damage Caused by Pissodes spp.

The damage caused by *Pissodes* species is most important in forest trees in plantation settings. Trees less than 1 m may be killed. On larger trees, larval feeding often kills 2–3 years of terminal growth. The destroyed terminals are replaced by lateral branches, which produces a crooked or forked stem.

Figure 13.17 Effects of *Pissodes* weevil feeding on form class of host. (U.S. Forest Service photograph.)

Trees experiencing this type of damage for a number of years become multistemmed and cabbage shaped. The most severe damage occurs in trees less than 25 years. Severe infestations substantially reduce usable volume at harvest and affect wood quality by producing cross grain, larger knots, and compression wood (Figure 13.17). Furthermore, adult feeding may serve as a portal for entry of plant diseases.

TWIG BORERS AND GIRDLERS

Although there are a large number of twig borers and girdlers, few are serious pests in forest ecosystems. Some species periodically are considered pests of ornamental trees. We do not consider twig borers and girdlers in great detail and only provide examples to illustrate their general life cycles and the damage they cause.

Many of the common twig borers and girdlers are Coleoptera belonging to the family Cerambycidae (roundheaded borers) and Buprestidae (flat-headed borers). Among the cerambycids there are important species in the genera *Oncideres*, *Oberea*, and *Elaphidionoides*. In the Buprestidae there are several important species belonging to the genera *Agrilus* and *Chrysobothris*. There are also several lepidopterous twig borers and girdlers, the most notable of which belongs to the family Olethreutidae.

Twig Girdler, *Oncideres cingulata* Say (Coleoptera: Cerambycidae)

This twig girdler is a common species that infests twigs of a variety of hosts, including oak, hickory, elm, as well as several other hardwood species. The insect is generally distributed throughout the eastern and midwestern United States. Adults of this species girdle twigs in the fall of the year (Figure 13.18). Eggs are deposited in the distal part of the stem, which later dries out and falls to the ground. Eggs hatch in the fall, and larvae remain in the twig during the winter months. The larvae develop throughout the summer, pupate, and adults emerge in the fall.

The genus *Oncideres* contains a number of twig borers and girdlers. These insects occur throughout the United States and Canada.

Twig Pruner, *Elaphidionoides villosus* (Fabricius) (Coleoptera: Cerambicidae)

The twig pruner is another common cerambycid that infests many of the same hosts as the twig girdler (Figure 13.19). It is found throughout the eastern United States. Adults oviposit eggs in slits in the bark at leaf axils near the tips of twigs and small branches in late spring. The developing

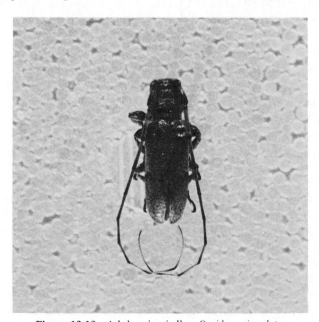

Figure 13.18 Adult twig girdler, *Oncideres cingulata.*

Figure 13.19   Adult twig prunner, *Elaphidionoides villosus.*

larvae feed towards the base of the twig. Late instar larvae sever the branch by making several concentric circular cuts from the center outward to the bark. These branches fall to the ground and provide food and habitat for the insect during the winter months. The larvae return upward in the fallen branch and form a cell between compacted fibrous frass where pupation takes place in either the fall or the spring of the year.

Cottonwood Twig Borer, *Gypsonoma haimbachiana* (Kearfott), (Lepidoptera: Olethreutidae)

Unlike most twig borers and girdlers, the cottonwood twig borer is a significant pest of eastern cottonwood and, indeed, can limit commercial production of the tree species in certain parts of its range. The insect is found in the Northeast, South, and Midwest, where it infests various *Populus* spp. Damage is caused by larvae tunneling and feeding in new terminals (Figure 13.20). Growth of young trees is stunted, and crowns become forked. In some cases damage is so great that it seriously threatens the economic production of cottonwood. Eastern cottonwood is a fast-growing tree species that is intensively cultured in the South in plantation settings. It is a species valued for its use as corestock in plywood, excelsior, magazine paper, packing crates, and newsprint. Its rapid growth makes harvest at an early age possible; therefore, damage by the cottonwood twig borer is of particular significance (Woessner and Payne 1971).

The natural history of the cottonwood twig borer has been investigated by Morris (1967) and Stewart and Payne (1975) and varies somewhat in

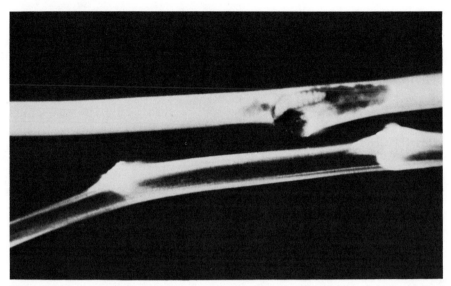

Figure 13.20   Larva of the cottonwood twig borer, *Gypsonoma haimbachiana*, infesting twig of cottonwood. (From Southern Forest Insect Work Conference Slide Series.)

different parts of the insect's range. For example, there is generally only one generation per year in the northern ranges of the insect, whereas there may be as many as four or five generations in the South. Eggs are oviposited on leaf surfaces. In general, larvae overwinter in shallow pits in margins of corky bark ridges, below leaf bases, or in depressions of leaf scars. Some larvae overwinter in hollowed-out terminal buds. In the spring, the younger larvae enter the new shoots and complete development. When the older larvae resume feeding in the spring, they frequently kill the bud and up to 5 cm of terminal. Lateral shoots result and are often attacked by subsequent generations during the same growing season.

ROOT FEEDING INSECTS

There are many forest insect species that spend a portion of the life cycle in or about the roots of trees. In this chapter, we have previously discussed some of these species, for example, the root collar weevils, the seedling debarking weevils, and the pine reproduction weevil. In Chapter 15 we indicated that certain bark beetle species [e.g., *Dendroctonus valens* LeConte; and *D. terebrans* (Olivier)] also utilize roots and the root collar for food and habitat. However, most of these species are considered to be pests for reasons other than their association with roots. For example, *D. terebrans* is primarily associated with the basal section of the bole of mature pine species.

However, there are certain species that damage primarily the root systems of hosts. The most notable species include the white grubs, *Phyllophaga* spp. (Coleoptera: Scarabeidae). These insects, which are known as May or June beetles, are sometimes damaging to forest nurseries and young plantations and are certainly pests of turf grass.

REFERENCES

Atkinson, T. H. 1979. Bionomics of *Pissodes nemorensis* (Coleoptera: Curculionidae) in north Florida. Ph.D. dissertation, University of Florida, Gainesville.

Baer, R. G. and C. W. Berisford. 1975. Species composition of pine tip moth, *Rhyacionia* spp., infestations in northeast Georgia. *J. Georgia Entomol. Soc.* **10**:64–67.

Berisford, C. W. 1974a. Comparisons of adult emergence periods and generations of the pine tip moths, *Rhyacionia frustrana* and *R. rigidana*. *Ann. Entomol. Soc. Am.* **67**:666–668.

Berisford, C. W. 1974b. Species isolation mechanisms in *Rhyacionia frustrana* and *R. rigidana*. *Ann. Entomol. Soc. Am.* **67**:292–294.

Berisford, C. W. and E. E. Brady. 1974. Specificity and inhibition of attraction of male *Rhyacionia frustrana* and *R. rigidana* to their female sex pheromone. *Nature* **241**:68–69.

Cade, S. C., A. M. Lynch, R. L. Hedden, and J. D. Walstad. 1981. Seedling debarking weevils: A site hazard-rating system case history. In Hedden, R. L., S. J. Barras, and J. E. Coster (Eds.), *Hazard-Rating Systems in Forest Insect Pest Management*. U.S. Forest Service General Technical Report WO-27.

Carolin, V. M. and G. E. Daterman. 1974. Hazard of European pine shoot moth to western pine forests. *J. For.* **72**:136–140.

Coulter, W. K. 1973. Emergence and premating behavior patterns of the adult European pine shoot moth in western Washington. U.S. Forest Service Research Paper PNW-168.

Daterman, G. E. 1970. Female sex attractant for survey trapping European pine shoot moth. *J. Econ. Entomol.* **63**:1406–1409.

Daterman, G. E. 1974. Synthetic sex pheromone for detection survey of European pine shoot moth. U.S. Forest Service Paper PNW-180.

Daterman, G. E., G. D. Daves, and R. G. Smith. 1975. Comparison of sex pheromones versus an inhibitor for disruption of pheromone communication in *Rhyacionia buoliana*. *Environ. Entomol.* **4**:944–946.

Doggett, C. A., C. R. Grady, H. J. Green, M. B. Kunselman, H. Layman, and S. Taylor. 1977. Seedling debarking weevils in North Carolina. North Carolina Forest Service Research Note 31.

Eaton, C. B. 1942. Biology of the weevil *Cylindrocopturus eatoni* Buchanan, injurious to ponderosa and jeffery pine reproduction. *J. Econ. Entomol.* **35**:20–25.

Finnegan, R. J. 1959. The pales weevil, *Hylobius pales*, in southern Ontario. *Can. Entomol.* **61**:664–670.

Franklin, R. T. and J. W. Taylor, Jr. 1970. Biology of *Pachylobius picivorus* (Coleoptera: Curculionidae) in the Georgia Piedmont. *Can. Entomol.* **102**:962–968.

Furniss, R. L. and V. M. Carolin. 1977. *Western Forest Insects*. U.S. Forest Service Miscellaneous Publication 1339.

Harris, J. W. E. and R. O. Wood. 1967. The European pine shoot moth, *Rhyacionia buoliana* (Lepidoptera: Olethreulidae), another introduced forest pest. *J. Entomol. Soc. Br. Columbia* **64**:14–17.

Hedlin, A. F., H. O. Yates III, D. Cibrian, B. H. Ebel, T. W. Koerber, and E. P. Merkel. 1980. *Cone and Seed Insects of North American Conifers.* Canadian Forestry Service, U.S. Forest Service, Section de Agricultura y Recurson Hidraulicus, Mexico.

Hertel, G. D. and D. M. Benjamin. 1975. Tip moth and webworm attacks in southwide pine seed source plantations. U.S. Forest Service Research Note SE-221.

Hertel, G. D. and D. M. Benjamin. 1977. Intensity of site preparation influences on pine webworm and tip moth infestations on pine seedlings in North Central Florida. *Environ. Entomol.* **6**:118–122.

Jennings, D. T. 1975. Life history and habits of the southwestern pine tip moth, *Rhyacionia neomexicana* (Dyar) (Lepidoptera: Olethreutidae). *Ann. Entomol. Soc. Am.* **68**:597–606.

Lashomb, J. H. and A. L. Steinhauer. 1974. *Nantucket Pine Tip Moth Damage in Maryland as Influenced by Moth Density, Host Preference, Generation Differences, and Life History.* Maryland Agriculture Experiment Station Miscellaneous Publication 87.

Lessard, G. and P. E. Buffam. 1976. Effects of *Rhyacionia neomexicana* on height and radial growth in ponderosa pine. *J. Econ. Entomol.* **69**:755–756.

Lessard, G. and D. T. Jennings. 1976. Southwestern pine tip moth damage to ponderosa pine reproduction. U.S. Forest Service Research Paper RM-168.

MacAloney, H. J. and D. C. Schmiege. 1962. Identification of conifer insects by type of tree injury, Lake States. U.S. Forest Service Lake States Forest Experiment Station Paper 100.

Merkel, E. P. 1963. A new southern pine tip moth. *J. For.* **61**:13.

Miller, W. E. 1960. A new pine tip moth (Olethreutidae) from the Gulf of Mexico region. *J. Lep. Soc.* **14**:231–236.

Miller, W. E. 1967a. Taxonomic review of the *Rhyacionia frustrana* group of pine-tip moths, with description of a new species (Olethreutidae). *Can. Entomol.* **99**:590–595.

Miller, W. E. 1967b. *The European Pine Shoot Moth—Ecology and Control in the Lake States.* Forest Science Monograph 14.

Miller, W. E. and L. F. Wilson. 1964. Composition and diagnosis of pine tip moth infestations in the Southeast. *J. Econ. Entomol.* **57**:722–726.

Morris, R. C. 1967. Biology of *Gypsonoma haimbachiana* (Lepidoptera: Olethreutidae), a twig borer in eastern cottonwood. *Ann. Entomol. Soc. Am.* **60**:423–427.

Pierson, H. B. 1921. The life history and control of the pales weevil, *Hylobius pales. Harvard For. Bull.* **3**.

Powell, J. A. and W. E. Miller. 1978. *Nearctic Tip Moths of the Genus Rhyacionia: Biosystematic Review.* Agriculture Handbook 514.

Smith, R. G., G. E. Daterman, G. D. Daves, K. D. McMurtrey, and W. G. Roelofs. 1974. Sex pheromones of the European pine shoot moth: Chemical identification and field tests. *J. Insect Physiol.* **20**:661–668.

Smith, S. G. and B. A. Sugden. 1969. Host trees and breeding sites of native North American *Pissodes* bark weevils, with a note on synonomy. *Ann. Entomol. Soc. Am.* **62**:146–148.

Speers, C. F. 1974. Pales and pitch-eating weevils: Development in relation to time pines are cut in the Southeast. U.S. Forest Service Research Note SE-207.

Speers, C. F. and J. L. Rauschenberger. 1971. Pales weevil. U.S. Forest Service Forest Pest Leaflet 104.

Stephen, F. M. and G. W. Wallis. 1981. *Dynamics of Nantucket Pine Tip Moth Populations in Intensively Managed Pine Plantations in Arkansas.* Proceedings of the IUFRO Conference, September 1980. Dornoch, Scotland.

Stevens, R. E. 1971. Pine reproduction weevil. U.S. Forest Service Forest Pest Leaflet 15.

Stevens, R. E. and D. T. Jennings. 1977. Western pine shoot borers: A threat to intensive management of ponderosa pine in the Rocky Mountain area and Southwest. U.S. Forest Service General Technical Report RM-45.

Stewart, J. W. and T. L. Payne. 1975. Seasonal abundance and impact of the cottonwood twig borer on cottonwood trees. *J. Econ. Entomol.* **68**:599–602.

Taylor, J. W., Jr. and R. T. Franklin. 1970. Biology of *Hylobius pales* (Coleoptera: Curculionidae) in the Georgia Piedmont. *Can. Entomol.* **102**:729–735.

Telerico, R. L. and H. J. Heikkenen. 1962. Stem injury to young red pine by the European pine shoot moth. *J. For.* **60**:403–406.

Thatcher, R. C. 1960. Influence of the pitch-eating weevil on pine regeneration in east Texas. *For. Sci.* **6**:354–361.

Williston, H. L. and S. J. Barras. 1977. *Impact of Tip Moth Injury on Growth and Yield of 16-Year old Loblolly and Shortleaf Pine.* U.S. Forest Service Research Note SO-221.

Wilson, L. F. and I. Millers 1983. *Pine Root Collar Weevil—Its Ecology and Management.* U.S. Forest Service Technical Bulletin 1675.

Woessner, R. A. and T. L. Payne. 1971. *An Assessment of Cottonwood Twig Borer Attacks.* Proceedings of the 11th Southern Conference on Forest Tree Improvement.

Yates, H. O. 1960. The Nantucket pine tip moth: A literature review. U.S. Forest Service, Southeastern Forest Experiment Station Paper 115.

14 | SEED AND CONE INSECTS

INTRODUCTION

The insect species that infest reproductive structures of host trees are considered to be among the most significant forest insect pests. Prior to the early 1960s few of the species were of particular importance to forestry as these insects were not generally a problem to natural regeneration of forests. However, seed- and cone-destroying insects earned a prominent position as pest species, with the intensified interest in production of genetically superior seeds for use in reforestation. Their most significant impact occurs in coniferous seed orchards and seed production areas. There are also a number of species that affect commercial production of nuts, such as pecans and almonds. Furthermore, nuts of many hardwood species in forests such as oaks, hickories, and walnuts are infested.

Our emphasis in this chapter will be directed primarily to the insects that are significant to the reproductive structures of coniferous hosts. We consider the following subjects: (1) an overview of major hosts affected and insects that have an important impact on the seed production process, (2) a description of the phenology of the seed production process in relation to insect pests, (3) a review of the major groups of seed and cone insects, (4) impact of insects on seed production, and (5) seed orchard IPM.

OVERVIEW OF MAJOR INSECT PESTS AND THEIR CONIFEROUS HOSTS

The presence of seed- and cone-destroying insects in a variety of coniferous hosts has been recognized for many years. Early work on western species and their hosts was reported by Miller (1914) and later greatly expanded by Keen (1958), Kinzer et al. (1972), and Hedlin (1974). Knowledge of the species that infest conifers in the southern United States increased rapidly during the decades 1960–1980 as a result of the widespread establishment of seed orchards and seed production areas. The southern species of seed and cone insects are among the most thoroughly studied. Literature on these insects has been reviewed and summarized by Ebel et al. (1975). Pest species and their impact on seed production in commercially valuable midwestern hosts have been reviewed by Lyons (1956, 1957a–c) and Mattson (1971, 1978). The most thorough compendium of information on seed and cone insects in North American conifers is reported by Hedlin et al. (1980). This valuable reference contains many excellent color photographs of the important insects as well as examples of the types of damage they cause, hosts infested, natural history, and distribution.

Most of the feeding groups into which we have classified insects, such as phloem feeders and tip and shoot feeders, contain pest species that occur in one or two of the insect orders. Seed and cone insects are atypical in this regard as there are important representatives in seven orders. These orders, along with important common names of pest species, include the following: Lepidoptera (coneworms and seedworms), Coleoptera (cone beetles), Hymenoptera (sawflies and seed chalcids), Diptera (cone midges), Hemiptera (seed bugs), Homoptera (aphids and scales), and Thysanoptera (thrips).

The host species infested by seed and cone insects include representatives from all 16 genera of conifers native to North America. The insects are considered primary pests in the commercially significant species of fir, spruce, pine, and Douglas-fir. Of these hosts, the 56 species of pines that occur in North America are most seriously affected. A number of different species of pine are commonly cultivated in seed orchards and seed production areas.

PHENOLOGY OF THE SEED PRODUCTION PROCESS IN RELATION TO INSECT PESTS

The seed production process in conifers takes place over a 1–2-year period and involves several different plant anatomic structures. The most complicated and lengthy cycle occurs in pines, where seed production takes about 15–20 months and spans two growing seasons. Seed production in fir, spruce, and Douglas-fir is completed in one season.

The seed production process in pines begins with an indeterminate bud or meristem. In the spring of the first year the indeterminate bud becomes determinate and produces either male or female strobili. The male and female strobili in the early stage of development are often referred to as "flowers." The male strobili produce pollen. The female strobili develop into first-year cones, which are also known as *conelets*. The conelets are pollinated during the spring and enlarge during the summer months. In the spring of the next year, the conelets are fertilized and development of the second-year cones, which contain the seeds, proceeds rapidly. The second-year cones mature in the fall. This process takes approximately 20 months. Insect damage to tips (meristems), male flowers, female flowers, conelets, second-year cones, and seed affects the ultimate seed yield for a tree. There are a number of different species of insects that feed on each of the anatomical structures involved in seed production. In the case of seed orchards there may be additional losses associated with harvesting the second-year cones and in the seed extraction process. Furthermore, if the seeds are planted in nurseries, there will be some seedling mortality.

In the case of fir, spruce, and Douglas-fir, the same plant anatomic structures are involved. However, the entire process takes place in 1 year. In forests, the cones and seeds of some species remain on the host for more than one season.

Because of the ephemeral nature of the various plant structures infested by seed and cone insects, the life cycles of many of the species are somewhat complicated. Alternative plant structures are often used by different life stages. Seed and cone insect populations are also prone to large fluctuations, as the cone production process is cyclic.

MAJOR GROUPS OF SEED AND CONE INSECTS

There are several hundred species of insects that infest the reproductive structures of host conifers. Some of the species are chronic pests that destroy cones and seeds, whereas others periodically cause damage or cosmetic defects. We emphasize the primary insect pests in this chapter.

Coleoptera

Cone Beetles, *Conophthorus* spp., Scolytidae

Cone beetles, *Conophthorus* spp., are by far the most notorious pests of cones within the Coleoptera. There are 11 species that infest pine cones in North America. These insects are generally distributed throughout the United States and Canada and are significant pests of most western and eastern pine species. However, cone beetles have not been reported from the Southeast and do not infest the commercially significant hard pine species grown in the region. This observation is somewhat surprising, as there is a rich fauna of scolytid bark beetles found in the South.

Conophthorus species are typical of other bark beetles in appearance. Adults range in size from 2.4 to 4.0 mm, are cylindrical shaped, and are shiny dark brown to black in color.

The general life history of *Conophthorus* is similar for all cone-infesting species (Figure 14.1). Adult females attack second-year cones in the late spring or early summer. Females initiate attack by boring into the cone stalk or side of the cone at the base. Males usually accompany the female after attack has been initiated. A pitch tube is formed at the entrance hole. The female excavates a gallery in the cone stalk that kills the cone by destroying conductive tissue. Eggs are deposited in the gallery. Infested cones may remain on the tree or drop to the ground. The life cycle is completed in the cone. Larvae develop in about a month, pupate, and transform to callow or teneral adults. The adults may overwinter in the cones or leave to attack shoots or conelets, where they feed and overwinter. There is one generation per year. In some species adults may diapause for an additional year (Hedlin et al. 1980).

Damage caused by *Conophthorus* species can be substantial in commercially valuable pine species. Successful colonization of the second-year cones ensures the death of the cone and thus the loss of all seeds. Larvae feed on immature seed, but this feeding is irrelevant to seed production as the seed in the infested cone would not develop. Infested cones are easily recognized by resin accumulation at the entrance hole, discolored cones,

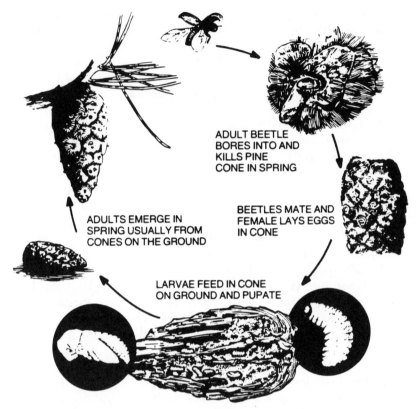

Figure 14.1 The general life history of cone beetles, *Conophthorus* species. (From Hedlin et al. 1980, courtesy of the Canadian Forestry Service.)

and reduced size of cones. The inside of the cone is packed with boring frass. Damaged cones are often found on the ground under trees.

Damage potential for *Conophthorus* species is substantial, as female beetles can attack more than one cone. Annual second-year cone mortality has been reported to be 80% or greater in some circumstances for commercially important tree species such as red pine and ponderosa pine (Mattson 1980, Kinzer et al. 1972).

Of the 11 species of *Conophthorus* that occur in North America, three are frequently serious pests. The white pine cone beetle, *C. coniperda* (Schwarz), infests primarily eastern white pine and occurs throughout the range of this host. It is particularly important in the Northeast. The red pine cone beetle, *C. resinosae* Hopkins, infests red pine and occurs in the Northeast and Midwest. It is a common and significant pest in red pine seed orchards and seed production areas. The ponderosa pine cone beetle, *C. ponderosae* Hopkins, infests primarily ponderosa pine, in the Southwest and West.

Lepidoptera

The order Lepidoptera contains four groups of insects that are among the most significant pests of cones and seeds. These pests include coneworms, *Dioryctria* spp., Pyralidae; cone moths, *Barbara* spp., Olethreutidae; cone borers, *Eucosma* spp., Olethreutidae; and seedworms, *Cydia* spp., Tortricidae.

Coneworms, *Dioryctria* spp., Pyralidae

Coneworms in the genus *Dioryctria* are the most important group of lepidopterous cone insects in North America. Hedlin et al. (1980) described 21 species that occur in the United States, Canada, and Mexico. These insects infest all commercially significant pines as well as spruce, fir, Douglas-fir, hemlock, and cypress. The primary damage caused by *Dioryctria* spp. is to second-year cones (Figure 14.2), although other host anatomic structures are also infested by some species (e.g., shoots, first-year cones, and galls). Damage, which is caused by larval feeding within the cones, can be substantial, as (in some species) larvae destroy more than one cone and there may be more than one generation per year. In general, all developing seeds within an infested cone will be destroyed. It is not possible to generalize about the life history of *Dioryctria* spp. because of the large number of members in the genus, the variety of hosts infested, and their wide geographic distribution. We provide individual case histories for two of the

Figure 14.2 Damage to second-year loblolly pine cone caused by the southern pine coneworm, *Dioryctria amatella*. (U.S. Forest Service photograph.)

prominent pest species of *Dioryctria*. The other species are treated in detail in Ebel et al. (1975) and Hedlin et al. (1980).

Southern Pine Coneworm, Dioryctria amatella (Hulst)

The southern pine coneworm, *D. amatella* (Figure 14.3), occurs in the south-eastern United States, where it infests a variety of pine species and is a primary pest in loblolly, longleaf, and slash pines. Adults have a wingspan of about 30 mm with the forewing base color of dark gray–brown shaded black and marked with sharply contrasting white patches and crossbands.

The life history of *D. amatella* is rather complicated (Figure 14.4). There are several overlapping generations per year. The insect infests flowers, shoots, second-year cones, rust [*Cronartium strobilinum* (Hedgecock and Hahn)]-infected first-year cones, branches, stems that have been infected with fusiform rust [*Cronartium fusiforme* (Hedgecock and Hunt),] and me-chanically injured tree trunks. The life history on slash and longleaf pine follows a path different from that observed on loblolly. Flowers and cones of slash and longleaf pine are first infested in late winter (February) at the time of flowering. Early instar larvae feed first in male and female flowers and then in new shoots. The larvae may mature in these structures or move to cones. Rust-infected first-year cones may also be attacked during May or June. Second-year cones are infested from summer to fall. The life cycle in late winter–early spring can follow an alternate route. The insect infests

Figure 14.3 Adult southern pine coneworm, *Dioryctria amatella*. (U.S. Forest Service photograph.)

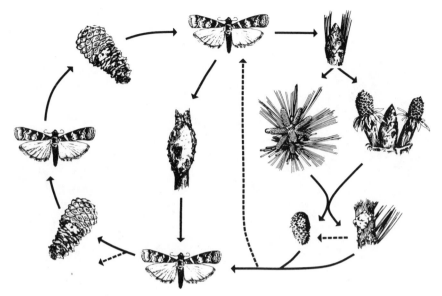

Figure 14.4   Diagram of major aspects of complex life cycle of *Dioryctria amatella*. On loblolly pine the cone to gall cycle (left) is typical; in slash and longleaf pine a variety of additional host parts may be fed on in the spring. (From Hedlin et al. 1980, courtesy of Canadian Forestry Service.)

fusiform galls on slash pine and produces a non-cone-infesting brood. Although fusiform galls and tree trunk wounds support a limited population throughout the summer, most adults that emerge from galls attacked in the spring probably lay eggs on cones in the early summer.

In loblolly pine, the spring generation occurs primarily in fusiform galls and is followed by repeated infestation of cones from summer to fall. Again, there are several overlapping generations (Hedlin et al. 1980, Ebel 1965, Coulson and Franklin 1970a,b).

The southern pine coneworm is considered to be the most serious pest of the southern *Dioryctria* species. It causes significant damage in seed orchards and seed production areas by feeding on flowers, buds, terminals, first- and second-year cones.

Webbing Coneworm, Dioryctria disclusa Heinrich

The webbing coneworm, *D. disclusa* (Figure 14.5), has a wide distribution, covering the eastern half of the United States and extending from the Gulf states into the Canadian provinces. The insect infests a large number of hosts, including loblolly, shortleaf, longleaf, slash, jack, Virginia, red pine, and white spruce. The adults have a wingspan of about 27 mm, with forewing coloration ranging from golden orange to reddish brown and containing white crossbands.

Various aspects of the life history of *D. disclusa* have been reported by

Figure 14.5   Adult webbing coneworm, *Dioryctria disclusa*. (U.S. Forest Service photograph.)

a number of workers: Ebel and Yates (1974), Hard (1964), Lyons (1957a), Nuenzig et al. (1964), and Mattson (1971). In the northern part of the range, first instar larvae overwinter. Male and female flowers are fed upon in early spring. Third instar larvae enter developing second-year cones. In southern ranges, cone infestation by the third instar larvae occurs in the early spring. Adults emerge from late spring to midsummer, depending on latitude. There is one generation per year (Hedlin et al. 1980).

Cones infested by *D. disclusa* can be identified by a characteristic mass of tightly webbed frass that covers the entry hole at the base of the cone. Primary damage occurs to young second-year cones in spring and early summer. As with *D. amatella*, *D. disclusa* can be an important pest in seed orchards and seed production areas.

Cone Moths, *Barbara* spp., Olethreutidae

Although the genus *Barbara* contains a small number of species, some members are important cone-destroying pests. The pest species occur in the West and Northwest.

Douglas-Fir Cone Moth, *Barbara colfaxiana* Kearfott

The Douglas-fir cone moth, *B. colfaxiana*, occurs throughout the range of Douglas-fir in British Columbia, the Pacific Coast states, and the Rocky Mountains. It infests cones of Douglas-fir. Adults have a wingspan of about 15–20 mm and are grayish brown with the forewings banded in gray, silver, and brown (Figure 14.6).

The life history of the insect has been reported by Hedlin (1960, 1964), Clark et al. (1963), and Nebeker (1977) (Figure 14.7). Adults emerge in

Figure 14.6 Adult Douglas-fir cone moth, *Barbara colfaxiana*. (From Hedlin et al. 1980, courtesy of Canadian Forestry Service.)

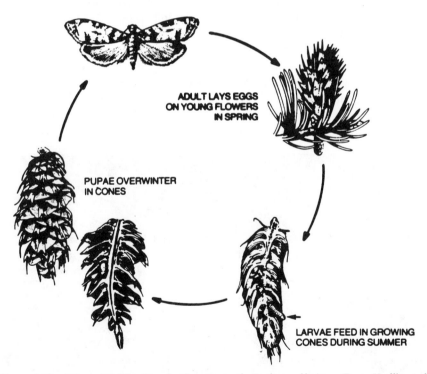

ADULT LAYS EGGS
ON YOUNG FLOWERS
IN SPRING

PUPAE OVERWINTER
IN CONES

LARVAE FEED IN GROWING
CONES DURING SUMMER

Figure 14.7 Life cycle of the Douglas-fir cone moth, *Barbara colfaxiana*. (From Hedlin et al. 1980, courtesy of Canadian Forestry Service.)

the spring (April and May) from cones infested the previous season. Eggs are oviposited on the outer surface of the cone bracts. Early instar larvae bore into the cone scales and feed for a short time. Later instar larvae bore into the cone center, where they feed around the cone axis and thereby destroy developing seeds. Several larvae are often found in a single cone. Pupation occurs within the cone during midsummer. Pupae overwinter in the cone that remains on the tree. Damage by *B. colfaxiana* is detectable by the presence of frass adhering to resin on the surface of the cone.

Cone Borers, *Eucosma* spp., Olethreutidae

The genus *Eucosma* contains a number of pest species that infest primarily cones of pines, although fir is also attacked. Insects in the genus are widely distributed in the United States and Canada, with representatives occurring in most of the commercially significant pine species. The natural history of *Eucosma* species cannot be easily generalized and we present case histories for two of the more significant pest species. Hedlin et al. (1980) consider seven species.

Shortleaf Pine Cone Borer, Eucosma cocana Kearfott

The shortleaf pine cone borer, *E. cocana*, is distributed in the Southeast and along the Eastern Seaboard, where it infests primarily shortleaf pine but occurs also in loblolly, Virginia, and pitch pine. The adults have a wingspan of about 18–22 mm and are colored in tan to reddish brown with gray shading (Figure 14.8).

The life history and habits of *E. cocana* have been described by Ebel and Yates (1973), Powell (1968), and Hedlin et al. (1980). In the Southeast, adults emerge in April and May. Eggs are oviposited in small groups on scales of the cone stalk. Early instar larvae bore into the cone (Figure 14.9), where they feed until food resources are depleted (Figure 14.10). The

Figure 14.8 Adult southern pine cone borer, *Eucosma cocana*. (U.S. Forest Service photograph.)

Figure 14.9 External damage to shortleaf pine cone caused by the southern pine cone borer, *Eucosma cocana*. (From Hedlin et al. 1980, courtesy of Canadian Forestry Service.)

larvae move to nearby cones, enter at the base, and resume feeding. Mature larvae drop to the ground in early summer and pupate in the soil, where they overwinter. There is only one generation per year (Hedlin et al. 1980).

Damage by *E. cocana* can be extensive and has been reported to cause as much as 20% cone loss on shortleaf pine. Larval feeding causes complete destruction on the cone, which is characteristically packed with frass.

Figure 14.10 Internal damage caused by larva of the southern pine cone borer, *Eucosma cocana*. (U.S. Forest Service photograph.)

Red Pine Cone Borer, *Eucosma monitorana* Heinrich

The red pine cone borer, *E. monitorana*, is distributed throughout the Northeast, Great Lake states, and adjacent Canadian provinces. It infests red pine and Virginia pine and damages second-year cones. The adults have a wingspan of about 15 mm and are colored reddish with tan and silver markings (Figure 14.11).

The natural history of *E. monitorana* has been studied by Barras and Norris (1969), Lyons (1957b), and Mattson (1971) and reviewed by Hedlin et al. (1980). Adults emerge in May and oviposit on or near second-year cones. Early instar larvae, which are gregarious, tunnel to the cone axis, and feed on immature seeds. A single cone can contain as many as 25 larvae. Later instar larvae move to adjacent cones, tunnel to the cone axis, and continue feeding. In midsummer, mature larvae exit the cones, drop to the ground and pupate in the litter. The pupal stage overwinters. There is one generation per year (Hedlin et al. 1980).

Damage caused by *E. monitorana* to second-year cones is of two types. Cones attacked by early instar larvae have multiple small surface holes, with the interior of the cone extensively foraged. Later instar larvae, that have moved to larger cones, excavate an oblong entrance hole at the base of the cone and then feed extensively within the cone. In both cases, seeds are destroyed.

Figure 14.11   Adult red pine cone borer, *Eucosma monitorana* [*Can. Entomol.* **89**(4), 153 (1957)].

Seedworms, *Cydia* spp., Tortricidae

The genus *Cydia* contains 11 species that are pests in a variety of conifers throughout North America. Insects in this group are called *seedworms* because larvae feed almost exclusively on seeds. In pines damage occurs in second-year cones, whereas in firs and spruces (where the cones mature in 1 year) flowers and conelets are also infested shortly after pollination.

Members of the genus *Cydia* were formerly classified as *Laspeyresia* spp. in the family Olethreutidae. This classification was changed by Brown (1979). There are many references in the literature that use the previous genus and family names. Adults have a wingspan of 10–20 mm, and most species are colored metallic gray with distinct white crossbands.

Generalized Life History for *Cydia* spp.

The life history for the cone-infesting *Cydia* is similar for all species and is closely synchronized with the cone development process (Figure 14.12).

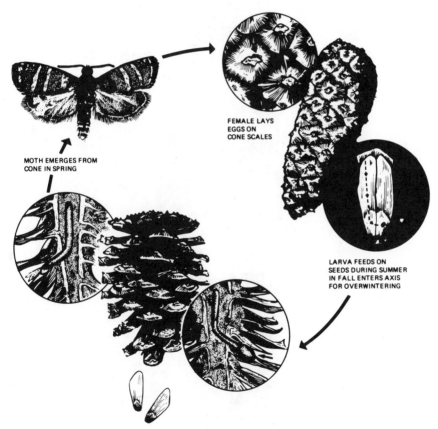

FEMALE LAYS
EGGS ON
CONE SCALES

MOTH EMERGES FROM
CONE IN SPRING

LARVA FEEDS ON
SEEDS DURING SUMMER
IN FALL ENTERS AXIS
FOR OVERWINTERING

Figure 14.12 Life cycle of cone-infesting *Cydia* species. (From Hedlin et al. (1980), courtesy of Canadian Forestry Service.)

The species that infest pines oviposit on the scales of cones or on the cone stalk. On spruce and fir the eggs are laid between the scales of female flowers. The early instar larva bores between cone scales, enters a seed, and feeds on its contents. Once a seed is consumed, the larva moves to an adjacent seed, leaving a silk-lined tunnel between the two of them. This process is repeated for successive seeds fed on. As the cone matures, the late instar larva burrows into the cone axis, where it overwinters in a tunnel. The larva excavates a passage to the surface of a previously hollowed out seed (or the cone surface on a serotinous cone—a cone that remains closed on the tree for several months to a year after maturity). This tunnel, which is sealed with a protective cap of host tissue, will be used later as an emergence hole for adults. The larva retreats into the cone axis. Pupation occurs in the spring. The pupa forces its way through the exit hole cover and adults emerge to start the cycle again (Hedlin et al. 1980).

Figure 14.13   Larva of *Cydia* infesting axis of Engelmann spruce cone. (U.S. Forest Service photograph.)

Most species of *Cydia* have a diapause, where a portion of the population takes 2 years to develop. Diapause in seed and cone insects is a common phenomenon and is interpreted to be a survival mechanism for periods when cone production is low.

Damages Caused by Cydia spp.

Larvae of *Cydia* feed directly on seeds. In most species 1–3 larvae infest a single cone but in some species there may be as many as 12 larvae (Figure 14.13). There is no external appearance of damage on the cone surface. Seedworm damage can be substantial in certain host species and has been reported to range from about 4–20% of the seed crop in loblolly and longleaf pines in the Gulf South.

Pest Species of Cydia

There are a number of *Cydia* spp. in North America that periodically have a significant impact on seed production. In the southern United States the longleaf pine seedworm, *C. ingens* (Heinrich), is a common pest of longleaf and loblolly pine (Figure 14.14). The eastern pine seedworm, *C. toreuta* (Grote), occurs throughout the East ranging from the Gulf Coast to the Canadian provinces (Figure 14.15). This species infests jack, loblolly, short-leaf, Virginia, red and lodgepole pine. The ponderosa pine seedworm, *C. piperana* (Kearfott), is a western species that infests primarily ponderosa and jeffrey pine (Figure 14.16). The most widely distributed of the *Cydia* species is the spruce seed moth, *C. strobilella* (Linnaeus). This insect was formerly classified as *C. youngana* (Kearfott) (Brown and Miller 1983). This insect has a transcontinental distribution and occurs throughout the Canadian provinces and along the West Coast (Figure 14.17). The primary

Figure 14.14   Adult longleaf pine seedworm, *Cydia ingens*. (From the Southern Forest Insect Work Conference Slide Series.)

Figure 14.15 Adult eastern pine seedworm, *Cydia torcuta*. (From the Southern Forest Insect Work Conference Slide Series.)

host is Englemann spruce, but black, blue, red, Sitka, and white spruce can be infested.

Other Important Lepidoptera

The genus *Choristoneura*, Tortricidae, which contains several noteworthy defoliators [e.g., the spruce budworm, *C. fumiferana* (Clemens)], also has a number of species that are periodically important in limiting production of cones and seeds. Insects in this genus often feed directly on

Figure 14.16 Adult ponderosa pine seedworm, *Cydia piperana*. (From Hedlin et al. 1980, courtesy of Canadian Forestry Service.)

Figure 14.17 Adult spruce seed moth, *Cydia strobilella*. (From Hedlin et al. 1980, courtesy of Canadian Forestry Service.)

flowers and young cones and are especially significant when population levels are high.

Hymenoptera

Within the Hymenoptera there are three general groups of insects that impact on seed production. These groups include conifer sawflies (Diprionidae), xyelid sawflies (Xyelidae), and torymids (Torymidae). The conifer sawflies are primarily defoliators, but periodically forage buds and flowers of various pine species. The xyelid sawflies infest male flowers but likely do not significantly affect pollen production. The torymids have species that are both parasitic on other insects as well as phytophagous on seeds. The most important seed infesting torymids belong to the genus *Megastigmus*, which are known as *seed chalcids*.

Seed Chalcids, *Megastigmus* spp.

The genus *Megastigmus* contains 11 species of seed chalcids that infest a large number of coniferous hosts. Adults are small wasps 5–7 mm in length with a large dilated and darkened stigma on the anterior margin of the forewing (Figure 14.18). Although the natural history of the various species is highly specialized, all cause the same type of damage to seeds.

Generalized Life History of Megastigmus spp.

The following life history is patterned after that of the Douglas-fir seed chalcid, *M. spermatrophus* Wachtl, which is a common pest of Douglas-fir in the West (Figure 14.19). This insect has been studied in detail (Hussey 1955, Hedlin 1974, Hedlin et al. 1980). Adults emerge over a period of

Figure 14.18 Adult *Megastigmus* species ovipositing in noble fir cone. (From Hedlin et al. 1980, courtesy of Canadian Forestry Service.)

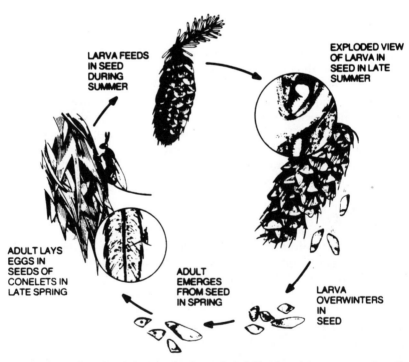

LARVA FEEDS
IN SEED
DURING
SUMMER

EXPLODED VIEW
OF LARVA IN
SEED IN LATE
SUMMER

ADULT LAYS
EGGS IN
SEEDS OF
CONELETS IN
LATE SPRING

ADULT
EMERGES
FROM SEED
IN SPRING

LARVA
OVERWINTERS
IN
SEED

Figure 14.19 Life cycle of the Douglas-fir seed chalcid, *Megastigmus spermatrophus*. (From Hedlin et al. 1980, courtesy of Canadian Forestry Service.)

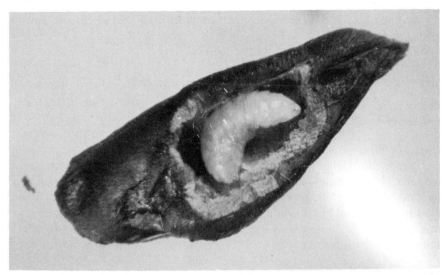

Figure 14.20   Larva of *Megastigmus pinus* infesting seed of red fir. (From Hedlin et al. 1980, courtesy of Canadian Forestry Service.)

about one month in the spring. Females, which may mate or reproduce parthenogenetically (without mating), oviposit through the scales of young cones and deposit eggs directly into developing seeds. Usually one egg is laid per seed. If more than one is laid only a single larva will survive. The larva develops within the seed in 6–8 weeks, during which time it consumes the entire contents of the seed (Figure 14.20). The mature larva overwinters in the seed and pupates in early spring. Some adults emerge at this time while others diapause in the larval stage for another year (Hedlin et al. 1980).

Damage Caused by Megastigmus

Feeding by *Megastigmus* spp. is not detectable by inspection of cones. Furthermore, infested seeds show no outward signs of feeding until the adult emerges, when a small exit hole is visible. Damaged seeds can be detected using radiographic techniques. Because of the difficulty in distinguishing healthy from infested seeds, insects in the genus have been widely distributed by transport of seeds used for commercial and ornamental plantings. Some of the more important species of *Megastigmus* have been reported to destroy as much as 2–15% of the seed crop of host trees.

Diptera

Within the order Diptera, the families Anthomyiidae and Cecidomyiidae contain a number of species that infest cones. The pest species occur throughout North America and are found in many different coniferous hosts.

Anthomyiidae

The family Anthomyiidae contains a single genus, *Hylemya*, with two species that are serious pests of spruce and fir cones: the spruce cone maggot, *H. anthracina* (Czerny), and the fir cone maggot, *H. abietis* Huckett. Adults of these insects are 6–9 mm in length, shiny brown to black, and superficially resemble house flies.

Hylemya anthracina occurs throughout Canada and Alaska and into the western United States. It infests a number of different spruce hosts. The natural history of this insect is known in some detail (Hedlin 1973, 1974; Hedlin et al. 1980; Furniss and Carolin 1977) (Figure 14.21). Adults emerge in early summer. Females lay eggs singly between scales of young conelets. Larvae feed within the cone by excavating a spiral tunnel around the cone

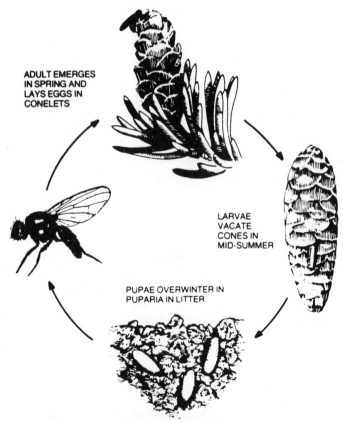

ADULT EMERGES
IN SPRING AND
LAYS EGGS IN
CONELETS

LARVAE
VACATE
CONES IN
MID-SUMMER

PUPAE OVERWINTER IN
PUPARIA IN LITTER

Figure 14.21   Life cycle of the spruce cone maggot, *Hylemya anthracina*. (From Hedlin et al. 1980, courtesy of Canadian Forestry Service.)

axis, which causes substantial damage to scales and seeds. After feeding for about 1 month, the larvae tunnel to the surface of the cone and drop to the ground, where they form a puparium. Pupation occurs in late summer and fall. The winter is spent as a pupa in the litter.

Hylemya abietis is a pest of cones in a number of species of firs in the West. The natural history and type of damage caused is similar to *H. anthracina*.

Cecidomyiidae

The family Cecidomyiidae contains several genera and many species that infest a large number of coniferous hosts. Adults in the family are delicate flies with relatively long antenna and legs and with reduced wing venation. Unlike the Anthomyiidae that infest cones, larvae of the Cecidomyiidae are not vigorous feeders. Damage to conelets and cones is usually indirect and results from gall formation on the seed scale, which prevents the seed from developing or prevents seed dispersal because scales are fused together. Often there will be several hundred larvae found in a single cone. At high population levels these insects are serious pests and cause significant damage to seed crops. There are important pest species in the following genera: *Asynapta, Cecidomyia, Contarinia, Dasineura,* and *Resseliella* (Figure 14.22).

Hemiptera

The Hemiptera (true bugs) contains two families that are significant pests of a number of coniferous species: Coreidae (coreid bugs) and Pentatomidae (stink bugs). The pest species feed on the ovules and seeds of pines and other conifers.

Coreidae

In the family Coreidae there is one genus (*Leptoglossus*, leaf-footed bugs) that has two important species of seed destroying insects: the southern pine seed bug, *L. corculus* (Say), and the western conifer seed bug, *L. occidentalis* Heidemann. These species are easily recognized by their laterally expanded and leaflike tibiae of the hind legs and the obvious spines on the femora. *Leptoglossus corculus* occurs in the eastern United States where it infests pine hosts and *L. occidentalis* is found in the West and infests pines as well as several other coniferous hosts. We discuss *L. corculus* as this species has been identified as a significant pest in southern pine seed orchards (DeBarr 1967, DeBarr and Ebel 1974). Koerber (1963) and Krugman and Koerber (1969) discuss *L. occidentalis*.

Southern Pine Seed Bug, Leptoglossus corculus (Say)

The southern pine seed bug is distributed throughout the East and Southeast and is a pest in most pines in these regions. It is particularly important

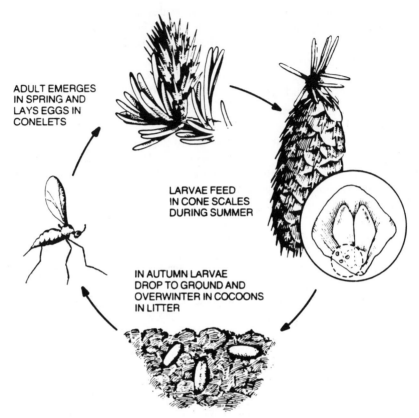

ADULT EMERGES
IN SPRING AND
LAYS EGGS IN
CONELETS

LARVAE FEED
IN CONE SCALES
DURING SUMMER

IN AUTUMN LARVAE
DROP TO GROUND AND
OVERWINTER IN COCOONS
IN LITTER

Figure 14.22   Life cycle of the Douglas-fir cone midge, *Contarinia oregonensis*, infesting Douglas-fir. (From Hedlin et al. 1980, courtesy of Canadian Forestry Service.)

in loblolly and shortleaf pine. The adults are elongated about 19 mm in length and colored reddish brown marked with black (Figure 14.23). The wings have distinctive whitish crossbands and the "leaf" on the hind tibia has an obvious white spot.

The natural history of *L. corculus* has been reviewed by Ebel et al. (1975), Hedlin et al. (1980), and Cameron (1981) (Figure 14.24). Adults become active in the late winter or early spring at about the time the host pines flower. Initially feeding is primarily on developing male flowers and later on succulent shoots, conelets, and young second-year cones. Females lay eggs in neat rows on pine needles. Young nymphs feed on conelets, whereas older nymphs and adults destroy seeds in cones. Development is continuous throughout the summer months. Adults hibernate during the winter. There are several generations per year.

Seed bugs feed on developing seeds by inserting their mouth parts be-

Figure 14.23 Adult southern pine seed bug, *Leptoglossus corculus*. (Courtesy of Texas Forest Service.)

tween scales on conelets or by puncturing scales in second-year cones. These insects are responsible for considerable conelet abortion and substantial seed mortality in second-year cones. Seed damage can be easily identified using radiography.

Pentatomidae

Within the Pentatomidae there is one important seed destroying insect, the shield-backed pine seed bug, *Tetyra bipunctata* (Herrich-Schäffer). This insect is distributed throughout the eastern United States and Canada, where it infests a wide variety of pines. Adults are 11–15 mm in length, yellowish to reddish brown with black markings, and shield shaped (Figure 14.25).

The natural history of *T. bipunctata* has been reviewed by Ebel et al. (1975) and Hedlin et al. (1980). Adults, which overwinter in the litter or under loose bark of logs, become active in early summer. Eggs are laid in double rows on pine needles or cones in groups of 8–14 (Figure 14.26). Nymphs feed on seeds of developing second-year cones (Figure 14.27). Later nymphal instars also feed on shoots. In the fall the new adults are gregarious and feed on maturing second-year cones. Adults hibernate during the winter. There is only one generation per year.

Damage by *T. bipunctata* is not distinguishable from that caused by *L. corculus*. Since there is only one generation per year, *T. bipunctata* probably does not have as large an impact on seed production as *L. corculus*.

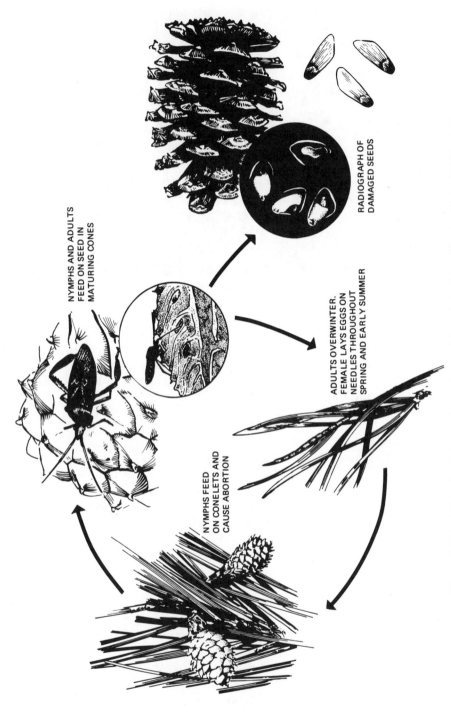

NYMPHS AND ADULTS FEED ON SEED IN MATURING CONES

RADIOGRAPH OF DAMAGED SEEDS

ADULTS OVERWINTER. FEMALE LAYS EGGS ON NEEDLES THROUGHOUT SPRING AND EARLY SUMMER

NYMPHS FEED ON CONELETS AND CAUSE ABORTION

Figure 14.24 Life cycle of the southern pine seed bug, *Leptoglossus corculus*. (From Hedlin et al. 1980, courtesy Canadian Forestry Service.)

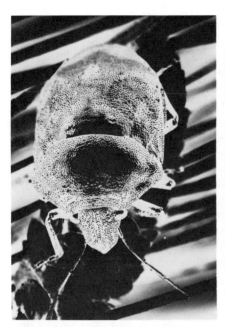

Figure 14.25 Adult shield-backed pine seed bug, *Tetyra bipunctata*. (Courtesy of Texas Forest Service.)

Figure 14.26 Eggs of the shield-backed pine seed bug, *Tetyra bipunctata*. (From Hedlin et al. 1980, courtesy of Canadian Forestry Service.)

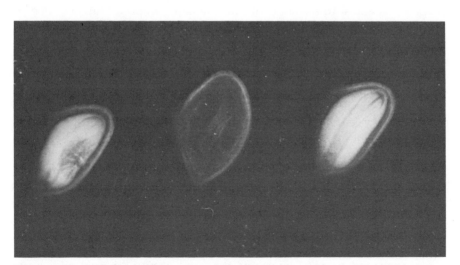

Figure 14.27 Radiograph of damage to slash pine seed caused by the shield-backed pine seed bug, *Tetyra bipunctata* (left = insect damaged, center = hollow seed, right = sound seed). (U.S. Forest Service photograph.)

IMPACT OF SEED AND CONE INSECTS

The primary impact of seed and cone insects occurs in seed orchards and seed production areas. Seed orchards are small areas of extremely valuable forest property that are managed for the single purpose of producing reliable supplies of genetically improved seed for use in reforestation. Seed production areas are, again, generally small areas containing trees of cone-producing size that have outstanding qualities such as growth rate, height, form class, and so on. Seed production areas are seldom as intensively managed as seed orchards.

Seed orchards and seed production areas now play an indispensable role in forestry. For example, in the South seed orchards produced more than 60 tons of genetically improved seed in 1977. Annual nursery production reached almost one billion seedlings and a total of 370 million or 41% of the seedlings grown in 1978 were genetically improved trees (DeBarr 1981). Seed and cone insects are the single most important external factor influencing seed production in seed orchards.

Until recently, the impact of seed and cone insects was not realized. Indeed, many of the species now known to be important, were unknown. Since the large-scale establishment of seed orchards and seed production areas, there have been a number of long-term studies conducted to appraise impact of seed and cone insects on several commercially valuable host trees. Examples of these studies include the following: Douglas-fir (Hedlin 1964), shortleaf pine (Ebel and Yates 1974), loblolly pine (Yates and Ebel 1978), slash pine (DeBarr and Barber 1975), and red pine (Mattson 1978).

In seed orchards we do not have the multiple use values (associated with forest ecosystems) to contend with in evaluating impact. Our sole focus is on factors affecting seed production. However, we know from our review of the phenology of seed production that insect damage can occur to indeterminate buds, determinate buds, male strobili, female strobili (conelets or first-year cones), second-year cones, and seeds. Furthermore, we have learned that there are many insects associated with each of these structures. Therefore, measuring impact involves consideration of the entire seed production cycle. One further complicating factor is that seed production is a cyclic phenomenon and thus results in large fluctuations in both seed quantity and insect populations. The life table format (see Chapter 6) has been used to catalogue mortality occurring to the various plant morphological structures involved in seed production. Mattson (1978) used this approach for red pine *cone production* (Table 14.1). Note the extremely low survival rate (S_x column in the life table). DeBarr and Barber (1975) constructed a life table to evaluate the effects of mortality agents on *seed yield* in slash pine (Table 14.2). In this case focus was directed to conelets, second-year cones, and seeds. Again, note the survival rate for seeds. This rate would be even lower if we added mortality resulting from nonviable seeds and mortality occurring in nursery plantings. The significant point, evident

Table 14.1 Partial Life Table Illustrating the Impact of Insects on Cone Production in Red Pine (1967–1971)

x	L_x	D_xF	D_x	$100q_x$	S_x
Age Interval	Number Alive per Branch	Mortality Factors Within x	Number Dying Within x	D_x as a Percent of L_x	Survival Rate Within x
Flowers	16.00	Defoliators[a]	4.15	25.97	
		D. zimmermani,	2.90	18.15	
		Conophthorus	0.20	1.28	
		unknown	0.62	3.87	
			7.87	49.27	0.5073
3-month conelets	8.12	Squirrels,	0.67	8.30	
		unknown			
			0.67	8.30	0.9170
11-month cones	7.45	Conophthorus	2.06	27.66	
		Dioryctria	3.25	43.64	
		Eucosma	0.49	6.53	
		Rubsaamenia	trace	0.07	
			5.82	77.90	0.2210
15-month cones	1.65	Size	0.39	23.86	
		Aborted embryo	0.15	9.25	
		Other insects	0.14	8.25	
		Laspeyresia	0.01	0.87	
			0.69	42.23	0.5777
Normal cones	0.95				

Source: Mattson (1978).

[a]Defoliators includes mortality as a result of *Dioryctria disclusa, Choristoneura pinus,* and other leaf-eating insects.

Table 14.2 Partial Life Table Illustrating the Impact of Insects on Seed Yields of Slash Pine in North Florida During 1967–69

Reproductive Structures	Cone Crop	Mean Potential Yield (Seed per Tree)[a]	Mortality Factor	Loss of Seed		
				Seeds per Tree	Percent Loss	Pounds per Tree[b]
Cones (June–September 1967)	1967	16,070	*Dioryctria* spp.	4760	29.6	0.397
			Abortion	560	3.5	0.047
			Midges	15	0.1	0.001
			Missing	270	1.7	0.023
			Total	5605	34.9	0.468
Seed		10,360	*Laspeyresia* spp.[c]	305	1.9	0.025
			Seedbugs[d]	545	3.4	0.045
			Empty	660	4.1	0.055
			Total	1510	9.4	0.125
Harvest = 8,950						
Conelets (June 1967)	1968	31,830	*Dioryctria* spp.	350	1.1	0.029
			Dioryctria (shoot)	3150	9.9	0.263
			Abortion	955	3.0	0.080
			Thrips	95	0.3	0.008
			Cone rust	65	0.2	0.005
			Missing	3630	11.4	0.303
			Total	8245	25.9	0.688

Cones (January 1968–September 1969)	23,585			
		Dioryctria spp.	2390	7.5	0.199
		Abortion	1590	5.0	0.133
		Missing	1530	4.8	0.128
		Total	5510	17.3	0.460
Seed	18,080	*Laspeyresia* spp.[c]	335	1.0	0.028
		Seedbugs[d]	1665	5.2	0.139
		Empty	1680	5.3	0.140
		Total	3680	11.5	0.307
Harvest = 14,400					
Conelets (January–September 1968)	1969 42,660	*Dioryctria*	130	0.3	0.011
		Dioryctria (shoot)	600	1.4	0.050
		Abortion	1320	3.1	0.110
		Thrips	6910	16.2	0.576
		Cone rust	85	0.2	0.007
		Missing	2860	6.7	0.238
		Total	11,905	27.9	0.992

Source: DeBarr and Barber (1975).

[a]Based on observations on 12 trees and assuming a potential of 100 seeds per cone.
[b]Assuming 12,000 seeds per pound.
[c]Assuming each *Laspeyresia* spp. larvae destroy six seeds per cone (Merkel 1967).
[d]Detectable damaged seed only.

from these studies, and those of Hedlin (1964), Ebel and Yates (1974), and Yates and Ebel (1978), is that insect-caused mortality in seed orchards and seed production areas is substantial.

In contrast to seed orchards and seed production areas, seed and cone insects likely play beneficial roles in forest ecosystems. Natural regeneration of stands is probably not limited by seed availability. The amount of seed produced by most forest trees will usually be in excess of that needed for regeneration. Mattson (1978) has suggested that heavy infestations of seed and cone insects in natural stands may be beneficial to general tree growth.

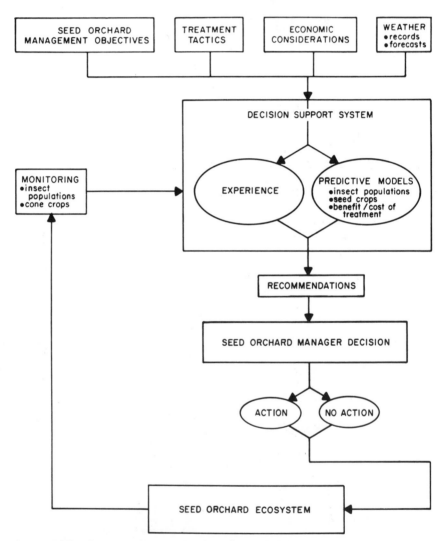

Figure 14.28 Diagrammatic representation of a seed orchard pest management system. (From Cameron 1981.)

Large fruit and cone crops preferentially mobilize and utilize an abundance of nutrients and photosynthate, which reduces cambial, shoot, root, and leaf growth. Mattson (1978) points out that cone insects can substantially reduce the amount of nutrients and photosynthates that are allocated to reproductive structures because they kill buds, conelets, and cones early in their development before such structures utilize large stores of energy and nutrients.

IPM IN SEED ORCHARDS

Because of the high value placed on genetically improved seed and the continually increasing demand for this seed, insect pests in seed orchards are particularly important. Integrated pest management practices in seed orchards are more like the practices used in traditional agriculture than for other forest properties. For example, seed orchards are routinely mowed, fertilized, subsoiled, pruned, and treated with insecticides.

Conceptually the principles of IPM outlined in Chapter 5 apply to seed orchards as well as forest ecosystems. Cameron (1981) defined a system structure for seed orchard IPM (Figure 14.28) that contains the same elements as defined in Figure 5.8 (Chapter 5). Operationally, the main dif-

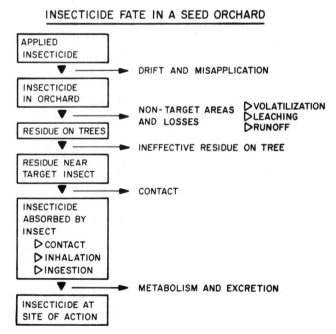

Figure 14.29   Fate of insecticides in seed orchards relative to the target insects. (From DeBarr 1981.)

ference between seed orchard and forest ecosystem IPM, at present, is the heavy dependence on the use of pesticides in seed orchards. This use is easily justified from an economic standpoint because of the value of the resource being protected.

Since one of the goals of seed orchard management is to produce a consistent and high seed yield, we create a condition where insect populations can flourish, because of abundant food supplies. Therefore, intensive remedial suppression tactics are required. The main developments in remedial tactics center on deployment of pesticides. Many seed orchards are now stocked with mature host trees, which presents a major problem in efficiently dispensing pesticides. Figure 14.29 illustrates the fate of insecticides in seed orchards relative to target pest species.

REFERENCES

Barras, S. J., and D. M. Norris. 1969. Bionomics of *Eucosma monitorana* (Lepidoptera: Tortricidae) attacking red pine cones in Wisconsin. *Ann. Entomol. Soc. Am.* **62**:1284–1290.

Brown, R. L. 1979. The valid generic and tribal names for the codling moth, *Cydia pomonella* (Olethreutinae: Tortricidae). *Ann. Entomol. Soc. Am.* **72**:565–567.

Brown, R. L. and W. E. Miller. 1983. Valid names of the spruce seed moth and a related *Cydia* species (Lepidoptera: Tortricidae). *Ann. Entomol. Soc. Am.* **72**:110–111.

Cameron, R. S. 1981. *Towards Insect Pest Management in Southern Pine Seed Orchards, with Emphasis on the Biology of Tetyra bipunctata (Hemiptera: Pentatomidae) and the Pheromone of Dioryctria clariorlas (Lepidoptera: Pyralidae)*. Texas Forest Service Publication 126.

Clark, E. C., J. A. Schenk, and D. L. Williamson. 1963. The cone-infesting moth *Barbara colfaxiana* as a pest of Douglas-fir in northern Idaho. *Ann. Entomol. Soc. Am.* **56**:246–250.

Coulson, R. N., and R. T. Franklin. 1970a. The biology of *Dioryctria amatella* (Lepidoptera: Phycitidae). *Can. Entomol.* **102**:679–684.

Coulson, R. N., and R. T. Franklin. 1970b. The occurrence of *Dioryctria amatella* and other insects in *Cronartium fusiforme* cankers. *Can. Entomol.* **102**:353–357.

DeBarr, G. L. 1967. Two new sucking insect pests of seed in southern pine seed orchards. U.S. Forest Service Research Note SE-78.

DeBarr, G. L. 1981. Seed orchard IPM. From presentation at the Southern Forest Insect Work Conference. August 19, 1980, Athens, Georgia.

DeBarr, G. L. and L. R. Barber. 1975. Mortality factors reducing the 1967–1969 slash pine seed crop in Baber Co. Fla.—a life table approach. U.S. Forest Research Paper SE-131.

DeBarr, G. L., and B. H. Ebel. 1974. Conelet abortion and seed damage of shortleaf and loblolly pines by a seed bug, *Leptoglossus corculus*. *For. Sci.* **20**:165–170.

Ebel, B. H. 1965. The *Dioryctria* coneworms of north Florida pines (Lepidoptera: Phycitidae). *Ann. Entomol. Soc. Am.* **58**:623–630.

Ebel, B. H., and H. O. Yates, III. 1973. Rearing and biological observations on a southern pine cone insect, *Eucosma cocana* Kearfott (Lepidoptera: Olethreutidae). *Ann. Entomol. Soc. Am.* **66**:88–92.

Ebel, B. H., and H. O. Yates, III. 1974. Insect-caused damage and mortality to conelets, cones, and seed of shortleaf pine. *J. Econ. Entomol.* **67**:222–226.

Ebel, B. H., T. H. Flavell, L. E. Drake, H. O. Yates III, and G. L. DeBarr. 1975. Seed and cone insects of southern pines. U.S. Forest Service, General Technical Report SE-8.

Furniss, R. L., and V. M. Carolin. 1977. *Western Forest Insects*. U.S. Forest Service, Miscellaneous Publication 1339.

Hard, J. S. 1964. The identification of primary red pine cone insects. U.S. Forest Service, Research Paper LS-12.

Hedlin, A. F. 1960. On the life history of the Douglas-fir cone moth, *Barbara colfaxiana* (Kft.) (Lepidoptera: Olethreutidae) and one of its parasites, *Glypta evetriae* Cush. (Hymenoptera: Ichneumonidae). *Can. Entomol.* **92**:826–834.

Hedlin, A. F. 1964. Results of a six year plot study on Douglas-fir cone insect population fluctuations. *For. Sci.* **10**:124–128.

Hedlin, A. F. 1973. Spruce cone insects in British Columbia and their control. *Can. Entomol.* **105**:113–122.

Hedlin, A. F. 1974. Cone and seed insects of British Columbia. Environment, Canada, Forest Service BC-X-90.

Hedlin, A. F., H. O. Yates III, D. Cibrian, B. H. Ebel, T. W. Koerber, and E. P. Merkel. 1980. Cone and Seed Insects of North American Conifers. Canada Forest Service, U.S. Forest Service, Section de Agricultura y Recurson Hidraulicus, Mexico.

Hussey, N. W. 1955. The life-histories of *Megastigmus spermotrophus* Wachtl (Hymenoptera: Chalcidoidea) and its principal parasite, with descriptions of the developmental stages. *Trans. Roy. Entomol. Soc. Lond.* **106**:133–151.

Keen, F. P. 1958. *Cone and Seed Insects of Western Forest Trees*. U.S. Forest Service, Technical Bulletin 1169.

Kinzer, H. G., B. J. Ridgill, and J. G. Watts. 1972. *Seed and Cone Insects of Ponderosa Pine*. New Mexico State University Agriculture Experiment Station Bulletin 594.

Koerber, T. W. 1963. *Leptoglossus occidentalis* (Hemiptera: Coreidae), a newly discovered pest of coniferous seed. *Ann. Entomol. Soc. Am.* **56**:229–234.

Krugman, S. L., and T. W. Koerber. 1969. Effect of cone feeding by *Leptoglossus occidentalis* on ponderosa pine seed development. *For. Sci.* **15**:104–111.

Lyons, L. A. 1956. Insects affecting seed production in red pine. I. *Conophthorus resinosae* Hopk. (Coleoptera: Scolytidae). *Can. Entomol.* **88**:599–608.

Lyons, L. A. 1957a. Insects affecting seed production in red pine. II. *Dioryctria disclusa* Heinrich, *D. abietella* (D. & S.), and *D. cambiicola* (Dyar) (Lepidoptera: Phycitidae). *Can. Entomol.* **89**:70–79.

Lyons, L. A. 1957b. Insects affecting seed production in red pine. III. *Eucosma monitorana* Heinrich, *Laspeyresia toreuta* Grote (Lepidoptera: Olethreutidae), *Rubsaamenia* sp. (Diptera: Cecidomyiidae), and other insects. *Can. Entomol.* **89**:150–164.

Lyons, L. A. 1957c. Insects affecting seed production in red pine. IV. Recognition and extent of damage to cones. *Can. Entomol.* **89**:264–271.

Mattson, W. J., Jr. 1971. Relationship between cone crop size and cone damage by insects in red pine seed-production areas. *Can. Entomol.* **103**:617–621.

Mattson, W. J., Jr. 1978. The role of insects in the dynamics of cone production of red pine. *Oecologia* **33**:327–349.

Mattson, W. J., Jr. 1980. Cone resources and the ecology of the red pine cone beetle, *Conophthorus resinosae*. *Ann. Entomol. Soc. Am.* **73**:390–396.

Merkel, E. P. 1967. Life history of the slash pine seedworm, *Laspeyresia anaranjada* Miller (Lepidoptera: Olethreutidae). *Fla. Entomol.* **50**:141–149.

Miller, J. M. 1914. *Insect Damage to the Cones and Seeds of Pacific Coast Conifers*. U.S. Department of Agriculture, Bulletin 95.

Nebeker, T. E. 1977. A partial life table for the Douglas-fir cone moth, *Barbara colfaxiana* (Lepidoptera: Olethreutidae). *Can. Entomol.* **109**:943–951.

Neunzig, H. H., E. D. Cashatt, and G. A. Matuza. 1964. Observations on the biology of four species of *Dioryctria* in North Carolina (Lepidoptera: Phycitidae). *Ann. Entomol. Soc. Am.* **57**:317–321.

Powell, J. A. 1968. Host associations and taxonomy of Nearctic conifer cone moths in the genus *Eucosma* (Lepidoptera: Tortricidae). *Hilgardia* **39**:1–36.

Yates, H. O. III and B. H. Ebel. 1978. Impact of insect damage on loblolly pine seed production. *J. Econ. Entomol.* **71**:345–349.

15 | PHLOEM BORING INSECTS

INTRODUCTION

Insects placed in the phloem boring feeding group utilize the phloem or inner bark region of the host for food and habitat during a portion of the life cycle. Both coniferous and hardwood species are infested. The phloem borers have representatives in three principal insect orders: Coleoptera, Lepidoptera, and Diptera. The most notorious species occur in the Coleoptera, which includes the families Scolytidae (bark beetles), Buprestidae (flatheaded borers), and Cerambycidae (roundheaded borers). Within these three families, the largest number of pest species occur in the Scolytidae. Indeed, this family contains several species that are considered to be among the most serious pests in forest ecosystems and urban forests. The Scolytidae are of particular importance to forest management as some species are capable of killing their hosts, which are usually mature trees. The Cerambycidae and Buprestidae are often found in association with Scolytidae and generally do not kill their hosts. Phloem borers in the Lepidoptera and Diptera rarely kill their hosts and are of lesser importance than the Coleoptera.

In this chapter we consider representative species of phloem boring insects in the Coleoptera, Lepidoptera, and Diptera. Major emphasis is placed on the Coleoptera and, in particular, the Scolytidae, because these insects are often disruptive to forest management practice. Common phloem borers in the Lepidoptera and Diptera are also considered.

BARK BEETLES (COLEOPTERA: SCOLYTIDAE)

The Scolytidae contains over 500 North American species. The family is often divided into two feeding groups: the ambrosia beetles, which are wood borers, and the bark beetles, which are phloem feeders. In this section we will consider several pest species of bark beetles. In particular, we will focus on representative species in the genera *Dendroctonus*, *Ips*, and *Scolytus*. Several species in these genera are among the most thoroughly studied forest insects.

The literature on bark beetles is extensive. There are a number of comprehensive reviews that treat various aspects of beetle behavior, ecology, and pest management, for example, Miller and Keen (1960), Rudinsky (1962), Stark and Dahlsten (1972), Borden (1974), Baumgartner (1975), Beaver (1977), Berryman et al. (1978), Coulson (1979), Cole and Amman (1980), Stephen et al. (1980), Thatcher et al. (1980), Mitton and Sturgeon (1982) and Amman and Cole (1983). The systematic arrangement of Scolytidae has been thoroughly revised by Wood (1982).

Natural History of Bark Beetles

Although there is great variation in the natural history of *Dendroctonus*, *Ips*, and *Scolytus* bark beetles, there are a number of generalizations that can be made about the three genera. Before examining representative species, we consider the following subjects: insect appearance and recognition, life cycle, hosts, and ecological roles in forests.

Insect Appearance and Recognition

Bark beetles have a characteristic appearance (Figure 15.1). The adults are hard-bodied, moderately elongate, cylindrical beetles. They are brown (callow) or black and range in size from 1.0 to 9.0 mm, but most species are only 1.0–3.0 mm in length. The antennae are geniculate (elbowed) and contain an elongate basal segment (scape), connected to a series of short segments (funicle), that attach to a distinct club (Figure 15.2). The elytra cover the abdomen and provide a useful characteristic for separating a number of common pest species. In some cases the distal end of the elytra (called the *elytral declivity*) is convex and in other cases concave with a distinct number of spines (Figure 15.3).

Because of their minute size, identification of bark beetles by use of morphological characteristics is a difficult task. However, it is possible to recognize most of the pest species by assembling several pieces of supportive evidence. For example, adult beetles excavate characteristic tunnels, termed *egg galleries*, in the phloem. Some species etch the xylem in the process of constructing their galleries. These species are termed *engravers*. Furthermore, the major pest species have distinct geographic ranges as well as preferred hosts. Therefore, it is possible to examine adult insects for gross

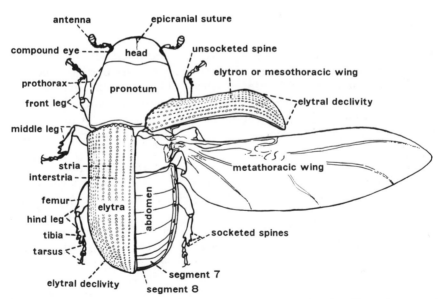

Figure 15.1 Dorsal view of the red turpentine beetle, *Dendroctonus valens*, illustrating general morphology of bark beetles. (From Mitten and Sturgeon 1982, courtesy of M. W. Stock; modified from Hopkins 1909.)

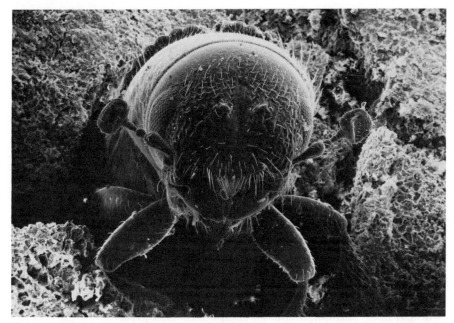

Figure 15.2 Frontal view of the southern pine beetle, *Dendroctonus frontalis*. Note structure of characteristic club-shaped antennae. (Courtesy of T. L. Payne.)

morphological characteristics (including size), the pattern of the galleries, the hosts infested, and the locality and determine with reasonable confidence the identity of the major pest species. This procedure is also useful for determining the identity of eggs, larvae, and pupae, which even taxonomic specialists cannot identify to the species level using morphological characteristics.

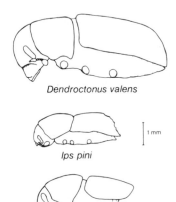

Dendroctonus valens

Ips pini

1 mm

Scolytus ventralis

Figure 15.3 Lateral view of common bark beetles illustrating variation in size and general morphology. Note the shape of the abdomen and elytra. (From Mitten and Sturgeon 1982, courtesy of M. W. Stock.)

Life Cycle

The life cycle for bark beetles can be divided into three general stages: (1) host selection and colonization, (2) brood development, and (3) dispersal. Details of the life cycle vary for each species.

Host Selection and Colonization

The life cycle begins with a small number of adult beetles locating a host tree. Initial discovery is termed *primary host selection*. The exact mechanism involved in initial host selection is unknown but may involve perception of the host by visual or olfactory means, random searching, or a combination of the two tactics. Once a host is selected, the adult beetles produce pheromones, which, in some cases, blend with host-produced volatile compounds, and results in attraction of large numbers of additional adults. In some cases, the females initiate the attack (e.g., *Dendroctonus* spp.) and in other cases it is the males that attack first (e.g., *Ips* spp.). This stage of colonization, that is, the response of adults to pheromones (and host-produced attractants), is termed *secondary host selection*. The population density of attacking adults arriving on the host is regulated in some species by production of additional volatile compounds that act to mask the pheromones and host attractants. These compounds are often termed *antiaggregation pheromones* or *inhibitors*. Many other insect species are capable of perceiving pheromones produced by the bark beetle. The term *kairomone* refers to a secretion from one species that is adaptively advantageous to another species, as in the case of a predator responding to the pheromone of its prey. Many of the parasites, predators, and other insect associates found with bark beetles have been demonstrated to perceive and respond to kairmones (Bordon 1974, 1982, Birch 1978, Wood 1982).

Once the adults arrive at the host, one of the sexes initiates entry through the bark into the phloem region and begins to excavate a gallery. The opposite sex enters the gallery later. Mating may take place in the gallery or in a cavity termed a *nuptial chamber*. Some bark beetles are monogamous (have only one mate, e.g., *Dendroctonus* spp.), whereas others are polygamous (have more than one mate, e.g., *Ips* spp.). Females excavate *egg galleries* that are characteristic for a particular species (see Figures 15.6, 15.7, 15.9, 15.11, 15.13, 15.16, 15.19, 15.23, 15.24, and 15.25). Eggs are oviposited in *niches* along the lateral walls of the gallery in most species. However, two species of *Dendroctonus* excavate chambers in the phloem and oviposit around the periphery of the chamber. Egg density within the host can be regulated by the attacking adult population in some species. At high adult density each female oviposits fewer eggs than at low density. This density-dependent regulation of oviposition is a survival mechanism that prevents over population of a particular host that would result in mortality to developing brood stages because of depletion of food and habitat. Beetles within the host communicate using auditory signals produced by stridulation (Barr 1969 and numerous references in Rudinsky's works, e.g., Rudinsky and Michael 1972, 1973).

Adult bark beetles carry with them a number of microorganisms, including fungi, yeasts, and bacteria. Some species have specialized structures, called *mycangia*, which are receptacles in the insect cuticle used especially for the transport of microorganisms. Attacking adults innoculate the host with the microorganisms. Certain fungi, particularly the blue-staining *Ceratocystis* and *Europhium* species, are extremely important in killing the host tree and perhaps in providing nutrition to later developmental stages. The symbiotic relationship between bark beetles and fungi is obligatory; that is, neither organism can survive without the other (see Whitney 1982 for a thorough review of the relationships between bark beetles and symbiotic microorganisms).

The final stage in the host selection–colonization process involves the fate of the attacking adult population. In some cases the adults die in the gallery. However, in other species the adults leave the host, a process called *reemergence*, and are capable of colonizing additional trees. These reemerging insects can perceive pheromones, produce pheromones once they reach a new host, and can produce viable eggs in the new host.

It is not uncommon for several species of bark beetles to inhabit the same host. Each species has a unique pheromone communication system and pattern of attack. Generally, the host tree is partitioned in the sense that a particular species will occupy or utilize a limited part of the host, for example, specific regions of the bole or the crown.

Brood Development

Following oviposition, the eggs hatch and first instar larvae mine at a right angle away from the egg gallery. Most bark beetles have three or four larval instars (Figure 15.4). In some cases all instars remain in the phloem region throughout development, whereas in other species the later instar larvae migrate into the outer bark (Figure 15.5). Pupation takes place in a small cell located at the end of the larval gallery. The pupae transform into callow or teneral adults. The brood adult bores a hole from the pupal chamber through the outer bark to emerge. This process is termed *emergence*. Feeding by the adults prior to emergence is termed *maturation feeding* and is required for the insect to obtain physiological maturity.

During brood development within the host many events involving a large number of other organisms are taking place. There are many species of insects and mites that have been associated with bark beetle-infested trees, as well as a number of different microorganisms. Bark beetles characteristically have a rich fauna of parasites and predators. Many of the associated organisms simply use the infested tree for habitat and food and are not directly involved in the development of the bark beetle. Other species, such as the buprestid and cerambycid phloem borers utilize the inner bark for larval development and are competitors with the bark beetles. Typically,

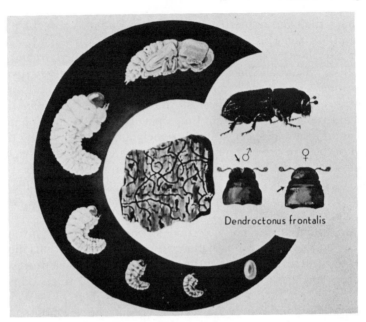

Figure 15.4 Life cycle of the southern pine beetle, *Dendroctonus frontalis*, illustrating the general pattern for bark beetles. (Modified from poster prepared by the Boyce Thompson Institute for Plant Research.)

80 to 98% of the initial brood established at oviposition will perish before emergence as a result of parasitization, predation, competition, disease, genetic defects, or weather-related disasters (see Dahlsten 1982 for a review of the relationships of bark beetles and their natural enemies).

Dispersal

Once the bark beetle emerges it must find another suitable host. Dispersal time is usually considered as the interval between leaving one host and successfully entering another. During this interval the beetles are in a particularly hazardous position. A large number of beetles perish as a result of not being able to locate a suitable host, predation, weather-related disasters (e.g., storms, high winds, etc.), and host resistance to attack.

Dispersal can be considered as a short-range or long-range phenomenon. In the case of the short-range circumstance, suitable hosts occur in the vicinity of the tree from which the beetles emerged. The process of secondary host selection, in response to pheromones and host attractants, guides dispersal. In the case of long-range dispersal, where suitable host trees are not available nearby, the mechanism of dispersal is unknown. Perception of volatile compounds over large distances does not appear to be an adequate explanation (Fares et al. 1980). However, there is little question that bark beetles do have the capacity to disperse over large dis-

Figure 15.5 Radiograph of bark containing late brood stages of the southern pine beetle, *Dendroctonus frontalis.* (U.S. Forest Service photograph.)

tances, successfully locate suitable host trees, and assemble a population large enough to colonize new hosts.

Generation time for bark beetles is usually calculated as the interval between production of adults in one generation to production of adults in the next generation. Therefore, generation time includes the period when the insect is in the host as well as the period of time involved in dispersal. Bark beetles spend, by far, the largest amount of time in the host. Dispersal time represents only a small fraction of the generation time. Most bark beetles have one or two generations per year. The most notable exception being the southern pine beetle, *Dendroctonus frontalis* Zimmermann, which can produce six to eight generations per year.

Hosts and Host Condition

Bark beetles infest both hardwood and coniferous hosts. By far the largest number of pest species are associated with commercially valuable species of pine, fir, and spruce. All bark beetles utilize their host as a habitat and food source. Therefore, variations in the condition of the host, such as tree size, tree age, bark thickness, phloem thickness, and resin production capacity, have an important influence on survival of a particular species. It is possible to classify bark beetles, in a general sense, according to their preference for a particular type of host condition. For example, the *Dendroctonus* bark beetles are often termed "aggressive" or "tree killing" species because they prefer living trees as hosts. Indeed, most *Dendroctonus* species require living hosts at the time of colonization if a brood is to develop successfully. The *Ips* bark beetles, by contrast, generally prefer hosts that have been recently killed or severely damaged. Therefore, trees damaged by wind or ice, logging slash, or freshly cut trees are colonized by the *Ips* species. Some species of bark beetles prefer dead hosts that are in early stages of deterioration, for example, some *Scolytus* species.

The condition of the host tree at the time of colonization can affect population dynamics of the bark beetle in two ways. First, if the tree is alive, the beetle must overcome host defenses (see Chapter 7). Most plants have defensive mechanisms that deter feeding by some groups of insects. In the case of pines, for example, the resin system is the primary defense against bark beetle colonization. When a bark beetle bores into the tree, resin exudes from the wound and in some cases prevents entry of the beetle into the host. The resin also can prevent establishment of fungal spores, which we indicated earlier are involved in tree death following bark beetle attack. Tree species and individual trees differ in their ability to resist colonization by bark beetles. The term *susceptibility* is used to describe the degree to which a tree can resist attack by a bark beetle (Cates and Alexander 1982). Any factor that affects the primary defense system of a host will increase susceptibility. For example, the following factors have been associated with increased susceptibility to bark beetle attack: tree senescence, flooding, drought, rootlet pathogens, air pollution, cultural damage to the tree, and so on. Vigorously growing trees, by contrast, are not as susceptible to bark beetle attack as the physiologically weakened trees. From the standpoint of beetle population dynamics, the insect must overcome tree resistance mechanisms in order to colonize the host (Berryman 1972). Failure to do so results in mortality to the insect (and survival of the host). The second way the host can affect populations of bark beetles is through *suitability* of the habitat for beetle development. The suitability of a particular host is determined by a number of factors, including bark thickness, phloem thickness, and nutritional quality.

Host susceptibility to colonization and suitability for brood development play major roles in the population dynamics of bark beetles. These factors operate in individual trees, but their effects on population are seen at the stand level of organization. Certain characteristics such as tree species composition, age, density, and soil type can be used as general indicators of stand vigor and, hence, host susceptibility and suitability. It has, therefore, been possible to classify stands according to their probable risk or hazard to bark beetle outbreaks (Coulson 1979, Hedden et al. 1981, Lorio 1980, Ferrell 1980, Moore et al. 1978).

Ecological Roles of Bark Beetles

Most bark beetles, particularly those considered as pest species, infest mature or senescent hosts or trees that are severely weakened or damaged. Given these circumstances, the primary role ascribed to bark beetles is in preparing the way for ecological succession in forests by selectively cropping certain age–classes of hosts (Amman 1977, Peterman 1978, Schowalter et al. 1981). Amman (1977) has suggested that the distribution of hosts can be regulated in certain parts of their natural range by the occurrence of bark beetles. The recycling of trees, through insect- and fungi-induced deterioration, releases bound nutrients (therefore serving as a type of forest fertilization), and changes plant competitive relationships by altering nutrient availability, light, and microclimates (Schowalter 1981).

It should be recognized that the occurrence of bark beetles in commercial forests constitutes a serious problem in forest management. In general, the infested hosts are of merchantable size and often are of greatest economic value (relative to other size–classes). Bark beetle outbreaks, therefore, are often disruptive to our planned use of forests. In the absence of forest management practices directed to wood and fiber production, bark beetle outbreaks are a major component of the process of ecological succession.

Dendroctonus Bark Beetles

The genus *Dendroctonus* is widely distributed throughout North America, Mexico, and Central America. All species infest coniferous hosts, with the most serious impact occurring on commercially valuable pines, spruces, firs, and Douglas-fir. Outbreaks of *Dendroctonus* bark beetles periodically cause great economic damage to forests. For this reason several species have been studied in considerable detail. Seven bark beetles are covered: southern pine beetle, *D. frontalis* Zimmermann; western pine beetle, *D. brevicomis* LeConte; mountain pine beetle, *D. ponderosae* Hopkins; spruce beetle, *D. rufipennis* (Kirby); Douglas-fir beetle, *D. pseudotsugae* Hopkins; black turpentine beetle, *D. terebrans* (Olivier); and red turpentine beetle, *D. valens* LeConte.

As the various species of *Dendroctonus* cannot be easily identified by nonspecialists, we will not provide detailed morphological characters to separate individual species. The general characteristics for adults in the genus are as follows: length, 3–8 mm; body, stout to elongate; elytral declivity, convex; antennae, geniculate; color, brown to black (Figure 15.1). Each species has a characteristic egg gallery pattern along with preferred host trees and geographic range. The student interested in the taxonomy of *Dendroctonus* bark beetles can refer to Wood (1963, 1982).

The *Dendroctonus* bark beetles colonize living hosts and must kill the tree, or a portion of it, if a brood is to develop. Colonization activity can be easily detected. When adults enter the host, fine boring dust is extruded and accumulates around the base of the tree, on the leaves of understory vegetation, and in spider webs. In host species that produce resin, a characteristic accumulation of resin, termed a *pitch tube*, accumulates at the beetle entrance hole. Once a host has been successfully colonized, the crown of the tree begins to discolor. The crown will gradually change from green to light brown ("fader") to red ("red top"), and finally the needles will drop to the ground. The rate of coloration change varies with season of the year, geographic location, and tree species. This characteristic crown coloration change is exploited by survey entomologists in that it is easily detected from aircraft and, therefore, can be used to identify the location and estimate the approximate size of infestations (based on the number of dead trees visible).

Although *Dendroctonus* bark beetles kill their hosts, the trees are not immediately rendered useless for the manufacture of wood products and pulp. The rate of tree deterioration following colonization varies according to when the tree was killed (season of the year) and geographic location. In the South trees may deteriorate beyond merchantability in as few as 3 months, whereas in the West the trees may be usable for 1–2 years after colonization. Although salvaging infested trees may be possible, in virtually all cases, the normal or planned harvest schedule is disrupted by bark beetle infestation.

Southern Pine Beetle, *Dendroctonus frontalis* Zimmermann

The southern pine beetle is the most important bark beetle pest in the southern United States. Literature on the southern pine beetle has been comprehensively reviewed and interpreted in Thatcher et al. (1980). Population dynamics of the insect has been treated by Coulson et al. (1979, 1980) and Stephen et al. (1980). Various procedures used in management of the pest are discussed in Coster and Searcy (1979). In addition, there are several U.S. Forest Service handbooks that were published during 1979–1982 that cover a variety of subjects ranging from damage recognition to identification of natural enemies.

In North America the southern pine beetle is distributed primarily through the southern states, with the range extending from Delaware south to Florida and west to Texas. The insect is capable of infesting all species of pine indigenous to this area but is considered to be a primary pest in loblolly, shortleaf, and slash pine. Longleaf pine is generally resistant to southern pine beetle colonization, presumably because of its high resin production capacity.

The southern pine beetle is the smallest of the pest species of *Dendroctonus*. It is 2–4 mm in length (average = 3.0 mm) and brownish to black in color. The head is broad and prominent, with median elevations that form a distinct frontal groove. The egg gallery pattern produced by the female is serpentine or "S" shaped (Figure 15.6). The insect normally infests the open bole of the tree from the base to the crown.

The life cycle of the insect follows the general pattern described earlier (Figure 15.4). Payne (1980) provides a detailed account of the life cycle.

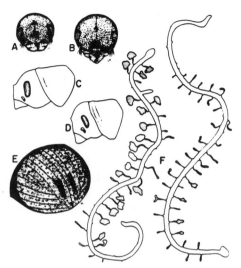

Figure 15.6 Egg gallery pattern and distinctive morphological characters of the southern pine beetle, *Dendroctonus frontalis:* A = female head, B = male head, C = male head and pronotum, D = female head and pronotum, E = elytral declivity, F = egg galleries. (Modified from Wood 1982, courtesy of S. L. Wood.)

The essential elements are as follows. After primary host selection, a tree is "mass attacked" by adults responding to pheromones and host attractants. Females initiate colonization and are followed by males. During colonization the tree is inoculated with microorganisms, principally blue-staining fungi, which aid in killing the host tree and in initiating the gradual degradation of the host. Mating takes place in the gallery excavated in the phloem. Each gallery (i.e., egg gallery) normally contains one pair of adults, termed a *mating pair*. The female continues to excavate the gallery and oviposits along both lateral walls of the gallery. Eggs are deposited singly in discrete cavities called *niches*. Once oviposition is completed, both males and females leave the host, a process called *reemergence*, and are capable of colonizing a new host. Eggs hatch and four larval instars follow. Larvae excavate the galleries, *larval galleries*, at a right angle away from the egg gallery. The larval galleries become progressively larger as the larvae mature. The first two larval instars remain in the phloem area, and the third instar migrates to the outer bark. The fourth instar larva pupates in the outer bark. The pupa transforms into a callow or teneral adult that bores to the outside and emerges. During summer months development is rapid, and there can be six to eight generations per year. Development often continues throughout winter months during periods of warm weather.

Southern pine beetle infestations have a pattern of development that is unique among bark beetles. The infestations develop continuously by the addition of newly colonized trees over a period ranging from weeks to several months. This pattern results because of the short development time and the common occurrence of the process of reemergence. Emerging adults and reemerging adults are often present at the same time, which provides a large population to colonize new hosts (Coulson 1979).

Periodic outbreaks of the southern pine beetle have been reported since the late 1800s. A number of factors contribute to the occurrence of outbreaks. In general, loblolly and shortleaf pines are most severely affected. The outbreaks typically occur in mature and overmature stands on lowland sites with poor drainage characteristics. The stands characteristically have high basal areas and exhibit poor growth rate, as indicated by radial increment of the trees. Stands with these characteristics are classified as having high hazard for beetle outbreaks. When beetle populations are present and favorable weather conditions prevail, these stands support rapid buildup of populations to epidemic proportions. During epidemics all host pines (saplings to mature trees) will be infested and killed. The term "spot" is often used to describe a local infestation. An epidemic is characterized by the presence of many spots distributed throughout a forest in a pattern that reflects centers of high stand susceptibility.

Western Pine Beetle *Dendroctonus brevicomis* LeConte

The western pine beetle is similar to the southern pine beetle in appearance, natural history, and destructiveness. Literature on the insect has been reviewed by Miller and Keen (1960), Stark and Dahlsten (1970), and Wood (1980).

The western pine beetle is distributed throughout the western United States and into southwestern Canada. The insect is a primary pest of ponderosa pine but infests Coulter pine as well.

The western pine beetle is similar in appearance to the southern pine beetle but can be distinguished by its larger size (2.5–5.0 mm, average 4.0

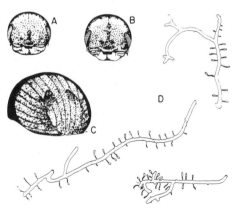

Figure 15.7 Egg gallery pattern and distinctive morphological characters for the western pine beetle, *Dendroctonus brevicomis:* A = male head, B = female head, C = elytral declivity, D = egg galleries. (Modified from Wood 1982, courtesy of S. L. Wood.)

mm), geographic location, and hosts infested. The egg gallery patterns for the two species are quite similar (Figure 15.7).

The life cycle of the western pine beetle follows the general pattern described earlier (Figure 15.8). Unique features are provided in Stark and Dahlsten (1970). Females initiate attack by boring through the bark to the

Figure 15.8 Life cycle of the western pine beetle, *Dendroctonus brevicomis:* A = adult, B = pitch tube, C = larva, D = pupa. (Courtesy of C. J. DeMars.)

phloem. The female begins excavation of a winding S-shaped gallery. The male joins the female in this gallery, where mating takes place. Pitch tubes, consisting of resin mixed with frass, form at the entrance hole. Mass colonization of the host is guided by pheromones and host-produced attractants (Wood 1972). The host is innoculated with microorganisms, primarily blue staining fungi. After mating, the female oviposits in niches cut in the lateral walls of the egg gallery. The males may remain in the gallery or exit (reemerge). After the eggs hatch, the larvae feed at right angles to the main egg gallery. Late instar larvae migrate from the phloem region into the outer bark where pupation takes place in a cell. Adults emerge by boring through the outer bark to the surface of the host.

The developmental rate of the western pine beetle is considerably slower than that of the southern pine beetle, because of the cooler climate characteristic of the range of the insect. There are 1.5–4 generations per year. Western pine beetles colonize the open bole of the hosts. However, it is not uncommon to observe only a portion of the bole colonized (e.g., the middle one-third), or for a patch on one side of a tree (termed a *patch kill*) to be infested.

Outbreaks of the western pine beetle have been associated with factors that contribute to poor tree vigor (and hence stand vigor). Mature and overmature stands of high basal area exposed to rootlet pathogens, air pollution, cultural damage, water stress, and so on are considered to be of high hazard for beetle outbreaks.

Mountain Pine Beetle, *Dendroctonus ponderosae* Hopkins

The mountain pine beetle is the most destructive western bark beetle species. For this reason, the insect has been studied in great detail and there is a wealth of available information on population dynamics, behavior, pest management, and other topics. Literature on the insect has been reviewed and summarized by Safranyik et al. (1974, 1975), Baumgartner (1975), Berryman et al. (1978), Berryman (1976), Amman (1977), Cole et al. (1976), Cole and Amman (1980), and Amman and Cole (1983).

The mountain pine beetle is distributed throughout the western United States from the Pacific Coast eastward through the Black Hills of South Dakota and from northern British Columbia and Western Alberta southward to northwestern Mexico. Its habitat ranges in altitude from 1600 m in the northern latitudes to 3350 m in southern California. The insect has four major host species: lodgepole, ponderosa, sugar, and western white pines. Lodgepole pine is generally considered to be the primary host (McCambridge et al. 1979).

Adult mountain pine beetles are 3.7–7.5 mm (average 5.5 mm) in length, 2.3 times as long as wide, and black in color. The egg galleries are vertical (to the long axis of the tree), have a slight hook at the bottom, and are packed with borings except for the terminal few centimeters (Figure 15.9). This gallery pattern, hosts infested, and geographic distribution are ade-

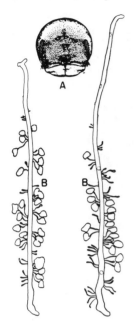

Figure 15.9   Egg gallery pattern and distinctive morphological characters for the mountain pine beetle, *Dendroctonus ponderosae:* A = female head, B = egg galleries. (Modified from Wood 1982, courtesy of S. L. Wood.)

quate characteristics for separating the mountain pine beetle from other western species.

The life cycle of the mountain pine beetle begins in midsummer, with adults colonizing host pines (Figure 15.10). Females initiate attack by boring through the bark to the phloem, where they begin construction of egg galleries. A male joins the female once the gallery is successfully started. Again, colonization is guided by pheromones and host attractants, and there are characteristic "pitch tubes" associated with attacked trees. Adult beetles inoculate the host with microorganisms (blue staining fungi) that aid in killing the host. Mating takes place in the gallery. Following mating the male may exit the host, that is, reemerge, or stay in the gallery. The female continues excavation of the vertical egg gallery and oviposits in niches along the lateral walls. Eggs hatch and the larvae mine horizontally away from the egg gallery. There are four larval instars. When fully grown, the larvae excavate oval cells in which they transform into pupae. Unlike the southern pine beetle and western pine beetle, all development takes place in the phloem region; that is, the larvae do not migrate to the outer bark. The pupae transform into adults, which feed before tunneling to the surface of the host to emerge. There is usually one generation per year, but at high elevations or more northern latitudes 2 years may be required for development.

The various conditions that contribute to development of outbreaks of the mountain pine beetle have been studied in great detail. During endemic periods, that is, periods when beetle populations are small and tree mor-

Figure 15.10   Life cycle of the mountain pine beetle, *Dendroctonus ponderosae:* (A) = egg, (B) = larva, (C) = pupa, (D) = adult. (U.S. Forest Service photograph.)

tality low, beetles infest weakened and injured trees and those hosts colonized by other species of bark beetles. Epidemics of mountain pine beetle, that is, large populations of the beetle and high tree mortality, occur in stands that have certain characteristics that are conducive for beetle reproduction and survival. The most prominent stand characteristics are as follows: (1) trees more than 80 years old, (2) average diameter more than 20 cm, (3) a substantial number of trees in the stand with diameter at breast height of 30 cm or more and phloem 0.25 cm thick or more, and (4) stand site at an elevation where temperatures are optimum for brood development (Amman 1978, Safranyik 1978, Safranyik et al. 1974, Cole and Amman 1980). Tree mortality in stands can occur as scattered individual trees, but more often entire groups of trees are killed. These groups expand with succeeding beetle generations, and eventually tree mortality may be extensive over large areas.

Douglas-Fir Beetle, *Dendroctonus pseudotsugae* Hopkins

The Douglas-fir beetle is the primary pest species of Douglas-fir throughout its range in western North America. The insect also infests western larch but is rarely a pest in this species.

Adult Douglas-fir beetles are dark brown to black with reddish elytra. The insect ranges in size from 4.4 to 7.0 mm (average = 5.5 mm). The egg galleries are excavated vertically (to the long axis of the tree) and are straight to slightly S shaped (Figure 15.11). Eggs are oviposited in grooves cut into lateral walls on alternate sides of the gallery. Each groove contains 5–12 eggs. These characteristics, along with the host information, are adequate for identification purposes.

The life history of the Douglas-fir beetle begins in the early summer (April to June), with adult beetles colonizing host trees (Figure 15.12). Females colonize the host first and initiate excavation of egg galleries. The females are joined later by males, and mating takes place in the gallery. Colonization is guided by pheromones and host attractants. Males are capable of reemerging to infest other hosts. Attacks by Douglas-fir beetles do not result in production of pitch tubes, characteristic of other *Dendroctonus* species discussed above. Red boring dust on the outside surface of the host provides evidence of attack. The adults inoculate the host with fungi. Females construct vertical galleries and excavate grooves in the lateral walls of the gallery, where they oviposit. The ensuing larvae mine horizontally away from the egg gallery. The larval galleries gradually increase in size as the larvae mature. There are four larval instars. The larvae do not migrate to the outer bark. Pupation occurs in a cell constructed by the last instar larva. The pupae transform into adults, which emerge by boring through the bark to the outside. There is only one generation per year (Furniss and Orr 1970, Furniss et al. 1979, Vité and Rudinsky 1957, Rudinsky 1966).

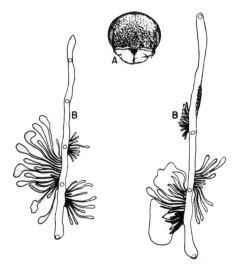

Figure 15.11 Egg gallery pattern and distinctive morphological characters for the Douglas-fir beetle, *Dendroctonus pseudotsugae:* A = male head, B = egg galleries. (Modified from Wood 1982, courtesy of S. L. Wood.)

Figure 15.12   Life history of the Douglas-fir beetle, *Dendroctonus pseudotsugae:* A = infestation, B = adult, C = eggs, D = larva, E = pupa, F = eggs in gallery, G = larval galleries. (U.S. Forest Service photograph.)

Douglas-fir beetles usually infest hosts that have been severely damaged, weakened, or diseased. The insect commonly occurs in trees felled by wind or snow. Under these conditions the insect occurs at endemic levels. When large volumes of timber are damaged, however, such as following a forest fire or wind or snow storm, populations can buildup to epidemic levels. Under these circumstances, living hosts can be infested and killed. The epidemics usually do not persist over long periods of time.

Spruce Beetle, *Dendroctonus rufipennis* (Kirby)

The spruce beetle is the most destructive insect pest of mature spruce. The insect is considered to be a pest of Englemann, Sitka, and white spruces. The distribution of the spruce beetle is transcontinental following the range of spruce forests throughout the western United States and Alaska, across the Canadian provinces, and into the northeastern United States.

The spruce beetle ranges in size from 4.5 to 7.0 mm (average = 5.5 mm) and is dark brown with reddish brown elytra. Old adults are uniformly black. The egg galleries are vertical (to the long axis of the tree) and straight (Figure 15.13).

The life cycle of the spruce beetle varies according to geographic location (Figure 15.14). In general, adults colonize hosts in midsummer. Females initiate attack by boring into the host and starting egg gallery construction. Males join the females, and mating takes place in the gallery. Colonization is guided by pheromones and host attractants. Adults inoculate the host with fungi. Attacking adults are capable of reemerging and colonizing additional hosts. The female elongates the egg gallery and oviposits along the lateral wall of the gallery. Eggs are placed in grooves cut into the wall. Early instar larvae mine as a group horizontally (to the long axis of the tree) away from the gallery. Later instar larvae construct individual larval galleries. This pattern of gallery construction by larvae results in a coalescence of galleries at the early stages of development. There are four larval instars. Pupation takes place in a chamber constructed by the last instar larva. Adults emerge by boring from the chamber to the outer surface of the host. The life cycle generally takes 2 years for completion. However, in warmer climates only 1 year may be required, whereas the life cycle may take 3 years in colder climates (Schmid and Beckwith 1975).

All recorded outbreaks by the spruce beetle have followed large-scale wind throw or large accumulations of artificially produced slash (Wygant and Lejeune 1967). The spruce beetle normally infests severely weakened

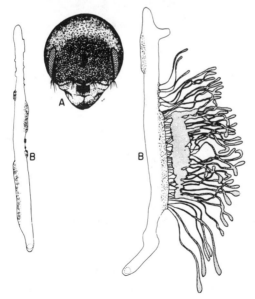

Figure 15.13 Egg gallery pattern and distinctive morphological characters for the spruce beetle, *Dendroctonus rufipennis:* A = female head, B = egg galleries. (Modified from Wood 1982, courtesy of S. L. Wood.)

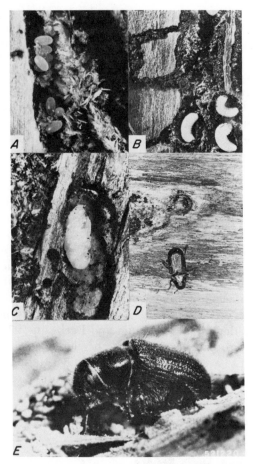

Figure 15.14 Life cycle of the spruce beetle, *Dendroctonus rufipennis:* A = eggs in gallery, B = larvae, C = pupa, D = adult, E = adult. (U.S. Forest Service photograph.)

or felled hosts. Under these circumstances populations persist at endemic levels. However, when there is a large accumulation of suitable host material, populations can increase to epidemic levels and standing trees are infested. Epidemic population levels normally do not persist for long periods of time (McCambridge and Knight 1972).

Black Turpentine Beetle, *Dendroctonus terebrans* (Olivier) and the Red Turpentine Beetle, *Dendroctonus valens* LeConte

The black turpentine beetle and red turpentine beetle are similar in appearance, natural history, and destructiveness. Both insects have a large geographic distribution and are among the more commonly observed forest insect pests. The black turpentine beetle ranges from 5.0 to 8.0 mm in length (average = 6.5 mm) and is dark brown to black in color (Figure

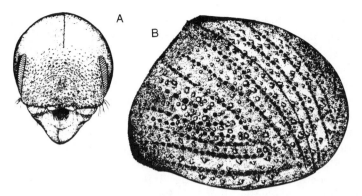

Figure 15.15 Distinctive morphological characters for the black turpentine beetle, *Dendroctonus terebrans:* A = female head, B = female declivity. (From Wood 1982, courtesy of S. L. Wood.)

15.15). The insect occurs throughout the eastern and southern United States, where it infests all species of pines. The red turpentine beetle is the largest of the *Dendroctonus* bark beetles and ranges in size from 5.4 to 9.0 mm (average = 8.0 mm). The adults are reddish brown in color (Figures 15.1 and 15.16). The insect has a wide distribution, occurring throughout

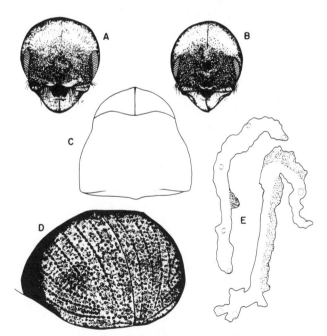

Figure 15.16 Egg gallery pattern and distinctive morphological characters for the red turpentine beetle, *Dendroctonus valens:* A = male head, B = female head, C = head and prontum, D = female declivity, E = egg galleries. The egg gallery pattern for the black turpentine beetle is the same. (From Wood 1982, courtesy of S. L. Wood.)

the western United States and Canadian provinces and eastward into the Great Lakes states and northeastern United States. The red turpentine beetle infests all species of pine within its range and occasionally spruce and larch. The two species can usually be distinguished by color, size, geographic distribution, and host infested.

The natural histories of the red and black turpentine beetles are quite similar. Colonization is initiated by the female and is usually restricted to the lower portion of the tree bole or root collar. The female initiates gallery construction and is joined by the male. Attacks by the adults produce large pitch tubes. Colonization is guided by pheromones and host attractants. The adults inoculate the host with fungi. It is not known whether the adults reemerge, but it is likely that they do. The female constructs a large vertical (to the long axis of the tree) egg gallery and oviposits in grooves cut into the lateral walls. Several eggs are placed in each groove. The early instar larvae feed gregariously away from the egg gallery, which results in the formation of a large cavity filled with resin and frass. Later instar larvae continue to enlarge the cavity and eventually excavate individual larval mines off the main chamber. Pupation takes place in a cell constructed by the last instar larva. Adults emerge by boring through the bark to the outside. For the brood to survive, the infested portion of the tree must die. Therefore, it is possible that the tree may survive attack, although it may be severely weakened and hence vulnerable to attack by other species of bark beetles. Depending on geographic location, there will be one to three generations per year.

Both species of turpentine beetles are attracted to freshly cut stumps, which are preferred breeding sites. It is not uncommon for large populations to build up following logging operations. Severely damaged or weakened trees are also readily colonized. When population levels are high, healthy standing trees are infested. The black turpentine beetle is occasionally a serious problem in gum naval stores production as the beetles are attracted to the wounds (faces) cut into the tree for turpentine extraction. The turpentine beetles are often found in conjunction with primary bark beetle species such as the southern pine beetle or western pine beetle.

Ips Engraver Beetles

There are about 25 North American species in the genus *Ips*. As with the *Dendroctonus* bark beetles, it is difficult (even for specialists) to identify with certainty the various species by using only morphological characters. In general, the adults are cylindrical in shape, usually dark brown to black in color, and range in length from 2.0 to 7.0 mm. The elytral declivity is concave. The lateral margins of the declivity each have three to six spines (Figure 15.17). These spines, along with the hosts infested, geographic location, and egg gallery pattern, are useful characteristics for identifying the important pest species. All species of *Ips* infest conifers, principally pine

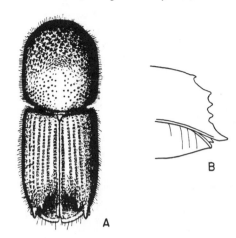

Figure 15.17 Pine engraver, *Ips pini:* A = adult, B = lateral view of the elytral declivity. (Modified from Wood 1982, courtesy of S. L. Wood.)

and spruce, but occassionally larch and fir. Furthermore, many of the pest species infest restricted areas of the host, including the crown, upper bole, and so on. The *Ips* bark beetles are often referred to as *engraver beetles* because the adults scar the outer surface of the xylem of the host when constructing galleries.

The *Ips* species are not usually considered to be primary pests as they rarely colonize and kill healthy trees. Severely weakened trees, felled trees, and logging slash are preferred breeding sites. Large populations can develop in stands where trees have been damaged by wind, ice, or snow storms. At high population levels, *Ips* bark beetles can colonize and kill healthy trees. *Ips* bark beetles are also commonly found in association with primary tree-killing *Dendroctonus* species. Under these circumstances, the *Dendroctonus* species may serve to condition the host for *Ips* colonization by overcoming tree resistance.

The life cycle of *Ips* bark beetles differs in several ways from the *Dendroctonus* species. Colonization is initiated by the male, which selects the host and bores through the bark to the phloem region. The male constructs a nuptial chamber and excavates rudimentary egg galleries. Once identified, a susceptible host is mass attacked by both males and females. Colonization is guided by production of insect pheromones and host attractants. The adults inoculate the hosts with blue-staining fungi and other microorganisms. *Ips* bark beetles are polygamous. Each male may service three to five females, which enter into the nuptial chamber. Mating takes place in the nuptial chamber. After mating, the female enters one of the prestarted egg galleries. The galleries are elongated in a vertical (to the long axis of the tree) direction and can develop toward the base or top of the host. The gallery patterns are often Y or H shaped with the nuptial chamber in the center, forming an axis (Figure 15.18). Eggs are oviposited singly along the lateral walls of the gallery in niches. When two galleries parallel one another, eggs often will be placed only on the outside of each gallery,

Figure 15.18   Gallery pattern for the pine engraver, *Ips pini*. The photograph illustrates the nuptial chamber, egg galleries, larval galleries, and pupal cells. (U.S. Forest Service photograph.)

thereby avoiding competition for space and food. Communication within the host is likely accomplished by using acoustic signals produced by stridulation. Although not documented for many species, it is likely that adults reemerge following oviposition. After the eggs hatch, the larvae mine away from the egg gallery. There are three or four larval instars. Larvae do not migrate into the outer bark. The last instar larvae construct a chamber in which pupation takes place. Adults emerge by boring through the outer bark. Most *Ips* species have one or two generations per year. Some species, that occur in regions with mild climates, may produce up to six generations per year.

Most of the *Ips* species have not been studied in as great a detail as the *Dendroctonus* species because they are not considered primary tree killing pests. Examples of several of the more important and widespread species are given in the following paragraphs.

Pine Engraver, *Ips pini* (Say)

The pine engraver is one of the most common and widely distributed bark beetles in North America. It occurs from South Carolina north to Maine and Quebec, westward across the northern United States and Canada to the interior of Alaska, and from there south through the Pacific Coast states and the Rocky Mountain region of northern Mexico. The insect infests a large number of species of pine and spruce. Because of the wide geographic range and the number of different hosts infested, the pine engraver has been known by several different scientific names (Lanier et al. 1972). The adults are brown to black, 3.5–4.5 mm in length, and there are four spines on each side of the declivity (Figure 15.17). The life cycle essentially follows the generalized biology described above, and the insect produces one to three generations per year (Figure 15.18). Damage caused by the pine engraver is associated with weakened host trees. Occasionally in-festations are restricted to crowns of mature trees, which produce *top-kills*. This type of damage often weakens the tree and may result in colonization by other species of bark beetles, which eventually kill the host (Sartwell et al. 1971).

California Fivespined Ips, *Ips paraconfusus* Lanier

The California fivespined ips is a common western species. It ranges from southern Oregon to southern California west of the summit of the Cascades and Sierra Nevada mountains and infests all species of pines within its range. The insect closely resembles the pinion ips, *Ips confusus* (LeConte), with which it was confused in the early literature. Adults are brown to black, range in size from 3.0 to 5.5 mm, and have five spines on each side of the elytral declivity (Figure 15.19). The life cycle follows the pattern described above, and there are one to five generations per year. The California fivespined ips generally infests weakened hosts in a range of size

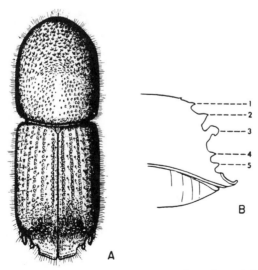

Figure 15.19 Adult California fivespined Ips, *Ips paraconfusus:* A = adult, B = lateral view of the elytral declivity. (Modified from Wood 1982, courtesy of S. L. Wood.)

classes, as do the other *Ips* species. It is also commonly associated with outbreaks of the western pine beetle.

Ips Species in the Southern United States

There are three common species of *Ips* found infesting pine in the southern United States: the small southern pine engraver, *Ips avulsus* (Eichhoff); the eastern fivespined ips, *Ips grandicollis* (Eichhoff); and the sixspined engraver, *Ips calligraphus* (Germar). Literature on the southern species of *Ips* has been identified by Wilkinson and Foltz (1980). These insects infest all species of pine in their range but are of particular importance in loblolly, shortleaf, and slash. The insects are often found infesting the same host and occur in trees colonized by the southern pine beetle. The small southern pine engraver, which is reddish brown to black in color, is the smallest of the eastern species of *Ips* (2.3–2.8 mm in length) (Figure 15.20). The elytral declivity contains four spines. This insect commonly infests the crown area of its host, although the upper portions of the bole are also utilized. The eastern fivespined ips is also reddish brown to black in color and ranges in size from 2.8 to 4.7 mm. It is intermediate in size relative to the other two species (Figure 15.21). The elytral declivity contains five spines on each side. This insect commonly infests the intermediate portions of the open bole of its host as well as large limbs in the crown. The sixspined engraver, which is also reddish-brown to black, is the largest of the southern *Ips* species, ranging in length from 3.5 to 6.5 mm (Figure 15.22). The elytral declivity contains six spines on each side. This species commonly infests the lower bole of the host. We have indicated that each of the three southern species of *Ips* selects a preferred section of the host for colonization and brood development. However, there is a great deal of overlap in the within-tree distributions. The southern species of *Ips* normally infest weakened hosts in a variety of size–classes (Figure 15.23). These insects are also commonly associated with outbreaks of the southern pine beetle. It is not uncommon to find all four species and the black turpentine beetle infesting the same host.

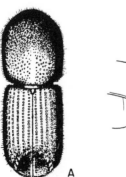

Figure 15.20 *Ips avulsus:* A = adult, B = lateral view of elytral declivity. (Modified from Wood 1982, courtesy of S. L. Wood.)

Figure 15.21 Adult *Ips grandicollis*. The elytral declivity for this insect is similar to that illustrated for *Ips paraconfusus* (Figure 15.19). (Modified from Wood 1982, courtesy of S. L. Wood.)

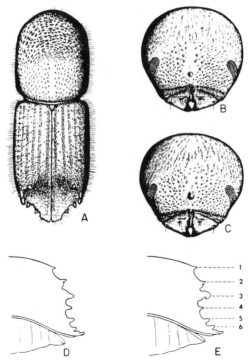

Figure 15.22 Adult *Ips calligraphus* and distinctive morphological characters: A = adult, B = female head, C = male head, D = female elytral declivity, E = male elytral declivity. (Modified from Wood 1982, courtesy of S. L. Wood.)

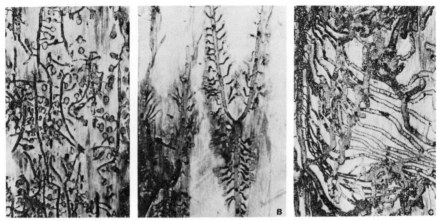

Figure 15.23   Egg gallery patterns: A = *Ips avulsus*, B = *Ips grandicollis*, C = *Ips calligraphus*.

Scolytus Bark Beetles

The genus *Scolytus* contains a large number of species that infest both coniferous and deciduous trees throughout North America. Members of the genus are short and thick bodied, brown to black in color, and 2–5 mm in length. The adults can be separated from other genera of bark beetles by inspecting the ventral surface of the abdomen, which ascends abruptly to the rear (i.e., is concave behind the thorax) (Figure 15.2). In some cases the elytral declivity is concave and contains spines. The outer edge of the fore tibia also contains a prominent spine. As with other genera, separation of species is difficult with the use of only morphological characters. Gallery pattern, hosts infested, and geographic distribution usually provide adequate evidence for general identification.

The generalized life cycle for *Scolytus* bark beetles differs from that of *Dendroctonus* and *Ips* in several ways. The female initiates colonization on the bole or larger limbs of the host and excavates a nuptial chamber in the phloem region. Each female is joined by one male. Colonization is guided by insect produced pheromones and perhaps host-produced attractants in some species. Mating takes place in the nuptial chamber. The females construct egg galleries by excavating either horizontally (Figure 15.24) or vertically (Figure 15.25) (depending on the particular species) away from the nuptial chamber. Typically there will be one or two galleries per nuptial chamber. When two galleries are present, they extend in opposite directions. The colonizing adults inoculate the host with fungi and other microorganisms. After the eggs hatch the larvae excavate galleries away from the egg gallery. There are usually three or four larval instars. Following pupation, adults emerge by boring through the bark to the outside. Gallery excavation by adults and larvae scores the sapwood and the *Scolytus* bark beetles are, therefore, known as "engraver beetles."

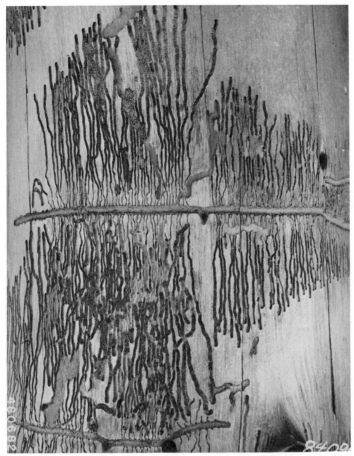

Figure 15.24 Egg gallery pattern for the fir engraver, *Scolytus ventralis*. (U.S. Forest Service photograph.)

Although there are a large number of *Scolytus* bark beetles, most are not considered to be primary pests and do not kill trees. However, the smaller European elm bark beetle, *Scolytus multistriatus* (Marsham) and the fir engraver *Scolytus ventralis* LeConte are important pests, and we will provide further details about these species.

Smaller European Elm Bark Beetle, *Scolytus multistriatus* (Marsham)

The smaller European elm bark beetle is an insect that was introduced into the eastern United States around 1909. The adults are dark reddish brown in color and about 2.0 mm in length (Figure 15.26). The abdomen is concave ventrally, and there is a prominent spine on the anterior half of the sternum. The insect infests all species of elm and now occurs throughout the United States and Canada in a pattern following the distribution of its hosts.

Figure 15.25 Egg gallery pattern for the smaller European elm bark beetle, *Scolytus multistriatus*. (U.S. Forest Service photograph.)

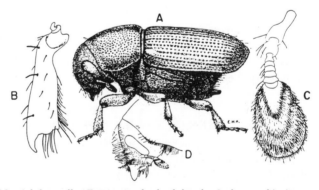

Figure 15.26 Adult smaller European elm bark beetle, *Scolytus multistriatus,* and distinctive morphological characters: A = adult, B = protibia, C = antenna, D = male head. (Modified from Wood 1982, courtesy of S. L. Wood.)

540

The smaller European elm bark beetle is considered to be a major pest species because it is a primary vector of the Dutch elm disease fungus *Ceratocystis ulmi* (Buism) C. Moreau, which is fatal to elms. The life cycle of the insect and transmission of the disease are closely linked. The smaller European elm bark beetle breeds in elms that are severely weakened, dying, or dead. Adult beetles are attracted to these types of habitats by perception of plant attractants and beetle-produced pheromones. The life cycle follows the generalized pattern provided above. The egg gallery is excavated in a vertical direction (to the long axis of the tree), and eggs are oviposited along the lateral walls (Figure 15.25). The developing larvae mine horizontally away from the egg gallery and produce a fanlike series of larval galleries. Pupation takes place in a chamber constructed by the last instar larva. Adults emerge by boring through to the outside surface. The adults carry with them on their body surfaces the spores of the Dutch elm disease. Before selecting a breeding habitat, the adults feed on small twigs (often in the axil of a branch) of healthy elms. This feeding can, and often does, result in the inoculation of the tree with the Dutch elm disease. After feeding, the adults enter their preferred breeding material. The adults are active in the spring of the year. There are usually one or two generations per year (Baker 1972, Meyer and Norris 1965).

The Dutch elm disease is also vectored by the native elm bark beetle, *Hylurgopinus rufipes* (Eichhoff). This insect also has the habit of feeding, as an adult, in the inner bark of branches and twigs of living elms. Therefore, it can transmit the Dutch elm disease in the same manner as the smaller European elm bark beetle (Gardiner 1981).

Fir Engraver, *Scolytus ventralis* LeConte

The fir engraver is an important pest of true firs in the western United States and southwestern Canada. The insect is among the largest species of *Scolytus*, approximately 4.0 mm in length (Figure 15.27). It is black in color and has the typical concave-shaped abdomen.

The life cycle of the fir engraver follows the general pattern presented above for this genus. Adults colonize their hosts during the summer months.

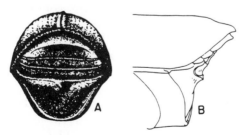

Figure 15.27 Distinctive morphological characters of the fir engraver, *Scolytus ventralis:* A = caudal aspect, B = profile of posterior area. (Modified from Wood 1982, courtesy of S. L. Wood.)

Colonization is guided by host attractants and insect-produced pheromones. Females attack the host first and excavate a nuptial chamber. Mating
takes place in the chamber, and egg galleries are constructed in a horizontal
direction (to the long axis to the tree) on both sides of the nuptial chamber.
Eggs are oviposited singly in niches on the lateral walls of the gallery (Figure
15.24). The tree is inoculated with fungi and other microorganisms that
produce discoloration in the area of the gallery. The larvae mine vertically
away from the egg gallery. The last instar larva constructs a chamber in
which pupation occurs. Adults emerge by boring through the bark to the
surface of the host. There is usually only one generation per year, but in
warmer areas there may be 1.5, and in cooler areas the life cycle may take
2 years (Stevens 1971).

The fir engraver infests standing living trees in a variety of size–classes
but can produce broods in freshly cut logs or trees felled by wind, snow,
or ice storms. On standing trees, the attacks are usually distributed over
the open bole of the host. The insect also is capable of killing sections,
strips, or patches of the tree without causing death to the tree (Berryman
1968a,b).

Outbreaks of the fir engraver have been associated with stressed trees
(Ferrell 1978). Population fluctuations are associated with conditions that
produce large quantities of highly susceptible hosts (such as water stress)
in combination with favorable weather conditions (Berryman 1973).

ROUNDHEADED PHLOEM BORERS (COLEOPTERA: CERAMBYCIDAE)

Although the family Cerambycidae is quite large, there are only a few pest
genera and species that are classified as phloem borers. Adult cerambycids
are known as "longhorned beetles" because of their characteristically long
antennae. The term "roundheaded borer" probably originated from the
habit of some species excavating round emergence holes. The larvae do
not have round heads, and they generally bore flat tunnels. Only the larvae
bore in the phloem. The North American species are not considered to be
primary pests as they seldom kill their hosts. Both coniferous and deciduous
hosts are infested. For this reason, we do not consider the roundheaded
phloem borers in any great detail. However, there are several species commonly associated with coniferous hosts that have been colonized and killed
by bark beetles, such as, *Monochamus, Acanthocinus,* and *Stenocorus* species.
Linsley (1959) provides a comprehensive review of the ecology of the family
Cerambycidae.

In general, round-headed phloem borers colonize coniferous hosts that
have been severely damaged or felled. Like the *Ips* and *Scolytus* bark beetles,
they commonly infest storm-damaged trees. The adults colonize the host
and generally oviposit through the bark into the phloem region. After the
eggs hatch, the larvae tunnel in the phloem region. Foraging generally

scores the xylem. In some species the late instar larvae bore into the xylem to pupate, whereas in other species, pupation occurs in a "chip cocoon" in the inner bark region. Adults emerge by boring a circular hole through the bark to the outer surface.

Southern Pine Sawyer, *Monochamus titillator* (Fabricius)

The southern pine sawyer is an example of a roundheaded phloem borer that has been studied in considerable detail. This insect is distributed throughout the eastern and southern United States. It infests pines that have been damaged by wind and ice storms, freshly cut, or infested by bark beetles. Adults are gray and brown in color and 18–30 mm in length. Antennae of the males are two to three times as long as the body. There is a pronounced spine on each side of the thorax, and the elytral sutures are prolonged into a prominent spine on both sides (Figure 15.28). Full-grown larvae are approximately 40 mm in length.

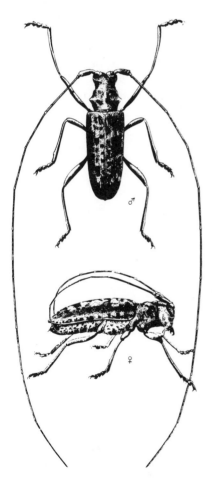

Figure 15.28 Adult southern pine sawyer, *Monochamus titillator*. (Original photograph by J. L. Webb, 1909.)

The life cycle of the southern pine sawyer begins with adults locating suitable breeding sites. Host selection is probably guided by perception of plant attractants but may be in response to kairomones or pheromones. Adults mate on the surface of the host. The female excavates an elyptical pit in the bark surface and oviposits through this pit into the phloem region. The eggs (6–12) are positioned in a circle around the pit. After the eggs hatch, the larvae begin to forage the inner bark region. The galleries are irregular and cavernous and increase in size with each larval instar (Figure 15.29). The last instar larva bores into the xylem and constructs a U-shaped tunnel. Foraging in the inner bark continues for a period of time following construction of the tunnel. Pupation occurs inside the tunnel, which is sealed with fibrous borings. Adults emerge by boring a circular hole to the outside. Because of its habit of foraging the inner bark and boring into the xylem, the southern pine sawyer is often classed in both the phloem boring and wood boring feeding groups.

When the insect occurs in hosts infested by the southern pine beetle and/or the *Ips* engraver beetles, the foraging activity of the larvae results in mortality to the immature bark beetle life stages. This mortality occurs because all species occur in the inner bark region at the same time (Coulson et al. 1976, 1980). When the larvae bore into the xylem of the host, the value of the tree is reduced and it is structurally weakened. This boring activity is also an early stage of ecological succession in the infested host that eventually leads to the degradation of the tree.

Figure 15.29 Gallery pattern produced by foraging by larvae of the southern pine Sawyer, *Monochamus titillator*.

FLATHEADED PHLOEM BORERS (COLEOPTERA: BUPRESTIDAE)

Like the Cerambycidae, the family Buprestidae is large and contains several genera and species that are classified in the phloem borer feeding group. Both coniferous and deciduous hosts are infested. However, insects in this group are not primary tree killers and prefer weakened hosts. The Buprestidae are commonly known as "metallic wood borers" or "flatheaded borers." The adults are hard bodied, compactly built, and are bullet shaped. They are often colored metallic blue, green copper, or black. The larvae are elongate in shape, and white in color, and most species have an enlarged and flattened prothorax with well-developed hardened plates on both the dorsal and ventral surfaces.

There is a great deal of variation in the life cycle of the flatheaded phloem borers. In general, weakened or severely damaged hosts are preferred. Adults oviposit on the surface of the host or in bark crevices. Larvae bore into the phloem, where they excavate irregular galleries that are oval shaped in cross section. The galleries contain tightly packed boring frass. Pupation occurs in the galleries or sometimes in the xylem. Adults emerge by boring through to the outer surface.

Most of the Buprestidae are better known as wood borers than phloem feeders. However, there are several species in the genera *Agrilus*, *Melanophila*, and *Chrysobothris* that are common, albeit of rather minor economic significance. We consider two case history examples: the bronze birch borer, *Agrilus anxius* Gory, and the California flatheaded borer, *Melanophila californica* Van Dyke.

Bronze Birch Borer, *Agrilus anxius* Gory

The bronze birch borer occurs throughout the United States and Canada in a pattern following the distribution of birch. It infests birch and breeds primarily in yellow and paper birch, with damaged or severely weakened hosts preferred. The adults are deep green–bronze in color and 6–12 mm in length. The front of the pronotum is coppery colored. In the males the front of the head is greenish, whereas in the females it is copper-bronze. The larvae are slender, flattened, and approximately 25 mm in length when mature (Baker 1972).

The life cycle of the bronze birch borer has been described by MacAloney (1968). Adults are active during the summer months. Eggs are oviposited in small groups underneath the bark. Larvae bore in the phloem region and intermittently into the xylem. The galleries are winding and tightly packed with boring frass. There are five larval instars. Mature larvae construct oblong cells in the xylem or thick bark where they overwinter and subsequently pupate. Adults emerge by boring to the outer surface. The life cycle takes 1 or 2 years depending on geographic location.

In general, the bronze birch borer cannot survive in healthy trees. Wounds created by unsuccessful attacks form a callus. The insect is capable of killing

Figure 15.30 Gallery pattern produced by larvae of the bronze birch borer, *Agrilus anxius.*

severely weakened trees, primarily as a result of girdling by larval mining (Figure 15.30).

California Flatheaded Borer, *Melanophila californica* Van Dyke

The California flatheaded borer occurs in the western United States, where it infests a variety of pine species, with ponderosa and Jeffrey pines being favored hosts. Adults are 7–11 mm in length, greenish bronze dorsally, and brassy green ventrally. The elytra may contain three small yellow markings (Figure 15.31).

The life cycle of the California flatheaded borer has been described by Lyon (1970) and Furniss and Carolin (1977). Adults are active in the early summer and feed on pine foliage, which is a requirement for females to produce viable eggs. The eggs are oviposited beneath bark scales and in crevices on the host. After the eggs hatch, the larvae bore into the phloem region, where they may forage for a few months to 4 years. This feeding behavior results in construction of galleries and scoring of the sapwood but does not produce appreciable damage to the host. If the host is not killed, the larvae will not complete development. If the host is killed, the larvae resume development and forage the inner bark region. Larvae move to the outer bark in late summer, where pupation takes place. Adults emerge the following year.

The California flatheaded borer prefers weakened hosts that occur on poor sites. Old growth, senescent, or diseased hosts are most susceptible to colonization, although healthy trees are not immune. The insect can weaken host trees and thereby increase susceptibility to attack by the western pine beetle and other bark beetle species.

Figure 15.31 California flatheaded borer, *Melanophila california:* A = adult, B = pupa (dorsal view), C = pupa (ventral view), D = eggs on underside of a bark scale, E = larva, F = prepupal larva in the outer bark. (U.S. Forest Service photograph.)

LEPIDOPTERA PHLOEM BORERS

The lepidoptera phloem borers are generally considered to be of minor importance in forests. However, there is one family, Sesiidae (clearwing borers), which contains a number of species that are pests in fruit trees, shelterbelt plantings, ornamental plantings, and nurseries. Adult clearwing borers bear a striking resemblance to bees and wasps. The wings are narrow and interlocking and often transparent because of the absence of scales (particularly the hind wings) (Figure 15.32). The larvae bore in the trunks, bark, stems, or roots of trees, shrubs, vines, and herbaceous plants.

Literature on the clearwing borers has been compiled by Solomon and Dix (1979) for species occurring in the United States and Canada. The most important genera in the family include *Paranthrene, Podosesia, Synanthedon,* and *Sesia*. Notes on the biology of the common species occurring in forests are provided in Baker (1972) and Furniss and Carolin (1977).

Figure 15.32   Adult clearwing borer. (U.S. Forest Service photograph.)

Johnson and Lyon (1976) provide information on species attacking shade trees.

DIPTERA PHLOEM BORERS

The Diptera are of little importance as phloem borers in forest trees. There is only one family with representatives that are classed in the phloem boring feeding group, the Agromyzidae, or leaf mining flies. As the common name implies, most of the insects in this family are leaf miners. The genus *Phytobia* contains species that mine in the cambium region of deciduous trees and shrubs. These insects are important only when infested host material is subsequently used in manufacturing finely finished wood products. Under these circumstances the wood may be blemished by the larval mines and thus unsuitable for use.

REFERENCES

Amman, G. D. 1977. The role of the mountain pine beetle in lodgepole pine ecosystems: Impact on succession. In Mattson, W. J. (Ed.), *The Role of Arthropods in Forest Ecosystems.* Springer-Verlag, New York.

Amman, G. D. 1978. The biology, ecology, and causes of outbreaks of the mountain pine beetle in lodgepole pine forests. In Berryman, A. A., G. D. Amman, R. W. Stark and D. L. Kibbee (Eds.), *Theory and Practice of Mountain Pine Beetle Management in Lodgepole Pine Forests.* Symposium Proceeding. University of Idaho, Moscow.

Amman, G. D. and W. E. Cole. 1983. *Mountain Pine Beetle Dynamics in Lodgepole Pine Forest Part II. Population Dynamics.* USDA Forest Service General Technical Report INT-145.

Baker, W. L. 1972. *Eastern Forest Insects.* USDA Forest Service Miscellaneous Publication 1175.

Barr, B. A. 1969. Sound production in Scolytidae (Coleoptera) with emphasis on the genus *Ips. Can. Entomol.* **101**:636–672.

Baumgartner, D. M., (Ed.) 1975. *Management of Lodgepole Pine Ecosystems.* Washington State University Cooperative Extension Service, Pullman.

Beaver, R. A. 1977. *Bark and Ambrosia Beetles in Tropical Forests.* Biotrop. Special Publication No. 2.

Berryman, A. A. 1968a. Distribution of *Scolytus ventralis* attacks, emergence, and parasites in grand fir. *Can. Entomol.* **100**:57–68.

Berryman, A. A. 1968b. Development of sampling techniques and life tables for the fir engraver, *Scolytus ventralis* (Coleoptera:Scolytidae). *Can. Entomol.* **100**:1138–1147.

Berryman, A. A. 1972. Resistance of conifers to bark beetle-fungus associations. *BioScience* **22**:598–602.

Berryman, A. A. 1973. Population dynamics of the fir engraver, *Scolytus ventralis* (Coleoptera: Scolytidae). I. Analysis of population behavior and survival from 1964 to 1971. *Can. Entomol.* **105**:1465–1488.

Berryman, A. A. 1976. Theoretical explanation of mountain pine beetle dynamics in lodgepole pine forests. *Environ. Entomol.* **6**:1225–1233.

Berryman, A. A., G. D. Amman, R. W. Stark, and D. L. Kibbee (Eds.). 1978. *Theory and Practice of Mountain Pine Beetle Management in Lodgepole Pine Forests.* Symposium proceedings. University of Idaho, Moscow.

Birch, M. C. 1978. Chemical communication in pine bark beetles. *Am. Sci.* **66**:409–419.

Borden, J. H. 1974. Aggregation pheromones in the Scolytidae. In Birch, M. C. (Ed.), *Pheromones.* North-Holland, Amsterdam.

Borden, J. H. 1982. Aggregation Pheromones. In Mitton, J. B. and K. B. Sturgeon (Eds.), *Bark Beetles in North American Conifers.* University of Texas Press, Austin.

Cates, R. and J. H. Alexander. 1982. Host resistance and susceptibility. In Mitton, J. B. and K. B. Sturgeon (Eds.), *Bark Beetles in North American Conifers.* University of Texas Press, Austin.

Cole, W. E. and G. D. Amman. 1980. *Mountain Pine Beetle Dynamics in Lodgepole Pine Forests.* Part 1: *Course of an Infestation.* USDA Forest Service General Technical Report INT-89.

Cole, W. E., G. D. Amman, and C. E. Jensen. 1976. Mathematical models for the mountain pine beetle-lodgepole pine interaction. *Environ. Entomol.* **5**:11–19.

Coster, J. E. and J. L. Searcy, (Eds.) 1979. *Evaluating Control Tactics for the Southern Pine Beetle.* USDA Forest Service Technical Bulletin 1613.

Coulson, R. N. 1979. Population dynamics of bark beetles. *Annu. Rev. Entomol.* **24**:417–447.

Coulson, R. N. 1980. Population dynamics. In Thatcher, R. C., J. L. Searcy, J. E. Coster, and G. D. Hertel, (Eds.), *The Southern Pine Beetle.* USDA Forest Service Technical Bulletin 1631.

Coulson, R. N., A. M. Mayyasi, J. L. Foltz, and F. P. Hain. 1976. Interspecific competition between *Monochamus titillator* (Fab.) and *Dendroctonus frontalis* Zimm. *Environ. Entomol.* **5**:235–247.

Coulson, R. N., D. N. Pope, J. A. Gagne, W. S. Fargo, P. E. Pulley, L. J. Edson, and T. L. Wagner. 1980. Impact of foraging by *Monochamus titillator* (Coleoptera: Cerambycidae) on within-tree populations of *Dendroctonus frontalis* (Coleoptera: Scolytidae). *Entomophaga* **25**:155–170.

Dahlsten, D. L. 1982. Relationships between bark beetles and their natural enemies. In Mitton, J. B. and K. B. Sturgeon (Eds.), *Bark Beetles in North American Conifers.* University of Texas Press, Austin.

Fares, Y., P. J. A. Sharpe, and C. E. Magnuson. 1980. Pheromone dispersion in forests. *J. Theo. Biol.* **84**:335–359.

Ferrell, G. T. 1978. Moisture stress threshold of susceptibility to fir engraver beetles in pole-size white firs. *For. Sci.* **24**:85–92.

Ferrell, G. T. 1980. *Risk Rating Systems for Mature Red Fir and White Fir in Northern California.* USDA Forest Service General Technical Report PSW-39.

Furniss, M. M. and P. W. Orr. 1970. Douglas-fir beetle. USDA Forest Service Forest Pest Leaflet 5.

Furniss, M. M., M. D. McGregor, M. W. Foiles, and A. D. Partridge. 1979. *Chronology and Characteristics of a Douglas-fir Beetle Outbreak in Northern Idaho.* USDA Forest Service General Technical Report INT 59.

Furniss, R. L. and V. M. Carolin. 1977. *Western Forest Insects.* USDA Forest Service Miscellaneous Publication 273.

Gardiner, L. M. 1981. Seasonal activity of the native elm bark beetle, *Hylugropinus rufipes*, in central Ontario (Coleoptera: Scolytidae). *Can. Entomol.* **113**:341–348.

Hedden, R. L., S. J. Barras, and J. E. Coster (Eds.). 1981. *Hazard-Rating Systems in Forest Insect Pest Management.* USDA Forest Service General Technical Report WO-27.

Johnson, W. T. and H. H. Lyon. 1976. *Insects that Feed on Trees and Shrubs.* Cornell University Press, Ithaca.

Lanier, G. N., M. C. Birch, R. F. Schmitz, and M. M. Furniss. 1972. Pheromones of *Ips pini* (Coleoptera: Scolytidae): Variation in response among three populations. *Can. Entomol.* **104**:1917–1923.

Linsley, E. G. 1959. Ecology of Cerambycidae. *Annu. Rev. Entomol.* **4**:99–138.

Lorio, P. L., Jr. 1980. Rating stands for susceptibility to SPB. In Thatcher, R. C., J. L. Searcy, J. E. Coster, and G. D. Hertel (Eds.), *The Southern Pine Beetle.* USDA Forest Service Technical Bulletin 1631.

Lyon, R. L. 1970. *California Flatheaded Borer.* USDA Forest Service Forest Pest Leaflet 24.

MacAloney, H. J. 1968. *The Bronze Birch Borer.* USDA Forest Service Forest Pest Leaflet 111.

McCambridge, W. F. and F. B. Knight. 1972. Factors affecting spruce beetles during a small outbreak. *Ecology* **53**:830–839.

McCambridge, W. F., G. D. Amman, and G. C. Trostle. 1979. Mountain pine beetle. USDA Forest Service Forest Insect and Disease Leaflet 2.

Meyer, H. J. and D. M. Norris, Jr. 1965. Dutch elm disease today. Proc. North Central Branch. *Entomol. Soc. Am.* **20**:102–105.

Miller, J. M. and F. P. Keen. 1960. *Biology and Control of the Western Pine Beetle.* U.S. Department of Agriculture Misc. Publ. 800.

Mitton, J. B. and K. B. Sturgeon (Eds.). 1982. *Bark beetles in North American Conifers.* University of Texas Press, Austin.

Moore, J. A., J. A. Schenk, and C. R. Hatch. 1978. Validation and refinement of a hazard rating model for fir engraver mortality in grand-fir stands. *For. Sci.* **24**:309–312.

Payne, T. L. 1980. Life history and habits (of the southern pine beetle). In Thatcher, R. C., J. L. Searcy, J. E. Coster, and G. D. Hertel (Eds.), *The Southern Pine Beetle.* USDA Forest Service Technical Bulletin 1631.

Peterman, R. M. 1978. The ecological role of mountain pine beetle in lodgepole pine forests. In Berryman, A. A., G. D. Amman, R. W. Stark, and D. L. Kibbee (Eds.), *Theory and Practice of Mountain Pine Beetle Management in Lodgepole Pine Forests.* Symposium Proceedings. University of Idaho, Moscow.

Rudinsky, J. A. 1962. Ecology of Scolytidae. *Annu. Rev. Entomol.* **7**:327–348.

Rudinsky, J. A. 1966. Host selection and invasion by the Douglas-fir beetle, *Dendroctonus pseudotsugae* Hopkins, in coastal Douglas-fir forests. *Can. Entomol.* **98**:98–111.

Rudinsky, J. A. and R. R. Michael. 1972. Sound production in Scolytidae: Chemostimulus of sonic signal by the Douglas-fir beetle. *Science* **175**:1386–1390.

Rudinsky, J. A. and R. R. Michael. 1973. Sound production in Scolytidae: Stridulation by female *Dendroctonus* beetles. *J. Insect Physiol.* **19**:689–705.

Safranyik, L. 1978. Effects of climate and weather on mountain pine beetle populations. In Berryman, A. A., G. D. Amman, R. W. Stark and D. L. Kibbee (Eds.), *Theory and Practice of Mountain Pine Beetle Management in Lodgepole Pine Forests*. Symposium Proceedings. University of Idaho, Moscow.

Safranyik, K. L., D. M. Shrimpton, and H. S. Whitney. 1974. *Management of Lodgepole Pine to Reduce Losses from the Mountain Pine Beetle*. Environment Canada, Forestry Service Forest Technical Report 1.

Safranyik, L., D. M. Shrimpton, and H. S. Whitney. 1975. An interpretation of the interaction between lodgepole pine, the mountain pine beetle, and its associated blue stain fungi in western Canada. In Baumgartner, D. M. (Ed.), *Management of Lodgepole Pine Ecosystems*, Washington State University Cooperative Extension Service, Pullman.

Sartwell, C. R., R. F. Schmitz, and W. J. Buckhorn. 1971. Pine engraver, *Ips pini*, in the Western States. USDA Forest Service Forest Pest Leaflet 122.

Schmid, J. M. and R. C. Beckwith. 1975. The spruce beetle. USDA Forest Service Forest Pest Leaflet 127.

Schowalter, T. D. 1981. Insect herbivore relationship to the state of the host plant: Biotic regulation of nutrient cycling through ecological succession. *Oikos* **37**:126–130.

Schowalter, T. D., R. N. Coulson, and D. A. Crossley, Jr. 1981. The role of southern pine beetle and fire in maintenance of structure and function of the southeastern coniferous forest. *Environ. Entomol.* **10**:821–825.

Solomon, J. D. and M. E. Dix. 1979. *Selected Bibliography of the Clearwing Borers (Sesiidae) of the U.S. and Canada*. USDA Forest Service General Technical Report SO-22.

Stark, R. W. and D. L. Dahlsten, (Eds.). 1970. Studies on the Population Dynamics of the Western Pine Beetle, *Dendroctonus brevicomis* LeConte. University of California Division of Agricultural Science, Berkeley.

Stephen, F. M., J. L. Searcy, and G. D. Hertel, (Eds.). 1980. *Modeling Southern Pine Beetle Populations*. Symposium Proceedings USDA Forest Service Technical Bulletin 1630.

Stevens, R. E. 1971. Fir engraver. USDA Forest Service Forest Pest Leaflet 13.

Thatcher, R. C., J. L. Searcy, J. E. Coster, and G. D. Hertel (Eds.). 1980. *The Southern Pine Beetle*. USDA Forest Service Technical Bulletin 1631.

Vité, J. P. and J. A. Rudinsky. 1957. Contribution toward a study of Douglas-fir beetle development. *For. Sci.* **3**:156–167.

Whitney, H. S. 1982. Relationships between Bark Beetles and Symbiotic Organisms. In Mitton, J. B. and K. B. Sturgeon (Eds.), *Bark Beetles in North American Conifers*, University of Texas Press, Austin.

Wilkinson, R. C. and J. L. Foltz. 1980. A selected bibliography (1959–1979) of three Southeastern species of *Ips* engraver beetles. *Bull. Entomol. Soc. Am.* **26**:375–380.

Wood, D. L. 1982. The role of pheromones, kairomones, and allomones in the host selection and colonization behavior of bark beetles. *Annu. Rev. Entomol.* **27**:411–446.

Wood, D. L. 1980. Approach to research and forest management for the western pine beetle. In Huffaker, C. B. (Ed.), *New Technology of Pest Control*. Wiley, New York.

Wood, D. L. 1972. Selection and colonization of ponderosa pine by bark beetles. In Van Emden, H. F. (Ed.), *Insect/Plant Relationships*, Blackwell, Oxford.

Wood, S. L. 1963. A revision of the bark beetle genus *Dendroctonus* Erichson. Great Basin Naturalist Memoirs 23.

Wood, S. L. 1982. The Bark and Ambrosia Beetles of North and Central America (Coleoptera: Scolytidae), a Taxonomic Monograph. Great Basin Naturalist Memoirs 6.

Wygant, N. D. and R. R. Lejeune. 1967. Engelmann spruce beetle *Dendroctonus obesus* (Mann.). In *Important Forest Insects and Diseases of Mutual Concern to Canada, the United States and Mexico*. Canada Department of Forestry and Rural Development Publication No. 1180, Ottawa.

16 | Wood Boring Insects

INTRODUCTION

Numerous and diverse groups of insects are wood borers. Marine organisms such as shipworms (phylum Mollusca) and wood lice (phylum Arthropoda, class Crustacea) also cause considerable damage to wood pilings in saltwater. Knight and Heikkenen (1980), Furniss and Carolin (1977), and Baker (1972) provide information on the marine wood borers.

Many wood borers obtain food and shelter from the wood, whereas others use only the wood for a shelter. Wood boring insects attack many different types of wood. Some species attack only old moist dead wood, whereas others survive only on dry seasoned wood. Many species of wood borers are attracted to dying trees or trees recently cut, whereas others attack only living trees. Insects attracted to living trees often spend a considerable amount of time feeding in the phloem before entering the wood. Insects described in Chapter 15 feed only or primarily in the phloem. The sawyer beetles in the genus *Monochamus* are described in both chapters because some species do most of their feeding in the phloem whereas other species in the genus feed both in the phloem and in the wood. An insect that feeds in the phloem and in the wood is often called a *phloem–wood borer*.

Some insects that attack dying trees, recently killed trees, or recently cut trees develop very slowly in dried wood. These insects often continue to develop in the wood after the wood has been dried and manufactured. Insects that are attracted to recently killed trees often start feeding directly into the wood. Wood boring insects such as ambrosia beetles live only in the wood. They may attack either living or dead trees and logs. Insects that attack moist wood such as subterranean termites or carpenter ants may be found in the dead moist heartwood of living trees and in moist wood on the ground but usually cause the most damage when they attack wood products. Powderpost beetles and drywood termites damage dry wood.

ORGANISMS INVOLVED

Wood boring insects that commonly damage forest and shade trees or wood products are present in the orders Coleoptera, Lepidoptera, Hymenoptera, and Isoptera. Hay and Soloman (1981) developed a bibliography for insects causing wood defects in eastern hardwoods.

Coleopterous Insects

Wood boring insects in the order Coleoptera include the roundheaded borers, flatheaded borers, ambrosia beetles, powderpost beetles, and timberworms. A few of the roundheaded borers and many of the flatheaded borers feed only in the phloem or are closely associated with phloem borers and are covered in Chapter 15.

Figure 16.1   Roundheaded borer larva, *Monochamus scutellatus*, feeding on another larva of same species in its excavation in balsam fir. (U.S. Forest Service photograph.)

Roundheaded Borers, Cerambycidae

The family Cerambycidae is a large and diverse family, with over 1200 species occurring in the United States (Linsley 1959). Most of the Cerambycidae are phloem–wood borers. Different species attack different types of trees. Most roundheaded borers prefer weakened and dying trees or freshly cut logs, but some species are attracted to living trees. Some species cause considerable damage to logs and wood products. However, as a group, the Cerambycidae are very important in helping to cycle minerals back into the soil since the galleries of many wood boring beetles provide avenues for the invasion of the wood rotting fungi.

The larvae, normally called "roundheaded borers," are elongated, cylindrical, fleshy, and white; many species have enlarged anteriors (Figure 16.1). Some of the cerambycids that feed only in the phloem have a very flattened shape. Adult Cerambycidae are called "longhorned beetles" and are elongated and cylindrical beetles with long antennae, often longer than the entire body. Many of the adults are very brightly colored insects. Seven species are discussed in the next section.

Locust Borer

The locust borer, *Megacyllene robiniae* (Forster), is a serious pest of black locust throughout the United States (Wollerman 1970). Adults are about 18 mm long and black, with narrow bright yellow crossbands on the elytra

Figure 16.2 Larva, pupa, and adult of the locust borer, *Megacyllene robiniae*. (U.S. Forest Service photograph.)

(Figure 16.2). They are commonly found feeding on the pollen of goldenrod flowers during late August to October. After mating, the female deposits eggs singly into bark crevices on black locust. Newly hatched larvae bore into the inner bark and construct small hibernation cells, where they overwinter. Larvae bore into the wood during the following spring. Adults emerge in August. One generation develops each year.

The locust borer prevents black locust trees from growing straight and tall on many sites. Vigorous trees on good sites produce unfavorable conditions for larval survival. If possible, black locust should be planted on the better sites. However, black locust will continue to be planted on eroded lands and mine spoils since it can provide a very quick cover. Silvicultural techniques that stimulate growth should be used after the trees are established on the poorer sites.

Red Oak Borer

The red oak borer, *Enaphalodes rufulus* (Haldeman), attacks most species of oaks throughout eastern North America. Northern red, black, and scarlet oak are especially subject to attack (Donley and Acciavatti 1980).

Adults are nocturnal (Figure 16.3) and present from mid-June to mid-August, primarily in odd years since the red oak borer has a 2-year synchronous life cycle. Eggs are deposited in cracks, under lichen, and vines of host trees (Donley 1978). Young larvae bore directly into the phloem and feed there until midsummer of the second year, when they move into the wood to feed. After mining into the heartwood for a maximum distance of 200 mm, larvae pupate in the heartwood. Adults emerge near the original oviposition sites by chewing oval exit holes through the bark.

The best evidence of infestation is the accumulation of granular frass and discoloration (i.e., "wet spots" caused by sap leakage) that occurs around the attack site. The major impact is damage from larval tunnels in the wood, which degrades lumber and veneer products (Figure 16.3). Tunnels cause further damage when they are used by other insects and diseases as sites of attack on the oak trees. For example, carpenterworms, timberworms, carpenter ants, and decay organisms often enter the tree through red oak borer tunnels.

The major silvicultural recommendation is removal of infested trees in pole-sized oak stands. The objective is to decrease borer numbers and to reduce the chances of subsequent attack in the residual stand throughout the rotation.

Poplar Borer

The poplar borer, *Saperda calcarata* Say, is distributed throughout North America and attacks poplars and willows. Adults are elongate, robust gray beetles with yellow markings on the thorax and elytra and are over 25 mm long (Figure 16.4). They emerge in late July and August. Females deposit eggs in small slits cut into the bark of the tree, often on the center bole portion of the tree. After 3 weeks, eggs hatch and larvae bore into the inner bark and sapwood, where they overwinter. During the following

(a)

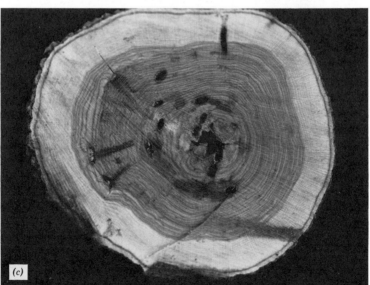

Figure 16.3 Red oak borer, *Enaphalodes rufulus:* (*a*) adult female, (*b,c*) damage. (U.S. Forest Service photograph, courtesy of J. Solomon.)

Figure 16.4　Adult poplar borer, *Saperda calcarata*. (U.S. Forest Service photograph.)

spring, larvae bore further into the sapwood and heartwood where they feed for 1 or 2 years. Larvae keep their tunnels fairly clean and maintain an opening into the bark where the eggs were laid by pushing their fibrous borings out of the entrance hole. Infested trees are recognized by swollen scars, holes, wet areas around entrance holes, and fibrous borings. Mature larvae construct pupal cells near the lower end of the larval gallery. Adults emerge in July or August. The life cycle is completed in 2–3 years over most of its range. Drouin and Wong (1975) report on the biology and damage that the poplar borer causes in western Canada when feeding at the junction of the root and stem of balsam poplar.

Larger trees are seldom killed directly, but they are very susceptible to wind breakage. Also, the numerous tunnels are sites for secondary injury from other insects and diseases such as several buprestid phloem borers and *Fomes igniarius*. The major impact is the large amount of defect present in certain logs and the increased susceptibility of infected trees to other insects and diseases.

Successful infestations appear to be concentrated on individual trees or groups of trees within a stand, often those exposed to abundant sunlight. In the Great Lakes states, infestations appear to increase with a decrease in stand density. The current recommendation in the Great Lakes states for minimizing damage by the poplar borer is to maintain fast-growing fairly dense stands on good sites and to clear-cut these stands at maturity.

Cottonwood Borer

The cottonwood borer, *Plectrodera scalator* (Fabricius), a pest of cottonwood and willows throughout the southeastern states, attacks the root collar and main roots. The most severe damage occurs in young natural stands growing in sandy soils along the Mississippi River (Morris et al. 1975). Adult borers, large (25–38-mm) black beetles with white cross stripes, emerge during late spring and early summer. First, they feed on the bark of tender shoots, causing the injured shoots to break and hang on the tree. These shriveled black shoots are obvious signs of an infestation. After mating, the females dig away the soil at the base of the tree, cut niches into the bark, and deposit one or more eggs. The emerging larvae mine downward into the phloem and then tunnel into the wood. Taproots of small trees may be completely hollowed by the larvae. The base of an infested tree may be completely mined with larval tunnels (Figure 16.5). Pupation occurs in the gallery. The life cycle is completed in 2 years.

Damage may be kept at a minimum by planting cottonwood on good sites and by using silvicultural techniques to maintain healthy trees.

Sawyers in the Genus Monochamus

Several species of sawyers in the genus *Monochamus* often cause heavy losses in wind-thrown or fire-killed conifers, conifer sawlogs left too long in the woods before milling, and improperly handled pulpwood. Prompt salvage and utilization of wind-thrown and dead or dying trees and not cutting logs during the egg-laying period are the best methods of reducing *Mon-*

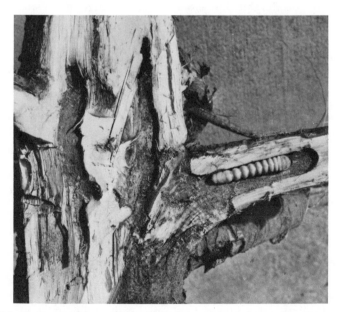

Figure 16.5 Cottonwood borer larva, *Plectrodera scalator* and tunneling damage of larva. (U.S. Forest Service photograph.)

ochamus populations in logging areas. Sawyer beetles feed both in the phloem and the wood. The life history of the southern pine sawyer, *Monochamus titillator* (Fabricius), was covered in Chapter 15 under the section on phloem borers.

Another common sawyer beetle is the whitespotted sawyer, *Monochamus scutellatus* (Say), which occurs throughout Canada and eastern and western United States. Its life cycle is similar to the southern pine sawyer (Wilson 1975).

Northern Spruce Borer

The northern spruce borer, *Tetropium parvulum* Casey, occurs in Alaska, the western Canadian provinces, and probably in some of the states in the western United States near the Canadian border (Raske 1973a,b). This phloem-wood borer has one generation per year with peak adult emergence in June. Adults oviposit under the bark scales of recently cut spruce logs or in dying spruce trees. Large-diameter logs (over 46 cm) already heavily infested with borers, and logs cut in the spring or early summer are preferred for oviposition. Larvae feed primarily in the phloem during mid to late summer. During late summer they make an L-shaped mine and form a pupal chamber. Most individuals overwinter as mature larvae within the pupal chamber. Pupation occurs during the following May or early June.

The larval galleries of the northern spruce borer penetrate into the log to a depth of 25–35 mm, sometimes up to 75 mm. Normally, this insect does not cause major economic damage because of its shallow boring habit. It has caused considerable damage to white and Engelmann spruce logs by degrading the lumber. Most of the larval galleries can be sawed off with slabs and edgings. However, larval densities can be so high that all the damage cannot be trimmed off the sawlogs.

Firtree Borer

The firtree borer, *Semanotus litigiosus* (Casey), is commonly found from Alaska to California and New Mexico, but it has also been recorded in New Jersey and Ontario. This insect can reach extremely high populations in the Pacific Northwest on wind-damaged coniferous trees, especially white fir and Douglas-fir (Wickman 1968a,b). The firtree borer can seriously degrade lumber manufactured from wind-damaged white fir.

After adults mate in early spring, females lay eggs in bark crevices of wind-thrown host trees or in cut logs of host trees. Young larvae excavate winding galleries into the phloem. By midsummer the mature larvae bore up to 75 mm into the wood to construct pupal chambers. Adults occur in September and overwinter within the pupal chamber.

Flatheaded Borers, Buprestidae

Many of the flatheaded borers feed only in the phloem; these were discussed in Chapter 15. In this section we discuss the flatheaded borers (Figure 16.6) that feed in both the phloem and the wood.

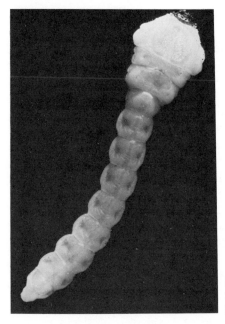

Figure 16.6 Flatheaded borer larva in the family Buprestidae. (U.S. Forest Service photograph.)

Western Cedar Borer

The western cedar borer, *Trachykele blondeli* Marseul, attacks western red cedar from British Columbia to California and New Mexico (Furniss and Carolin 1977). Females lay their eggs under bark scales on branches of living trees. Larvae bore from the branches into the main bole, where they feed primarily in the heartwood for several years (Figure 16.7). Mature

Figure 16.7 Western cedar borer, *Trachykele blondeli,* larval galleries in western red cedar lumber. (U.S. Forest Service photograph.)

larvae move to near the surface of the wood and pupate there. Adults emerge in the spring of the year.

Considerable damage is found in some forests. Larval galleries degrade lumber from the logs and make it useless for products requiring sound wood such as boats, shingles, and furniture.

Golden Buprestid

The golden buprestid, *Buprestis aurulenta* Linnaeus, normally attacks the pitchy wood in fire scars, lightning scars, and mechanical wounds of primarily ponderosa pine and Douglas-fir. Eggs are laid in cracks in the wood. Larvae feed in both the phloem and the wood (Figure 16.8). Under forest conditions, the life cycle is usually completed in 2–4 years. Most of the larval mining in houses and all that in finished wood products results from infestations present in the wood prior to the manufacture of the wood. Larvae have spent 30–50 years completing development in manufactured wood within buildings (Smith 1962).

Turpentine Borer

The turpentine borer, *Buprestis apricans* Herbst, once a serious pest of southern pines used for the production of naval stores, attacks injured pines with exposed dry wood. Modern turpentining methods have in-

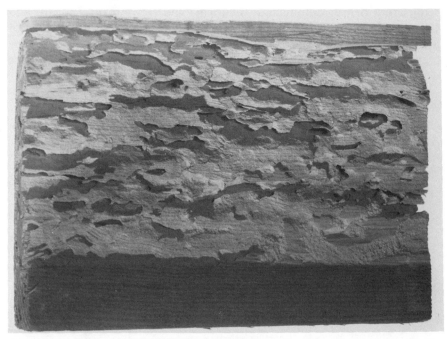

Figure 16.8   Feeding damage by golden buprestid, *Buprestis aurulenta*, larvae on Douglas-fir timber. (U.S. Forest Service photograph.)

creased gum flow and eliminated the dry face on trees in the southern turpentine orchards. The turpentine borer is now only a minor pest found in fire scars and in mechanical wounds that damage the bark and expose bare wood at the base of standing trees.

Ambrosia Beetles, Scolytidae, Platypodidae

Certain insects in the family Scolytidae and all members of the family Platypodidae are called "ambrosia beetles" because the larvae and adults feed on a fungus called "ambrosia." Some are closely related to bark beetles, although they do not feed between the bark and wood. Ambrosia beetles are often called "pinhole borers" by log scalers and lumber graders because the damage caused by their galleries usually consists of small pinholes surrounded by a dark stain (Figure 16.9). This damage seriously reduces the quality of the lumber and eliminates the potential for utilization of infested wood in certain products such as furniture.

Ambrosia beetles are primarily pests of green lumber, usually preferring recently cut trees, logs, pulpwood, or stumps. A considerable amount of moisture is required for development of these beetles, which do not attack green lumber unless the moisture content is at least 48% (Christian 1939). The greatest damage in the United States occurs in the southern and western coastal areas. Ambrosia beetles in the family Platypodidae are serious pests, but they occur primarily in the tropics and subtropics. Several species, belonging to the genus *Platypus*, are found in the United States.

A generalized life cycle for ambrosia beetles begins with males boring directly into the wood of a recently cut tree where they begin gallery construction. Females join them and construct most of the tunnels, which are either a simple, branched, or compound type of tunnel or gallery (Figure 16.10). Simple tunnels often penetrate deeply into the wood and are unbranched so the eggs, larvae, and pupae are all found together [(i.e., *Xy-*

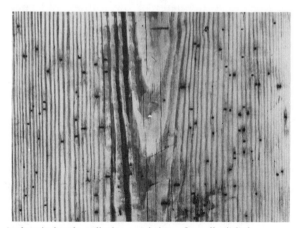

Figure 16.9 Ambrosia beetle galleries consisting of small pinholes surrounded by a dark stain. (U.S. Forest Service photograph.)

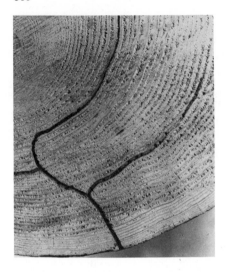

Figure 16.10   Tunnels of the ambrosia beetle, *Gnathotrichus sulcatus*. (U.S. Forest Service photograph.)

leborus xylographus (Say)]. Branched tunnels penetrate deeply into the wood and then divide into several branches that extend in various directions within the same plane (i.e., *Pterocyclon* spp.). Compound tunnels branch off from a single entrance gallery, but egg niches extend from the tunnel sides [i.e., *Trypodendron lineatum* (Olivier)].

After forming the egg gallery, a female either lays eggs in the main gallery or cuts an egg niche next to the main gallery. Larvae of some species live in the main adult beetle galleries, whereas other species excavate a special chamber called a *larval cradle* for each larva. The larval fungal food is brought into the gallery in specialized structures called *mycangia*, located on the head or thorax of the adult. Each group of beetles have their own specific fungus. The fungus is grown in pure cultures on specialized beds and on the walls of the tunnels (Batra 1968).

The shape of the insect, diameter of the tunnel, and character of the wood borings ejected from the tunnels are often used to identify the insect or damage to the genus or species level (Johnson 1958). Two species of ambrosia beetles are discussed in the following paragraphs.

Columbian Timber Beetle

The Columbian timber beetle, *Corthylus columbianus* Hopkins, seriously degrades lumber and veneer of hardwoods, such as maples, sycamore, and tulip poplar, in the eastern United States. In North America this is the only ambrosia beetle that attacks healthy trees. It is found on practically any size tree, but it does not kill the tree. The damage caused by the defects, often referred to as "grease spots" or "steamboats," renders the wood useless for veneer or furniture.

The life cycle of the Columbian timber beetle, including the fungi and staining associated with it, is described by Nord and McManus (1972) and Kabir and Giese (1966a,b). Adults become active in May and June and enter the wood through bark crevices on the main trunk near the base of the tree. Galleries are bored straight into the wood until the tunnels come close to the heartwood, where the beetles bore to the left or the right (Figure 16.11). Short egg cradles are cut in the sides of the main tunnels. Eggs are laid in these cradles, and larvae develop in these chambers. Pupae and/or adults overwinter in the galleries. There are two to three generations per year.

Striped Ambrosia Beetle

The striped ambrosia beetle, *Trypodendron lineatum* (Olivier), breeds in a wide range of conifers throughout Canada and the northern United States. This species is the most damaging ambrosia beetle in the West and is a major economic concern in British Columbia, where heavy infestations can occur on logs of Douglas-fir, true firs, western hemlock, and cedars (Figure 16.12).

Adult striped ambrosia beetles build up large populations by developing broods in wind-thrown and fire-killed trees, at the base of bark beetle–killed trees, in logging slash, and in logs stored for a long time. They emerge in the spring of the year and cause the most economic damage when attacking logs that were cut the previous fall or early spring (Chapman and Dyer 1969, Dyer and Chapman 1965). Shaded sides and undersides of logs lying on the ground and exposed surfaces of logs floating in water are generally attacked by the striped ambrosia beetle. Oviposition begins in the spring, and new adults emerge in about 2 months. In mid to late summer, adults emerge from the logs and fly to nearby forest margins where they overwinter in the duff and litter on the forest floor (Dyer and Kinghorn 1961). Normally only one generation occurs per year, but some of the emerging vigorous adults may reattack and deposit eggs for a second late-season generation.

An annotated bibliography on the striped ambrosia beetle was prepared by Nijholt (1979). A pheromone-based suppression program for ambrosia beetles, in the genus *Trypodendron* and *Gnathotrichus*, in industrial timber processing areas is discussed at the end of this chapter.

Powderpost Beetles

The term "powderpost" refers to damage that reduces the interior of the wood to a flourlike powder. Many small exit holes are often present on the surface of the wood. Powderpost beetle damage is found in the sapwood or heartwood of hardwoods and softwoods. Many species in the families Lyctidae, Anobiidae, Bostrichidae, and the old house borer in the family Cerambycidae cause this damage (Table 16.1).

Lyctid Beetles, Lyctidae

Lyctid beetles, the most destructive of the powderpost beetles, are found in tropical and warm temperate areas (Gerberg 1957). These powderpost beetles primarily cause damage to products manufactured from sapwood of hardwood trees (e.g., ash, hickory, oak, and walnut). Survival of larvae

Figure 16.11 Evidence of infestation and damage caused by the Columbian timber beetle, *Corthylus columbianus:* (*a*) fresh entrance hole, (*b*) wet spots indicating unhealed galleries in red maple, (*c*) damaged log of red maple, (*d*) maple rotary veneer showing cross sections of

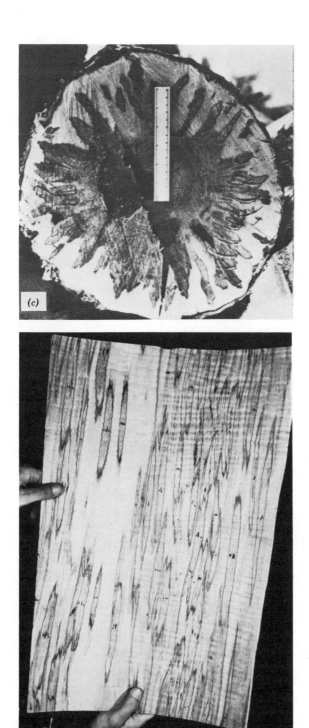

beetle galleries and associated stains (*a–c*—U.S. Forest Service photographs; *d*—from Southern Forest Insect Work Conference Slide Series).

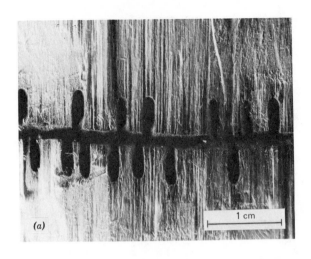

Figure 16.12 Striped ambrosia beetle, *Trypodendron lineatum:* (*a*) dark-stained gallery in sapwood of Douglas-fir, (*b*) pinhole defect (*a*—courtesy of R. Long, Simon Fraser University, *b*—U.S. Forest Service photograph).

Table 16.1   Common Types of Powderpost Beetle

Family and Common Names	Description of Damaged Wood	Type and Age of Wood
Lyctidae true powderpost beetle, lyctus beetle	Galleries are loosely filled with a talcumlike powder; small round exit holes (3 mm in diameter)	Primarily found in sapwood of dry seasoned hardwoods of high starch content; found primarily in newer homes
Bostrichidae false powderpost beetle, bostrichid beetle, branch and twig borers	Galleries are tightly packed with a coarse boring dust; small to medium round exit holes (3–9 mm in diameter); exit holes usually larger in size than those made by lyctids and anobiids; bostrichid tunnels vary greatly in size and shape	Found primarily in sapwood of hardwoods; few attack conifers; often found in imported bamboo products
Anobiidae deathwatch beetle, furniture beetle, anobiids	Galleries are tightly packed with very small frass pellets (less powdery in appearance than lyctids or bostrichids); small round exit holes (3 mm in diameter)	Found primarily in sapwood and heartwood of conifers or hardwoods; usually found in older homes
Cerambyciidae old house borer	Galleries are tightly packed with powdery borings and small frass pellets; medium oval exit holes (6 mm in diameter)	Found primarily in recently seasoned sapwood of conifers (especially pine and spruce); usually found in newer homes

and adults is greatest in hardwoods with at least 3% starch. Also, the females can lay their eggs in the large pores (Williams 1973). Damage commonly occurs in stored lumber, flooring, furniture, tool handles, and other hardwood products. The life cycle is similar for all lyctid beetles.

The southern lyctus beetle, *Lyctus planicollis* LeConte, the most destructive powderpost beetle found in this country, is distributed throughout the United States but causes the most damage in the South. In the more northern parts of its range, this species has one generation per year and overwinters in the larval stage with adults emerging primarily in early spring (Wright 1960). Eggs are laid in the open end of pores in the sapwood.

Young larvae tunnel irregular winding galleries that are parallel to the grain. While tunneling, the larvae loosely pack the galleries behind them with a talcumlike powder (Figure 16.13). Mature larvae pupate after boring a tunnel close to the surface of the wood. Emerging adults chew their way out of the wood. Heavily infested wood is riddled with round exit holes, about 3 mm in diameter. The southern lyctus beetle may complete two generations per year in the South under very favorable conditions such as high temperatures and high starch content.

Bostrichid Beetles, Bostrichidae

Bostrichid beetles are very abundant and cause serious damage to felled trees, buildings, and furniture in the tropics (Fisher 1950). These beetles do not cause as much damage in the temperate areas of the United States as do the lyctids, anobiids, or the old house borer. Bostrichid beetles mainly attack the sapwood of hardwoods, but a few species infest conifers. Some attack freshly cut wood, whereas others infest wood that has been cut for a long time.

Xylobiops basilaris (Say), a common species in the eastern and southern United States, often infests hickory, persimmon, and pecan (Figure 16.14). Occasionally, it causes serious damage to wood products such as rustic furniture and handles.

The bamboo powderpost beetle, *Dinoderus minutus* (Fabricius), a very common pest of bamboo in the West Indies, is now found in Florida and Louisiana. Frequently it is intercepted at ports of entry into the United States on bamboo products.

Anobiid Beetles, Anobiidae

About 280 species of anobiids occur in the United States; most feed on dead wood (White 1971, Simeone 1962). Under forest conditions, many species breed in twigs or larger branches. None are major pests in the forest, but some are significant pests of older wooden structures. Anobiids attack old, dry sapwood and heartwood of both conifers and hardwoods. Galleries of anobiids are tightly packed, with very small frass pellets; the galleries are less powdery in appearance than galleries formed by lyctid or bostrichid beetles (Figure 16.15). Many small (3-mm) round exit holes are present on material heavily damaged by anobiids. Usually these beetles are found in wood that has been in a wood structure for 10 or more years.

Xyletinus peltatus (Harris), a serious pest of structural timber in the southeastern United States, occurs from eastern Canada to Michigan and south to Arkansas and Florida. Under natural conditions, adults probably breed in dead branches and lightning scars unprotected by bark. In buildings, *X. peltatus* infestations usually begin in exposed untreated wood in crawl spaces under buildings. Damage is normally most severe with moderate temperatures and high relative humidities in the crawl spaces.

Adult emergence begins in mid-April and peaks in late May or early

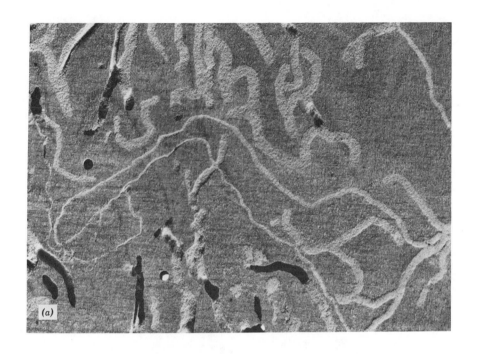

Figure 16.13 Lyctus powderpost beetle damage: (*a*) frass-packed tunnels and the round exit holes of adult beetles, (*b*) on arm of an upholstered piece of furniture. (U.S. Forest Service photograph.)

Figure 16.14 Bostrichid powderpost beetle damage. Piece of hickory with the bark and a little wood removed, revealing the tunnel of an adult powderpost beetle, *Xylobiops basilaris*. Entrance hole is shown at tip of arrow, and the gallery is seen extending on each side. Larvae, pupae, and emerging adults are shown in their cells. (U.S. Forest Service photograph.)

June in the deep South (Williams and Waldrop 1978). *Xyletinus pletatus* beetles prefer rough surfaces for oviposition. Larvae feed and pupate in the wood, usually being confined to the springwood. They most often damage softwood timbers in buildings, but also prefer porous hardwoods such as yellow poplar, maple, and beech (Williams and Mauldin 1974). Temperature and relative humidity influence the natural geographic distribution of *X. peltatus*. Severity of damage by this species to the interior of a building is probably controlled by temperature, wood moisture content, host wood species, and building construction characteristics (Williams 1977). The life cycle of *X. peltatus* may be completed in 1 year with favorable moisture and temperature conditions, but often conditions necessitate 3–5 years to complete its life cycle.

The Pacific powderpost beetle, *Hemicoelus gibbicollis* (LeConte) significantly damages buildings along the Pacific Coast from Alaska to California by attacking structural timbers and subflooring of older buildings without basements. This anobiid beetle prefers well-seasoned unrotted sapwood of both conifers and hardwoods (Figure 16.15).

Other anobiids occasionally encountered in scattered locations throughout the United States can cause heavy localized damage to wood: the fur-

Figure 16.15 Anobiid powderpost beetle damage. Shotholes and pulverizing of structural wood by the Pacific powderpost beetle, *Hemicoelus gibbicollis*. (U.S. Forest Service photograph.)

niture beetle, *Anobium punctatum* (De Geer) damages antique furniture and structural wood, and the deathwatch beetle, *Xestobium rufovillosum* (De Geer) damages structural wood in older buildings, primarily in the northeastern states.

Old House Borer, Cerambycidae

The old house borer, *Hylotrupes bajulus* (Linnaeus), accidentally introduced into North America over 200 years ago, can cause severe damage to buildings in the eastern United States (Figure 16.16). Contrary to its name, in North America the old house borer usually damages new buildings constructed with recently seasoned sapwood of pine and spruce, but sometimes this borer attacks lumber from hemlock, Douglas-fir, and true firs (Cannon and Robinson 1981, McIntyre 1976). The major signs of an old house borer infestation are a rasping or ticking sound by boring larvae, blistering of wood when larvae are tunneling close to the wood surface, boring dust on timber surface, and broad oval exit holes about 6 mm in cross section.

Females lay eggs in crevices, holes, cracks, and checks in the wood. Young

Figure 16.16 Old house borer, *Hylotrupes bajulus*. (U.S. Forest Service photograph.)

larvae feed near the surface of the wood, whereas older larvae bore tunnels and cause serious damage in the sapwood. Wood timbers can be severely damaged but appear sound since the larvae avoid breaking through the surface of the wood. Larval galleries are tightly packed with powdery borings and small frass pellets. Depending on temperature, relative humidity, wood moisture content, and nutrient content of wood, the old house borer generally spends 3–5 years completing its life cycle in the South and 5–8 years in the North.

Timberworms, Lymexylonidae, Brentidae

Timberworms, found in the eastern United States, make pinholes in the wood that can be separated from those caused by ambrosia beetles. The boring holes caused by timberworm larvae vary in size from 1 to 3 mm in diameter, the galleries are kept free of borings, and the gallery walls are seldom stained like those of the ambrosia beetles.

Pinholes made in the wood by timberworm larvae, such as the oak timberworm, *Arrhenodes minutus* Drury, severely degrade the wood so that it looses much of its economic value (Buchanan 1960).

Timberworms attack living trees, fresh logs, and dying hardwood trees such as oaks, beech, poplar, and birch. Females of different species of timberworms either lay eggs in cracks or deposit the eggs in deep holes chewed into the wood. Emerging larvae bore deeply into the sapwood and heartwood. The larva life cycle is usually completed in 2–4 years.

Lepidopterous Insects

Wood boring insects in the order Lepidoptera include the carpenterworms and clearwing moths. All carpenterworms cause considerble amount of damage to the wood, whereas some clearwing moths only feed in the phloem (Chapter 15), and others feed both in the phloem and the wood.

Carpenterworms, Cossidae

Approximately 50 species of carpenterworms occur in North America. Carpenterworm larvae bore into the phloem and wood of deciduous trees. Three species of carpenterworm are presented.

Carpenterworm

The carpenterworm, *Prionoxystus robiniae* (Peck), widely distributed throughout most of the United States and southern Canada, is considered a major pest of southern hardwoods (Solomon and Hay 1974). Host preference varies by location and host availability: oaks, especially the red oak group in the eastern and southern states; green ash in the prairie states, poplar in the Rocky Mountain region, and California live oaks and elms in California. Maples and black locust are also attacked by this wood borer. Carpenterworms attack small and large live trees but are particularly attracted to trees growing in open areas. Trees are seldom killed by the boring damage from the wood boring larvae, but lumber cut from infested trees is seriously degraded as a result of the large feeding tunnels, stain, and wood decays associated with the tunnels.

Length of the life cycle varies from 2 years in the extreme southern states to 4 years in the northeastern states and southern Canada. The large gray moths, with a wingspread of about 75 mm (Figure 16.17), emerge, mate, and deposit eggs in early summer (Solomon and Neel 1972, 1973, 1974). Female moths prefer to lay their 200–800 eggs in deep, narrow bark crevices, under vines or lichens, or near wounds and scars on the trunk or major limbs (Hay and Morris 1970). After about 2 weeks eggs hatch and larvae begin feeding in the cambium and then enter the sapwood and heartwood within 2 and 4 months, respectively. Tunnels are kept open by the larvae. The feeding tunnel eventually becomes 150–225 mm long, with a diameter of about 15 mm, and the tunnel is always stained light gray to dark brown or black by wood-rotting fungi (Figure 16.17). Mature larvae have a green-white body and brown head and reach a length of 50–75 mm (Figure 16.17). Pupation occurs in the newest end of the tunnel.

Other Cossids

The little carpenterworm, *Prionoxystus macmurtrei* (Guérin), widely distributed in eastern United States and eastern Canada, attacks oaks. Infestations are very local, and the life cycle and habits are similar to those of *P. robiniae*.

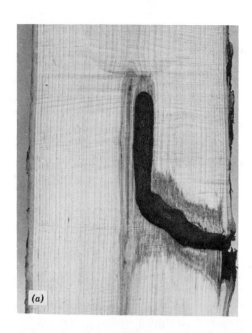

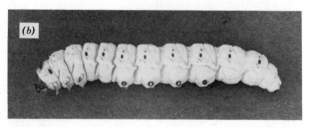

Figure 16.17 Carpenterworm, *Prionoxystus robiniae:* (*a*) boring damage on green ash, (*b*) larva, (*c*) adult female (left) and adult male (right). (U.S. Forest Service photograph, courtesy of J. Solomon.)

The leopard moth, *Zeuzera pyrina* (Linnaeus), an introduced pest found throughout the northeastern United States has been reared from over 125 deciduous hosts. The life cycle is similar to *P. robiniae*. The leopard moth is not a major pest because it seldom occurs in large numbers.

Clearwing moths, Sesiidae

Larvae of some clearwing moths such as the dogwood borer, *Synanthedon scitula* (Harris), are phloem feeders. Other clearwing moth larvae such as the lilac borer, *Podosesia syringae syringae* (Harris), and the ash borer, *Podesesia syringae fraxini* (Lugger), feed in the phloem and wood. Clearwing moths are pests when the larvae bore into the roots, trunks, and branches of ornamental trees and shrubs. Solomon and Dix (1979) compiled a list of references for this family. Two examples of clearwing moths that cause damage to the phloem and wood are presented in this chapter.

Lilac Borer

The lilac borer, *Podosesia syringae syringae* (Harris), a pest of lilac and privit throughout the eastern half of the United States and southern Canada, produces one generation per year. Adults emerge in late spring or early summer (Figure 16.18). Eggs are laid on the rough or scarred bark of lilac. Larvae first feed on the sapwood and then on the heartwood, overwintering in the heartwood.

Ash Borer

The ash borer, *Podosesia syringiae fraxini* (Lugger), is a pest of ornamental ash in the midwestern states, Rocky Mountain states, Texas, and into Manitoba and Saskatchewan. The life cycle and damage of the ash borer is similar to the lilac borer.

Figure 16.18   Lilac borer, *Podosesia syringae syringae,* the female moth; an example of a clearwing moth in the family Sesiidae. (U.S. Forest Service photograph, courtesy of J. Solomon.)

Hymenopterous Insects

Wood boring insects in the order Hymenoptera include carpenter ants, carpenter bees, and horntails. Carpenter ants and carpenter bees do not eat wood but only use it as a shelter. Some horntails actually digest the food.

Carpenter Ants, Formicidae

Ants belonging to the genus *Camponotus* are called "carpenter ants" because they tunnel into wood of standing live and dead trees, rotting logs, stumps, telephone poles, and certain wooden parts of houses (Figure 16.19). Carpenter ants are large ants, 5–15 mm long, and are black or black and red (Figure 16.19). The black carpenter ant, *Camponotus pennsylvanicus* (De Geer), is the most common species in the eastern United States. The Florida carpenter ant, *C. abdominalis* (Fabricius), ranging throughout the southern United States is one of the most important house-infesting pests in Florida. Several species of *Camponotus* occur commonly in the western United States.

(a)

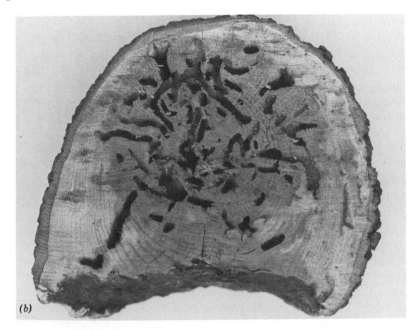

(b)

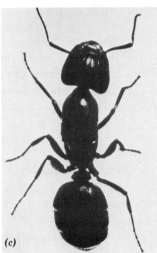

(c)

Figure 16.19 Carpenter ants damage the wood by cutting across the grain, but chambers or cavities are left clean: (a) damaged wood, (b) damage to trunk of oak shade tree, (c) adult (a,b—U.S. Forest Service photographs, c—from Southern Forest Insect Work Conference Slide Series).

Carpenter ants are considered as important pests as termites in the Pacific Northwest.

Carpenter ants are social insects that live in colonies consisting of thousands of individuals. There are three castes of adults: winged males, winged females, and workers. In the spring or early summer, young winged males and females leave the nest in a mating flight. Males die shortly after mating. Each queen mates only once but produces offspring throughout her 2–15-year life span. The young female may be taken into an established colony to replace a queen, or she may bore into a suitable piece of wood and establish a new colony. She then lays about 20 eggs and cares for the emerging larvae by feeding them a material secreted from her salivary glands. It takes about 2 months to complete development from egg to adult stage. Workers produced during the first years are all small. These small workers cut parallel galleries longitudinally through the wood to make a nest for the enlarging colony. Workers enlarge and clean the nest; forage for food; and care for the eggs, larvae, and queen.

Carpenter ants do not eat wood, but remove the wood to form galleries that serve as a nest. Usually carpenter ants initially attack a decayed or damaged spot even though they can tunnel into sound wood. Carpenter ants feed on other insects, honeydew produced by aphids, sap, juices of ripe fruit, meat, and refuse. Carpenter ants commonly invade houses and feed on molasses, honey, and other types of refuse.

Honeycomb wood boring damage caused by carpenter ants can be distinguished from termite damage because galleries of the carpenter ant run across the grain, are sandpaper smooth, and are free of frass (Figure 16.19). Coarse, fibrous borings are pushed out of the galleries and may accumulate around the infested wood. Major signs of a carpenter ant infestation inside of a building are swarms of large black, winged ants during the spring, piles of sawdustlike borings, and holes in woodwork such as window and door casings.

Carpenter ants usually enter live trees through cracks, scars, knot holes, or decay. Once inside the tree, damage may occur only at the base, or the ants may move higher into the tree. Infested forest and shade trees often become so weakened that they incur wind breakage (Fowler and Roberts 1982). Additional information on carpenter ants in forested areas is presented by Sanders (1964, 1970).

Carpenter Bees, Xylocopidae

Carpenter bees, belonging to the genus *Xylocopa*, are usually minor pests of wood structures because adults tunnel into the solid wood of beams, bridges, poles, posts, and wooden structures. Superficially, carpenter bees resemble bumblebees but are usually metallic blue–black rather than yellow and red, have a shiny smooth abdomen rather than a hairy one, and do not have pollen baskets on the hind legs.

Seven species of carpenter bees occur in the United States; there are five species in the West and two in the East. The carpenter bee, *Xylocopa virginica* (Linnaeus), is the most common species in the East, whereas *X. tabaniformis* Smith causes the most damage in the West.

The life cycle is similar for both species (Balduf 1962, Hurd 1955). In the spring, adult bees emerge and mate, whereupon the female bee bores in the wood and constructs a nest for rearing a brood. The female cuts an entrance hole straight into the wood for about 25 mm and then tunnels at a right angle for 300 mm or more. The removed wood is never eaten.

After the female completes the tunnel, she collects pollen and nectar to form a pollen–nectar food mass near the closed end of the gallery. She places an egg on the food mass and then seals it off from the rest of the tunnel by cementing chips of wood together. This process is continued until the gallery is filled with provisioned cells. A young larva feeds on the pollen and nectar for about 2 months until pupation. The young adult usually remains in its chamber until the following spring. There is one generation per year.

All species of dry seasoned wood may be used for nests, but the softer woods such as cedar, cypress, pines, fir, and redwoods are preferred hosts. Carpenter bees are not serious pests, but structural damage can occur in wood structures if the tunnels are used continuously for nesting.

Horntails, Siricidae

Horntails, also called "woodwasps," are large, often 25 mm or more in length, thick-waisted, wasplike insects. Adults are predominantly metallic blue or black in color, but most species have yellow or orange markings. Both sexes have a short hornlike process at the end of the abdomen.

Adults of most horntails emerge in late spring and early summer. They usually attack recently killed trees or fresh logs. Trees scorched by spring fires are the most attractive to the adults. Females use their long ovipositor to insert eggs into the solid wood of both coniferous and hardwood trees. Horntail larvae bore round tunnels about the size of a pencil through the heartwood of host trees. The wood passes through the digestive tract of the larva and is packed behind them in the tunnel. The life cycle of the horntail is normally completed in 1–2 years, depending on the climatic conditions and the moisture content of the wood. Mature larvae construct their pupal cells in the phloem. The exit holes bored by the emerging adults are round.

The blue horntail, *Sirex cyaneus* Fabricius, is a common species that attacks spruce and pine in southern Canada, northeastern United States and from California to British Columbia. Several species of horntails aid in the penetration and establishment of fungal pathogens in dying or dead balsam fir. The sap stain fungus, *Stereum chailletii*, is transmitted by horntails. The pigeon tremex, *Tremex columba* (Linnaeus), one of the largest and best known horntails in neartic America, breeds on a wide variety of hardwoods such as beech, maple, birch, elm, hickory, and oak (Stillwell 1967). Morgan (1968), Cameron (1965), and Middlekauff (1960) provide additional information on horntails.

Isopterous Insects

Information on this important and interesting group of insects is presented in six parts: general information; identification; caste system; interactions between termites, wood, and fungi; life cycles; and organisms involved.

General Information

Termites are one of the oldest and most primitive insect groups. Because they feed on cellulose, obtained primarily from wood, termites both benefit and harm human settlements and industry. In forested areas termites play a major role in the breakdown of forest litter and the subsequent reincorporation of the material into the soil. Much of the world's forested area would be an impenetrable mass of fallen trees and stumps without termites and decay fungi. Large numbers of termites are almost always present in the southern and southwestern United States and the tropics. They are found in stumps, fallen trees, and in other deadwood material in contact with the ground.

Termites seldom injure or kill live trees but can be very destructive to buildings, telephone poles, fences, and other wood products, particularly in the tropics and in the southern United States. Damage and cost of controlling termites in the United States is estimated to be between a half billion and a billion dollars per year.

Literature on termites is extensive. A number of comprehensive books have been published on the natural history, ecology, evolution, and control of termites (Brian 1978, Behnke 1977, Krishna and Weesner 1969–1970, Kofoid et al. 1934).

Identification

Common signs associated with termite infestations are (Figures 16.20–16.22): (1) appearance of winged adult termites in the house or termite wings on window sills, (2) honeycomb wood boring damage, (3) the presence of earthen tubes between the soil and some wooden structure under the house (i.e., subterranean termites), and (4) piles of fecal pellets on the outside of finished wood (i.e., drywood termites).

Sometimes termites are called "white ants." However, it is fairly easy to separate termites from ants. Termites are soft bodied and usually light colored, whereas ants are hard bodied and usually dark colored. A termite's thorax is broadly jointed to the abdomen, whereas the thorax and abdomen of an ant are jointed by a narrow waist called a *petiole*. Termite antennae are straight and beadlike (i.e., moniliform or filiform), whereas ant antennae are elbowed (i.e., geniculate). Front and hind wings of termites have many small veins and are similar in size, shape, and pattern, whereas in ants the front wings are larger than the hind wings and have more veins. Termites hold their wings flat over the abdomen when at rest; ants usually hold their wings above the body when at rest.

Caste System

Termites are social insects with a well-developed caste system (Figure 16.20) consisting of primary reproductives, supplementary reproductives, workers, and soldiers (Lüscher 1977, Wilson 1971). Primary reproductives (kings and queens) have fully developed wings, are usually heavily pigmented,

Figure 16.20 Eastern subterranean termite, *Reticulitermes flavipes:* (a) winged reproductive, (b) worker, (c) soldier. (U.S. Forest Service photograph.)

and are the most highly developed individuals sexually. Kings and queens are usually produced in large numbers during certain seasons of the year. Primary reproductives leave the colony in a swarm for a very short flight, mate, and then drop their wings. Because of high predation by birds and other insects, only a few primary reproductives (kings and queens) survive and establish a new colony and produce eggs. Supplementary reproductives are capable of reproducing and perpetuating the life of the colony if the king and queen die. In large colonies they may carry on extensive reproduction in addition to that of the king and queen.

The worker caste consists of nymphs and sterile adults that are pale in color, usually lack compound eyes, and have small mandibles. This caste performs most of the work of the colony. Workers feed on the wood and by regurgitation and excretion provide food for the very young larvae, soldiers, and queen. Also, the workers build the nest's passageways, tunnels, and galleries.

Soldiers, sterile adults with greatly enlarged and armored heads and

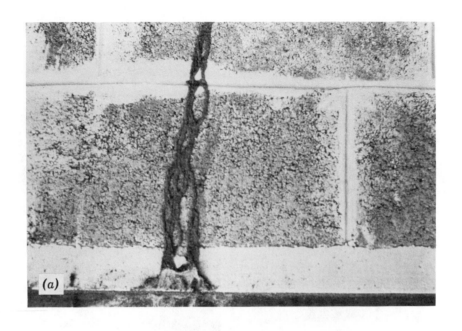

Figure 16.21 Signs and damage caused by the eastern subterranean termite, *Reticulitermes flavipes:* (*a*) shelter tube, (*b*) termite damage follows the grain; chambers are left cluttered with gray–brown excretion, (*c*) damage to a house, (U.S. Forest Service photographs.)

mandibles, attack invaders of the colony. These soldiers also signal the other colony members that there is danger by striking their heads against the side of tunnels.

Only two castes, soldiers and reproductives, are present in some of the primitive species of termites. The work of the colony is performed by the immature termites of these two castes.

Interactions Between Termites, Wood, and Fungi

Termites can ingest cellulose from wood and other plants because protozoa and bacterial organisms in their gut convert the cellulose to digestible smaller units. Digestion of the cellulose often begins before the termites are attracted to the wood. Decay fungi are normally present on the wood and start breaking the cellulose into smaller units. The heartwood becomes a preferred feeding and nesting site for termites after the toxins and repellent resins are broken down by the brown cubical rots. Subterranean termites are attracted to wood by an olfactory attractant produced by the brown rot fungus, *Gloeophyllum trabeum*. Amburgey and Beal (1977) showed that white rot decay fungi inhibits attack by subterranean termites. Amburgey (1979) provided a review on the interaction between wood-inhabiting fungi and subterranean termites.

Sound wood can be ingested by termites, but the presence of certain decay fungi accelerates their intake of wood. Termites need all the protozoan species present in their gut. Experiments have shown that removing only one species of protozoan from the gut of termites will cause death

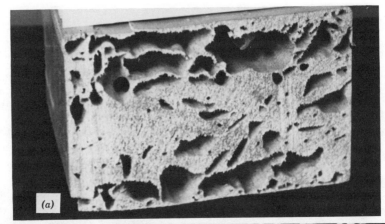

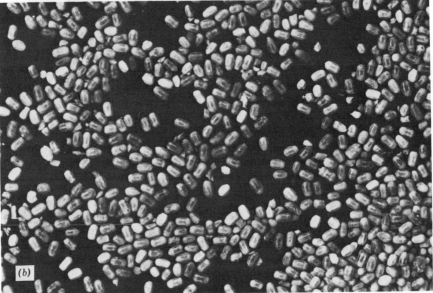

Figure 16.22 Drywood termites: (A) damage, (B) excreted pellets. (U.S. Forest Service photograph.)

from starvation because the wood cannot be digested by the termites. Microorganisms in the termite's gut are shed when it molts to the next instar. However, the microorganisms are reestablished immediately after molting by proctodeal feeding on other members of the colony that have not molted recently.

Life Cycle

The life cycle of subterranean termites in the genus *Reticulitermes* is typical of most termites. The time of colonizing flights usually varies by species but often occurs after a warm rain during early spring. Winged reproductives leave en masse, fly a short distance, mate, and shed their wings.

A few of the individuals survive and start new colonies. The growth of a new colony from a pair of primary reproductives is slow. The female lays 6–12 eggs. It takes about a year before the first nymphs reach maturity. Then soldiers and reproductive nymphs appear in the colony. Under very favorable conditions, flights of primary reproductives do not occur until the third or fourth year. As the colony becomes well established, supplementary reproductives greatly help to increase the size of the colony. The average *Reticulitermes flavipes* (Kollar) colony in southern Mississippi contains about 250,000 termites (Howard et al. 1982). In the colonies, workers predominate (84%), followed by larvae (9%), nymphs (5%), soldiers (2%), and supplementary reproductives (0.1%), respectively (Howard and Haverty 1981). Additional general information on colony formation, life cycle, and control of subterranean termites is presented by Haverty (1976a,b), Ebeling (1968, 1975), Johnston et al. (1972), and Weesner (1956, 1960).

Organisms Involved

There are 40 termite species that are native to the continental United States, 15 in the East and 25 in the West. There are four groups based on their habits: dampwood termites, subterranean termites, drywood termites, and powderpost termites.

Dampwood Termites

Dampwood termites attack moist wood; they do not require contact with the ground, but require wood with a high moisture content. These termites usually occur in dead, damp, rotting logs but frequently damage poles, pilings, and buildings in the Pacific Coast region, especially in very foggy areas.

The most common dampwood termites include three species in the genus *Zootermopsis* (family Hadotermidae) that are found along the Pacific Coast from British Columbia to Baja, California. *Zootermopsis* species commonly attack dead and fallen trees, houses, and other wooden structures. They cause damage to wooden structures, but their presence in large numbers indicates a basic rot problem with the particular structure. The Pacific dampwood termite, *Zootermopsis angusticollis* (Hagen), is the common dampwood termite of the Pacific Coast forests that normally colonizes most dead and down trees and untreated wood products in contact with the ground. The Nevada dampwood termite, *Zootermopsis nevadensis* (Hagen), is similar in appearance and habits to the Pacific dampwood termite but tends to occur in the more cooler, drier, and higher areas from southern British Columbia to central California and east to Montana.

Several species of dampwood termites are present in the families Kalotermitidae and Rhinotermitidae. These species belong to the genera *Neotermes*, *Paraneotermes*, and *Prorhinotermes* and are found in Florida and the southwestern United States. They cause minor damage since moist dead wood or tree roots are preferred hosts. Occasionally they will girdle living plants such as young citrus trees and grape vines below the soil line in desert areas.

Subterranean Termites

Subterranean termites, family Rhinotermitidae, are the most common group of termites in the continental United States and also cause the greatest damage to wood structures. These termites require a constant supply of moisture. Their colonies are located in the ground, but they may feed in wood located some distance from the nest. To feed above ground, these termites must construct covered passageways, called *earthened tubes* or *sheltered tubes*, from the nest to the feeding site.

Subterranean termites always leave the covering shell of the wood intact so that they are not exposed to desiccation or light. They feed primarily on the springwood and leave the harder summerwood in ribbons (Figure 16.21). Mud is always present in the honeycomb wood boring damage caused by subterranean termites.

Most subterranean termites in the United States are in the genus *Reticulitermes*, but one other genus, *Coptotermes*, was recently accidentally introduced into the continental United States. Four subterranean termite species are of major concern to the United States public.

The eastern subterranean termite, *Reticulitermes flavipes* (Kollar), the most destructive of all termites in the continental United States, occurs from the Gulf of Mexico north to Ontario and from the Great Plains to the East Coast. It does not occur in the far West. The generalized life cycle and caste system of subterranean termites were described at the beginning of this section. More detailed information on the eastern subterranean termite is presented by Howard et al. (1982) and Howard and Haverty (1980, 1981).

The western subterranean termite, *Reticulitermes hesperus* Banks, the major termite pest in the far western United States, ranges from southern British Columbia south to western Mexico and east to Idaho and Nevada. The life cycle and damage is similar to *R. flavipes* (Ebeling 1975, Kofoid et al. 1934).

The aridland subterranean termite, *Reticulitermes tibialis* Banks, probably the most widely distributed species of subterranean termites in the United States, is found primarily in the western United States, but it also occurs in the northern central states and as far east as the Chicago area (Baker 1972). Life cycle and damage is similar to *R. flavipes* (Kofoid et al. 1934).

The Formosan subterranean termite, *Coptotermes formosanus* Shiraki, is a destructive oriental species that was first found in the continental United States, in 1965 in Houston, Texas. It is now found in Hawaii, Texas, Louisiana, and South Carolina. This insect is a widespread pest in the tropical and subtropical areas of Asia. Life cycle and damage is similar to the other subterranean termites. This termite can be extremely destructive because the queen can lay up to 1000 eggs per day. In Hawaii the walls of new buildings have been destroyed in 3 months. This termite also feeds on living and dead standing trees in Texas and Louisiana.

Drywood Termites

Drywood termites belong to the family Kalotermitidae. They are extremely serious pests in the tropics but occur in the United States only along the coastal or border states from Virginia into California. The drywood termites are major pests in the United States in Florida, Arizona, California, and Hawaii. These termites do not need any contact with the soil. Once established in a region through shipment of infested wood, they can enter other buildings by going under shingles, through cracks in windows, or through screen vents in the attic. At swarming time, drywood termites fly directly to and enter untreated wood. The major signs of attack of drywood termites are piles of brown fecal pellets below the infested wood (Figure 16.22) and swarms of winged adults within the infested building. These drywood termites establish their colonies, live, and cause damage in sound nondecayed wood that contains very little moisture (Ebeling 1968, Kofoid et al. 1934).

The western drywood termite, *Incisitermes minor* (Hagen), is a major pest in southern California, parts of Arizona, and Mexico. This insect is commonly found in the dead limbs of orchard trees, especially walnut, and in the upper portions of buildings. Colonies are usually much smaller in size than subterranean termites; thus the damage in buildings usually occurs less rapidly than with subterranean termites. These colonies consist only of the primary reproductive pair, a few supplementary reproductives, some soldiers, and primary immature forms (i.e., nymphs). The immatures do the major work of the colony and there is no true worker caste.

In the southeastern United States, the southeastern drywood termite, *I. snyderi* (Light), is the most common species. The life cycle and type of damage is similar to *I. minor*, but it is not as severe a pest.

Powderpost Termites

The powderpost termites usually attack drywood, do not have a ground contact, and can reduce the wood to a powder. These termites occur in the southern United States. The most common species is *Cryptotermes brevis* (Walker), which was accidentally introduced into the United States. This species is now well established in Hawaii, Florida, and Louisiana (Ebeling 1975). This species is not established in any natural habitat in the continental United States, where it occurs only in buildings. It was probably introduced in furniture and can cause severe damage to floors, woodwork, furniture, and small wooden objects.

MANAGEMENT APPROACHES USED AGAINST WOOD BORING INSECTS

The two major approaches used against wood boring insects are prevention and control. In this section we present examples of each. Additional information on management approaches is presented by Ebeling (1975),

Smythe and Williams (1974), Johnston et al. (1972), Schread (1971), and Williams and Johnston (1971).

Prevention

There are a number of prevention techniques that can be used to lessen the damage caused by wood boring insects. Numerous silvicultural techniques can be used to reduce the susceptibility of forest stands to certain wood boring insects. Stands of healthy, vigorous fast-growing poplar and black locust sustain very little damage from the poplar borer and locust borer, respectively. The removal and destruction of trees with numerous signs of red oak borers in pole-sized oak stands reduces the chances of subsequent attack in the residual stand. The prompt salvage and utilization of windthrown, dead, and dying trees will reduce the impact for many wood boring beetles such as sawyer beetles and the firtree borer.

Prevention techniques for reducing ambrosia beetle damage concentrates on the removal of the logs from the forest before they are attacked during the beetle flight season and minimizing storage time in dryland sorts and sawmill yards. Water misting has proved to be very effective in protecting high-value logs in a small area (Nijholt 1978). Another prevention technique that can be used against ambrosia beetles is to use trap logs or pheromone-baited traps to suppress ambrosia beetle populations.

The damage from lyctid beetles can be prevented or reduced considerably in lumber yards and manufacturing plants by frequent inspections of the wood, rapid turnover and utilization of the hardwood lumber, burning or removing all scrap material, and by using old stock first to reduce the breeding sites of lyctid beetles. Another method of protecting material from lyctid beetles is to treat the wood with a sealer such as linseed oil, varnish, or paint. Early detection of lyctid beetle damage in homes allows the homeowner to control the insect by replacement and destruction of the damaged material.

With bostrichid beetles, the best techniques to prevent damage is the rapid utilization of hardwood logs and the removal of the bark from wood being used as house timbers or for rustic material. With anobiids, use of treated lumber and maintenance of adequate ventilation around buildings, especially in crawl space, aids in prevention of damage. The old house borer can be controlled by using properly stored kiln dry material.

Subterranean and drywood termites require somewhat different types of prevention and control techniques. Proper construction techniques help to prevent both subterranean and drywood termite infestations. The following techniques are helpful in preventing termite infestations in buildings. Remove all tree roots, stumps, or other wood debris from the building site before starting construction of the building. Prevent moisture from accumulating in the soil beneath the building by using techniques to promote drainage (i.e., drainage tile around outside of buildings with basements, use of eave gutters). Treat the soil with a registered insecticide before pouring the foundation. Concrete foundations should be rendered impervious to termites to prevent hidden attack on any wood associated with the building (Haverty 1976b, Johnston et al. 1972). The ventilation openings in foundation walls beneath wooden structures with crawl space should be evenly distributed and large enough to prevent the formation of dead-air pockets where relative humidity conditions favor subterranean termites. The lumber in the building should be prevented from becoming wet as a result of rain, condensation, leaking pipes, and dripping faucets. Buildings should be inspected once a year in areas where termites cause major damage.

Drywood termites infest drywood, and the prevention techniques are different. Prevention techniques for drywood termites begin with construction practices that result in tightly sealed buildings. Painting of all exposed wood surfaces and annual inspection of the building in areas where drywood termites are a problem also prevent serious damage.

Control

Chemical control techniques for wood boring insects in wood products involves the use of registered insecticides such as chlorinated hydrocarbons and fumigants against insects such as termites and powderpost beetles. If termites or powderpost beetles or other insects in wooden structures are observed, proper identification of the insect is the first step in deciding on a treatment tactic or strategy. If these insects cannot be easily removed by replacing damaged boards, a responsible pest control operator or extension specialist can be consulted for advice. Reliable representatives of the structural pest control industry can apply treatments.

Pheromone-Based Suppression Program for Ambrosia Beetles at a Commercial Sawmill

Ambrosia beetles play an important primary role in helping to break down deadwood in the forests of the Pacific Northwest. The three most important species of ambrosia beetles are *Trypodendron lineatum* (Olivier), *Gnathotrichus sulcatus* (LeConte), and *G. retusus* (LeConte). In the spring these species infest the sapwood of coniferous trees that died the previous winter. Males of *Gnathotrichus* species and females of *T. lineatum* initiate the attack and produce aggregation pheromones that bring about mass attack on suitable hosts. Under natural conditions this process ensures maximum utilization of suitable dead and dying host material. However, these ambrosia beetles also can build up to high population levels in and around dryland log sorting areas and sawmills. Under these conditions ambrosia beetles can cause damage to logs and green lumber (McLean and Borden 1977).

Borden and McLean (1981) and McLean and Borden (1979) described an operational pheromone-based suppression program for the ambrosia

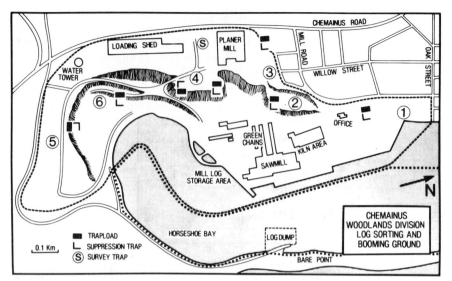

Figure 16.23 Map of the MacMillan Bloedel, Chemainus Division Sawmill, Vancouver Island, British Columbia, Canada, showing numbered study locations and appropriate position in 1976 of the suppression traps and adjacent trap loads, and the survey trap in location 4. The dashed line indicates the working area of the sawmill including the log storage area, and the dotted line indicates the position of Horseshoe Bay used for dumping, sorting, and booming logs from the Chemainus Woodlands Division. (From McLean and Borden, 1979.)

Figure 16.24 The Lindgren multiple-dash funnel pheromone trap that is currently being used to mass trap ambrosia beetles at sawmills and dryland sorts in British Columbia, the Pacific Northwest, and Alaska. (Courtesy of R. Long, Simon Fraser University.)

beetle, *G. sulcatus,* in a commercial sawmill in British Columbia. *Gnathotrichus sulcatus* can complete its life cycle and cause degrade in green lumber (McLean and Borden 1975). It also has been intercepted in countries importing lumber from British Columbia.

A management strategy was needed that would intercept the adult ambrosia beetle at the sawmill before they reached their intended hosts (logs, green lumber). This strategy would reduce the amount of degrade and prevent expensive quarantine measures in the importing country. Sticky traps baited with the synthetic aggregating pheromone of the male *G. sulcatus* were set out in a commercial sawmill in 1976 (Figure 16.23). An estimated 65% of the total population was captured in the traps (Figure 16.24). Complete suppression was not achieved, but mill personnel evaluated the attack rate on lumber as very low in comparison to past experiences. The suppression trapping program is fairly inexpensive, and the mill has incorporated this suppression program into its normal quality control operations.

REFERENCES

Amburgey, T. L. 1979. Review and checklist of the literature on interactions between wood-inhabiting fungi and subterranean termites: 1960–1978. *Sociobiology* **4**:279–296.

Amburgey, T. L. and R. H. Beal. 1977. White rot inhibits termite attack. *Sociobiology* **3**:35–38.

Baker, W. L. 1972. *Eastern Forest Insects*. U.S. Department of Agriculture Forest Service Miscellaneous Publication 1175.

Balduf, W. V. 1962. Life of the carpenter bee, *Xylocopa virginica* (Linn.) (Xylocopidae: Hymenoptera). *Annu. Rev. Entomol.* **55**:263–271.

Batra, L. R. 1968. Ambrosia fungi: A taxonomic revision, and nutritional studies of some species. *Mycologia* **59**:976–1017.

Behnke, F. L. 1977. *A Natural History of the Termites*. Charles Scribner's Sons, New York.

Borden, J. H. and J. A. McLean. 1981. Pheromone-based suppression of ambrosia beetles in industrial timber processing areas. In Mitchell E. R. (Ed.), *Management of Insect Pests with Semiochemicals: Concepts and Practice*. Plenum Press, New York.

Brian, M. V. (Ed.). 1978. *Production Ecology of Ants and Termites*. Cambridge University Press, Cambridge.

Buchanan, W. D. 1960. Biology of the oak timberworm. *J. Econ. Entomol.* **53**:510–513.

Cameron, E. A. 1965. The siricinae (Hymenoptera: Siricidae) and their parasites. *Commonwealth Inst. Biol. Control Bull.* **5**:1–31.

Cannon, K. F. and W. H. Robinson. 1981. Wood consumption and growth of *Hylotrupes bajulus* (L.) larvae in three environments. *Environ. Entomol.* **10**:458–461.

Chapman, J. A. and E. D. A. Dyer. 1969. Characteristics of Douglas-fir logs in relation to ambrosia beetle attack. *For. Sci.* **15**:95–101.

Christian, M. B. 1939. Experiments on the prevention of ambrosia beetle damage in hardwoods. *S. Lumberman* **159**:110–112.

Donley, D. E. 1978. Oviposition by the red oak borer, *Enaphalodes rufulus* Coleoptera: Cerambycidae. *Ann. Entomol. Soc. Am.* **71**:496–498.

Donley, D. E. and R. E. Acciavatti. 1980. Red oak borer. U.S. Department of Agriculture Forest Service Forest Insect and Disease Leaflet 163.

Drouin, J. A. and H. R. Wong. 1975. Biology, damage, and chemical control of the poplar borer (*Saperda calcarata*) in the junction of the root and stem of balsam poplar in western Canada. *Can. J. For. Res.* **5**:433–439.

Dyer, E. D. A. and J. M. Kinghorn. 1961. Factors influencing the distribution of overwintering ambrosia beetles, *Trypodendron lineatum* (Oliv.). *Can. Entomol.* **93**:746–759.

Dyer, E. D. A. and J. A. Chapman. 1965. Flight and attack of the ambrosia beetle *Trypodendron lineatum* (Oliv.) in relation to the felling date of logs. *Can. Entomol.* **97**:42–57.

Ebeling, W. 1968. *Termites, Identification, Biology, and Control of Termites Attacking Buildings.* California Agricultural Experiment Station Extension Service Manual 38.

Ebeling, W. 1975. *Urban Entomology.* Division of Agricultural Science, University of California, Berkeley.

Fisher, W. S. 1950. *A Revision of the North American Species of Beetles Belonging to the Family Bostrichidae.* U.S. Department of Agriculture Miscellaneous Publication 698.

Fowler, H. G. and R. B. Roberts. 1982. Carpenter ant (Hymenoptera: Formicidae) induced wind breakage in New Jersey shade trees. *Can. Entomol.* **114**:649–650.

Furniss, R. L. and V. M. Carolin. 1977. *Western Forest Insects.* U.S. Department of Agriculture Forest Service Miscellaneous Publication 1339.

Gerberg, E. J. 1957. *A Revision of the New World Species of Powder-Post Beetles Belonging to the Family Lyctidae.* U.S. Department of Agriculture Technical Bulletin 1157.

Haverty, M. I. 1976a. Termites. *Pest Control* **44**:12–17, 46–49.

Haverty, M. I. 1976b. *You Can Protect Your Home from Termites.* U.S. Department of Agriculture Forest Service (unnumbered bulletin).

Hay, C. J. and R. C. Morris. 1970. Carpenterworm. U.S. Department of Agriculture Forest Service Forest Pest Leaflet 64.

Hay, C. J. and J. D. Solomon. 1981. *A Selective Bibliography on Insects Causing Wood Defects in Living Eastern Hardwood Trees.* U.S. Department of Agriculture, Bibliography and Literature of Agriculture 15.

Howard, R. W. and M. I. Haverty. 1980. Reproductives in mature colonies of *Reticulitermes flavipes* (Kollar): Abundance, sex-ratio, and association with soldiers. *Environ. Entomol.* **9**:458–460.

Howard, R. W. and M. I. Haverty. 1981. Seasonal variation in caste proportions of field colonies of *Reticulitermes flavipes* (Kollar). *Environ. Entomol.* **10**:546–549.

Howard, R. W., S. C. Jones, J. K. Mauldin, and R. H. Beal. 1982. Abundance, distribution, and colony size estimates for *Reticulitermes* spp. (Isoptera: Rhinotermitidae) in southern Mississippi. *Environ. Entomol.* **11**:1290–1293.

Hurd, P. D. 1955. The carpenter bees of California (Hymenoptera: Apoidea). *Calif. Insect Surv. Bull.* **4**(2):35–72.

Johnson, N. E. 1958. Field identification of ambrosia beetles attacking coniferous timber in the Douglas-fir region. *Can. Entomol.* **90**:236–240.

Johnston, H. R., V. K. Smith, and R. H. Beal. 1972. *Subterranean Termites, Their Prevention and Control in Buildings.* U.S. Department of Agriculture, Home and Gardens Bulletin 64.

Kabir, A. K. M. F. and R. L. Giese. 1966a. The Columbian timber beetle, *Corthylus columbianus* (Coleoptera: Scolytidae). I. Biology of the beetle. *Ann. Entomol. Soc. Am.* **59**:883–894.

Kabir, A. K. M. F. and R. L. Giese. 1966b. The Columbian timber beetles, *Corthylus columbianus* (Coleoptera: Scolytidae). II. Fungi and staining associated with the beetle in soft maple. *Ann. Entomol. Soc. Am.* **59**:894–902.

Knight, F. B. and H. J. Heikkenen. 1980. *Principles of Forest Entomology.* McGraw-Hill, New York.

Kofoid, C. A., S. F. Light, A. C. Horner, and Others. 1934. *Termites and Termite Control.* University of California Press, Berkeley.

Krishna, K. and F. M. Weesner (Eds.). 1969–1970. *Biology of Termites,* Vol. 1 and 2. Academic Press, New York.

Linsley, E. G. 1959. Ecology of Cerambycidae. *Annu. Rev. Entomol.* **4**:99–138.

Lüscher, M. (Ed.). 1977. *Phase and Caste Determination in Insects: Endocrine Aspects.* Pergamon Press, New York.

McIntyre, T. 1976. The old house borer. U.S. Department of Agriculture Leaflet 501.

McLean, J. A. and J. H. Borden. 1975. *Gnathotrichus sulcatus* attack and breeding in freshly sawn lumber. *J. Econ. Entomol.* **68**:605–606.

McLean, J. A. and J. H. Borden. 1977. Suppression of *Gnathotrichus sulcatus* with sulcatol-baited traps in a commercial sawmill and notes on the occurrence of *G. retusus* and *Trypodendron lineatum. Can. J. For. Res.* **7**:348–356.

McLean, J. A. and J. H. Borden. 1979. An operational pheromone-based suppression program for an ambrosia beetle, *Gnathotrichus sulcatus,* in a commercial sawmill. *J. Econ. Entomol.* **72**:165–172.

Middlekauff, W. W. 1960. The siricid wood wasps of California (Hymenoptera: Symphyta). *Calif. Insect Surv. Bull.* **6**(4):59–77.

Morgan, F. D. 1968. Bionomics of Siricidae. *Annu. Rev. Entomol.* **13**:239–256.

Morris, R. C., T. H. Filer, J. D. Solomon, F. I. McCracken, N. A. Overgaard, and M. J. Weiss. 1975. *Insects and Diseases of Cottonwood.* U.S. Department of Agriculture Forest Service General Technical Report SO-8.

Nijholt, W. W. 1978. *Evaluation of Operational Watermisting for Log Protection from Ambrosia Beetle Damage.* Canadian Forestry Service, Pacific Forest Research Centre Report BC-P-22-78.

Nijholt, W. W. 1979. *The Striped Ambrosia Beetle, Trypodendron lineatum (Oliver): An annotated Bibliography.* Canadian Forestry Service, Pacific Forest Research Centre Report.

Nord, J. C. and M. L. McManus. 1972. The Columbian timber beetle. U.S. Department of Agricultural Forest Service Forest Pest Leaflet 132.

Raske, A. G. 1973a. Notes on the biology of *Tetropium parvulum* (Coleoptera: Cerambycidae) in Alberta. *Can. Entomol.* **105**:757–760.

Raske, A. G. 1973b. *Tetropium parvulum* elevated to species rank and contrasted to *T. cinnamopterum* in morphology and host preference (Coleoptera: Cerambycidae) in Alberta. *Can. Entomol.* **105**:745–755.

Sanders, C. J. 1964. The biology of carpenter ants in New Brunswick. *Can. Entomol.* **96**:894–909.

Sanders, C. J. 1970. The distribution of carpenter ants in colonies in the spruce-fir forests of northwestern Ontario. *Ecology* **51**:865–873.

Schread, J. C. 1971. *Control of Borers in Trees and Woody Ornamentals.* Connecticut Agriculture Experiment Station Circular 241.

Simeone, J. B. 1962. Survey of wood-feeding Anobiidae in northeastern United States including a study of temperature and humidity effects on egg development of *Hadrobregmus carinatus* Say. *Proceedings of the Eleventh International Congress on Entomology,* Vienna, 2nd Section, pp. 326–335.

Smith, D. N. 1962. Prolonged larval development in *Buprestis aurulenta* L. (Coleoptera: Buprestidae). A review with new cases. *Can. Entomol.* **94**:586–593.

Smythe, R. V. and L. H. Williams. 1974. Structural pest control regulations. U.S. Department of Agriculture Forest Service Research Paper SO-93.

Solomon, J. D. and M. E. Dix. 1979. *Selected Bibliography of the Clearwing Borers (Sesiidae) of the U.S. and Canada.* U.S. Department of Agriculture Forest Service General Technical Report SO-22.

Solomon, J. D. and C. J. Hay. 1974. *Annotated bibliography of the carpenterworm, Prionoxystus robiniae.* U. S. Department of Agriculture Forest Service General Technical Report SO-4.

Solomon, J. D. and W. W. Neel. 1972. Emergence behavior and rhythms in the carpenterworm moths, *Prionoxystus robiniae. Ann. Entomol. Soc. Am.* **65**:1296–1299.

Solomon, J. D. and W. W. Neel. 1973. Mating behavior in the carpenterworm moth, *Prionoxystus robiniae* (Lepidoptera: Cossidae). *Ann. Entomol. Soc. Am.* **66**:312–314.

Solomon, J. D. and W. W. Neel. 1974. Fecundity and oviposition behavior in the carpenterworm, *Prionoxystus robiniae. Ann. Entomol. Soc. Am.* **67**:238–240.

Stillwell, M. A. 1967. The pigeon tremex, *Tremex columba* (Hymenoptera: Siricidae), in New Brunswick. *Can. Entomol.* **99**:685–689.

Weesner, F. M. 1956. The biology of colony foundation in *Reticulitermes hesperus* Banks. *Univ. Calif. Publ. Zool.* **61**:253–306.

Weesner, F. M. 1960. Evolution and biology of the termites. *Annu. Rev. Entomol.* **5**:153–170.

White, R. E. 1971. Key to North American genera of Anobiidae, with phylogenetic and synonymic notes (Coleoptera). *Ann. Entomol. Soc. Am.* **64**:179–191.

Wickman, B. E. 1968a. Fir tree borer. U.S. Department of Agriculture Forest Service Forest Pest Leaflet 115.

Wickman, B. E. 1968b. The biology of the fir tree borer, *Semanotus litigiosus* (Coleoptera: Cerambycidae) in California. *Can. Entomol.* **100**:208–220.

Williams, L. H. 1973. Identifying wood-destroying beetles. *Pest Control* **41**(5):30,32,34,36, 38,40.

Williams, L. H. 1977. Responses of *Xyletinus peltatus* [(Harris) Coleoptera: Anobiidae] larvae to favorable and unfavorable temperatures. *Mater. Org.* **12**:59–67.

Williams, L. H. and H. R. Johnston. 1971. Controlling wood-destroying beetles in buildings and furniture. U.S. Department of Agriculture Leaflet 558.

Williams, L. H. and J. K. Mauldin. 1974. Anobiid beetle, *Xylentinus peltatus* (Coleoptera: Anobiidae), oviposition on various woods. *Can. Entomol.* **106**:949–955.

Williams, L. H. and J. D. Waldrop. 1978. *Xyletinus peltatus* seasonal flight, diel activity, and associated environmental influences. *Ann. Entomol. Soc. Am.* **71**:567–574.

Wilson, E. O. 1971. *The Insect Societies.* Harvard University Press, Cambridge.

Wilson, L. F. 1975. Whitespotted sawyer. U.S. Department of Agriculture Forest Service Pest Leaflet 75.

Wollerman, E. H. 1970. The locust borer. U.S. Department of Agriculture Forest Service Forest Pest Leaflet 71.

Wright, C. G. 1960. Biology of the southern Lyctus beetle, *Lyctus planicollis. Ann. Entomol. Soc. Am.* **53**:285–292.

17 | Gall Makers

INTRODUCTION

When feeding on plant tissues, many insects and mites inject or secrete a chemical substance into the plant that causes the plant to grow abnormally and produce a gall. Stimulus for gall formation is usually provided by the feeding stage of the insect, but in some insects the ovipositing female provides the stimulus when she lays eggs on the plant. The exact cause of gall formation is poorly understood, but the stimulus for gall formation is believed to be a growth-regulating chemical. Aphids, causing galls, probably affect plant growth by secreting a substance in their saliva that decreases plant growth hormones and increases growth inhibitors. If the insect or mite dies or leaves the host, the plant resumes normal growth.

Galls may be found on leaves, buds, stems, or roots. Plant galls are caused by insects, mites, nematodes, bacteria, fungi, and viruses, but most galls are produced by insects and mites. Galls are caused by insects such as cynipid wasps and sawflies (Hymenoptera); by gall adelgids, aphids, and psyllids (Homoptera); by gall midges (Diptera); and by a few twig borers (Coleoptera, Lepidoptera). The greatest majority of galls are produced by cynipid wasps in the family Cynipidae, gall midges in the family Cecidomyiidae, and eriophyid mites in the class Arachnida, order Acari, and family Eriophyidae.

Insects and mites causing galls are not considered economically important pests of forest stands. Gall makers are considered serious pests on certain ornamental trees and shrubs, and a few are pests on Christmas trees. The forester or natural resource specialist must be able to recognize the common galls and to advise the landowner or homeowner whether the particular gall maker is or is not a pest. Usually control techniques are not needed for gall makers, but they are useful in certain situations such as Christmas tree plantations and ornamentals.

Each species of insect or mite produces a characteristic gall on a certain part of a specific plant. Identification of the organism causing the gall by using the shape of the gall and the species of host plant is extremely important because these insects and mites are often extremely small and very difficult to identify at the species level. Hutchins (1969), Mani (1964), and Felt (1925, 1940) provide useful information for identifying many gall maker species.

Biological information on the most common arthropods causing galls is presented in this chapter and, when appropriate, information on control of gall-forming organisms.

ORGANISMS INVOLVED

Most common insects and mites causing galls on forest and shade trees are found in six orders: Hymenoptera, Diptera, Homoptera, Coleoptera, Lepidoptera, and Acari (class Arachnida).

Hymenopterous Insects

Hymenopterous insects in three families (i.e., Cynipidae, Tenthredinidae, Eurytomidae) commonly cause galls on forest and shade trees. Cynipid wasps, often called gall wasps, are the most common.

Cynipid Wasps, Gall Wasps, Cynipidae

Most cynipid wasps are "gall makers," and approximately 80% are found on oak. Galls are found on all parts of host tree, but most are found on leaves and branches. Galls range from 1 to over 50 mm and vary from round to irregular in shape. Adult wasps are 1–6 mm long, antlike, usually black insects that are recognized by their characteristic shape and wing venation pattern (Figure 17.1).

Many gall wasps have complex life cycles, with two different generations per year (Figure 17.1). One generation of parthenogenetic females develop during the early summer in one type of gall. They lay eggs that hatch, and these larvae cause an entirely different type of gall. Male and female adults emerge and mate; eggs are deposited in twigs or leaves depending on the species. At first glance, galls and adults from the two generations of one species often appear to be different species (Evans 1972). Most gall wasps cause no damage to forest or shade trees. Some species produce irregularly shaped galls on twigs and branches that result in unsightly trees. Heavy population densities of gall wasps can eventually cause branch and tree mortality. Gall makers in four common genera of Cynipidae are described.

Callirhytis spp.

The majority of cynipid gall wasps cause no significant impact, but two species of gall makers in the genus *Callirhytis* can cause severe injury, even mortality, in oak shade trees (Johnson and Lyon 1976). Gouty oak gall, caused by *C. punctata* Osten Sacken, is commonly found on the twigs and branches of scarlet, red, pin, and black oaks from southern Canada to Georgia. Horned oak gall, caused by *C. cornigera* Osten Sacken, is found over the same geographic range as the gouty oak gall, but attacks pin, scrub, black, blackjack, and water oak. Horned oak and gouty oak galls (Figure 17.2) are similar, except that the mature horned oak galls have horns protruding through the surface. These galls can be as large as 50 mm in diameter and often grow together to form a mass that can be up to 1 m long.

Life cycles of these two gall wasps are complex and not well known. A pictorial life cycle of the horned oak gall is presented (Figure 17.1).

Amphibolips spp.

All of the species (over 100) in this genus occur on oaks. The best known species cause large applelike galls on the leaves, leaf petioles, or twigs of oak trees (Figure 17.3). *Amphibolips confluenta* Harris is found throughout

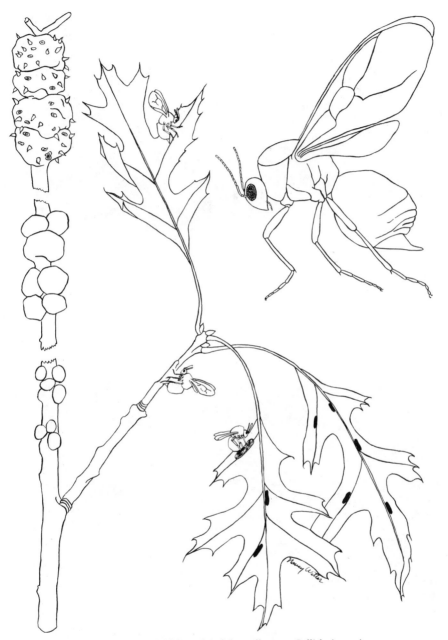

Figure 17.1 Pictorial life cycle of the gall wasp, *Callirhytis cornigera*.

Figure 17.2 Gouty oak galls caused by *Callirhytis punctata*, a gall wasp. (North Carolina Agricultural Extension Service photograph.)

Figure 17.3 Oak apple gall caused by a gall wasp in the genus *Amphibolips*. (University of California Cooperative Extension photograph.)

the eastern regions of the United States primarily on red, black, and scarlet oaks, whereas *A. californicus* Ashmead is found in Washington, Oregon, and California on white oaks. Both species produce apple galls that are large, 15–50 mm in diameter, and green to brown in color depending on the age. They are filled with a spongy mass of fibers that contains a single larva inside a small and very hard central capsule. Life histories of these species are not fully documented. *Amphibolips* species do not cause any measurable damage to their hosts.

Mealy Oak Gall Wasp, Disholcaspis cinerosa Bass

The gall caused by *D. cinerosa* is found on live oaks in Texas, Louisiana, and Mexico but causes no measurable damage (Morgan et al. 1978, Frankie et al. 1977). Homeowners often are concerned about spherical shape galls with diameters of 10–30 mm that are commonly found on the branches of live oak trees. Some trees are much more susceptible than others. Some people have expressed an interest in the potential use of the gall in decorative arrangements.

Mealy oak gall wasp produces two generations per year on live oak. Spherical galls of the first generation are located on the branches. Parthenogenetic adults emerge from these stem galls in early winter and oviposit into the swollen leaf buds. Larvae hatch from the eggs and feed within leaf buds, causing bud galls about 3–4 mm long. Male and female gall wasps emerge from these galls and mate; the females oviposit into the branches in early spring. Feeding by the larvae of cynipid wasps in the branches causes the formation of spherical galls.

Jumping Oak Gall Wasp, Neuroterus saltatorius (H. Edwards)

The jumping oak gall wasp produces ovoid mustard-seed-like galls, about 1 mm long, on the underside of white oak leaves in Arizona, Oregon, and California (Furniss and Carolin 1977). These galls often are very abundant but generally cause little damage to trees. However, these galls attract the attention of humans because of the behavior patterns of the mature gall wasp larvae. Galls containing mature larvae drop to the ground, where movement of mature larvae causes the galls to jump about like Mexican jumping beans.

Euura Sawflies, Tenthredinidae

The genus *Euura* contains species of tenthredinid sawflies that produce galls on the buds, leaf petioles, and stems of willow (Smith 1968, 1970). The most common species, *E. exiguae* E. L. Smith, causes elongated brown stem galls on willow in California.

Eurytomids, Eurytomidae

Several species in the genus *Eurytoma* cause galls on the branches of young ponderosa, Scots, and jack pine trees. Stark and Koehler (1964) reported that *E. tumoris* Bugbee caused swellings on the terminal and lateral branches of Scots pine Christmas trees in California.

Dipterous Insects

Several families contain species that produce galls, but only gall midges in the family Cecidomyiidae commonly cause galls on trees and shrubs.

Gall Midges, Cecidomyiidae

Adult gall midges are tiny delicate flies that resemble mosquitoes. These gall midges have long legs, relatively long antennae, and reduced wing venation. Larvae are usually orange, pink, or yellow. Approximately two-thirds of the species in this family cause galls that are found almost anywhere on the tree, but most are present on leaves, needles, buds, seeds, cones, or twigs. Most form a characteristic gall (Figure 17.4) on a specific part of a particular tree species (Felt 1940). Gall midges are a pest on Christmas trees but are not considered major forest pests, although they can kill ornamental and forest trees, reduce seed crops, and cause unsightly damage to ornamental trees. Five examples of gall midges are presented in this chapter.

Balsam Gall Midge, Paradiplosis tumifex Gagńe

The balsam gall midge is found on balsam fir and Fraser fir; it is recognized by the swollen, oval galls, 3 mm in diameter, that occur at the bases of needles. A major problem caused by the balsam gall midge on Christmas trees is premature dropping of galled needles in late fall, causing a severe reduction in the number of needles on the tree.

Balsam gall midge produces one generation per year and overwinters

Figure 17.4 Needle galls caused by gall midges. (Vermont Department of Forests, Parks, and Recreation, courtesy of R. Kelly.)

as a pupa in the soil beneath infested host trees. In Wisconsin, adults emerge in mid-May and mate, and females lay eggs in the developing needles of balsam fir. Larvae emerge from the eggs and start feeding on the new needles. Almost immediately, the needle responds and a gall-like swelling encloses the larva. Larvae emerge from the galls in late fall and drop to the soil, where they pupate. Additional information on the biology and ecology of this gall midge is provided by Giese and Benjamin (1959) and Osgood and Gagné (1978). Until recently it was believed that *Dasineura balsamicola* (Lint) was the midge that caused the gall on balsam fir needles. Osgood and Gagné (1978) determined the galls were initiated by the larvae of *Paradiplosis tumifex* and that *D. balsamicola* occurred within the galls and caused 100% mortality of *P. tumifex* by early October.

Needle Galls on Douglas-Fir Caused by Three Species of Contarinia

Contarinia cuniculator Condrashoff, *C. constricta* Condrashoff, and *C. pseudotsuga* Condrashoff cause development of galls on the new needles of Douglas-fir.

C. pseudotsuga is the most abundant species and has the greatest distribution range of the three species (Condrashoff 1962a). It renders Douglas-fir Christmas trees unsalable in the dry-belt, open-grown, interior forests of British Columbia (Condrashoff 1962b). Adults emerge from the soil beneath Douglas-fir in early May and lay their eggs on the lower surface of new needles. Several yellow-colored larvae per needle feed in new needles until October or early December, when mature larvae drop to the ground to overwinter in the soil. Pupation occurs in the spring completing the cycle of one generation per year. Galls are first noticeable in early June, when they are soft and pliable, becoming much darker and harder during the summer, and brown and brittle by fall. Heavy populations of this midge cause the needles of Douglas-fir to drop prematurely, usually by December, and also cause twig mortality.

Birch Midge, Oligotrophus papyriferae Gagné

The birch midge causes either petiole-bud or petiole-stem galls (Figure 17.5) on paper birch in the Great Lakes states (Wilson 1968). In Michigan this midge produces one generation per year and overwinters as a mature larva in a cocoon in the duff or topsoil underneath infested trees. Pupation occurs in May, adults emerge in mid-May and mate, and then the females deposit eggs on the underside of the birch leaves near the petiole. Larvae bore into and down the petiole and then enter the stem or a bud. After larvae feed in these tissues all summer, the galls become noticeable in August. Mature larvae leave the gall in late September. Large galls can kill buds, twigs, and entire branches. Damage occurs on trees 1–10 m high, badly deforming some younger trees. Although this species is not a major forest pest, it is an excellent example of a typical life history of a cecidiomyid midge that causes a bud or stem gall.

Figure 17.5 Petiole–stem galls caused by the birch midge, *Oligotrophus papyriferae* (U.S. Forest Service photograph, courtesy of L. Wilson.)

Honeylocust Pod Gall Midge, Dasineura gleditschiae (Osten Sacken)

This midge causes a podlike leaf deformation on several varieties of honeylocust. When abundant, galled leaflets drop prematurely and the host tree appears very unsightly. Many generations occur each year. The honeylocust pod gall midge overwinters as an adult outside of the pod (Johnson and Lyon 1976).

Maple Leaf Spot Gall Midge, Cecidomyia ocellaris (Osten Sacken)

The gall caused by this midge (Figure 17.6) superficially resembles a fungal leaf spot on leaves of red maple. On the upper surface of the red maple leaf, the gall is small, about 1 mm in diameter, and appears as a black elevated spot. On the underside of the leaf, the gall is about 8 mm in diameter and varies in color from yellow to yellow with a red border to brown depending on the stage of development (Johnson and Lyon 1976). No significant damage is caused by the maple leaf spot midge even though it can be extremely abundant in localized areas.

Homopterous Insects

Certain species in the families Phylloxeridae, Aphididae, and Psyllidae cause galls on forest and shade trees. None of these insects are important forest pests, but all can damage shade trees and ornamentals. Gall adelgids also are important Christmas tree pests.

Figure 17.6 Maple leaf spot gall caused by the maple leaf spot gall midge, *Cecidomyia ocellaris* (North Carolina Agricultural Extension Service photograph.)

Gall Makers in the Family Phylloxeridae

Insects in the family Phylloxeridae were formerly placed in the families Chermidae and Adelgidae and had common names such as gall aphids, pine aphids, or woolly aphids. Now these insects are commonly referred to as *gall adelgids, pine adelgids,* or *woolly adelgids,* and only insects in the family Aphididae are referred to as *aphids.* Gall adelgids are described in this chapter; woolly adelgids were described in Chapter 12.

Gall Adelgids in the Genus Adelges

Individual species in this genus form cone-shaped galls on spruce and normally are recognized on other host trees by white cottony material on the bark, branches, twigs, or needles. The Cooley spruce gall adelgid, *Adelges cooleyi* (Gillette), and the eastern spruce gall adelgid, *A. abietis* Linnaeus, are the two most important species of *Adelges* in North America, which form distinct cone-shaped galls on spruce. Other gall adelgids in the genus *Adelges* or *Pineus* produce galls on spruce that could be mistaken for the two above species. Lindquist (1971) provides a key for the identification of galls on spruce. The pine leaf adelgid, *Pineus pinifoliae* (Fitch), also forms loose, terminal cone-shaped galls on spruce, but seldom causes much damage on spruce. Dimond and Bishop (1968) and Balch and Underwood (1950) present detailed information about the pine leaf adelgid, including damage caused by this adelgid while feeding on young white pine trees.

The Cooley spruce gall adelgid is found on spruce throughout southern Canada and the northern United States. Primary hosts for the Cooley spruce gall adelgid are white, Engelmann, Sitka, and Colorado blue spruce, whereas Douglas-fir serves as an alternate host. The Cooley spruce gall adelgid is identified by the elongated pineapple or conelike swellings (Figure 17.7), which are 25–75 mm long and located at the tips of new twigs.

The biology of the Cooley spruce gall adelgid is very complicated. After overwintering at the base of spruce or Douglas-fir buds, the immature nymphs become adults in the spring. Females then lay eggs under a mass of cottony material. Eggs hatch within a week, and young nymphs feed at the base of young needles. Galls, caused by the nymphs' feeding, begin to form immediately and soon enclose the nymphs. Young galls are green or purple and later turn brown. Nymphs mature in July or August, and winged females fly to either Douglas-fir or spruce and lay eggs on the needles. Eggs hatch and this generation overwinters as nymphs. During the following summer, these adelgids continue to live on either Douglas-fir or spruce. Galls are not formed by Douglas-fir when this adelgid feeds at the base of needles. The major sign of Cooley spruce gall adelgid on Douglas-fir is the white cottony material on the needles, new shoots, and cones (Figure 17.8).

The complete life cycle, including the alternation of generations between hosts, takes 2 years (Cumming 1959). However, the Cooley spruce gall

Figure 17.7 Gall caused by the Cooley spruce gall adelgid, *Adelges cooleyi* (U.S. Forest Service photograph.)

Figure 17.8 Cottony material of the Cooley spruce gall adelgid, *Adelges cooleyi* on Douglas-fir. (U.S. Forest Service photograph.)

adelgid is capable of producing continuous parthenogenic life cycles on spruce or Douglas-fir. Two generations per year are produced on the needles of Douglas-fir when spruce is absent or scarce. A 1-year parthenogenic life cycle is found on spruce in Alberta and Saskatchewan (Cumming 1962).

The Cooley spruce gall adelgid does not significantly damage forest trees but can reduce the value of spruce and Douglas-fir raised for Christmas trees and seriously damage ornamental spruce.

Eastern spruce gall adelgid is found primarily on Norway spruce but also occurs on Colorado blue, white, and red spruce in southern Canada and the eastern United States. Eastern spruce gall adelgid is identified by the small pineapple- or conelike galls (Figure 17.9) that are 10–18 mm long and located at the base of new twigs (Plumb 1953). In the spring, after overwintering as small nymphs at the base of spruce buds, nymphs become adults. Females lay eggs on spruce needles. Eggs hatch in 1–2 weeks. Small nymphs feed at the base of new spruce needles and stimulate the formation of galls. Winged adult females, which emerge from the galls in August and September, lay eggs on spruce needles. Nymphs hatch in about 2 weeks and crawl to overwintering sites. The eastern spruce gall adelgid does not significantly damage spruce trees in forests but can reduce the value of spruce as Christmas trees and seriously damage ornamental spruce.

Figure 17.9   Gall caused by the eastern spruce gall adelgid, *Adelges abietis* (U.S. Forest Service photograph.)

The balsam woolly adelgid, *A. piceae* (Ratzeburg), can be found on the boles, twigs, nodes, and bark scales of true firs in North America. Feeding on twigs and buds often causes gall-like formation and calluses (see Chapter 12).

Gall Makers in the Genus *Phylloxera*

Several species of *Phylloxera* produce galls on leaf blades, petioles, and occasionally on rapidly growing twigs of hickory. All species overwinter in the egg stage in bark cracks and crevices. In the spring nymphs emerge from eggs and crawl to feeding sties on leaf stems or midribs of leaflets. A hollow gall is formed immediately around an individual nymph. When the female matures, she lays numerous eggs within the gall. After the eggs hatch, nymphs develop, and winged adults emerge from the gall. Adults fly to a summer host, where several generations occur during the summer. In the fall, winged adults return to hickory and deposit eggs (Johnson and Lyon 1976). Phylloxeran gall makers are not important forest pests, but branches on hickory trees dieback when heavily infested.

Gall Makers in the Family Aphididae

Woolly gall makers in the genus *Eriosoma*, gall makers in the genus *Pemphigus*, and the poplar vagabond aphid, *Mordvilkoja vagabunda* (Walsh), the most common gall makers in this family, do not cause significant damage to forest stands but can reduce the aesthetic value of ornamental and shelterbelt trees.

Woolly Gall Makers, Eriosoma spp.
These insects usually alternate between a primary host, usually a tree or shrub, and a secondary host, an herbaceous plant or tree. The woolly apple aphid, *Eriosoma lanigerum* (Hausmann), is an example of these gall makers. This aphid overwinters as eggs in bark crevices of elm trees, the primary host. In the spring, nymphs emerge from the eggs and feed on the new terminal leaves, causing them to curl or to appear in the form of rosettes. Only the females become adults. Several generations of wingless females are produced on elm trees, followed by a winged generation that appears during early summer and disperses to summer hosts such as apple, hawthorn, mountain ash, and pyracantha (Johnson and Lyon 1976). Woolly apple aphids colonize their summer hosts and feed on twigs, branches, or roots. In the fall, the woolly apple aphid leaves its summer host and a bisexual generation is produced on elm.

Pemphigus spp.
Life cycles of most insects in the genus *Pemphigus* are poorly understood. They appear to have alternate generations between the leaves, petioles, or twigs of poplar trees and herbaceous hosts (Harper 1959). For example, the sugarbeet root aphid, *P. populivenae* Fitch, a pest on the roots of sugarbeets, also forms an elongated gall on the midvein of the upper side of poplar leaves.

Poplar Vagabond Aphid, Mordvilkoja vagabunda (Walsh)
The poplar vagabond aphid causes the formation of convoluted galls on the tips of cottonwood twigs (Figure 17.10) throughout most of the northern United States. It does not normally kill ornamental cottonwoods but can severely reduce their aesthetic value. Poplar vagabond aphids overwinter as eggs within the old galls. Most of the eggs are found in the larger galls located on branches in the upper half of the tree. Nymphs emerge from the eggs in late spring and feed gregariously on the tips of twigs, which form a gall within a week. Two generations of aphids are produced within the gall. Adult aphids leave the gall in July for an unknown secondary host. Several generations are produced on the alternate host before adults of the poplar vagabond aphid migrate back to the old galls on cottonwood, where they lay eggs (Ignoffo and Granovsky 1961). The poplar vagabond aphid can be controlled on ornamental cottonwood by removing all old galls in early spring before the eggs hatch.

Gall Makers in the Family Psyllidae
Psyllid adults are 1–5 mm long and resemble miniature cicadas or small aphids, but unlike aphids, they have stout legs and bodies adapted for

Figure 17.10   Galls caused by the poplar vagabond aphid, *Mordwilkoja vagabunda*. (U.S. Forest
Service photograph, courtesy of L. Wilson.)

jumping. The psyllids are plant feeders, and some cause galls. Most psyllids
that cause galls are in the genus *Pachypsylla*. They produce primarily leaf
galls on hackberry. Adult psyllids often emerge in large numbers during
late summer and early fall. These adults cluster around screen doors, buildings, and ears, becoming extremely annoying to people during September.

Hackberry Psyllids

There are at least eight species of psyllids that attack hackberry. Most of
these psyllids cause leaf galls (Figure 17.11), but the budgall psyllid, *P.
celtidisgemma* Riley, causes a bud gall (Walton 1960); the petiolegall psyllid,
P. venusta (Osten Sacken), causes a petiole gall (Baker 1972); and one species
causes galls under the bark of twigs. The two most common hackberry
psyllids causing galls are the hackberry blister gall maker, *P. celtidisvesicula*
Riley and the hackberry nipplegall maker, *P. celtidismamma* (Riley).

The hackberry blister gall is 3–4 mm in diameter and only slightly raised
from the leaf surface, whereas the hackberry nipple gall is about 4 mm in
diameter and about 6 mm high. The life cycle and habits of the two gall
makers are similar. They produce one generation per year and overwinter
as adults in protected places such as in bark crevices on hackberry, under
litter on the ground, and inside buildings (Smith 1953). Adults are often
observed flying about or crawling on the terminal twigs of hackberry during
early spring. The females deposit eggs on the underside of developing
leaves. Nymphs hatch from the eggs and begin feeding on the leaves.
Abnormal growth of plant occurs immediately with galls forming around
the nymphs. The nymphs live inside of the gall during the entire summer.
Adults emerge in the fall.

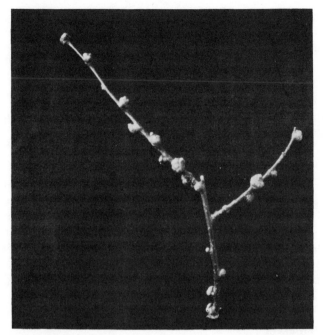

Figure 17.11   Galls on hackberry caused by psyllids in the genus *Pachypsylla*. (Connecticut Agricultural Experiment Station photograph.)

Coleopterous Insects

A few coleopterous insects cause galls or swellings on forest and shade trees.

Gall Makers in the Family Cerambycidae
There are several gall makers in this family that are often found on poplar and maple. None are considered major forest pests.

Saperda spp.
Several species of *Saperda* bore into the twigs and stems of young poplars and willows primarily throughout the United States. The poplar gall saperda, *Saperda inornata* (Say), is a very common eastern species that produces globose galls on the twigs and stems of poplar.

Maple Gall Borer, Xylotrechus aceris Fisher
The maple gall borer causes the formation of galls or swellings around wounds on maple trees. Generally, this gall borer has a 2-year life cycle. The maple gall borer does not kill trees outright but can seriously weaken maple trees. Eggs are deposited at bases of small dead twigs along the bole or in wounds. Larvae first bore into the sapwood, and as they grow larger,

the larvae construct tunnels in the heartwood. Galls or swellings form around the wounds caused by the feeding of the larvae in the sapwood and heartwood.

Lepidopterous Insects

A few lepidopterous insects in the family Olethreutidae cause galls or swellings on shade trees. None are considered major forest pests.

Boxelder Twig Borer, Proteoteras willingana (Kearfott)

This borer is a pest of boxelder shade trees in shelterbelts in the Midwest, Great Plains, and southern Canada, especially in Manitoba, Saskatchewan, Alberta, and North Dakota (Peterson 1958). The major damage is caused by the smaller larvae, which destroy dormant leaf buds in the fall and early spring, and by the larger larvae, which burrow into succulent twigs, causing the formation of spindle-shaped galls. Infested twigs dry out, become woody, and usually prevent further terminal growth. Secondary branching results, and further insect damage of these twigs leads to bushy trees.

Arachnid Gall Makers

Numerous mite species feed on the leaves, buds, stems, flowers, and fruit of deciduous trees. Many produce blisterlike or pouchlike galls on leaves or twigs. Other mites cause a crimson or yellow felt patch to occur on the

Figure 17.12 Maple bladder gall caused by an eriophyid mite in the genus *Vasates*. (North Carolina Agricultural Experiment Station photograph.)

upper and lower surface of leaves. Some mites cause woody galls to occur around the buds on tree species such as aspen and birch. A few mite species feed inside the bud, causing the bud to swell or enlarge, a condition known as "big buds." Other mite species cause galls to form on the needles, buds, and twigs of conifers.

Figure 17.13 (a,b) Maple spindle gall caused by an eriophyid mite in the genus *Vasates*. (North Carolina Agricultural Extension Service photograph.)

Eriophyid Mites in the Family Eriophyidae

Eriophyid mites are tiny (0.2–0.5 mm), elongated, translucent organisms. Most are highly specific, attack only a few different tree species, do not cause any significant damage to trees, and produce very distinctive galls (Krantz 1970). The galls produced by various species of eriophyid mites can be very abundant in localized areas. They are often extremely spectacular due to their bright colors.

Gall Mites on Maple

Several species of gall mites cause bladder galls, spindle galls, or felt patches of hairy or beadlike growth on maple leaves (Keifer 1946, 1952; Hodkiss 1930). The maple bladdergall mite, *Vasates quadripedes* Shimer, produces a pouchlike or bladderlike gall on the upper side of silver and sugar maple leaves (Figure 17.12). The galls are yellowish green when first formed but later turn red or black. Heavily infested maple leaves become distorted or curled. The maple spindle gall mite, *Vasates aceris-crumena* (Riley), causes a slender, spindle-shaped gall, about 5 mm long, on the upper surface of silver and red maple leaves (Figure 17.13). Several species of eriophyid mites in the genus *Eriophyes* produce a crimson felt patch of hairy or beadlike growth, often called "erineum," on the upper and lower sides of maple leaves (Figure 17.14).

Eriophyid mites producing galls on maple trees generally overwinter as adults under bark scales. In the spring these mites move to the developing leaves and begin feeding. A slight depression immediately forms at the feeding site, followed by a bladder or spindle gall that encloses the mite. The mite continues to feed and lays numerous eggs within the gall. Mature mites leave the gall, crawl to new leaves, and start feeding.

Figure 17.14 Erineum gall caused by eriophyid mite in the genus *Eriophyes*. (Courtesy of D. Allen, N.Y. State University, Syracuse.)

MANAGEMENT APPROACHES USED AGAINST GALL MAKERS

Few gall making insects cause enough damage to require any type of control. In the past, insecticides often have been used by Christmas tree growers and homeowners to reduce population numbers and subsequent damage of gall makers such as the Cooley spruce gall adelgid, eastern spruce gall adelgid, balsam fir gall midge, and gall midges in the genus *Contarinia*. Contact or systemic insecticides are used to control immature or adult gall makers. Contact the Cooperative Extension Service in your state for updated insecticide recommendations for specific gall makers.

REFERENCES

Baker, W. L. 1972, *Eastern Forest Insects*. U.S. Department of Agriculture Forest Service Miscellaneous Publication 1175.

Balch, R. E. and G. R. Underwood. 1950. The life-history of *Pineus pinifoliae* (Fitch) (Homoptera: Phylloxeridae) and its effect on white pine. *Can. Entomol.* **82**:117–123.

Condrashoff, S. F. 1962a. Bionomics of three closely related species of *Contarinia* Rond. (Diptera: Cecidomyiidae) from Douglas-fir needles. *Can. Entomol.* **94**:376–394.

Condrashoff, S. F. 1962b. *Douglas-Fir Needle Midges—Pest of Christmas Trees in British Columbia*. Canadian Department of Forestry, Ottawa (unnumbered leaflet).

Cumming, M. E. P. 1959. The biology of *Adelges cooleyi* (Gill.) (Homoptera: Phylloxeridae). *Can. Entomol.* **91**:601–617.

Cumming, M. E. P. 1962. A monomorphic cycle of *Adelges cooleyi* (Gill.) (Homoptera: Phylloxeridae) living only on spruce. *Can. Entomol.* **94**:1190–1195.

Dimond, J. B. and R. H. Bishop. 1968. *Susceptibility and Vulnerability of Forests to the Pine Leaf Aphid, Pineus pinifoliae (Fitch) (Adelgidae)*. Maine Agricultural Experiment Station Bulletin 658.

Evans, D. 1972. Alternate generations of gall cynipids (Hymenoptera; Cynipidae) on Garry oak. *Can. Entomol.* **104**:1805–1818.

Felt, E. P. 1925. *Key to Gall Midges*. New York State Museum Bulletin 257.

Felt, E. P. 1940. *Plant Galls and Gall Makers*. Comstock, Ithaca, NY.

Frankie, G. W., D. L. Morgan, M. J. Gaylor, J. G. Benskin, W. E. Clark, H. C. Reed, and P. J. Hamman. 1977. *The Mealy Oak Gall on Ornamental Live Oaks in Texas*. Texas Agricultural Experiment Station MP-1315.

Furniss, R. L. and V. M. Carolin. 1977. *Western Forest Insects*. USDA Forest Service Miscellaneous Publication 1339.

Giese, R. L. and D. M. Benjamin. 1959. The biology and ecology of the balsam gall midge in Wisconsin. *For. Sci.* **5**:193–208.

Harper, A. M. 1959. Gall aphids on poplar in Alberta. I. Descriptions of galls and distributions of aphids. *Can. Entomol.* **91**:489–496.

Hodgkiss, H. E. 1930. *The Eriophyidae of N.Y. II. The Maple Mites*. New York Agricultural Experiment Station Technical Bulletin 163.

Hutchins, R. E. 1969. *Galls and Gall Insects*. Dodd, Mead, New York.

Ignoffo, C. M. and A. A. Granovsky. 1961. Life history and gall development of *Mordwilkoja vagabonda* (Homoptera: Aphidae) on *Populus deltiodes*. *Ann. Entomol. Soc. Am.* **54**:486–499.

Johnson, W. T. and H. H. Lyon. 1976. *Insects that Feed on Trees and Shrubs*. Cornell University Press, Ithaca.

Keifer, H. H. 1946. A review of North American economic eriophyid mites. *J. Econ. Entomol.* **39**:563–570.

Keifer, H. H. 1952. The eriophyid mites of California (Acarina: Eriophyidae). *Calif. Insect. Surv. Bull.* **2**(1):1–23.

Krantz, G. W. 1970. *A Manual of Acarology*. Oregon State University Book Stores, Corvallis.

Lindquist, O. H. 1971. The Adelgids (Homoptera) on forest trees in Ontario with key to galls on spruce. *Proc. Entomol. Soc. Ontario* **102**:23–27.

Mani, M. S. 1964. *Ecology of Plant Galls*. Junk, Hague.

Morgan, D. L., G. W. Frankie, and M. J. Gaylor. 1978. Potential for developing insect-resistant plant materials for use in urban environments. In Frankie, G. W. and C. S. Koehler (Eds.). *Perspectives in Urban Entomology*. Academic Press, New York.

Osgood, E. A. and R. J. Gagńe. 1978. Biology and taxonomy of two gall midges (Diptera: Cecidomyiidae) found in galls on balsam fir needles with description of a new species of *Paradiplosis*. *Ann. Entomol. Soc. Am.* **71**:85–91.

Peterson, L. O. T. 1958. The boxelder twig borer, *Proteoteras willingana* (Kearfott), (Lepidoptera: Olethreutidae). *Can. Entomol.* **90**:639–646.

Plumb, G. H. 1953. *The Formation and Development of the Norway Spruce Gall Caused by Adelges abietis L*. Connecticut Agricultural Experiment Station Bulletin 566.

Smith, E. L. 1968. Biosystematics and morphology of Symphyta. 1. Stem-galling *Euura* of the California region, and a new female genitalic nomenclature. *Ann. Entomol. Soc. Am.* **61**:1389–1407.

Smith, E. L. 1970. Biosystematics and morphology of gall-making nematine sawflies in the California region. *Ann. Entomol. Soc. Am.* **63**:36–51.

Smith, R. C. 1953. The biology and control of the hackberry psyllids in Kansas. *Kans. Entomol. Soc.* **26**:103–115.

Stark, R. W. and C. S. Koehler. 1964. Biology of the gall wasp, *Eurytoma tumoris*, on Scots pine (Hymenoptera: Eurytomidae). *Pan.-Pac. Entomol.* **40**:41–46.

Walton, B. C. J. 1960. The life cycle of the hackberry gall-form, *Pachypsylla celtisgemma* (Homoptera: Psyllidae). *Ann. Entomol. Soc. Am.* **53**:265–277.

Wilson, L. F. 1968. Life history, habits, and damage of a gall midge, *Oligotrophus papyriferae* (Diptera: Cecidomyiidae), injurious to paper birch in Michigan. *Can. Entomol.* **100**:663–669.

18 ARTHROPOD PESTS IN RECREATIONAL AREAS

INTRODUCTION

Arthropods that bite or sting humans and their domesticated animals have been a recurring danger and annoyance for all civilizations. Their greatest impacts have been as vectors of diseases and stimulators of allergic reactions. Epidemics such as malaria, yellow fever, and trypanosomiasis (sleeping sickness) are serious problems in many areas in South America, Africa, and Southeast Asia. Fortunately, epidemics of plague, malaria, and yellow fever are no longer common in North America. More deaths are usually now reported each year in North America from allergic reactions or toxicity caused by bites or stings than from arthropod spread diseases. Over the past 25 years increasing emphasis has been placed on the importance, magnitude, and effect of arthropod pests in North American recreational areas. This increased concern about arthropod pests on recreational lands parallels the increased demand for outdoor recreational areas and substantial change in people's recreational habitats. These changes are due to a shift from a primarily rural society to an urban and suburban society. Approximately 75% of the population of the United States now lives in urban areas. An urban society is generally not as prepared psychologically or physically for arthropod pests, especially biting insects, which are present in great numbers in many rural or undeveloped outdoor recreational areas.

The objectives of this chapter are to provide (1) an understanding of the various human reactions to insects and their damage in recreational areas, (2) biological information on the most common arthropod pests in recreational areas, and (3) information on the various management approaches used against arthropod pests in recreational areas.

HUMAN RESPONSES TO ARTHROPODS AND THEIR DAMAGE IN RECREATIONAL AREAS

Humans react in different ways to arthropods that bite, sting, or cause some kind of nuisance to them or their animals while they are using recreational areas. Response to arthropods and their damage is influenced by a person's background and experience, the species of arthropods, and population densities of the pests. Land managers often encounter five different types of responses from recreationists: (1) dead insect syndrome, (2) perfect leaf syndrome, (3) entomophobia, (4) environmental, and (5) no reaction. These responses are briefly discussed to assist the forester or natural resource specialist to better understand the reactions of recreationists to arthropod pests.

Dead Insect Syndrome

Negative or defensive human reactions to insects such as flies, cockroaches, and yellowjackets have ingrained in our society the conclusion that "the only good insect is a dead insect." This generalization is reinforced by radio and television advertisements that depict the pest exterminator by using insecticides to kill household pests or the farmer applying insecticides to protect crops from insect pests. Many Americans' responses are still characterized by the dead insect syndrome. The automatic response of many recreationists is to spray around the recreational vehicle or automobile and nearby picnic table as soon as the user steps onto the recreational site. Also, many modern campers demand immediate action and effective control measures when confronted with nuisance insects on recreational lands.

Perfect Leaf Syndrome

Urban pest managers often receive phone calls concerning minor leaf feeding damage (i.e., hole feeding, leaf galls) or aesthetically unpleasing damage such as web-enclosed foliage on urban trees. This public concern is raised by expectations of the "perfect apple" or the "perfect leaf" with no blemishes or insects. Many individuals will not spray for this minor damage once they understand that these insects will not severely damage or kill important tree species. Recreation managers experience a similar response from recreationists after they have convinced these people that the insects will not permanently damage trees or harm humans.

Entomophobia

The extreme end of the spectrum of negative attitudes is one of hysterical dislike or a true entomophobia response. This profound aversion to insects may involve only biting or stinging insects or all insects. The basic entomophobia response is primarily one of fear of contamination, penetration, and filth (Olkowski and Olkowski 1976). People with severe entomophobia frequently become quite distressed merely by thinking about contact with a caterpillar or adult insect. They feel the best solution to this problem is to disinfect their backyards or campsites.

Environmentalist Response

Some environmentalists present extreme viewpoints about the use of insecticides and feel that insecticides should not be used in any situation on recreational lands. Other environmentalists realize that there are certain circumstances where insecticides are necessary or at least one logical solution to the pest problem.

No Reaction

Many recreationists understand that tolerance of biting and stinging insects is necessary to experience the satisfaction they derive from various outdoor activities. Eavy et al. (1979) reported that most users of facilities in Michigan's Porcupine Pine Mountain Wilderness State Park would return to the area again in spite of biting insect problems such as mosquitoes, deer flies, horse flies, stable flies, and "no-see-ums."

ORGANISMS INVOLVED

The most common organisms that bother humans in recreational areas are divided into three groups: biting arthropods, stinging arthropods, and other nuisance arthropods.

Biting Arthropods

A number of arthropods bite humans and other animals. Some species are only a nuisance, whereas others cause discomfort, sickness, and even death to humans as well as wild and domesticated animals. Information is presented on the biology of mosquitoes, black flies, biting midges, deer flies, horse flies, stable flies, fleas, ticks, chiggers, and spiders.

Mosquitoes, Diptera: Culicidae

Adult mosquitoes are very small (normally 3–6 mm) insects with scales along the wing veins and posterior wing margin and a long proboscis (Figure 3.20). Ninety-four of the 124 species of mosquitoes in North America belong to three genera: *Aedes, Anopheles,* and *Culex* (Merritt and Cummins 1984).

Egg-laying habits vary by genera and species, but most species of *Anopheles* and *Culex* deposit eggs directly on the surface of water whereas most species of *Aedes* deposit their eggs in moist depressions in the ground. Mosquito eggs laid in water usually hatch in 2 or 3 days, whereas those laid in moist ground may remain dormant for months or several years until water covers the site. Mosquito larvae require water to complete their development, and larvae of most species feed on algae and organic debris. The number of generations per year ranges from one to five or more and varies by species and climatic conditions. Few adult mosquitoes fly far from their breeding sites. For example, most *Anopheles* remain within 1 km of their breeding sites. However, many *Aedes* fly 16 km or more from their breeding sites. Both sexes obtain food from plant juices; only female mosquitoes are bloodsuckers. Female mosquitoes obtain blood meals from either birds, reptiles, or mammals.

In North America, mosquitoes can act as vectors of several human diseases (i.e., the encephalitis viruses and occasionally malaria). Wild birds are the primary reservoirs of several encephalitis viruses such as St. Louis encephalitis, eastern equine encephalitis, and western equine encephalitis. Certain species of mosquitoes are involved in transmitting the virus from bird to bird or, in some cases, from an overwintering host (e.g., snowshoe hare or ground squirrel) to bird. The same species, or a different species may be important in the transmission of the virus from birds to humans (McLintock and Iversen 1976). During the 1975 outbreak of St. Louis encephalitis, there were more than 2000 confirmed cases in humans in 30 different states, with 95 known human deaths (Knight and Heikkenen 1980).

Mosquito-transmitted diseases are seldom considered important recurring problems in recreational areas in North America (Merritt and Newson 1978). However, all land managers and pest managers concerned with natural resources must be aware of the potential problems, adverse publicity, and severe economic impact that an epidemic of an arthropod-borne disease can have on a recreational area. For example, it was estimated that the hotels in Atlantic City, New Jersey, suffered a $2 million revenue loss in 1959 because the tourists were afraid to visit the area after hearing about a local outbreak of eastern equine encephalitis (Newson 1977).

Mosquitoes are vectors of dog heartworm, *Dirofilaria immitis* (Leidy), a nematode that commonly causes sickness in dogs in the eastern and southeastern United States. Adult nematodes invade the heart and pulmonary arteries of dogs and often cause death. Several species of mosquitoes present in most parts of the United States are capable of transmitting this parasite. Campgrounds with large mosquito populations and campers with dogs provide an excellent opportunity for transmission of dog heartworm (Newson 1977).

Mosquitoes are the most widespread and serious biting arthropod pest in many recreational areas throughout North America. Everyone is familiar with the blood feeding habits of female mosquitoes (Figure 18.1). Wagner and Newson (1975) found that park visitors in Michigan avoided recreation areas in forested regions (i.e., nature trails) when average biting counts of mosquitoes were greater than two per minute. The visitors stayed in areas that had good prevailing winds and lacked a forest canopy such as beach areas and open fields. Park visitors utilized the forested areas when mosquito counts were less than one per minute.

Black Flies, Diptera: Simulidae

Black flies are small (1–5 mm long), usually dark-colored insects with stout, humpback bodies, short legs, and broad wings (Figure 18.2). After mating, females of most species of black flies lay their eggs in habitats with running water ranging from small trickling streams to large rivers. After hatching, individuals of most species attach themselves to stones, aquatic vegetation, or partly submerged objects such as old logs. Pupation occurs in cone-shaped cases at or near the larval feeding sites. Adults emerge in large numbers during the spring and summer in many parts of Canada and the northern areas of the United States, including Alaska. Most species produce one generation per year, but some produce several generations per year.

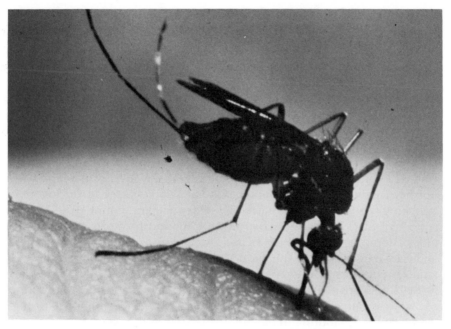

Figure 18.1 Adult female mosquito, *Culex tarsalis,* feeding on a human. (Photograph courtesy of R. Merritt, Michigan State University.)

Figure 18.2 Adult black fly, family Simulidae. (Photograph courtesy of R. Merritt, Michigan State University.)

Adult male and female black flies feed on the nectar of flowers. Females of most species of black flies also require a blood meal to produce eggs. Some species are quite vicious bloodsuckers. Individual species are often discriminatory in host selection, with birds and mammals, including humans, serving as hosts. The flight range, approximately 11 km, of many species of black flies is greater than most species of mosquitoes. Black flies can sometimes be a problem in recreation areas located some distance from their breeding sites.

Black fly adults can be extremely annoying to their hosts because of their habit of swarming around the head and over the eyes, ears, and nostrils. Domestic and wild animals have been killed in western Canada and the northern United States, including Alaska, as a result of blood loss from the biting activity of female black flies (Harwood and James 1979). Several species of black flies are vectors of an important protozoan disease that infects domestic and wild ducks and geese such as mallards, black ducks, and Canada geese in the northern United States and Canada. No black fly adults are vectors of human diseases in North America.

Black flies are active only during the day. The females of certain species of black flies attack humans on exposed parts of the body or crawl through openings in the clothing to bite on other parts of the body. Some humans are immune to black fly bites, but black fly bites usually produce allergic responses ranging from temporary local irritations to severe swellings in the area of the bite. Some humans have additional reactions to the bite, including extreme swelling, which requires hospitalization (Newson 1977).

Even a few black flies can discourage most humans from staying in a recreational area. Large numbers of black flies present during the spring and early summer can drive many people, including avid fishermen, indoors. Sleeper (1975) reported that a "Black Fly Control Committee" was established in Maine during the 1970s to determine control methods for a species of black fly not previously collected there. The species, *Simulium penobscotensis* (Snoddy and Bauer), is making life miserable for residents and tourists in many recreational areas in Maine (Boobar and Granett 1980). Merritt and Newson (1978) suggested that effective antipollution measures to clean up Maine's rivers may be partly responsible for these recent outbreaks.

Biting Midges, Diptera: Ceratopogonidae

The common name "no-see-ums" indicates the very small size of many species of biting midges (i.e., 0.6–5.0 mm). The members of this family, known as "no-see-ums," "punkies," or "sand flies," are serious pests in many recreational areas in North America. The blood-feeding species that attack humans bite mainly during the evening and early morning. They breed in a wide range of habitats such as coastal salt marshes; intertidal zones; bottoms of freshwater ponds, streams, and swamps; accumulations of moist leaves; and in wet clay or mud (Kwan and Morrison 1974, Linley 1976).

These biting midges are extremely abundant in some coastal areas of the southeastern United States, especially Florida. They are also common in many inland recreational areas throughout the United States and in some mountainous areas such as the Adirondack Mountains of New York state (Kettle 1977). Suitable breeding habitats are often very localized in inland recreational areas. The adults are weak fliers, which restricts these biting insects to areas near suitable breeding habitats. However, biting midges occur over very extensive areas along the southeastern U.S. coastline because of the contiguous and extensive breeding sites in the intertidal areas and in the salt marshes.

Sand flies have been a major problem in the growth of tourism on the Caribbean islands and in parts of Florida. Research work conducted by the Bahamian government, the Jamaican government, and the State of Florida has led to a number of fairly effective methods of reducing sand fly populations (Linley and Davies 1971). Tourism has increased dramatically in areas where sand fly populations have been reduced by various pest management techniques.

Deer Flies and Horse Flies, Diptera: Tabanidae

Their are approximately 300 species of tabanid flies in North America, with over half of the species in two genera: *Tabanus* (horse flies) and *Chrysops* (deer flies) (Merritt and Cummins 1984). Tabanids are moderately large (6–25 mm), stout-bodied, bristleless flies (Figure 18.3). They are strong fliers and are persistent, and the females are vicious biters. The females suck blood and are often serious pests of horses, cattle, deer, and other

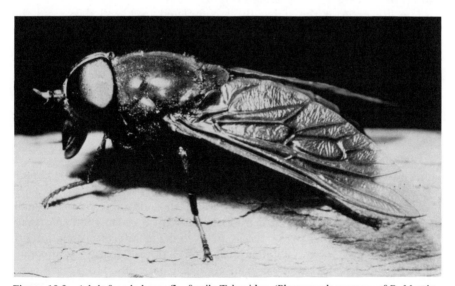

Figure 18.3 Adult female horse fly, family Tabanidae. (Photograph courtesy of R. Merritt, Michigan State University.)

warm-blooded animals, including humans. Some species of horse flies and deer flies in North America serve as vectors of diseases, such as tularemia and anthrax and as vectors of eastern equine encephalitis in states bordering the eastern Seaboard and Gulf Coast (Axtell 1976).

The female horse fly or deer fly lays eggs on leaves of aquatic plants or on objects hanging near or over water in swamps and marshes. On hatching, the larvae drop into the water or damp soil. Larvae of horse flies are primarily predators and feed on insect larvae, crustaceans, earthworms, and other soft-bodied organisms, whereas larvae of deer flies are primarily vegetarians (Harwood and James 1979). Some tabanid flies will spend 1–3 years in the immature stage, but most species produce one generation per year. Deer flies and horse flies are serious pests in recreational areas because they bite humans, transmit diseases, and are nuisances because of their irritating buzzing flight.

Stable Fly, Diptera: Muscidae

The stable fly, *Stomoxys calcitrans* (Linnaeus), is very similar in size and color to the house fly, *Musca domestica* Linnaeus. However, the daggerlike proboscis of the stable fly, which is used to draw out blood from the host, distinguishes the stable fly from the house fly, which has sponging–biting mouthparts. Although named for their role as pest of livestock, stable flies have important adverse affects on the tourist industry along the northwestern Gulf Coast in Florida, along New Jersey beaches, on some reservoirs constructed by the Tennessee Valley Authority (TVA), and along the Lake Superior shoreline (Merritt and Newson 1978). The female flies do the biting, preferring legs and ankles (Figure 18.4).

The life cycle of the stable fly is completed in 13–33 days, and the number of generations per year varies by location (Harwood and James 1979). Stable fly immatures readily develop in manure and straw associated with livestock management operations, in decaying grasses and marine algae deposited on Florida and New Jersey beaches, on peanut farming wastes in Georgia, and in rotting mayfly corpses along the TVA lakes (Newson 1977). The suspected breeding sites of stable flies along the Lake Superior shoreline are farms and stables.

Fleas, Siphonaptera

The most important disease transmitted by fleas (Figure 3.21) in the United States is sylvatic plague, *Yersinia pestis*, a bacillus disease. In the western United States, the bacillus normally circulates in a natural reservoir of small rodents such as white-footed mice and meadow mice, causing little mortality (Merritt and Newson 1978). Occasionally, plague infects populations of other more susceptible small mammals such as prairie dogs, ground squirrels, chipmunks, and wood rats, causing heavy mortality. Humans in rural recreational areas in the western areas of the United States can be exposed to bites of infected fleas.

Plague is widespread through the world and generally endemic in the

Figure 18.4 Adult female stable flies, family Muscidae, often prefer legs and ankles. (The University of Michigan photograph.)

United States. However, sylvatic plague is of increasing significance in the western third of the United States as more people use outdoor recreational facilities and as suburbs are constructed in areas near sylvatic plague foci such as mountainous areas and foothills of Albuquerque and Sante Fe, New Mexico, and various areas in California (Nelson 1978).

During the last three decades, most of the human cases of plague in the United States have occurred in the Rocky Mountain states (Merritt and Newson 1978). An outbreak of plague among prairie dogs in 1971 at a major fishing and camping resort area in south central Colorado necessitated closing the facility for most of the season. More recently, a large epizootic of plague affecting ground squirrels and chipmunks occurred in a newly developed U.S. Forest Service campground in Plumas Co., California. The resulting population buildup of susceptible rodents was due to tourists who constantly fed the ground squirrels and chipmunks in an area that had a foci of the enzootic plague in mice.

Potential problems could arise in areas where highly susceptible plague hosts coexist with the highly mobile tourist population. The greatest possible danger to the public exists when domestic rats are exposed to infection from wild mammals in areas near human communities. In such a situation, an outbreak of plague among domestic rats would expose many persons in these urban areas to infected fleas.

Ticks, Arachnida: Ixodidae, Argasidae
Ticks in North America occur in two families: Ixodidae, the hard-bodied ticks (Figure 18.5), and Argasidae, the soft-bodied ticks. Ticks are parasitic

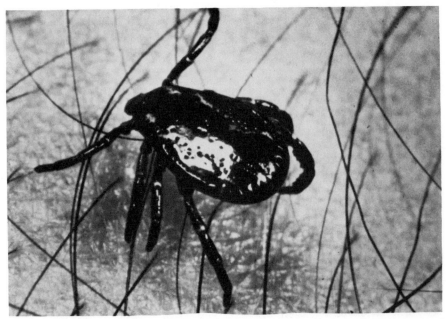

Figure 18.5   Hard-bodied tick, family Ixodidae, genus *Dermacentor*. (Photograph courtesy of R. Merritt, Michigan State University.)

and feed on the blood of mammals such as humans, birds, and reptiles. Those species of ticks that attack humans are very annoying pests. The recreation-seeking public prefers areas with low tick populations. Also, the forester, land manager, and recreationist must be aware that ticks are vectors of four diseases that are endemic in many recreational areas in the United States. These are Rocky Mountain spotted fever, Colorado tick fever, tick-borne relapsing fever, and tularemia.

Rocky Mountain spotted fever is commonly found throughout the eastern, southeastern, south central, and western United States (Harwood and James 1979). This disease is primarily a wild animal infection that is maintained and spread by numerous species of hard-bodied ticks in the family Ixodidae. The two principal vectors are the Rocky Mountain wood tick, *Dermacentor andersoni* Stiles and the American dog tick, *Dermacentor variabilis* (Say).

The ecology of these two species of ticks is different. The Rocky Mountain wood tick is found in the western United States and is common in sagebrush thickets along streams and in cutover mountainous areas. In the West, Rocky Mountain spotted fever is considered a rural occupational and recreational disease that occurs most frequently among farmers, foresters, road construction workers, hunters, fishermen, campers, and hikers. The disease is most common during April, May, and June, when adult Rocky Mountain wood ticks are most active (Burgdorfer 1975). In contrast, Rocky

Mountain spotted fever in the eastern and southeastern United States is common in both rural and urban areas during the summer months, when its primary vector, the American dog tick, is most active. The American dog tick is commonly found in small woodlots, in abandoned farmland, in old fields, and along edges of fields and forests. Many cases of Rocky Mountain spotted fever in the East and South occur in children and women because of their close association with tick-infested household pets, especially dogs.

Colorado tick fever is an acute virus disease that occurs primarily in the mountainous areas of the western United States and Canada. It is normally a relatively mild virus disease of humans but appears to be much more common and widespread than formerly realized (Merritt and Newson 1978). The disease is transmitted to forest workers and outdoor recreationists through the bite of the Rocky Mountain wood tick. Colorado tick fever normally occurs from April to August, when its vector is most active. Normally it is a very localized disease that is correlated with the presence of its rodent hosts such as ground squirrels.

Tick-borne relapsing fever is usually considered a sporadic endemic disease found in mountainous recreational areas in the western United States (Gelman 1961). The disease is caused by a spirochete, *Borrelia* sp., and the principal vectors are soft-bodied ticks in the family Argasidae. Rodents are the usual hosts, but humans can become infected with this disease when bitten by an infected soft-bodied tick. Normally the victim is not aware of the bite and the tick leaves the host shortly after having a blood meal.

An outbreak of tick-borne relapsing fever developed in 1973 at the northern rim of Grand Canyon National Park. There were 45 confirmed cases on humans during the outbreak. A rare interaction between two diseases, plague and relapsing fever, was discovered. The rodent populations were very high in 1972 and were decimated in 1973 by an undetected outbreak of plague that occurred prior to the relapsing fever outbreak. After the rodent dieoff, the soft ticks present in the rodent nests moved onto humans and while feeding, transmitted the tick-borne relapsing fever disease (Merritt and Newson 1978).

Tularemia is a plaguelike disease that occurs throughout North America and is fatal to rabbits. The causal agent is a rod-shaped bacterium, *Francisella tularensis*, which is transmitted from infected to susceptible rabbits by means of ticks. In humans, the pathogen is usually transmitted to a person through the feeding of an infested tick or deer fly or by direct inoculation of a scratch or wound coming into contact with a diseased animal (i.e., skinning an infected rabbit). An average of 180 human cases a year have been detected in the United States during the last 10 years (Merritt and Newson 1978). Seasonal peaks of tularemia are normally associated with hunting and outdoor activities and large populations of infected ticks or deer flies.

Chiggers, Acari: Trombicullidae

Chiggers, sometimes called "redbugs," are tiny ectoparasitic mites on vertebrates, including humans, during the larval stage. The larvae of chiggers tend to concentrate in the shaded portions of vegetation such as briar patches, grasses, and low shrubs. They remain quiescent in these locations until stimulated by an air current containing carbon dioxide such as would be associated with a vertebrate host. The chiggers do not suck blood or burrow into the skin. The six-legged larvae attach themselves to the skin and inject a digestive fluid that penetrates the skin and disintegrates the cells into disorganized cytoplasm and fragmented nuclei. It is probably the action of the digestive fluid that causes the "bite" to itch 3–6 hours after attack. The irritated spot usually swells and can continue to itch for several days to a week. When the larva is engorged with tissue fluid, normally in 4–6 hours, it leaves the host and transforms into a quiescent prenymphal stage. Nymphs and adults have eight legs and are free living. The food habits of the nymphs and adults are unknown.

Chiggers are present throughout North America but are extremely abundant in the central and southern United States. There is generally one generation per year in the temperate zone, with three or more generations per year in the southern areas.

Spiders, Arachnida: Araneae

There are over 2500 species of spiders in North America, but very few bite humans. Spiders have a venomous bite, but usually their mouthparts are unable to penetrate the skin of humans. Only a few are dangerous with bites that may be fatal to some humans. These are the widow spiders, *Latrodectus mactans* (Fabricius), *L. variolus* (Walckenaer), and *L. hesperus* (Chamberlin and Ivie), and the brown recluse spider, *Loxosceles reclusa* Gertsch and Mulaik.

The females of the widow spiders are about 10–15 mm in size and dark black with reddish-orange markings on the underside of the abdomen. The males are seen less frequently than the females, and males of *L. mactans* and *L. variolus* are similar to the females in size and color. *Latrodectus mactans* and *L. variolus* occur in the eastern United States, being most abundant in the southern states, whereas *L. hesperus* occurs in the western United States. Widow spiders are quite venomous but rarely bite people. They tend to try to escape when disturbed rather than attack. Generally they are found in sheltered, somewhat dark places such as under stones, in stumps, around outbuildings, and in similar places.

The brown recluse spider is commonly found around homes and farm buildings in the central and southern United States. Its bite can be serious enough to require medical attention. This spider is not aggressive, and it prefers to hide in dark, quiet places, but it will sometimes bite humans if handled or trapped in clothing. The bite of the brown recluse spider is especially dangerous to children and elderly persons, but death is rare.

Death of humans from the bite is very rare. Normal symptoms of a bite from a brown recluse spider is intense local pain, blistering, inflammation of the affected area, and an ulcerated sore.

Stinging Arthropods

A number of arthropods sting humans and other animals. Some are only a nuisance, whereas others cause discomfort, sickness, and death to humans and wild and domestic animals. In the next section, information is presented about the biology of the most important stinging arthropods.

Wasps (Primarily Yellowjackets and Hornets), Hymenoptera: Vespidae

There are about 15,000 species of stinging wasps in the world, but 95% of these are nonaggressive and solitary species that use the stinger primarily for subduing prey. Venom from these species usually causes only slight pain, and the stingers of many are too small to penetrate human skin. Most wasp stings affecting humans in North America are inflicted by eusocial wasps in the family Vespidae, subfamily Vespinae. This includes yellowjackets (genera *Vespula* and *Dolichovespula*) and the baldfaced hornet, *Dolichovespula maculata* (Linnaeus). The nest of the baldfaced hornet and some yellowjackets consist of a number of hexagonal paper cells, enclosed in a paper envelope (Figure 18.6). Yellowjackets in the genus *Vespula* usually build subterranean nests, whereas yellowjackets in the genus *Dolichovespula*

Figure 18.6 Aerial nest of a yellowjacket in the genus *Vespula*. (Photograph courtesy of R. Merritt, Michigan State University.)

and the baldfaced hornet usually build aerial nests. Yellowjackets are the most common.

Yellowjacket colonies are initiated by a single fertilized queen, the only member of the colony that can survive the winter conditions. During early spring, the queen emerges from diapause and searches for a nesting site. At this time, the queen assumes all duties of foraging for construction materials, building the nest, laying eggs, and foraging for arthropod prey to feed the young larvae. Once the first workers emerge, they assume the duties of the colony. The queen rarely leaves the nest, where her only duty is to lay eggs. New broods of workers are reared in a constantly expanding nest. In late summer the workers build large reproductive cells that contain immature males and queens. New queens and males emerge and leave the nest. After mating, the fertilized females hibernate and the males die. The cycle is repeated each spring. More information on the life history of yellowjackets is found in Spradbery (1973), Akre and Davis (1978), Davis (1978), and Akre et al. (1981).

Twelve species of *Vespula* and five species of *Dolichovespula* are found in North America. Yellowjackets present serious recreational problems throughout most of the United States. The species involved varies by region, but usually only one or two species are pests in a given area. The genus *Vespula* is divided into two groups: the *V. rufa* (Linnaeus) species group and the *V. vulgaris* (Linnaeus) species group. The *V. rufa* species group forages only for live prey, whereas the *V. vulgaris* species group forages for live prey and scavenges for protein on dead animals, picnic tables, and garbage cans (Akre and Davis 1978). The most important pest yellowjackets are the *V. vulgaris* species group because they also act as scavengers. The workers of this species group become a serious problem when the colonies start to decline in late summer and early fall. They have reduced foraging responsibilities for feeding young, and their sources of live food becomes depleted, forcing them to scavenge more. These changes cause them to become more aggressive and more likely to sting a larger animal or human.

Severity of the yellowjacket problem varies as a result of fluctuations in the population densities of yellowjackets. Akre and Reed (1981) reported that 1973, 1977, and 1979 were outbreak years for *V. vulgaris* or *V. pensylvanica* (Saussure) throughout most of the Pacific Northwest. They showed that the spring (April or June) weather conditions during colony formation appeared to be the major factor determining outbreak populations. Outbreak populations have not occurred since 1971 unless the spring period was warm and dry.

Most vespid wasps are beneficial because they are predators of insects such as lepidopterous caterpillars, grasshoppers, and adult flies. However, most people's attitude toward yellowjackets is very negative because of the few pest species. Wagner and Reierson (1969) reported that the density at which yellowjacket populations become pests is entirely subjective and dependent on the attitudes of the users. In the state of Washington, Davis

(1978) reported that 7–10 yellowjackets per hour annoying people constituted a nuisance. When the above densities were reached, park personnel received many complaints from park users. At that level of incidence, people became frightened or annoyed. They then attempted to kill yellowjackets and often received unnecessary stings.

Bees (Primarily Honeybees and Bumblebees), Hymenoptera: Apidae

Honeybees and bumblebees are also capable of stinging humans. The stings of bees and wasps are painful, often resulting in swelling of the affected area. Anaphylactic shock or even death can occur in people who are very allergic to bee or wasp stings. Parrish (1963) reported an average annual mortality in the United States of 23 individuals per year from bee and wasp stings, divided approximately equally between bees and wasps.

Imported Fire Ants, Hymenoptera: Formicidae

The red imported fire ant, *Solenopsis invicta* Buren, and the black imported fire ant, *Solenopsis richteri* Forel are important nuisance and agricultural pests in the southeastern United States. The red imported fire ant is much more common and is now found in the coastal southeastern states from North Carolina to Texas. The black imported fire ant is found in a relatively small area of northeastern Mississippi and northwestern Alabama.

The workers of the imported fire ants are 3–6 mm in length and reddish-brown in color. The nests of the colony are hard-crusted earthen mounds that may be as large as 1 m high and 1 m wide (Figure 18.7). Over 100,000 individuals may be found in a large nest (Lofgren et al. 1975).

Figure 18.7 Earthen mounds of the red imported fire ant, *Solenopsis invicta*. (Photograph courtesy of S. B. Vinson, Texas A&M University.)

There are several important economic impacts of imported fire ants. These insects are hazards to human health because of their stings, which may cause systemic reactions or complications from secondary infections. They feed on agricultural plants, particularly seedlings or germinating seeds. Livestock may be stung. Farm machinery that strikes mounds is often damaged, and grazing areas may be rendered useless. Workers may refuse to enter heavily infested agricultural fields. Certain recreational areas may have reduced useage. Bluegill sunfish may be killed as a result of ingestion of imported fire ants. Eggs and newly hatched chicks of birds such as quail may be destroyed (Lofgren et al. 1975, Harwood and James 1979). Immunotherapy of individuals who are highly sensitive to fire ant stings has met with good success (Rhodes et al. 1975).

Caterpillars, Lepidoptera

A number of lepidopterous families contain species with larvae possessing stinging hairs and spines that serve as effective defense mechanisms. These stinging hairs contain toxins that are very irritating to the skin, eyes, and respiratory tracts of many individuals. During recent outbreaks of the gypsy moth and Douglas-fir tussock moth, some homeowners, recreationists, and forest workers developed various dermal and respiratory problems when they came into contact with the stinging hairs from these two species of lymantriid caterpillars. Perlman et al. (1976) presented detailed information on human reactions to the Douglas-fir tussock moth.

Scorpions, Arachnida: Scorpiones

Scorpions occur primarily in the southern and western United States where they are nocturnal predators of many types of arthropods. They are easily recognized by their flattened, lobsterlike appearances and by the long, fleshy five-segmented, tail-like, postabdomen that terminates with a stinger.

Scorpions rarely attack humans but will sting quickly if disturbed. They are largely nocturnal and hide in protected places during the day. There are over 40 species of scorpions in the United States, but only one, *Centruroides sculpturatus* (Ewing), is very venomous, and its sting may be fatal. The stings of most of the other species of scorpions in the United States are not dangerous, but painful, and often accompanied by local discoloration and swelling.

C. sculpturatus is believed to occur only in Arizona and is locally abundant. It is slender, approximately 60 mm in length, and usually straw yellow in color with two irregular black stripes down the back. One must be careful when picking up boards, rocks, and other objects in areas where scorpions are common.

Other Nuisance Insect Pests

Many nonbiting and nonstinging nuisance insects are short-term problems, regional in scope, and often difficult to control, because of social and political reasons. Insect pests that occur in recreational areas are grouped as: (1) shade and forest tree pests and (2) other insect pests.

Shade Tree and Forest Pests

Many different types of insects live and feed in recreational areas. Most of these insects are unnoticed by the public until they reach outbreak numbers or cause noticeable or aesthetically unpleasing damage. All the insects described in Chapters 11–17 can cause problems in recreational areas, but specific examples of defoliators and other forest insects that can cause enormous impact in recreational areas are given.

Epidemic population levels of immature gypsy moth, *Lymantria dispar* (Linnaeus) or forest tent caterpillar, *Malacosoma disstria* (Hübner), often defoliate entire stands of preferred host trees and then the mature larvae disperse into nearby areas looking for food. The dead bodies of these insects can cause slippery spots on highways and make driving hazardous for motorists. Large numbers of caterpillars crawling around recreational areas, and on vehicles and buildings, upset many people.

Large numbers of adults of certain forest pests and their natural enemies often congregate in certain areas. This can cause distress to humans. For instance, forest tent caterpillar adults are often a nuisance when they congregate around light sources and their dead bodies accumulate on the surrounding surfaces. Also, large numbers of adult parasites, such as the flesh fly, *Sarcophaga aldrichi* (Parker), associated with forest tent caterpillar outbreaks, can be more of a nuisance than the defoliating insect. These flesh flies do not bite, but they are attracted to people's skin and also congregate around light-colored objects such as cars, sheets, and towels. Large numbers of adult forest pests or beneficial natural enemies that occur along the shoreline or in the water at swimming beaches can have a disastrous effect on its recreational usage. For example, adults of the oblong leaf weevil, *Phyllobius oblongus* (Linnaeus), were so numerous around and in the lakes that the use of certain swimming areas in the western part of Michigan's Upper Peninsula was greatly limited in late June during the early 1970s.

Insect products, signs, and remains are upsetting or aesthetically unpleasing to many recreationists. They often complain loudly to park officials about the honeydew produced by aphid, scales, and leafhoppers, especially when the honeydew falls on their cars or other personal equipment. The silk shelter of the eastern tent caterpillar, *Malacosoma americanum* (Fabricius), and the web-enclosed foliage of the fall webworm, *Hyphantria cunea* (Drury), are aesthetically unpleasing to many recreationists.

Defoliated and dead trees in recreational areas are aesthetically unpleasing to many people. The reduction of shade caused by temporary or permanent damage from insects on shade trees often leads to the temporary unsuitability of certain areas for many recreational uses. Dead trees killed by insects may fall or be blown down and injure people or their property. Some users are aware of this danger and may avoid using hazardous recreational areas. Foresters and land managers must constantly be on the lookout for trees that might cause injury to users.

Other Insect Pests

There are numerous other insects, besides shade tree and forest pests, that occasionally become nuisances in recreational areas. Adult mayflies and caddisflies sometimes emerge in such large numbers along major rivers (i.e., Mississippi River, St. Lawrence Seaway) that they interfere with planned outdoor activities and with highway traffic (Jamnback 1969). These adults are often attracted to lights near the rivers and may become extremely numerous around store windows and resorts. Also, large amounts of scales, hair, and other insect parts produced by these insects may cause allergic reactions such as eczema and asthma in some humans (Shulman 1967).

Similarly, some species of nonbiting midges (Diptera: Chironomidae) can emerge by the millions from lakes, especially lakes that are oxygen poor and nutrient rich. Emerging adults of a nonbiting midge called the "Clear Lake gnat," *Chaoborus astictopus* Dyar and Shannon, have been a major problem for residents and tourists around Clear Lake, Lake Company, California (Grodhaus 1963). These small midges enter the eyes, nostrils, and mouths of humans. Generally, the major annoyance consists of personal discomfort, but large numbers of midges and gnats have been responsible for creating traffic hazards, ruining paint on buildings, fouling swimming pools, causing a nuisance inside homes, causing human allergies, increasing density of spiders and webs on houses, and causing unpleasant odors when piles of dead midges begin to rot (Merritt and Newson 1978).

Any insect that is present in large numbers or is attracted to food will cause nuisance problems in recreation areas. Ants and house flies around picnic areas and garbage cans are classic examples. The house fly, *Musca domestica* Linnaeus, can be quite bothersome because of its feeding habits, reproductive success, and because it can transmit pathogens that cause various human diseases such as dysentery and typhoid fever.

MANAGEMENT APPROACHES USED AGAINST ARTHROPOD PESTS IN RECREATIONAL AREAS

The impact that biting or stinging arthropods have depends on the user's socioeconomic background, experiences, expectations, as well as the species of pest, and pest population densities. The real impact these pests have on the public's use of recreational areas is difficult for a recreation manager to evaluate. Park managers have daily use records, refund records, and injury records, which contain information on major impacts of insect pests such as severe black fly or stable fly days and injuries or deaths from stinging insects such as yellowjackets. However, most pests have less dramatic impact on recreationists, and these impacts are more difficult to measure accurately.

Ownership, state and federal regulations, type of user, popularity of the recreational area, pest species, and pest population densities determine the management approaches used to reduce insect pest problems on recreational areas. Private owners, catering to clients from urban and suburban areas, tend to keep biting and stinging insects at low population levels. In many cases, state or federal regulations will not allow chemical spraying in state or national parks. Sometimes, chemical insecticides can be used in state or national parks. Often chemical insecticides can be used, but the park manager will not use them except to control an arthropod vector of a human disease. Also, the type of user will affect the management approach implemented by a park manager. Intensive pest control is not employed in walk-in access campgrounds or in back-country fishing resorts because the user tolerates some discomfort from biting and stinging arthropods. Users of recreational vehicles or luxury resorts generally have much less tolerance for biting and stinging arthropods and demand that the population densities of arthropod pests be kept at low levels. The greatest amount of pest control is usually found in busy metropolitan parks and fewer management techniques are generally used in rural recreational sites.

The following management approaches have been used against arthropod pests in recreational areas: (1) no control or very limited hazard removals, (2) educational techniques, (3) chemical insecticides, (4) natural enemies, (5) cultural techniques, (6) managerial techniques, (7) personal protective mechanisms, and (8) integrated pest management.

No Control or Very Limited Hazard Removals

Arthropod pests are not controlled on most federal, state, and industrial lands. Very limited hazard removals are conducted when fallen logs, dead trees, or overhanging "stressed" trees are located on or near roads, trails, or parking areas. Busy recreational areas may be more intensively managed to reduce arthropod pest problems.

Educational Techniques

Numerous educational techniques have been used effectively by land managers to educate the public about arthropod pests and how to cope with these pests. Many techniques are commonly used to inform the public about pest problems. Newspaper and magazine articles, radio spots and television announcements, and advisory radio pest alert announcements can reach wide audiences. Pamphlets distributed at the check-in office of a park, pest advisory alerts, displays at nature centers, and other information posted on bulletin boards at campground offices help to inform the recreationists directly. Campfire and nature talks, slide–tape shows presented at campfire talks, and solicited advice on recommended recreational activities are informal methods used to educate the public. The objective of all these educational techniques is to present the pest information to the public in a clear and concise manner. An educated public will be better prepared mentally and physically to enjoy their outdoor activity with minor annoyance from arthropod pests. Recreationists have a choice of changing their recreational activity or to move to a location with low populations of arthropod pests.

Chemical Insecticides

Chemical larvicides or adulticides have often been used from the ground with power sprayers, mist machines, and thermal foggers, or sprayed from the air to reduce biting and stinging arthropod pests. Currently, the majority of chemical insecticides used in recreational areas are for control of mosquitoes and biting midges. Few approved chemical insecticides provide long-lasting effectiveness. These approved chemical insecticides must be applied every 7–14 days during the mosquito season to adequately treat the larval habitats (i.e., standing water) of mosquitoes. Often treatment or elimination of all mosquito-producing water sites within the flight range of the adult mosquito is impossible. Two approaches are available to reduce the invasion of adult mosquitoes from nearby habitats: (1) treat vegetation in campground or picnic areas with a residual insecticide to kill mosquitoes that remain long enough to obtain a lethal dose or (2) apply an insecticidal fog or mist to areas where adults are flying or resting. For current information on controlling all biting and stinging insects, including mosquitoes, contact a nearby county extension office.

It is impossible to cover all the ways chemical insecticides have been used against arthropod pests during the last 25 years. The following five examples represent a wide range of arthropod pests, different methodologies, various problems, and possible solutions.

Spraying window screens with a chemical insecticide is one method of reducing the number of biting midges. Jamnback (1961) showed that spraying window screens with an organic phosphate insecticide such as Malathion was still very effective in killing exposed biting midges 21 days after treatment. Presently, treating window screens, door screens, and tent screens with a residual chemical insecticide is a common method of reducing the number of midges, gnats, and no-see-ums.

Insect growth regulators also reduce the number of nonbiting midges and mosquitoes in artificially created recreational lakes and wastewater oxidation lakes. The periodic appearance of large numbers of gnats, midges, and mosquitoes over the summer has been a long-term problem for many residents of large artificially created lakes, natural lakes, and for inhabitants near tidal marshes. In certain areas, such as Clear Lake, Lake Company, California, and the Long Island, New York, tidal marshes, chemical treatment of these pest insects has been demanded for many years. These long-term spraying programs resulted in insects resistant to chemical insecticides and the biological magnification of insecticides in fish and carnivorous birds.

Promising new techniques for reducing mosquito and midge populations in man-made recreational lakes involve insect growth regulators. Several of these materials have shown high activity against mosquitoes and midges with little effect on nontarget organisms (Mulla et al. 1976).

Insecticides are applied in certain situations to reduce the number of fleas on wild rodents. Good control of fleas on wild rodents has been obtained by dusting rodent burrows with insecticides, by using insecticide bait traps where rodents treat themselves with an insecticidal dust while feeding, and by impregnating rodent baits with systemic insecticides or fumigants such as dichlorvos (Barnes et al. 1972, 1974, Miller et al. 1975, Cole et al. 1976). These methods of chemical control can be used in recreational areas against fleas or ticks that are important vectors of human diseases and have rodent hosts.

Granules or concentrated sprays of acaricides such as Chlorpyrifos and Stirofos can be used to reduce tick populations in recreational areas (Mount 1981a,b). Mount (1981b) demonstrated that one tractor-mounted, air-blast sprayer, using acaricides against free-living nymphs and adults of the lone star tick, *Amblyomma americanum* (Linnaeus), could treat all camping and picnic areas in almost any of the parks in the Ozark–Ouachita highlands in 8 hours or less. These, or similar chemical control methods, are available for park managers to use in recreational areas where ticks are a major arthropod pest.

Various chemical treatments are often used to reduce yellowjacket populations in recreational areas during August, September, or October. The best method of controlling yellowjackets in recreational areas involves the proper management of human litter and garbage. Frequent garbage pickup, along with attaching a dichlorvos strip to the inside of trash can lids or the spraying of trash containers with a chemical insecticide, have worked well in some recreational areas (Wagner 1961, Akre and Retan 1973).

One promising new approach is a meat bait with encapsulated insecticide to reduce yellowjacket populations. This approach was used very successfully in California against *V. pensylvanica* (Davis 1978). Additional biological and behavior studies on other species of yellowjackets in various parts of North America are needed to develop integrated pest management programs for other species of yellowjackets.

Natural Enemies

Very seldom have natural enemies been managed to reduce population numbers of biting and stinging arthropod pests. One exception is the introduction of fish such as *Gambusia* species into artificially created water systems to reduce mosquito populations. The fish have been successful in certain situations in Virginia, California, and Hawaii. However, fish mortality from cold water, cost of rearing the fish, effects on populations of native fish, and survival of mosquitoes in ephemeral breeding sites have reduced the effectiveness of these introduced natural enemies. Legner et al. (1974) and Coppel and Mertins (1977) provide more detailed information on introducing fish to reduce mosquito populations.

Cultural Techniques

Various cultural techniques were used long before the advent of chlorinated hydrocarbons to reduce the number of biting and stinging arthropods. Many of the cultural techniques used today to reduce the number of biting and stinging arthropods are preventive methods and not stopgap methods to use after the pest becomes a problem. Gerhardt et al. (1973), Linley and Davis (1971), and NAS (1969) present details on the numerous cultural techniques used to reduce arthropod pests in recreational areas. Examples of five cultural methods that reduce arthropod pest populations are described in the following paragraphs.

Elimination or Reduction of Suitable Breeding Sites

Reduction or elimination of mosquito breeding sites, such as standing water, within or near recreational areas effectively lowers local mosquito populations. All trash that might hold water, such as containers, tires, and abandoned cars, should be removed from recreational areas. Several species of mosquitoes also breed in standing water in hollow stumps. All rot holes and hollow stumps in recreational areas should be removed or filled with sand or concrete to destroy breeding areas for tree hole mosquitoes. Small ponds, seepage areas, or undesirable swamps are often drained, filled, or graded to reduce the number of mosquito breeding sites. Increasing the rate of flow and reducing water surface areas in shallow-sluggish streams and ditches will decrease mosquito breeding sites. Chemical or mechanical removal of emergent vegetation that protects mosquito larvae and pupae from wave action and natural enemies can also be used to reduce local mosquito populations.

Presently mosquito control is an integral part of wetlands management. Likewise, house fly and stable fly populations can be greatly reduced by the destruction of numerous breeding sites for these two recreational pests.

Removal or Reduction of Favorable Sites for Biting and Stinging Arthropods

No-see-ums are very weak fliers and are greatly inhibited by even light to moderate wind. Increasing the amount of light and moderate wind around human and animal habitations by mowing grass and removing shrubs and low vegetation around campsites and buildings can reduce the number of no-see-ums. Mowing or removing vegetation within a half meter along either side of paths used by humans and dogs, including adjacent dog exercise areas in roadside parks destroys cover for ticks and small animals. Proper management of garbage and litter, keeping garbage containers clean and emptied regularly, and removing litter from recreational sites will reduce the number of feeding sites for yellowjackets.

Removal or Blockage of a Wasp Nest
A subterranean nest can be eliminated by pouring gasoline or kerosene into the entrance hole and blocking it. Do not ignite the fuel. An aerial nest can be destroyed at night by using an aerosol product that propels a quick-knockdown insecticide from distances of 3–5 m.

Elimination of Dangerous Trees and Limbs in Recreational Areas
Techniques for managing shade and forest tree pests in recreational areas have been discussed in other chapters of this book. However, a key sanitation technique for recreational areas is the removal of hazardous trees and limbs, regardless of whether they were damaged by insects, disease, weather, or humans.

Use of Mechanical Barriers or Traps
No-see-um proof screening on tents and window screens is commonly recommended for preventing no-see-ums, mosquitoes, and midges from entering. Many types of mechanical fly traps are often used by homeowners and recreationists to reduce population numbers of house flies, deer flies, horse flies, and stable flies.

Managerial Techniques

Several managerial techniques should be considered when making decisions about arthropod pests in recreational areas. First, employees should be trained to be familiar with local biting and stinging arthropods and "updated" on techniques that can be used to reduce these pests. Second, land managers should plan new recreational areas in locations as free of arthropod pests as possible. For example, recreational sites should be set in breezy areas and away from wet spots, areas with drainage problems, and areas near major breeding grounds for black flies, biting midges, and no-see-ums. Third, unpopular campsites or recreational areas that have a long history of serious arthropod pest populations can be closed. Fourth, alternative campsites and recreational activities can be recommended to the user when biting or stinging arthropod populations are at extremely "high" nuisance levels in localized camping or recreational areas. Fifth, the recreational area can be closed at certain times of the year or reschedule the opening or closing of a recreational site, or hunting season, around arthropod pest life cycles. For example, many campsites in the northern United States, excluding Alaska, do not open until after the peak black fly emergence period. Land managers may close a recreational area when several cases of an epizootic human disease, such as the St. Louis strain of equine encephalitis or plague, are reported locally. Human contact with infected rabbits, ticks, and deer flies during peak tularemia periods can be minimized through education and thoughtful scheduling of hunting seasons and recreational activities. Sixth, always consider what effects various modifications in a recreational area will have on arthropod pest populations.

Personal Protection

Human contact with biting and stinging arthropods is difficult to avoid in many recreational areas. Properly informed individuals can reduce their discomfort and annoyance caused by arthropod pests. First, an individual should be informed of pests that are vectors of disease and when possible avoid areas or situations where arthropod-borne disease occurs commonly. For example, contact with sick or dying rodents in the western United States should be avoided. Second, care should be taken when working in areas where stinging arthropods are common. Third, proper clothing can protect an individual working or recreating where biting arthropods are present. Protective clothing includes clothing of closely woven fabric, through which insects cannot bite, tightly fastened clothing with pants tucked into the boots, a long sleeve shirt, and a hat. Head nets and gloves are often very useful, especially in northern areas, where warm, moist weather conditions are not so common. Fourth, insect repellents containing N,N-diethylmethatoluamide applied on exposed skin offer fairly good protection against biting arthropods such as mosquitoes, black flies, stable flies, horse flies, and deer flies. Most repellents will not prevent biting midges from trying to feed, but some repellents will entrap them like flypaper so that they cannot reach the skin. Fifth, individuals should obtain medical information about major arthropod pests and have emergency equipment available. Sixth, careful self-examination and removal of ticks after working in a tick-infested area is highly recommended. Seventh, good sanitation procedures such as a bath or a shower after working in the field may help reduce the number of chigger bites. Eighth, anyone working in areas where Rocky Mountain spotted fever is common should consider being immunized against this tick-borne disease.

Integrated Pest Management

Many of the described management approaches are commonly used against arthropod pests in recreational areas. However, most recreational areas do not have management programs for all or even a few arthropod pests. Mosquito abatement programs are a widely applied approach and have been developed for some cities, metropolitan areas, and counties throughout the United States. Integrated pest management programs for some recreation areas will undoubtedly be developed in the future as local, state, and national agencies become more interested in recreational areas. Several detailed conceptual IPM models have been developed for particular insect pests, but none are completely operational. Two examples of currently used IPM programs are presented.

IPM for Flies on Mackinac Island, Michigan

Mackinac Island, approximately 1000 hectares in size, is located between the upper and lower peninsulas of Michigan where Lake Huron and Lake Michigan meet to form the Straits of Mackinac. The island attracts over 750,000 visitors a year, who enjoy its scenery, Victorian architecture, and atmosphere. No automobiles are allowed on the island. The only transportation available is horse-drawn carriages and bicycles. Each summer 500–600 horses are brought to the island to provide transportation for the tourists.

Manure produced by the horses provides breeding sites for two pests, the house fly and the stable fly. The flies breed in the disturbed manure that has been mixed with straw and urine. Large populations of flies have persisted around and in stables and adjacent barns despite efforts to dispose of the manure. These populations are a nuisance to the public and spread outbreaks of dysentery. Biting stable flies cause carriage horses to become skittish and some humans to panic. Sanitation was the major control method used against these flies until 1945.

A DDT–fly control study was established in 1945 on Mackinac Island because state governors had chosen to meet there for a national conference. The fly control program was successful, and DDT, a chlorinated hydrocarbon insecticide, was used for control until 1949, when the fly built up a resistance to the chemical insecticide. Other chlorinated hydrocarbons were used in various combinations with DDT during 1949–1954, but all gave unsatisfactory results because the flies developed resistance to these insecticides. Malathion and Dimethoate (Cygon), organic phosphate insecticides, were used effectively against the flies during 1954–1964 and 1964–1977, respectively. During 1978, two major problems developed on the island: flies were becoming more resistant to Dimethoate, and an outbreak of the European fruit lecanium scale, *Lecanium corni* (Bouché), was seriously damaging many shade and fruit trees on the island.

Residents of Mackinac Island asked specialists at Michigan State University for advice about pest management. Kennedy and Merritt (1980) found that the Dimethoate spray operators routinely directed the mist blower spray into the lower crowns of trees. The scale insect was not susceptible to the spray, but its natural enemies were killed by the chemical insecticide. The chemical control program directed at the primary pest, the flies, had induced an outbreak of a secondary pest, the European fruit lecanium scale. The pest management specialists proposed an IPM program to city council and the Mackinac Island Commission, which incorporated cultural, chemical, and biological techniques instead of continuing to control pests with only chemical insecticides as had been done for the past 30 years on Mackinac Island (Kennedy and Merritt 1980).

After lengthy discussion and debate, they voted to support the IPM program for a 1-year trial program. An educational program involving newspaper stories, a movie, and informal discussions was used to explain the biology of the insects to the public. Residents more readily implemented a sanitation program once they understood that the major breeding site of the house flies and stable flies was disturbed manure. Surveys were conducted to determine major larval breeding sites and adult fly densities. Information from these surveys indicated where the effort should be concentrated and provided a basis for evaluation of the IPM program. A detailed sanitation program was recommended to stable and store owners that included cleaning manure from barns and stables once a week, removing fallen feed from cracks in horse stalls and applying rock salt or lime to these sites to prevent larval development, covering trash cans, providing flyproof screens for store windows and doors, laying a cement floor where manure wagons were parked to eliminate breeding areas and facilitate cleanup, and composting manure to prevent larval and pupal development of flies (Kennedy and Merritt 1980).

Public opinion surveys showed that the flies were not as serious a problem for tourists as they were to the residents. Adult stable fly populations declined 25% in selected areas, and the amount of Dimethoate insecticide applied was reduced from 235 gallons to less than 1 gallon by the end of the first year of the IPM program. Very significant decreases in the adult stable fly and housefly populations also occurred throughout the island during the second year. The broad-scale insecticide program was completely eliminated, which reduced the amount of environmental contamination. The sanitation program was enhanced considerably by the passage of an ordinance that imposed fines on those not complying with established sanitation measures. City and state park personnel were trained and are now administering the IPM program.

IPM for Mosquitoes in a California Salt Marsh

The Petaluma Salt Marsh is located between the San Francisco Bay and the hills and pastures of Marin and Sonoma Counties of northern California. Areas near the marsh were considered undesirable for recreational sites and housing because of swarms of mosquitoes originating from the marsh. Suburban sprawl eventually reached the areas near the marsh. Suburbanites demanded mosquito control, and the marsh received five aerial applications per year of the insecticide parathion. However, the citizens still complained about the mosquitoes.

Entomologists from the Marin Mosquito Abatement District investigated the biological aspects of the problem before developing an IPM program for the marsh (Flint and van den Bosch 1981). A commonly asked question was "Why did the marsh have such high populations of mosquitoes?" The marsh lacked the stability of a typical mosquito breeding area because the San Francisco Bay tide flushed the sloughs and channels of the marsh twice a day. District entomologists discovered that mosquitoes were breeding only in potholes created mainly by dummy bombs dropped into this practice bombing range during World War II. These potholes were unconnected by drainage channels to tidal sloughs and were not flushed regularly but existed as stagnate mosquito breeding sites.

Entomologists from the Marin Mosquito Abatement District attached a ditch-digging tool to an all-terrain vehicle and created drainage ditches, a cultural technique, between all the potholes and main channels of the marsh. Now all potholes received two daily tidal flushes, which reduced the number of mosquito breeding sites. Larger pools and ditches were stocked with gambusia fish. These fish and other mosquito predators such as spiders, birds, and insects reduced mosquito populations to lower levels.

Potential trouble areas occasionally develop, so district personnel regularly travel through the marsh in a modified ditch buggy to monitor larval population levels in the breeding pools. Chemical insecticides are applied only to areas where larval populations reach levels that might be troublesome if the adult mosquitoes emerge. Approximately 2 gallons of chemical insecticide are now used each year to treat the entire 810-ha marsh. This IPM program has very successfully reduced the cost of the mosquito control program, reduced the environmental effects of massive spraying on the wetland, and reduced the number of mosquitoes normally found in nearby recreational, urban, and farming areas.

REFERENCES

Akre, R. D. and H. G. Davis. 1978. Biology and pest status of venomous wasps. *Annu. Rev. Entomol.* **23**:215–238.

Akre, R. D. and H. C. Reed. 1981. Population cycles of yellowjackets (Hymenoptera: Vespinae) in the Pacific northwest. *Environ. Entomol.* **10**:267–274.

Akre, R. D. and A. H. Retan. 1973. *Yellowjackets and Paper Wasps.* Washington State University Cooperative Extension Service Bulletin 643.

Akre, R. D., A. Greene, J. F. MacDonald, P. J. Landolt, and H. G. Davis. 1981. *The Yellowjackets of America North of Mexico.* USDA Agriculture Handbook 552.

Axtell, R. C. 1976. Horse flies and deer flies (Diptera: Tabanidae). In Cheng, L. (Ed.), *Marine Insects.* North-Holland, Amsterdam.

Barnes, A. M., L. G. Ogden, and E. G. Campos. 1972. Control of the plague vector *Opisocrostis ludovicianus,* by treatment of prairie dog (*Cynomys ludovicianus*) burrow with 2% carbaryl dust. *J. Med. Entomol.* **4**:330–333.

Barnes, A. M., L. J. Ogden, W. S. Archibald, and E. G. Campos. 1974. Control of plague vectors of *Peromiscus maniculatus* by use of 2% carbaryl dust in bait stations. *J. Med. Entomol.* **11**:83–87.

Boobar, L. R. and J. Granett. 1980. *Simulium penobscotensis* (Diptera: Simuliidae) habitat characteristics in the Penobscot River, Maine. *Environ. Entomol.* **9**:412–415.

Burgdorfer, W. 1975. A review of Rocky Mountain spotted fever (tick-borne typhus), its agent, and its tick vectors in the United States. *J. Med. Entomol.* **12**:269–278.

Cole, M. M., W. C. Bennett, G. N. Graves, J. R. Wheeler, B. E. Miller, and P. H. Clark. 1976. Dichlorvos bait for control of fleas on wild rodents. *J. Med. Entomol.* **12**:625–630.

Coppel, H. C. and J. W. Mertins. 1977. *Biological Insect Pest Suppression.* Springer-Verlag, New York.

Davis, H. G. 1978. Yellowjacket wasps in urban environments. In Frankie, G. W. and C. S. Koehler (Eds.), *Perspectives in Urban Entomology.* Academic Press, New York.

Eavy, L., K. Ankli, C. Brandell, J. Greager, L. Higginbottom, S. Kane, S. Miller, and S. Voice. 1979. Biology, economics, and management of the stable fly as a recreational pest. Final Technical Report, University of Michigan, School of Natural Resources Stable Fly Study Project, Ann Arbor.

Flint, M. L. and R. van den Bosch. 1981. *Introduction to Integrated Pest Management.* Plenum Press, New York.

Gelman, A. C. 1961. The ecology of relapsing fevers. In May, J. M. (Ed.), *Studies in Disease Ecology.* Hafner, New York.

Gerhardt, R. R., J. C. Dukes, J. M. Fatler, and R. C. Axtell. 1973. *Public Opinion on Insect Pest Management in Coastal North Carolina.* North Carolina Agriculture Extension Service Miscellaneous Publication 97.

Grodhaus, G. 1963. Chronomid midges as a nuisance. II. The nature of the nuisance and remarks on its control. *Calif. Vector Views* **10**:27–37.

Harwood, R. F. and M. T. James. 1979. *Entomology in Human and Animal Health.* Macmillan, New York.

Jamnback, H. 1961. The effectiveness of chemically treated screens in killing annoying punkies, *Culicoides obsoletus. J. Econ. Entomol.* **54**:578–580.

Jamnback, H. 1969. Bloodsucking flies and other outdoor nuisance arthropods of New York State. New York Museum of Science Service Memo 19.

Kennedy, M. K. and R. W. Merritt. 1980. Horse and buggy island. *Nat. Hist.* **89**:34–40.

Kettle, D. 1977. Biology and bionomics of bloodsucking ceratopogonids. *Annu. Rev. Entomol.* **22**:35–51.

Knight, F. B. and H. J. Heikkenen. 1980. *Principles of Forest Entomology.* McGraw-Hill, New York.

Kwan, W. E. and F. O. Morrison. 1974. A summary of published information for field and laboratory studies of biting midges, *Culicoides* species (Diptera: Ceratopogonidae). *Ann. Entomol. Soc. Quebec* **19**:127–137.

Legner, E. F., R. D. Sjogren, and I. M. Hall. 1974. The biological control of medically important arthropods. *CRC Crit. Rev. Environ. Control* **4**:85–113.

Linley, J. R. 1976. Biting midges of mangrove swamps and salt-marshes (Diptera: Ceratopogonidae). In Cheng, L. (Ed.), *Marine Insects.* North-Holland, Amsterdam.

Linley, J. R. and D. B. Davies. 1971. Sandflies and tourism in Florida and the Bahamas and Caribbean areas. *J. Econ. Entomol.* **64**:264–278.

Lofgren, C. S., W. A. Banks, and B. M. Glancey. 1975. Biology and control of imported fire ants. *Annu. Rev. Entomol.* **20**:1–30.

McLintock, J. and J. Iversen. 1976. Mosquitoes and human disease in Canada. *Can. Entomol.* **107**:695–704.

Merritt, R. W. and K. W. Cummins (Eds.). 1984. *An Introduction to the Aquatic Insects of North America.* Kendall/Hunt, Dubuque, Iowa.

Merritt, R. W. and H. D. Newson. 1978. Ecology and management of arthropod populations in recreational lands. In Frankie, G. W. and C. S. Koehler (Eds.), *Perspectives in Urban Entomology.* Academic Press, New York.

Miller, B. E., W. C. Bennett, G. N. Graves, and J. R. Wheeler. 1975. Field studies of systemic insecticides. I. Evaluation of phoxim for control of flies on cotton rats. *J. Med. Entomol.* **12**:425–430.

Mount, G. A. 1981a. *Amblyomma americanum*: Area control of overwintering nymphs and adults in Oklahoma with acaricides. *J. Econ. Entomol.* **74**:24–26.

Mount, G. A. 1981b. *Amblyomma americanum:* Control in Oklahoma Parks with air-blast sprayer applications of acaricides. *J. Econ. Entomol.* **74**:27–29.

Mulla, M. S., W. L. Kramer, and D. R. Barnard. 1976. Insect growth regulators for control of chironomid midges in residential–recreational lakes. *J. Econ. Entomol.* **69**:285–291.

National Academy Sciences. 1969. *Insect–Pest Management and Control,* Vol. 3, National Academy of Sciences, Washington, DC.

Nelson, B. C. 1978. Ecology of medically important arthropods in urban environments. In Frankie, G. W. and C. S. Koehler (Eds.), *Perspectives in Urban Entomology.* Academic Press, New York.

Newson, H. D. 1977. Arthropod problems in recreation areas. *Annu. Rev. Entomol.* **22**:333–353.

Olkowski, H. and W. Olkowski. 1976. Entomophobia in the urban ecosystem, some observations and suggestions. *Bull. Entomol. Soc. Am.* **23**:313–317.

Parrish, H. M. 1963. Analysis of 460 fatalities from venomous animals in the United States. *Am. J. Med. Sci.* **245**:129–141.

Perlman, F., E. Press, G. A. Googins, A. Malley, and H. Poarea. 1976. Tussockosis: Reactions to the Douglas-fir tussock moth. *Ann. Allerg.* **36**:302–307.

Rhodes, R. B., W. L. Schafer, W. H. Schmidt, P. F. Wubbena, R. M. Dozier, A. W. Townes, and H. J. Wittig. 1975. Hypersensitivity to the imported fire ant. A report of 49 cases. *J. Allergy Clin. Immunol.* **56**:84–93.

Sasa, M. 1961. Biology of the chiggers. *Annu. Rev. Entomol.* **6**:221–244.

Shulman, S. 1967. Allergic responses to insects. *Annu. Rev. Entomol.* **12**:323–346.

Sleeper, F. 1975. Visit from a small monster. *Sports Illus.* **43**:46–49.

Spradbery, J. P. 1973. *Wasps: An Account of the Biology and Natural History of Solitary and Social Wasps.* University of Washington Press, Seattle.

Wagner, R. E. 1961. Control of the yellowjacket, *Vespula pensylvanica* in public parks. *J. Econ. Entomol.* **54**:628–630.

Wagner, R. E. and D. A. Reierson. 1969. Yellowjacket control by baiting. 1. Influence of toxicants and attractants on bait acceptance. *J. Econ. Entomol.* **62**:1192–1197.

Wagner, V. C. and H. D. Newson. 1975. Mosquito biting activity in Michigan State parks. *Mosq. News* **35**:217–222.

SUBJECT INDEX

SPECIES INDEX